Lecture Notes in Computer Science 5008

Commenced Publication in 1973
Founding and Former Series Editors:
Gerhard Goos, Juris Hartmanis, and Jan van Leeuwen

Antonios Gasteratos   Markus Vincze
John K. Tsotsos (Eds.)

Computer
Vision Systems

6th International Conference, ICVS 2008
Santorini, Greece, May 12-15, 2008
Proceedings

 Springer

Volume Editors

Antonios Gasteratos
Democritus University of Thrace
Department of Production and Management Engineering
University Campus, Kimmeria, 671 00 Xanthi, Greece
E-mail: agaster@pme.duth.gr

Markus Vincze
Vienna University of Technology
Automation and Control Institute
Gusshausstraße 27/376, 1040 Vienna, Austria
E-mail: vincze@acin.tuwien.ac.at

John K. Tsotsos
York University
Department of Computer Science and Engineering
4700 Keele St., Toronto, ON M3J 1P3, Canada
E-mail: tsotsos@cse.yorku.ca

Library of Congress Control Number: 2008925840

CR Subject Classification (1998): I.4, I.2.0, I.2.6, I.5.4-5, I.3.1-2, D.2

LNCS Sublibrary: SL 1 – Theoretical Computer Science and General Issues

ISSN   0302-9743
ISBN-10   3-540-79546-4 Springer Berlin Heidelberg New York
ISBN-13   978-3-540-79546-9 Springer Berlin Heidelberg New York

Springer is a part of Springer Science+Business Media

springer.com

© Springer-Verlag Berlin Heidelberg 2008
Printed in Germany

Typesetting: Camera-ready by author, data conversion by Scientific Publishing Services, Chennai, India
Printed on acid-free paper   SPIN: 12264100   06/3180   5 4 3 2 1 0

Preface

In the past few years, with the advances in microelectronics and digital technology, cameras became a widespread media. This, along with the enduring increase in computing power boosted the development of computer vision systems. The International Conference on Computer Vision Systems (ICVS) covers the advances in this area. This is to say that ICVS is not and should not be yet another computer vision conference. The field of computer vision is fully covered by many well-established and famous conferences and ICVS differs from these by covering the systems point of view. ICVS 2008 was the 6th International Conference dedicated to advanced research on computer vision systems. The conference, continuing a series of successful events in Las Palmas, Vancouver, Graz, New York and Bielefeld, in 2008 was held on Santorini.

In all, 128 papers entered the review process and each was reviewed by three independent reviewers using the double-blind review method. Of these, 53 papers were accepted (23 as oral and 30 as poster presentation). There were also two invited talks by David Hogg and by Heinrich H. Bülthoff. The presented papers cover all aspects of computer vision systems, namely: cognitive vision, monitor and surveillance, computer vision architectures, calibration and registration, object recognition and tracking, learning, human—machine interaction and cross-modal systems.

The theme of the conference was 'Vision for Cognitive Systems', and thus in conjunction with ICVS 2008 two workshops were organized:

The 4th International Cognitive Vision Workshop—ICVW 2008, organized by Barbara Caputo and Markus Vincze, aimed at studying issues such as multi-cue integration, embodied categorization, and behavior / skill acquisition.

The 5th International Workshop on Attention in Cognitive Systems—WAPCV 2008, organized by Lucas Paletta and John Tsotsos, aimed at selective attention and its importance for the organization of behaviors for control and interfacing between sensory and cognitive information processing and for the understanding of individual and social cognition in humanoid artifacts.

We wish to thank the Workshop Chair, Antonis Argyros, for his assistance and his constructive comments during the workshop selection. We also owe a great thank you to Dimitris Chrysostomou and Stamatina Gika for their valuable efforts in organizing this event. Thanks also to EuCognition network and the Greek Ministry of Education for sponsoring this event.

May 2008

Antonios Gasteratos
Markus Vincze
John Tsotsos

Conference Committee

Conference General Chair

Antonios Gasteratos (Democritus University of Thrace, Greece)

Program Co-chairs

Markus Vincze (TU Vienna, Austria)
John Tsotsos (York University, Canada)

Workshop Chair

Antonis Argyros, (University of Crete and FORTH, Greece)

Program Committee

Balasundram P. Amavasai (Sheffield Hallam University, UK)
Nick Barnes (National ICT, Australia)
Christian Bauckhage (Deutsche Telekom AG, Berlin, Germany)
Carlos Beltran Gonzalez (University of Genoa, Italy)
Alexandre Bernardino (Instituto Superior Técnico, Portugal)
Horst Bischof (Technical University Graz, Austia)
Alain Boucher (IFI Hanoi, Vietnam)
François Bremond, (INRIA Sophia Antipolis, France)
Jorge Cabrera (University of Las Palmas de Gran Canaria, Spain)
Régis Clouard (GREYC Laboratory, France)
Patrick Courtney (Perkin Elmer Life Science, UK)
James Crowley (I.N.P. Grenoble, France)
Kostas Daniilidis (University of Pennsylvania, USA)
Larry Davis (University of Maryland, USA)
Alberto Del Bimbo (University of Florence, Italy)
Rachid Deriche (INRIA Sophia Antipolis, France)
Bruce Draper (Colorado State University, USA)
James Ferryman (University of Reading, UK)
Bob Fisher (School of Informatics, University of Edinburgh, UK)
Gian Luca Foresti (University of Udine, Italy)
Jannik Fritsch (Honda Research Institute Europe GmbH, Germany)
Vassilios Gatos (National Center for Scientific Research 'Demokritos,' Greece)
Riad Hammoud (Delphi Corporation, USA)
Jesse Hoey (University of Dundee, UK)
David Hogg (University of Leeds, UK)

Vaclav Hvalac (Czech Technical University in Prague, Czech Republic)
Rick Kjeldsen (IBM T.J. Watson Research Center, USA)
Edgar Koerner (Honda Research Institute Europe GmbH, Germany)
Yiannis Kompatsiaris (ITI CERTH, Greece)
Costas Kotropoulos (Aristotle University of Thessaloniki, Greece)
Ales Leonardis (University of Ljubljana, Slovenia)
Dimitrios Makris (Kingston University, UK)
Bärbel Mertsching (University of Paderborn, Germany)
Giorgio Metta (Instituto Italiano di Technologia, Italy)
Bernd Neumann (University of Hamburg, Germany)
Ramakant Nevatia (University of Southern California, USA)
Lucas Paletta (Joanneum Research, Austria)
Nikolaos Papamarkos (Democritus University of Thrace, Greece)
Chung Pau-Choo (National Cheng Kung University, Taiwan)
Justus Piater (University of Liege, Belgium)
Claudio Pinhanez (IBM T.J. Watson Research Center, USA)
Axel Pinz (Graz University of Technology, Austria)
Fiora Pirri (University of Rome 'La Sapienza,' Italy)
Ioannis Pratikakis (National Center for Scientific Research 'Demokritos,' Greece)
Paolo Remagnino (Kingston University, UK)
Gerhard Sagerer (University of Bielefeld, Germany)
Gerald Schaefer (Aston University, UK)
Bernt Schiele (TU Darmstadt, Germany)
Athanasios Skodras (Hellenic Open University, Greece)
Anastasios Tefas (Aristotle University of Thessaloniki, Greece)
Monique Thonnat (INRIA Sophia Antipolis, France)
Panagiotis Trahanias (University of Crete, Greece)
Sofia Tsekeridou (Athens Information Technology, Greece)
Sergio Velastin (Kingston University, UK)
Sven Wachsmuth (University of Bielefeld, Germany)
Christian Wöhler (DaimlerChrysler Group Research, Ulm, Germany)
Sebastian Wrede (University of Bielefeld, Germany)

Local Administration

Dimitris Chrysostomou (Democritus University of Thrace, Greece)

Additional Reviewers

Angelos Amanatiadis
Alexander Andreopoulos
Neil Bruce
Dimitris Chrysostomou
Andrew Dankers
Petros Daras

Konstantinos Derpanis
James Elder
Pantelis Ellinas
Ehsan Fazl-Ersi
Michael Jenkin
Anastasios Kesidis

Table of Contents

III Computer Vision Architectures

IV Calibration and Registration

V   Object Recognition and Tracking

VI   Learning

VII   Human Machine Interaction

VIII   Cross Modal Systems

Part I

Cognitive Vision

Part I

Cognitive Vision

Visual Search in Static and Dynamic Scenes Using Fine-Grain Top-Down Visual Attention

Muhammad Zaheer Aziz and Bärbel Mertsching

GET Lab, University of Paderborn, Pohlweg 47-49, 33098 Paderborn, Germany,
<last name>@get.upb.de
http://getwww.upb.de

Abstract. Artificial visual attention is one of the key methodologies inspired from nature that can lead to robust and efficient visual search by machine vision systems. A novel approach is proposed for modeling of top-down visual attention in which separate saliency maps for the two attention pathways are suggested. The maps for the bottom-up pathway are built using unbiased rarity criteria while the top-down maps are created using fine-grain feature similarity with the search target as suggested by the literature on natural vision. The model has shown robustness and efficiency during experiments on visual search using natural and artificial visual input under static as well as dynamic scenarios.

1 Introduction

Finding a robust, flexible, and efficient solution for visual search in real-life scenes has been a topic of significant interest for researchers in the field of machine vision. In the recent years emphasis has been increased on vision systems engineered according to the role model of human or natural vision in order to achieve generic solutions able to perform competently independent of the input complexity. Visual attention is one of the prominent attributes of natural vision that contributes into its efficiency and robustness. Computational models of this phenomenon has been built and applied to many vision-based problems.

A majority of the existing attention models have demonstrated visual search as a primary area of application for their models. Most of these models have utilized manipulation on bottom-up (BU) saliency maps in order to let the search target pop-out early. We argue that the top-down (TD) tasks of attention have a different nature and require a separate mechanism for computing saliency. The models of human vision such as [1] suggest target related feature processing in the V4 area of brain. Similarly the models on feature and conjunction search, for example [2], also presume excitation and inhibitions on particular feature magnitudes rather than whole channels. Results of psychophysical experiments reported by [3], [4], and [5] also support our argument. The work of [3] has shown that a population of neurons encoding the target color and/or orientation gets a gain while others get suppressed. According to [4], each feature channel can adopt many values that are evaluated by a specialized layer of neurons in the human brain. The experiments reported by [5] explicitly declare fine-grain nature

A. Gasteratos, M. Vincze, and J.K. Tsotsos (Eds.): ICVS 2008, LNCS 5008, pp. 3–12, 2008.

of TD attention showing that particular feature values are highlighted by human vision rather than the whole feature channel. These findings suggest that the TD saliency mechanism constructs task dependant maps to allow quick pop-out of the target rather than using the BU saliency maps, hence we propose to model the top-down pathway independent of the bottom-up process.

This paper introduces an approach that applies influence of the active attention behavior at the early stage of saliency map construction in contrast to the existing models that apply TD influences at a later stage. Processes for construction of BU and TD saliency maps are separated from each other in the proposed model. The major significance of this work is the proposal of a model of TD attention based upon fine-grain saliency maps, which has been done for the first time as per knowledge of the authors. Another highlight is the experiments on visual search using dynamic scenes carried out by active vision systems as the existing models of TD attention have mostly experimented with static images, rarely addressing true active vision in attentional search applications.

2   Related Work

Early computational models of visual attention such as [6] and [7] have proposed a comprehensive mechanism for determining BU saliency using some feature channels but they use the same BU saliency maps for search task as well. They apply high weight to the feature channel that facilitates highlighting the search target. Even the recent developments by the same group in this context [8][9] apply a similar strategy. The model of [10] determines weights for the feature maps that would highlight the target in a learning stage and applies them in the searching stage. Although [11] has separate components for BU and TD pathways in the model but the same saliency maps are used to deal with the TD pathway. The model presented in [12] also applies attentional bias towards the target by learning weights for the conspicuity maps that would make the required object prominent. Such approaches are likely to show inefficiency when distractors are also salient in the same feature channel.

The work presented in [13] has provided a search mechanism to detect the target by looking for its constituent parts. This approach can be considered close to fine-grain search but the methodology is inclined towards pure machine vision rather than following a biologically inspired approach. Using gist of the whole view to apply a TD influence to restrict search locations as proposed by [14] is also a useful concept that can accelerate biologically plausible visual search. This concept deals with signature of the whole image rather than individual items.

The object-based attention models such as [15] seem to have similarity with the fine-grain nature of attention because objects are defined by particular feature values. Existing object-based models have concentrated on finding only BU saliency using objects as a fundamental unit. Hence TD saliency maps based upon fine-grain concept still remains untried.

The proposed region-based methodology for attention modeling has developed as an evolutionary process. The earlier model from our group [16] introduced attentional tracking in dynamic scenes but it had high computation time and lacked robustness in visual search. The first prototype [17] for the region-based approach used convex hulls of the segmented regions. After enabling the segmentation algorithm to produce an optimized input for use of attention [18], new methods were developed to compute BU saliency using channels of color [19] and other features [20]. Methods for applying inhibition of return (IOR) and determining pop-out in the region-based paradigm were proposed in [21], groundwork for using fine-grain saliency using color channel was established in [22], and solution for handling bottom-up attention and IOR in dynamic scenarios was proposed in [23]. Here we extend the model by introducing other feature channels in the TD pathway and propose methods for TD map fusion and IOR on both TD and BU saliency maps.

3 Proposed Region-Based Approach

The proposed model groups pixels of the visual input possessing similar color attributes into clusters using a robust segmentation method [18] before starting attention related processes. Assigning fine grain attributes to these regions allows using them as units to be processed by attention procedures. Some models such as [16] perform a clustering step in the final saliency map but such late clustering becomes less effective and inefficient because most of the feature magnitudes related to the actual objects get faded away at this stage because of processing on fine and coarse scales of input.

The proposed model separates the steps of feature magnitude computation and saliency evaluation as shown in figure 1. The primary feature extraction function F produces a set of regions $\Re$ consisting of n regions each represented as R_i and feeds each R_i with data regarding location, bounding rectangle, and magnitudes of each feature ϕ_i^f ($f \in \Phi$). As five channels of color, orientation, eccentricity, symmetry and size are considered in the current status of our model hence we have $\Phi = \{c, o, e, s, z\}$.

Computation of the BU saliency using the rarity criteria is performed by the process S whose output is combined by W that applies weighted fusion of these maps to formulate a resultant BU map. The function G consideres the given TD conditions to produce fine grain saliency maps that are combined by the function C into a resultant TD map. The function P applies appropriate weights to the resultant saliency maps according to the active attention behavior, combines them into a master conspicuity map, and applies a peak selection mechanism to choose one pop-out at a time. The focus of attention at a particular time t is stored in the inhibition memory using which the process of IOR suppresses the already attended location(s) at time $t+1$ in order to avoid revisiting of the same location. The memory management function M decides whether to place the recent focus of attention in inhibition memory or excitation memory according to the active behavior and sets the weights of inhibition.

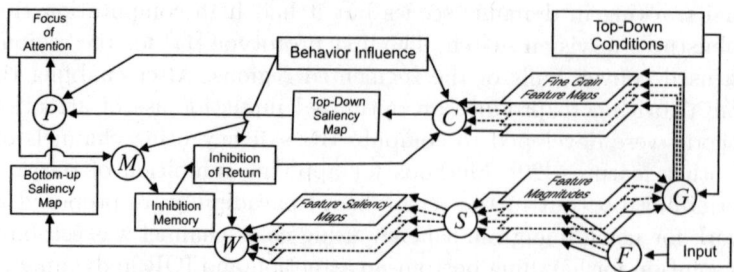

Fig. 1. Architecture of the proposed region-based attention model

3.1   Fine-Grain Top-Down Saliency Maps

The process G from the architecture diagram shown in figure 1 is responsible for construction of fine-grain saliency maps for each feature channel f considered in the model. The search target is defined as a set of top-down feature values F_{td} in which the individual features are referred as F_{td}^f. For constructing the saliency map with respect to color ($f = \{c\}$), we define D^h as the difference of hue that can be tolerated in order to consider two colors as similar, D^s as the tolerable saturation difference, D^I as the allowed intensity difference for equivalent colors, and ϕ_i^c as the magnitude of the color feature for R_i. Now, the TD color saliency γ_i^c of each region R_i is determined as follows:

$$
\gamma_i^c = \begin{cases}
\frac{a(D^h - \Delta_i^h)}{D^h} + \frac{b(D^s - \Delta_i^s)}{D^s} + \frac{c(D^I - \Delta_i^I)}{D^I} & \text{for } \Delta_i^h < D^h \text{ \& chromatic } \phi_i^c, F_{td}^c \\
\frac{(a+b+c)(D^I - \Delta_i^I)}{D^I} & \text{for } \Delta_i^I < D^I \text{ \& achromatic } \phi_i^c, F_{td}^c \\
0 & \text{otherwise}
\end{cases}
$$

where a, b, and c are weighting constants to adjust the contribution of each color component into this process. Δ_i^h, Δ_i^s, and Δ_i^I are magnitudes of the difference between ϕ_i^c and F_{td}^c in terms of hue, saturation, and intensity respectively. We take $a = 100$, $b = 55$, and $c = 100$ because the saliency values of a region lie between the range of 0 and 255 in our model. The value of b is kept smaller in order to keep more emphasis on the hue and intensity components. Hence a perfect match would result in a saliency value equal to 255.

The color map had specific requirements being a composite quantity whereas the other feature channels consist of single-valued quantities; hence they can be processed using a simpler procedure. Having Θ^f as the normalized ratio of the feature magnitudes ϕ_i^f and F_{td}^f (for $f \neq \{c\}$) defined as

$$
\Theta^f = \begin{cases}
\phi_i^f / F_{td}^f & \text{for } \phi_i^f < F_{td}^f \\
F_{td}^f / \phi_i^f & \text{otherwise}
\end{cases}
$$

which always keeps $1 \geq \Theta^f \geq 0$. Now the TD saliency γ_i^f of a region R_i with respect to a feature f ($f \in \Phi, f \neq \{c\}$) will be computed as

$$
\gamma_i^f = \begin{cases}
k\Theta^f & \text{for } \Theta^f > D^\Theta \\
0 & \text{otherwise}
\end{cases}
$$

where k is a scaling constant and D^{Θ} is the ratio above which the two involved quantities may be considered equivalent. We take $k = 255$ because the maximum amount of saliency can be 255 in our implementation and $D^{\Theta} = 0.91$.

3.2 Map Fusion and Pop-Out

In this paper we are concerned with the TD portion of the model hence we explain the map fusion function C that produces a resultant TD saliency map. We take W_{td}^{f} as the TD weight for the map of feature channel f that gets a value depending upon the active behavior of the vision system. Under search behavior, high weights are set for color channel while keeping low weights for other shape-based features because the target could be in an arbitrary size or orientation in the given input. Under track behavior other feature channels also gain high weight because the target has to match strict criteria. The resultant TD saliency $\gamma_i(t)$ of a region R_i at time t is computed as follows

$$\gamma_i(t) = \sum_{}^{\forall f \in \Phi} \left(W_{td}^{f} \gamma_i^{f} \right) / \sum_{}^{\forall f \in \Phi} W_{td}^{f}$$

Resultant of BU saliency is obtained as $\beta_i(t)$ for which details can be seen in [21]. The function P combines the BU and TD saliency maps to produce the final conspicuity map. The active behavior again plays an important role at this step by adjusting weights of these two maps. Under explore behavior the major emphasis remains on the BU map while during other behaviors, like search or track, high weight goes to the TD channel. Denoting the behavior dependant weight for TD map as W_{td}^{b} and for BU map as W_{bu}^{b}, the final saliency $S^i(t)$ of each R_i at time t is given as

$$S^i(t) = \left(W_{bu}^{b} \beta_i(t) + W_{td}^{b} \gamma_i(t) \right) / \left(W_{bu}^{b} + W_{td}^{b} \right)$$

3.3 Inhibition Using Saccadic Memory

After having attended a region at time $t - 1$, the saliency value of that region with respect to each feature f is inhibited for use at time t. Instead of using an inhibition map as done by existing methods we use a memory oriented mechanism. As our application area is mobile active vision systems, previously attended locations may get relocated in subsequent frames of input. We propose to put the attended regions into a spatial inhibition memory M_{inh}^{s} able to remember p regions. An item is inserted into M_{inh}^{s} as M_{k}^{s} where the age k is set to 1 for freshly arrived item and the older entries get an increment in their values of k on arrival of a new item. In order to deal with the problem of relocation of regions in context of the view-frame, we use the world coordinates of the regions calculated using the head angles and the position of regions within the view-frame.

We apply the inhibition right after formulation of region saliency in order to make the model efficient. We take the time at which the freshly arriving regions get their saliency as $t-1$ and the time after going through the inhibition process as t. Hence, at time t, for each R_i with BU and TD saliency values with respect to a feature f, represented as $\beta_i^f(t)$ and $\gamma_i^f(t)$ respectively, are updated from $\beta_i^f(t-1)$ and $\gamma_i^f(t-1)$ as follows:

$$\beta_i^f(t) = \delta_1^k \beta_i^f(t-1) \text{ when } D^s(R_i, M_k^s) < r^{inh} \forall k \in \{1..p\}$$
$$\gamma_i^f(t) = \delta_2^k \gamma_i^f(t-1) \text{ when } D^s(R_i, M_k^s) < r^{inh} \forall k \in \{1..p\}$$

where r^{inh} is the radius in which inhibition takes effect and $D^s(R_i, M_k^s)$ is the spatial distance between the considered region R_i and the region in the memory location M_k^s. δ_1^k and δ_2^k are inhibition factors both having a value between 0 and 1. The value of δ_1^k becomes closer to 1 as the age of M_k^s increases, hence suppression on recently attended items is stronger than the older ones. δ_2^k remains the same for all items in the memory because under TD attention, such as search, once the target is found at a location then that location has to be strongly inhibited during the next few saccades of further search.

4   Results

Experiments were performed to test the search capabilities of the proposed method by using three scenarios. In each scenario the search target was given to the system in form of an image containing the isolated target over a blank background. In the current status the system is able to work with single regions at a time rather than composite objects hence the system picks the largest region from the picture of the target as the region to search. The first scenario of experiments was the search in static scenes in which the attention mechanism was allowed to mark as many occurrences of the target as possible. These experiments tested the ability of the system to select all relevant locations. Figure 2(a) reflects this scenario with the search field as a still scene viewed through the camera of the mobile vision system available in our laboratory and four occurrences the target (a dull blue box) in the scene. In the second scenario a simulated vision system was set into motion and it was required to mark the locations matching the search target one location per frame. This scenario was useful to test the ability of inhibition of return in dynamic scenes. Figure 2(b) represents this scenario in the simulation framework developed in our group [24]. In the third scenario the attention mechanism was required to perform overt attention

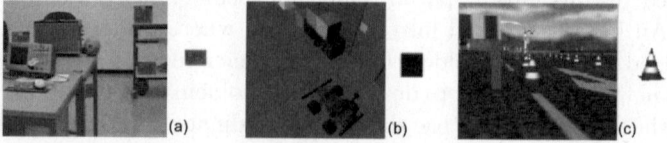

Fig. 2. Samples from visual input used in experiments. (a) Search field and target used as static scenario (b) Search environment and target used for dynamic scene scenario (c) Search environment and target used to test overt attention.

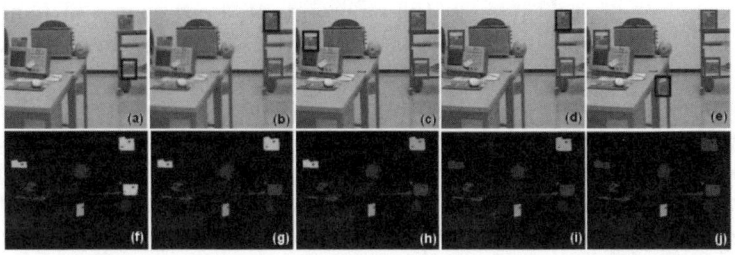

Fig. 3. Top row: Fixated (black) and inhibited (blue) locations for static scenario given in figure 2(a). Bottom row: Top-down saliency maps at time of each fixation.

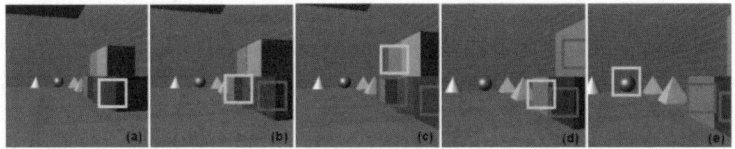

Fig. 4. Fixated (yellow) and inhibited (blue) locations for dynamic scenario given in figure 2(b)

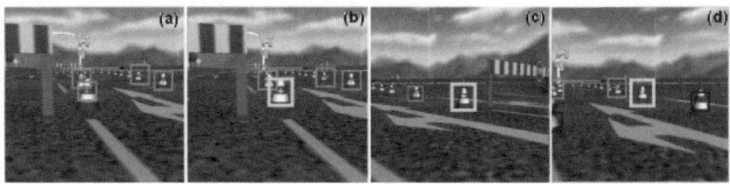

Fig. 5. Target locations brought into center of camera view (yellow), salient locations (green), and inhibited locations (blue) for overt attention scenario given in figure 2(c)

to the best matching location by bringing the target into center of camera view. Hence one selection per saccade was allowed. These experiments tested the ability of the system to locate the (estimated) position of the search target in three dimensional space. Figure 2(c) shows a sample input for this scenario.

Figure 3 demonstrates output of attentional search for the test case given in figure 2(a). Results of first five fixations by the attention system ($t = 1$ to $t = 5$) are reported here. The current focus of attention is marked with a black rectangle while blue rectangles are drawn at the inhibited locations. It may be noted that the four target locations are marked in the first five fixations in which the extra fixation is due to a repeated saccade on an object that had such a high top-down saliency that it still remained higher than the fourth object, which had relatively less similarity with the target, even after inhibition. This aspect can be noticed in the saliency maps provided in the second row of figure 3. Results of search in a dynamic scene performed by the vision system in motion are shown in figure 4.

The occurrences of the target in the environment, both shown in figure 2(b), are marked by the vision system working in the simulation framework. After fixating on the best matches, the system tries to pick target locations even when they have less similarity with the target, for example, the later fixations are done based only upon color similarity. Figure 5 demonstrates the results of overt attention in which the vision system maneuvers its camera head to bring the search target into to fovea area (center of view). Salient locations are marked with green rectangles, the attended locations brought into the center of view with yellow, and inhibited ones with blue.

5   Evaluation and Conclusion

In order to quantitatively evaluate the performance of our model, we carried out experiments using some specially designed visual data apart from the visual input consisting of natural and virtual reality images. Five occurrences of a predefined search target were embedded in each test image that contained distractors offering quantified amount of complexity. In the simplest case, as shown in images labeled as 1 and 1-D in figure 6, the distractors possessed high difference of features (Color, orientation, and size) from the target. The rest of the samples were created using different combinations of feature differences as shown in table 1 where H represents a high difference from target and L stands for low difference, hence the inputs labeled 8 and 8-D offer the maximum amount of complexity. The samples labeled as 1-D to 8-D contain extra distractors possessing high bottom-up saliency and the occurrences of the targets were distorted by introducing gradually rising blur (increasing from right to left in each image).

Table 1. Feature differences between target and distractors used for figure 6

Image label	1 / 1-D	2 / 2-D	3 / 3-D	4 / 4-D	5 / 5-D	6 / 6-D	7 / 7-D	8 / 8-D
Color	H	H	H	H	L	L	L	L
Orientation	H	H	L	L	H	H	L	L
Size	H	L	H	L	H	L	H	L

A comparison of attentional search models is given in [12] using the criteria of time taken and number of fixations to reach the target. Similarly [10] uses the average hit number to reach the target as a measure of search efficiency. Evaluation of our model in terms of these two metrics using the test cases given in figure 6 is shown in figure 7. The proposed model was able to locate the search target in the first fixation in all experiments (hence, 1 fixation per search). Average time to fixate on the first target location was 23.6 milliseconds in these evaluation experiments while average search time in the natural images was 69.3 ms on Linux based 3 Ghz Pentium 4 machine. This time includes segmentation and feature computation processes. None of the distractors possessing high BU saliency were fixated in all experiments. The time reported by [12] for an average search is 1.1 seconds on Linux based dual Opteron machine with minimum 2.2

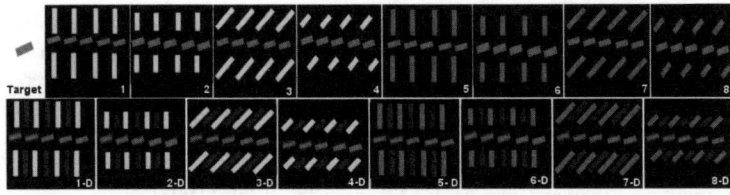

Fig. 6. Search target and sample input, having distractors offering different levels of complexity, used for quantitative evaluation

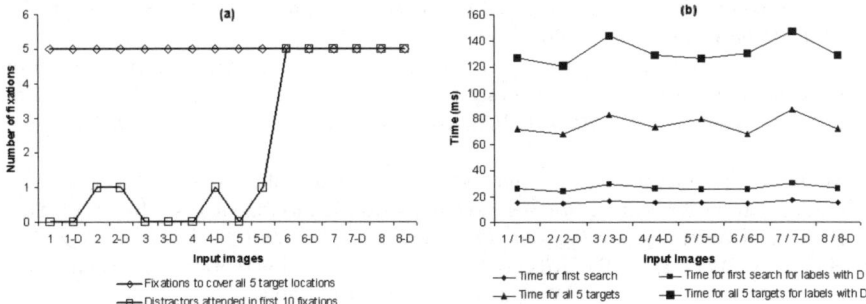

Fig. 7. Results of experiments using evaluation data given in figure 6

GHz clock speed while they have reported the average search time of the model of [7] to be 1.43 seconds on the same machine. In terms of fixations per search, the model of [7] has an average of 4.03, [12] has 2.73, and [10] has reported an average of 1.45 in best cases and 3.39 in worst cases.

It may be concluded that the region-based methodology with the innovation of constructing the fine-grain saliency maps separate from the bottom-up maps, using the concepts taken from the recent literature on research in natural visual attention, is an efficient and robust alternative to the existing approaches. The proposed method is also immune to bottom-up saliency of distractors in every feature channel and does not require any tuning of parameters or adjusting of weights. The memory based inhibition mechanism has also shown success in static as well as dynamic scenarios.

References

1. Lanyon, L., Denham, S.: A model of object-based attention that guides active visual search to behaviourally relevant locations. In: Paletta, L., Tsotsos, J.K., Rome, E., Humphreys, G.W. (eds.) WAPCV 2004. LNCS, vol. 3368, pp. 42–56. Springer, Heidelberg (2005)
2. Laar, P., Heskes, T., Gielen, S.: Task-dependent learning of attention. Neural Networks 10, 981–992 (1997)
3. Hamker, F.H.: Modeling attention: From computational neuroscience to computer vision. In: Paletta, L., Tsotsos, J.K., Rome, E., Humphreys, G.W. (eds.) WAPCV 2004. LNCS, vol. 3368, pp. 118–132. Springer, Heidelberg (2005)

4. Deco, G.: The computational neuroscience of visual cognition: Attention, memory and reward. In: Paletta, L., Tsotsos, J.K., Rome, E., Humphreys, G.W. (eds.) WAPCV 2004. LNCS, vol. 3368, pp. 100–117. Springer, Heidelberg (2005)
5. Navalpakkam, V., Itti, L.: Top-down attention selection is fine-grained. Journal of Vision 6, 1180–1193 (2006)
6. Itti, L., Koch, U., Niebur, E.: A model of saliency-based visual attention for rapid scene analysis. Transactions on PAMI 20, 1254–1259 (1998)
7. Itti, L., Koch, C.: A saliency based search mechanism for overt and covert shifts of visual attention. Vision Research, pp. 1489–1506 (2000)
8. Navalpakkam, V., Itti, L.: Modeling the influence of task on attention. Vision Research, pp. 205–231 (2005)
9. Navalpakkam, V., Itti, L.: Optimal cue selection strategy. In: NIPS 2006, pp. 1–8. MIT Press, Cambridge (2006)
10. Frintrop, S., Backer, G., Rome, E.: Goal-directed search with a top-down modulated computational attention system. In: Kropatsch, W.G., Sablatnig, R., Hanbury, A. (eds.) DAGM 2005. LNCS, vol. 3663, pp. 117–124. Springer, Heidelberg (2005)
11. Michalke, T., Gepperth, A., Schneider, M., Fritsch, J., Goerick, C.: Towards a human-like vision system for resource-constrained intelligent cars. In: ICVS 2007, Bielefeld University eCollections, Germany, pp. 264–275 (2004)
12. Hawes, N., Wyatt, J.: Towards context-sensitive visual attention. In: Second International Cognitive Vision Workshop (ICVW 2006) (2006)
13. Tagare, H.D., Toyama, K., Wang, J.G.: A maximum-likelihood strategy for directing attention during visual search. Transactions on PAMI 23, 490–500 (2001)
14. Peters, R.J., Itti, L.: Beyond bottom-up: Incorporating task-dependent influences into a computational model of spatial attention. In: CVPR 2007, IEEE, Los Alamitos (2007)
15. Sun, Y., Fischer, R.: Object-based visual attention for computer vision. Artificial Intelligence 146, 77–123 (2003)
16. Backer, G., Mertsching, B., Bollmann, M.: Data- and model-driven gaze control for an active-vision system. Transactions on PAMI 23, 1415–1429 (2001)
17. Aziz, M.Z., Mertsching, B., Shafik, M.S., Stemmer, R.: Evaluation of visual attention models for robots. In: ICVS 2006, IEEE, New York (2006) index–20
18. Aziz, M.Z., Mertsching, B.: Color segmentation for a region-based attention model. In: 12. Workshop Farbbildverarbeitung (FWS 2006), pp. 74–83 (2006)
19. Aziz, M.Z., Mertsching, B.: Color saliency and inhibition in region based visual attention. In: WAPCV 2007, Hyderabad, India, pp. 95–108 (2007)
20. Aziz, M.Z., Mertsching, B.: Fast and robust generation of feature maps for region-based visual attention. In: IEEE Transactions on Image Processing (2008)
21. Aziz, M.Z., Mertsching, B.: Pop-out and IOR in static scenes with region based visual attention. In: WCAA-ICVS 2007, Bielefeld University eCollections (2007)
22. Aziz, M.Z., Mertsching, B.: Region-based top-down visual attention through fine grain color map. In: 13 Workshop Farbbildverarbeitung (FWS 2007), pp. 83–92 (2007)
23. Aziz, M.Z., Mertsching, B.: Color saliency and inhibition using static and dynamic scenes in region based visual attention. In: Attention in Cognitive Systems. LNCS (LNAI), vol. 4840, pp. 234–250 (2007)
24. Kutter, O., Hilker, C., Simon, A., Mertsching, B.: Modeling and Simulating Mobile Robots Environments. In: 3rd International Conference on Computer Graphics Theory and Applications (GRAPP 2008) (2008)

Integration of Visual and Shape Attributes
for Object Action Complexes

K. Huebner, M. Björkman, B. Rasolzadeh, M. Schmidt, and D. Kragic

KTH – Royal Institute of Technology, Stockholm, Sweden
Computer Vision & Active Perception Lab
{khubner,celle,babak2,schm,danik}@kth.se
http://www.csc.kth.se/cvap

Abstract. Our work is oriented towards the idea of developing cognitive capabilities in artificial systems through Object Action Complexes (OACs) [7]. The theory comes up with the claim that objects and actions are inseparably intertwined. Categories of objects are not built by visual appearance only, as very common in computer vision, but by the actions an agent can perform and by attributes perceivable. The core of the OAC concept is constituting objects from a set of attributes, which can be manifold in type (e.g. color, shape, mass, material), to actions. This twofold of attributes and actions provides the base for categories. The work presented here is embedded in the development of an extensible system for providing and evolving attributes, beginning with attributes extractable from visual data.

Keywords: Cognitive Vision, Object Action Complexes, Object Attribution.

1 Introduction

In cognitive systems, like we want robots to become, representation of objects plays a major role. A robot's local world is built by objects that are ought to be recognized, classified, interpreted or manipulated. Though also *things*, as untreated basic sensory features, might help for some of these tasks, the semantic representation of an *object* seems to be more intuitive. Nevertheless, the question arises what makes an object an object, what makes Peter's cup being Peter's cup? There has been plenty of research on this issue, most of which concentrates on example-based recognition of objects by learned features, may they be visual or shape-based. In such systems, Peter's cup has been shown to the robot and can thus be recognized again. However, this does not make the robot identify arbitrary cups it has never seen before.

Due to this demerit of model-based recognition, another approach which is focussed on the functionalities or affordances of objects is motivated. Peter's cup will not only be Peter's cup, because the color or the texture of the specific instance has been learned, but because the concept of attributes (e.g. *solid, hollow*) shall be learned to be connected to a set of actions (e.g. *pick up, fill, drink*). Peter's cup is solid, it can stand stable and it is hollow so it can keep coffee, and is mainly used for filling or drinking. Maybe each other object that holds the same attributes can also be used as a 'drinking device' or 'filling device', which humans might name a cup. However, the 'filling device' property

A. Gasteratos, M. Vincze, and J.K. Tsotsos (Eds.): ICVS 2008, LNCS 5008, pp. 13–22, 2008.

is alone more general and allows Peter to put in flowers, which would make one name it a vase instead. Technically, these attributes can be various in type, e.g. color, shape and mass. While color might be perceived by visual processes only, interaction greatly supports the recognition of shape by vision, e.g. in case of hollowness. Mass probably is an attribute that is perceivable by strong interaction with the object only. On the other hand, attributes can be a result of higher-level reasoning, e.g. that the cup is full or empty. This line of argument from attributes and actions to objects is formalized into an upcoming concept, the Object Action Complexes (OACs). We refer to [7] on the theory of OACs and the formalization of objects and actions, while we here present a system which is able provide a variety of attributes from visual sensory input to support OACs. We link to several fields of research that relate to our work.

1.1 Cognitive Vision Systems

One of the major requirements of a cognitive robot is to continuously acquire percep- tual information to successfully execute mobility and manipulation tasks [5,13,17]. The most effective way of performing this is if it occurs in the context of a specific task. This was, for a long time, and still is the major way of thinking in the field of robotics. Focus is usually put on the on task-specific aspects when processing sensor data which may reduce the overall computational cost as well as add to the system robustness. However, in most cases this leads to the development of special-purpose systems that are neither scalable nor flexible. Thus, even if significant progress has been achieved, from the view of developing a general system able to perform various tasks in domestic environments, research on autonomous manipulation is still in its embriotic stage.

In this work, we treat the development of active vision paradigms and their relation of how to exploit both kinematic and dynamic regularities of the environment. Early work recognized that a robot has the potential to examine its world using causality, by performing probing actions and learning from the response [11]. Visual cues were used to determine what parts of the environment were physically coherent through in- terplay of objects, actions and imitations. Our interest is very similar, but geared to the development of a more advanced vision system necessary for such an application.

[16] examines the problem of object discovery defined as autonomous acquisition of object models, using a combination of motion, appearance and shape. The authors discuss that object discovery is complicated due to the lack of a clear definition of what constitutes an object. They state that rather than trying for an all-encompassing definition of an object that would be difficult or impossible to apply, a robot should use a definition that identifies objects useful for it. From the perspective of the object- fetching robot, useful objects would be structures that can be picked up and carried. Similar line of thinking is pursued in our work, while we go one step forward by also extracting a set of object attributes that can be used for manipulation purposes or further learning of object properties in future work.

Such a system has been presented in [15] with an objective of learning visual con- cepts. The main goal is to learn associations between automatically extracted visual features and words describing the scene in an open-ended, continuous manner. Unfor- tunately, the vision system is very simple and the experimental evaluation is performed with homogeneous objects of simple and easy distinguishable shapes.

In relation to representation of object properties, there is a close connection to *anchoring* [4] that connects, inside an artificial system, the symbol-level and signal-level representations of the same physical object. Although some nice ideas about the representations are proposed, there is no attempt of developing the underlying vision system necessary for extraction of symbols.

2 From Visual Sensors to Attributes

Our original system was purely top-down driven, with top-down information given in terms of visual search tasks [1]. These tasks were represented as precomputed models, typically one model for each possible requested object. Given a task the system scanned the environment for suitable new fixation points and at each visited such point the attended region was compared to the model corresponding to the task. Due to its dependence on precomputed models, the original system had a number of key weaknesses. It could not generalize beyond the scope of the models and it was unable to explore the environment so as to learn new models. The aim of the work presented here is to go beyond these limitations and open up for scenarios in which all objects are not necessarily known beforehand. The attentional system in Section 2.1 is based on top-down as well as bottom-up cues and can be tuned towards either exploration or visual search. With attention driven by generalizable attributes as explained in Section 2.3, rather than models of known objects, tasks can be expressed in more general terms.

As already introduced, our work is oriented towards the idea of Object Action Complexes (OACs). Categories of objects are not built by visual appearance only, as very common in computer vision, but by the actions an agent can perform, as also by attributes linked to them. This twofold of attributes and actions provides the base for categories, where even bins or vases might be seen as a cup in terms of the actions one can perform with them. In this context, our aim here is the development of an extensible system for providing and evolving early Object Action Complexes, beginning with attributes extractable from visual data in Section 2.1. After this, basic shape primitives are introduced by 3D segmentation in Section 2.2.

2.1 Visual Attributes from Attentional Cues

It has been suggested that objects present in a scene possess a certain intrinsic ranking or "interestingness" with regards to that scene. For a visual observer this means that a dynamic combination of both top-down (task-dependent) and bottom-up (scene-dependent) control is available for selecting and attending regions in the scene [14]. Salience-based models in computational attention became largely popular after the work of Koch and Ullman [9]. A topic of research has been in explaining, with a computational model, how the top-down mechanism works. Recent work in the field include models where top-down modulations of attention are learnt with an ART-network [2]. Another attempt has been to train a bottom-up attention model towards detection of particular target objects by displaying these objects in different backgrounds [12].

Our system uses a model similar to the VOCUS-model [6] which has a top-down tuned saliency map that can be "controlled" through a set of weights. Weights are

Fig. 1. Top row: Objects in use: car, giraffe, mug, dog, sugar box, peach can and mango can. Bottom row: Three exemplary visual attribute searches depicted by their saliency maps.

applied to each feature and conspicuity map used in the computation of the salience map. Four broadly tuned color channels (R, G, B and Y) calculated as in Itti's NVT model [10], an intensity map, and four orientation maps, computed by Gabor filters, are weighted individually. Following the original version, we create scale-space pyramids for all nine maps and form conventional center-surround differences by across-scale-subtraction, followed by normalization. This leads to the final conspicuity maps for intensity, color and orientation. As a final set of weight parameters we introduce one weight for each of these maps, constructing the final modulated top-down saliency map.

The purpose of the attentional system is twofold. First of all, attention is used to control the stereo head so that objects of interest are placed in the center of the visual field. The second purpose is to derive visual attributes to describe objects in scene, objects that can later be revisited and possibly manipulated. In the current version of the system, the visual attributes of an object are represented by the weights that make this object stand out in the top-down salience map (see Fig. 1). From previous searches for the object, weights are optimized through gradient descent, with the influence of context modelled using a neural network [14].

2.2   Shape Attribution from 3D Segmentation

3D Segmentation without Table Plane Assumption. Image data needs to be grouped into regions corresponding to possible objects in the 3D scene, for shape attributes to be extracted and manipulation performed. The attentional system, as described in Section 2.1, does no such grouping, it only provides hypotheses of where such objects may be located in image space. However, from binocular disparities the extent of hypotheses can be determined also in 3D space. Disparities can be considered as measurements in 3D space, clustered around points of likely objects. To find such clusters we applied a kernel-based density maximization method, known as Mean Shift [3]. Clustering is done in image and disparity space, using a 3D Gaussian kernel with a size corresponding to the typical 3D size of objects that can be manipulated. The maximization scheme is iterative and relies on initial center point estimates. As such estimates we use the hypotheses from the attentional system. Examples of segmentation results using this approach can be seen in the second row of Fig. 3.

The Mean Shift approach has a number of weaknesses that tend to complicate the extraction of shape attributes. First of all, the approximate size of objects has to be known. Elongated objects tend to be broken up into parts, typically on either side of the object. The most important weakness, however, is the fact that an object can not be reliably segregated from the surface it is placed on, if there is no evidence supporting such a segregation. Without any additional assumption on surface shape or appearance there is no way of telling the surface from the object. However, in many practical scenarios it might be known to the robotic system that objects of interest can in fact be expected to be located on flat surfaces, such as table tops.

3D Segmentation with Table Plane Assumption. As an alternative approach we therefore test a parallel solution, i.e. segmentation is done independently of the attentional system. The dominant plane in the image is the table top. Using a well-textured surface, it is possible to find the main plane and cut it with a 3D version of the Hough transform. Since the Hough transform requires relatively long computation time of a few seconds, we assume in this scenario that the setup, i.e. camera and table position, does not change. The plane has therefore only to be computed once and can be re-used afterwards. An additional advantage of this solution in contrast to online computation of the dominant plane is that 3D information of objects which greatly occlude the table will not effect the plane clipping. Following the table assumption the 3D points are mapped onto a 2D grid to easily find segments and basic attributes.

The result of transformation and clipping on the scene given in Fig. 2(a) can be seen in Fig. 2(b). The segmentation of objects is computed on the 2D grid with a simple region growing algorithm grouping pixels into larger regions by expanding them bottom up. The recursive algorithm uses an 8-neighborhood on the binary 2D grid. This procedure is depicted in Fig. 2(c). Since the grid is thereby segmented, simple shape-based attributes of each segment can be determined and the segments reprojected to 3D points or to the image plane (see Fig. 2(d)). Note that dilation has been applied for the reprojected segments for the later application of point-based object hypotheses verification. The dilation, the grid approach, as also noisy and incomplete data from stereo cause that reprojections are often little larger or not completely covering the bodies.

2.3   Attribution of Segments

Each of the produced segments is just a *thing* according to our definition, as the step to an *object* longs for semantics. One way to identify the semantics of a thing in order to derive an object is to link attributes to it. Attributes can be divided in two different groups, which are named intrinsic and extrinsic. Intrinsic attributes are object-centered and thereby theoretically viewpoint-independent (e.g. physical size, color, mass). Extrinsic attributes describe the viewpoint-dependent configuration of an object (e.g. position, orientation), which mostly is measured in the quantitative domain. In our system, the basic intrinsic attributes of covered area, length (along the dominant axis), width (perpendicular to the dominant axis) and height can be qualitatively determined for each segment. The discretization, i.e. if an object is *small* or *large* in size, is adapted to our table manipulation scenario at hand. Additionally, the centroid position of a

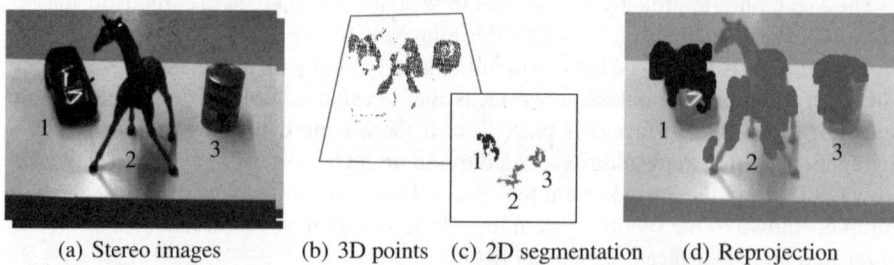

| (a) Stereo images | (b) 3D points | (c) 2D segmentation | (d) Reprojection |

Fig. 2. Segmentation under the table plane assumption. Disparity information from the stereo images (a) produces 3D points (b). Having defined the dominant plane, the points can be projected onto this plane, where distinctive segments are computed (c) and reprojected to the image (d).

segment is calculated. Its 3D point cloud is kept available for optional further application, e.g. shape approximation and grasping, as we proposed in [8].

3   Experimental Evaluation

Experiments are performed on a Yorick stereo head with four degrees of freedom: neck pan and tilt, and an additional tilt for each camera. The cameras used are 1.3 Mpixel cameras from Allied Vision. The head is controlled so that the cameras are always fixating on something in the center of view. Given commands from the attentional system, the fixation point can be changed through rapid gaze shifts, a process that takes about half a second. Since the extrinsic camera parameters are constantly in change, camera calibration is done on-line. The work presented here is integrated into an existing software system, modularized and containing modules for frame grabbing, camera calibration, binocular disparities, attention, foveated segmentation, recognition and pose estimation. Modules are implemented as CORBA processes that run concurrently, each module at a different speed. Using a 2.6 GHz dual dual-core Opteron machine, cameras are calibrated and disparities computed at a rate of 25 Hz, while foveated segmentation and recognition is done only upon request.

Based on the hypotheses produced by the attentional system from Section 2.1, we will validate these by introducing the segmentation information. As discussed in Section 2.2, segmenting with the table plane assumption can be made in parallel and initially independent of the attentional system. Results of six different scenarios of the segmentation are presented in Fig. 3. The plane was previously computed by using a textured table top in order to apply table clipping throughout the experiments. However, we removed the textured top to provide a clearer comparison of the two segmentation techniques we evaluated.

Although distortion and uncertainty in the disparity calculation clearly influence the results, it can be seen that segmentation in terms of 3D distinction of the objects in the scene works well in general. The errors arising, like oversegmentation (Fig. 3d), undersegmentation (Fig. 3e) or occlusion in height due to the vertical projection (Fig. 3f), can partially be solved by the attribution issues shown in Fig. 4. While the segmentation

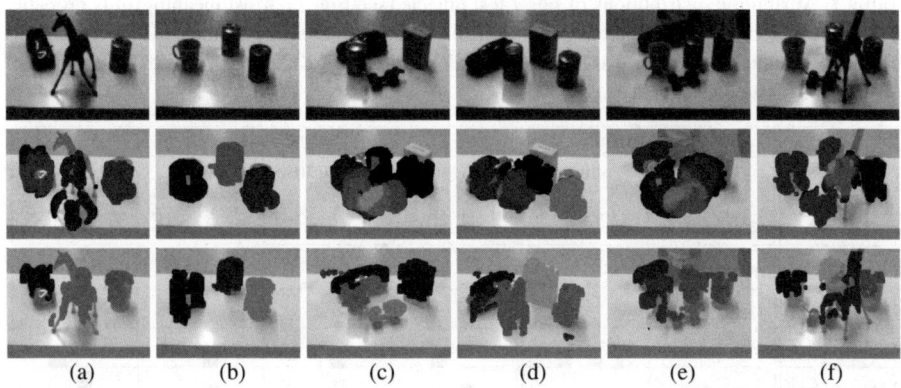

(a)   (b)   (c)   (d)   (e)   (f)

Fig. 3. Sample scenario segmentations (best viewed in color). Original images are shown in the first row. The second row shows results using the Mean Shift segmentation, the bottom row those using the table plane assumption (see Section 2.2). In the latter, (a) and (b) seem well segmented and in (c) there is just some noise at the table edge. Problems arise for (d)-(f): (d) two segments for the car, (e) one segment for two cans, and (f) the unnoticed dog underneath the giraffe.

presented in Fig. 3 (bottom row) depicts segments reprojected to the image plane, the important step inbetween has been the segmentation in the $2\frac{1}{2}$D table plane space. Here, also the attribution of segments, as presented in Section 2.3, takes place. As a simple and neat set, we only use the intrinsic attributes aligned in Tab. 1. The table also shows the distribution on how segments have been attributed along the sample scenarios. Note that the identification of a segment as a specific object has been performed manually to establish the distribution. Though the number of attributes is sparse and the quantification into four levels per attribute is coarse, one can detect differences and similarities of objects. While the car and the dog are mostly attributed *almost flat* (afl) in height, the cans and the mug are usually *medium high* (med) and the giraffe and the sugar box *high* (hig). Also note that the mango can, the mug and the peach can are attributed almost alike. This is quite reasonable, as they are very similar in the rough shape domain that we span with these four attributes.

3.1 Validation

We can now combine results of both visual and shape attribution. On the one hand, our set gives an extensible base for attribution of things to make them objects. The framework that takes care of the management of attribute sets and connecting them to actions is implemented as an extensible system. On the other hand, we can show in our practical experiment how an extended set of attributes improves the results of object interpretation. Three examples of such validations are shown in Fig. 4.

In Fig. 4(a), we focus on the visual attribute "car-like", i.e. on hypotheses that the attentional system rates similar to the car model in terms of color and gradients. As it can be seen, the top-ranked hypotheses are on the car in the image (left image). By combining this result with the segmentation, hypotheses can be grouped and also neglected (right image). Finally, five hypotheses fall in one segment. Comparing the shape

Table 1. Attribution distributions of our 7 test objects (see Fig. 1). Most meaningful is probably distribution of color and shape attributes. For the latter, checking the identity of the objects has been done manually over our 6 scenes (see Fig. 3); in brackets, each object carries the number of appearance along the sequence.

Object	Visual Attributes		Shape Attributes			
	Color	Orientation	Area	Length	Width	Height
	R G B Y	0° 45° 90° 135°	tin sml lrg hug	sht med lng vln	thn med wid vwd	afl med hig vhg
Car (4x)	(12,5,40,10)					
Dog (3x)	(35,22,11,13)					
Giraffe (2x)	(64,1,24,48)					
Mango (6x)	(12,60,21,23)					
Mug (2x)	(57,83,29,113)					
Peach (4x)	(13,8,15,12)					
Sugar (2x)	(28,6,2,14)					

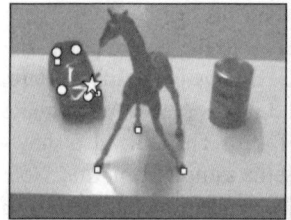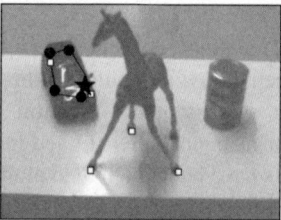

5 best 'car-like' in one segment.
shape: [lrg,med,med,afl]
→ very car-like (Tab. 1)

(a) *"Find the 'car'-like."* (source Fig. 3(a))

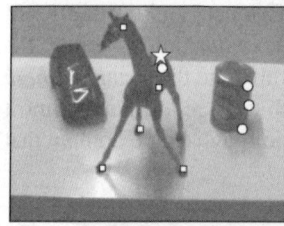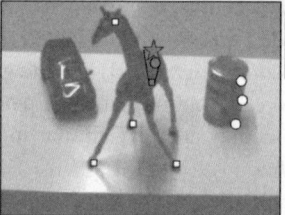

3 'dog-like' in one segment.
shape: [lrg,med,med,hig]
→ very dog-unlike (Tab. 1)

(b) *"Find the 'dog'-like."* (source Fig. 3(a))

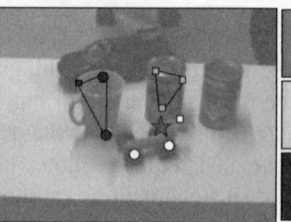

Best 'can-like' in one segment.
shape: [sml,sht,thn,afl]
→ quite can-unlike (Tab. 1)
3 'can-like' in one segment.
shape: [lrg,lng,med,med]
→ length not can-alike (Tab. 1)
3 'can-like' in one segment.
shape: [lrg,med,med,med]
→ very can-alike (Tab. 1)

(c) *"Find the 'mango can'-like."* (source Fig. 3(e))

Fig. 4. Top-level tasks corresponding to Fig. 1 (continued). Left: The 10 best hypotheses (star = best hypothesis, circles = hypotheses ranked 2-5, small squares = hypotheses ranked 6-10). Right: visual and shape attribute information is merged (connected and colored hypotheses).

attributes of this segment to the distribution shown in Tab. 1 clearly affirms that this segment corresponds to a car-like object. Note that the same process results in a negative response for example Fig. 4(b). We look for a "dog-like" object, though there is no dog in the image. While the attention returns ten hypotheses for this search, the shape attribute check clearly neglects that the only group of hypotheses corresponding to a segmented area is "dog-like". In Fig. 4(c), the process returns three selected segments. The first one with the strongest hypothesis from the visual attributes is declined by shape attributes again. Both the other segments are very similar and only differ in one shape attribute. However, the interesting result is that there are two objects, both the mango can and the mug, which are very "mango-can"-like. If one would aim at distinguishing between those, this might be approached by new attributes (e.g. more detailed shape and hollowness). On the other hand, both objects are truely can-like in terms of color and shape. Hence, they would fall in one category of actions performable on them in this example.

4 Conclusion

We presented a visual subsystem in which we integrated both visual and shape attributes towards the concept of OACs. The overall vision system in which we embed our attribute determination is more general and supports also other applications, as briefly proposed in Section 2.1. In this paper, we focus on the issue of meaningful attributes that constitute an object as opposed to a thing. While finding complex attributes like hollowness or emptiness is hard, very basic visual 2D and 3D attributes are collected by the system using common techniques. We are planning to include manipulation attributes, e.g. weight, by object interaction in future work. When a 'weight' detector is made available, its integration is simple, as the framework consists of a server database which holds an extensible set of attribute classes (e.g. height, size, color) and corresponding attribute instances (e.g. small, medium, large for size). The vision system client can access this server, ask for available attributes classes, as also insert or request a detected attribution, i.e. an object category. The system server can now reply if this attribution has been seen before. However, as we have not yet introduced manipulative capabilities in practice, the system is not yet able to connect attributions to actions, but offers a fundamental technique to produce the necessary attributes for issues of learning.

Besides the buildup of this system, the improvement of combining pure visual attributes with shape attributes has been exemplified. In our experiment, visual hypotheses were checked and tested according to shape attributes. Hereby, it is possible to neglect wrong hypotheses, to cluster and affirm the good ones, or even to distinguish between a car-like object and the plain image of it.

We also compared two types of 3D segmentation techniques for shape attribute generation. The specificity of our system towards table set scenarios with high camera view on the objects supports the table plane assumption. In particular, it has the advantages of a reference system (which is the table) and the hereby introduced spatial arrangement, as most objects are placed next to another than on one another on a table. If this assumption does not hold, manipulation might help by picking up or moving something around. Though the system was kept fixed in combination with an a-priori table plane detection here, our future goal is to dissolve this constraint by a 3D acceleration sensor on the camera head, linking the vertical gravity vector to mostly horizontal table planes.

Acknowledgments

This work was supported by EU through the project PACO-PLUS, IST-FP6-IP-027657.

References

1. Björkman, M., Eklundh, J.-O.: Foveated Figure-Ground Segmentation and Its Role in Recognition. In: British Machine Vision Conference, pp. 819–828 (2005)
2. Choi, S.B., Ban, S.W., Lee, M.: Biologically Motivated Visual Attention System using Bottom-Up Saliency Map and Top-Down Inhibition. Neural Information Processing - Letters and Review 2 (2004)
3. Comaniciu, D., Meer, P.: Mean Shift: A Robust Approach toward Feature Space Analysis. IEEE Transactions on Pattern Analysis and Machine Intelligence 24(5), 603–619 (2002)
4. Coradeschi, S., Saffiotti, A.: An Introduction to the Anchoring Problem. Robotics and Autonomous Systems, Special Issue on Perceptual Anchoring 43(2-3), 85–96 (2003)
5. Edsinger, A., Kemp, C.C.: Manipulation in Human Environments. In: IEEE/RSJ International Conference on Humanoid Robotics, pp. 102–109 (2006)
6. Frintrop, S.: VOCUS: A Visual Attention System for Object Detection and Goal-Directed Search. LNCS (LNAI), vol. 3899. Springer, Heidelberg (2006)
7. Geib, C., Mourao, K., Petrick, R., Pugeault, N., Steedman, M., Krüger, N., Wörgötter, F.: Object Action Complexes as an Interface for Planning and Robot Control. In: IEEE RAS International Conference on Humanoid Robots (2006)
8. Huebner, K., Ruthotto, S., Kragic, D.: Minimum Volume Bounding Box Decomposition for Shape Approximation in Robot Grasping. In: IEEE International Conference on Robotics and Automation (to appear 2008)
9. Koch, C., Ullman, S.: Shifts in Selective Visual Attention: Towards the Underlying Neural Circuitry. Human Neurobiology 4, 219–227 (1985)
10. Koch, C., Itti, L., Niebur, E.: A Model of Saliency-Based Visual Attention for Rapid Scene Analysis. Transactions on Pattern Analysis and Machine Intelligence 20, 1254–1259 (1998)
11. Metta, G., Fitzpatrick, P.: Better Vision Through Experimental Manipulation. In: 2nd International Workshop on Epigenetic Robotics: Modeling Cognitive Development in Robotic Systems, vol. 11, pp. 109–128 (2002)
12. Navalpakkam, V., Itti, L.: Sharing Resources: Buy Attention, Get Recognition. In: International Workshop on Attention and Performance in Computer Vision (2003)
13. Neo, E.S., Sakaguchi, T., Yokoi, K., Kawai, Y., Maruyama, K.: Operating Humanoid Robots in Human Environments. In: Workshop on Manipulation for Human Environments, Robotics: Science and Systems (2006)
14. Rasolzadeh, B.: Interaction of Bottom-Up and Top-Down Influences for Attention in an Active Vision System. Master's thesis, KTH – Royal Institute of Technology, Stockholm, Sweden (2006)
15. Skočaj, D., Berginc, G., Ridge, B., Štimec, A., Jogan, M., Vanek, O., Leonardis, A., Hutter, M., Hewes, N.: A System for Continuous Learning of Visual Concepts. In: International Conference on Computer Vision Systems (ICVS 2007) (2007)
16. Southey, T., Little, J.J.: Object Discovery using Motion, Appearance and Shape. In: AAAI Cognitive Robotics Workshop (2006)
17. Sutton, M., Stark, L., Bowyer, K.: Function from Visual Analysis and Physical Interaction: A Methodology for Recognition of Generic Classes of Objects. Image and Vision Computing 16, 746–763 (1998)

3D Action Recognition and Long-Term Prediction of Human Motion

Markus Hahn, Lars Krüger, and Christian Wöhler

Daimler AG Group Research
Environment Perception
P.O. Box 2360, D-89013 Ulm, Germany
{Markus.Hahn,Lars.Krueger,Christian.Woehler}@daimler.com

Abstract. In this contribution we introduce a novel method for 3D trajectory based recognition and discrimination between different working actions and long-term motion prediction. The 3D pose of the human hand-forearm limb is tracked over time with a multi-hypothesis Kalman Filter framework using the Multiocular Contracting Curve Density algorithm (MOCCD) as a 3D pose estimation method. A novel trajectory classification approach is introduced which relies on the Levenshtein Distance on Trajectories (LDT) as a measure for the similarity between trajectories. Experimental investigations are performed on 10 real-world test sequences acquired from different viewpoints in a working environment. The system performs the simultaneous recognition of a working action and a cognitive long-term motion prediction. Trajectory recognition rates around 90% are achieved, requiring only a small number of training sequences. The proposed prediction approach yields significantly more reliable results than a Kalman Filter based reference approach.

Keywords: 3D tracking, action recognition, cognitive long-term prediction.

1 Introduction

Today, industrial production processes in car manufacturing worldwide are characterised by either fully automatic production sequences carried out solely by industrial robots or fully manual assembly steps where only humans work together on the same task. Up to now, close collaboration between human and machine is very limited and usually not possible due to safety concerns. Industrial production processes can increase efficiency by establishing a close collaboration of humans and machines exploiting their unique capabilities. A safe interaction between humans and industrial robots requires vision methods for 3D pose estimation, tracking, and recognition of the motion of both human body parts and robot parts. To be able to detect a collision between the human worker and the industrial robot there is a need for reliable long-term prediction (some tenths of a second) of the motion. This paper addresses the problem of tracking and recognising the motion of human body parts in a working environment. The results of action recognition are used for the long-term prediction of complex motion patterns.

A. Gasteratos, M. Vincze, and J.K. Tsotsos (Eds.): ICVS 2008, LNCS 5008, pp. 23–32, 2008.

Our 3D tracking and recognition system consists of three main components: the camera system, the model based 3D tracking system, and the trajectory based recognition system. The input images are captured at 20 fps with a trinocular grey scale camera at VGA resolution.

2 Related Work

Previous work in the field of human motion capture and recognition is extensive, Moeslund et al. [11] give a detailed introduction and overview. Bobick and Davis [3] provide another good introduction. They classify human motion using a temporal template representation from a set of consecutive background subtracted images. A drawback of this approach is the dependency on the viewpoint.

Li et al. [10] use Hidden Markov Models (HMMs) to classify hand trajectories of manipulative actions and take the object context into account. In [4] the motion of head and hand features are used to recognise Tai Chi gestures by HMMs. Head and hand are tracked with a real time stereo blob tracking algorithm. HMMs are used in many other gesture recognition systems due to their ability to probabilistically represent the variation in the training data. However, in an application with only a small amount of training data and the need for a long-term prediction of the motion, HMMs are not necessarily the best choice.

A well known approach is the one by Black and Jepson [2], who present an extension of the CONDENSATION algorithm and model gestures as temporal trajectories of the velocity of the tracked hands. They perform a fixed sized linear template matching weighted by the observation densities. Fritsch et al. [6] extend their work by incorporation of situational and spatial context. Both approaches merely rely on 2D data. Hofemann [8] extends the work of Fritsch et al. [6] to 3D data by using a 3D body tracking system. The features used for recognition are the radial and vertical velocities of the hand with respect to the torso.

Croitoru et al. [5] present a non iterative 3D trajectory matching framework that is invariant to translation, rotation, and scale. They introduce a pose normalisation approach which is based on physical principles, incorporating spatial and temporal aspects of trajectory data. They apply their system to 3D trajectories for which the beginning and the end is known. This is a drawback for applications processing a continuous data stream, since the beginning and end of an action is often not known in advance.

3 The 3D Tracking System

We rely on the 3D pose estimation and tracking system introduced in [7], which is based on the Multiocular Contracting Curve Density algorithm (MOCCD). A 3D model of the human hand-forearm limb is used, made up by a kinematic chain connecting the two rigid elements forearm and hand. The model consists of five truncated cones and one complete cone. Fig. 1(a) depicts the definition of the cones by nine parameters. The 3D point $\mathbf{p}_1$ defines the beginning of the forearm. The wrist position $\mathbf{p}_2$ is computed based on the orientation of the forearm

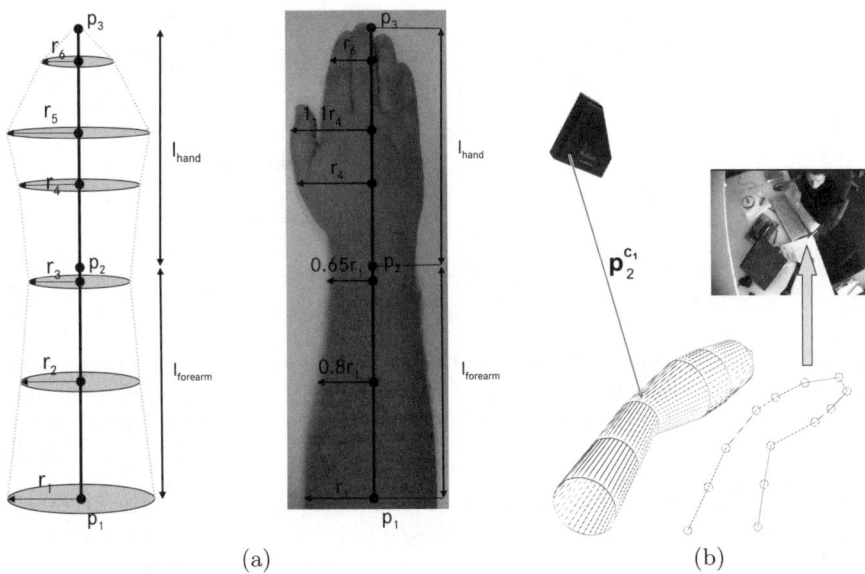

(a)   (b)

Fig. 1. (a) Definition of the model cones and the dependencies of the radii derived from human anatomy. (b) Extraction and projection process of the 3D contour model.

and its predefined length l_{forearm}. The computation of the 3D point $\mathbf{p}_3$ in the fingertip is similar. The radii of the cones are derived from human anatomy, see Fig. 1(a) (right). As the MOCCD algorithm adapts a model curve to the image, the silhouette of the 3D model in each camera coordinate system is extracted and projected into the camera images (Fig. 1(b)). The MOCCD algorithm fits the parametric curve to multiple calibrated images by separating the grey value statistics on both sides of the projected curve.

To start tracking, a coarse initialisation of the model parameters at the first timestep is required. In the tracking system we apply three instances of the MOCCD algorithm in a multi-hypothesis Kalman Filter framework. Each MOCCD instance is associated with a Kalman Filter and each Kalman Filter implements a different kinematic model, assuming a different object motion. The idea behind this kinematic modelling is to provide a sufficient amount of flexibility for changing hand-forearm motion. It is required for correctly tracking reversing motion, e.g. occurring during tightening of a screw. A Winner-Takes-All component selects the best-fitting model at each timestep. For a more detailed description refer to [7].

4   Recognition and Prediction System

The working action recognition system is based on a 3D trajectory matching approach. The tracking stage yields a continuous data stream of the 3D position

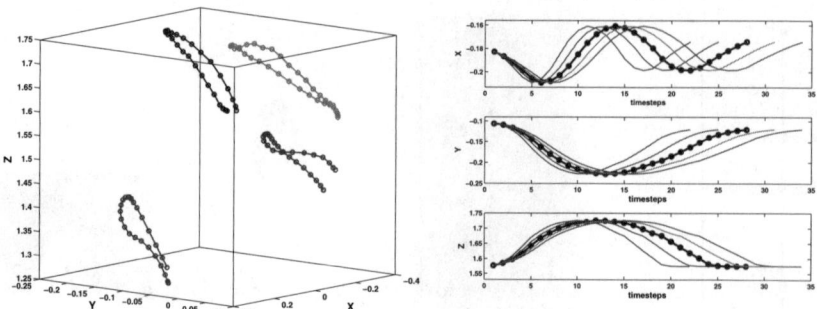

Fig. 2. Left: 3D reference trajectories of the working action class "tightening". Right: Time scaling (-20% (green), -10%(red), ±0% (blue), +10% (cyan), +20% (magenta)) of the blue (upper left) 3D reference trajectory. All 3D coordinates are depicted in mm.

of the tracked 3D hand-forearm limb. Our trajectories are given by the 3D motion of the wrist point $\mathbf{p}_2$. A sliding window is used to match the sequence of 3D points with a set of hypotheses generated from labelled reference trajectories.

4.1 Determining the Reference Trajectories

In contrast to other previously presented approaches [3], our system relies on a small number of reference trajectories. They are defined by manually labelled training sequences. The beginning and the end of a reference action are manually determined and the resulting 3D trajectory is stored with the assigned class label. To cope with different working speeds, the defined reference trajectories are scaled in the temporal domain (from -20% to +20% of the total trajectory length) using an Akima interpolation [1]. Fig. 2 (left) shows example 3D trajectories of the working action class "tightening". In Fig. 2 (right) time scaled reference trajectories are depicted.

After labelling and temporal scaling of the reference trajectories, we construct a set of M model trajectories $\left\{\mathbf{m}^{(i)}, i = 1, \cdots, M \right\}$, which are used to generate and verify trajectory hypotheses in the recognition and prediction process.

4.2 Recognition Process

In our system the beginning and the end of a trajectory are not known a priori, which is different from the setting regarded in [5]. To allow an online trajectory matching on the continuous data stream we apply a sliding window approach which enables us to perform a working action recognition and simultaneously a long-term prediction of the human motion patterns. In contrast to the probabilistic method of [2] we deterministically match a set of pre-defined non-deformable reference trajectories (Sec. 4.1) over time and discriminate between the different classes of reference trajectories.

In a preprocessing step, noise and outliers in the trajectory data are reduced by applying a Kalman Filter based smoothing process [5]. The kinematic model

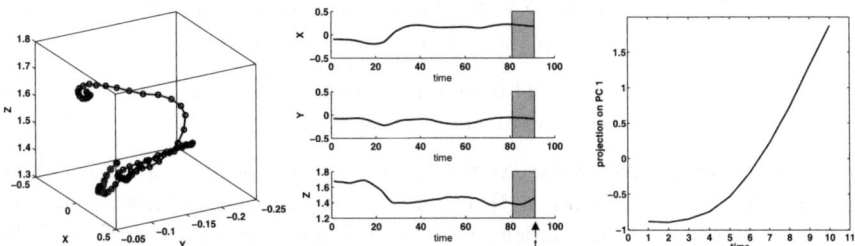

Fig. 3. Left: Smoothed 3D input trajectory, the values in the current sliding window are red, all other blue. Middle: 3D data for each coordinate and a sliding window of length 10 frames. Right: PCA normalised data in the sliding window.

of the Kalman Filter is a constant-velocity model. Fig. 3 depicts the smoothed 3D trajectory, the current sliding window of size $W = 10$ frames, and the values in the sliding window normalised by a whitened Principal Component Analysis (PCA). The 3D data are projected only on the first principal component (PC 1), since the energy of the first eigenvector is always above 90%.

Our sliding window approach consists of five essential operations: (i) generate trajectory hypotheses, (ii) verify hypotheses, (iii) delete hypotheses, (iv) classify remaining hypotheses, and (v) use a hypothesis for a long-term prediction of the 3D motion.

Generate Trajectory Hypotheses: At timestep t we compare the current input trajectory $\mathbf{Z}_t$,

$$\mathbf{Z}_t = \left[(X_{(t-W+1)}, Y_{(t-W+1)}, Z_{(t-W+1)})^T, \ldots, (X_t, Y_t, Z_t)^T \right] , \qquad (1)$$

consisting of the last W elements of the continuous data stream, with the first W elements of all reference trajectories. The compared trajectories always have the same length W and are matched with the 3D trajectory matching approach described in Sec. 4.3. The trajectory matching returns a similarity value for the two compared trajectories. If this value is smaller than a threshold Θ_{sim} the reference trajectory is assigned to the set of hypotheses and the current matching phase ϕ in the reference trajectory is set to $(W + 1)/N$. Every hypothesis is characterised by a current phase ϕ, $0 \leq \phi \leq 1$, within the reference trajectory of length N. The sub-trajectory, defined by phase ϕ and length W, aligns the model data with the current input data in the sliding window. The next essential operation is to verify the generated hypotheses and move the sliding window within the model trajectory.

Verify Trajectory Hypotheses: In this step all trajectory hypotheses, generated at timestep $(t - 1)$ or earlier, are verified. The 3D data $\mathbf{Z}_t$ in the current sliding window is matched with the current sub-trajectory in all hypothesis trajectories. The current sub-trajectory in a hypothesis trajectory is defined by its phase ϕ and length W. If the 3D trajectory matching approach (Sec. 4.3) returns a similarity value smaller than Θ_{sim}, the hypothesis is kept and the current phase ϕ

in the model is incremented by $1/N$. If a hypothesis does not pass the verification step, the no-match counter γ of the hypothesis is incremented by one.

Delete Trajectory Hypotheses: This operation deletes all hypotheses for which the no-match counter exceeds a threshold Θ_{noMatch}.

Classify Remaining Hypotheses: At timestep t we search all hypotheses which have a phase ϕ of more than a threshold Θ_{recog}. If there is more than one hypothesis and different class labels are present, the no-match counter γ and the sum of all similarity values during the matching process are used to determine the winning reference trajectory. After the decision the last N elements of the input trajectory are labelled with the class label of the winning reference trajectory of total length N.

Cognitive Prediction: The action recognition result is used for a long-term prediction ("cognitive prediction"). At timestep t we search all hypotheses which having a phase ϕ of more than a threshold Θ_{pred}. For all hypotheses found we predict the 3D position k timesteps ahead based on the underlying reference trajectory. Accordingly, the phase $(\phi + k/N)$ in the reference trajectory is projected on the first principal component (PC 1) based on the PCA transformation of the current sliding window in the reference trajectory. This transformed value is then projected to a 3D point by applying the inverse PCA transformation of the input data $\mathbf{Z}_t$ in the sliding window. In the case of multiple significant hypotheses, the effective prediction is given by the mean of all predicted 3D points. Typical cognitive prediction results are shown in Fig. 5.

4.3   3D Trajectory Matching

In this section we describe our 3D trajectory matching algorithm, which is used in the recognition process (Sec. 4.2) to determine the similarity between an input trajectory and a reference trajectory. Our trajectory matching approach consists of two stages: First, we compare the travelled distances along both trajectories. Then, in the second stage, we apply the Levenshtein Distance on Trajectories (LDT) to determine a similarity value. In this framework, a 3D trajectory $\mathbf{T}$ of length N is defined as

$$\mathbf{T} = \left[(X_1, Y_1, Z_1)^T, \ \ldots, (X_N, Y_N, Z_N)^T \right] \quad . \tag{2}$$

The travelled distance $TD(\mathbf{T})$ along the trajectory $\mathbf{T}$ is given by:

$$TD(\mathbf{T}) = \sum_{t=2}^{N} \| \mathbf{T}_t - \mathbf{T}_{(t-1)} \| \quad . \tag{3}$$

In the first stage we assume that two trajectories $\mathbf{S}$ and $\mathbf{T}$ are similar if the travelled distances of both trajectories $TD(\mathbf{S})$ and $TD(\mathbf{T})$ are similar. If $\mathbf{S}$ and $\mathbf{T}$ have a similar travelled distance they are PCA normalised and matched with the Levenshtein Distance on Trajectories (LDT). If they have no similar travelled distance the process stops at this first stage and returns the maximum length of both trajectories.

Normalisation: In our application we rely on a small number of reference trajectories extracted from a small number of training sequences. It is possible that the same working action is performed at different positions in 3D space, e.g. tightening a screw at different locations of an engine. Therefore the normalisation step should achieve an invariance w.r.t. translation, rotation, and scaling. Hence we apply a whitened PCA, which ensures the required invariances. Since we use a sliding window technique, the length of the matched trajectories is small, thus we project the data only on the first principal component (PC 1), defined by the most significant eigenvector, as the energy of PC 1 is always above 90 %. In the next step the trajectory based similarity measure is computed.

Levenshtein Distance on Trajectories (LDT): At this point, we introduce a new similarity measure for trajectories by extending the Levenshtein distance [9]. The Levenshtein distance $LD(S_1, S_2)$ is a string metric which measures the number of edit operations (insert, delete, or replace) that are needed to convert string S_1 into S_2. We extend this approach to d-dimensional trajectories by using the following algorithm:

```
int LDT(trajectory S[1..d,1..m], trajectory T[1..d,1..n], matchingThresh)
   // D is the dynamic matrix with m+1 rows and n+1 columns
   declare int D[0..m, 0..n]
   for i from 0 to m   D[i, 0] := i
   for j from 1 to n   D[0, j] := j

   for i from 1 to m
       for j from 1 to n
           if(L2Norm(S[1..d,i] - T[1..d,j]) < matchingThresh)
               then subcost := 0
               else subcost := 1
           D[i, j] := min(D[i-1, j] + 1,         // deletion
                          D[i, j-1] + 1,         // insertion
                          D[i-1, j-1] + subcost)// substitution
   return D[m, n]
```

$LDT(\mathbf{S}, \mathbf{T})$ returns the number of edit operations required to transform $\mathbf{S}$ into $\mathbf{T}$ and offers the capability to handle local time shifting. The matching threshold maps the Euclidean distance between two pairs of elements to 0 or 1, which reduces the effect of noise and outliers. Fig. 4 depicts a PCA normalised reference trajectory, an input trajectory, and the point correspondences between the trajectories. In this example the number of edit operations to transform the reference trajectory into the input trajectory is two.

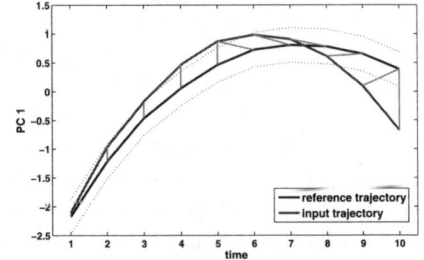

Fig. 4. PCA normalised reference trajectory (blue), the matching borders (dotted), a PCA normalised input trajectory (red) and the point correspondences (green) between both trajectories. The required number of edit operations is two.

Table 1. Action recognition results

Action	Training Trajectories (#)	Test Trajectories (#)	Recognised (%)
tightening a screw	4	36	92
transfer motion	6	54	89
plugging	2	18	89

5 Experimental Investigations

The system is evaluated by analysing 10 trinocular real-world test sequences acquired from different viewpoints. These sequences contain working actions performed by five different test persons in front of a complex cluttered working environment. Each sequence contains at least 900 image triples. The mean distance of the test persons to the camera system varies from 1.5m to 2m. Each sequence contains the actions listed in Table 1. All actions are performed with the right hand. The actions were shown to the test persons by a teacher in advance. All sequences were robustly and accurately tracked at virtually all timesteps with our 3D tracking system described in Sec. 3. Similar to [6] we incorporate spatial context for the actions "tightening" and "plugging", since it is known where the worker has to tighten the screw and to place the plug and these positions are constant during the sequence. The 3D positions of the screws and holes are obtained from the 3D pose of the engine, which was determined by bundle adjustment [12] based on the four reference points indicated in Fig. 5. We utilise the following thresholds defined in Sec. 4: $\Theta_{sim} = 3$, $\Theta_{noMatch} = 3$, and $\Theta_{recog} = 0.9$. In the experiments we assume that if the system recognises the class "tightening" at two consecutive timesteps, the worker tightens a screw. As can be seen from Table 1, the system achieves recognition rates around 90% on the test sequences. The recognition errors can be ascribed to tracking errors and motion patterns that differ in space and time from the learned motion patterns. Higher recognition rates may be achieved by using more training sequences, since the scaling in the temporal domain of the reference trajectories is not necessarily able to cope with the observed variations of the motion patterns. Our recognition rates are similar to those reported by Croitoru et al. [5] and Fritsch et al. [6]. Croitoru et al. use segmented 3D trajectories in their experiments, which is different from our approach. Fritsch et al. [6] rely on 2D data and their method is not independent of the viewpoint.

An additional experiment was performed to determine the accuracy of the long-term prediction ($k = 5$, corresponding to 0.25 s). We utilise $\Theta_{pred} = 0.6$ as a prediction threshold. As a ground truth for this experiment, we use the results of the 3D tracking system. Table 2 shows the mean and standard deviation of the Euclidean distance between the long-term prediction result and the ground truth for all test sequences. The values in Table 2 are plotted in millimetres for the proposed cognitive prediction approach and a Kalman Filter with a constant-velocity model as a reference method. As can be seen from Table 2, our long-term prediction achieves more reliable results than the Kalman Filter method. While the mean deviations are smaller about one third the random fluctuations, represented by the standard deviation are reduced by a factor of about 2 by our approach. Especially

Table 2. Long-term prediction results

Name	mean dist	mean dist KF	std dist	std dist KF
Kia2	61	77	32	55
Markus1	79	105	50	94
Markus2	90	118	63	101
Markus3	71	86	34	64
Stella1	63	89	33	63
Stella2	86	113	58	106
Lars1	66	81	43	86
Lars2	60	93	40	88
Christian1	67	89	35	75

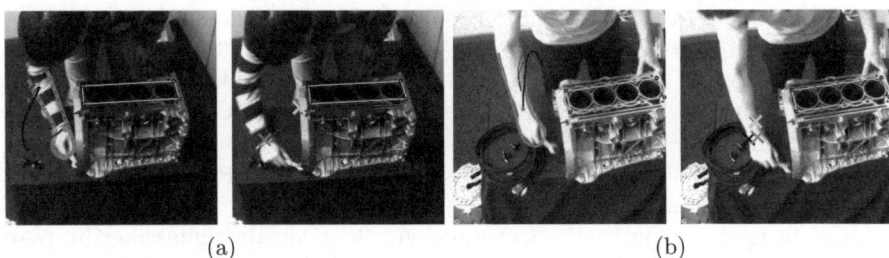

(a)   (b)

Fig. 5. Cognitive prediction results for reversing motion (a) and transfer motion (b). In (a) and (b), the left image shows the input image at timestep t with the adapted hand-forearm model (green) and the trajectory (blue: transfer motion; red: tightening; cyan: unknown). The right image shows the image at timestep $t + 5$ with the ground truth position of the wrist (green cross), the cognitive prediction result (red or blue cross, depending on the action), and the Kalman Filter result with constant velocity model (yellow cross). The four linked points are reference points on the engine.

for reversing motion, e.g. while tightening a screw or plugging, the proposed prediction technique is highly superior to the Kalman Filter (cf. Fig. 5).

6   Summary and Conclusion

We have introduced a method for 3D trajectory based action recognition and long-term motion prediction. Our approach allows a classification and discrimination between different working actions in a manufacturing environment. The trajectory classification relies on a novel similarity measure, the Levenshtein Distance on Trajectories (LDT). Our experimental investigations, regarding 10 long real-world test sequences, have shown that our recognition system achieves recognition rates around 90%, requiring only a small number of training trajectories. The proposed trajectory recognition method is viewpoint independent. Intermediate results of the action recognition stage are used for the long-term prediction of complex motion patterns. This cognitive prediction approach yields metrically more accurate results than a Kalman Filter based reference approach.

Future work may involve online learning of reference trajectories and the integration of HMMs, provided that an adequate number of training sequences are available.

References

[1] Akima, H.: A new method of interpolation and smooth curve fitting based on local procedures. Journal of the Association for Computing Machinery 17(4), 589–602 (1970)

[2] Black, M.J., Jepson, A.D.: A probabilistic framework for matching temporal trajectories: Condensation-based recognition of gestures and expressions. In: Burkhardt, H.-J., Neumann, B. (eds.) ECCV 1998. LNCS, vol. 1406, pp. 909–924. Springer, Heidelberg (1998)

[3] Bobick, A.F., Davis, J.W.: The recognition of human movement using temporal templates. IEEE Trans. Pattern Anal. Mach. Intell. 23(3), 257–267 (2001)

[4] Campbell, L.W., Becker, D.A., Azarbayejani, A., Bobick, A.F., Pentland, A.: Invariant features for 3-d gesture recognition. In: FG 1996: Proceedings of the 2nd International Conference on Automatic Face and Gesture Recognition (FG 1996), Washington, DC, USA, p. 157. IEEE Computer Society Press, Los Alamitos (1996)

[5] Croitoru, A., Agouris, P., Stefanidis, A.: 3d trajectory matching by pose normalization. In: GIS 2005: Proceedings of the 13th annual ACM international workshop on Geographic information systems, Bremen, Germany, pp. 153–162. ACM Press, New York (2005)

[6] Fritsch, J., Hofemann, N., Sagerer, G.: Combining sensory and symbolic data for manipulative gesture recognition. In: Proc. Int. Conf. on Pattern Recognition, vol. 3, pp. 930–933. IEEE, Cambridge (2004)

[7] Hahn, M., Krüger, L., Wöhler, C., Gross, H.-M.: Tracking of human body parts using the multiocular contracting curve density algorithm. In: 3DIM 2007: Proceedings of the Sixth International Conference on 3-D Digital Imaging and Modeling, Washington, DC, USA, pp. 257–264. IEEE Computer Society Press, Los Alamitos (2007)

[8] Hofemann, N.: Videobasierte Handlungserkennung für die natürliche Mensch-Maschine-Interaktion. Dissertation, Universität Bielefeld, Technische Fakultät (2007)

[9] Levenshtein, V.I.: Binary codes capable of correcting deletions, insertions, and reversals. Soviet Physics Doklady 10(8), 707–710 (1966)

[10] Li, Z., Fritsch, J., Wachsmuth, S., Sagerer, G.: An object-oriented approach using a top-down and bottom-up process for manipulative action recognition. In: Franke, K., Müller, K.-R., Nickolay, B., Schäfer, R. (eds.) DAGM 2006. LNCS, vol. 4174, pp. 212–221. Springer, Heidelberg (2006)

[11] Moeslund, T.B., Hilton, A., Krüger, V.: A survey of advances in vision-based human motion capture and analysis. Computer Vision and Image Understanding 104(2), 90–126 (2006)

[12] Triggs, B., McLauchlan, P.F., Hartley, R.I., Fitzgibbon, A.W.: Bundle adjustment - a modern synthesis. In: ICCV 1999: Proceedings of the International Workshop on Vision Algorithms, pp. 298–372. Springer, London (2000)

Tracking of Human Hands and Faces through Probabilistic Fusion of Multiple Visual Cues

Haris Baltzakis[1], Antonis Argyros[1,2], Manolis Lourakis[1], and Panos Trahanias[1,2]

[1] Foundation for Research and Technology – Hellas,
Heraklion, Crete, Greece
[2] Department of Computer Science, University of Crete,
Heraklion, Crete, Greece
{xmpalt,argyros,lourakis,trahania}@ics.forth.gr

Abstract. This paper presents a new approach for real time detection and tracking of human hands and faces in image sequences. The proposed method builds upon our previous research on color-based tracking and extends it towards building a system capable of distinguishing between human hands, faces and other skin-colored regions in the image background. To achieve these goals, the proposed approach allows the utilization of additional information cues including motion information given by means of a background subtraction algorithm, and top-down information regarding the formed image segments such as their spatial location, velocity and shape. All information cues are combined under a probabilistic framework which furnishes the proposed approach with the ability to cope with uncertainty due to noise. The proposed approach runs in real time on a standard, personal computer. The presented experimental results, confirm the effectiveness of the proposed methodology and its advantages over previous approaches.

1 Introduction

Real time segmentation of human hands and faces in image sequences is a fundamental step in many vision systems, including systems designed for tasks such as human-computer and human-robot interaction, video-enabled communications, visual surveillance, etc. A variety of approaches have been employed to achieve this task. Several of them rely on the detection of skin-colored areas [1,2,3,4]. The idea behind this family of approaches is to build appropriate color models of human skin and then classify image pixels based on how well they fit to these color models. On top of that, various segmentation techniques are used to cluster skin-colored pixels together into solid regions that correspond to human hands and/or human faces.

A second family of approaches tries to differentiate between static and moving regions based on background subtraction techniques [5,6,7,8]. These techniques involve the calculation of a background model and the comparison (subtraction) of each new frame against this model. Human parts and/or other non-static objects are extracted by thresholding the result.

Both families of approaches have advantages and disadvantages: color based approaches generally work better on constant lighting and predictable background

A. Gasteratos, M. Vincze, and J.K. Tsotsos (Eds.): ICVS 2008, LNCS 5008, pp. 33–42, 2008.

conditions but are unable to distinguish between skin-colored human body parts and similarly-colored objects in the background. On the other hand, background subtraction techniques are not suitable for applications requiring a moving camera. Moreover, depending on the application at hand, additional processing may be required to further-process foreground regions and/or utilize additional information cues in order to distinguish humans from other moving objects and/or distinguish human hands or faces [9,10,11].

In this paper we build upon our previous research on color-based, multiple objects tracking [3]. Based on this, we propose a broader probabilistic framework that allows the utilization of additional information cues (image background model, expected spatial location, velocity and shape of the detected and tracked segments) to efficiently detect and track human body parts, classify them into hands and faces, and avoid problems caused by the existence of skin-colored objects in the image background. Thus, contrary to other color based approaches, the proposed approach operates effectively in cluttered backgrounds that contain skin-colored objects. All information cues are combined by means of a graphical model (bayes network) which provides a clean mathematical formalism that makes it possible to explicitly model the probabilistic relationships among the involved quantities.

The proposed approach runs in real time on a conventional personal computer. Experimental results presented in this paper, confirm the effectiveness of the proposed methodology and its advantages over our previous approach.

The rest of the paper is organized as follows. For completeness purposes, Section 2 provides an overview of the existing approach to color based tracking, on which the new, proposed approach is based. In Section 3 the proposed approach and its individual components are presented in detail. Experimental results are presented in Section 4. Finally, in Section 5, conclusions and hints for future work are given.

2   The Skin-Color Based Tracker

The proposed approach, builds on our previous research on color-based tracking of multiple skin-color regions [3]. According to this approach, tracking is facilitated by three processing layers.

2.1   Processing Layer 1: Assign Probabilities to Pixels

Within the first layer, the input image is processed in order to estimate and assign likelihood values to pixels for depicting skin colored regions like human hands and faces. Assuming that S is a binary random variable that indicates whether a specific pixel depicts skin and C is the random variable that indicates the color of this pixel and c is a perceived color, the probability $P(S=1|C=c)$ can be estimated according to the Bayes law as:

$$P(S=1|C=c) = \frac{P(C=c|S=1)P(S=1)}{P(C=c)} \qquad (1)$$

C is assumed to be two dimensional and discrete, i.e. encoding the Y and U components of the YUV color space within $[0..255]^2$. In the above equation, $P(S=1)$ and $P(C=c)$

are the prior probabilities of a pixel depicting skin and of a pixel having a specific color c, respectively. $P(C{=}c|S{=}1)$ is the conditional probability of a pixel having color c, given that it depicts skin. All these three probabilities are computed off-line during a separate training phase. A procedure for on-line adaptation of these three priors is also described in [3].

2.2 Processing Layer 2: From Pixels to Blobs

This layer applies hysteresis thresholding on the probabilities determined at layer 1. These probabiliies are initially thresholded by a "strong" threshold T_{max} to select all pixels with $P(S{=}1|C{=}c) > T_{max}$. This yields high-confidence skin pixels that constitute the seeds of potential skin-colored blobs. A second thresholding step, this time with a "weak" threshold T_{min}, along with prior knowledge with respect to object connectivity to form the final blobs. During this step, image points with probability $P(S{=}1|C{=}c) > T_{min}$ where $T_{min} < T_{max}$, that are immediate neighbours of skin-colored image points are recursively added to each blob.

A connected components labeling algorithm is then used to assign different labels to pixels that belong to different blobs. Size filtering on the derived connected components is also performed to eliminate small, isolated blobs that are attributed to noise and do not correspond to meaningful skin-colored regions.

Finally, a feature vector for each blob is computed. This feature vector contains statistical properties regarding the spatial distribution of pixels within the blob and will be used within the next processing layer for data association.

2.3 Processing Layer 3: From Blobs to Object Hypotheses

Within the third and final processing layer, blobs are assigned to object hypotheses which are tracked over time. Tracking over time is realized through a scheme which can handle multiple objects that may move in complex trajectories, occlude each other in the field of view of a possibly moving camera and whose number may vary over time. To achieve this goal, appropriate hypothesis management techniques ensure: (a) the generation of new hypotheses in cases of unmatched evidence (unmatched blobs), (b) the propagation and tracking of existing hypotheses in the presence of multiple, potential occluding objects and (c) the elimination of invalid hypotheses (i.e. when tracked objects disappear from the scene of view).

3 Proposed Approach

As with our previous approach, the proposed approach is organized into three layers as well. These layers are depicted in Fig. 1 and are in direct correspondence with the ones described in the previous section. A major difference is that the first layer is completely replaced by a new layer that implements the pixel model that will be described in the following section. This new pixel model allows the computation of probabilities for human hands and faces instead of skin. That is, distinguishing between hands and faces is facilitated directly from the first layer of the architecture proposed in this paper.

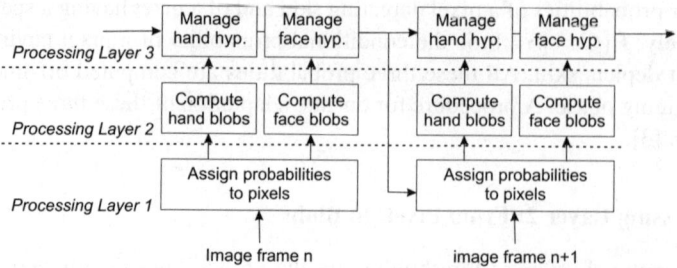

Fig. 1. Block diagram of the proposed approach. Processing is organized into three layers.

The second and the third layers consist of the same components as the ones used in [3]. However, they are split into two different parallel processes, the first being responsible for managing hand blobs and hypotheses and the second for managing face blobs and hypotheses. Another notable difference between our previous approach and the current one is signified by the top-down dependence of the 1st processing level of frame $n + 1$ from the 3rd processing layer of frame n (see Fig. 1). This dependence is essentially responsible for bringing high-level information regarding object hypotheses down to the pixel level.

In the following section, we will emphasize to the new approach for realizing the fist processing layer of Fig. 1 which constitutes the most important contribution of this paper. Details regarding the implementation of the other two layers can be found in [3].

3.1 Notation

Let $\mathcal{U}$ be the set of all pixels of an image. Let $\mathcal{M}$ be the subset of $\mathcal{U}$ corresponding to foreground pixels (i.e a human body) and $\mathcal{S}$ be the subset of $\mathcal{U}$ containing pixels that are skin colored. Accordingly, let $\mathcal{H}$ and $\mathcal{F}$ stand for the sets of pixels that depict human hands and faces, respectively. The relations between the above mentioned sets are illustrated in the Venn diagram in Fig. 2(a). Notice the convention that both $\mathcal{F}$ and

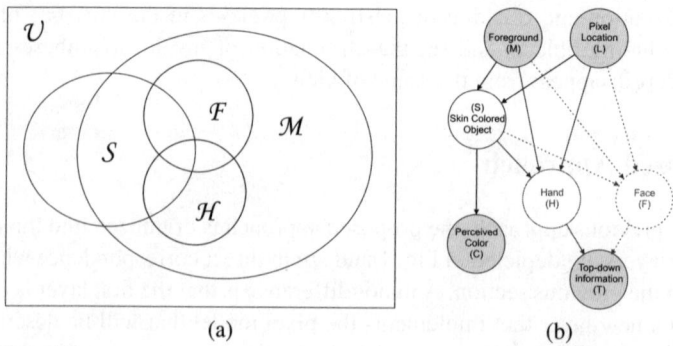

(a)   (b)

Fig. 2. The proposed approach. (a) Venn diagram representing the relationship between the pixel sets $\mathcal{U}$, M, S, H and F. (b) The proposed Bayes net.

$\mathcal{H}$ are assumed to be subsets of $\mathcal{M}$ (i.e all pixels depicting hands and faces belong to the foreground). It is also important that $\mathcal{F}$ and $\mathcal{H}$ are not mutually exclusive, i.e. a foreground pixel might belong to a hand, to a face or to both (i.e in the case of occlusions). Last but not least, the model does not assume that all hands and face pixels are skin-colored.

3.2   The Pixel Model

Let M, S, F and H be binary random variables (i.e taking values in $\{0, 1\}$), indicating whether a pixel belongs to set $\mathcal{M}$, $\mathcal{S}$, $\mathcal{F}$ and $\mathcal{H}$, respectively. Let L be the 2D location vector containing the pixel image coordinates and let T be a variable that encodes a set of features regarding the currently tracked hypotheses. Note that the source of this piece of information lies in the third processing layer, i.e. the layer that is responsible for the management and the tracking of face and hand hypotheses over time, hence this piece of information traverses the model in a 'top-down" direction.

The goal is to compute whether a pixel belongs to a hand and/or a face, given (a) the color c of a single pixel, (b) the information m on whether this pixel belongs to the background (i.e. $M=m$) and, (c) the values l, t of L and T, respectively. More specifically, we need to estimate the conditional probabilities $P_h = P(H=1|C=c, T=t, L=l, M=m)$ and $P_f = P(F=1|C=c, T=t, L=l, M=m)$.[1]

To perform this estimation, we use the Bayesian network shown in Fig. 2(b). The nodes of the graph are random variables that represent degrees of belief on particular aspects of the problem. The edges are parameterized by conditional probability distributions that represent dependencies between the involved variables. A notable property of the network of Fig. 2(b) is that if $P(H)$ and $P(F)$ are assumed to be independent, then the network can be decomposed into two different networks one for the computation of hand probabilities and the other for face probabilities. The first one corresponds to what remains from Fig. 2(b) when the red dotted components are excluded and the second one is the one with the blue components excluded.

Regarding the hands, we know that:

$$P(H=1|c, t, l, m) = \frac{P(H=1, c, t, l, m)}{P(c, t, l, m)} \tag{2}$$

By marginalizing the numerator over both possible values for S and the denominator over all four possible combinations for S and H (the values of S and H are expressed by the summation indices s and h, respectively), Eq. (2) can be expanded as:

$$P_h = \frac{\displaystyle\sum_{s \in \{0,1\}} P(H=1, s, c, t, l, m)}{\displaystyle\sum_{s \in \{0,1\}} \sum_{h \in \{0,1\}} P(h, s, c, t, l, m)} \tag{3}$$

---

[1] Note that capital letters are used to indicate variables and small letters to indicate specific values for these variables. For brevity, we will also use the notation $P(x)$ to refer to probability $P(X=x)$ where X any of the above defined variables and x a specific value of this variable.

By applying the chain rule of probability and by taking advantage of variable independence as the ones implied by the graph of Fig. 2(b), we easily obtain:

$$P(h, s, c, t, l, m) = P(m)P(l)P(t|h)P(c|s)P(s|l, m)P(h|l, s, m) \qquad (4)$$

Finally, by substituting to Eq. (2), we obtain:

$$P_h = \frac{P(t|H=1) \sum_{s \in \{0,1\}} P(c|s)P(s|l, m)P(H=1|l, s, m)}{\sum_{h \in \{0,1\}} P(t|h) \sum_{s \in \{0,1\}} P(c|s)P(s|l, m)P(h|l, s, m)} \qquad (5)$$

Similarly, for the case of faces, we obtain:

$$P_f = \frac{P(t|F=1) \sum_{s \in \{0,1\}} P(c|s)P(s|l, m)P(F=1|l, s, m)}{\sum_{f \in \{0,1\}} P(t|f) \sum_{s \in \{0,1\}} P(c|s)P(s|l, m)P(f|l, s, m)} \qquad (6)$$

Details regarding the estimation of the individual probabilities that appear in Eq. (5) and in Eq. (6) are provided in the following paragraphs.

Foreground segmentation. It can be easily verified that when $M = 0$ (i.e. a pixel belongs to the background), the numerators of both Eq. (5) and Eq. (6) become zero as well. This is because, as already mentioned, hands and faces have been assumed to always belong to the foreground. This convention simplifies computations because Equations (5) and (6) should only be evaluated for foreground pixels.

In order to compute M, we apply the background subtraction technique proposed by Stauffer and Grimson [6,7] that employs an adaptive Gaussian mixture model on the background color of each image pixel. The number of Gaussians, their parameters and their weights in the mixture are computed online.

The color model. $P(c|s)$ is the probability of a pixel being perceived with color c given the information on whether it belongs to skin or not. This probability is the same as the one in Eq. (1) and can be obtained off-line through a separate training phase with the procedure described in [3]. The result is encoded in the form of two two-dimensional look-up tables; one table for skin-colored objects ($s = 1$) and one table for all other objects ($s = 0$). The rows and the columns of both look-up tables correspond to the Y and U dimensions of the YUV color space.

Top-down information. In this work, for each tracked hypothesis, a feature vector t is generated which is propagated in a "top-down" direction in order to further assist the assignment of hand and face probabilities to pixels at processing layer 1. The feature vector t consists of two different features:

1. The average vertical speed v of the hypothesis, computed as the vertical component of the speed of the centroid of the ellipse modeling the hypothesis. The rationale behind the selection of this feature is that hands are expected to exhibit considerable average vertical speed v compared to other skin colored regions such as heads.

2. The ratio r of the perimeter of the hypothesis contour over the circumference of a hypothetical circle having the same area as the area of the hypothesis. The rationale behind the selection of this feature is that hands are expected to exhibit high r compared to faces. That is, $r = \frac{1}{2}\rho/\sqrt{\pi\alpha}$, where ρ and α are the length of the hypothesis contour and the area, respectively.

Given v and r, $P(t|h)$ and $P(t|f)$ are approximated as:

$$P(t|h) \approx P(v|h)P(r|h) \tag{7}$$
$$P(t|f) \approx P(v|f)P(r|f) \tag{8}$$

In our implementation, all $P(v|h)$, $P(r|h)$, $P(v|f)$ and $P(r|f)$ are given by means of one-dimensional look-up tables that are computed off-line, during training. If there is more than one hypothesis overlapping with the specific pixel under consideration, the hypothesis that yields maximal results is chosen separately for $P(t|h)$ and $P(t|f)$. Moreover, if there is no overlapping hypothesis at all, all of the conditional probabilities of Equation (7) are substituted by the maximum values of their corresponding look-up tables.

The spatial distribution model. A spatial distribution model for skin, hands and faces is needed in order to evaluate $P(s|l, m)$, $P(h|l, s, m)$ and $P(f|l, s, m)$. All these three probabilities express prior probabilities that can be obtained during training and stored explicitly for each each location L (i.e for each image pixel). In order to estimate these probabilities, a set of eight different quantities are computed off-line during a training phase. These quantities are depicted in Table 1 and indicate the number of foreground pixels found in the training sequence for every possible combination of s and h or f. As discussed in Section 3.2, only computations for foreground pixels are necessary. Hence, all training data correspond to $M = 1$. We can easily express $P(s|l, M{=}1)$,

Table 1. Quantities estimated during training for the spatial distribution model

h=0				h=1			
$f = 0$		$f = 1$		$f = 0$		$f = 1$	
$s = 0$	$s = 1$	$s = 0$	$s = 1$	$s = 0$	$s = 1$	$s = 0$	$s = 1$
s_{000}	s_{001}	s_{010}	s_{011}	s_{100}	s_{101}	s_{110}	s_{111}

$P(h|l, s, M{=}1)$ and $P(f|l, s, M{=}1)$ in terms of the eight quantities of Table 1.

$$P(s|l, M{=}1) - \frac{P(s, M{=}1, l)}{P(M{=}1, l)} = \frac{s_{00s} | s_{01s} + s_{10s} + s_{11s}}{s_{000} + s_{001} + s_{010} + s_{011} + s_{100} + s_{101} + s_{110} + s_{111}} \tag{9}$$

Similarly:

$$P(h|l, s, M{=}1|) = \frac{P(h, s, M{=}1, l)}{P(s, M{=}1, l)} = \frac{s_{h0s} + s_{h1s}}{s_{00s} + s_{01s} + s_{10s} + s_{11s}} \tag{10}$$

$$P(f|l, s, M{=}1|) = \frac{P(h, s, M{=}1, l)}{P(s, M{=}1, l)} = \frac{s_{0fs} + s_{1fs}}{s_{00s} + s_{01s} + s_{10s} + s_{11s}} \tag{11}$$

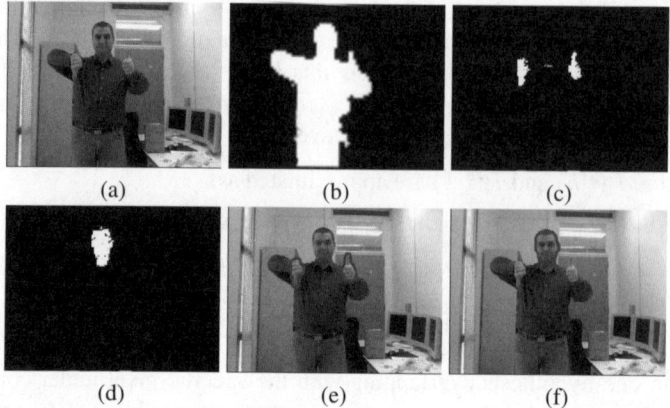

Fig. 3. The proposed approach in operation. (a) original frame, (b) background subtraction result, (c),(d) pixel probabilities for hands and faces, (e),(f) contours of hand and face hypotheses.

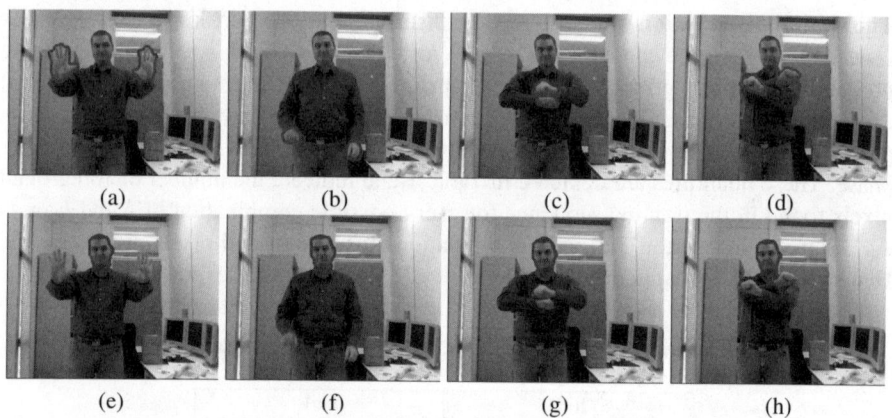

Fig. 4. Four frames for a sequence depicting a man performing gestures in an office environment (a,b,c,d) hand hypotheses, (e,f,g,h) face hypotheses

4   Results and Discussion

The proposed approach has been assessed using several video sequences containing people performing various gestures in indoor environments. Several videos of example runs are available on the web[2].In this section we will present results obtained from a sequence depicting a man performing a variety of hand gestures. The resolution of the sequence is 320×240 and it was obtained with a standard, low-end web camera at 30 frames per second. Figure 4 depicts various intermediate results obtained at different stages of the proposed approach. A frame of the test sequence is shown in Fig. 4(a).

---

[2] http://http://www.ics.forth.gr/ xmpalt/research/bayesfuse/index.html

Figure 4(b) depicts the result of the background subtraction algorithm, i.e $P(M)$. In order to achieve real-time performance, the background subtraction algorithm operates at down-sampled images of dimensions 160×120.

Figures 4(c) and 4(d) depict P_h and P_f i.e. the results of the first processing layer of the proposed approach. The contours of the blobs that correspond to hand and face hypotheses are shown in Figures 4(e) and 4(f), respectively. As can verified, the algorithm manages to correctly identify both hands and the face of the depicted man. Notice also that, in contrast to what would happen with the original tracking algorithm of [3], the skin-colored books are not detected.

Figure 4 shows additional four frames out of the same sequence. Figures on the left column depict the resulting hand hypotheses, while figures on the right column depict face hypotheses. In all cases, the proposed approach has been successful in correctly identifying the face and the hands of the person. The presented results were obtained at a standard 3GHz personal computer which was able to process images of size 320×240 at 30Hz.

5   Summary

We have presented an approach for visual detection and tracking of human faces and hands. The proposed approach builds on our previous research on color-based, skin-color tracking and extends it towards building a system capable of distinguishing between human hands, faces and other skin-colored regions in the background. This is achieved by the exploitation of additional information cues including motion information as well as spatial location, velocity and shape of detected and tracked objects. All information cues are combined under a probabilistic framework which furnishes the proposed approach with the ability to cope with uncertainty due to noise. Experimental results presented in this paper, confirm the effectiveness of the proposed approach. The resulting system combines the tracking robustness of the approach presented in [3] together with the new capability of discriminating hands from faces. Additionally, the proposed system is not influenced by the presence of skin-colored background objects. These features, together with the maintained real-time performance characteristics, constitute a very attractive framework for building more complex and ambitious vision systems.

Acknowledgements. This work has been partially supported by EU-IST NoE MUS-CLE (FP6-507752), the Greek national project XENIOS and the EU-IST project IN-DIGO (FP6-045388).

References

1. Jones, M.J., Rehg, J.M.: Statistical color models with application to skin detection. International Journal of Computer Vision 46(1), 81–96 (2002)
2. Sigal, L., Sclaroff, S., Athitsos, V.: Skin color-based video segmentation under time-varying illumination. IEEE Trans. Pattern Analysis and Machine Intelligence 26(7), 862–877 (2004)
3. Argyros, A.A., Lourakis, M.I.A.: Real-time tracking of multiple skin-colored objects with a possibly moving camera. In: Proc. European Conference on Computer Vision, Prague, Chech Republic, May 2004, pp. 368–379 (2004)

4. Nickel, K., Seemann, E., Stiefelhagen, R.: 3d-tracking of head and hands for pointing gesture recognition in a human-robot interaction scenario. In: Proc. IEEE International Conference on Automatic Face and Gesture Recognition, Seoul, Korea, May 2004, pp. 565–570 (2004)
5. Haritaoglu, I., Harwood, D., Davis, L.: W4s: A real time system for detecting and tracking people in 2.5 d. In: Proc. European Conference on Computer Vision, Freiburg, Germany, June 1999, pp. 877–892 (1999)
6. Grimson, W.E.L., Stauffer, C.: Adaptive background mixture models for real time tracking. In: Proc. IEEE Computer Vision and Pattern Recognition (CVPR), Ft. Collins, USA, June 1999, pp. 246–252 (1999)
7. Stauffer, C., Grimson, W.E.L.: Adaptive background mixture models for real-time tracking. In: Proc. IEEE Computer Vision and Pattern Recognition (CVPR), Ft. Collins, USA, June 1999, pp. 2246–2252 (1999)
8. Elgammal, A., Harrwood, D., Non-parametric, L.D.: model for background subtraction. In: Proc. European Conference on Computer Vision, Dublin, Ireland (June 2000)
9. Wren, C.R., Azarbayejani, A., Darrell, T., Pentland, A.: Pfinder: Real-time tracking of the human body. IEEE Trans. Pattern Analysis and Machine Intelligence 19(7), 780–785 (1997)
10. Yoon, S.M., Kim, H.: Real-time multiple people detection using skin color, motion and appearance information. In: Proc. IEE International Workshop on Robot and Human Interactive Communication (ROMAN), Kurashiki, Okayama Japan, September 2004, pp. 331–334 (2004)
11. Zhou, J., Hoang, J.: Real time robust human detection and tracking system. In: Proc. IEEE Computer Vision and Pattern Recognition (CVPR 2005) III, pp. 149–149 (2005)

Enhancing Robustness of a Saliency-Based Attention System for Driver Assistance

Thomas Michalke[1], Jannik Fritsch[2], and Christian Goerick[2]

[1] Darmstadt University of Technology, Institute for Automatic Control
D-64283 Darmstadt, Germany
thomas.michalke@rtr.tu-darmstadt.de
[2] Honda Research Institute Europe GmbH, D-63073 Offenbach, Germany
{jannik.fritsch,christian.goerick}@honda-ri.de

Abstract. Biologically motivated attention systems prefilter the visual environment for scene elements that pop out most or match the current system task best. However, the robustness of biological attention systems is difficult to achieve, given e.g., the high variability of scene content, changes in illumination, and scene dynamics. Most computational attention models do not show real time capability or are tested in a controlled indoor environment only. No approach is so far used in the highly dynamic real world scenario car domain. Dealing with such scenarios requires a strong system adaptation capability with respect to changes in the environment. Here, we focus on five conceptual issues crucial for closing the gap between artificial and natural attention systems operating in the real world. We show the feasibility of our approach on vision data from the car domain. The described attention system is part of a biologically motivated advanced driver assistance system running in real time.

Keywords: driver assistance, top-down / bottom-up saliency, cognitive systems, real world robustness.

1 Introduction

The most important sensory modality of humans with the highest information density is vision. The human vision system filters this high abundance of information by attending to scene elements that either pop out most in the scene (i.e., objects that are visually conspicuous) or match the current task best (i.e., objects that are compliant to the current mental status or need/task of the subject), while suppressing the rest. For both attention guiding principles psychophysical and neurological evidence exist (see [1,2]). Following this principle, technical vision systems have been developed that prefilter a scene by decomposing it into basic features (see [3]) and recombining these to a saliency map that contains high activation at regions that differ strongly from the surroundings (i.e., bottom-up (BU) attention, see [4]). More recent system implementations additionally include the modulatory influence of task relevance into the saliency

A. Gasteratos, M. Vincze, and J.K. Tsotsos (Eds.): ICVS 2008, LNCS 5008, pp. 43–55, 2008.

(i.e., top-down (TD) attention, see [5] as one of the first and [6,7] as the most recent and probably most influential approaches).

In these systems, instead of scanning the whole scene in search for certain objects in a brute force way, the use of TD attention allows a full scene decomposition despite restraints in computational resources. In principle the vision input data is serialized with respect to the importance for the current task. Based on this, computationally demanding processing stages higher in the architecture work on prefiltered data of higher relevance, which saves computation time and allows complex real-time vision applications.

In the following, we present a TD tunable attention system we developed that is the front end of the vision system of an advanced driver assistance system (ADAS) described in [8], whose architecture is inspired by the human brain. The design goals of our TD attention subsystem comprised the development of an object and task-specific tunable saliency suitable for the real world car domain. In this contribution we present new robustness enhancements in order to cope with the challenges our system is faced with when using saliency on real outdoor scenes. Important aspects discriminating real world scenes from artificial scenes are the dynamics in the environment (e.g., changing lighting and weather conditions, highly dynamic scene content) as well as the high scene complexity (e.g., cluttered scenes).

In Section 2 we will describe specific challenges that the mentioned aspects provoke on an attention system under real world conditions. Section 3 will describe our attention subsystem in detail pointing out the solutions to the denoted challenges and relates its structure to other attention approaches. Section 4 underlines the potential of the described solutions based on results calculated on different real world scenes after which the paper is summarized.

2   Real World Challenges for TD Attention Systems

In the following paragraph we describe challenges a TD attention system is faced with when used on real world images.

① **High feature selectivity:** In order to yield high hit rates in TD search an attention system needs high feature selectivity to have as much supporting and inhibiting feature maps as possible. For this the used features must be selected and parameterized appropriately. Even more important for high selectivity is the use of modulatory TD weights on *all* subfeature maps and scales. Many TD attention approaches allow TD weighting only on a high integration level (e.g., no weighting on scale level [9]) or without using the full potential of features (e.g., no on-off/off-on feature separation [6]) which leads to a potential performance loss. Our system fulfills both aspects. Based on the extended selectivity of our attention subsystem, we can handle specific challenges of the car domain, as dealing with the horizon edge present in most images.

② **Comparable TD and BU saliency maps:** Typically the TD and BU attention maps are combined to an overall saliency, on which the Focus of

Attention (FoA) is calculated. The combination requires comparable TD and BU saliency maps, making a normalization necessary. Humans undergo the same challenge when elements popping out compete with task-relevant scene elements for attention. A prominent procedure in literature normalizes each feature map to its current maximum (see [6] that is based on [10]), which has some drawbacks our approach avoids.

③ **Comparability of modalities:** Similarly, the combination of different a priori incomparable modalities (e.g., decide on the relative importance of edges versus color) must be achieved. We realize this by the biological principle of homeostasis that we define as the reversible adaptation of essential processes of a (biological) system to the environment (see e.g., [11]).

④ **Support of conjunctions of weak object features in the TD path:** Another important robustness aspect is the support of conjunction of weak object features in the TD path of the attention subsystem. That is, an object having a number of mediocre feature activations but no feature map popping out should still yield a clear maximum when combined on the overall saliency.

⑤ **Changing lighting conditions:** In a real world scene changing lighting conditions influence the features the saliency is composed of and hence the attention system performance heavily. As the calculated TD weights are based on the features of the training images, the TD weights are illumination dependent as well. Put differently, the TD weights are optimal for the specific illumination and thereby contrast that is present in the training images. Using the TD weights on test images with a differing illumination will then lead to an inferior TD search performance. Therefore, a local exposure control is needed to adjust the contrast of the training images as well as the test images before applying TD weight calculation and TD search.

3   Modeling Attention: From a Robustness Point of View

Section 3.1 focuses on the processing steps of our attention system that are crucial for solving the challenges described in Chapter 2. In Section 3.2 our system is compared to other state-of-the-art attention systems.

3.1   Description of the ADAS Attention Subsystem

The organization of Section 3.1 is led by the consecutive processing steps of the current ADAS attention subsystem as depicted in Fig. 1. After a short description of the general purpose of the BU and TD pathways, their combination to the overall saliency is described. Following this overview, the used modalities (feature types) are specified followed by the entropy measure that is used for the camera exposure control. Next, the different steps of the feature postprocessing are described. The TD feature weighting, the homeostasis process to get the conspicuity maps comparable, as well as the final BU/TD saliency normalization are the final processing steps in our attention architecture.

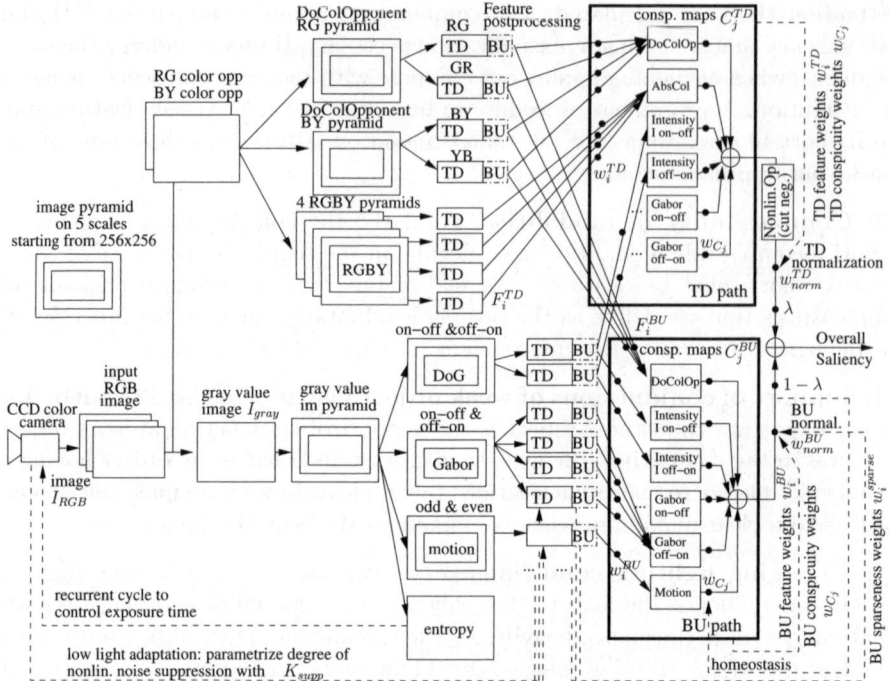

Fig. 1. Visual attention sub-system (dashed lines correspond to TD links)

The attention system consists of a BU and a TD pathway. The TD pathway (on top) allows an object- and task-dependent filtering of the input data. All image regions containing features that match the current system task well are supported (excitation), while the others are suppressed (inhibition) resulting in a sparse task-dependent scene representation. Opposed to that, the BU pathway (on bottom) supports an object- and task-unspecific filtering of input data supporting scene elements that differ from their surroundings. The BU pathway is important for a task-unspecific analysis of the scene supporting task-unrelated but salient scene elements.

The BU and TD saliency maps are linearly combined to an overall saliency on which FoAs are generated that determine the scene elements higher system layers will work on. The combination is realized using parameter λ (on the right hand side in Fig. 1) that is set dependent on the system state emphasizing the BU and/or TD influence. Due to this combination the system also detects scene elements that do not match the current TD system task and are hence suppressed in the TD pathway (to prevent inattentional blindness, i.e. complete perceptual suppression of scene elements as described in [12]).

Turning to the processing details, the following modalities are calculated on the captured color images: RGBY color (inspired from [7]), intensity by a Difference of Gaussian (DoG) kernel, oriented lines and edges by a Gabor kernel, motion by differential images and entropy using structure tensor.

In the following, these modalities are described in more detail, after which the entropy feature is specified that is used to set the camera exposure. The features motion and color are used differently for the BU and TD path. The BU path uses double color opponency from RGBY colors by applying a DoG on 5 scales on the RG and BY color opponent maps. The filter results are separated into their positive and negative parts (on-off/off-on separation, whose importance is emphasized in [7]) leading to 4 pyramids of double color opponent RG,GR,BY and YB-channels. The TD path uses the same color feature but additionally 4 pyramids of the absolute RGBY maps. Absolute RGBY colors do not support the BU popout character and are hence not used in the BU path. A DoG filter bank is applied on 5 scales separating on-off and off-on effects. Furthermore a Gabor filter bank on 4 orientations $(0, \pi/4, \pi/2, 3/4\pi)$ and 5 scales is calculated separately for lines and edges (even and odd Gabor). The realized Gabor filter bank ensures disjoint decomposition of the input image. The detailed mathematical formulation of the used Gabor filter bank can be found in [13]. Motivated from DoG the concept of on-off/off-on separation is transferred to Gabor allowing e.g., the crisp separation of the sky edge or of street markings from shadows on the street. Motion from differential images on 5 scales is used in the BU path alone. Since this simple motion concept cannot separate static objects from self-moving objects, it is not helpful in TD search. The entropy T is based on the absolute gradient strength of the structure tensor A on the image I_{gray} (see Equation (1)). The matrix A is calculated using derivatives of Gaussian filters G_x and G_y and a rectangular filter of size W. We use the entropy as a means to adapt the camera exposure and not as a feature yet.

$$G_x(x,y) = -\frac{x}{2\pi\sigma^4}exp(-\frac{x^2+y^2}{2\sigma^2}), \quad G_y(x,y) = -\frac{y}{2\pi\sigma^4}exp(-\frac{x^2+y^2}{2\sigma^2})$$

$$A=\begin{bmatrix} \Sigma_W(G_x * I_{\mathrm{gray}})^2 & \Sigma_W(G_x * I_{\mathrm{gray}})(G_y * I_{\mathrm{gray}}) \\ \Sigma_W(G_y * I_{\mathrm{gray}})(G_x * I_{\mathrm{gray}}) & \Sigma_W(G_y * I_{\mathrm{gray}})^2 \end{bmatrix}, T=\frac{det(A)}{trace(A)} \quad (1)$$

The local exposure control works on the accumulated activation $T_{sum} = \Sigma_{RoI}T$ on an image region of interest (RoI) (e.g., coming from the appearance based object tracker that is part of our ADAS, for details see [8]). Here we get inspiration from the human local contrast normalization. The exposure time is recursively modified in search of a maximum on T_{sum}, which maximizes the contrast on

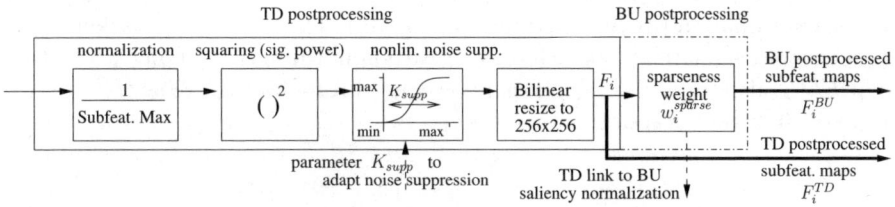

Fig. 2. Postprocessing of feature maps in BU and TD path

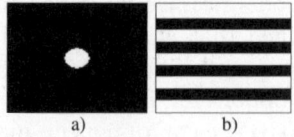

Fig. 3. Input patterns that maximize the filter response. The maximum of this filter response is used for subfeature normalization: a) Ideal DoG input pattern, b) Ideal 0° even Gabor input pattern.

the defined image regions. In sum, the system disposes of 130 independently weightable subfeature maps.

Following the calculation of the modalities a postprocessing step on all subfeature maps is performed (see Fig. 2). The feature postprocessing consists of 5 steps. First all subfeatures are normalized to the maximal value that can be expected for the specific subfeature map (not the current maximum on the map). For example, for DoG and Gabor this is done by determining the filter response for the ideal input pattern, maximizing the filter response. The ideal input pattern is generated by setting all pixels to 1 whose matching pixel positions in the filter kernel are bigger than 0. Figure 3 shows the resulting ideal DoG and 0° even Gabor input patterns that are derived from the known filter kernels. This procedure ensures comparability between subfeatures of one modality. Next, the signal power is calculated by squaring and a dynamic neuronal suppression using a sigmoid function is applied for noise suppression. A parameter K_{supp} shifts the sigmoid function horizontally, which influences the degree of noise suppression respectively the sparseness of the resulting subfeature maps. After a bilinear resize to the resolution 256x256 for later feature combination, for the BU feature postprocessing a sparseness weight w_i^{sparse} is multiplied that ensures popout by boosting subfeature maps with sparse activation (see Equation (2)).

$$w_i^{sparse} = \sqrt{\frac{2^s}{\sum\limits_{\forall x,y \text{ with } F_{i,k}(x,y) > \xi} F_{i,k}(x,y)}} \quad \text{for } s = [0,4] \text{ and } \xi = 0.9 \cdot Max(F_{i,k}) \tag{2}$$

The sparseness operator is not used in the TD path (see TD branch in Fig. 2) in order to prevent the suppression of weak object features.

Later in the TD path a weighting realizing inhibition and excitation on all 130 subfeature maps takes place. The TD weights w_i^{TD} are calculated in an offline step using Equation (3) (inspired by Frintrop [9]). The average activation in the object region is related to the average activation in the surround on each feature map F_i^{TD} taken only the N_i pixels above the threshold $K_{conj}Max(F_i^{TD})$ with $K_{conj} = (0,1]$ into account:

$$w_i^{TD} = \begin{cases} SNR_i & \forall \ SNR_i \geq 1 \\ -\frac{1}{SNR_i} & \forall \ SNR_i < 1 \end{cases} \quad \text{with } SNR_i = \frac{\frac{\sum(F_{i,obj}^{TD} > K_{conj}Max(F_i^{TD}))}{N_{i,obj}}}{\frac{\sum(F_{i,surr}^{TD} > K_{conj}Max(F_i^{TD}))}{N_{i,surr}}} \tag{3}$$

In the BU path only excitation ($w_i^{\mathrm{BU}} >= 0$) takes place, since without object or task knowledge in BU nothing can be inhibited. For a more detailed discussion of feature map weighting see [7,8].

The subfeature normalization procedure ensures intra-feature comparability, but for the overall combination, comparability between modalities is required as well. We solve this by dynamically adapting the conspicuity weights w_{C_j} for weighting the BU and TD conspicuity maps C_j^{BU} and C_j^{TD}. This concept mimics the homeostasis process in biological systems (see e.g., [11]), which we understand as the property of a biological system to regulate its internal processes in order to broaden the range of environmental conditions in which the system is able to survive. More specifically, the $\tilde{w}_{C_j}(t)$ are set to equalize the activation on all $j = 1..M$ BU conspicuity maps (see Equation (4)), taking only the N_j pixel over the threshold $\xi = 0.9 \cdot Max(C_j^{BU})$ into account. Exponential smoothing (see Equation (5)) is used to fuse old conspicuity weights $w_{C_j}(t-1)$ with the new optimized ones $\tilde{w}_{C_j}(t)$. The parameter α sets the velocity of the adaptation and could be adapted online dependent on the gist (i.e. basic environmental situation) via a TD link. In case of fast changes in the environment α could be set high for a brief interval e.g., while passing a tunnel or low in case the car stops. Additionally we use thresholds for all M conspicuity maps based on a sigma interval of recorded scene statistics to avoid complete adaptation to extreme environmental situations.

$$\tilde{w}_{C_j}(t) = \frac{1}{\frac{1}{N_j} \sum_{\forall x,y \text{ with } C_j^{BU}(x,y)>\xi} C_j^{BU}(x,y)} \text{ and } \xi = 0.9 \cdot Max(C_j^{BU}) \qquad (4)$$

$$w_{C_j}(t) = \alpha \tilde{w}_{C_j}(t) + (1-\alpha)w_{C_j}(t-1) \text{ for } j = 1..M \qquad (5)$$

Before combining the BU and TD saliency using the parameter λ a final normalization step takes place. Like the subfeature maps, the saliency maps are normalized to the maximal expected value. For this we have to step back through the attention subsystem taking into account all weights ($w_i^{\mathrm{sparse}}, w_i^{\mathrm{BU}}, w_i^{\mathrm{TD}}, w_{C_j}$) and the internal disjointness/conjointness of the features to determine the highest value a single pixel can achieve in each conspicuity map. We define a feature as internally disjoint (conjoint), when the input image is decomposed without (with) redundancy in the subfeature space. In other words the recombination of disjoint (conjoint) subfeature maps of adjacent scales or orientations is equal to (bigger than) the decomposed input image. Since DoG and Gabor are designed to be disjoint between scales and orientations the maximum pixel value on a conspicuity map j is equal to the maximum of the product of all subfeature and/or sparseness weights of the subfeatures it is composed of (w_i^{sparse} and w_i^{BU} for BU as well as w_i^{TD} for TD). Motion is conjoint between scales, therefore we sum up the product of all subfeature motion weights w_i^{BU} and their corresponding w_i^{sparse} to get the maximally expected value on the motion conspicuity map. The contribution of the color feature to the saliency normalization weight is similar but more complex. Since there is disjointness between conspicuity maps the maximum possible pixel values for all BU and TD conspicuity maps, calculated as described above, are multiplied with the corresponding w_{C_j} and added to achieve the normalization weights w_{norm}^{TD} and w_{norm}^{BU}. Using this approach w_{norm}^{TD} will adapt when the TD weight set changes.

3.2   Comparison to Other TD Attention Models

Taken the abundance of computational attention models (see [14] for a review) we selected the two related approaches of Navalpakam [6] and Frintrop [7] for a detailed structural comparison, since these impacted our work most. Then, we summarize what makes our approach particularly appropriate for the real world car domain.

The system of **Navalpakam** [6] is based on the BU attention model Neuromorphic Vision Toolkit (NVT) [10] but adds TD to the system. Each feature map is normalized to its current maximum, resulting in a loss of information about the absolute level of activity and a boosting of noise in case the activation is low. Taken such a normalization procedure and the object dependence of the TD weights, the BU and TD saliency maps are not comparable, since the relative influence of the TD map varies when the TD weight set is changed. Additionally, the BU and TD saliency maps are not weighted separately for combination. As features a speed-optimized RGBY (leading to an inferior separability performance), a DoG intensity feature and Gabor filter on 4 orientations (both without on-off/off-on or line/edge separation) are used on 6 scales starting at a resolution of 640x480. The system uses TD weights on all subfeature maps resulting in 42 weights that allow reasonable selectivity. A DoG-based normalization operator (see [10]) is applied for popout support and to diminish the noise resulting from the used feature normalization. However the absolute map activation is lost.

The system of **Frintrop** [7] integrates BU and TD attention and is real-time capable (see [15]). It was evaluated mainly on indoor scenes. The system normalizes the features to their current maximum, resulting in the same problems as described above. The BU and TD saliency maps are weighted separately for combination. Following the argumentation above the used normalization makes these combination weights dependent on the used TD weight set and thereby object-dependent. As features the system uses double color opponency based on an efficient RGBY color space implementation, a DoG intensity feature (with on-off/off-on separation), and a Gabor with 4 orientations starting from 300x300 resolution. A total of 13 TD-weights are used on feature (integrated over all scales) and conspicuity maps. For popout support a uniqueness operator is used.

Most important differences comparing the systems: We obtain high selectivity by decomposing the DoG (on-off/off-on separation) and Gabor (on-off/off-on separation, lines and edges) features without increasing the calculation time. Furthermore, the usage of TD weights on all subfeature maps and scales increases the selectivity. The resulting scale variance of the TD weights is not a crucial issue in the car domain. The RGBY is used as color and double color opponency. In contrast to [6,7], we use motion to support scene dynamics. All subfeature maps and the BU respectively TD saliency maps are normalized without loosing information or boosting noise and by that preventing false-positive FoAs. Comparability of modalities is assured via homeostasis. The attention subsystem works on 5 scales starting at a resolution of 256x256. In the car domain bigger image sizes do not improve the attention system performance.

Our system supports conjunction of weak features since the sparseness operator is not used in the TD path. Illumination invariance is reached by image region specific exposure control that is coupled tightly to the system.

4   Results

In the following, we evaluate the system properties related to the challenges of Section 2. All results are calculated on five real world data sets (cars, reflexion poles, construction site, inner city stream, toys in an indoor scene) accessible in the internet (see [16]).

① **High feature selectivity:** In the car domain the search performance is strongly influenced by the horizon edge present in most images of highways and country roads. This serves as example problem for showing the importance of high feature selectivity. Typically, the horizon edge is removed by mapping out the sky in the input image, which might not be biological plausible. Based on the high selectivity of the attention features, we instead suppress the horizon edge directly in the saliency by weighting the subfeature maps. The gain of this approach is depicted in Fig. 4 that shows the diminished influence of the horizon edge on the (TD modified) BU saliency of the real world example in Fig. 5b). Table 1 shows the significant performance gain of attentional sky suppression versus no horizon edge handling on the average FoA hit number ($\overline{Hit}$) and

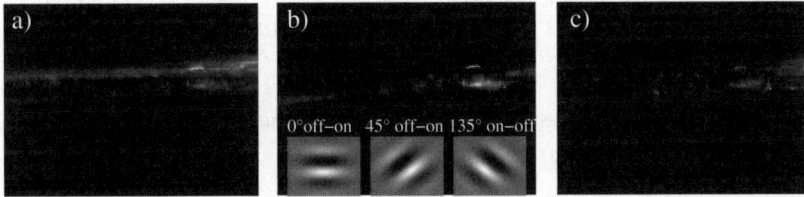

Fig. 4. Evaluation of selectivity (based on the input image depicted in Fig. 5b). a)Original BU saliency, b)modified BU saliency with attentional sky suppression (TD influence), using suppressive odd Gabor filter kernels in low scales, c)BU saliency, masked sky

Table 1. Benefit of attentional sky suppression on real world data

Search target	# test images	a) original BU $\overline{Hit}$ ($\overline{DRate}$)	b) attentional sky supp. $\overline{Hit}$ ($\overline{DRate}$)	c) sky masked $\overline{Hit}$ ($\overline{DRate}$)
Cars	54	3.06 (56.3%)	2.19 (71.4%)	2.47 (71.4%)

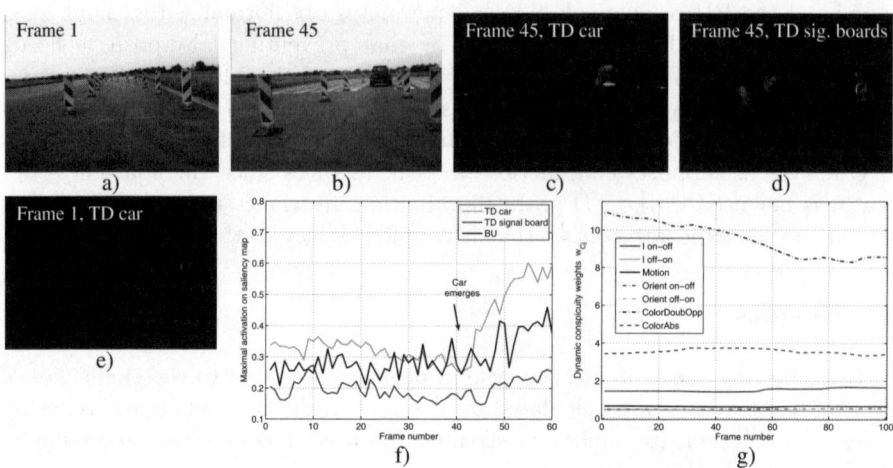

Fig. 5. Evaluation of normalization: a),b) Input images c)TD saliency tuned to cars, d)TD saliency tuned to signal boards, e)TD saliency tuned to cars (noise, since no car is present), f)Maximal saliency activation level on BU, TD signal board, and TD car map (the TD car curve is rising, when the car comes into view) g) Dynamically adapted conspicuity weights w_{C_j} (homeostasis) for the M=7 modalities

Table 2. Linear combination of BU and TD saliency, influence on search performance ($\lambda = 0$ equals pure BU and $\lambda = 1$ pure TD search)

Target	# Test im (obj)	# Trai- ning im	Aver. FoA hit number (and detection rate [%])		
			$\lambda = 0$ (BU)	$\lambda = 0.5$ (BU & TD)	$\lambda = 1$ (TD)
Cars	54 (58)	54 (selftest)	3.06 (56.9%)	1.56 (93.1%)	1.53 (100%)
		3	3.06 (56.9%)	1.87 (89.7%)	1.82 (96.6%)
Reflection poles	56 (113)	56 (self test)	2.97 (33.6%)	1.78 (59.8%)	1.85 (66.3%)
		3	2.97 (33.6%)	2.10 (51.3%)	2.25 (52.2%)

detection rate ($\overline{DRate}$) (see [7] for definition of these measures) based on our real world benchmark data.

② **Comparable TD and BU saliency maps:** The used feature normalization prevents noise on the saliency map and ensures the preservation of the absolute level of feature activation. Using a TD weight set that supports certain object-specific features our normalization hence ensures that the TD map will show high activation if and only if the searched object is really present. Figure 5f) shows that the maximal attention value on the TD saliency map for cars rises when the car comes into view (see [16] for downloadable result stream). The influence combining the now comparable TD and BU saliency maps is depicted in Tab. 2, showing that TD improves the search performance considerably. However, the influence of task-unspecific saliency (i.e., $\lambda < 1$) has to be preserved to avoid inattentional blindness.

Table 3. Comparability of modalities via homeostasis

Traffic-relevant objects	#images (obj)	SNR$_{obj}$ using static w_{C_j}	SNR$_{obj}$ using dynamic w_{C_j}
Inner city stream	20 (26)	2.56	2.86 (+11.7%)

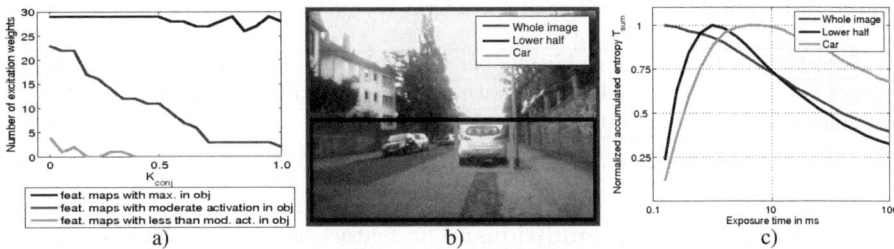

Fig. 6. Evaluation of illumination influence: a)# of excitatory TD weights depending on K_{conj}, b)Image regions used for exposure optimization (whole image, lower half, car), c)Energy function: Accumulated entropy T_{sum} with object-dependent optima

③ **Comparability of modalities:** The used dynamic adaptation of w_{C_j} (homeostasis, see Equation (5)) causes a twofold performance gain. First, the a priori incomparable modalities can be combined yielding a well balanced BU and TD saliency map. Secondly, the system adapts to the dynamics of the environment preventing varying modalities from influencing the system performance (e.g., in the red evening sun the R color channel will not be overrepresented in the saliency). Figure 5g) depicts the dynamically adapted w_{C_j}. Table 3 shows a noticeable SNR gain on the overall saliency for 26 traffic relevant objects (e.g., traffic light, road signs, cars), comparing the dynamically adapted w_{C_j} vector with a locally optimized static w_{C_j} vector.

④ **Support of conjunctions of weak object features in the TD path** is assured since w_i^{sparse} is used in BU only. Evaluation on 54 images with cars as TD search object shows that the average object signal to noise ratio ($\overline{\text{SNR}}_{obj}$) on the TD saliency map (defined as the mean activation in the object versus its surround) decreases by 9% when w_i^{sparse} is also used in the TD path. For evaluation we define weak object feature maps as having the current maximum outside the object region but still having object values of at least 60% of the maximum within the object. For the used 54 traffic scene images 11% of all feature maps are weak. In case weak feature maps are used to optimally support the TD saliency in an excitatory way $\overline{\text{SNR}}_{obj}$ on the TD saliency map increases by 25%. The results are aggregated in Tab. 4. Figure 6a) shows that the number of excitatory TD weights w_i^{TD} decreases the bigger K_{conj} is. An object-dependent trade-off exists since the TD saliency map gets sparser the bigger K_{conj} is.

Table 4. Improvement due to support of weak feature conjunctions

TD search target	# test image	SNR_{obj} with w_i^{sparse}	SNR_{obj} without w_i^{sparse}	SNR_{obj} with optimal weak feat. excitation
Cars	54	6.72	7.32 (+9%)	8.41 (+25%)

Table 5. Illumination invariance of TD weight sets using dedicated exposure control

Target	# Test im (obj)	Average hit number (and detection rate [%]), TD search $\lambda = 1$				
Toys in a complex in-		Traning illu- mination 75 lx	without expos. control		with expos. control	
			150 lx	15 lx	150 lx	15 lx
door setup	20 (20)	1.95 (100%)	2.74 (95%)	2.83 (30%)	1.80 (100%)	2.0 (100%)

⑤ **Changing lighting conditions:** The feature activation of an image region depends on the illumination. Hence the TD weight set is only optimal for the lighting conditions of the training images and the TD search performance decreases when illumination changes without an adaptation of the camera exposure. It is important to note that in a real world scene the optimal exposure in varying illumination is different for all objects (see Fig. 6b and c), making the exposure control dependent on the current task of the system. Evaluation based on a complex indoor test setting where we were able to control the illumination shows that the realized exposure control leads to illumination invariance of the TD weight sets (see Tab. 5).

5   Summary

This paper describes a flexible biologically motivated attention subsystem that is used as the front end of an ADAS. The real world requirements of the car domain have resulted in an improved system performance by incorporating modulating TD links.

The key enhancements of our attention subsystem are: high feature selectivity, a normalization leading to comparable BU and TD saliency maps enabling their combination with a linear combination weight λ that is independent of the used TD weight set, the comparability of the used modalities, the conjunction support of weak object features in the TD path and an exposure control that depends on the object in focus or a task relevant image region. These principles lead to a robust system suitable for the dynamic real world environment.

Using a purely vision based situation analysis that worked on TD prefiltered vision data provided by an earlier version of the attention subsystem described here, we showed the real time capability of our system in a real world test setup, where our prototype car was reliably able to brake autonomously (see [8]).

References

1. Corbetta, M., Shulman, G.: Control of goal-directed and stimulus-driven attention in the brain. Nature Reviews Neuroscience 3, 201–215 (2002)
2. Egeth, H.E., Yantis, S.: Visual attention: control, representation, and time course. Annual Review of Psychology 48, 269–297 (1997)
3. Wolfe, J.M., Horowitz, T.S.: What attributes guide the deployment of visual attention and how do they do it? Nat. Reviews Neuroscience 5(6), 495–501 (2004)
4. Koch, C., Ullman, S.: Shifts in selective visual attention: towards the underlying neural circuitry. Human Neurobiology 4(4), 219–227 (1985)
5. Tsotsos, J.K., Culhane, S.M., Wai, W.Y.K., Lai, Y., Davis, N., Nuflo, F.: Modeling visual attention via selective tuning. Artificial Intelligence 78(1-2), 507–545 (1995)
6. Navalpakkam, V., Itti, L.: Modeling the influence of task on attention. Vision Research 45(2), 205–231 (2005)
7. Frintrop, S.: VOCUS: A Visual Attention System for Object Detection and Goal-Directed Search. PhD thesis, University of Bonn Germany (2006)
8. Michalke, T., Gepperth, A., Schneider, M., Fritsch, J., Goerick, C.: Towards a human-like vision system for resource-constrained intelligent cars. In: Int. Conf. on Computer Vision Systems, Bielefeld (2007)
9. Frintrop, S., Backer, G., Rome, E.: Goal-directed search with a top-down modulated computational attention system. In: DAGM-Symposium, pp. 117–124 (2005)
10. Itti, L., Koch, C., Niebur, E.: A model of saliency-based visual attention for rapid scene analysis. IEEE Trans. Pattern Anal. Mach. Intell. 20(11), 1254–1259 (1998)
11. Hardy, R.N.: Homeostasis, Arnold (1983)
12. Simons, D., Chabris, C.: Gorillas in our midst: Sustained inattentional blindness for dynamic events. British Journal of Developmental Psychology 13, 113–142 (1995)
13. Trapp, R.: Stereoskopische Korrespondenzbestimmung mit impliziter Detektion von Okklusionen. PhD thesis, University of Paderborn Germany (1998)
14. Heinke, D., Humphreys, G.: Computational models of visual selective attention: a review. In: Houghton, G. (ed.) Connectionist Models in Psychology, pp. 273–312. Psychology Press (2005)
15. Frintrop, S., Klodt, M., Rome, E.: A real-time visual attention system using integral images. In: Int. Conf. on Computer Vision Systems, Bielefeld (2007)
16. BenchmarkData: (2007)
    http://www.rtr.tu-darmstadt.de/~tmichalk/ICVS2008_BenchmarkData/

Covert Attention with a Spiking Neural Network

Sylvain Chevallier[1,2] and Philippe Tarroux[2,3]

[1] Université Paris-Sud XI, France
[2] LIMSI-CNRS UPR 3251, Orsay, France
[3] École Normale Supérieure, Paris, France
{sylvain.chevallier,philippe.tarroux}@limsi.fr

Abstract. We propose an implementation of covert attention mechanisms with spiking neurons. Spiking neural models describe the activity of a neuron with precise spike-timing rather than firing rate. We investigate the interests offered by such a temporal code for low-level vision and early attentional process. This paper describes a spiking neural network which achieves saliency extraction and stable attentional focus of a moving stimulus. Experimental results obtained using real visual scene illustrate the robustness and the quickness of this approach.

Keywords: spiking neurons, precise spike-timing, covert attention, saliency.

1 Introduction

Understanding the neural mechanisms underlying early attentional processes can open novel ways of solving some artificial vision problems. Neurobiology and cognitive psychology produce evidence for an early information selection: the brain handles only a small part of the visual scene at a time. Spiking neural networks offer interesting properties since they seem to capture important characteristics of biological neuron with relatively simple models. We propose a bio-inspired spiking neural network (SNN) which selects such a small visual area and focuses on it, using saliency extraction. The focusing mechanism relies on the spatio-temporal continuity of the stimulus and is robust to small movements.

The different approaches used for modeling visual attention and the motivations leading to place this work in a bio-inspired framework are explained in 1.1. The properties of the different spiking neural models that can be used in the present context are detailled in 1.2. The network set up to extract saliencies and focus on a moving stimulus is described in Sect. 2 and experimental results are given in Sect. 3. The experimental validation and the obtained results are given in Sect. 3. The spike coding used in this network is discussed in Sect. 4. Section 5 concludes this paper.

1.1 Modeling Visual Attention and Saliency

Visual attention is a sequential mechanism: the brain concentrates only on a small region at a time as *change blindness* experiments demonstrate (see

A. Gasteratos, M. Vincze, and J.K. Tsotsos (Eds.): ICVS 2008, LNCS 5008, pp. 56–65, 2008.
© Springer-Verlag Berlin Heidelberg 2008

O'Regan [1] for example). It is often said that the complexity of the visual world exceeds the brain ability to process a whole visual scene. This hypothesis can be questioned regarding the unmatched computational power of the brain's massively parallel architecture. This sequential process may have been kept by evolution because it brings some benefits. The questions of what these benefits are and whether they are relevant for artificial vision are seldom addressed and have no simple answer. However, for instance, a sequential process endows the system with what Tsotsos calls an "hypothesize-and-test" mechanism [2] leading to inferential abilities that could have been the target of the natural selection process.

The spatial attention is expressed by two mechanisms : overt and covert attention. Overt attention refers to situation where the eye makes a saccade to focus a saliency. It is opposed to covert attention, which involves no saccadic moves, addressed in this paper. The attentional process selects a part of the visual input and is a top-down process, i.e. involving task-dependent or context-dependent influences. Pre-attention is a similar process, but in a bottom-up (BU) or data-driven manner. The rest of this paper deals only with BU processes: there is no assumption on learning or categorizing objects. A specific region of a visual scene, selected by a pre-attentional process, is referred to as a saliency. The saliencies are then gathered on saliency map whose existence is commonly accepted but remains unproven [3]. Many models describe visual attention mechanisms and a significative part rely on saliencies. Saliency-based models can be separated in three main approaches: psychological models, image processing systems and bio-inspired approaches.

Computational models set up by psychologists are closely linked to experimental data, trying to explain or predict the behavior resulting from neuropsychological disorders [4]. Whereas these goals diverge from computational ones, some findings are interesting: Treisman [5] and Wolfe [6] have proved the existence of visual features. These features are the different modalities of vision: color, luminance, movement, orientation, curvature, among others. Treisman proposed a theory [5] in which features are extracted in a parallel way during the pre-attentive stage and then combined on a saliency map. Psychological models help to build a theory of perception although these models cannot be part of an artificial perceptual system dealing with real world situation.

Salient regions can also be seen as "meaningful" descriptors of an image. This formulation leads the image processing community to propose other ways for extracting saliency points. Image processing models use information theory (local complexity or unpredictability, [7]) or pixel distribution (local histograms, [8]). Such descriptors are used to recognize known objects or object classes and give their best performance in controlled environments. Image processing systems can handle real world data but they are often constrained by strong hypothesis and are not suited for generic situation or open environment.

The bio-inspiration way aims at bringing together natural solutions and computational efficiency. Realistic biological or psychological models try to reproduce or explain every observation. Image processing systems seek efficient solutions and are well suited for specific situations. On the contrary, bio-inspired models seek a compromise and try to capture only key properties. Itti and Koch [9] proposed an image processing based model inspired by low-level biological visual processing. There are many other bio-inspired models (described in [10]) which rely on similar principles and share the notion of a saliency map. The existence of a saliency map neural correlate is broadly discussed [3]. We use the following definition of a saliency: a region in a visual scene which is locally contrasted in terms of visual features and globally rare in the visual scene. Bio-inspired approaches offer a good framework for designing efficient and robust methods for extracting saliencies. In a bio-inspired framework, visual attention problems can be addressed at two levels. At a system level, Bayesian approaches model or reproduce a global behavior. At the opposite, at a unit level, neural-based approaches specify the local properties enabling the emergence of a global behavior. These two approaches follow different methods, explicative model for the former and global analysis for the latter, but can benefit from each other.

We experiment the contribution of a neural-based system, with simple spiking models, not suited for precise modelling but adequate for real-time computation. We choose to investigate the explicative models of bio-inspired visual attention rather than the descriptive ones.

1.2   Spiking Neural Networks

Maass [11] described spiking neurons as the "third generation" of neural models. Spiking neurons capture fundamental aspect of the neural functionality: the ability to code the information as discrete events whereas the underlying equation are reasonably simple. A spiking neuron unit [12,13] models the variation of the membrane potential and fires a spike if the membrane crosses the threshold. The main difference between a spiking unit and a classical sigmoid unit reside in the way of handling time. The membrane potential V_i of neuron i is driven by a differential equation and takes into account the precise time of the incoming spikes. The learning ability of spiking neural networks are actively investigated [14,15,16,17].

A single spiking neuron can exhibit two behaviors: it can either integrate the information over a predefined temporal window or act as a synchrony detector, i.e. emitting spikes when inputs are condensed in a small period of time.

2   Model Description

We use a Leaky Integrate-and-Fire (LIF) model characterized by the following equation:

$$\begin{cases} \tau \dot{V}_i = g_{\text{leak}}(V_i - E_{\text{leak}}) + \text{PSP}_i(t) + \text{I}(t), \text{ if } V \leq \vartheta \\ \text{spike and reset } V \text{ otherwise} \end{cases} \tag{1}$$

where τ is the membrane time constant, g_{leak} is the membrane leak conductance, ϑ is the threshold and E_{leak} is the membrane resting potential [13]. $\text{I}(t)$ represents the influence of an external input current (as in Chap. 4.1.1 of [13]). The $\text{PSP}(t)$

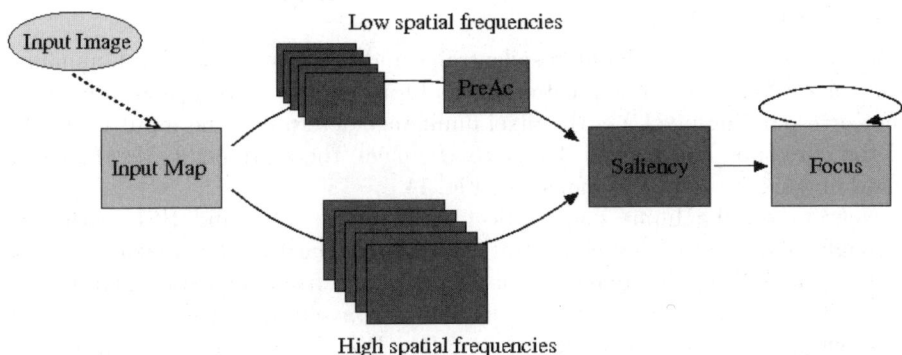

High spatial frequencies

Fig. 1. Architecture of a set of feed-forward connected neural maps, which extract saliencies from an input image and focus on the most salient region. The image is processed both at low spatial frequencies (LSF) and high spatial frequencies (HSF).

is the synaptic input function, describing the influence of incoming spikes on membrane potential. Among the different PSP models that can reflect complex synaptic variations (as in [18,19]), we have chosen a simple one for achieving fast computation. Thus we use a PSP model without synaptic conductance (as in [20]). Formally, incoming PSPs from neuron j are denoted by:

$$S_j(t) = \sum_f \delta(t - t_j^{(f)} + d_j) \qquad (2)$$

where $\delta(x)$ is the Dirac distribution, with $\delta(x) = 0$ for $x \neq 0$ and $\int_{-\infty}^{\infty} \delta(x)\mathrm{d}x = 1$, $t_j^{(f)}$ is the spike emission time and d_j the synaptic delay. Since we use a model without synaptic conductance, the influence of incoming PSPs on membrane potential is given by the simple relation:

$$\mathrm{PSP}_i(t) = \sum_j w_{i,j} S_j(t) \qquad (3)$$

These computations was handled in a clock-based sequential simulator which not distributed. This simulator process only the active neurons, i.e. neurons integrating PSPs [21].

The SNN represented on Fig. 1 is a set of neural maps (2D neural layer) which is divided in two main pathways for processing high and low spatial frequencies. Visual modalities of an input image are decomposed with neural filters, explained in Sect. 2.1, and we combine all the obtained visual modalities on the Saliency map, detailed in Sect. 2.2. This combination relies on the temporal processing of spiking neurons, low spatial frequencies being gathered on PreAc map (on Fig. 1), which pre-activates the Saliency map neurons. The Focus map selects the most intense saliency as the focus of attention is described in Sect. 2.3.

2.1 Neural Filter

The input image is translated in spike trains and the network handles luminance and color information. Each neuron of the Input map (Fig. 1) is associated with the corresponding pixel, i.e. the pixel luminance determines the input term $I(t)$ of the corresponding neuron. For a LxM image, there are eight MxM neural maps and six $\frac{L}{2}x\frac{M}{2}$ neural maps (see Fig. 1).

Neurons on the Input map project on both the LSF and HSF pathways through connection masks as illustrated on Fig. 2. These masks are static weight matrices with delay and define a generic projection from one neural map to another. The weight matrix values are similar to convolution kernel used in image processing. We use difference of Gaussian (DoG) and four Gabor orientated kernels as connection masks between Input map and maps in both HSF and LSF pathways.

This network achieves an image filtering similar to a classical kernel convolution. However the "convolution" realized by PSPs propagation through connection masks is applied in an order depending on the input value, i.e. the most important filter coefficient being processed first. Furthermore, the lowest input values are not processed: due to the discrete nature of spiking neurons, only above threshold information is propagated into the network (depending on g_{leak} and $I(t)$ values). This functional filtering and the fact that our implementation processes only the neurons receiving PSPs lead to a fast execution (see Sect. 3).

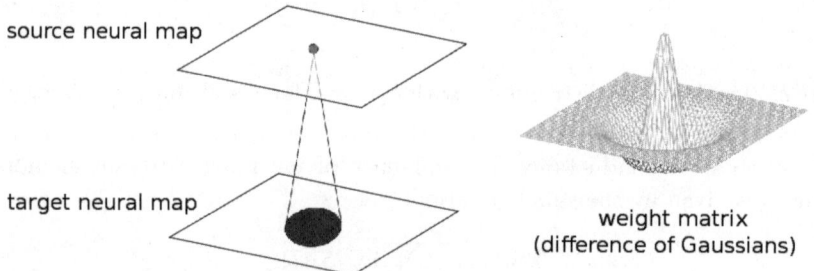

Fig. 2. A neuron (in green or light grey) emits a spike and sends PSPs to all red (or dark grey) neurons. The weight of each PSP is given by the weight matrix, represented on the right. The weight matrix values are similar to convolution kernel used in image processing. Here, a difference of Gaussian.

2.2 Saliency Map

The Saliency map (Fig. 1) gathers all information from visual features on different spatial frequencies. The Saliency map neurons are tuned to implement synchrony detectors, i.e. they emit spikes only if PSPs are gathered in a small time window. Thus, saliencies are emerging from saliency map only if a spatial location generates spikes on different neural maps coding for different visual features.

A saliency point is represented by a spike emited by a neuron of the Saliency map. Thus saliencies are temporally coded and arise in hierarchical order. The neuron corresponding to the most salient location is the first to emit a spike, and so on. Others bio-inspired approaches extract visual features, combining them on a saliency map, eventually using a Winner-Takes-All (WTA) algorithm to choose the most intense saliency. To find the second saliency, the previous saliency must be inhibited and the whole computation is to be started again. On the contrary, the present implementation uses a recurrent map for implementing selection process and the experimental results show that this kind of network implements a fast and implicit WTA.

2.3   Covert Attention

When a saliency is detected, the output spikes from saliency map are sent to the self-connected Focus map, see Fig. 1. This self-connection mask is a DoG, which excites adjacent neighbours and inhibits distant ones. This self-connection needs the Saliency map spikes to keep a stable activity and is not sufficient to maintain a constant activity alone. As the saliency moves, the activity on the Focus map follows as long as the saliency stays in the positive part of the DoG [22].

3   Experimental Results

Real world images were used for the evaluation of this SNN. We used a Sony EVID31 pan-tilt camera for the acquisition and a Khepera robot as the moving stimulus. A 30 frames sequence has been recorded (see Fig. 3). During this sequence, the network focused on the moving stimulus and let the focus change quickly when the camera made a saccade. Note that this saccadic move was driven externally and does not rely on the activity of the network.

The frames are 760x570 pixels wide images and are reduced to 76x56 pixels for the input of the SNN. As one pixel of the input frame corresponds to one neuron, the network was composed of ~53,000 neurons ($L = 76$ and $M = 56$). In this set of experiment, we only used the luminance information.

The first frame was presented to the network for 20 integration steps. This bootstrap stage let the network activity emerge and the spikes propagate through each neural maps. At the 20th integration step, the Focus map emited spikes. Each frame was then presented during N integration steps. The results for different N values are shown in Fig. 4 and 5.

To check the performance of the SNN, we computed the euclidean distance between the stimulus centroid and the centroid of the activity as an error measure. Stimulus centroid was computed as the centroid of the stimulus pixel, for a given frame. The activity centroid is defined as the centroid of all emitted spikes by the focus map during the N integration steps of the image presentation.

Figure 4 shows that the error decreased when the network had more time (integration steps) to process each frame. The error level decreased rapidly when

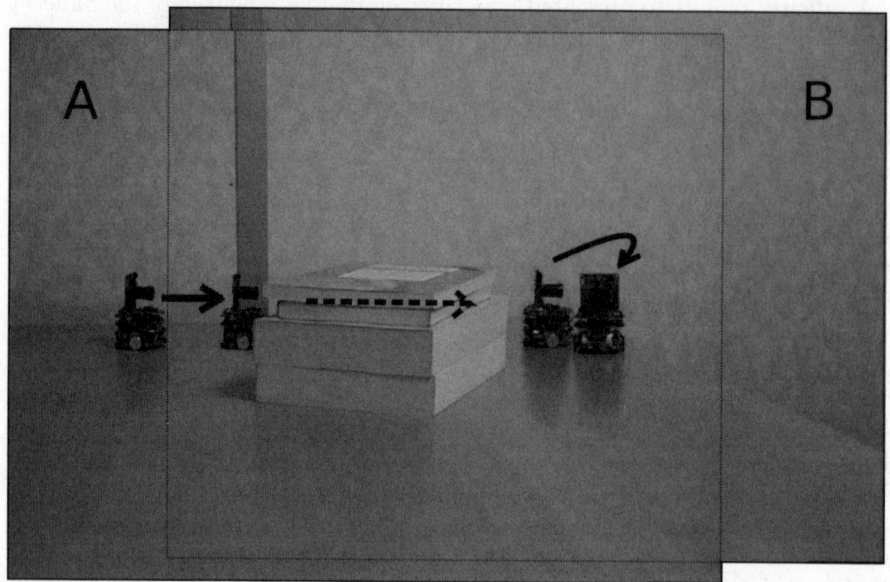

Fig. 3. Representation of the input video sequence. The mobile stimulus (a Khepera robot) moves from left to right. As it reappears, after being hidden behind the books, the camera makes a saccade from frame A to frame B for focusing the stimulus.

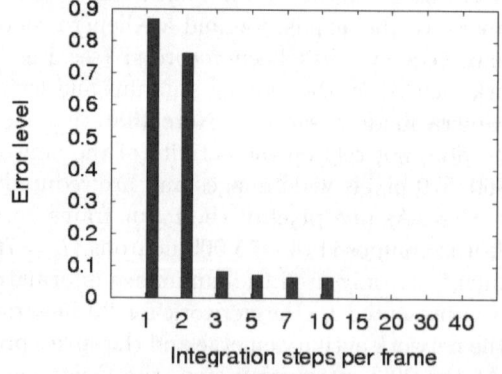

Fig. 4. Error level for the 30 frames video sequence

there is a sufficient number of computation steps per frame. One can notice that the error is still very low for only 3 integration steps per frame. This is an interesting result especially given the computation time which are shown on Fig. 5.

All the results presented on Fig. 5 have been obtained with an desktop Intel Core2Duo (1.86GHz). The total run time and the overall activity evolves

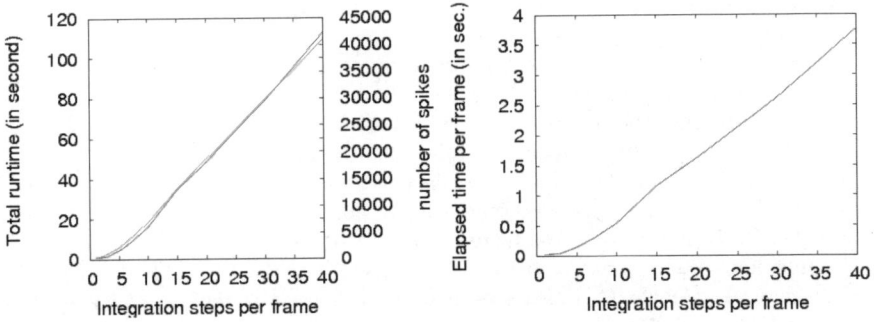

Fig. 5. *Left*: Runtime of our program, including building and ending process, is indicated by the green curve. Overall activity load of the network is displayed by the red curve, as the total number of spikes emitted by the network. *Right*: time taken to process one frame, given the number of integration steps per frame.

linearly as the number of steps per frame increases, as shown on left part of Fig. 5. The time needed to process a frame is very promising (Fig 5, right), as with 3 integration steps per frame, the network process ~20 frames/second. These results confirm that SNN are suitable for visual computation in a real-time framework.

4   Discussion

Thorpe [23] shows that monkeys and humans were able to detect the presence of animals in a visual scene in an extremely short time, leaving neurons just enough time to fire a single spike. Information is condensed in the precise time of each spike and the relative latency between the spikes. This first spike code can been used to recognize a previously learned pattern in real world images [24,25] or to characterize natural images [26]. The network described in this paper uses spike train for detecting the spatio-temporal continuity of a stimulus, which is not possible with a unique first spike.

5   Conclusion

In this contribution, we build a SNN able to compute saliencies and to focus on the most important one. Thanks to the coincidence detector properties of the Saliency map spiking neurons, we show that this SNN can extract saliencies. The implementation of a covert attention process rely on the temporal computation of the spiking neuron. This network was evaluated on real data (a video sequence) and was able to focus on a moving target. The mesured computation time shows that this network is suitable for a real-time application.

References

1. O'Regan, K.J., Noë, A.: A sensorimotor account of vision and visual consciousness. Behavioral and Brain Sciences 24, 939–1031 (2001)
2. Tsotsos, J.K.: On the relative complexity of active v.s. passive visual search. International Journal of Computer Vision 7(2), 127–141 (1992)
3. Fecteau, J.H., Munoz, D.P.: Salience, relevance, and firing: a priority map for target selection. Trends in Cognitive Sciences 10(8), 382–390 (2006)
4. Heinke, D., Humphreys, G.W.: Connectionist Models in Cognitive Psychology. In: Connectionist Models in Cognitive Psychology, Routledge, pp. 273–312 (2005)
5. Treisman, A., Gelade, G.: A feature-integration theory of attention. Cognitive Psychology 12(1), 97–136 (1980)
6. Wolfe, J.: Visual attention. In: Seeing, 2nd edn. pp. 335–386. Academic Press, London (2000)
7. Kadir, T., Brady, M.: Scale, saliency and image description. International Journal of Computer Vision 45(2), 83–105 (2001)
8. Schmid, C., Mohr, R., Bauckhage, C.: Evaluation of interest point detectors. International Journal of Computer Vision 37(2), 151–172 (2000)
9. Itti, L., Koch, C.: Computational modeling of visual attention. Nature Reviews Neuroscience 2(3), 194–203 (2001)
10. Itti, L., Rees, G., Tsotsos, J. (eds.): Models of Bottom-Up Attention and Saliency. In: Neurobiology of Attention, San Diego, CA, January 2005, pp. 576–582. Elsevier, Amsterdam (2005)
11. Maass, W.: Networks of spiking neurons: the third generation of neural network models. Neural Networks 10, 1659–1671 (1997)
12. Maass, W., Bishop, C.M. (eds.): Pulsed neural networks. MIT Press, Cambridge (1999)
13. Gerstner, W., Kistler, W.: Spiking Neuron Models: An Introduction. Cambridge University Press, New York (2002)
14. Maass, W., Natschläger, T., Markram, H.: Real-time computing without stable states: A new framework for neural computation based on perturbations. Neural Computation 14(11), 2531–2560 (2002)
15. Jaeger, H., Maass, W., Principe, J.: Introduction to the special issue on echo state networks and liquid state machines. Neural Networks 20(3), 287–289 (2007)
16. Maass, W.: Liquid Computing. In: Cooper, S.B., Löwe, B., Sorbi, A. (eds.) CiE 2007. LNCS, vol. 4497, pp. 507–516. Springer, Heidelberg (2007)
17. Cios, K.J., Swiercz, W., Jackson, W.: Networks of spiking neurons in modeling and problem solving. Neurocomputing 61, 99–119 (2004)
18. Rudolph, M., Destexhe, A.: On the use of analytic expressions for the voltage distribution to analyze intracellular recordings. Neural Computation (2006)
19. Brette, R.: Exact simulation of integrate-and-fire models with synaptic conductances. Neural Computation 18(8), 2004–2027 (2006)
20. Brunel, N.: Dynamics of sparsely connected networks of excitatory and inhibitory spiking neurons. Journal of Computational Neuroscience 8, 183–208 (2000)
21. Chevallier, S., Tarroux, P., Paugam-Moisy, H.: Saliency extraction with a distributed spiking neural network. In: Proc. of European Symposium on Artificial Neural Networks, Bruges, Belgium, pp. 209–214 (2006)

22. Chevallier, S., Tarroux, P.: Visual focus with spiking neurons. In: Proc. of European Symposium on Artificial Neural Networks, Bruges, Belgium (2008)
23. Thorpe, S., Fize, D., Marlot, C.: Speed of processing in the human visual system. Nature 381, 520–522 (1996)
24. Delorme, A., Gautrais, J., VanRullen, R., Thorpe, S.J.: Spikenet: a simulator for modeling large networks of integrate-and-fire neurons. Neurocomputing 26-27, 989–996 (1999)
25. Thorpe, S.J., Guyonneau, R., Guilbaud, N., Allegraud, J.-M., VanRullen, R.: Spikenet: Real-time visual processing with one spike per neuron. Neurocomputing 58-60, 857–864 (2004)
26. Perrinet, L.: Finding independent components using spikes: a natural result of hebbian learning in a sparse spike coding scheme. Natural Computing 3(2), 159–175 (2004)

Salient Region Detection and Segmentation

Radhakrishna Achanta, Francisco Estrada, Patricia Wils, and Sabine Süsstrunk

School of Computer and Communication Sciences (I&C),
Ecole Polytechnique Fédérale de Lausanne (EPFL)
{radhakrishna.achanta,francisco.estrada,patricia.wils,
sabine.susstrunk}@epfl.ch
http://ivrg.epfl.ch/

Abstract. Detection of salient image regions is useful for applications like image segmentation, adaptive compression, and region-based image retrieval. In this paper we present a novel method to determine salient regions in images using low-level features of luminance and color. The method is fast, easy to implement and generates high quality saliency maps of the same size and resolution as the input image. We demonstrate the use of the algorithm in the segmentation of semantically meaningful whole objects from digital images.

Keywords: Salient regions, low-level features, segmentation.

1 Introduction

Identifying visually salient regions is useful in applications such as object based image retrieval, adaptive content delivery [11,12], adaptive region-of-interest based image compression , and smart image resizing [2]. We identify salient regions as those regions of an image that are visually more conspicuous by virtue of their contrast with respect to surrounding regions. Similar definitions of saliency exist in literature where saliency in images is referred to as local contrast [9,11].

Our method for finding salient regions uses a contrast determination filter that operates at various scales to generate saliency maps containing "saliency values" per pixel. Combined, these individual maps result in our final saliency map. We demonstrate the use of the final saliency map in segmenting whole objects with the aid of a relatively simple segmentation technique. The novelty of our approach lies in finding high quality saliency maps of the same size and resolution as the input image and their use in segmenting whole objects. The method is effective on a wide range of images including those of paintings, video frames, and images containing noise.

The paper is organized as follows. The relevant state of the art in salient region detection is presented in Section 2. Our algorithm for detection of salient regions and its use in segmenting salient objects is explained in Section 3. The parameters used in our algorithm, the results of saliency map generation, segmentation, and comparisons against the method of Itti et al. [9] are given in Section 4. Finally, in Section 5 conclusions are presented.

A. Gasteratos, M. Vincze, and J.K. Tsotsos (Eds.): ICVS 2008, LNCS 5008, pp. 66–75, 2008.
© Springer-Verlag Berlin Heidelberg 2008

2 Approaches for Saliency Detection

The approaches for determining low-level saliency can be based on biological models or purely computational ones. Some approaches consider saliency over several scales while others operate on a single scale. In general, all methods use some means of determining local contrast of image regions with their surroundings using one or more of the features of color, intensity, and orientation. Usually, separate feature maps are created for each of the features used and then combined [8,11,6,4] to obtain the final saliency map. A complete survey of all saliency detection and segmentation research is beyond the scope of this paper, here we discuss those approaches in saliency detection and saliency-based segmentation that are most relevant to our work.

Ma and Zhang [11] propose a local contrast-based method for generating saliency maps that operates at a single scale and is not based on any biological model. The input to this local contrast-based map is a resized and color quantized CIELuv image, sub-divided into pixel blocks. The saliency map is obtained from summing up differences of image pixels with their respective surrounding pixels in a small neighborhood. This framework extracts the points and regions of attention. A fuzzy-growing method then segments salient regions from the saliency map.

Hu et al. [6] create saliency maps by thresholding the color, intensity, and orientation maps using histogram entropy thresholding analysis instead of a scale space approach. They then use a spatial compactness measure, computed as the area of the convex hull encompassing the salient region, and saliency density, which is a function of the magnitudes of saliency values in the saliency feature maps, to weigh the individual saliency maps before combining them.

Itti et al. [9] have built a computational model of saliency-based spatial attention derived from a biologically plausible architecture. They compute saliency maps for features of luminance, color, and orientation at different scales that aggregate and combine information about each location in an image and feed into a combined saliency map in a bottom-up manner. The saliency maps produced by Itti's approach have been used by other researchers for applications like adapting images on small devices [3] and unsupervised object segmentation [5,10].

Segmentation using Itti's saliency maps (a 480x320 pixel image generates a saliency map of size 30x20 pixels) or any other sub-sampled saliency map from a different method requires complex approaches. For instance, a Markov random field model is used to integrate the seed values from the saliency map along with low-level features of color, texture, and edges to grow the salient object regions [5]. Ko and Nam [10], on the other hand, use a Support Vector Machine trained on the features of image segments to select the salient regions of interest from the image, which are then clustered to extract the salient objects. We show that using our saliency maps, salient object segmentation is possible without needing such complex segmentation algorithms.

Recently, Frintrop et al. [4] used integral images [14] in VOCUS (Visual Object Detection with a Computational Attention System) to speed up computation of center-surround differences for finding salient regions using separate feature maps of color, intensity, and orientation. Although they obtain better resolution saliency maps as compared to Itti's method, they resize the feature saliency maps to a lower scale, thereby losing resolution. We use integral images in our approach but we resize the filter at each scale instead of the image and thus maintain the same resolution as the original image at all scales.

3   Salient Region Detection and Segmentation

This section presents details of our approach for saliency determination and its use in segmenting whole objects. An overview of the complete algorithm is presented in Figure 1. Using the saliency calculation method described later, saliency maps are created at different scales. These maps are added pixel-wise to get the final saliency maps. The input image is then over-segmented and the segments whose average saliency exceeds a certain threshold are chosen.

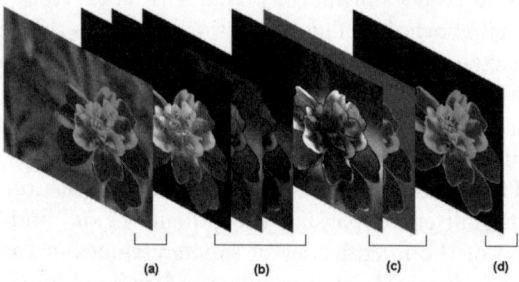

(a)   (b)   (c)   (d)

Fig. 1. Overview of the process of finding salient regions. (a) Input image. (b) Saliency maps at different scales are computed, added pixel-wise, and normalized to get the final saliency map. (c) The final saliency map and the segmented image. (d) The output image containing the salient object that is made of only those segments that have an average saliency value greater than the threshold T (given in Section 3.1).

3.1   Saliency Calculation

In our work, saliency is determined as the local contrast of an image region with respect to its neighborhood at various scales. This is evaluated as the distance between the average feature vector of the pixels of an image sub-region with the average feature vector of the pixels of its neighborhood. This allows obtaining a combined feature map at a given scale by using feature vectors for each pixel, instead of combining separate saliency maps for scalar values of each feature. At a given scale, the contrast based saliency value $c_{i,j}$ for a pixel at position (i,j) in the image is determined as the distance D between the average vectors of pixel features of the inner region R_1 and that of the outer region R_2 (Figure 2) as:

$$c_{i,j} = D\left[\left(\frac{1}{N_1}\sum_{p=1}^{N_1}\mathbf{v}_p\right), \left(\frac{1}{N_2}\sum_{q=1}^{N_2}\mathbf{v}_q\right)\right] \tag{1}$$

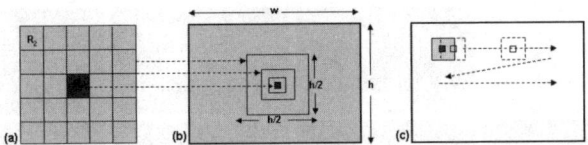

Fig. 2. (a) Contrast detection filter showing inner square region R_1 and outer square region R_2. (b) The width of R_1 remains constant while that of R_2 ranges according to Equation 3 by halving it for each new scale. (c) Filtering the image at one of the scales in a raster scan fashion.

where $N1$ and N_2 are the number of pixels in R_1 and R_2 respectively, and $\mathbf{v}$ is the vector of feature elements corresponding to a pixel. The distance D is a Euclidean distance if $\mathbf{v}$ is a vector of uncorrelated feature elements, and it is a Mahalanobis distance (or any other suitable distance measure) if the elements of the vector are correlated. In this work, we use the $CIELab$ color space [7], assuming sRGB images, to generate feature vectors for color and luminance. Since perceptual differences in $CIELab$ color space are approximately Euclidian, D in Equation 1 is:

$$c_{i,j} = \|\mathbf{v}_1 - \mathbf{v}_2\| \tag{2}$$

where $\mathbf{v}_1 = [L_1, a_1, b_1]^T$ and $\mathbf{v}_2 = [L_2, a_2, b_2]^T$ are the average vectors for regions R_1 and R_2, respectively. Since only average feature vector values of R_1 and R_2 need to be found, we use the integral image approach as used in [14] for computational efficiency. A change in scale is affected by scaling the region R_2 instead of scaling the image. Scaling the filter instead of the image allows the generation of saliency maps of the same size and resolution as the input image. Region R_1 is usually chosen to be one pixel. If the image is noisy (for instance if high ISO values are used when capturing images, as can often be determined with the help of Exif data (Exchangeable File Information Format [1]) then R_1 can be a small region of $N \times N$ pixels (in Figure 5(f) N is 9).

For an image of width w pixels and height h pixels, the width of region R_2, namely w_{R_2} is varied as:

$$\frac{w}{2} \geq (w_{R_2}) \geq \frac{w}{8} \tag{3}$$

assuming w to be smaller than h (else we choose h to decide the dimensions of R_2). This is based on the observation that the largest size of R_2 and the smaller ones (smaller than $w/8$) are of less use in finding salient regions (see Figure 3). The former might highlight non-salient regions as salient, while the latter are basically edge detectors. So for each image, filtering is performed at three different scales (according to Eq. 3) and the final saliency map is determined as a sum of saliency values across the scales S:

$$m_{i,j} = \sum_S c_{i,j} \tag{4}$$

$\forall i \in [1, w], j \in [1, h]$ where $m_{i,j}$ is an element of the combined saliency map $\mathbf{M}$ obtained by point-wise summation of saliency values across the scales.

Fig. 3. From left to right, original image followed by filtered images. Filtering is done using R_1 of size one pixel and varying width of R_2. When R_2 has the maximum width, certain non salient parts are also highlighted (the ground for instance). It is the saliency maps at the intermediate scales that consistently highlight salient regions. The last three images on the right mainly show edges.

3.2   Whole Object Segmentation Using Saliency Maps

The image is over-segmented using a simple *K-means* algorithm. The K seeds for the *K-means* segmentation are automatically determined using the hill-climbing algorithm [13] in the three-dimensional *CIELab* histogram of the image. The

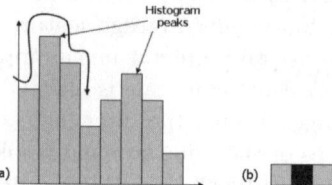

Fig. 4. (a) Finding peaks in a histogram using a search window like (b) for a one dimensional histogram

hill-climbing algorithm can be seen as a search window being run across the space of the d-dimensional histogram to find the largest bin within that window. Figure 4 explains the algorithm for a one-dimensional case. Since the *CIELab* feature space is three-dimensional, each bin in the color histogram has $3^d - 1 = 26$ neighbors where d is the number of dimensions of the feature space. The number of peaks obtained indicates the value of K, and the values of these bins form the initial seeds.

Since *K-means* algorithm clusters pixels in the *CIELab* feature space, an 8-neighbor connected-components algorithm is run to connect pixels of each cluster spatially. Once the segmented regions r_k for $k = 1, 2 ... K$ are found, the average saliency value V per segmented region is calculated by adding up values in the final saliency map $\mathbf{M}$ corresponding to pixels in the segmented image:

$$V_k = \frac{1}{|r_k|} \sum_{i,j \in r_k} m_{i,j} \tag{5}$$

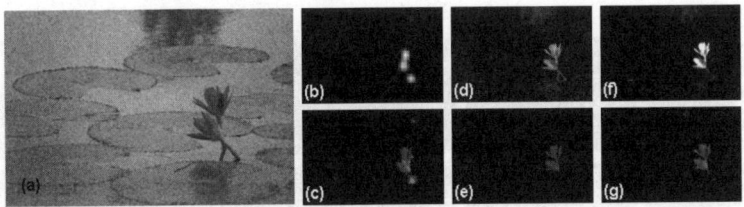

Fig. 5. (a) Original image with 5db gaussian noise. (b) Itti's saliency map. (c) Segmentation result using map (b). (d) Saliency map with our method using R_1 of size 1×1. (e) Segmentation result using map (d). (f) Saliency map with our method using R_1 of size 9×9. (g) Segmentation result using map (f).

where $|r_k|$ is the size of the segmented region in pixels. A simple threshold based method can be used wherein the segments having average saliency value greater than a certain threshold T are retained while the rest are discarded. This results in an output containing only those segments that constitute the salient object.

4 Experiments and Results

Experiments were performed on images from the Berkely database and from flickr[TM, 1]. The saliency maps for Itti's model[2] were generated using iLAB Neuromorphic Vision Toolkit[3]. The results of salient region segmentation from our method[4] are compared with those from Itti's model for the same input image and same segmentation algorithm. For segmentation, a window size of $3 \times 3 \times 3$ is used for the hill-climbing search on a $16 \times 16 \times 16$ bin $CIELab$ histogram. The average saliency threshold used for selecting segments T is set at 25 (about 10% of the maximum possible average saliency in the normalized final saliency map) based on observations on about 200 images. This threshold is not too sensitive and can be varied by 10% of its value without affecting the segmentation results. The results[5] in Figures 6 and 7 show that salient pixels using our computational

Table 1. Table comparing time (in seconds) required to find salient regions for different sizes of input images. The two algorithms were run on an Intel Dual Core 2.26 GHz machine with 1GB RAM.

Algorithm used	320x240	640x480	800x600	1024x768
Itti-Koch Method	0.75	2.54	4.40	7.50
Our algorithm for saliency	0.12	0.46	0.68	1.29

[1] http://www.flickr.com/

[2] Since Itti's model generates very small saliency maps relative to the original input image, in Figures 6 and 7 these images are shown up-scaled.

[3] http://ilab.usc.edu/toolkit/

[4] http://ivrg.epfl.ch/~achanta/SalientRegionDetection/SalientRegionDetection.html

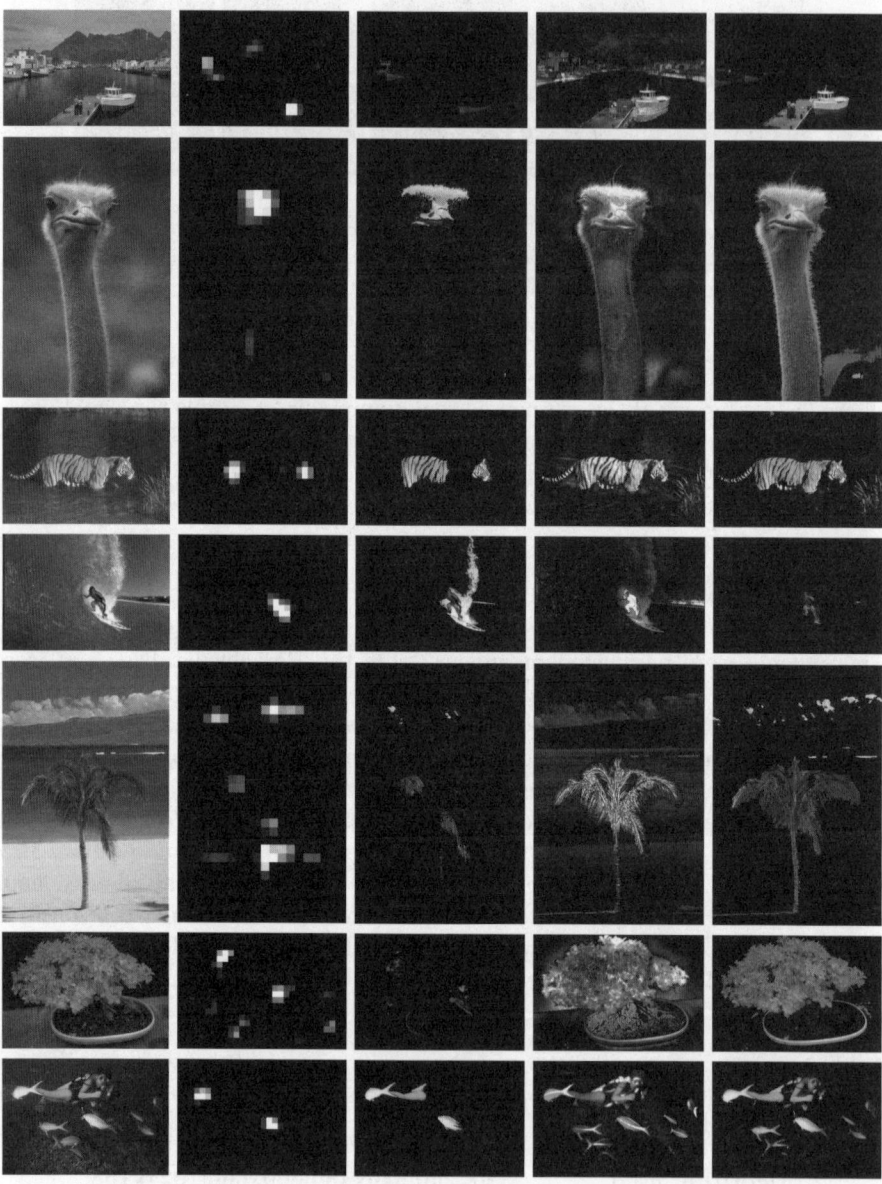

Fig. 6. Visual attention region detection results on images from the Berkeley database. From left to right: Original image, Itti's saliency map, segmentation using Itti's map, saliency map using our method, and segmentation using our saliency map. Note that the regions of saliency in Itti's maps and our maps are often the same, however, in our maps, the detail is much greater and the regions are well defined.

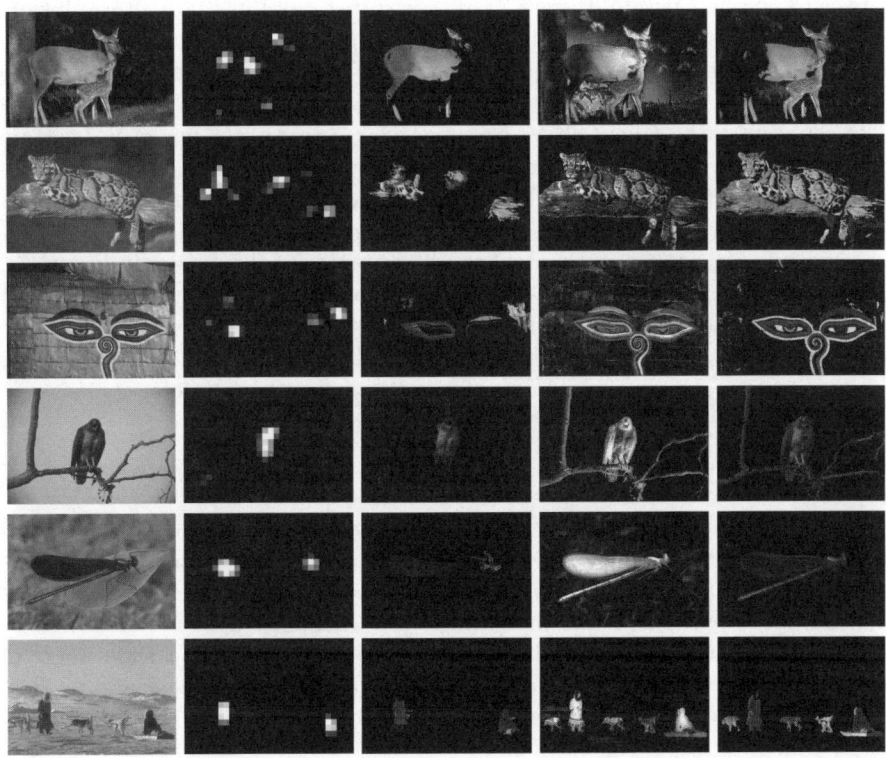

Fig. 7. Visual attention region detection results on images from the Berkeley database. From left to right: Original image, Itti's saliency map, segmentation using Itti's map, saliency map using our method, and segmentation using our saliency map.

method correspond closely to those using Itti's method, which is based on a biological model. In addition, because of the high resolution of the saliency maps, the entire salient region is clearly highlighted (Figures 6 and 7, column 3). This facilitates a clean segmentation of semantically more meaningful whole objects without having to use an overly complex segmentation algorithm.

We compared speed of salient map generation of our proposed method against that of Itti's method. The results are shown in Table 1. Our algorithm is at least five times faster in generation of saliency maps for a given image size. Although both algorithms have roughly have a complexity of $O(n)$ (which is also evident from the speeds vs. image size values in Table 1), there is a lot more processing taking place in Itti' method, where apart from color and luminance maps several orientation maps are also created. As opposed to this only three maps created by our method for the features of color and luminance treated as one vector value. Itti's method computes center-surround differences by performing subtraction

---

[5] The saliency maps from Itti's method as well as our method shown in the results are contrast-stretched for better print quality.

between Gaussian pyramid levels. This speedup results in a loss of resolution. Our method instead changes the size of the filter at each scale through the use of integral images, which achieves even greater speed without lowering the resolution.

In cases when the salient object occupies a large part of the image or if certain parts of the salient objects do not show sufficient contrast w.r.t their surroundings (eg. the back of the deer in Figure 7), the salient object segmentation is not satisfactory. At times there are some holes left in the salient objects or some extra segments are present in the final result (eg. spots of the Jaguar in Figure 7). These can be handled in a post-processing step. In the experiments done with noisy images it was observed that (see Figure 5), for moderate amounts of noise (less than 1dB), one pixel size for R_1 suffices. The size of R_1 can be increased in the presence greater amount of noise for better salient region detection.

5   Conclusions

We presented a novel method of finding salient regions in images, using low level features of color and luminance, which is easy to implement, noise tolerant, and fast enough to be useful for real time applications. It generates saliency maps at the same resolution as the input image. We demonstrated the effectiveness of the method in detecting and segmenting salient regions in a wide range of images. The approach is at least five times as fast as a prominent approach to finding saliency maps and generates high resolution saliency maps that allow better salient object segmentation.

Acknowledgements

This work is supported by the National Competence Center in Research on Mobile Information and Communication Systems (NCCR-MICS), a center supported by the Swiss National Science Foundation under grant number 5005-67322, and the European Commission under contract FP6-027026 (K-Space, the European Network of Excellence in Knowledge Space of semantic inference for automatic annotation and retrieval of multimedia content).

References

1. Digital still camera image file format standard (exchangeable image file format for digital still cameras: Exif) Version 2.1, Specification by JEITA (June 1998)
2. Avidan, S., Shamir, A.: Seam carving for content-aware image resizing. ACM Transactions on Graphics 26(3), 10 (2007)
3. Chen, L., Xie, X., Fan, X., Ma, W.-Y., Zhang, H.-J., Zhou, H.: A visual attention model for adapting images on small displays. ACM Transactions on Multimedia Systems 9, 353–364 (2003)
4. Frintrop, S., Klodt, M., Rome, E.: A real-time visual attention system using integral images. In: International Conference on Computer Vision Systems (ICVS 2007) (March 2007)

 5. Han, J., Ngan, K.N., Li, M., Zhang, H.J.: Unsupervised extraction of visual attention objects in color images. IEEE Transactions on Circuits and Systems for Video Technology 16(1), 141–145 (2006)
 6. Hu, Y., Xie, X., Ma, W.-Y., Chia, L.-T., Rajan, D.: Salient region detection using weighted feature maps based on the human visual attention model. In: Aizawa, K., Nakamura, Y., Satoh, S. (eds.) PCM 2004. LNCS, vol. 3332, pp. 993–1000. Springer, Heidelberg (2004)
 7. Hunt, R.W.G.: Measuring Color. Fountain Press (1998)
 8. Itti, L., Koch, C.: Comparison of feature combination strategies for saliency-based visual attention systems. In: SPIE Human Vision and Electronic Imaging IV (HVEI 1999), May 1999, pp. 473–482 (1999)
 9. Itti, L., Koch, C., Niebur, E.: A model of saliency-based visual attention for rapid scene analysis. IEEE Transactions on Pattern Analysis and Machine Intelligence 20(11), 1254–1259 (1998)
10. Ko, B.C., Nam, J.-Y.: Object-of-interest image segmentation based on human attention and semantic region clustering. Journal of Optical Society of America A 23(10), 2462–2470 (2006)
11. Ma, Y.-F., Zhang, H.-J.: Contrast-based image attention analysis by using fuzzy growing. In: Proceedings of the Eleventh ACM International Conference on Multimedia, November 2003, pp. 374–381 (2003)
12. Setlur, V., Takagi, S., Raskar, R., Gleicher, M., Gooch, B.: Automatic image retargeting. In: Proceedings of the 4th International Conference on Mobile and Ubiquitous Multimedia (MUM 2005), October 2005, pp. 59–68 (2005)
13. Ohashi, T., Aghbari, Z., Makinouchi, A.: Hill-climbing algorithm for efficient color-based image segmentation. In: IASTED International Conference On Signal Processing, Pattern Recognition, and Applications (SPPRA 2003) (June 2003)
14. Viola, P., Jones, M.: Rapid object detection using a boosted cascade of simple features. In: Proceedings of IEEE Conference on Computer Vision and Pattern Recognition (CVPR 2001), December 2001, vol. 1, pp. 511–518 (2001)

Part II

Monitor and Surveillance

The SAFEE On-Board
Threat Detection System

N.L. Carter and J.M. Ferryman

Computational Vision Group, School of Systems Engineering,
The University of Reading, Reading, U.K., RG6 6AY
{N.L.Carter,J.M.Ferryman}@reading.ac.uk

Abstract. Under the framework of the European Union Funded SAFEE project[1], this paper gives an overview of a novel monitoring and scene analysis system developed for use onboard aircraft in spatially constrained environments. The techniques discussed herein aim to warn on-board crew about pre-determined indicators of threat intent (such as running or shouting in the cabin), as elicited from industry and security experts. The subject matter experts believe that activities such as these are strong indicators of the beginnings of undesirable chains of events or scenarios, which should not be allowed to develop aboard aircraft. This project aimes to detect these scenarios and provide advice to the crew. These events may involve unruly passengers or be indicative of the precursors to terrorist threats. With a state of the art tracking system using homography intersections of motion images, and probability based Petri nets for scene understanding, the SAFEE behavioural analysis system automatically assesses the output from multiple intelligent sensors, and creates recommendations that are presented to the crew using an integrated airborn user interface. Evaluation of the system is conducted within a full size aircraft mockup, and experimental results are presented, showing that the SAFEE system is well suited to monitoring people in confined environments, and that meaningful and instructive output regarding human actions can be derived from the sensor network within the cabin.

Keywords: Scene Recognition, Tracking, Planar Homographies.

1   Introduction

In this paper, we present an overview of the SAFEE project, which brings together 31 European partners with the aim, among other objectives, to provide a systematic solution to monitoring people within enclosed spaces and in the presence of heavy occlusion, analyse these observations and derive threat intentions. These threats are then conveyed to the crew and may include unruly passenger behaviour (due to intoxication, etc.), potential hijack situations, and numerous other events of importance to both flight crew and ground staff.

---

[1] EU Funded SAFEE project (Grant Number:AIP3-CT-62003-503521).

A. Gasteratos, M. Vincze, and J.K. Tsotsos (Eds.): ICVS 2008, LNCS 5008, pp. 79–88, 2008.

The indicators of such events have been compiled and verified by independent subject matter experts (SMEs) and the resultant pre-determined indicators of threat (PDIs), such as running in the cabin or shouting, have been incorporated into the tracking and understanding modules of the system to allow for automatic computerised analysis of potential threats.

Many different SMEs have also given technical input into this project[2], and their contributions (e.g. audio surveillance systems and low-level visual stress detections systems) are fed into the scene-understanding module. This module (as discussed in Section 3) produces a synergised and reasoned output from the various sections and subsections of this project.

In order to correctly analyse the actions of passengers on board an aircraft, information, such as the identity and positions of people within the cabin area, vapour analysis of explosive materials, key word and audio analysis (searching for sound patterns) and low level stress analysis of people at the seat level, must be collected by intelligent sensors. For reasons of brevity, this paper, while acknowledging the contribution from other technical partners, will focus mainly on global object tracking and scene understanding within the SAFEE project.

2 Threat Detection System

Real time tracking and analysis of multiple moving targets using computer vision is difficult in open and uncluttered environments with low inter-object occlusion. The task is made many times more difficult in enclosed and confined environments with high levels of occlusion [6]. In these types of environment, canonical tracking approaches are problematic to implement and often give sub-optimal localisation output, as shown in Section 4. This type of output may also be more susceptible to occlusion related issues. The framework presented within this paper address these problems, and the results presented reinforce the applicability of this approach.

To adequately test and demonstrate the potential of the proposed system, a realistic approximation of the cabin environment was required. For this reason, a full-scale aircraft mock-up was used. A cabin seating configuration of the highest density possible was chosen, in order to test the system under extreme occlusion conditions. For the global tracking system, an array of six cameras was used to gain an adequate coverage of all key areas of the cabin environment. This arrangement is extensible and can generalise to larger aircraft and alternate aircraft configurations. The current arrangement is shown in Figure 1.

This project uses Point Grey Research Dragonfly 2 cameras, with 2.1mm focal length lenses, producing a fish-eye type image. This focal length was required as cameras could not be placed at a great enough distance from the viewing area (given the constraints of the environment) to create a large and fully view-overlapping surveillance area.

---

[2] Additional information regarding other project partners may be found at www.safee.info.

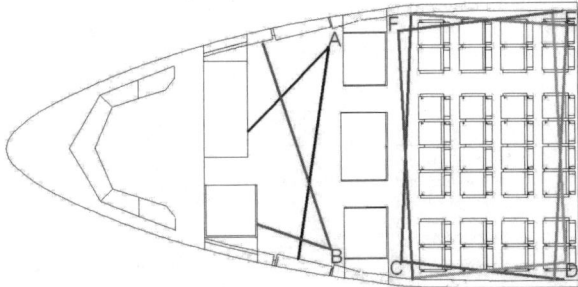

Fig. 1. Camera Placement Within the Aircraft Mock-up. Cameras A and B View the Cockpit Door, Cameras C-F View the Cabin Area.

To process the resultant camera images, a set of five custom built computers were used. For every two cameras, one computer node was used to capture images. Using a variety of background segmentation methodologies (see Section 2.1) the images are segmented to produce binary motion images. This data is then sent via a Huffman encoded database connection to another processing unit, which performs homography-based fusion and tracking [4]. The output from this processing unit is sent to the last unit, where scene understanding and final subsystem output is created. This information flow is represented diagrammatically in Figure 2.

2.1   Motion Segmentation

We implemented three segmentation approaches based on the colour, mean and variance concept given in [2], the Wallflower concept [3] and Gaussian Mixture Model [9]. It has been noted by [7] that each of the segmentation approaches have specific advantages and disadvantages where spurious readings and background noise is concerned, but that the main objects of interest within a given scene normally appear as foreground in each approach, especially when stable scenes are used. As our aim is to create a background segmentation system that is robust to background noise and spurious readings, a combinatory approach was taken, which fused the three techniques together. This is shown experimentally to outperform the individual techniques in isolation.

To achieve fusion of disparate segmentation schemes, each motion segmentation module in the system, (see Figure 2), takes input from one of the overlapping camera views. This data is then sent to a central store (via the Huffman encoded database link), where it is processed by the Homography Fusion Module (see Section 2.2).

The images are co-registered through planar homography calibrations, the individual segmentation data can be projected from each view to any other view, so that the motion data overlaps. Due to the co-registered nature of the combinatorial approach, any type of motion segmentation system can be employed and then fused at a later stage.

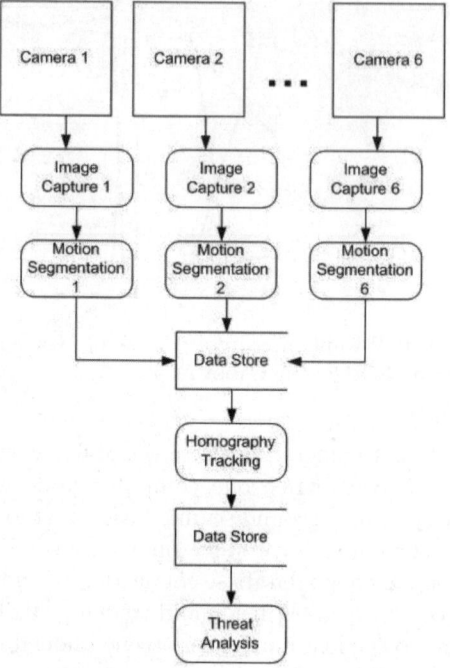

Fig. 2. Data Flow Diagram For the Person Tracking Sub-System

The fusion system has the extremely important benefit of removing spurious readings (detection noise) from each technique during the fusion stage, leaving only the actual objects of interest, and improves upon the results obtained using any of the techniques in isolation (see Section 4).

2.2 Homography Based Tracking

Given the motion segmentation output, which should contain objects of interest, the goal now is to fuse the motion data, extract individual objects that are of interest and are not background clutter (seats, reflections, shadows, etc), and can be separated spatially to localise separate objects[4]. For this purpose, homography intersections can be used. Khan and Shah introduced the concept of using planar homographies for motion tracking.

Homographies can be used to map a plane in one image to a plane in another image by calibrating image pairs based on known pixel correspondences. This quality makes them highly useful in combining pictorial information. This combinatorial prowess allows motion images to be combined in our method, whilst simultaneously resolving inter-object image occlusion and motion segmentation inaccuracies [4].

If one were to create a homography matrix, but calibrate using only co-planar calibration points, the homography would then be constrained to a projection

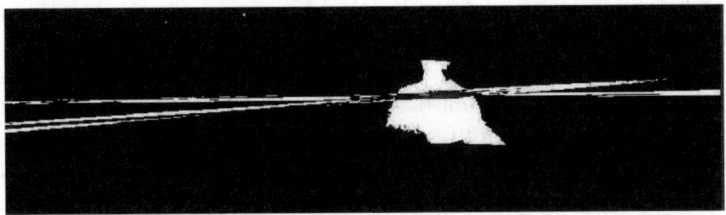

Fig. 3. Homography Fusion: White Areas Show Projected Motion From Segmentation, Red and Blue Show High Levels of Camera Agreement

upon a designated plane within an image pair. The homography matrix can be used to transform pixels in one image to fall upon a plane in another image (e.g. the ground plane).

If one image view was arbitrarily chosen as a reference view, and planar homographies were extrapolated in the way previously suggested, each pixel in the reference view could be projected to a plane in every other image view. Planar parallax states that co-planar pixel locations transformed in such a way will fall upon the same plane in every correctly calibrated image, and that all points not on the plane in the reference image will miss-align upon the plane of any other calibrated image [4]. This reduces the complexity of combination drastically, as areas of high agreement correspond to locations of objects that all cameras agree are on the plane. Agreement in this case can be viewed as density of pixel overlap. This concept is shown graphically in Figure 3.

As planar homographies do not form correctly in fish-eye type images, an image dewarping step was also performed. The planar homographies could in fact be calibrated correctly in most cases without image dewarping, however radial distortion could introduce some unpredictable behaviour if the dewarping step was not performed.

2.3   Environmental Considerations

In previous homography based tracking tasks, such as Khan and Shah [4], the ground plane was used for calibration. This is normally a sound choice of calibration plane in outdoor and uncluttered environments, as it is readily observable by all cameras and usually forms a planar surface upon which all cameras can be calibrated. In the SAFEE environment, the ground plane is unsuitable for tracking. Heavy occlusion caused by the solid seats in the cabin does not allow all cameras to reliably view the ground area. This plane is also more susceptible to shadow effects and specularities, not only in cabin environment, but in many other environments as well.

Another issue found when using the ground plane is that a more complicated tracking system must be employed to determine the actual location of a person. This is due to the ground plane based trackers reliance on foot position. As these are free to move independently, they may not accurately represent the torso (centre of balance) position of the person. Khan and Shah solve this problem by using the assumption that feet are normally closer to each other (over a prolonged period) than to other objects. This approach naturally assumes a look ahead / look behind system based on a temporal build up of observations. This approach may fail in highly cluttered environments such as an aircraft aisle, as the fundimental precept can be violated (peoples feet may in fact be closer to others than to each other).

We propose that the issue can be more elegantly solved by raising the homography calibration plane away from the ground. When tracking people, use of a plane at standing chest height means only one object (the torso) is to be tracked. This also alleviates the issues that may be caused by shadow effects and specularity, which are most prevalent on the ground plane.

2.4   Object Tracking

Once the Homography based tracking system has localised the objects within the scene, solved the occlusion issues and reduced or eliminated the shadows and specularity, object tracking is performed. This allows a global threat level to be maintained, with previous actions adding to the overall threat assessment of a passenger.

Though the objects in the scene should therefore rarely fuse, the tracking system must still reason about direction of travel when people come into close contact. This is performed by a Nearest Neighbour Data Association Filter (NNDAF) [8]. This technique relies solely on spatial information to create associations.

3   Behavioural Analysis

When considering the suitability of behavioural analysis techniques for this project, several strong contenders are evident. Bayesian networks provide a good framework for combining numerous pieces of information in a probabilistic framework, and provides a probability based output. However, these networks have no readily available state based information, so system state would not be easy to obtain [5]. Markov chains by contrast provide good state based information, but are less suited to combining numerous low level variables [6,7].

A technique proposed by Carter et. al. [7] aimed to fuse Bayesian networks and Markov chain methodologies. This technique was implemented and tested, however, a more temporally and concurrent approach was required (see Section 4). Petri nets [5], as a technique originally designed to analyse system concurrency, are an obvious choice for consideration. Petri nets allow collections of variables to be combined in a temporal manner (in specialised temporal Petri nets), and can even use probability based transitions to maintain a probability based output.

Using Petri nets, collections of basic PDIs are arranged and ordered, so that their combination can be used to reason about more complex scenarios. In this way simple PDIs such as running can form higher level scenarios such as running

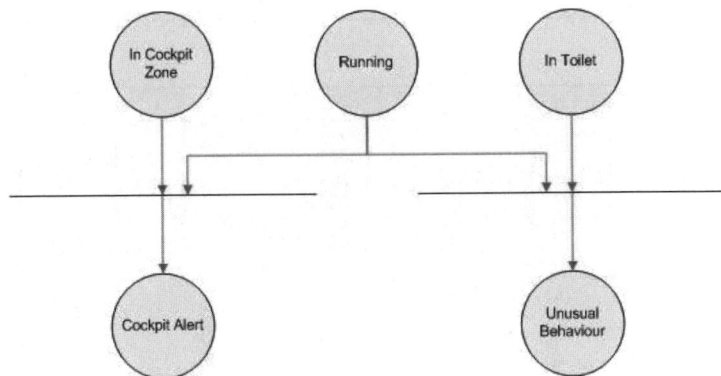

Fig. 4. Simplified Example of A SAFEE Petri Net. Shows the Combination of Pre-Defined Indicators to Build Outputs.

to cockpit door, prolonged time in toilet or running to toilet. When additional information, such as the state of the cockpit door (open / closed / locked / unlocked) is taken into account, the threat probabilities can be further altered and refined.

Within the SAFEE project, information can be obtained from the global position of passengers within the scene. Some of these are listed:

- Standing (and standing while the seatbelt sign is on)
- Being within a predefined zone (e.g. cockpit entry zone)
- Running (within the aisle zone)
- Multiple people standing at the same time

These observations can be combined with other partner's output, some of which are shown in the following list:

- Aggressive behaviour
- Nervous behaviour
- Suspicious sounds (breaking glass, weapons fire, etc.)
- Bomb vapour analysis
- Information about the plane (seat belt sign status, smoke alarm, door status, etc.)

Using a probability based Petri net, state information can be utilised as well as final output. This allows compound decisions based on multiple events to be reasoned about, and can reduce network complexity, when contrasted against other network structures.

4   Evaluation

In this section we present experimental results for the SAFEE threat detection sub-systems. We demonstrate the increased accuracy available when using a

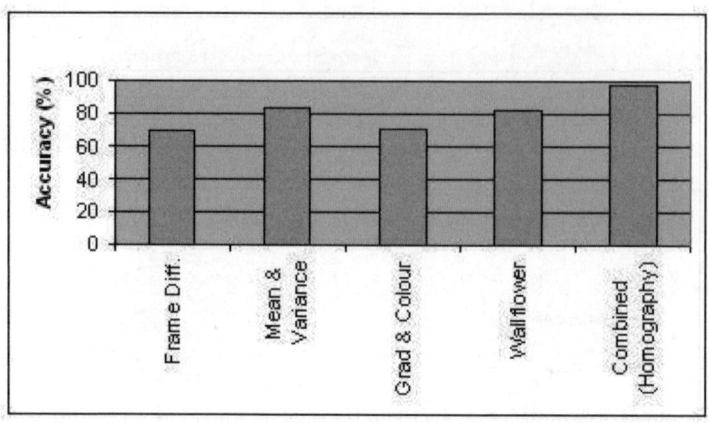

Fig. 5. Comparison of Motion Segmentation Approaches

combination of fused background segmentation approaches. We also show the overall accuracy of the homography based tracker, as the central system for generating tracking based warnings and alarms.

4.1   Segmentation through Motion

Figure 5 highlights the effect of using different motion segmentation techniques as a pre-processing step to motion tracking. The different segmentation approaches are contrasted against the effect of fusing all of the motion segmentation techniques together through Homography based filtering. The combined homography based result outperforms all individual segmentation results. Figure 5 shows (on the y-axis) the percentage of motion detected within ground truthed "moving" objects in experimental video frames.

4.2   Generation of Warnings and Alarms

From the global tracking output, and other available partners' outputs (e.g. audio cues), the behavioural recognition system, as described in Section 3, is required to reason about the state of the aircraft and provide warnings and alarms where necessary to the crew and ground staff. These warnings and alarms can be sequenced to create scenarios, or can be used in isolation and passed to other interpretation systems within the SAFEE project. Table 1 provides results showing the number of actual (ground truthed) threat actions presented to the system, with the recognition rates shown for each. This table shows the accuracy of the recognition sub-system explicitally, and the accuracy of the homography implicitly.

As can be seen from Table 1, standing up indicators are highly robust, as are the restricted standing up events (an extension of the basic standing behaviour).

Table 1. Analysis of Indicator Output (Focusing on Tracking)

Indicator	Tests(#)	Recognition(%)	Data
Stands	52	100%	Real
Stands (Restricted Time)	28	100%	Real/Synthetic
Running	20	70%	Real
In Zone (e.g. Cockpit)	81	100%	Real
Long Time in Toilet	10	90%	Synthetic

Zone indicators, which locate a person in a pre-defined area of the aircraft, are similarly robust. The lowest scoring indicator (running) is correspondingly the hardest indicator to detect, as it requires robust tracking over time, and a concept of distance. This indicator is adversely influenced by the frame rate of the system (6-7 fps). Increasing the system frame rate should increase the accuracy of running detection.

5   Conclusion

A systematic approach to tracking and scene understanding in confined locations is presented, building upon previous homography tracking theory to increase accuracy and applicability to spatially confined surveillance areas.

The main contributions of this paper include:

- An overview of the SAFEE project and tracking in constrained environments
- A flexible fusion technique to combine different background segmentation techniques in a complimentary way, that also aids in the reduction of occlusion
- An extension to previous homography tracking approaches, which more elegantly solves the tracking problem without the need for temporal information
- Real-time homography tracking through the use of a distributed architecture
- Deployment of an integrated system for behavioural analysis in a real world environment

Though the system is demonstrated within the scope of cabin surveillance, the techniques and structures can be generalised to other complex tracking domains such as buses, trains and confined public spaces. To our knowledge, this is the first major project to use homography based tracking, and fuse background segmentation schemes. The degree of occlusion tolerance provided by this approach is far superior to many canonical techniques in the tracking domain.

6   Future Work

The main limitation of the system described in this paper is its reliance upon motion segmentation based on pre-calculated background models. Lighting and vibrations heavily influence the systems robustness. We can currently detect corruptions to the background model in real time and correct this through fast background updates. This approach is not optimal, however, as information during the update is lost. This kind of approach is curative, when a preventative measure would be more appropriate. For this reason, we are investigating applications of lighting invariant background models, especially those based on homography reasoning. We would also like to investigate the optimal way to assign background segmentation methodologies to camera views, and the effect of clutter and occlusion to the segmentation fusion results.

References

1. Fusier, F., Valentin, V., Bremond, F., Thonnat, M., Borg, M., Thirde, D., Ferryman, J.: Video Understanding for Complex Activity Recognition. The Journal of Machine Vision and Applications 18(3-4), 167–188 (2007)
2. Aguilera, J., Wildernauer, H., Kampel, M., Borg, M., Thirde, D., Ferryman, J.: Evaluation of motion segmentation quality for aircraft activity surveillances. In: Proc. Joint IEEE Int. Workshop on VS-PETS, Beijing, October 2005, pp. 293–300 (2005)
3. Toyama, K., Krumm, J., Brumitt, B., Meyers, B.: Wallflower: Principles and Practice of Background Maintenance. In: International Conference on Computer Vision, Corfu, September 1999, pp. 255–261 (1999)
4. Khan, S., Shah, M.: A Multiview Approach to Tracking People in Crowded Scenes using a Planar Homography Constraint. In: European Conference on Computer Vision, Austria, 2006, pp. 1025–1039 (2006)
5. Vu, V., Bremond, F., Thonnat, M.: Automatic Video Interpretation: A Recognition Algorithm for Temporal Scenarios Based on Pre-compiled Scenario Models. In: International Conference on Visual Systems, pp. 523–533 (2003)
6. Carter, N., Young, D., Ferryman, J.: Supplementing Markov Chains with Additional Features for Behavioural Analysis. In: AVSS, IEEE International Conference on Video and Signal Based Surveillance (AVSS 2006), Hong Kong, pp. 65–71 (2006)
7. Carter, N., Young, D., Ferryman, J.: A Combined Bayesian Markovian Approach for Behaviour Recognition, icpr. In: 18th International Conference on Pattern Recognition (ICPR 2006), pp. 761–764 (2006)
8. Song, T., Lee, D., Ryu, J.: A probabilistic nearest neighbor filter algorithm for tracking in a clutter environment. Signal Processing 85(10), 2044–(2053)
9. Friedman, N., Russell, S.: Image segmentation in video sequences: a probabilistic approach. In: Proceedings of the Thirteenth Annual Conference on Uncertainty in Artificial Intelligence (UAI-1997), pp. 175–181. Morgan Kaufmann Publishers, Inc, San Francisco (1997)

Region of Interest Generation in Dynamic Environments Using Local Entropy Fields

Luciano Spinello and Roland Siegwart

Autonomous Systems Lab, ETH Zurich, Switzerland
{luciano.spinello,roland.siegwart}@mavt.ethz.ch

Abstract. This paper presents a novel technique to generate regions of interest in image sequences containing independent motions. The technique uses a novel motion segmentation method to segment optical flow using a local entropies field. Local entropy values are computed for each optical flow vector and are collected as input for a two state Markov Random Field that is used to discriminate the motion boundaries. Local entropy values are highly informative cues on the amount of information contained in the vector's neighborhood. High values represent significative motion differences, low values express uniform motions. For each cluster a motion model is fitted and it is used to create a multiple hypothesis prediction for the following frame. Experiments have been performed on standard and outdoor datasets in order to show the validity of the proposed technique.

1 Introduction

Region of interest (ROI) generation in image sequences has a considerable importance in a number of mobile robotics applications using vision, especially in object detection and tracking in dynamic and outdoor environments. The aim of this paper is to segment regions of interest that contain independent relative motions in the optical flow and to use these moving regions to further enhance the segmentation in the following frames.

Several approaches can be found in literature to segment motions in image sequences including layered based analysis [1][2][3], multi-body factorization [4], motion eigenvectors analisys [5][6][7] or methods that exploit the 3D information contained in n-image sequences [8][9] to obtain precise results with computationally demanding algorithms.

The technique explained in this paper generates a motion segmentation within two frames and it is designed to work in sequences with moving observers and moving objects. Such kind of segmentation can be used in mobile robotics where waiting for n-frames for an hypothesis can represent a drawback.

The novelty of this paper is given as follows:

- Neighborhood definition in the motion vector field through the use of a Delaunay triangulation: The arcs of the graph define the neighbor search path.

A. Gasteratos, M. Vincze, and J.K. Tsotsos (Eds.): ICVS 2008, LNCS 5008, pp. 89–98, 2008.

- Generation of a local entropy field to compute motion difformities in the optical flow: for each node of the graph a local entropy value measures the information quantity of the vector's neighborhood motion.
- Use of a two states Markov Random Field (MRF) for defining uniform motion boundaries: the class $\mathcal{H}$ define the boundaries of the clusters that are then labeled using a graph cut approach.
- Segmentation enhancement in following frames using a multiple hypothesis motion prediction scheme.

The algorithm is also built considering a practical implementation with compact memory usage, suitable for mobile robotics.

The structure of the paper is the following. The motion field neighbourhood and topology is explained in Sec. 2. The local entropies field is described in Sec. 3. The design of the Markov random field for the problem is explained in Sec 4. The multiple hypotheses motion prediction is explained in the following Sec 5 and the experimental results are shown in Sec 6. A schematic explanation of the technique presented in this paper is given in fig. 1.

2   Motion Field Neighbourhood

A sparse optical flow method based on the work of Kanade, Lucas and Tomasi [10] is here used (KLT) in order to overcome disadvantages of dense optical flow techniques in outdoor environments In the sparse optical flow the velocity vectors

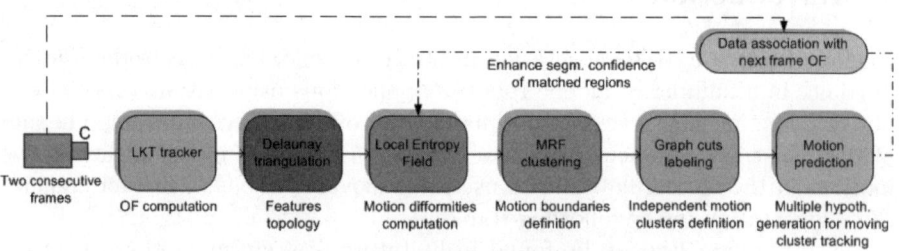

Fig. 1. Overview of the proposed technique

are scattered in the image plane. The neighborhood information is expressed through the use of a Delaunay triangulation. The origins of the velocity vectors of the computed optical flow are used as the set P of points that define the vertices of the triangulation. The edges of the graph defined by the Delaunay triangulation define the search path among features. Delaunay triangulation has been selected for its low computational complexity and unique tessellation of the space.

3 Local Entropies Field

In this paper the optical flow is considered for a local entropies field computation. The dual of a Delaunay triangulation, the Voronoi decomposition, is used to tessellate the optical flow in cells. A local entropy value is computed for each cell's neighborhood, defined by the adjacent cells using the information theory.

Let's consider an information source emitting n symbols $A = \{a_1, a_2, \ldots, a_n\}$ with probability $\mathbf{u} = [P(a_1), P(a_2), \ldots, P(a_n)]$. Having modeled the information source, we can develop the input-output characteristics of the information channel. Because we modeled the source as a discrete random variable, the information transferred to the output of the channel is also a discrete random variable. Given the channel symbol alphabet $B = \{b_1, b_2, \ldots, b_n\}$ the probability of the event that symbol b_k is presented to the information user is $P(b_k) = \sum_j^n P(b_k|a_j)P(a_j)$. The probability distribution for the complete output alphabet can be computed from:

$$\mathbf{v} = Q\mathbf{z}; \qquad Q = \begin{bmatrix} P(b_1|a_1) & P(b_1|a_2) & \cdots & P(b_1|a_n) \\ P(b_2|a_1) & \vdots & \cdots & \vdots \\ \vdots & \vdots & \ddots & \vdots \\ P(b_k|a_1) & P(b_k|a_2) & \cdots & P(b_k|a_n) \end{bmatrix} \tag{1}$$

The matrix Q is referred to as *forward channel transition matrix*. In our case the alphabet A considered is defined by the difference between salient values for motion segmentation. Salient values in the optical flow for relative motion segmentation are defined by the vector angle α, the vector norm m, and the L_1 distance between the origin of two vectors l. Values of α and m give an information about motion difference between two vectors, l is useful to avoid grouping of distant vectors in the motion field.

For each cell an histogram is built using the salient value differences between the reference vector and the neighborhood. The probability set $\mathbf{u}$ is computed using this histogram. High uncertainty is given to conditional probability relative to symbols expressing large differences in the matrix channel Q. This means that probabilities emitted from the source expressing large differences are considered more noisy, therefore they contribute more to the channel output entropy value $H(\mathbf{v}) = -\sum_j^n P(b_j) \log P(b_j)$, effectively highlighting motion difformities in the cell's neighborhood.

For each cell $c(i)$ its local channel output entropy value is computed using the salient values α, l, m in the neighborhood $N(c(i))$:

$$H_c(i) = c_1 \underbrace{\sum_{j \in N(c(i))} P(b_j)^\alpha \log_2 P(b_j)^\alpha}_{angle} + c_2 \underbrace{\sum_{j \in N(c(i))} P(b_j)^m \log_2 P(b_j)^m}_{norm} +$$

$$+ c_3 \underbrace{\sum_{j \in N(c(i))} P(b_j)^l \log_2 P(b_j)^l}_{dist} \tag{2}$$

where c_1, c_2, c_3 represent the weighting factors. The cell local entropy value expresses the amount of information present in its neighborhood, using the cell as reference value. The smaller the value $H_c(i)$ is the stronger the evidence is that the cell is contained in a similar motion region. Cluster boundaries are cells in which the entropy is substantially bigger. An example of a computed local entropy field is shown in Fig.9. Intuitively, the motion segmentation algorithm has to segment local minima in the local entropy field to obtain a correct clustering.

4   Clustering with a Two State MRF

We model the clustering problem of motion segmentation with a pairwise Markov random field (MRF). Well known methods already exist to achieve clustering with MRF, but most of them are computationally expensive or memory demanding. In Fig.2 the circles represent network nodes and the lines indicate the statistical dependencies among nodes. With x_i we indicate the states and with y_i the observations. The problem is formalized using only two states instead of defining one for each cluster. This improves the convergence speed and the memory compactness of the algorithm. The considered state space is defined by:

$$x_i \in \{\mathcal{H}, \ \mathcal{L}\} \tag{3}$$

where $\mathcal{H}$ defines a cluster boundary (high entropy) and $\mathcal{L}$ a cluster element (low entropy). Instead of retrieving from the clustering phase the segmented clusters, as the classical cluster approach, we retrieve the boundaries of the clusters defined by the state $\mathcal{H}$. We let the observations y_i be proportional to

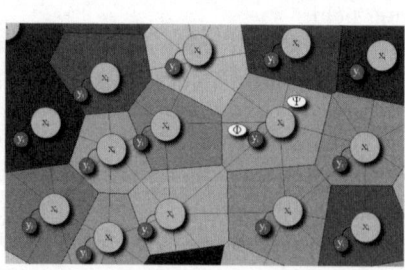
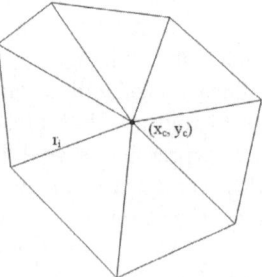

Fig. 2. Pairwise Markov Random Field connected through Delaunay triangulation graph

Fig. 3. Shape descriptor

the observed local entropy values $H_c(i)$ explained in the previous section. For this network, the overall joint probability of the nodes x_i and the observations y_i is proportional to the product of all sets of compatibility matrix Ψ, relating the possible states of each pair of neighboring hidden nodes, and the vectors Φ, relating each observation to the underlying hidden states:

$$p(\{x\}, \{y\}) = \frac{1}{Z} \prod_{(ij)} \Psi_{ij}(x_i, \ x_j) \prod_i \Phi(x_i, y_j) \tag{4}$$

where Z is a normalization constant, and the first product is over all neighboring pairs of nodes, i and j.

The compatibility function $\Psi_{ij}(x_i, \ x_j)$ is specified to have an high compatibility if the states are the same and a low value if they are different. It is defined by a distance measure:

$$\Psi_{ij}(x_i, \ x_j) = e^{\left(-\frac{d_{ij}(x_i, \ x_j)}{2\sigma^2} \right)} \tag{5}$$

where d_{ij} is defined with respect to the mean entropy value. This MRF model has similarities with the case of image noise removal with MRF [11]. The method aims to suppress boundary cells that have just small support from their neighbors. This compromises the segmentation of clusters having a very small area, because the MRF considers them as noise. The compatibility function $\Phi(x_i, y_j)$ enhances high values of $H_{c(i)}$ as strong evidences of $\mathcal{H}$ and low values of $H_{c(i)}$ as strong evidences of $\mathcal{L}$.

Finding the exact solution of Eq.4 can be computationally intractable, but good results are obtained using an approximate solution based on a fast, iterative algorithm called loopy belief propagation (BP) [12]. The standard belief-propagation algorithm updates messages m_{ij} from node i to node j, which are vectors of two elements (the dimensionality of the state).

The messages are determined self-consistently by the message update rules:

$$m_{ij} = \sum_{x_i} \Phi(x_i, y_j) \Psi_{ij}(x_i, \ x_j) \prod_{k \in N(i)/j} m_{ki}(x_i) \tag{6}$$

where $N(i)$ denotes the nodes neighboring i. Furthermore the belief at node i is proportional to the product of the local compatibility function at that node and all the messages coming into the node i:

$$b_i(x_i) = \mu\Phi(x_i, y_j) \prod_{j \in N(i)} m_{ij}(x_i) \tag{7}$$

where μ is the normalization constant (the beliefs must sum 1). If we consider the observation y_i fixed and we focus on the joint probability distribution of x_i in Eq.4, the belief propagation in fact gives the exact marginal probabilities for all the nodes in any singly-connected graph. Even though the convergence of belief propagation algorithm is not guaranteed [13] in graph with loops, it is often used in literature to solve marginalization problems (i.e. [14]). Markov random field marginalization defines only boundaries thus a labeling procedure is needed to define motion blobs in the image. A *marching line*-like algorithm is run among border nodes in order to distinct the different hulls.

5   Multiple Hypothesis Motion Prediction

The motion segmentation obtained using two frames is used to augment the information of the following frames. This is achieved using a multiple hypothesis motion prediction. The idea is to use the motion clusters at time t to enhance the motion segmentation in the following frame, matching clusters with similar motions. An affine motion model is fitted to the motion vectors contained in each blob using a least squares fitting method. A shape descriptor is used to describe the convex hull of a cluster:

$$s_d = \{x_c, y_c, r_1, \dots, r_n\} \tag{8}$$

where (x_c, y_c) is the centroid of the convex hull and r_i the radii connecting it to the boundary points, as shown in Fig.3. The set of possible shape hypotheses N_h we want to generate for each cluster is created adding to each radius a Gaussian noise. The affine motion model of each cluster is applied to the centroid coordinates of the N_h shapes generated. The multiple hypotheses set of time t is then compared with the unsegmented optical flow of frame $(t + 1)$. A greedy nearest neighbor data association technique is applied to check which hypothesis fits better to the data. If the data association problem is satisfied the old motion model reinforces the local potentials $\Phi(x_i, y_j)$ of the nodes covered by the predicted cluster, increasing the value of the $\mathcal{L}$ state.

6   Experimental Results

The algorithm was tested on several image sequences taken from PETS2000-PETS2001 standard dataset [15] and a real-world outdoor dataset.

Image sequences which show close relative motion have been selected from PETS2000 and PETS2001 datasets in order to show significative and not trivial results. 800 tracking features are computed between two consecutive images. In fig. 4(a), fig. 4(b), fig. 5(a) and fig. 5(b) moving objects are correctly segmented but due to lack of stable tracking features some parts of the objects are outside of the convex hull. In order to obtain a quantitative result a sequence detection rate is evaluated. The sequence detection rate is given by the sum of detections rate for each frame divided by number of frames. A correct detection is defined as that segmented moving region bounding box that overlaps at least 70% of the annotated one. 15 frames are considered for each of the sequences shown in fig. 6; this frame quantity has been selected in order to complete a crossing between shown objects. Detection rate for 4(a) is 80.0%, for 4(b) is 93.3%, for 5(a) is 93.3% and 5(a) is 86.6%. We did not consider a false positive rate analysis because this algorithm is designed to be an hypothesis generator therefore false positives (a clustered moving region that do not correspond to an annotated moving part) have to be considered in later stages (i.e. object detection) and are not included in the scope of this paper.

The mobile platform Smartter [16], used to acquire the outdoor datasets, is based on a Daimler-Chrysler Smart vehicle equipped with several active and

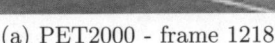

(a) PET2000 - frame 1218   (b) PET2001 - frame 424

Fig. 4. a) Two semented pedestrians are moving in the street in different directions. Due to the lack of features the moving convex hull does not cover completely the moving pedestrians b) A car and a pedestrian are moving in opposite directions; well defined separation is shown.

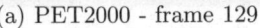

(a) PET2000 - frame 129   (b) PET2001 - frame 563

Fig. 5. a) A car is moving on a street. A small incorrectly segmented moving region is found (green area - false positive). b) A car and a pedestrian are moving in opposite directions; well defined separation is shown.

passive sensors (fig. 10). The camera used is a Sony 910XCR firewire camera mounted behind the windscreen equipped with a wide field of view lens.

A moving dataset and a static dataset are retrieved from our mobile platform Smartter to show the performance of the algorithm in different real-world conditions.

In the dataset 1, the Smartter is moving and several cars are passing in the other lane. The cars are segmented together due the similar motion due to the settings in the algorithm that prefers to cluster together similar motion than doing overclustering. In a bigger cluster it is more probable to find objects than in many fragmented blobs. In fig. 6(a) the Voronoi tessellation and local potentials are shown, the overlayed motion clusters are depicted in fig. 6(b).

In the dataset 2, the Smartter is still in front of a red traffic light. The car in the other lane is correctly segmented. In fig. 7(a) the optical flow, the triangulation and local potentials are shown, the overlayed motion clusters are depicted in fig. 7(b).

(a) Local entropy fields (set1)   (b) Moving clusters (set1)

Fig. 6. [Outdoor set 1: moving observer/moving objects] a) Local entropies field and Voronoi tessellation. Two low entropy zones are in the field (in blue), in the gray zone a below than 1px optical flow is detected. b) Moving clusters detected. Two cars in the left lane are segmented together; the right cluster segments the features of the right part of the road. The dotted central cluster depicts a static cluster in which the optical flow is negligible.

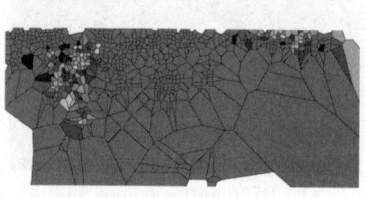

(a) Local entropy fields (set1)   (b) Moving clusters (set1)

Fig. 7. [Outdoor set 2: static observer/moving objects] a) Local entropies field and Voronoi tessellation. Only the cells associated with left car show a coherent motion. b) Moving clusters detected. The car in the other lane is correctly segmented.

In both datasets Markov random field steady state is always reached less than 30 message propagations. Another experiment was performed to test the scalability of the algorithm with respect to the number of extracted features. The optical flow information is consequently decreased but, as shown in fig. 8(a), the motion segmentation scales gracefully with respect to the features quantity. The motion segmentation algorithm here described has been also used as a constraint for an AdaBoost cascade based car detection. An Haar feature based Adaboost classifier is trained with a car data set (trunk/front) to obtain car detection. Classically, the trained classifier searches all over the image for classified features at different scales [17]. This extensive search is now constrained in the segmented motion clusters. This enhances the execution speed and potentially reduces the false positive rate because the car is only searched in a relative motion area. The area constrained detection is shown in fig. 8(b).

(a) Scalability

(b) Application example: AdaBoost Haar features cascade based car detection.

Fig. 8. a) Scalability of the proposed technique with respect to the number of tracked features. b) The classification algorithm is run only in the segmented moving regions. The overlayed yellow boxes depict a car detection.

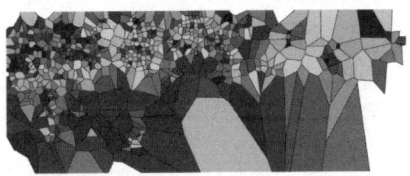

Fig. 9. A local entropies field. The magnitude of the entropy in the image is depicted using a color space from blue (low value) to red (high value).

Fig. 10. Smartter platform: mobile platform for autonomous navigation, mapping and perception

7   Conclusions

This paper presented a novel technique to segment region of interest based on independent motion detection. Optical flow is segmented using local entropy values for each motion vector computed on a Delaunay graph and it is then clustered using a two states Markov Random Field. The clusters motion information is used to create a multiple hypothesis prediction for the following frames in order to influence the clustering.

Experiments have been conducted on different datasets to show that independent motion regions are correctly segmented. Moreover a scalability test shows that the segmentation detail scales gracefully with the number of features. This technique has been already used to constraint an Adaboost based method for car detection with promising results.

The method presented in this paper does not use heavily computationally expensive or memory demanding techniques therefore it represents a suitable choice for mobile robotics applications.

References

1. Wang, J., Adelson, E.: Representing moving images with layers. IEEE Transactions on Image Processing 3(5), 625–638 (2004)
2. Weiss, Y., Adelson, E.H.: A unified mixture framework for motion segmentation: Incorporating spatial coherence and estimating the number of models. In: IEEE Conf. on Computer Vision and Pattern Recognition, pp. 321–326 (1996)
3. Xiao, J., Shah, M.: Accurate motion layer segmentation and matting. In: IEEE Conference on Computer Vision and Pattern Recognition (2005)
4. Ke, Q., Kanade, T.: A subspace approach to layer extraction. In: IEEE Conference on Computer Vision and Pattern Recognition, pp. 255–262 (2001)
5. Shi, J., Malik, J.: Motion segmentation and tracking using normalized cuts. In: 6th Intl. Conference on Computer Vision, pp. 1154–1160 (1998)
6. Cremers, D., Soatto, S.: Motion competition: a variational approach to piecewise parametric motion. Intl. Journal of Computer Vision 62(3), 249–265 (2005)
7. Rothganger, F., Lazebnik, S., Schmid, C., Ponce, J.: Segmenting, modeling, and matching video clips containing multiple moving objects. In: IEEE Conference on Computer Vision and Pattern Recognition (2004)
8. Tong, W.-S., Tang, C.-K., Medioni, G.: Simultaneous two-view epipolar geometry estimation and motion segmentation by 4d tensor voting. IEEE Trans. Pattern Anal. Mach. Intell. 26(9), 1167–1184 (2004)
9. Vidal, R.: Multi-subspace methods for motion segmentation from affine, perspective and central panoramic cameras. In: IEEE International Conference on Robotics and Automation (ICRA 2005) (2005)
10. Shi, J., Tomasi, C.: Good features to track. In: IEEE Conference on Computer Vision and Pattern Recognition (CVPR 1994), Seattle (1994)
11. Felzenszwalb, P., Huttenlocher, D.: Efficient belief propagation for early vision. In: IEEE Conference on Computer Vision and Pattern Recognition (2004)
12. Yedidia, J., Freeman, W., Weiss, Y.: Exploring Artificial Intelligence in the New Millennium. Understanding Belief Propagation and Its Generalizations, pp. 236–239. Morgan Kaufmann, San Francisco (2003)
13. Pearl, J.: Probabilistic Reasoning in Intelligent Systems: Networks of Plausible Inference. Morgan Kaufmann, San Francisco (1988)
14. Freeman, W., Jones, T., Carmichael, O.: Example-based super-resolution. IEEE Image-Based Modelling, Rendering, and Lighting, March-April 2002, 21 (2002)
15. Young, D.P., Ferryman, J.M.: Pets metrics: On-line performance evaluation service. In: ICCCN 2005: Proceedings of the 14th International Conference on Computer Communications and Networks (2005)
16. Kolski, S., Macek, K., Spinello, L.: Secure autonomous driving in dynamic environments: From object detection to safe driving. In: Workshop on Safe Navigation in Open and Dynamic Environments (IROS 2007) (2007)
17. Viola, P., Jones, M.: Robust real-time object detection. International Journal of Computer Vision (2002)

Real-Time Face Tracking for Attention Aware Adaptive Games

Matthieu Perreira Da Silva, Vincent Courboulay, Armelle Prigent, and Pascal Estraillier

Université de La Rochelle,
Laboratoire Informatique Image Interaction,
17071 La Rochelle cedex 9, France
mperreir@univ-lr.fr

Abstract. This paper presents a real time face tracking and head pose estimation system which is included in an attention aware game framework. This fast tracking system enables the detection of the player's attentional state using a simple attention model. This state is then used to adapt the game unfolding in order to enhance user's experience (in the case of adventure game) and improve the game attentional attractiveness (in the case of pedagogical game).

1 Introduction

Usually, computer software has a very low understanding of what the user is actually doing in front of the screen. It can only collect information from its mouse and keyboard inputs. It has no idea of whether the user is focused on what it is displaying, it doesn't even know if the user is in front of the screen. One of the first steps to making computer software more *context aware* is to make it *attention aware*. In [1] attention aware systems are defined as

Systems capable of supporting human attentional processes.

From a functional point of view, it means that these systems are thought as being able to provide information to the user according to his estimated attentional state. This definition shares some objectives with the definition of adaptive systems [2] which are system that are able to adapt their *behaviour* according to the *context*. An attention aware system must be an adaptive system.

According to [1], one of the best ways to estimate user's attention is using gaze direction. Consequently, building good adaptive attention aware system requires estimating reliably user's gaze, but in an unconstrained environment this is a very difficult task. To overcome this problem we propose, in a first step, to use head pose as an estimator for gaze direction. Head pose provides less accurate but more robust gaze estimation.

In this paper, we present a real time vision based face tracking and head pose estimation system coupled with a simple inattention model that will allow an adaptive game to detect attentional shifts and adapt its unfolding accordingly.

A. Gasteratos, M. Vincze, and J.K. Tsotsos (Eds.): ICVS 2008, LNCS 5008, pp. 99–108, 2008.

This model is implemented in two different types of systems (see 1):

- A pedagogical game in which information about the user's attention is used to adapt the game unfolding in order to refocus the player's attention. It is used as a tool for pedo-psychiatrists working with children with autism in the pedo-psychiatric hospital of La Rochelle in order to improve children's attention.
- An adventure game in which user's attentional state helps modifying the game scenario in order to make the game more immersive and fun to play.

In the next section we introduce the attention aware adaptive game framework which is using our head pose based gaze estimation algorithm.

Fig. 1. Left: A screen capture of the adventure game prototype. Right: a screen capture of the pedagogical game together with a preview of the head tracking system.

2   An Attention Aware Adaptive Game Framework

Adaptive game is a subcategory of adaptive systems that can take good advantage of being attention aware. They are designed to react and adapt their unfolding according to the players (explicit) actions. Thus, being able to *see* if the player is facing the screen and is attentive allows the game to adapt its actions to the situation.

2.1   Attention

Attention is historically defined as follows [3]:

> Everyone knows what attention is. It is the taking possession by the mind in clear and vivid form, of one out of what seem several simultaneously possible objects or trains of thought...It implies withdrawal from some things in order to deal effectively with others.

Thus, attention is the cognitive process of selectively concentrating on one thing while ignoring other things. In spite of this single definition, it exists several types of attention [4]: awakening, selective attention, maintained attention, shared attention, internal or external absent-mindedness and vigilance. For an interactive task, we are mainly interested in *selective and maintained attention*.

The analysis of the first one allows knowing whether people are involved in the activity. The second one enables us to assess the success of the application.

It has been proven that the same functional brain area were activated for attention and eye movements [5]. Consequently, the best attention marker we can measure is undoubtedly eyes and gaze behaviour. A major indicator concerning another type of attention, *vigilance*, named PERCLOS [6] is also using such markers. In continuity of such studies, we based our markers on gaze behaviour, approximated by head pose, to determine selective and maintained attention. A weak hypothesis is that a person involved in an interesting task focuses his/her eyes on the salient aspect of the application (screen, avatar, car, enemy, text...) and directs his/her face to the output device of the interactive application (screen). Nevertheless, if a person does not watch the screen, it does not necessarily mean that he/she is inattentive; he/she can be speaking with someone else about the content of the screen [7].

In order to treat these different aspects, we have decided to adopt the following solutions: if the user does not watch the screen during a time t, we conclude to inattention. In the following subsection, we present how t is determined. If inattention is detected, we inform the application.

A simple model of human inattention. The goal of this model is to define the delay after which the application tries to refocus the user on the activity. Actually, we easily understand that in this case, an interactive application does not have to *react* the same way if people play chess, role player game or a car race. Until now, this aspect of the game was only directed by the time during which nothing was done on the paddle or the keyboard.

We based our model of what could be named *inattention* on two parameters:

1. the type of application;
2. the time spent using the application.

The last parameter depends itself on two factors:

1. a natural tiredness after a long time
2. a disinterest more frequent during the very first moments spent using the application than once attention is focused, this time corresponds to the delay of *immersion*.

Once the parameters are defined, we propose the following model in order to define the time after which the application try to refocus the player who does not look at the screen.

Potential of attention. As we mentioned, potential of attention depends mainly on two parameters, tiredness and involvement. We have decided to model arousal (the opposite of tiredness), or potential of attention, by a sigmoid curve parameterized by a couple of real number β_1 and β_2. β_2 represents the delay after which the first signs of fatigue will appear and β_1 is correlated to the speed of apparition of tiredness (Figure 2).

$$P_{arousal} = \frac{\exp^{-\beta_1 t + \beta_2}}{1 + \exp^{-\beta_1 t + \beta_2}}, \qquad (1)$$

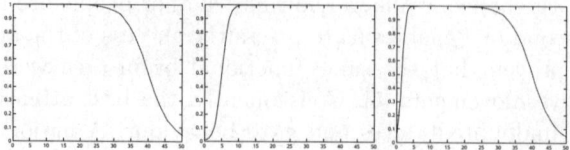

Fig. 2. Left: model of tiredness evolution. Middle: model of interest probability. Right: model of potential of attention. Abscissa represents time in minutes. Each curve is designed for a single person involved in an unique activity. ($\alpha_1 = 1$, $\alpha_2 = 3$, $\beta_1 = 0.3$, $\beta_2 = 12$)

where β_1 and β_2 are two real parameters.

For the second parameter, we have once again modelled involvement, or interest probability, by a sigmoid. We started from the fact that activity is *a priori* fairly interesting, but if the person is involved after a certain time ruled by α_2, we can consider that interest is appearing at a speed correlated to α_1 (Figure 2).

$$P_{interest} = \frac{1}{1 + \exp^{-\alpha_1 t + \alpha_2}}. \tag{2}$$

For our global model of potential of attention, we couple both previous models in order to obtain:

$$P_{attention} = P_{interest} * P_{arousal}, \tag{3}$$

Delay of inattention. Once this model is defined, we are able to determine the time after which the software has to react (if the person still does not look at the screen). Here, it is an arbitrary threshold γ guided by experience, which characterizes each application. The more the application requires attention, the higher this coefficient is. The model we have adopted is an exponential function.

$$D_{game} = exp^{\gamma(t) * P_{attention}}, \tag{4}$$

γ is a function of time because we have estimated that it can exist several *tempo* in an application (intensive, stress, reflection, action ...). As a conclusion, we can summarize our model of inattention by the two following steps (Figure 3):

- depending on the time elapsed from the beginning of the application, we estimate the potential of attention $P_{attention}(t)$;
- depending on this potential and the application, we estimate the delay $D_{\gamma(t)}(P_{attention}(t))$ after which the software has to refocus the inattentive player.

Please note that this model was validated on only five children and still need to be validated on more people. Nevertheless, the first tests are quite promising.

2.2 An Adaptive Framework

As we already mentioned, our objective is to implement a system that interacts in a smart way with the person using the application. It consists in establishing a multi-mode and multimedia dialogue between the person and the system.

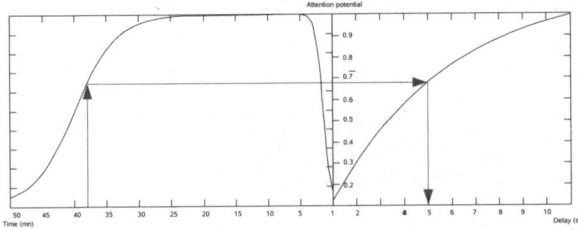

Fig. 3. Curves used to determine the delay of software interaction

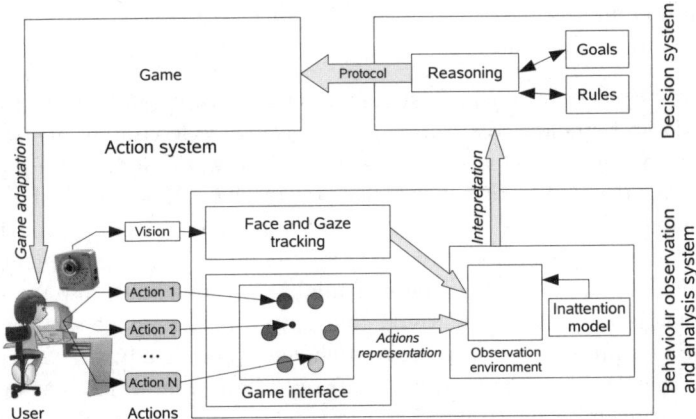

Fig. 4. General architecture

Consequently, the conception of the platform, represented Figure 4, was guided by the following constraints:

– it must track gaze behaviour, determined as the best markers of attention;
– it must allow to focus user attention and be able to refocus it if necessary;
– it must not perturb the user by inopportune interaction.

The system can be divided into three sub-parts:

– *the system of observation and behaviour analysis*: monitors the player's attention;
– *the decision system*: adapts the execution of games;
– *the action system*: runs the game.

This architecture needs a fast and robust gaze estimation system in order to respond to its environment in an adaptive and dynamic manner. To achieve this goal, we have built a fast tracking system dedicated to adaptive systems. This system is described in the following section.

3   Face Tracking for Adaptive Games

3.1   Constraints

As the system is designed to be used by a wide range of applications and users (from educational games for children with autism to adventure games for "common gamers"), some constraints have emerged:

- non invasive material;
- low cost;
- single user;
- recordable information;
- standard computer;
- unconstrained environment.

Our system is based on a low cost ieee-1394 camera connected to a standard computer. Despite its low cost, this camera captures video frames of size 640x480 at 30 frames per second which are suitable characteristics for both accurate face features localization and efficient face features tracking. The choice of a grayscale camera instead of a more common colour camera is driven by the fact that most of the aimed applications are performed in an indoor environment. In such an environment, the amount of light available is often quite low, as grayscale cameras usually have more sensitivity and have a better image quality (as they don't use Bayer filters), they are the best choice. Another advantage of grayscale cameras is that they can be used with infra-red light and optics that don't have infra-red coating in order to improve the tracking performance by the use of a non invasive more frontal and uniform lightning.

3.2   Architecture

The tracking algorithm we have developed is built upon four modules which interoperate together in order to provide a fast and robust face tracking system (see Figure 5). The algorithm contains two branches: one for face detection and a second for face tracking. At run time, the choice between the two branches is made according to a confidence threshold, evaluated in the *face checking and localization* module.

Pre-processing. Before face or radial symmetry detection, the input image must be pre-processed in order to improve face and face feature detection performance. The main pre-processing steps are image rescaling and lightning correction, also called contrast normalization. The input image is rescaled so that low resolution data is available for radial symmetry detection algorithms. Contrast normalisation consists in adapting each pixel intensity according to the local mean intensity of its surrounding pixel. As this task is performed by humans retina, several complex models have been developed to mimic this processing [8]. As our system needs to be real-time, we have chosen to approximate this retinal processing by a very simple model which consists in the following steps:

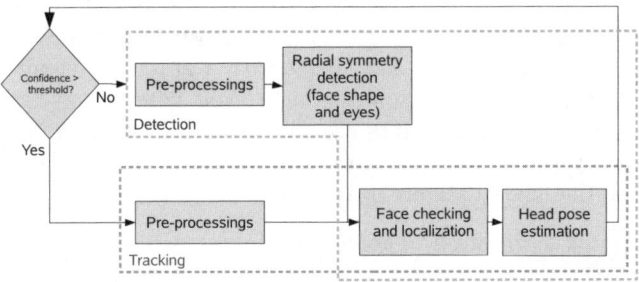

Fig. 5. Architecture of the face tracking and pose estimation system

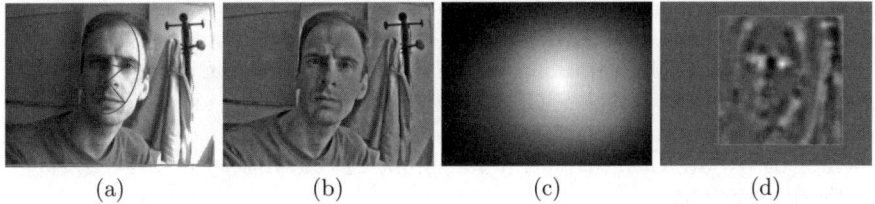

(a)   (b)   (c)   (d)

Fig. 6. a) Tracking result of a side lit scene. b) Source image after lightning correction. c) Result of face ovoid detection (Hough Transform). d) Result of eyes detection (Loy and Zelinsky Transform).

1. For each image pixel, build a weighted mean $M_{x,y}$ of its surrounding pixels. In our implementation we used first order integral filtering (Bartlett Filter) in order to achieve fast filtering. Note that first order integral filters are an extension of the commonly used zero order integral filters (box filters). For more information about generalized integral images see [9].
2. Calculate the normalized pixel intensity:

$$I_{x,y} = \frac{S_{x,y}}{(M_{x,y} + A)}$$

with S the source image, I the normalized image, and A a normalization factor.

Figure 6 shows the result of our simple contrast normalization algorithm on a side lit scene.

Radial symmetry detection for face shape and eye detection. Once the image is pre-processed, we use a set of radial symmetry detector in order to localize a face region candidate that will be further checked by the *face checking and localization* module. Once again our real-time constraint guided the choice of the algorithms we used.

Face ovoid shape is detected in low resolution version of the input image (typically 160x120) using an optimized version of the Hough transform (Fig. 6.c) whereas eyes are detected using an optimized version of the Loy and Zelinsky transform [10](Fig. 6.d). In order to speed up both transforms, the following improvements have been made: only pixels with a gradient magnitude above a pre-defined threshold are processed, the algorithms vote in only one accumulator for all radius and accumulators are smoothed only once at the end of the processing. Using these two symmetry map and a set of face geometry based rules we define the face candidate area.

Face checking and localization. This module serves two purposes:

- When called from the face detection branch, it checks if the face candidate area really contains a face and outputs the precise localization of this face.
- In the case of face tracking, it only finds the new position of the face.

In both cases, the module outputs a confidence value which reflects the similarity between the interface face model and the real face image.

Face checking and localization is based on the segmentation of the face candidate image into several blobs. The source frame is first filtered by a DoG filter; the result image is then adaptively thresholded. The resulting connected components (blobs) are then matched on a simple 2D face model in order to check and localize the face.

Head pose estimation. Similarly to previous research we use triangle geometry for modelling a generic face model. For example, [11] resolves equations derived from triangle geometry to compute head pose. Since we favour speed against accuracy, we use a faster and simpler direct approximation method based on side length ratios.

3.3   Performance and Robustness

Processing time. We measured the processing time of he algorithm on a laptop PC equipped with a 1,83GHz *Intel Core Duo* processor. We obtained the following mean processing times:

- Face detection: 30 milliseconds (first detection or detection after tracking failure).
- Face tracking: 16 milliseconds

Processing time include all processing steps, from pre-processing to head pose estimation. Since image capture is done at 30fps and the algorithm is using only one of the two processor cores, our system uses 50% of processor time for face detection and 25% of processor time for face tracking. Consequently, the algorithm is fast enough to enable running a game in parallel on a standard middle-end computer.

Robustness. As can be seen from the tracking example shown on figure 7, the algorithm can handle a broad range of head orientation and distance. The contrast

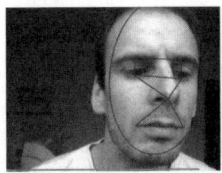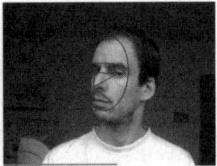

Fig. 7. Left: Result of the tracking algorithm for different face distances and orientation

normalization step also allows the algorithm to run under different illumination conditions. However, this algorithm is designed to be fast, as a consequence tracking performances still need to be improved under some lightning conditions (backlit scene, directional lighting casting hard shadows, etc.). A future version of the algorithm may use a colour camera and skin colour detection algorithms (as in [12] or [13]) to improve face detection and tracking robustness. This modification would however prevent us from using infra-red light to improve the algorithm performances under poor lightning conditions. Another possibility would be to add an infra-red lightning and adapt the current algorithm to this new lightning in order improve the robustness of the system.

4   Discussion and Future Work

We described a complete framework for attention aware adaptive games. This framework uses a fast face tracking and head pose estimation algorithm coupled with a simple model of human inattention in order to generate feedback information about the attentional state of the player. This system is currently implemented in an adventure and a pedagogical game.

In order to improve this framework, we are currently working at building a more complex and realistic attentional model which would not only react to attentional shifts but could also predict them. We are also working at using colour information to enhance the accuracy and robustness of our face tracking system as it can provide performance improvements without impacting too much processing time.

Acknowledgement

This research is partly funded by the French Poitou-Charentes county and the Orange Foundation.

The authors would also like to thank doctor Mr. D. Lambert Head of Department of Child Psychiatry of La Rochelle hospital (France) and his team, in particular: Mr. V. Gabet for their useful advices regarding the rehabilitation methods dedicated to children with autism.

References

1. Roda, C., Thomas, J.: Attention Aware Systems: Theories, Applications, and Research Agenda. Computers in Human Behavior, vol. 22, pp. 557–587. Elsevier, Amsterdam (2006)
2. Weibelzahl, S.: Evaluation of Adaptive Systems. PhD thesis, University of Education, Freiburg (October 2002)
3. James, J.: The Principles of Psychology (1890 (1983))
4. Mohamed, A.O., Courboulay, V., Sehaba, K., Menard, M.: Attention analysis in interactive software for children with autism. In: Assets 2006: Proceedings of the 8th international ACM SIGACCESS conference on Computers and accessibility, pp. 133–140. ACM Press, New York (2006)
5. Corbetta, M., Akbudak, E., Conturo, T.E., Snyder, A.Z., Ollinger, J.M., Drury, H.A., Linenweber, M.R., Petersen, S.E., Raichle, M.E., Van Essen, D.C., Shulman, G.L.: A common network of functional areas for attention and eye movements. Neuron 21(4), 761–773 (1998)
6. Dinges, D., Mallis, M., Maislin, G., Powell, J.: Evaluation of techniques for ocular measurement as an index of fatigue and the basis for alertness management. Technical Report Report No. DOT HS 808 762, Final report for the USDOT, National Highway Traffic Safety Administration(NHTSA) (1998)
7. Kaplan, F., Hafner, V.V.: The challenges of joint attention. Interaction Studies 7(2), 129–134 (2006)
8. Beaudot, W.: The neural information in the vertebra retina: a melting pot of ideas for artifical vision. PhD thesis, TIRF Laboratory, Grenoble, France (1994)
9. Derpanis, K., Leung, E., Sizintsev, M.: Fast scale-space feature representation by generalized integral images. Technical Report CSE-2007-01, York University (January 2007)
10. Loy, G., Zelinsky, A.: Fast radial symmetry for detecting points of interest. IEEE Trans. Pattern Anal. Mach. Intell. 25(8), 959–973 (2003)
11. Kaminski, J.Y., Teicher, M., Knaan, D., Shavit, A.: Head orientation and gaze detection from a single image. In: International Conference Of Computer Vision Theory And Applications (2006)
12. Schwerdt, K., Crowley, J.L.: Robust face tracking using color. In: FG 2000: Proceedings of the Fourth IEEE International Conference on Automatic Face and Gesture Recognition 2000, Washington, DC, USA, p. 90. IEEE Computer Society Press, Los Alamitos (2000)
13. Séguier, R.: A very fast adaptive face detection system. In: International Conference on Visualization, Imaging, and Image Processing (VIIP) (2004)

Rek-Means:
A k-Means Based Clustering Algorithm

Domenico Daniele Bloisi and Luca Iocchi

Sapienza University of Rome
Dipartimento di Informatica e Sistemistica
via Ariosto 25, 00185 Rome, Italy
{bloisi,iocchi}@dis.uniroma1.it
http://www.dis.uniroma1.it/~bloisi

Abstract. In this paper we present a new clustering method based on
k-means that has been implemented on a video surveillance system. Rek-
means does not require to specify in advance the number of clusters to
search for and is more precise than k-means in clustering data coming
from multiple Gaussian distributions with different co-variances, while
maintaining real-time performance. Experiments on real and synthetic
datasets are presented to measure the effectiveness and the performance
of the proposed method.

Keywords: data clustering, k-means, image segmentation.

1 Introduction

Data clustering techniques are used to accomplish a multitude of tasks in many
fields, such as artificial intelligence, data mining, computer vision, data compression, and others. There are a series of well known algorithms that perform the
task of clustering data: k-means, Fuzzy C-means, Hierarchical clustering, EM,
and many others [1]. It can be shown that there is no absolute best criterion
which would be independent of the final aim of the clustering [2]. Consequently,
the user must supply this criterion, in such a way that the result of the clustering
will suit his/her needs. For instance, we could be interested in finding representatives for homogeneous groups (data reduction), in finding natural clusters and
describe their unknown properties (natural data types), in finding useful and
suitable groupings (useful data classes) or in finding unusual data objects (outlier detection). While the above discussed characteristic is common to all the
clustering methods, it is possible to compare techniques with respect to time
efficiency and solution quality. Among these methods, k-means is the most efficient in terms of execution time [1]. However, k-means requires to specify in
advance the number of clusters k, it converges only to a locally optimal solution,
and the solution depends from the initialization step.

The aim of this paper is to present an extension of k-means, called Rek-means
which has the following features:

1. it provides better results in clustering data coming from different Gaussian
   distributions;

A. Gasteratos, M. Vincze, and J.K. Tsotsos (Eds.): ICVS 2008, LNCS 5008, pp. 109–118, 2008.

2. it does not require to specify k beforehand;
3. it maintains real-time performance.

In the rest of the paper, we will first present a brief overview of the AR-GOS project, then we will describe the proposed algorithm, and finally we will illustrate implementation details and experimental results.

2 ARGOS Project

The ARGOS project (Automatic Remote Grand Canal Observation System) [3] has been launched in early 2006 by the Municipal Administration of Venice and it is in full operation since September 2007.

The system provides for boat traffic monitoring, measurement and management along the Grand Canal of Venice based on automated vision techniques. The Venice Grand Canal (about 4 km length and 80 to 150 meters width) is monitored through 14 observation posts (Survey Cells), each composed by three perspective cameras and a PTZ camera. Boats are identified by background subtraction techniques and tracked with a set of multi-hypotheses Kalman Filters. All the information from the 14 survey cells are communicated to a central server that shows an integrated view of all the Grand Canal and of the traffic within it. The system allows for traffic statistics, event detection (e.g., speed limit and wrong ways) and is in use by Venice Administration in order to evaluate and monitor boat navigation rules.

While a more detailed presentation of the system is given in [3], in this paper we focus on data clustering step that is performed to refine segmentation of the images. Background subtraction is used to first distinguish foreground (i.e., boats) from background. However, with respect to other surveillance applications (like for example people tracking in indoor environment or car tracking on streets), our system has to deal with a significantly higher noise, mostly due to waves and sun reflections on the water, and with high number of boats in the scene. Therefore, we have implemented an optical flow step after background subtraction, in order to reduce the effects of under-segmentation due to boats being close each other and errors due to waves. Moreover, everything must be done in real-time and due to project constraints we need to process in real-time the image streams coming from three high-resolution cameras (1280x960) on a single PC with an Intel Core 2 Duo 2.4 GHz CPU.

The first approach to cluster data was based on k-means and gave us poor results, while more sophisticated approaches, like EM algorithm, were not compatible with real-time constraints we have in the project. The algorithm proposed in this paper has shown very good performance in clustering while maintaining real-time performance.

3 K-Means Limitations

K-means [4] is a very simple and fast algorithm for solving the clustering problem. Unfortunately k-means requires that the user knows the exact number of clusters (k) beforehand. When clustering a dataset, the right number k of clusters to use is often not obvious, and choosing k automatically is a hard algorithmic problem [12]. Furthermore k-means is not guaranteed to return a global optimum: The quality of the final solution depends largely on the initial set of centroids, and may, in practice, be much poorer than the global optimum.

Thus, in using k-means, one encounters a major difficulty, i.e., how to choose the k initial clusters. If we do it at random, k-means can in fact converge to the wrong answer (in the sense that a different and optimal solution to the minimization function above exists). As an example, Fig. 1 shows a bad result of k-means (shown by "plus" symbols) with random initialization, even in the case in which the number of cluster ($k = 5$) is correctly specified. In order to overcome the above mentioned limitation, our algorithm is designed to work without an *a priori* knowledge on the number of clusters (k) and to be robust with respect to a random initialization.

Fig. 1. Centroids found by k-means with random initialization (+) and true ones (×)

4   Rek-Means

Rek-means been developed for clustering data coming from a supposed Gaussian distribution and extends k-means algorithm by using small rectangular areas first to over cluster the data, then to efficiently merge them in the final clusters. The prefix "Re" in Rek-means stands thus for rectangle.

4.1   Rek-Means Algorithm

The Rek-means algorithm (shown in Table 1) performs 5 steps. Suppose we have n 2D-points to cluster (see Fig. 2a). We may choose a distance d that is the maximal distance between two points in order to consider them belonging to the same cluster. We may choose also a minimal dimension $dimC$ so that a cluster is considered of interest. As a first step, we compute k-means with $k = n/4$ taking the n points we have to cluster as input (see Fig. 2b). The choice of this number k is a trade-off between speed of execution for this step

Table 1. The Rek-means algorithm

Rek-means Algorithm
1. (*over-clustering step*) Compute k-means with $k = n/4$ where n is the number of points to cluster.
2. (*cutting step*) Discard every centroid c_i having $dim(c_i) \leq 2$.
3. (*discretizing step*) For each of the remaining centroids c_j, consider a rectangle $\text{RECT}(c_j)$ containing all the points belonging to c_j.
4. (*associating step*) If $dist(\text{RECT}(c_i), \text{RECT}(c_j)) \leq d$ then merge clusters c_i and c_j.
5. (*validating step*) When the associating step is terminated, apply a validating test for each found cluster.

and the number of clusters that will be associated in the next steps. Our choice ($k = n/4$) gave us good results in our application. In this step, we perform an over clustering of the data, thus we need to reduce the number of clusters.

The second step consists on discarding too small clusters, by eliminating centroids c_i having $dim(c_i) \leq 2$. Since we have initialized $k = n/4$, we expect that each cluster contains in average 4 points: if a cluster has a number of points < 4, then it is likely that such a cluster is far from the true centroid we are searching for. In fact an outlier or a point far from the center is isolated and k-means tends to assign it a centroid c_o with dimension $dim(c_o) = 1$. Furthermore, this discarding rule is useful in presence of noise between two distinct clusters (see Fig. 3a).

In the third step, Rek-means builds a rectangle around each remained centroid c_r (see Fig. 2c). One of the rectangle vertices has coordinates ($minX$, $minY$), while the opposite rectangle vertex has coordinates ($maxX$, $maxY$) where $minX$

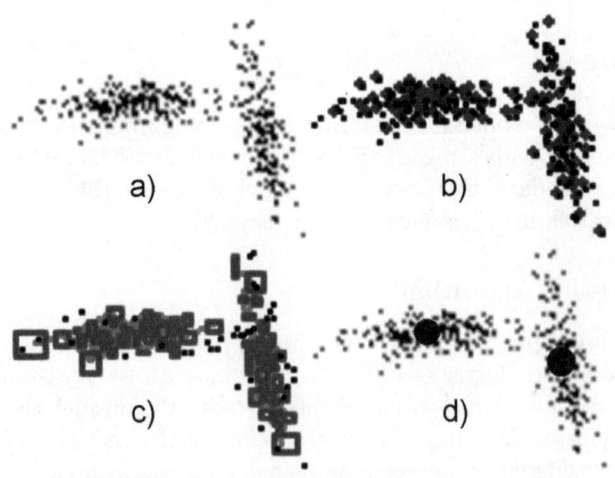

Fig. 2. Rek-means example

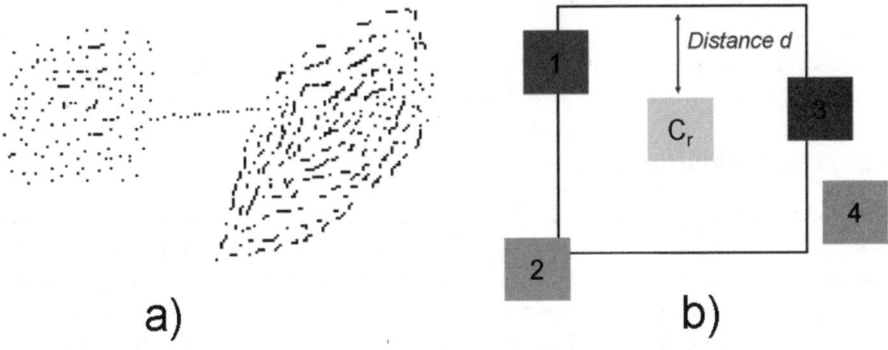

Fig. 3. a) Two clusters not well-separated; b) The associating rule: C_r is associated with 1, 2 and 3 but not with 4. When the algorithm will process 3, it will be associated with 4 and then C_r will be associated with 4 also.

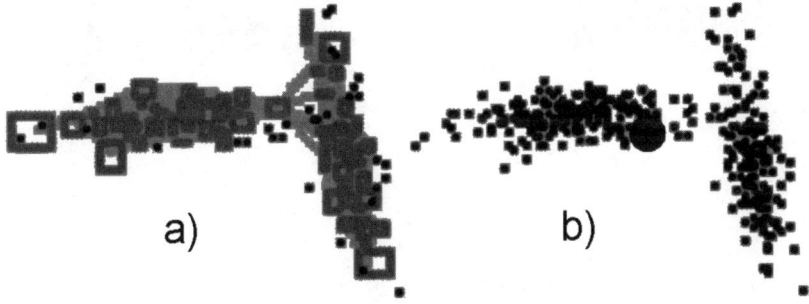

Fig. 4. Under clustering example

and $maxX$ are the minimal and the maximal x values for the points belonging to c_r, $minY$ and $maxY$ are the minimal and the maximal y values for the points belonging to c_r.

In the forth step Rek-means associates clusters with respect to a distance d. In particular, if $dist(RECT(c_i), RECT(c_j)) \leq d$ then clusters c_i and c_j are associated. In Fig. 3b such associating step is depicted in an intuitive manner, while in Fig. 2c a line links the rectangles that are close enough. This step produces larger *macro*-clusters and subsequently a new set of centroids for these *macro*-clusters are computed, by merging the points contained in the associated rectangles (see Fig. 2d). Rek-means uses rectangles to discretize the cluster dimension since it is computationally efficient to compare the relative distance between rectangle as depicted in Fig. 3b.

The above presented algorithm works on 2D data, but it can be generalized for three or more dimensions: For instance, in 3D it is possible to use parallelepipeds instead of rectangles without modifying the algorithm core.

As one can note, the associating algorithm heavily depends on the value chosen for the distance d: If we choose a large value for d, then we may obtain an incorrect output (see Fig. 4). In order to avoid an under clustering caused by a wrong choice for d, we apply a validating test as the final step of the algorithm.

4.2   The Validating Step

The validating step is useful if the data to cluster are not well-separated, for example if we have to deal with overlapping clusters. A possible approach consists in applying a statistical test in order to discover if the points belonging to a found cluster follow a particular statistical distribution. There exist a series of one-dimensional statistical test that are effective and simple to apply (for example, the Kolmogorov-Smirnov test [5], the K-L divergence [6], etc.).

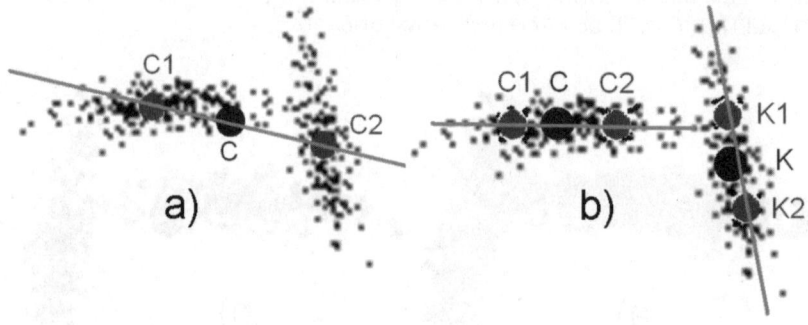

Fig. 5. Projection examples

Since we are manipulating 2D data, we can either use a two dimensional statistical test (e.g., Peacock test [7], FF test [8], etc.) or reduce 2D-points to one dimension. The currently known 2D tests are not fast (the fastest has $O(n \log n)$ time complexity [9]) and easy to use as the 1D ones, so we have chosen to apply a mono-dimensional test through a projection. Rek-means assumes that the data to cluster follow a Gaussian distribution and uses the Anderson-Darling (AD) statistics [10,11] to test the data with the confidence level α set to 0.0001. This one-dimensional test has been shown empirically to be the most powerful normality test that is based on the empirical cumulative distribution function (ECDF) [12]. As already mentioned, to apply this test we need to project 2D points over a line. The projection details are depicted in Fig. 5.

The simple idea [12] consists in taking the points belonging to a centroid C and then applying k-means with $k = 2$ with such points as input in order to find two new centroids $C1$ and $C2$ (see Fig. 5). If C is a correct centroid, the projected points over the line connecting $C1$ and $C2$ must have a Gaussian distribution in 1D and thus the projected points pass the statistical test (see Fig. 5b). If C is not a correct centroid, the points projected over the line connecting $C1$ and $C2$ are not sampled from a Gaussian distribution and so the statistical test rejects them

Table 2. The validating procedure

The Validating Procedure
Let S be the set of centroids found by the associating algorithm.
For every $c_i \in S$:
1. Find c_i^1 and c_i^2 (applying k-means with $k = 2$),
project the points belonging to c_i onto the line connecting c_i^1 and c_i^2,
translate, normalize and do the AD test.
2. If the test is successful then c_i is a true centroid and discard it from S,
otherwise add c_i^1 and c_i^2 to S.
Repeat until S is empty.

(see Fig. 5a). In case of rejection, the Rek-means algorithm performs k-means over the subsets of data that do not pass the validating test with incrementing k, and then re-apply the AD test, until the test is satisfied. Fig. 5 can be viewed as a graphical explanation of two iterations made by the validating step: Fig. 5a depicts the first iteration with a negative test, while Fig. 5b depicts the second iteration with two positive tests. As a difference with [12], Rek-means applies the projection over a selected set of points (the one selected by the association step), minimizing in this way the possible errors due to the k-means initialization. Table 2 summarizes the operations made in the validating procedure. Note that it terminates always since the AD test for a single point is trivially positive.

4.3   Rek-Means Time Complexity

The Rek-means time complexity can be analyzed considering the complexity of each single step:

1. over clustering step
2. cutting step
3. discretizing step
4. associating step
5. validating step

The first step has a complexity equal to the k-means complexity, i.e., $O(kn)$ (a particular exception for the k-means time complexity has been showed in [14]). The second and the third steps have $O(1)$ complexity. The forth step has $O(n^2)$ complexity if the rectangles to be compared are not sorted, but if we sort them (for example, simply with respect to the x-coordinate), we can reduce such a complexity to $O(n \log n)$, i.e., the time needed to sort the data $O(n \log n)$ plus the time of a binary search $O(\log n)$. The fifth step has $O(n \log n)$ time complexity, since we have to apply two geometrical transformations to project onto the x-axis and to compute the AD test with sorted samples. Summarizing, the overall complexity of the algorithm is $O(n \log n)$.

5   Implementation and Experiments

Rek-means has been designed for solving the problem of segmenting real images in real-time. The segmentation is made exploiting optical flow computation that yields a sparse map (see Fig. 6). Unfortunately, we cannot know in advance how many boats are in the image in a given moment and even if we suppose to know such number, k-means can produce poor results on data coming from the characteristic elliptic shape of boats (Fig. 6).

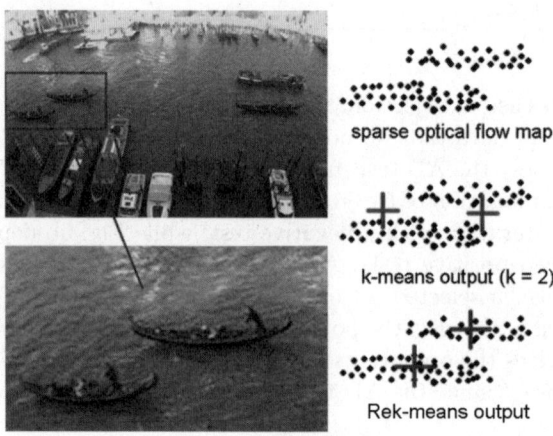

sparse optical flow map

k-means output (k = 2)

Rek-means output

Fig. 6. Rek-means vs k-means in a real scenario

The algorithm presented in this paper runs within the core of the ARGOS video-surveillance system in a very effective and efficient way. The overall system processes three high resolution (1280×960) image streams on a single PC with an Intel Core 2 Duo 2.4 GHz CPU, with an average frame rate of about 7 fps.

ARGOS is regularly evaluated by user inspection and several tests show the effectiveness of the system in image segmenting and tracking of all the boats in the channel. The main achievement, that is related to the Rek-means algorithm presented here, is the ability of the system of correctly distinguishing boats that are very close (see Fig. 7).

We also tested the algorithm on a synthetic dataset obtained by a Gaussian random number generator (developed by Elkan and Hamerly [12]). It is made of 100 distinct images (with resolution 2000×2000), each containing data from 5 different Gaussian distributions with an eccentricity = 4, in order to simulate the typical shape of a boat. For every image Rek-means algorithm finds the correct number and position of the centroids. The experiment was repeated using k-means with k = 5 (using the OpenCV implementation [13]). The results of the comparison are showed in Table 3.

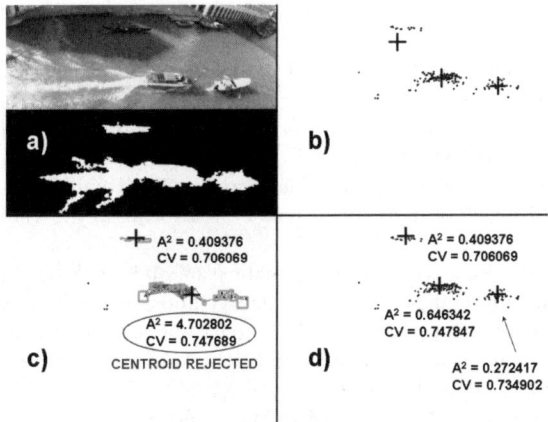

Fig. 7. a) a real frame and the corresponding foreground; b) k-means output with k = 3. c) Rek-means output before the validating step (A^2 is the AD value while CV is the critical value); d) Rek-means output after the validating step.

Table 3. A comparison between Rek-means and k-means

Algorithm	Percentage of Correct Output	CPU Time (ms)
Rek-means	100	29
k-means	59	< 1

6 Conclusion

In this paper we have presented Rek-means, a new clustering method based on k-means that has been implemented on a video surveillance system. Rek-means aims at overcoming the main limitations of k-means, which consist in the dependence of the result to the initial configuration and in its need to guess the correct number of centroids (k) as input.

As shown by experimental results, Rek-means returns better results than k-means in clustering data coming from n-dimensional multiple Gaussian distributions with different co-variances, while maintaining real-time performance.

Acknowledgments. The project has been realized thanks to the view of the future and to the active participation of the City Council of Venice. In particular, special thanks to Lord Vice-Major of Venice, On. Michele Vianello, for his foresight in applying innovative technologies in the delicate and complex historical city of Venice. We are also grateful to the Responsible Manager Arch. Manuele Medoro and his staff for their constant support and commitment. We finally thank Ing. Luigi Tombolini and Ing. Luca Novelli for their valuable help on this research work.

References

1. Jain, A.K., Murty, M.N., Flynn, P.J.: Data Clustering: A Review. ACM Computing Surveys 31(3), 264–323 (1999)
2. Orlowska, M.E., Sun, X., Li, X.: Can exclusive clustering on streaming data be achieved? SIGKDD Explorations 8(2), 102–108 (2006)
3. Bloisi, D., Iocchi, L., Leone, G.R., Pigliacampo, R., Tombolini, L., Novelli, L.: A Distributed Vision System for Boat Traffic Monitoring in the Venice Grand Canal. In: VISAPP 2007, pp. 549–556 (2007)
4. MacQueen, J.B.: Some Methods for classification and Analysis of Multivariate Observations. In: Proceedings of 5-th Berkeley Symposium on Mathematical Statistics and Probability, vol. 1, pp. 281–297. University of California Press, Berkeley (1967)
5. Chakravarti, Laha, Roy,: Handbook of Methods of Applied Statistics, vol. I, pp. 392–394. John Wiley and Sons, Chichester (1967)
6. Kullback, S., Leibler, R.A.: On information and sufficiency. Royal Astronomical Society, Monthly Notices 202, 79–86 (1983)
7. Peacock, J.A.: Two-dimensional goodness-of-fit testing in astronomy. Annals of Mathematical Statistics 22, 615–627 (1951)
8. Fasano, G., Franceschini, A.: A Multidimensional Version Of The Kolmogorov-Smirnov Test. Monthly Notices of the Royal Astronomical Society 225, 155–170 (1987)
9. Lopes, R.H., Reid, I., Hobson, P.R.: The two-dimensional Kolmogorov-Smirnov test. In: XI International Workshop on Advanced Computing and Analysis Techniques in Physics Research (2007)
10. Anderson, T.W., Darling, D.A.: Asymptotic theory of certain "goodness-of-fit" criteria based on stochastic processes. Annals of Mathematical Statistics 23, 193–212 (1952)
11. Stephens, M.A.: EDF Statistics for Goodness of Fit and Some Comparisons. Journal of the American Statistical Association 69, 730–737 (1974)
12. Hamerly, G., Elkan, C.: Learning the k in k-means. In: Proceedings of the seventeenth annual conference on neural information processing systems (NIPS), pp. 281–288 (2003)
13. Open Computer Vision Library (OpenCV):
    http://opencvlibrary.sourceforge.net/
14. Arthur, D., Vassilvitskii, S.: How slow is the k-means method? In: Symposium on Computational Geometry, pp. 144–153 (2006)

Smoke Detection in Video Surveillance: A MoG Model in the Wavelet Domain

Simone Calderara, Paolo Piccinini, and Rita Cucchiara

DII, University of Modena and Reggio Emilia, Italy
{calderara.simone,piccinini.paolo,cucchiara.rita}@unimore.it

Abstract. The paper presents a new fast and robust technique of smoke detection in video surveillance images. The approach aims at detecting the spring or the presence of smoke by analyzing color and texture features of moving objects, segmented with background subtraction. The proposal embodies some novelties: first the temporal behavior of the smoke is modeled by a Mixture of Gaussians (MoG) of the energy variation in the wavelet domain. The MoG takes into account the image energy variation due to either external luminance changes or the smoke propagation. It allows a distinction to energy variation due to the presence of real moving objects such as people and vehicles. Second, this textural analysis is enriched by a color analysis based on the blending function. Third, a Bayesian model is defined where the texture and color features, detected at block level, contributes to model the likelihood while a global evaluation of the entire image models the prior probability contribution. The resulting approach is very flexible and can be adopted in conjunction to a whichever video surveillance system based on dynamic background model. Several tests on tens of different contexts, both outdoor and indoor prove its robustness and precision.

Keywords: Smoke detection, Image processing, MoG, DWT.

1 Introduction

Smoke detection in video-surveillance systems is still an open challenge for computer vision and pattern recognition communities. It concerns the definition of robust approaches to detect, as soon as possible, spring and fast propagation of smoke possibly due to explosions, fires or special environmental conditions. Smoke detection module can enrich standard video surveillance systems for both indoor and outdoor monitoring. These systems can replace standard smoke and fire sensors, which cannot be applied in large and open spaces. Moreover, detecting smoke by visual cues could allow fast and reactive alarms also in some specific situations, where smoke is growing in unconventional directions, so that the time-to-alarm of normal sensors could become unacceptable.

The video analysis tasks for smoke detection are not trivial due to the variability of shape, motion and texture patterns of smoke, which appearance is dependent on the luminance conditions, the background manifolds and colors of

A. Gasteratos, M. Vincze, and J.K. Tsotsos (Eds.): ICVS 2008, LNCS 5008, pp. 119–128, 2008.
© Springer-Verlag Berlin Heidelberg 2008

the scene. Since smoke modifies the visual cues of the background, typically background suppression techniques are adopted, followed by validation/classification tasks. The smoke identification becomes more challenging in presence of other moving objects and shadows and whenever the background is variable too.

The problem of smoke detection has been discussed in the past in some works where local features of pixels in the images or measures on the shape temporal variations are exploited. In an early work, Kopilovic et al. [1] took advantage of irregularities in motion due to non-rigidity of smoke. They computed optical flow field using two adjacent images, and then used the entropy of the motion directions distribution as key feature to differentiate smoke motion from non-smoke motion. Similarly, motion was exploited in [2] where local motions from cluster analysis of points in a multidimensional temporal embedding space are extracted. The goal was to track local dynamic envelopes of pixels, and then use features of the velocity distribution histogram to discriminate between smoke and various natural phenomena such as clouds and wind-tossed trees that may cause such envelopes. In this work, the presence of other moving objects, typical of video-surveillance scenes, has not taken into account.

Recently, Chen, Yin et al. [3] present a smoke detection approach working on pixel-level classification after motion segmentation based on frame difference. Pixels can be initially classified as a smoke-pixel with a very simple chromaticity-based static decision rule; it is based on two thresholds in the color space assuming that smoke usually displays grayish colors. A Further dynamic decision rule is dependent on the spreading attributes of smoke: the ratio between the sums of circumferences of smoke regions segmented and the number of smoke-pixel extracted can give a measure of disorder in the segmented objects. Similarly other works evaluate the contours of the object that are candidate to be classified as smoke. In [5], smoke detection is based on four steps: background subtraction, flickering extraction, contour initialization, and contour classification using both heuristic and empirical knowledge about smoke. Background subtraction uses the Stauffer and Grimson algorithm [4]. Then a measure of flickering is provided. They state that flickering frequency of turbulent flame has shown experimentally to be around 10Hz and it could be as low as 2 or 3 Hz for slowly-moving smoke. The temporal periodicity can be calculated using Fast Fourier Transform (FFT), Wavelet Transform or Mean Crossing Rate (MCR). They adopt the Mean Crossing Rate (MCR). Finally as in [3], a measure of the shape complexity given by the ratio between edge length and area is provided to achieve classification. Also in this work, only qualitative measure are provided.

An interesting and robust approach has been defined by Toreyin et. al. [6] and further improved in [7]. They use the Collins background subtraction method to extract moving objects [8]. Then as in previous work a flickering analysis and a measure of turbulence is provided by evaluating the edge and texture variation using the Wavelet Transform. In each block of the sub-image resulting after the wavelet decomposition the variation of energy is computed. The energy is given by the sum of the high-frequency components in the wavelet domain. Finally two thresholds are given to measure an acceptable energy variation. The dynamism of the variation is modeled with a simple three state Random Markov Model (RMM), trained with smoke and non-smoke pixels. Finally, an analysis of smoke shape complexity is provided as in [3] and [5], based on the distance between the contour points and the center of mass of the shape. This approach is quite robust in the given examples, but a precise evaluation of the different features contributions is not provided. However in our experiments, we observed that sometimes a strong shape variation and edge complexity of smoke regions cannot be visually revealed due to both camera field of view and wind direction. For this reason we avoid to use this feature.

Instead, we tested an higher discriminative power of wavelet with respect to Mean Crossing Rate, thus we adopt this transform for energy analysis. In our approach, moving objects are extracted with a standard background suppression technique and blobs subsequently classified as real objects or artifacts due to the smoke. The energy is computed using the coefficients of the Wavelet Transform; the RMM is substituted with a different statistical approach which takes into account the energy time-variability using a MoG computed with the online mixture model approach also used in [4]. In addition, the MOG classification is improved in a Bayesian model accounting the chromaticity variations by means of a blending function.

Differently from most of the previous approaches we do not make any assumptions both on the external conditions and on the field of view of the camera making our system flexible enough to be applied on different setups. Several tests have been carried out also taking videos form the Web. We evaluate the system performance measuring both the detection rate and the time to detect. The video used as test set are publicly available with annotation on the website *http://imagelab.ing.unimore.it/visor*. The paper is structured as follows. Section 2 describes the feature used for smoke detection and the adopted Bayesian Classifier. Finally Section 3 details all the system parameters and discuss the experiments carried out.

2   Smoke Detection for Foreground Object Classification

The proposed model evaluates the joint contribution coming from the graylevel image energy and color intensity attenuation to classify an object as possible smoke. We assume that when smoke grows and propagates in the scene its image energy is attenuated by the blurring effect of smoke diffusion.

We firstly detect possible candidate objects by means of a motion segmentation algorithm. When a new foreground object is detected we analyze its energy using the Wavelet Transform coefficients and evaluate its temporal evolution. The color properties of the object are analyzed accordingly to a smoke reference color model to detect if color changes in the scene are due to a natural variation or not. The input image is then divided in blocks of fixed sized and each block is evaluated separately. Finally a Bayesian approach detect whether a foreground object is smoke.

2.1   Energy Analysis Using the Direct Wavelet Transform

An efficient way to evaluate the energy variation of an intensity image is the discrete wavelet transform DWT [10].

The DWT is obtained convolving the image signal with several banks of filters obtaining a multiresolution decomposition of the image. Given the input image I_t the decomposition produces four subimages, namely the compressed version of the original image C_t, the horizontal coefficient image H_t, the vertical coefficient image V_t and the diagonal coefficient image D_t. An example decomposition is computed with the algorithm proposed in [10] is shown in Fig. 1.

Fig. 1. Example of discrete wavelet transform. The leftmost image is the original image. The right image is the transformed one. The components are: top left compressed image C_t, top right horizontal coefficient image H_t, bottom left vertical coefficient image V_t and bottom right diagonal coefficient image D_t.

The energy is evaluated blockwise dividing the image in regular blocks of fixed size and summing up the squared contribution coming from each coefficient image:

$$E(b_k, I_t) = \sum_{i,j \in b_k} V_t^2(i,j) + H_t^2(i,j) + D_t^2(i,j) \tag{1}$$

where b_k is the kth block in the input image I^t.

The energy value of a specific block varies significantly over time in presence or absence of smoke, Fig. 2. When the smoke covers part of the scene the edges are smoothed and the energy consequently lowered. This energy drop can be

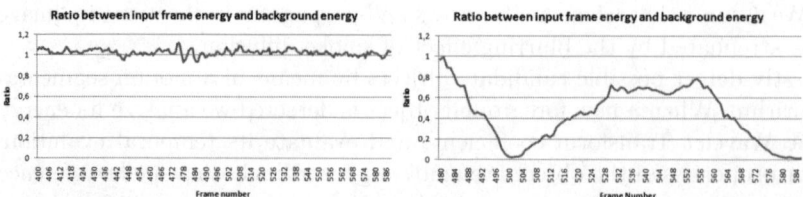

Fig. 2. Left figure: the energy ratio trend of a non smoke block. Right figure: the energy ratio trend of a smoke block. In presence of smoke the energy ratio is subjected to gradual drops in its value.

further emphasized computing the ratio $r(B_k)$ between the image energy of the current input frame and the one of the background model. The energy ratio has the advantage of normalizing the energy values and allowing a fair comparison between different scenes where the block energy itself can vary significantly. The ratio of the block b_k is given by:

$$r(b_k, I_t, Bg_t) = \frac{E(b_k, Bg_t)}{E(b_k, I_t)} \qquad (2)$$

where Bg_t is the background model up to time t and I_t is the input frame.

The analysis of the energy ratio is performed in two different context to account for both global and local energy drops.

Firstly the image energy variation is computed frame by frame to bias the detection using global information. Several clips containing a smoke events have been analyzed and the global energy ratio of the scene computed by sum the block energy. The *Parzen window* technique is adopted to build a non parametric distribution from global energy ratio values computed on several clips. The parzen window method is a kernel density estimator that computes a non parametric distribution from a set of iid samples $X = \{x_i \,|\, i = 1 \ldots N\}$ of a random variable x. Adopting a specific kernel distribution the approximated pdf is computed summing the kernel for all the sampled values:

$$\widehat{f} = \frac{1}{N\,h} \sum_{i=1}^{N} K(x - x_i) \qquad (3)$$

using a standard Gaussian kernel function $K = \frac{1}{2\pi} e^{-\frac{1}{2} x^2}$.

Secondly each block is then locally evaluated to capture the temporal evolution of the energy ratio.

When an energy drop is observed for a significant period of time an edge smoothing process occurs. The edge smoothing process can be affected by noise due to light variation in the scene. A Mixture of Gaussian model is adopted to improve the analysis robustness.

The MoG has the great advantage to correctly catch variations for multimodal distributions. To compute the probability for each frame the on-line expectation maximization algorithm proposed in [11] is used.

In detail, for all blocks b_k of the image I_t at time t the value $r(b_k, I_t, Bg_t)$ is computed and the MoG of block b_k updated using a selective update method.

This process have a main advantage. The mixture component reweighting process is able to catch slow and gradual variations of energy ratio. Values that do not occur frequently are filter out and assigned to the least probable Gaussian of the mixture. This property is helpful for evaluating the gradient intensity lowering process of smoking regions that has the peculiarity of being slow and continuous in time, Fig. 3.

To capture the time variation of the energy ratio the Gaussian Mixture Model was preferred to a Hidden Markov model (HMM). Although HMMs are widely adopted to classify and model temporal stochastic processes, the data values

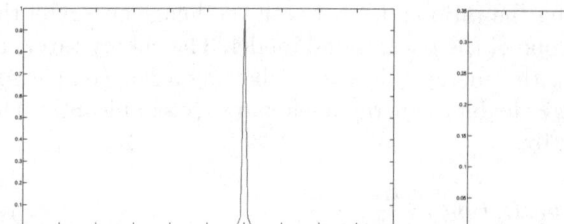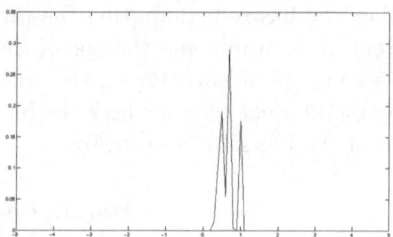

Fig. 3. Gaussian mixtures obtained observing energy ratio values at a single block. The left plot shows the mixture when there is no smoke in the block. The right plot shows how the mixture changes when smoke is in the scene. It is worth noting that when a block is covered by smoke the mixture components mean values move gradually towards 0.

sequence is crucial to obtain a good classification. Instead, as previously stated, the block energy ratio is subject to strong fluctuations of energy values due to noise and natural scene lighting. This reason makes the lowering sequence unpredictably variable in different setups; thus the specific energy drop trajectory can produce misleading results. On the contrary is interesting to analyze the global trend.

2.2   Color Analysis to Detect Blended Smoke Regions

When a smoke event occurs, scene regions covered by smoke change their color properties. The smoke can either be completely opaque or partially transparent. In the former case the covered region changes completely its color while in the latter case the color of the covered region appears to be blended with the smoke color.

This simple observation remains valid in all the observed cases and intuitively suggests a hint to characterize the color of a smoke region.

The proposed model simply adopts an evaluation based on a blending function mutuated from computer graphics. A reference color model is chosen in the RGB color space to represent the color of the smoke in the scene. The model is selected by analyzing the different color tones produced combusting different materials. For explanatory purposes is possible to concentrate the analysis to the case of a light gray color model as the smoke in the leftmost image of Fig. 1. Each pixel $I_t(i,j)$ of the input frame at time t is then checked against the smoke model and the background model Bg_t to evaluate the reference color presence computing the blending parameter bl using equation 4. The evaluation takes into account the case where the scene color and the smoke color are mixed together.

$$bl(i,j,I_t,Bg_t,S) = \frac{I_t(i,j) - Bg_t(i,j)}{S - Bg_t(i,j)} \qquad (4)$$

where Bg_t is the current backround model at time t and S is the smoke reference color model.

To filter out the errors and possible measurements inaccuracy the blending value is computed for each image block as the average of bl values in the block:

$$\beta_{b_k}(I_t, Bg_t, S) = \frac{1}{N^2} \sum_{i,j \in \,,b_k} \frac{I_t(i,j) - Bg_t(i,j)}{S - Bg_t(i,j)} \qquad (5)$$

where block size is $N \times N$.

In conclusion the β measure quantifies how much each block globally shares chromatic properties with the reference color model.

2.3 A Bayesian Approach for Classification

In the previous subsections the blockwise energy ratio measure r and the color blending measure β have been presented as possible discriminant features to identify a smoke region in the scene. A Bayesian formulation has been chosen to identify whether a block b_k is likely to belong to a smoke region. For each block the posterior probability of smoke presence, the event $f = 1$, considering the block b_k is defined:

$$P(f = 1|b_k) \propto P(b_k|f = 1)P(f = 1) \qquad (6)$$

The likelihood value is obtained by combining both the contributions coming from energy ratio and color information. These terms are considered probabilistically independent to simplify the treatment.

$$P(b_k|f = 1) = P(r_{b_k}, \beta_{b_k}|f = 1) = P_r(b_k|f = 1) \cdot P_\beta(b_k|f = 1) \qquad (7)$$

The likelihood contribution due to energy ratio decay is obtained by summing the weighted Gaussians of the MOG having mean value below a considered threshold th_1 computed empirically observing the mean energy ratio value in smoke regions.

$$P_r(b_k|f = 1) = \sum_{i-1}^{K} w_i N(r(b_k, I_t, Bg_t)|\mu_i \, \sigma_i) \qquad (8)$$

when the ith Gaussian mean value $\mu_i < th_1$.

The color contribution to the likelihood value is directly computed as the block color blending measure β_{b_k} according to equation 5.

$$P_\beta(b_k|f = 1) = B_k(I_t, Bg_t, S) \qquad (9)$$

The classification is biased making use of prior knowledge acquired observing several clips containing smoke. The prior probability of a smoke event in the current frame is directly related to the mean energy ratio value of the scene and computed using the non parametric distribution obtained by equation 3.

$$P(f = 1) = \widehat{f}(\frac{1}{M} \sum_{\forall b_k \in I_t} r(b_k, I_t, Bg_t)) \qquad (10)$$

where I_t is composed by M blocks.

The posterior probability value is thresholded to identify a candidate smoke block. The test for smoke presence is performed after foreground object segmentation. For any segmented object in the scene the number of candidate blocks intersecting the object's blob is computed. Finally an object is classified as smoke when the 70% of its area overlays candidated smoke blocks.

3 Experimental Results and Discussion

The proposed smoke detection system can be used in conjunction with a whichever video surveillance system providing moving object segmentation using a background model. The background model should be updated regularly but smoke regions should not be included in the background. This can be achieved choosing a slow background update rate and avoiding updating the background model areas where a smoke object is detected. The tests were performed using both the Stauffer and Grimson background model with selective update [4] and the SAKBOT median background model with knowledge based update [9]. Although the results did not vary significantly changing the background model and object detection technique, the second method has been preferred since discriminates the presence of possible shadows objects too.

Movie Name	Frame Number	Outdoor/Indoor	Temporal Analysis		Color Analysis		Gloabal Analysis	
			Time To Detect	False positive	Time To Detect	False positive	Time To Detect	False positive
movie_01	165	Outdoor	22	-	1	-	1	-
movie_02	210	Indoor	18	-	1	-	1	-
movie_03	2200	Outdoor	28	-	34	-	20	-
movie_04	3005	Indoor	212	-	273	-	185	-
movie_05	1835	Indoor	87	-	100	3	52	-
movie_06	2345	Outdoor	129	-	161	-	116	-
movie_07	2024	Indoor	57	3	99	-	35	-
movie_08	2151	Outdoor	88	2	88	-	42	-
movie_09	1880	Outdoor	59	-	56	-	45	-
movie_10	2953	Outdoor	457	-	498	-	300	-
movie_11	1485	Indoor	62	-	x	5	62	-
movie_12	499	Outdoor	43	-	8	-	16	-
movie_13	195	Indoor	53	-	23	-	27	-
movie_14	1226	Outdoor	77	-	370	-	69	-
movie_15	109	Outdoor	29	-	x	1	3	-

Fig. 4. Experimental results of the proposed system on reference clips

In all the tests carried out the learning rate α, [4], of the MoGs used to model the energy ratio decay was set to 0.1. Although changing this parameter does not have major effects on the system performance, a fast learning rate is preferable to detect energy ratio variations rapidly. The system was tested on 50 clips of varying length in both indoor and outdoor setups where moving objects such as people or vehicles were present in the scene during the smoke event. Each clip contained a smoke event. Part of the dataset is publicly available at

Fig. 5. Snapshots of the proposed system working on several clips in different conditions. The blue area in the images is detected as smoke.

website *http://imagelab.ing.unimore.it/visor*. Each likelihood term was evaluated separately to measure the impact on the system performance.

The table in Fig. 4 summarizes the results obtained on 15 reference clips.

The first column of the table reports the video type and its frame-length. The average clips framerate is 25fps. The remaining columns report the results obtained using each likelihood term separately and finally the results of the whole system. The detection time after the smoke event occurs is reported for all the test clips. The table clearly shows that the likelihood term due to temporal analysis (eq.8) is effective in most of the observed cases. The main problem is the long detection time. This is caused by the time based statistics used to capture the energy ratio decay. Although the likelihood contribution due to color blending has the advantage of speed up the detection process it tends to detect much false positives if used alone. See seventh column of Fig. 4. Observing the last two columns of Fig. 4 we can state that the complete approach is fast and reliable enough even in situations where each likelihood contribution fails. The overall system results on the 50 clips used for testing purposes report a detection rate of 77% 3 seconds later the smoke event occurs, 98.5% 6 seconds later and finally 100% 10 seconds later with an average true positive rate of 4%. Fig. 5 shows some snapshots of the system working on different conditions.

4   Conclusions and Acknowledgments

In conclusion we propose a system capable of detecting if foreground objects are smoke or not using both wavelet transform energy coefficients and image color properties. The proposed Bayesian approach has been extensively evaluated on public data and results in term of detection rate and time to detect have been reported. The adoption of a two-contribution likelihood measure solves most of the emerged problems of each chosen feature and boosts up significantly the detection process. The system well performed in all the tested scenarios and results are very robust.

This work is partially supported by the project BESAFE (Behavior lEarning in Surveilled Areas with Feature Extraction) funded by NATO Science for Peace programme and by the project FREE SURF funded by Italian MIUR Ministry.

References

1. Kopilovic, I., Vagvolgyi, B., Sziranyi, T.: Application of panoramic annular lens for motion analysis tasks: surveillance and smoke detection. In: Proceedings of 15th International Conference on Pattern Recognition, September 3-7, 2000, vol. 4, pp. 714–717. IEEE, Los Alamitos (2000)
2. Vicente, J., Guillemant, P.: An image processing technique for automatically detecting forest fire. In:International Journal of Thermal Sciences 41(12), 1113–1120 (2002)
3. Chen, T.-H(C.-H.)., Yin, Y.-H., Huang, S.-F., Ye, Y.-T.: The Smoke Detection for Early Fire-Alarming System Base on Video Processing. In: International Conference on Intelligent Information Hiding and Multimedia, pp. 427–430 (2006)
4. Stauffer, C., Grimson, W.E.L.: Adaptive Background Mixture Models for Real-Time Tracking. In: Proceedings IEEE Conference on Computer Vision and Pattern Recognition, pp. 246–252. IEEE, Los Alamitos (1999)
5. Xiong, Z., Caballero, R., Wang, H., Finn, A., Lelic, M.A., Peng, P.: Video-based Smoke Detection: Possibilities, Techniques, and Challenges Suppression and Detection Research and Applications. In: A Technical Working Conference (SUPDET 2007), Orlando, Florida (March 5-8, 2007)
6. Toreyin, B.U., Dedeoglu, Y., Cetin, A.E.: Flame detection in video using hidden Markov models. In: IEEE International Conference on Image Processing, IEEE, Los Alamitos (2005)
7. Toreyin, B.U., Dedeoglu, Y., Cetin, A.E., Fazekas, D., Chetverikov, T., Amiaz, N., Kiryati, N.: Dynamic texture detection, segmentation and analysis In:Conference On Image And Video Retrieval, pp. 131–134. ACM, New York (2007)
8. Collins, R.T., Collins, A.J., Lipton, K.T.: A system for video surveillance and monitoring. In: 8th International Topical Meeting on Robotics and Remote Systems. American Nuclear Society (1999)
9. Cucchiara, R., Grana, R., Piccardi, C., Prati, M.: A. Detecting Moving Objects, Ghosts and Shadows in Video Streams. IEEE Transactions on Pattern Analysis and Machine Intelligence. IEEE 25(10), 1337–1342 (2003)
10. Mallat, S.G.: A theory for multiresolution signal decomposition: The wavelet representation. IEEE Transactions on Pattern Recognition and Machine Intelligence IEEE 11(7), 674–693 (1989)
11. Sato, M.: Fast learning of on-line EM algorithm. In: Technical Report TR-H-281, ATR Human Information Processing Research Laboratories

Part III

Computer Vision Architectures

Feature Extraction and Classification by Genetic Programming

Olly Oechsle and Adrian F. Clark

VASE Laboratory, Department of Computing and Electronic Systems
University of Essex, Colchester, CO4 3SQ, UK

Abstract. This paper explores the use of genetic programming for constructing vision systems. A two-stage approach is used, with separate evolution of the feature extraction and classification stages. The strategy taken for the classifier is to evolve a set of partial solutions, each of which works for a single class. It is found that this approach is significantly faster than conventional genetic programming, and frequently results in a better classifier. The effectiveness of the approach is explored on three classification problems.

1   Introduction

Computer vision researchers have explored a vast range of approaches and techniques in order to produce working vision systems. Many of the early approaches, perhaps typified by the convolution with masks of the 1970s and early 1980s, did little more than emphasize features for subsequent human processing. These were refined into techniques such as edge and corner detectors that did a much better job in the late 1980s and early 1990s. The last decade or so, however, has seen an increasing emphasis being placed on approaches that learn a solution from the data; not surprisingly, these tend to out-perform less adaptive approaches.

Just as there is a wide range of techniques for extracting information from images, there are many learning algorithms that can be employed. However, almost all of these are unable to operate directly on the pixel data, requiring some preceding feature extraction stage. One technique that can work directly with the pixels is genetic programming (GP) [1], essentially an adaption of the classic genetic algorithm [2] to evolve programs (parse trees) rather than sets of numerical coefficients.

GP has, of course, been applied to a number of problems in the vision domain, and work in this respect is reviewed briefly in Sect. 2. The authors are exploring the extent to which GP can be used to develop complete solutions to vision problems, from feature extraction right through to classification; indeed, our work is focused towards problems involving several classes. The major attraction of the GP approach is that — given truly representative training data and enough training — the evolution of the solution can be tailored to the performance requirements of the system. This paper presents what is essentially a framework that allows a vision system to be trained on a fairly wide variety of vision tasks with only a modicum of human control being involved in defining the problem and the general nature of a solution. The overall vision system is built up from two stages, each evolved independently. A novel feature of this approach is a training

A. Gasteratos, M. Vincze, and J.K. Tsotsos (Eds.): ICVS 2008, LNCS 5008, pp. 131–140, 2008.

strategy that allows the classification stage to be evolved significantly more rapidly than in conventional GP, and usually resulting in a more accurate classifier. As well as reducing training time dramatically, the training strategy also allows the system to be applied to problems with a larger number of classes than have been reported to date using GP-based approaches.

It is assumed that the reader is familiar with the basic concepts of GP. Following a brief review of previous work on the use of GP in computer vision in Sect. 2, the overall architecture of the authors' framework is presented in Sect. 3. Sect. 4 describes the approach that has been developed for fast evolution of classifiers. A range of problems to which the system has been applied is presented in Sect. 5, along with comparisons with a well-established GP engine and a conventional classifier. Finally, conclusions are drawn in Sect. 6.

2   Previous Work

Since its first application to a recognizably computer vision problem, for recognising targets in military environments [3], GP has been employed on a wide range of computer vision tasks. It has been used for face detection using a multi-scale windowed approach [4]; for detecting cracks using an image exploring agent [5]; and has been used to tackle segmentation problems, such as the segmentation of skin lesions to aid the detection of melanoma (skin cancer) [6], the recognition of features from remotely-sensed multi-spectral images [7] and the classification of texture [8]. GP has also been applied to some of the classic problems tackled by computer vision researchers, namely colour constancy [9], edge detection [10] and optical character recognition [11].

Results of approaches using generic features which are designed to solve a range of vision problems were published by [12] (recognising vehicles and ships from satellite images), [13] (coins, shapes and retinal images) and [14] (triangles and pasta shapes). Various schemes have been used in GP for classification, some of which were compared by [15], further details about two of which are presented in Sect. 3.1.

3   System Architecture

While the majority of GP vision researchers have leaned toward evolving several programs that each perform *the entire task*, this work takes a rather different approach. Here, the feature extraction and classification stages are separated and evolved independently. Although this is fairly conventional for vision system architectures, it does not appear to have been attempted previously by GP.

In order to train the feature extraction stage, the developer identifies regions of 'feature' and 'non-feature' using a graphical user interface. A program is then evolved to do this automatically. The output of this program yields the regions of interest within a given image which are to be classified. The developer marks each region with the expected class to produce a second training set. After identifying these training data and choosing a set of measures that the classification stage may use, the work of tailoring the classifier is left to the software.

Intellectually, procedures to calculate the feature measures can be thought of as being included in the set of functions made available to the classifier. In practice however, the authors have found it better to calculate them independently and provide them in a table to the classifier stage — this is effectively a speed optimization analogous to the caching of common sub-trees to avoid re-calculation [16]. Hence, a typical system architecture produced by our framework is shown diagrammatically in Fig. 1.

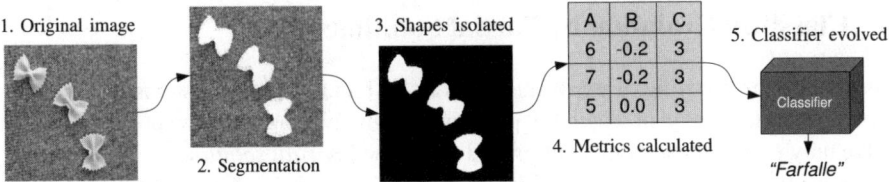

Fig. 1. The Vision System Used for the Experimental Work

Feature extraction is evolved using conventional GP, but it is found that this approach works poorly for the classifier, which is often more complicated and takes longer to evolve, especially for multi-class problems. The reason for this is that standard GP aims to evolve *a single program* to solve the problem defined by the training data — and the result is usually a large program. However, the nature of the crossover and mutation operators used means the probability that adding new features to large programs without causing some damage to the existing solution decreases as the program size increases, a feature of the so-called stability-plasticity dilemma, which was demonstrated empirically in [17]. In effect, GP becomes more difficult as evolution progresses. Hence, the authors have developed a somewhat different scheme for evolving the classifier, termed *partial-solution GP*. A full description of the technique will be published elsewhere but an overview is given in Sect. 4.

3.1 Existing GP Approaches

Two different classification strategies were explored for comparison, the first using evolved decision trees (DT), and the second using dynamic range selection (DRS). A decision tree typically consists of a number of nested if-then-else statements. Each branch of the if-statement may contain either a further if-statement or return a particular class, coded by a number. A Boolean expression determines which branch in the if statement should be executed. The expression may be as simple as a basic threshold, although GP is capable of expressing more complicated Boolean logic through use of operators such as AND, OR and NOT, and comparative functions such as less and more. As decision trees output the class directly, there is no need to make further interpretation. However, this can make the trees inflexible and unable to make subtle changes without damaging fitness.

A second GP approach is dynamic range selection, where each individual is represented as an evolved mathematical function. The output is typically a floating-point number producing a set of continuous values. This output is translated into a classification using a mapping that is calculated and optimized for each individual. In our experiments, the individual's average output for each class in the training data was cal-culated and stored. These values could then be used for classification: the associated class of the nearest mean value to any new output was returned. Dynamic range selec-tion allows programs to be smaller as it removes the need to evolve thresholds. In a comparison of several classification representations dynamic range selection was found to be the most effective strategy [15].

4   Classifier Evolution by Partial Solutions (PS)

Inspired by the boosting of weak classifiers in [18] and classifier systems in general, a scheme was developed in which GP programs are evolved as simple expressions which solve only part of the overall solution and are termed *partial solutions*.

As useful partial solutions are identified (see below for details) they are added to a separate, 'strong' classifier which exists outside of the GP system (see Fig. 2). The scheme continues to evolve partial solutions until the strong classifier is capable of a certain level of accuracy.

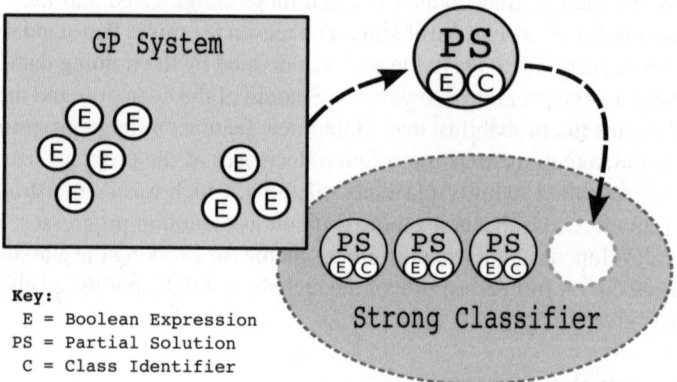

Fig. 2. GP by Partial Solutions creates a strong classifier from a number of smaller solutions

As each partial solution is not expected to solve the whole problem, the programs are small and so may be discovered and evolved quickly. Once a partial solution is identified as being useful – that is, it can solve part of the problem that has not already been solved – it is saved in the strong classifier and the problem is redefined to include only the remaining training data. This removes the need for already-solved data to be continuously re-evaluated, as is the case with standard GP, and also ensures that the 'knowledge' of the partial solution is protected[1].

Each partial solution is treated as a binary classifier with respect to a class C. The kinds of nodes used to create Boolean expressions of this type were mentioned in Sect. 3.1. C is chosen by evaluating the partial solution with respect to each class c in the problem and choosing the value of c for which it has best fitness.

---

[1] The actions of genetic operators and the sampling effect inherent in tournament selection may each cause useful subtrees to be destroyed or lost inadvertently in standard GP.

The fitness with regard to a particular class c is calculated by dividing the total number of correct classifications T_c by the total number of training samples N added to the number of missed classifications F_c, as shown below:

$$\text{fitness}_c = \frac{\alpha T_c}{N + \beta F_c} \tag{1}$$

The factors α and β allows the fitness measure to be adjusted to affect the individuals' sensitivity or specificity.

Fitness is used to drive the evolution. However, in order to decide whether a partial solution should be added to the strong classifier — that is to say that it is able to solve a new part of the overall solution — four criteria were devised:

1. *Does the partial solution discriminate?* If the solution returns only 'true' or only 'false' it is not capable of making decisions. GP often evolves this kind of lazy solution in response to training data that are weighted in favour of one particular class. GP by partial solutions avoids this form of code bloat.
2. *Is the partial solution unique?* If the classifier returns the same results for every instance as another partial solution that has already been chosen, then this classifier is usually discarded[2].
3. *Does the partial solution return 'true' for data that have not yet been solved?* Each item of training data has a field indicating whether it has already been solved. Each candidate partial solution has to identify at least one instance that has not yet been solved in order to be used.
4. *Does the partial solution return 'false' for data in other classes?* If a classifier returns 'true' for instances of one class, it should return 'false' for all instances of other classes. However, it *may* return 'true' mistakenly for other classes provided that they have already been completely solved by other partial solutions. We describe this solution as being *dependent* on the other classes.

If the partial solution matches all these criteria, it is added to the strong classifier. Several partial solutions may be discovered during the course of a single generation – another feature which makes GP by partial solutions faster.

A version of island selection is used with crossover only occurring between parents with the same value of C which are more likely to share some similarity.

The strong classifier produces classifications by evaluating each of its partial solutions in turn (starting with the first added). If the partial solution returns 'true' for a given input vector, the class C associated with the partial solution is returned, otherwise the next partial solution is executed and so forth.

5   Experiments and Results

A series of experiments has been conducted to explore the practicality and effectiveness of the approach outlined above, namely colour recognition, hand gesture identification,

---

[2] Unless it is smaller or less dependent than the existing one, in which case the existing solution is replaced.

and a standard image classification benchmark. These are deliberately rather different in nature and are discussed in the following sub-sections. The authors' own GP engine, SXGP, forms a common base for the different GP-based schemes discussed to ensure that the comparisons are meaningful; the performance of the popular GP engine ECJ [19] (using dynamic range selection) is also presented to aid comparison. Genetic Programming parameters are summarised in Table 1. The table also highlights any differences between conventional GP and GP by partial solutions[3].

Table 1. Genetic Programming Parameters

Parameter	Standard GP	Partial Solutions
P(crossover)	0.80	Same
P(mutation)	0.15	Same
Selection Method	Tournament Selection ($t = 2$)	Same
Max Tree Size	575 nodes	100
Population Size	500	1500
Time Limit	600 seconds per run	Same

5.1 Colour Recognition

Problems of this type typically represent the first evolved stage of our vision system. Here, we are concerned the recognition of seven different colours (red, green, blue, black, silver, white, yellow), with sample pixels taken from photographs of different vehicles. Although the number of classes involved is not large in absolute terms, it represents roughly the upper limit of classes to which GP has been reported successfully to date.

The classification algorithms were provided with a feature set which consisted of basic colour information about each sample pixel, such as its red/green/blue components and corresponding hue/saturation/lightness. Further features included data about the distribution of these components in a 3×3 region around the central pixel, including the mean, standard deviation and range. Equivalent measures for the entire image were also included for context.

A training set of 213 samples was created, and a further set of 10,470 samples was used to test the evolved solutions. The training set and test set are disjoint, consisting of pictures taken on different days and in different weather conditions. The images were all taken with a Nikon D70 camera using the camera's automatic white balance function.

A comparison of the performances of different GP-based approaches is given in Table 2. For each experiment we present the performance of the best-evolved classifier from each approach on training and test data, averaged over 10 runs. The $\pm$ marks indicate the standard deviation from the mean. The average evolution time to evolve the individual is also given.

---

[3] In GP by partial solutions a larger population size is used to ensure each 'island' has sufficient individuals. As each partial solution is intended to be smaller, the maximum tree size for each is reduced.

Table 2. Colour Recognition Performance

Technique	Training %	Testing %	Time
SXGP (PS)	100.0 ± 0.0	96.9 ± 1.9	60 secs
SXGP (DRS)	80.4 ± 3.3	77.3 ± 3.5	603 secs
SXGP (DT)	72.1 ± 9.7	70.2 ± 9.9	603 secs
ECJ (DRS)	82.3 ± 7.5	78.4 ± 8.7	599 secs

Comparing the performances obtained using dynamic range selection (DRS) and decision trees (DT), it is apparent that dynamic range selection yields rather better results on average, and appears to do so more consistently. However, when the same GP engine is used with the 'partial solutions' (PS) approach, all the training data are recognised and the performance on unseen test data increases to $> 95\%$. Although the evolution times cannot be directly compared – as the non partial solutions approaches never discover an optimal individual within the given time period – it is clear that Genetic Programming by partial solutions is substantially faster, in this case by an order of magnitude.

The average performances of ECJ and SXGP on this problem appear broadly similar, although ECJ is able to evaluate individuals more rapidly. Both ECJ and SXGP are written in Java and executed on the same platform, so this is a meaningful comparison.

5.2 Hand Gestures

This experiment represents the kind of problem tackled in the second stage of our vision system. The experiment involved the recognition of ten different hand gestures[4] from images captured using a webcam. Although this kind of problem has been tackled very effectively by researchers using other learning techniques [20], it has not previously been investigated using Genetic Programming.

In the feature extraction stage a program was evolved to segment the hand from the background by colour (using a program similar to those evolved in the first experiment). Some 22 generic features about the shape of each hand were computed and supplied to the classifier, including metrics approximating the circularity, number of corners, density etc. Using these features, a classifier was evolved to recognise the different gestures. Some 100 samples were used for training with a further 200 samples being used for testing.

The relative performances are summarized in Table 3. Here, results from a K-nearest neighbour (K-NN) classifier are also included as a benchmark algorithm. Again, the partial solution approach is the most effective, and was evolved dramatically faster than the ones using conventional GP. Interesting, the K-NN algorithm was unable to solve the problem acceptably, perhaps indicating that the training data are difficult or noisy.

The authors have also tackled other shape classification and optical character recognition tasks using the same framework. The metrics which produced the feature set for this experiment are suitably generic to solve a variety of tasks, although the results show that they are not yet sufficient to develop highly accurate classifiers.

---

[4] Open-Palm, Fist, Thumbs-Up, Live-Long, Pinch, Closed-Palm, Point1, Point2, Okay and Bang; more information is available on our website.

Table 3. Hand Gesture Performance

Technique	Training %	Testing %	Time
SXGP (PS)	100.0 ± 0.0	81.4 ± 2.7	28 secs
SXGP (DRS)	75.4 ± 7.9	67.2 ± 8.4	603 secs
SXGP (DT)	55.6 ± 6.3	51.6 ± 7.0	603 secs
ECJ (DRS)	86.1 ± 3.8	73.7 ± 6.2	599 secs
K-NN ($k = 1$)		52.5	

5.3 The SatImage Classification Benchmark

This experiment explores a benchmark in image classification, the Statlog SatImage data set [21]. This database was generated from Landsat Multi-Spectral Scanner image data; it consists of the values of each pixel in a 3×3 neighbourhood across four spectral bands, thus producing 36 features in total. Using these data, the central pixel is classified into one of six classes pertaining to the kind of soil present. There are 4,435 items of training data and 2,000 samples of test data. Performance figures are summarized in Table 4, here consisting of the best individual from each method after 10 runs. Here, the partial solutions approach was trained on a reduced sample of 250 examples; consequently, it is again the fastest to evolve by a factor of about 10 yet still offers a performance commensurate with the other techniques reported on the Statlog website.

Table 4. Statlog SatImage Performance

Technique	Training %	Testing %	Time (ms)	Error
SXGP (PS)	NA	83.9	57 secs	0.161
SXGP (DRS)	74.9	73.4	606 secs	0.192
SXGP (DT)	63.7	63.3	601 secs	0.196
ECJ (DRS)	73.0	72.1	599 secs	0.279
K-NN	91.1	90.6	NA	0.094

6 Concluding Remarks

We have shown in this paper that GP provides an excellent foundation for the creation of vision systems. With some initial guidance from the vision system developer, it is possible for complete systems to be evolved in a comparatively short space of time, and these systems have performance commensurate with those obtained using other learning techniques.

In further work, the authors are keen to see whether it is possible to dispense with the human development of measures that are applied to extracted features and passed on to the classification stage. Ideally, the authors would prefer to develop a system which uses purely evolved features, which may be tailored to each solution and would be both appropriate for the data set and the kind of constraints that are imposed on any practical application.

All our software, training data and further detail about our experiments which could not be included are available at: `http://vase.essex.ac.uk/papers/icvs2008`

References

1. Koza, J.R.: Genetic Programming. MIT Press, Cambridge (1992)
2. Goldberg, D.E.: Genetic Algorithms in Search, Optimization and Machine Learning. Addison-Wesley, Reading (1989)
3. Tackett, W.A.: Genetic programming for feature discovery and image discrimination. In: Proceedings of the Fifth International Conference on Genetic Algorithms, pp. 303–309 (1993)
4. Winkeler, J.F., Manjunath, B.S.: Genetic programming for object detection. In: Koza, J.R., Deb, K., Dorigo, M., Fogel, D.B., Garzon, M., Iba, H., Riolo, R.L. (eds.) Proceedings of the Second Annual Conference on Genetic Programming, Morgan Kaufmann, San Francisco (1997)
5. Koppen, M., Nickolay, B.: Design of image exploring agent using genetic programming. In: Proc. IIZUKA 1996, Iizuka, Japan, pp. 549–552 (1996)
6. Roberts, M.E., Claridge, E.: An artificially evolved vision system for segmenting skin lesion images. In: Ellis, R.E., Peters, T.M. (eds.) MICCAI 2003. LNCS, vol. 2878, pp. 655–662. Springer, Heidelberg (2003)
7. Brumby, S.P., Theiler, J., Perkins, S., Harvey, N.R., Szymanski, J.J.: Genetic programming approach to extracting features from remotely sensed imagery. In: FUSION 2001: Fourth International Conference on Image Fusion, Montreal, Quebec, Canada (2001)
8. Song, A., Ciesielski, V.: Texture analysis by genetic programming. In: Proceedings of the IEEE Congress on Evolutionary Computation, pp. 2092–2099 (2004)
9. Ebner, M.: Evolving color constancy for an artificial retina. In: Miller, J., Tomassini, M., Lanzi, P.L., Ryan, C., Tetamanzi, A.G.B., Langdon, W.B. (eds.) EuroGP 2001. LNCS, vol. 2038, pp. 11–22. Springer, Heidelberg (2001)
10. Zhang, Y., Rockett, P.I.: Evolving optimal feature extraction using multi-objective genetic programming: a methodology and preliminary study on edge detection. In: GECCO 2005: Proceedings of the 2005 conference on Genetic and evolutionary computation, Washington DC, USA, vol. 1, pp. 795–802. ACM Press, New York (2005)
11. Spivak, P.K.: Discovery of optical character recognition algorithms using genetic programming. In: Koza, J.R. (ed.) Genetic Algorithms and Genetic Programming at Stanford 2002, Stanford Bookstore, Stanford, California, 94305-3079 USA, pp. 223–232 (2002)
12. Roberts, S.C., Howard, D.: Evolution of Vehicle Detectors for Infra-red Linescan Imagery. In: Poli, R., Voigt, H.-M., Cagnoni, S., Corne, D.W., Smith, G.D., Fogarty, T.C. (eds.) EvoIASP 1999 and EuroEcTel 1999. LNCS, vol. 1596, pp. 110–125. Springer, Heidelberg (1999)
13. Zhang, M., Ciesielski, V.: Genetic programming for multiple class object detection. In: Foo, N. (ed.) Proceedings of the 12th Australian Joint Conference on Artificial Intelligence, pp. 180–192. Springer, Heidelberg (1999)
14. Roberts, M.E., Claridge, E.: A multistage approach to cooperatively coevolving feature construction and object detection. In: Rothlauf, F., Branke, J., Cagnoni, S., Corne, D.W., Drechsler, R., Jin, Y., Machado, P., Marchiori, E., Romero, J., Smith, G.D., Squillero, G. (eds.) EvoWorkshops 2005. LNCS, vol. 3449, Springer, Heidelberg (2005)
15. Loveard, T., Ciesielski, V.: Representing classification problems in genetic programming. In: Proceedings of the Congress on Evolutionary Computation, vol. 2, pp. 1070–1077. IEEE Press, Los Alamitos (2001)

16. Roberts, M.E.: The effectiveness of cost based subtree caching mechanisms in typed genetic programming for image segmentation. In: Raidl, G.R., Cagnoni, S., Cardalda, J.J.R., Corne, D.W., Gottlieb, J., Guillot, A., Hart, E., Johnson, C.G., Marchiori, E., Meyer, J.-A., Middendorf, M. (eds.) EvoIASP 2003, EvoWorkshops 2003, EvoSTIM 2003, EvoROB/EvoRobot 2003, EvoCOP 2003, EvoBIO 2003, and EvoMUSART 2003. LNCS, vol. 2611, pp. 444–454. Springer, Heidelberg (2003)

17. Banzhaf, W., Nordin, P., Keller, R.E., Francone, F.D.: Genetic programming: an introduction: on the automatic evolution of computer programs and its applications. Morgan Kaufmann Publishers Inc, San Francisco (1998)

18. Freund, Y., Schapire, R.E.: A decision-theoretic generalization of on-line learning and an application to boosting. In: European Conference on Computational Learning Theory, pp. 23–37 (1995)

19. Luke, S.: A Java-based evolutionary computation research system, vol. 14 (2008), http://cs.gmu.edu/~eclab/projects/ecj/

20. Starner, T., Weaver, J., Pentland, A.: Real-time american sign language recognition using desk and wearable computer based video. IEEE Transactions on Pattern Analysis and Machine Intelligence 20, 1371–1375 (1998)

21. Asuncion, A., Newman, D.J.: UCI machine learning repository (2007)

GPU-Based Multigrid:
Real-Time Performance in High Resolution
Nonlinear Image Processing

Harald Grossauer and Peter Thoman*

Department of Computer Science
Universität Innsbruck
Technikerstraße 21a
A-6020 Innsbruck, Austria
harald.grossauer@uibk.ac.at,
peter.thoman@uibk.ac.at
http://infmath.uibk.ac.at

Abstract. Multigrid methods provide fast solvers for a wide variety of problems encountered in computer vision. Recent graphics hardware is ideally suited for the implementation of such methods, but this potential has not yet been fully realized. Typically, work in that area focuses on linear systems only, or on implementation of numerical solvers that are not as efficient as multigrid methods. We demonstrate that nonlinear multigrid methods can be used to great effect on modern graphics hardware. Specifically, we implement two applications: a nonlinear denoising filter and a solver for variational optical flow. We show that performing these computations on graphics hardware is between one and two orders of magnitude faster than comparable CPU-based implementations.

Keywords: GPGPU, multigrid methods, optical flow, partial differential equations.

1 Introduction

Many important building blocks of computer vision algorithms, like denoising and dense optical flow calculation, necessitate solving complex systems of nonlinear Partial Differential Equations (PDEs). *Multigrid methods* [12,18,4,5] belong to the fastest and most versatile schemes available for the numerical solution of such systems. In addition to their fast convergence, multigrid methods have another advantage: they can be composed of operations that are completely data-parallel and are thus able to benefit immensely from parallel hardware architectures.

Recent efforts in *General Purpose computation on Graphics Processing Units* (GPGPU) aim to use one ubiquitous type of such parallel hardware: modern graphics processors. However, despite the suitability of multigrid methods to GPUs,

---

* Supported by FSP Project S9203-N12.

A. Gasteratos, M. Vincze, and J.K. Tsotsos (Eds.): ICVS 2008, LNCS 5008, pp. 141–150, 2008.

there have only been a very limited number of publications attempting to combine the two [3,11,16]. Furthermore, multigrid methods for nonlinear systems – in the form of *Full Approximation Schemes* (FAS) [4] – have not appeared in the GPGPU literature at all.

In this paper, we demonstrate the possibilities offered by FAS on GPUs. We present in detail an implementation of variational optical flow computation on standard consumer graphics hardware which achieves rates of up to 17 dense high quality flow fields per second at a resolution of 511^2 pixels, more than 30 times as fast as comparable CPU-based implementations.

1.1   Background

GPGPU. Since the introduction of user-programmable shaders (see [13]) interest in using the vast computational capabilities offered by GPUs for tasks not directly related to graphics rendering has been on the rise. Modern graphics hardware is comprised of a large number of parallel floating point units paired with high-bandwidth memory and a cache structure optimized for 2D locality. Evidently, such a hardware architecture should be well suited to image processing.

Multigrid Methods. The mathematical basis of our work is provided by multigrid methods, in particular FAS since we deal with nonlinear problems. In this context we use the standard terminology as provided in Brandt [4] and Trottenberg et al. [18].

Nonlinear PDEs in Image Processing. To demonstrate the wide applicability of FAS schemes – and thus also of our GPGPU implementation – in computer vision we chose two common problems that lead to nonlinear PDEs. The first, relatively simple process is denoising using a nonlinear filter based on the model developed by Rudin, Osher, and Fatemi (ROF) [15]. We solve the resulting system of equations using a FAS scheme with a damped Jacobi smoother.

The second, far more complex and computationally intensive task is optical flow computation. The best models proposed in the literature [8] use variational formulations that lead to coupled PDEs with a large number of nonlinear terms. We will describe the mathematical foundation of such an approach in the next section, and discuss our GPU-based implementation of this algorithm after that.

Previous Work. Durkovic et al. [9] explored optical flow computation on GPUs, and demonstrated the performance advantages compared to CPUs. However, their work has two decisive drawbacks. Firstly, in terms of quality, the methods they implemented (the modified Horn-Schunck and Nagel algorithms presented in [2]) do not achieve results comparable to the most recent algorithms. Secondly, in terms of performance, they do not use a multigrid solver – these have been proven (in [7]) to give speedups of factor 200 to 2000 for optical flow calculation compared to standard iterative methods. In contrast, we implement one of the leading optical flow estimators in literature and use a multigrid method.

2   Optical Flow Model

In this section we review the variational model used in our implementation, which is essentially based on [8]. We also present some necessary adaptations of the numerical scheme to make the process more tractable on data-parallel architectures such as GPUs.

2.1   The Approach of Bruhn et al.

Let $I(\boldsymbol{x})$ be a presmoothed image sequence with $\boldsymbol{x} = (x, y, t)^T$. Here, $t \geq 0$ denotes the time while (x, y) denotes the location in the image domain Ω. Let $\boldsymbol{u} = (u, v, 1)^T$ be the unknown flow field between two frames at times t and $t+1$. Bruhn et al. [8] compute the optical flow as minimizer of the energy functional

$$E(\boldsymbol{u}) = E_{D_1}(\boldsymbol{u}) + \alpha E_{D_2}(\boldsymbol{u}) + \beta E_S(\boldsymbol{u}) \tag{1}$$

with the data and smoothness terms

$$E_{D_1}(\boldsymbol{u}) = \int_\Omega \psi(|I(\boldsymbol{x} + \boldsymbol{u}) - I(\boldsymbol{x})|^2) \, d\boldsymbol{x} \,, \tag{2}$$

$$E_{D_2}(\boldsymbol{u}) = \int_\Omega \psi(|\nabla I(\boldsymbol{x} + \boldsymbol{u}) - \nabla I(\boldsymbol{x})|^2) \, d\boldsymbol{x} \,, \tag{3}$$

$$E_S(\boldsymbol{u}) = \int_\Omega \psi(|\nabla u|^2 + |\nabla v|^2) \, d\boldsymbol{x} \tag{4}$$

and weighting parameters $\alpha, \beta \geq 0$. Thus the first data term E_{D_1} models the grey value constancy assumption, and the second data term E_{D_2} adds a constancy assumption of the spatial image gradient ∇I to improve robustness against varying illumination. The term E_S provides for spatial smoothness of the flow field. All three terms are modified by the non-quadratic penalizer

$$\psi(s^2) = \sqrt{s^2 + \epsilon^2} \,. \tag{5}$$

The Numerical Scheme. From the Euler-Lagrange equations corresponding to the energy functional outlined above, Bruhn et al. derive the finite difference approximation

$$0 = \Psi_{D_1 i}(S_{11i} du_i + S_{12i} dv_i + S_{13i}) + \alpha \Psi_{D_2 i}(T_{11i} du_i + T_{12i} dv_i + T_{13i})$$
$$- \beta \sum_{j \in \mathcal{N}(i)} \frac{\Psi_{Si} + \Psi_{Sj}}{2} \frac{u_j + du_j - u_i - du_i}{h^2} \,, \tag{6}$$

$$0 = \Psi_{D_1 i}(S_{12i} du_i + S_{22i} dv_i + S_{23i}) + \alpha \Psi_{D_2 i}(T_{21i} du_i + T_{22i} dv_i + T_{23i})$$
$$- \beta \sum_{j \in \mathcal{N}(i)} \frac{\Psi_{Si} + \Psi_{Sj}}{2} \frac{v_j + dv_j - v_i - dv_i}{h^2} \tag{7}$$

with the symmetric tensors

$$S := \boldsymbol{I}_\nabla \boldsymbol{I}_\nabla^T \,, \tag{8}$$

$$T := \boldsymbol{I}_{\nabla x} \boldsymbol{I}_{\nabla x}^T + \boldsymbol{I}_{\nabla y} \boldsymbol{I}_{\nabla y}^T \tag{9}$$

and abbreviations

$$\Psi_{D_1} := \Psi((du, dv, 1)^T S(du, dv, 1)) , \qquad (10)$$

$$\Psi_{D_2} := \Psi((du, dv, 1)^T T(du, dv, 1)) , \qquad (11)$$

$$\Psi_S := \Psi(|\nabla(u + du)|^2 + |\nabla(v + dv)|^2) \qquad (12)$$

containing nonlinear terms. In (6) and (7) the set $\mathcal{N}(i)$ denotes the spatial neighbours of pixel i. In (8) and (9) we use the definitions $\boldsymbol{I}_\nabla := (I_x, I_y, I_z)^T$, $\boldsymbol{I}_{\nabla x} := (I_{xx}, I_{yx}, I_{zx})^T$ and $\boldsymbol{I}_{\nabla y} := (I_{xy}, I_{yy}, I_{zy})^T$, with subscripts x and y denoting spatial derivatives and $I_z := I(\boldsymbol{x} + \boldsymbol{u}) - I(\boldsymbol{x})$.

2.2   Adaptations of the Numerical Scheme

Instead of using a Gauss-Seidel method (as in [8]) to solve the nonlinear system of equations given by (6) and (7) we adopt a damped Jacobi solver, retaining the coupled point relaxation and frozen coefficients approach proposed in [10]. While offering slightly better convergence rates, a standard Gauss-Seidel solver can not be efficiently implemented on current GPUs because it accesses values computed in the current iteration step and is thus not fully data-parallel. An alternative would be a Gauss-Seidel solver with Red/Black ordering of grid points (see [18]), but the access pattern required by such a method would greatly reduce the GPU cache efficiency. As the main purpose of the iterative solver in a multigrid application is reducing high-frequency error components, using a damped Jacobi scheme does not significantly decrease the efficiency of the algorithm (see [5]).

Using a point coupled damped Jacobi method the system of equations that must be solved for each pixel i at iteration step n is given by

$$\begin{pmatrix} du^{n+1} \\ dv^{n+1} \end{pmatrix} = \frac{1}{3} \begin{pmatrix} du^n \\ dv^n \end{pmatrix} + \frac{2}{3} (M^n)^{-1} \begin{pmatrix} r_u^n \\ r_v^n \end{pmatrix} \qquad (13)$$

with matrix entries

$$M_{11}^n = \Psi_{D_1 i}^n S_{11i}^n + \alpha \Psi_{D_2 i}^n T_{11i}^n + \beta \sum_{j \in \mathcal{N}(i)} \frac{\Psi_{Si}^n + \Psi_{Sj}^n}{2h^2} , \qquad (14)$$

$$M_{22}^n = \Psi_{D_1 i}^n S_{22i}^n + \alpha \Psi_{D_2 i}^n T_{22i}^n + \beta \sum_{j \in \mathcal{N}(i)} \frac{\Psi_{Si}^n + \Psi_{Sj}^n}{2h^2} , \qquad (15)$$

$$M_{12}^n = M_{21}^n = \Psi_{D_1 i}^n S_{12i}^n + \alpha \Psi_{D_2 i}^n T_{12i}^n \qquad (16)$$

and right hand side

$$r_u^n = -\Psi_{D_1 i}^n S_{13i}^n + \alpha \Psi_{D_2 i}^n T_{13i}^n + \beta \sum_{j \in \mathcal{N}(i)} \frac{\Psi_{Si}^n + \Psi_{Sj}^n}{2} \frac{u_j + du_j^n - u_i}{h^2} , \qquad (17)$$

$$r_v^n = -\Psi_{D_1 i}^n S_{23i}^n + \alpha \Psi_{D_2 i}^n T_{23i}^n + \beta \sum_{j \in \mathcal{N}(i)} \frac{\Psi_{Si}^n + \Psi_{Sj}^n}{2} \frac{v_j + dv_j^n - v_i}{h^2} . \qquad (18)$$

2.3   Our Multigrid Algorithm

Our multigrid algorithm is derived by reformulating (6) and (7) as

$$A^h(\boldsymbol{x}^h) = \boldsymbol{f}^h \tag{19}$$

with h denoting the discretization width, A^h a nonlinear operator and the vectors $\boldsymbol{x}^h = ((du^h)^T, (dv^h)^T)^T$ and $\boldsymbol{f}^h = ((f_1^h)^T, (f_2^h)^T)^T$. We use a standard FAS approach, with (13) serving as a smoother. The grid hierarchy is created by standard coarsening with full weighting as restriction operator and bilinear interpolation as prolongation method.

It is important to note that, unlike Bruhn et al. [8], we use V-cycles. While W-cycles or other variations may offer slightly better convergence rates, they require significantly more computations at very small grids where the parallelization advantages of GPUs are reduced, as shown in Table 3.

3   Optical Flow GPU Implementation

Implementing an algorithm on the GPU requires mapping the necessary data structures to textures and reformulating the computation as a series of pixel shader applications. When aiming to develop a high-performance GPU implementation, special attention must be paid to the flow and storage of data through the individual computational steps. We will now describe the data structures and the most important shader programs used in our implementation.

Data Structures. The number of texture reads and buffer writes has a significant impact on the throughput of a shader program. For this reason, it is very advantageous to pack related data values into 4-component (RGBA) textures to minimize the amount of read and write accesses to different buffers required in the shaders.

Our final implementation uses four buffers that are exclusive to the finest grid level, storing $[I; J]$, $[I_x; I_y; J_x; J_y]$, $[I_z; I_{xz}; I_{yz}]$ and $[I_{xx}; I_{xy}; I_{yy}]$ with $J :=I(\cdot, \cdot, t + 1)$. Furthermore, on each grid level ten buffers are required. Three of them store the symmetric tensors S and T (with six independent components each), three are general purpose buffers used for different types of data throughout the computation, and the last four store $[du; dv; un; vn]$, $[\Psi_{D_1}; \Psi_{D_2}; \Psi_S]$, $[f_1; f_2; u; v]$ and $[A(u); A(v)]$. These values correspond to the formulas provided in Section 2, except for $un := u + du$ and $vn := v + dv$, which are stored to speed up the computation and greatly reduce the number of texture reads required.

Shader Programs. The actual computation of our GPU implementation takes place in shader programs, the six most important of which we will now describe. There are a few helper programs used in our application, but those only implement basic mathematical operations or are used to move and restructure data.

- `calcIdJd` calculates the spatial derivatives of the source images.
- `calcIzIxzIyz` computes the differences between the first image relocated by the current flow field and the second image.

- `calcST` calculates the tensors S and T.
- `calcdpsi` calculates the nonlinearities Ψ_{D_1}, Ψ_{D_2} and Ψ_S.
- `calcAuAv` is used to compute the residual and right hand side for each coarser grid level. It calculates $A(u)$ and $A(v)$.
- `coupledJacobi` is the most complex shader program, performing one step of point-coupled damped Jacobi relaxation.

Computation. We shall now illustrate how the shader programs and data objects described above are used to perform the optical flow calculation. Figure 1 shows the computations required before starting each V-cycle of the multigrid solver. The spatial derivatives of the images are calculated, and the tensors S and T are computed from them. These operations are only performed at the finest grid level – the tensors are subsequently restricted to the coarser grids. In the following we will call a cycle of the algorithm that includes the recomputation of these tensors an *outer cycle*.

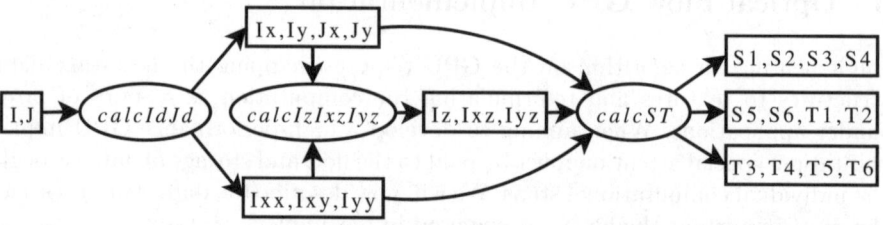

Fig. 1. Computations performed before starting each V-Cycle. Boxes represent data buffers, ellipses denote pixel shaders.

Pre- and postsmoothing operations at each level of the hierarchy follow the outline provided in Fig. 2. Note that this depiction is somewhat simplified: GPUs do not allow writing to an input buffer, therefore 2 alternating buffers are used for $[du; dv; un; vn]$.

At each grid level, after some steps of presmoothing have been applied, `calcAuAv` is used in a similar manner to `coupledJacobi` above. However, the resulting values

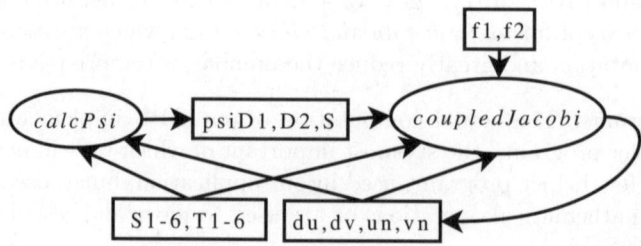

Fig. 2. Applying one smoothing iteration on the GPU. *S1-6, T1-6* is an abbreviated form which actually represents 3 separate buffer objects.

$[A(u); A(v)]$ are required to compute the residual, which is subsequently restricted to a coarser grid level. There, f_1 and f_2 are calculated and the cycle is restarted at this coarser grid. Once the computation is complete, the correction is prolongated to the next finer grid and a number of postsmoothing steps are performed.

4 Results

The focus of our optical flow implementation is to achieve high performance, however doing so is meaningless unless the high quality of the flow field provided by the original algorithm of Bruhn et al. [8] is maintained. To evaluate this aspect we measure the average angular error (see [2]) achieved by our method on the well-known *Yosemite* test sequence.

Table 1 shows the qualitative performance of our algorithm and compares it to some of the best results that can be found in literature. **GPU** refers to our implementation using ten outer cycles composed of two V-cycles each and demonstrates the optimum accuracy possible using our approach, without real-time capability at high resolutions. **GPU-RT** uses five outer cycles with a single V-cycle each. This setting represents a good trade-off between accuracy and real-time performance. In both cases two pre- and postsmoothing iterations are used. The weighting parameters α and β do not change the execution time, but have a significant impact on the quality of the result and have to be chosen carefully depending on the scene and computation method. For **GPU** we use $\alpha = 0.1$ and $\beta = 0.08$, for **GPU-RT** $\alpha = 0.15$ and $\beta = 0.06$.

Table 1. Accuracy compared to results from literature. Table adapted from Bruhn et al. [8] AAE = average angular error STD = standard deviation.

Method	AAE	STD
Horn-Schunck, mod. [2]	9.78	16.19
Uras et al. [2]	8.94	15.61
Alvarez et al. [1]	5.53	7.40
Mémin-Pérez [14]	4.69	6.89
GPU-RT	**3.48**	**7.75**
GPU	**2.65**	**7.12**
Brox et al. [6]	2.46	7.31
Bruhn et al. [8]	2.42	6.70

The slight loss in accuracy compared to Bruhn et al. can be explained by a variety of factors. In terms of the numerical scheme, they use a fourth-order approximation for spatial derivatives, while we use a second-order approximation. Also, on GPUs, our computations are limited to single-precision (32 bit) floating point values. Finally, the built-in hardware linear texture filtering we use to determine values of $I(\boldsymbol{x} + \boldsymbol{u})$ is not as accurate as a software implementation on the CPU.

Despite these minor drawbacks, we have established that a GPU-based solver can come very close in quality to the best results found in literature. We will now move on to examining the quantitative performance of our method.

All times in the following tables have been measured on a standard desktop PC with a Geforce 8800 GTX graphics card. Table 2 shows that our implementation achieves rates of more than 17 dense flow fields per second at a resolution of 511 pixels squared. In terms of flow vectors per second, this is a 35-fold speedup compared to the results shown by Bruhn et al. using their CPU-based implementation. Note however that this gain comes with a slight decrease in the quality of the result.

Table 2. Time required and FPS achieved for GPU-RT optical flow

Resolution (pixels)	Time (ms)	FPS
255^2	33.192	30.128
511^2	57.409	17.419
1023^2	206.107	4.852

One surprising fact that can be seen in Table 2 is that calculating a 255^2 flow field is only about twice as fast as calculating a field with four times as many flow vectors. This means that while the computational effort increases nearly fourfold, the computation also gets twice as efficient on the larger grid. Conversely, switching over from 511^2 to 1023^2 causes the theoretically expected change of a factor of four.

To better understand this behaviour, Table 3 shows the performance of our implementation on image sequences different sizes. Evidently, at grids up to and including 255^2, *our algorithm is not completely limited by GPU performance.* Rather, external factors like driver interaction and housekeeping operations seem to dominate the computation time, as it increases at a nearly constant pace with the number of grid levels required. The time per pixel values support this notion: realizing the full potential performance of the GPU implementation is only possible at image sizes of 511^2 and beyond.

The largest drawback of this performance profile is that it renders the Full Multigrid (FMG) algorithm (see [18]) much less attractive, as that method requires a higher number of cycles at very small grid sizes to achieve its theoretical performance advantage. To weaken the impact of this overhead and parallelization problem, one interesting option is the development of a combined GPU/CPU solving strategy that performs the computations on small grids on the CPU. For simple linear problems this was shown to be effective in [17].

To demonstrate the versatility of the FAS on GPU approach we would like to add some results for the denoising filter described in Section 1.1. For this algorithm, we measure 14.2 ms for filtering 511^2, and 49.8 ms for 1023^2 RGBA color images. This translates to 80 megapixels per second of single-component throughput and enables the real-time filtering of high-resolution color video

Table 3. Performance at various resolutions with 6 pre-/postsmoothing iterations. *Outer Cycles* contain a single V-Cycle.

Grid Levels	Resolution (pixels)	V-cycle (ms)	Outer cycle (ms)	Time/Pixel (μs)
1	1^2	0.325	0.519	519.350
2	3^2	1.509	1.916	212.867
3	7^2	2.686	3.337	68.101
4	15^2	3.957	4.478	19.902
5	31^2	5.193	6.126	6.375
6	63^2	6.193	7.566	1.906
7	127^2	7.751	9.045	0.561
8	255^2	8.979	10.520	0.162
9	511^2	20.465	22.785	0.087
10	1023^2	76.942	84.388	0.081

streams with spare performance for subsequent processing. Note that, due to the multigrid approach used, these computation times are much less dependent on the filtering strength than explicit Euler time stepping or standard iterative implicit solvers.

5   Summary and Conclusions

By implementing a state-of-the-art optical flow algorithm on graphics hardware and achieving unprecedented performance, we have demonstrated that multigrid solvers for nonlinear PDEs are well suited to data-parallel architectures like GPUs. We achieved a 35-fold speedup with only small losses in accuracy compared to the best CPU-based implementations in literature. Additionally, we implemented a fast ROF-based denoising filter as another example showing the applicability of GPU-based FAS to image processing.

We hope that our contributions enable further development in two distinct ways: Firstly, the real-time application of complex nonlinear filters to high-resolution video streams should prove beneficial in the field of computer vision. Here, using mostly the graphics hardware and keeping CPU cycles free for subsequent processing is an additional advantage. Secondly, any research in using GPGPU techniques for solving nonlinear systems of equations should also be encouraged by our findings.

References

1. Alvarez, L., Weickert, J., Sanchéz, J.: Reliable estimation of dense optical flow fields with large displacements. International Journal of Computer Vision 39(1), 41–56 (2000)
2. Barron, J.L., Fleet, D.J., Beauchemin, S.S.: Performance of Optical Flow Techniques. International Journal of Computer Vision 12(1), 43–77 (1994)

3. Bolz, J., Farmer, I., Grinspun, E., Schroeder, P.: Sparse Matrix Solvers on the GPU: Conjugate Gradients and Multigrid. ACM Transactions on Graphics 22, 917–924 (2003)
4. Brandt, A.: Multi-Level Adaptive Solutions to Boundary-Value Problems. Mathematics of Computation 31(138), 333–390 (1977)
5. Briggs, W.L., Henson, V.E., McCormick, S.F.: A Multigrid Tutorial, 2nd edn. Society for Industrial and Applied Mathematics (2000)
6. Brox, T., Bruhn, A., Papenberg, N., Weickert, J.: High accuracy optical flow estimation based on a theory for warping. In: Proc. 8th European Conference on Computer Vision, Prague, Czech Republic (2004)
7. Bruhn, A., Weickert, J., Kohlberger, T., Schnrr, C.: A Multigrid Platform for Real-Time Motion Computation with Discontinuity-Preserving Variational Methods. Int. J. Comput. Vision 70(3), 257–277 (2006)
8. Bruhn, A., Weickert, J.: Towards Ultimate Motion Estimation: Combining Highest Accuracy with Real-Time Performance. In: Proc. 10th IEEE international Conference on Computer Vision (Iccv 2005), Washington, DC, vol. 1, pp. 749–755. IEEE Computer Society, Los Alamitos (2005)
9. Durkovic, M., Zwick, M., Obermeier, F., Diepold, K.: Performance of Optical Flow Techniques on Graphics Hardware. In: IEEE International Conference on Multimedia and Expo, 9–12, pp. 241–244 (2006)
10. Frohn-Schnauf, C., Henn, S., Witsch, K.: Nonlinear Multigrid Methods for Total Variation Denoising. Computation and Visualization in Science 7(3–4), 199–206 (2004)
11. Goodnight, N., Woolley, C., Lewin, G., Luebke, D., Humphreys, G.: A Multigrid Solver for Boundary Value Problems using Programmable Graphics Hardware. Siggraph 2003. In: Proceedings of SIGGRAPH, pp. 102–111 (2003)
12. Hackbusch, W.: Multigrid methods and applications. Springer, Heidelberg (1985)
13. Lindholm, E., Kilgard, M., Moreton, H.: A user-programmable vertex engine. Siggraph 2001. In: Proceedings of SIGGRAPH, pp. 149–158 (2001)
14. Mémin, E., Pérez, P.: A multigrid approach for hierarchical motion estimation. In: Proc. 6th International Conference on Computer Vision, Bombay, India (1998)
15. Osher, S., Rudin, L.I., Fatemi, E.: Nonlinear total. variation based noise removal algorithms. Physica D 60, 259–268 (1992)
16. Rehman, T., Pryor, G., Tannenbaum, A.: Fast Multigrid Optimal Mass Transport for Image Registration and Morphing. In: British Machine Vision Conference (2007)
17. Thoman, P.: GPGPU-based Multigrid Methods. Master Thesis, University of Innsbruck (2007)
18. Trottenberg, U., Oosterlee, C.W., Schüller, A.: Multigrid. Academic Press, San Diego (2001)

Attention Modulation Using Short- and Long-Term Knowledge

Sven Rebhan, Florian Röhrbein, Julian Eggert, and Edgar Körner

Honda Research Institute Europe GmbH,
Carl-Legien-Strasse 30,
63073 Offenbach am Main, Germany

Abstract. A fast and reliable visual search is crucial for representing visual scenes. The modulation of bottom-up attention plays an important role here. The knowledge about target features is often used to bias the bottom-up pathway. In this paper we propose a system which does not only make use of knowledge about the target features, but also uses already acquired knowledge about objects in the current scene to speed up the visual search. Main ingredients are a relational short term memory in combination with a semantic relational long term memory and an adjustable bottom-up saliency. The focus of this work is to investigate mechanisms to use the memory of the system efficiently. We show a proof-of-concept implementation working in a real-world environment and performing visual search tasks. It becomes clear that using the relational semantic memory in combination with spatial and feature modulation of the bottom-up path is beneficial for speeding up such search tasks.

Keywords: scene representation, attention, semantic memory.

1 Introduction

The representation of important objects in a visual scene is essential for intelligent systems in real-world scenarios. In this context, important objects are defined as things that are required to solve a given task. Building up such representations comprises three main steps: acquiring task-relevant objects, keeping their position up-to-date and gathering properties like color, identity and shape.

Many state-of-the-art models only solve the task of acquiring objects and make use of an adjustable bottom-up saliency computation to speed up visual search tasks. The features of the target object are normally provided in a top-down manner. Newer approaches also learn the background statistics of the current scene to further improve the signal to noise ratio (SNR) between the target object and the background [1,2]. All these models show that one is able to gain a huge speed up in search tasks by using this kind of modulation.

There are only few models trying to tackle the remaining aspects of a scene representation as mentioned above. In [3] an architecture is shown which provides a framework for representing objects in a scene. However, it only considers long

A. Gasteratos, M. Vincze, and J.K. Tsotsos (Eds.): ICVS 2008, LNCS 5008, pp. 151–160, 2008.
© Springer-Verlag Berlin Heidelberg 2008

term knowledge, like the features of an object. The short term memory (STM), containing information of already seen objects in the current scene, is not used. This means that information gathered on these objects, especially if they do not match the target object, is completely lost. Furthermore the spatial arrangement of objects, which would be helpful especially for immobile objects is ignored.

We show that using short and long term knowledge is important for a more realistic scenario which includes varying tasks in a real environment without starting the system from scratch every time a new task arrives. Regarding the architecture and layout of our system we stick to our idea of an intentional vision system [4] as proposed previously. Such a system is top-down driven and organizes the underlying information acquisition processes dynamically. Furthermore we use a biologically inspired relational semantic memory [5]. Even though we do not make use of this biological background in this work directly it provides a huge potential for further extensions of our system. It is also important to mention that the STM has the same relational structure as the long-term memory (LTM) which makes it easy to transfer novel knowledge to the LTM later.

In the following section we describe the three use-cases we have identified during our work and introduce our overall system architecture. In Sect. 3 we describe the basic components of the system more in detail. After this we show some results on a real-world scene in Sect. 4. Finally we discuss the results and give a brief outlook on our future work.

2   System Architecture

The aim of our work is to create a system that is able to represent a dynamic visual scene with respect to a given task. Currently the set of possible tasks is reduced to search tasks for known objects. These objects and their corresponding appearance are stored in the LTM. The system we propose follows the principles described in [4] and can be seen in Fig. 1. The main components of the system are the relational semantic memory, a tunable saliency similar to [1] and a feature extraction module. The functionality of all components is described in Sect. 3. As can be seen in Fig. 1 there are two inputs to the system: the images of the stereo camera head (to get depth information) and the task, which is directly passed to the LTM and activates the target object. One can identify three different use-cases for the system:

1. no target object is specified
2. target object is specified and already stored in the short-term memory
3. target object is specified, but not yet stored in the short-term memory

In the first case we simply search for interesting objects (in this case colorful and close) with a default modulation of the saliency in the current scene. The positions found for these objects are inhibited and stored in the STM together with their measured appearance (color, size, etc).

In the second and third case a target object is specified, meaning that an object with its corresponding features has been activated in the LTM. Now we

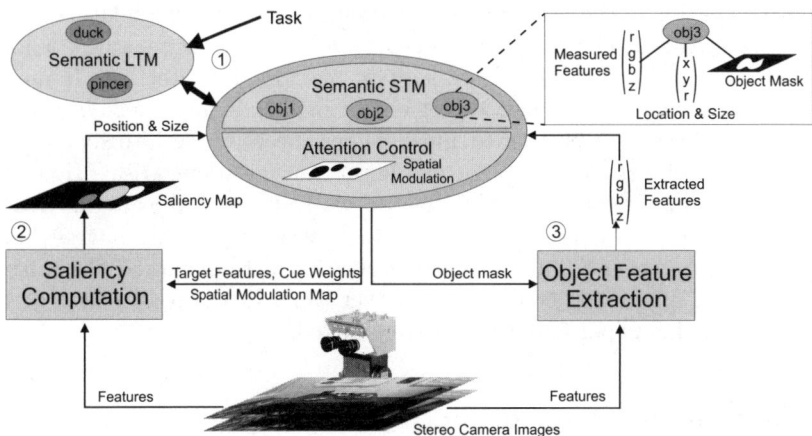

Fig. 1. The overall system architecture consists of three main ingredients: the semantic memory(1), the tunable saliency(2) and a feature extraction component(3)

have to decide if we have already seen the target object or not. Therefore we first search in the set of already seen objects stored in the STM for a matching object. To decide if an object matches the target, we compare the features given for the target object with the measured features of the already seen object. If a distance measure (e.g. Euclidian distance in feature space) is below a chosen static threshold, the object is considered to be the target object (case two). The previously measured features and the last known location of the matching object are used to modulate the bottom-up saliency both in the feature and spatial domain to regain the object in the current input image.

If the search in the STM was not successful (case three), the bottom-up saliency is biased by using the features of the target object retrieved from LTM. An eventually stored preferred location of the object can also be incorporated, which is especially helpful for immobile objects. The tuning of the low-level visual components towards the features of the target object is done in a similar fashion as proposed in [1] and [2].

In all cases the modulated saliency map computes a candidate map for a given bias. Additionally to the location, a rough size estimate is given by the saliency (a detailed description is given in Sect. 3) for the candidates. Now the most promising candidate is selected from the map using a WTA algorithm to create an "object blob" in the STM, containing the candidate's location and estimated size. Even if the saliency map is tuned towards the features of a target object, it might still be possible that the selected candidate is a false positive. To eliminate this possibility we extract the candidate's features at its location including a size related surrounding. This is done in the feature extraction module. The measured features are also attached to the "object blob" and the candidate is checked using an Euclidian distance measure. If the candidate is verified successfully, we assume it is the searched object. Otherwise we keep the rejected object in the STM and inhibit its location in the input image. By doing so the next candidate is selected in the saliency map. The procedure is repeated until the target object is found.

The false positive candidates are kept in memory for later use. If the task for the system changes, the new target object might already reside in the STM and the search can be performed much faster, because we already know the position of the object. At this point two important questions arise: "How do we forget objects in the STM?" and "How do we learn new objects and transfer them to the LTM?". Forgetting is important because we only have a limited storage capacity in our STM. Our current strategy is to memorize the existence of the objects, but to forget its features over time. Learning of new objects is not subject of this paper and is therefore omitted.

3   Component Description

As described in the previous section, our system is comprised of three main modules: the relational semantic memory (STM and LTM), a tuneable saliency map and a feature extraction module. Having looked at the interplay between the modules in the last section, the modules themselves and their functionality are described in this section.

3.1   Relational Semantic Memory

To represent relational and concept knowledge we have developed a graphical model which combines ideas from classical semantic networks and processing principles of the cortical minicolumn (see [5]). A sketch of this model can be seen in Fig. 2. An important aspect of our approach is that we only use one uniform node type in the network, which is the representational entity of all concepts, both in STM and LTM. This node type represents "saliency blobs",

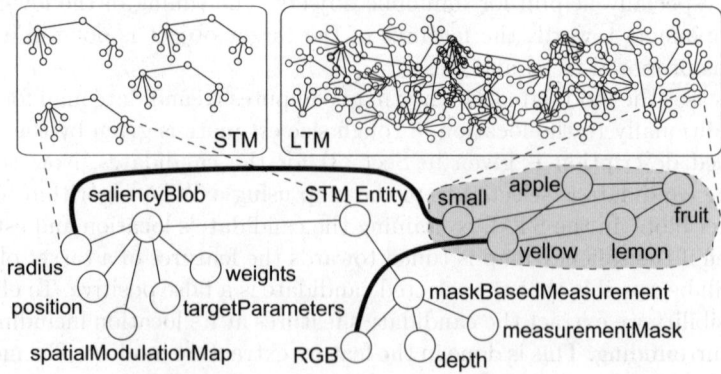

Fig. 2. The activated object in the LTM (here *lemon*) is instantiated in the STM, where all known properties of the object are inherited (e.g. *small*, *yellow*)

sensory measurements, properties, instances, categories and even relations between nodes. A relation in general is represented explicitly via nodes. For example *MadeOf(Table,Wood)* requires the five nodes *Table, Object, MadeOf, Material* and *Wood* (for more details see [6]). Very few basic relations like partonomic ones, for which we think biological evidence exist, are coded directly with specific link types, making our approach quite different from standard AI systems like [7].

For our current system we use a rather flat ontology consisting of a few objects and properties. The entities consist of a node "saliencyBlob" and a node "maskBasedMeasurement", which resembles the two information pathways in the system (saliency and feature extraction as shown in Fig. 1). To these nodes properties like position and color are attached, together with their modulatory influences (e.g. weights or masks). We provide an entity prototype, which is specialized into a new instantiation each time a task requires the generation of a new entity. This instantiation inherits all procedures and default values of the prototype which can be overwritten by objects activated in the LTM. In a next step, the attached values are passed down to the saliency computation and measurement process as modulatory inputs. All incoming measurements are stored in the corresponding nodes of the object.

3.2 Saliency Computation and Size Estimation

In our system the saliency map provides locations of possible object candidates and their estimated size. As shown in Fig. 3 the saliency computation can be separated into three steps: tuning of the cues (blue), center-surround contrast calculation (yellow) and computation of the lateral dynamics (green). First input features are modulated to enhance the contrast of the target object against the

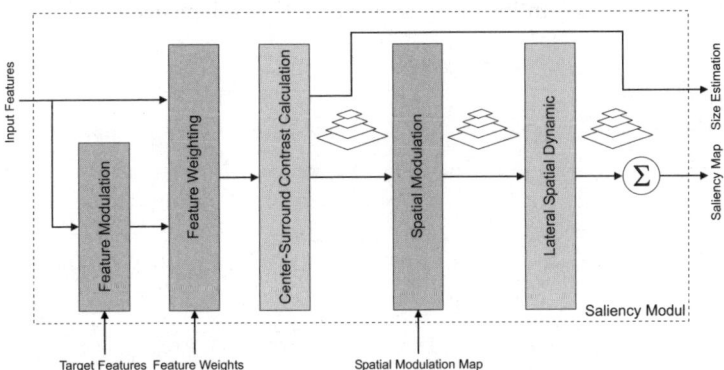

Fig. 3. The input features are modulated and weighted according to the modulatory inputs (bottom). After the contrast computation, spatial modulation and lateral dynamic which work on spatial pyramids, the resulting pyramid is integrated into a final saliency map. In addition center-surround contrast is also used to roughly estimate the object size (see Fig. 4).

background. This is done by calculating the similarity between the input vector f and the top-down provided Gaussian target distributions (t, σ).

$$\hat{f} = e^{-\frac{1}{2} \sum_n \frac{(f_n - t_n)^2}{\sigma_n^2}} . \tag{1}$$

Here n is the n-th channel of the vectors. In the case of RGB-color this reads as

$$\hat{f}_{rgb} = e^{-\frac{1}{2} \left(\left(\frac{f_r - t_r}{\sigma_r} \right)^2 + \left(\frac{f_g - t_g}{\sigma_g} \right)^2 + \left(\frac{f_b - t_b}{\sigma_b} \right)^2 \right)} . \tag{2}$$

After tuning the features, the center-surround contrast over all features within the same spatial scale is computed. Therefore the Euclidian distance between the center and the surround part of the feature vector is calculated for each channel of f and different sizes

$$c_s = \| \left(F_s^{center} - F_s^{surround} \right) * f \|^2 , \tag{3}$$

where s is a certain size of the filter F. For choosing the size of the center and the surround the scheme proposed in [8] is used. Each filter is normalized to have a mean of zero. The contrast maps are now biased with the spatial modulation map, provided in a top-down manner.

To calculate the size estimation at a certain position the distribution over all filter scales is used as shown in Fig. 4. Here we exploit the fact that we use Gaussian filters with different sizes to calculate the contrast. If we assume that an object is circular and homogeneously structured, the response stays constant for increasing sizes of the filter until the filter exceeds the object size. At this point the structure changes because of the object boundaries and so does the filter response. Using the standard deviation of the corresponding filter plus a constant scaling factor we are able to generate an initial hypothesis of the object size.

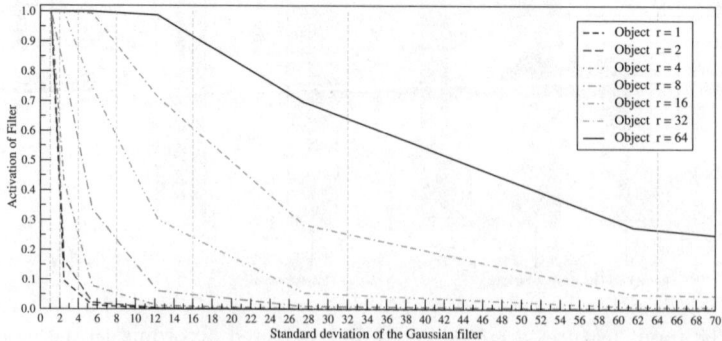

Fig. 4. The Gaussian filter response stays nearly constant until the filter exceeds the object size. Beyond this point the filter response decreases rapidly. This property can be used to estimate the object size.

After calculating the contrast on different scales we perform a lateral spatial competition within each scale with the aim to enhance the SNR. Contrary to the dynamic in [8], we use an Amari dynamic [9], which shows a hysteresis over time that is controllable by different parameters. We use this behavior to model a sensory memory for the saliency map. Finally the maps of different scales are combined to one single saliency map, which contains the location of the candidates for the target object.

3.3 Feature Extraction

The feature extraction module measures the features of an object in the current input using a given segmentation mask of the object. So far a segmentation process is not part of our system, so we use the location with an object-size dependent surrounding (see Sect 3.2) as the mask. The measurement itself is done by calculating the mean and standard deviation in each feature channel of the input image. The top-down provided object mask is used to exclude parts of the image which do not belong to the object.

4   Results

In this section we show how the system behaves in a real scene. In Fig. 5 one can see the first of the three cases (see Sect. 2). Without a given task the system sequentially acquires knowledge about its environment over time until all locations in the input image are inhibited. In each timestep the STM is filled with the one

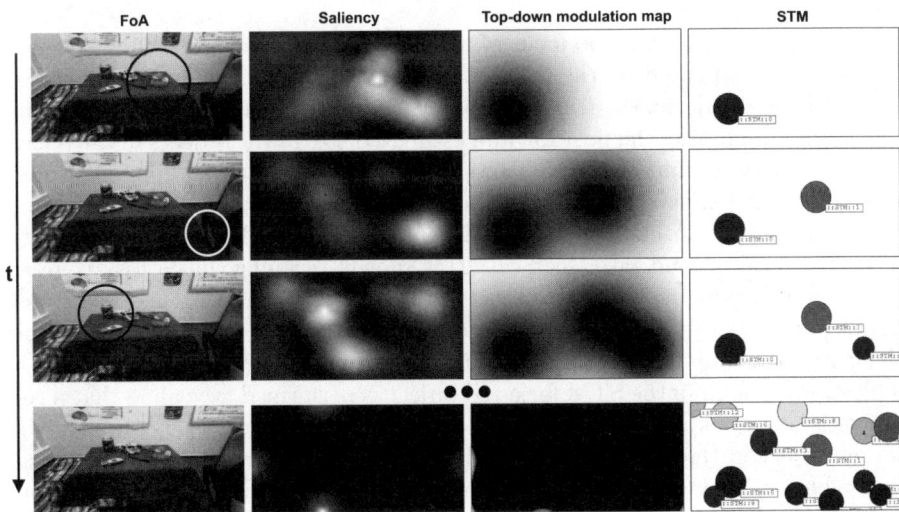

Fig. 5. The STM is filled over time, without a specific target. The internal state of the STM is shown on the right, representing all known objects with their measured color and size. The spatial modulation map is generated from all known objects in the STM.

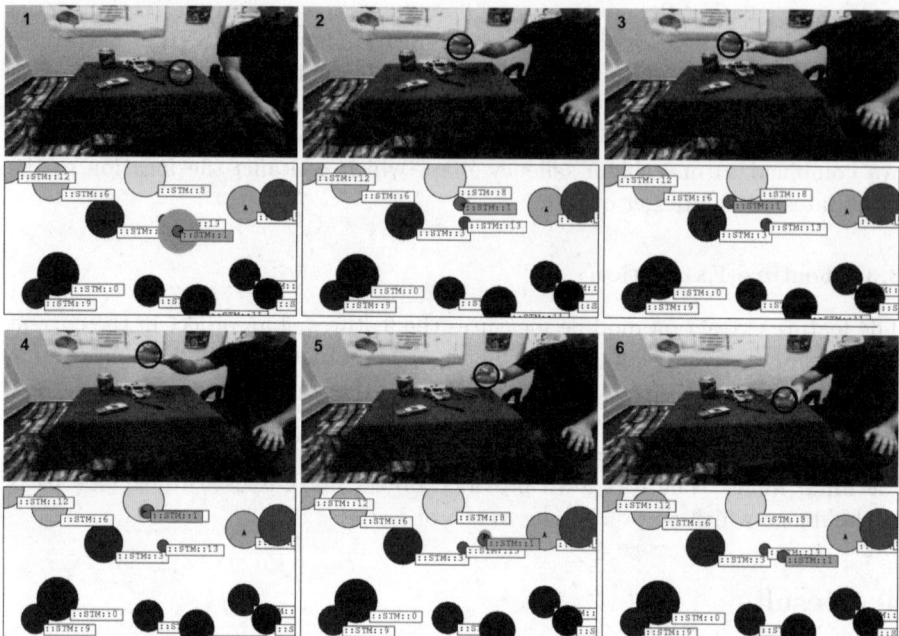

Fig. 6. The task is to find the red duck. The object was found in STM (marked with a green text label) and its features (color, depth and position) were used to bias the saliency. In this sequence one can see that even while moving the object the content of the STM (size, position, depth and color) is continuously updated.

object that currently has the focus of attention (FoA). The underlying saliency map is only modulated by the top-down spatial modulation map to inhibit the already known objects, the features are not modulated. The modulation map itself is generated using the position and estimated size of the objects in the STM. The rightmost column of Fig. 5 shows a dump of the STM at different times. Here the position, size and color of the "object blobs" represent the measured properties of the objects, the measured depth is attached but not shown.

In Fig. 6 the second case (see Sect. 2) is shown, meaning that a task is given to the system and the searched object is already in the STM. This case is not handled in state-of-the-art systems. In our example we specified the task to find the duck. A lookup in the LTM shows that our duck is red ($r = 1.0, g = 0.0, b = 0.0$). Now a search in the STM for a red object is performed, revealing that a red object is already known to the system (marked green in Fig. 6). By finding the target object in the STM all information about the object are instantaneously accessible without referring to the bottom-up saliency or feature extraction. However, to keep track of the changes in features and position we now bias the saliency, both in feature and spatial domain, to concentrate on the object found and verify the properties at the known position. The feature bias is performed using the color of the object found in the STM, similarly the position and size is used to generate an excitatory spatial bias at the last known position. As can be seen in the first image of Fig. 6, the biasing of the saliency also leads to a better size estimation. After verifying that the object is still there and that the measured properties match the target criteria, we concentrate the system's attention on the object found and keep a reference to this object in the STM. To concentrate the attention we keep the current biasing of the system (spatial and feature). By keeping the attention on the object we are able to continuously update its position, depth, size and color. After each update of a property, the modulation for the corresponding property is updated. If for example the size decreases, the spatial bias becomes more narrow (as in the first image of Fig. 6). The same is done for the position of the object. By continuously updating the object's position in the STM, a tracking of simple objects is possible as shown in the sequence of Fig. 6.

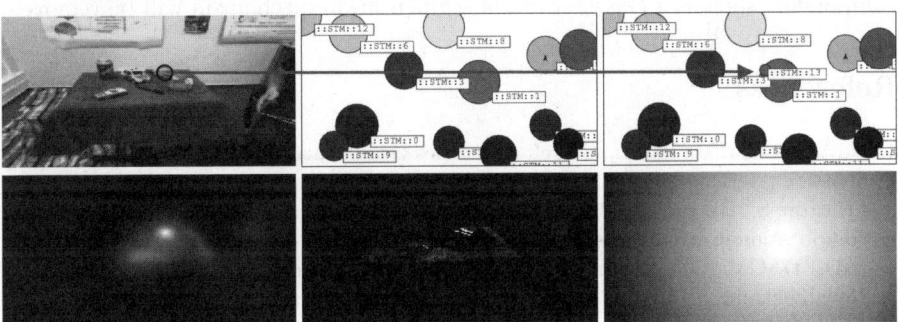

Fig. 7. The task is to find the cyan pincer. Therefore we bias the features to highlight cyan objects (second row middle). Additionally we provide the system with a spatial hint (second row right), because pure color information is not enough to exceed the WTA threshold. The final saliency can be seen on the left hand side of the second row. The STM content (first row) before and after finding the object shows that the pincer has been added.

In Fig. 7 the third case (see Sect. 2) is shown, meaning that a task is given to the system and the searched object is not yet in the STM. In this example the task is to find the pincer in the scene. Given this task, a search in the LTM for features of the pincer is performed, revealing that it has the color cyan ($r = 0.0, g = 1.0, b = 1.0$). Because a search in the STM for a cyan object was not successful we bias the features of the saliency map to prefer cyan objects. The result of this biasing can be seen in the middle of the second row of Fig. 7. The biasing of the feature channels is not sufficient to exceed the threshold of the WTA selection, therefore we additionally give a spatial hint to the system, indicating that the searched object is on the right hand side of the current scene. Using this hint the system is able to find the object and adds it to the STM.

5 Discussion

In the system we propose, the short-term memory plays a crucial role. We showed that by using the knowledge about already seen objects, we are able to instantaneously access the information about a given target object if it is already stored in the short-term memory. Otherwise, we used knowledge about the object's features and potential locations, coming from the long-term memory, to find "difficult" objects like the pincer as well. We furthermore showed that by deliberately directing attention to a certain object and continuously updating its properties in memory, a simple tracking mechanism can be established.

To cover highly dynamic scenes which are not covered yet, our future systems will use a more elaborated tracking system, together with a more powerful modulation-mechanism for the saliency. Good examples for such mechanisms were shown in [1] and [2]. However, a mandatory step to go is the learning of new objects and its properties to fill the long-term memory. For this, additional components such as a classifier and a segmentation mechanism will be required.

References

1. Navalpakkam, V., Itti, L.: Search goal tunes visual features optimally. Neuron 53(4), 605–617 (2007)
2. Frintrop, S., Backer, G., Rome, E.: Goal-directed search with a top-down modulated computational attention system. In: Kropatsch, W.G., Sablatnig, R., Hanbury, A. (eds.) DAGM 2005. LNCS, vol. 3663, pp. 117–124. Springer, Heidelberg (2005)
3. Navalpakkam, V., Arbib, M.A., Itti, L.: Attention and scene understanding. In: Neurobiology of Attention, pp. 197–203 (2005)
4. Eggert, J., Rebhan, S., Körner, E.: First steps towards an intentional vision system. In: Proceedings of the 5th International Conference on Computer Vision Systems (ICVS 2007) (2007)
5. Roehrbein, F., Eggert, J., Körner, E.: A cortex-inspired neural-symbolic network for knowledge representation. In: Proceedings of the IJCAI Workshop on Neural-Symbolic Learning and Reasoning (accepted, 2007)
6. Roehrbein, F., Eggert, J., Körner, E.: Prototypical relations for cortex-inspired semantic representations. In: Proceedings of the 8th International Conference on Cognitive Modeling, pp. 307–312 (2007)
7. Brachman, R., Levesque, H.: Knowledge Representation and Reasoning. Morgan Kaufmann Publishers Inc. San Francisco (2004)
8. Itti, L., Koch, C.: A saliency-based search mechanism for overt and covert shifts of visual attention. Vision Research 40(10–12), 1489–1506 (2000)
9. Amari, S.: Dynamics of pattern formation in lateral-inhibition type neural fields. Biological Cybernetics 27, 77–87 (1977)

PCA Based 3D Shape Reconstruction of Human Foot Using Multiple Viewpoint Cameras

Edmée Amstutz[1], Tomoaki Teshima[1], Makoto Kimura[2], Masaaki Mochimaru[2], and Hideo Saito[1]

[1] Graduate School of Science and Technology, Keio University,
3-14-1 Hiyoshi Kohoku-ku, Yokohama 223-8522, Japan
{eamstutz,tomoaki,saito}@ozawa.ics.keio.ac.jp
http://www.hvrl.ics.keio.ac.jp
[2] Digital Human Research Center, AIST
2-41-6 Ohmi Koto-ku, Tokyo, 125-0064, Japan
{makoto.kimura,m-mochimaru}@aist.go.jp
http://www.aist.go.jp

Abstract. This article describes a multiple camera based method to reconstruct a 3D shape of a human foot. From a feet database, an initial 3D model of the foot represented by a cloud of points is built. In addition, some shape parameters, which characterize any foot at more than 92%, are defined by using Principal Component Analysis. Then, the 3D model is adapted to the foot of interest captured in multiple images based on "active shape models" methods by applying some constraints (edge points' distance, color variance for example). We insist here on the experiment part where we demonstrate the efficiency of the proposed method on a plastic foot model, and on real human feet with various shapes. We compare different ways to texture the foot, and conclude that using projectors can improve drastically the reconstruction's accuracy. Based on experimental results, we finally propose some improvements regarding to the system integration.

Keywords: Foot shape reconstruction, Multiple cameras, PCA.

1 Introduction

In the past 70 years, there had been a quick and significant change in the humans' height evolution, which is called "secular change" [1]. This has led to an important development of anthropometric methods and projects. The CAESAR project [2], a survey of body measurements for people in three countries, is one of them. One of their goals is the construction of a database, which could be used to study the variability of people or to design some equipments specifically for a certain type of people. There are many other interesting application fields for anthropometry like human recognition, or medical assistance (design of prosthesis for instance). In this framework, our research focuses on the human foot. The secular change has particularly led to some huge differences between feet' size and shape among people of various generations. This is the reason why some

A. Gasteratos, M. Vincze, and J.K. Tsotsos (Eds.): ICVS 2008, LNCS 5008, pp. 161–170, 2008.

shoe makers and sellers want to be able to reconstruct especially the 3D foot shape of each client so that they can develop and sell the most adapted shoes to each person. One of our motivating applications is also the possibility for each person to purchase some shoes on the Internet by transmitting his personal foot data, stored on a small ID card.

One of the most classical methods to measure the shape of the human body is the use of laser, like the method described by Weik [3]. Some systems, like IN-FOOT system [4], which allows translating a laser along the foot to acquire the exact shape, have already proven their efficiency. However, this method presents two problems: first, the system which consists of a laser and some mechanical devices to allow the translation is very expensive. The second problem is a psychological one: some people are afraid of laser and refuse to use this kind of system. To solve these two issues, our goal is the development of a new system to reconstruct the shape of a human foot in 3D by using only multiple USB cameras and computer vision techniques [5].

One of the most interesting methods for 3D shape reconstruction is called "deformable models", studied by McInerney and Terzopoulos [6]. Cootes et al. [7] proposed to combine the deformable models theory with a statistical approach, which consists in defining the ways the model can be deformed by analyzing the variability of shapes among a training set. Based on this idea and the work on statistical approach developed by Wang and Staib [8], Wang et al. [9,10] proposed a method to reconstruct the shape of a human foot by using principal component analysis. However, in [10], they use synchronized cameras to achieve the reconstruction.

In the following, we describe our method, which is based on similar principles than [10], but can work with simple USB cameras. Then, we insist on the experiment part, where we test our method on a plastic foot model, but also on 17 different human feet. We show the ability of the method to reconstruct feet with various shapes, and we compare different ways to texture the foot of interest. Finally, we propose two methods to improve the accuracy of our reconstruction.

2   Method Proposed

Based on the active shape models theory [7], the general approach consists in adapting an initial 3D model of a foot to the real foot, by analyzing the initial model's projection in the images of the real foot and applying some constraints.

2.1   From the Feet Database

From a feet database, we define the initial 3D model, which is a cloud of vertices, and we determine the 12 most important shape parameters which characterize a foot, by using Principal Component Analysis.

Construction of the initial model. Each foot of the n feet database ($n = 397$) is described by the same m vertices ($m = 372$), which have been defined by anatomy's specialists. v_i represents the position of ith vertex in a 3D model $\mathbf{F}$

that represents a foot shape. The initial 3D model ($\mathbf{F}^{average}$) is defined as the average of each database foot($\mathbf{F}^{database}$).

$$\mathbf{F} = [v_1, v_2, ..., v_m] \tag{1}$$

$$\mathbf{F}^{average} = \frac{1}{n} \sum_{k=1}^{n} \mathbf{F}_k^{database} \tag{2}$$

Definition of the shape parameters. Principal Component Analysis is a powerful method to describe the statistical relationship among a set of objects. Here, this method is used among a feet database to determine the shape parameters which mostly define any foot.

First, the covariance matrix, which basically represents the variation of each foot from the average foot, is calculated and the eigenvectors of this matrix are computed. Then, the most important variation modes can be found easily: they correspond to the eigenvectors associated to the largest eigenvalues. By applying this theory to our feet database, we have found that the 12 first eigenvectors define the statistical relationship among the feet at 92%, which is the best compromise between computation cost and information gained.

A new foot $\mathbf{F}^{new}$ can be obtained by using the following formula:

$$\mathbf{F}^{new} = \mathbf{F}^{average} + \sum_{j=1}^{12} w_j \mathbf{F}_j^{eigen} \tag{3}$$

where $\mathbf{F}_j^{eigen}$ is the jth column of the $3m \times 3m$ matrix which contains the eigenvectors of covariance matrix, and w_j represents the weight of the jth variation mode.

2.2 Camera Calibration

We use a multiple cameras system to acquire images of the human foot we want to reconstruct in 3D. The camera calibration is done by using the Calibration Toolbox provided by MATLAB [11]. We use 5 images per camera of a simple marked pattern to obtain the intrinsic parameters. Secondly, we fixed the multiple cameras on their definitive position, and we take a last image per camera of the pattern in one fixed position, in order to obtain the extrinsic parameters. To solve the problem of small oscillations which can occur between many captures, one of our future goal is to develop an interface to recompute the extrinsic parameters easily before each utilization.

2.3 Input Images of the Human Foot we Want to Reconstruct

During the image acquisition, color images (24 bit color depth) are taken. For the 3D shape reconstruction, the binary (foot/background) and edge images of the foot are also necessary. The binary images are obtained using a background segmentation program. Some images sometimes require manual correction. The background segmentation program begins with a background subtraction and uses some morphological operations to smoothen the results. The edge images are directly obtained from the binary images.

2.4   Deformation of the Initial 3D Model to Fit the Real Foot

First adjustment of the real foot and the model. The registration between the coordinates system of the calibration and the one in which the initial model is described is done approximately. After applying some 90 rotations to make axes correspond, we search a translation to roughly put the initial model on the foot of interest. To do this, the idea is to make the two gravity centers (initial model and real foot) correspond. Since we don't have any 3D data of the real foot (but only the acquired images' information), we define a 2D gravity center in each binary image which is basically the barycenter of the white pixels (i.e. foot area). Then, the distance between projected center of the initial 3D model and 2D gravity center of the foot of interest, for each image, is minimized.

Adaptation by successive optimizations. The 3D shape reconstruction of the foot of interest is done as follows: first, the initial 3D model is projected on the 3 types of input images (color, binary and edge) by using the camera calibration results. Then, an evaluation function which represents the error between the projected model and the real foot is calculated. Finally, by repeating some optimization processes, this evaluation function is minimized by changing the initial model. Modifying the initial model consists in applying a translation, a rotation and a scale and changing the 12 most important shape parameters defined by the PCA (i.e. changing the vector of parameters' weights w defined in formula (3)). There are two different optimizations: the first one concerns the 6 pose parameters and the scale, and the second one, the shape parameters. These optimizations are performed by using a least square method.

Criteria used in the evaluation function. Three different criteria are used to represent the error between the adapting 3D model and the real foot. Each of them uses one of the three types of input images.

Binary images. This criterion consists in counting the number of vertices of the adapting model which are projected in the foot area in the multiple binary images. A penalization is applied when a vertex is projected outside the foot area. For each camera, the error between the model and the foot is expressed as follows:

$$e_{bin} = \left(1 - \sum_m b_m\right) + nb_{outside}\alpha \qquad (4)$$

Where m is the number of vertices, b_m is the pixel's value at the model point projection in binary images. $nb_{outside}$ is the number of vertices projected outside the foot area and α is the penalization applied to each of those vertices.

Edge images. For each camera, the sum of the 2D distances between each edge point of the adapting model $EP_{model,m}$ and the nearest edge point of the real foot $EP_{foot,m}$ is minimized. (Concerning the adapting model, a point is an edge point if it is not projected in any faces of the foot.) For each camera, the error is expressed with the following formula:

$$e_{edge} = \sum_m \text{dist}\left(EP_{model,m} - EP_{foot,m}\right) \tag{5}$$

Color images. The last criterion consists in calculating a variance between pixels' color. First, for each vertex of the adapting model, we calculate the average of pixel's values of this vertex projected in multiple color images. Then, considering one camera, the difference between the color intensity of each projected vertex in this camera and its average intensity calculated previously, is minimized. There are two conditions to use this criterion efficiently. First, the foot has to be textured in color images, so that there can be some differences of pixels' values according to the localization of projected vertices. Secondly, the foot's shape must be already quite well approximated. For each camera, the error is the sum of each vertex's variance:

$$e_{color} = \sum_m p_m - \bar{c}_m \tag{6}$$

Where p_m is the pixel's value at the model vertex's projection, and $\bar{c}_m$ is the average of pixels' values of this same vertex projected in all color images.

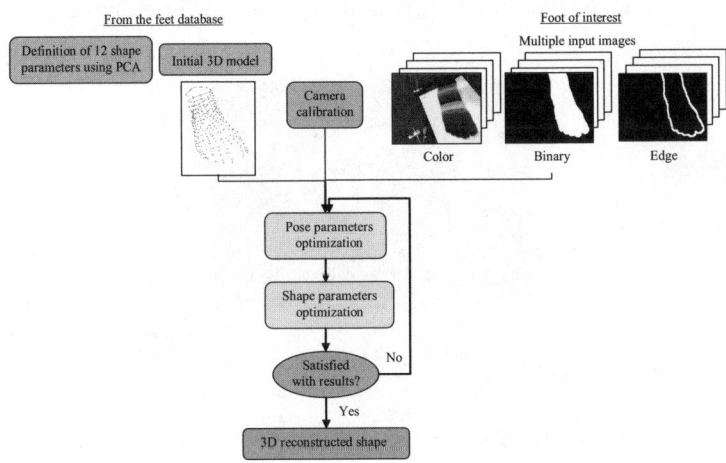

Fig. 1. Overall method for the 3D reconstruction

Weights according to the criterion. Some weights are applied to each criterion, so that their influence can be changed to obtain a better result. Those weights are defined according to the type of optimization and the number of iterations already performed. We explain in more details what is the best combination of the 3 criteria (found empirically) in the experiments and results part.

Occlusion problem. Some vertices can be occluded by other faces, depending on the considered view. To find those occluded vertices, we first calculate if a projected vertex is inside or outside a face, and then if it is inside, we compare the 3D distances from the camera center to the vertex and from the camera center to the face. To avoid the occlusion problem, we simply don't take into account the occluded points in the calculation of the evaluation function.

3   Experiments and Results

Experiments are performed on a plastic foot model and also on 17 human feet. We compare different ways to texture the feet and discuss the influence of criteria weights. Based on the experiments results, we also propose two ways to improve the accuracy of the reconstruction.

3.1   Multi Cameras System

The acquisition system is composed of a small box on top of which a human can put his foot Fig.(2). On the four sides of this box, 10 USB cameras are fixed with sticks so that the entire foot can be captured from each of them. Ten cameras seem to be a good compromise between accuracy (6 are not suffcient to cover the whole foot well) and the computation time. All cameras are connected to one PC, which captures still images of the foot model with a resolution of 640 x 480. Those cameras are not synchronized. The database used is composed of 397 right feet of male and female, which have been captured by laser scanning.

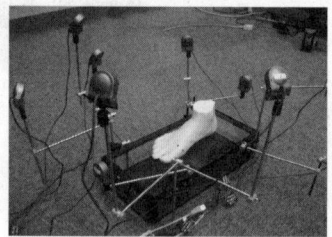

Fig. 2. Photo of the system used

3.2   Different Ways to Texture the Foot of Interest

Those experiments have for objectives to validate the global reconstruction method and to try different ways to texture the foot, needed for a good efficiency of the color criterion. Two different ways are tested: the first one is simply to wear some colored socks during the images' acquisition. The second one consists in using two projectors to apply a pattern on both sides of the foot. The advantage of using projectors is that the nude foot can be captured, so that the reconstruction can be more accurate. However, the drawback is the need to use at least two projectors to texture the entire foot and avoid occluded areas.

On plastic foot model. The plastic foot model is captured by 10 cameras. First, we evaluate the influence of criteria' relative weights. Then, we try the different ways to texture the foot of interest, and compare them.

First, this experiment shows that the relative weights between the three criteria have a significant influence on the 3D reconstruction. Fig.(3) shows the reconstructed shape obtained when the binary criterion is too important compared to the edges' criterion. The scale of the adapting 3D model becomes too small due to the important binary constraint. Empirically, we found that the best combination is an edges' criterion with a larger weight than the two other criteria in both optimization processes. The same weights are applied for the binary and color criteria. The relative weights of each criterion can be changed throughout the process.

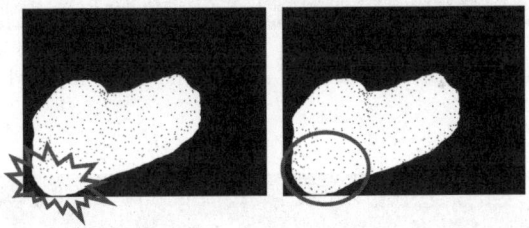

Fig. 3. Illustration of the influence of relative weights between criteria

Secondly, for each texturing method and for the nude foot, the accuracy of the computed shape is calculated. The 3D data of this plastic model are known, so we can calculate a 3D distance error between the computed foot and the real one. By using projectors, we can improve drastically the accuracy: from 3.30mm of error with a nude foot, we obtain 3.06mm with socks and only 0.51mm of error with projectors. Results obtained by using projectors are presented in Fig.(4) where the 3D shape is projected on 6 input images. The reconstruction process, coded in MATLAB, takes 45 minutes when using 10 cameras.

On real human feet. In this second series of experiment, 16 different feet are captured by 6 cameras. 8 of them are textured by projectors whereas the 8 others are wearing colored socks. We check the method's validity while we reconstruct various feet shapes.

Fig.(5) illustrates the final 3D computed shapes of two feet projected in color images. The visual results show a very good adaptation of the model to the real foot, even if we can observe some model points outside the foot. Since we don't have any 3D data of the real feet, we can only define a matching difference (relative surface difference) from the results' images. The average matching differences for feet with colored socks and feet textured by projectors are respectively 6.48% and 5.66%. The first experiment's conclusion is confirmed. Moreover, a last experiment is performed on a human foot with 10 cameras. The accuracy achieved by our method is 1.57mm (obtained by comparison with the 3D data computed

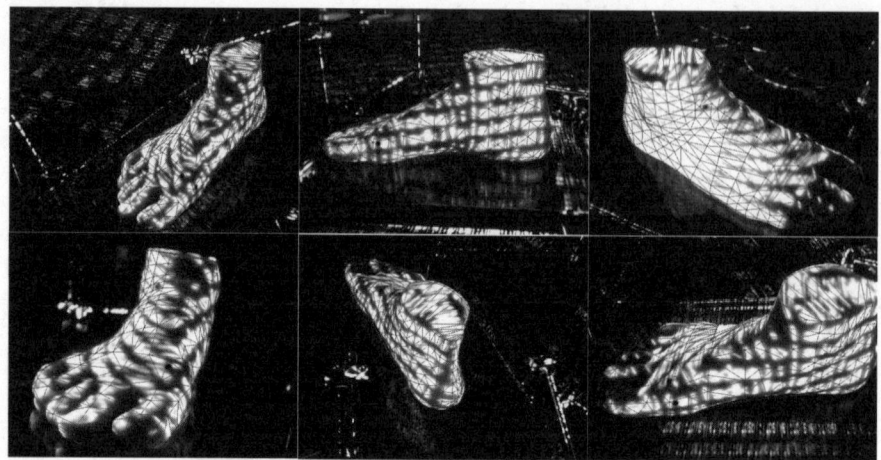

Fig. 4. Final results for the plastic foot model: the 3D computed shape (in red) is projected in 6 cameras

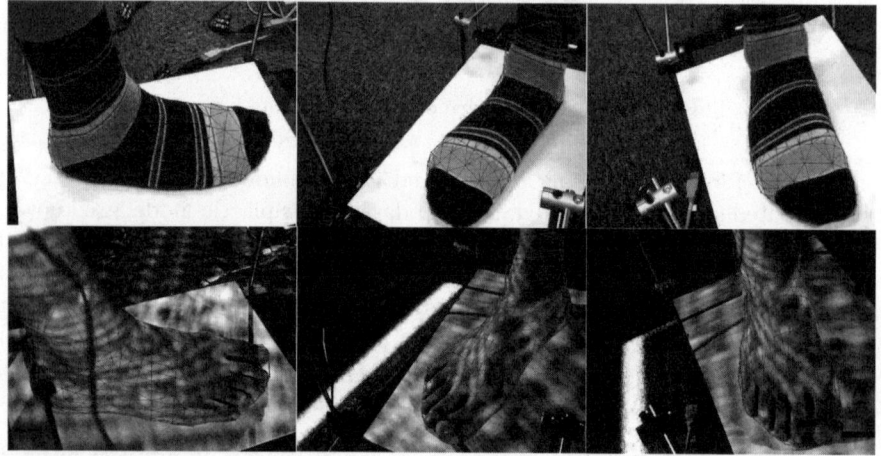

Fig. 5. Final results for 2 human feet: the 3D computed shape (in red) is projected in 3 cameras when using socks (top) or using projectors (bottom)

by a laser based system). From the viewpoint of a computer vision system, the results are very satisfactory, but we still want to improve the reconstruction's accuracy to reach our future objectives.

This experiment makes appear some difficulties which cannot be seen in an ideal experiment: the leg occlusion is one of them. To solve this problem, the leg is manually removed in input images and consequently, vertices which belongs to the upper part of the ankle are not taken into account in the optimizations, so that the manual removal does not induce reconstruction errors. We believe that it is not a major problem considered that most of shoes stop just before the ankle.

3.3   System Integration: Two Ways of Improvement

The error caused in our method can be explained by various reasons. The first one concerns the human's posture. Since the system is not really ergonomic, the person tends to relax his foot and the angle between the foot and the leg becomes too important. The small number of vertices in the initial model (372) can also be an important issue. We are currently developing two solutions to solve those issues.

To improve the system ergonomy, we have placed a small box near the main one, so that the human can put his left foot on it during capture of the right foot. According to humans' anatomy specialists, it is very important to reduce the distance between the 2 feet during the capturing. One drawback of this position is that the left foot will occlude a large part of the right foot. However, we believe that we can overcome this issue by placing the left side cameras very close to the right foot, and reconstruct the foot shape even if we don't see the entire foot in all cameras. We are currently running those experiments.

Moreover, the database used contains male and female feet, where each foot is described by 372 vertices. The sparsity of the model could explain the differences between our computed shape and INFOOT data. Thus, we have decided to create 2 separate databases for male and women, and we have computed a denser model for each foot of the male database by using a software called Homologous Body Modeling, available at the AIST, Japan. This software divides each mesh into 4 new meshes at each iteration, by fitting to some landmarks defined on the foot. We obtain a new model with 1482 vertices instead of only 372. Fig. (6) illustrates the proposed improvements.

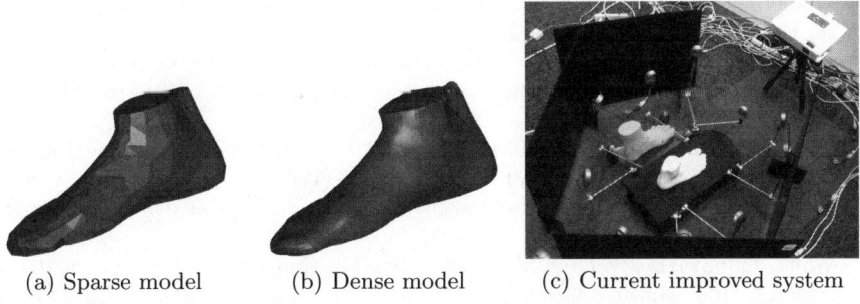

(a) Sparse model   (b) Dense model   (c) Current improved system

Fig. 6. Improvements considering system integration

4   Conclusion and Future Works

Compared to many multiview reconstruction approaches which are based on the matching of features on images, our method takes advantage of the use of a feet database to adapt an initial model and make it fit the captured images. Many experiments have been performed and prove that the method works well even with various human feet, when using unsynchronized USB cameras. Using projectors to texture the foot can improve the reconstruction's accuracy. We are currently working on the densification of database's models and the improvement of the system's ergonomy.

Acknowledgment

The authors would like to thank Makiko Kouchi at Digital Human Research Center for providing the plastic foot model, and also Mr. Kimura, Mr. Utsumi at I-Ware Laboratory Co., Ltd. and Mr. Tsuchiyama at Tachibana Eletech for designing the prototype of the foot system. This work was supported by Grant-in-Aid for Scientific Research (C) (17500119).

References

1. http://www.dh.aist.go.jp/research/centered/index.php.en
2. Robinette, K.M., Daanen, H., Paquet, E.: The Caesar Project: A 3D Surface Anthropometry Survey. In: Proc. in 3D Digital Imaging and Modeling, pp. 380–386 (1999)
3. Weik, S.: A passive full body scanner using shape from silhouettes. In: ICPR 2000, pp. 1750–1753 (2000)
4. Kouchi, M., Mochimaru, M.: Development of a low cost foot-scanner for a custom shoe making system. In: 5th ISB Footwear Biomechanics, Zurich, Switzerland, pp. 58–59 (2001)
5. Hartley, R., Zisserman, A.: Multiple View Geometry in Computer Vision. Cambridge University Press, Cambridge (2000)
6. McInerney, T., Terzopoulos, D.: Deformable Models in Medical Image Analysis. In: Proc. of MMBIA, pp. 171–180 (1996)
7. Cootes, T.F., Taylor, C.J., Cooper, D.H., Graham, J.: Active shape models-their training and application. Computer Vision Image Understanding 61(1), 38–59 (1995)
8. Wang, Y., Staib, L.H.: Boundary Finding with Correspondence Using Statistical Shape Models. In: Proc. in CVPR, pp. 338–345 (1998)
9. Wang, J.: Research on 3D surface reconstruction by deformable model-based methods (2005)
10. Wang, J., Saito, H., Kimura, M., Mochimaru, M., Kanade, T.: Human Foot Reconstruction from Multiple Camera Images with Foot Shape Database. IEICE Trans. Inf. and Syst. E89-D(5) (May 2006)
11. http://www.vision.caltech.edu/bouguetj/calib_doc/

An On-Line Interactive Self-adaptive Image Classification Framework

Davy Sannen[1], Marnix Nuttin[1], Jim Smith[2], Muhammad Atif Tahir[2],
Praminda Caleb-Solly[2], Edwin Lughofer[3], and Christian Eitzinger[4]

[1] Katholieke Universiteit Leuven, Department of Mechanical Engineering,
Celestijnenlaan 300B, B-3001 Heverlee (Leuven), Belgium
{davy.sannen,marnix.nuttin}@mech.kuleuven.be
[2] University of the West of England, Bristol Institute of Technology, Department of
Computer Science, Bristol, BS16 1QY, UK
{james.smith,muhammad.tahir,praminda.caleb-solly}@uwe.ac.uk
[3] Johannes Kepler University Linz, Department of Knowledge-based Mathematical
Systems, Altenbergerstrasse 69, A-4040 Linz, Austria
edwin.lughofer@jku.at
[4] Profactor GmbH, Im Stadtgut A2, A-4407 Steyr-Gleink, Austria
christian.eitzinger@profactor.at

Abstract. In this paper we present a novel image classification framework, which is able to automatically re-configure and adapt its feature-driven classifiers and improve its performance based on user interaction during on-line processing mode. Special emphasis is placed on the generic applicability of the framework to arbitrary surface inspection systems. The basic components of the framework include: recognition of regions of interest (objects), adaptive feature extraction, dealing with hierarchical information in classification, initial batch training with redundancy deletion and feature selection components, on-line adaptation and refinement of the classifiers based on operators' feedback, and resolving contradictory inputs from several operators by ensembling outputs from different individual classifiers. The paper presents an outline on each of these components and concludes with a thorough discussion of basic and improved off-line and on-line classification results for artificial data sets and real-world images recorded during a CD imprint production process.

Keywords: Image classification, feature extraction, on-line adaptation and evolution, resolving contradictory inputs, classifier ensembles.

1 Introduction

In many machine vision applications, such as inspection tasks for quality control, an automatic system tries to reproduce human cognitive abilities. The most efficient and flexible way to achieve this is to learn the task from a human expert. This training process involves the adaptation of object recognition methods, feature extraction algorithms and classifiers. While a lot of research has been done on each of these topics, simply plugging all of these methods together does not

A. Gasteratos, M. Vincze, and J.K. Tsotsos (Eds.): ICVS 2008, LNCS 5008, pp. 171–180, 2008.
© Springer-Verlag Berlin Heidelberg 2008

necessarily lead to a working machine vision system. We will thus focus on integration issues and on topics that are specific to quality control applications. Object recognition in the field of inspection systems is mainly about locating a fault on a surface. Faults are characterized by the fact that they deviate from the normal appearance of the surface. The most basic recognition methods are grey-level thresholding or locally adaptive thresholds [1] either applied to the original image or to a deviation image [2]. Whenever the surface has an irregular high-contrast structure, much more complicated methods from the field of texture analysis, such as texture fault detection [3] or texture segmentation [4] are required. These methods usually identify the statistics of the faultless texture and detect any significant deviation. In most cases, this means that the algorithms are application-specific and developed for very special needs, although generic adaptive methods have recently been reported [5]. Once the deviating pixels in the image have been identified, the standard procedure is to group these pixels together, such that each group constitutes a single fault. Various methods exist to detect and group relevant regions [6]. We apply clustering methods [7] on the binarized images for finding regions of arbitrary shape, which is usually quite promising. For each of these regions a set of features is calculated, which is usually specific for each application. Each of the feature vectors is then processed by data-driven classifiers [8] built up based on some off-line or on-line recorded and labelled images. Confidence measures for each decision are a useful tool to indicate the reliability of the currently trained classifier.

After analyzing a large number of image quality control approaches, e.g. [9], we have found the following relevant topics that have not yet been investigated in sufficient detail:

- Classifiers usually operate on single feature vectors of fixed dimension. Quite often this is insufficient for an inspection task, because frequently an undetermined number of faults needs to be judged as a whole group.
- Most of the approaches implement a (small) specific set of features, appropriate to the given types of images; here we go a step further towards more generic applicability by defining a wide range of possible features and performing automatic feature selection within the classifier's training process.
- A fully automatic incorporation of operator's feedback into the classifier during online processing. This includes the adaptation and extension of already trained classifiers with incremental and evolving learning schemes.
- Usually, several experts are involved in performing the inspection tasks. Their decisions will be inconsistent and the classifier system has to deal with these contradictions in a constructive way.

We begin with a description of the framework of our approach (Section 2). Following this, we explain object recognition and feature extraction and how to handle a variable number of objects (Section 3). Section 4 describes the different types of classifier that we have implemented within our approach, and the methods used for dimension reduction. Where appropriate, we also discuss how these classifiers have been adapted to permit on-line training. Section 5 discusses the way in which our approach deals with the fact that the data used to train the

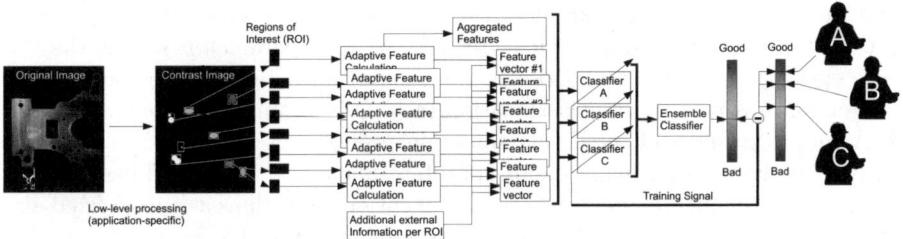

Fig. 1. Classification framework for classifying images into good and bad

classifiers may be contradictory. In Section 6 we will present an evaluation of the whole image classification framework based on artificial and real-world data sets. Section 7 concludes this paper with an outlook of further improvements.

2 The Framework

The whole framework is shown in Figure 1. Starting from the original image (left) a so called "contrast image" is calculated. The gray value of each pixel in the contrast image correlates to the deviation from the normal appearance of the surface. Thus the image is mostly black, with the faults highlighted by non-zero gray values. The contrast image serves as an interface to the subsequent processing steps in order to remove the application-dependent elements. From the contrast image regions of interest (ROIs) are extracted, each of which contains a single object which is a potential fault. The features of each object are calculated and complemented by three additional data sources: information about the region of interest, information about the status of the production process and aggregate features characterizing images as a whole. The feature vectors are then processed by a trained classifier system that generates a final good/bad decision for the whole image. This result is compared to the input of one or more human experts and a feedback loop adapts the classifier system. In order to consider the inputs of different experts, one classifier will be set up for each expert and an ensemble method will combine them to generate the final decision.

3 Object Recognition and Feature Extraction

In our image classification framework, the object recognition component reduces to finding regions of interest (ROIs) in the "contrast image". These are usually represented by a concentration of pixels that visually belong together. Within the framework various methods are implemented for detecting ROIs such as connected components, morphology [10] and iterative prototype-based clustering. For the applications described here hierarchical clustering [11] performed best among these with respect to the noise level in the features. A large number of object features are extracted from the recognized ROIs to characterize their appearance, such as area, brightness, homogeneity or roundness of objects, etc., and we then applied automatic feature selection (Section 4.1). Special attention was given to so-called adaptive features [12]: we used parameters during the feature extraction process to maximize the separation between the good and the bad class, thus making the classification task more simple and robust.

A major problem of image classification problems is the fact that it is not known in advance how many regions of interests may be segmented from images occurring in the future, and yet most classification algorithms assume a fixed-size input data space. Initial analysis reveals a number of possible approaches to this issue. The first of these is to only consider aggregated features which describe the image as a whole. These might include the total number of ROIs detected, their density, and descriptors of the grey levels detected within the image. For time-critical high-throughput applications this approach may be considered preferable since it requires significantly less processing. It also presents a much lower dimensional space to the classifiers which will often be beneficial. A second approach is to augment the aggregate features with statistics describing distribution of values for each of the object-level features for a given image. This approach provides more information, but also creates the problem of knowing what type of techniques should be used for data modelling. A third approach involves preprocessing the object feature vectors through a learning system which assigns each of them to one of a small, fixed number of groups, and then presenting the outputs of that system as an additional image-level information. For example, if the data is labelled at the object-level, then supervised object-level classifiers can be built or alternatively if object labels are not available, unsupervised clustering methods can be used [5] to build up cluster structures.

4   Building Up the Classifier

4.1   Dimension Reduction

For dimension reduction we apply both redundancy deletion and feature selection. The redundancy deletion algorithm automatically detects linear dependencies between two or more features through linear regression (hyperplane) modelling and then discards the dependent features, taking into account cross-links between different hyper-planes. This usually improves the transparency of a classifier as reducing the number of input variables, but never decreases the accuracy of the classifier as pointed out in [13].

Feature selection algorithms have three goals: 1.) to reduce the cost of extracting the features, 2.) to improve the classification accuracy and 3.) to improve the reliability of the estimation of the performance since a reduced feature set requires less training samples in the training process of a pattern classifier [14]. Feature selection algorithms can be broadly divided into three categories [13]: *filters*, *wrappers* and *embedded* approaches. Embedded approaches are a part of the classifiers training mechanism itself. The filter approach evaluates the relevance of each feature or feature subset using the data set alone and without using any machine learning algorithm. On the other hand, wrapper approaches use machine learning algorithms to evaluate the relevance of feature subset. The choice of an algorithm for selecting the features from an initial set depends on the number of examples it contains [15]. In this paper we used as a wrapper approach a specific Tabu Search algorithm [16] for selecting the most appropriate features for classifier training, see Section 6.

4.2   Batch Training and On-Line Evolution of Classifiers

For an initial off-line batch training of the classifiers we exploit two approaches, namely 1.) decision tree-based classifiers based on the well-known approaches C4.5 [17] and CART [18] both of which support a quite transparent and readable structure and 2.) k-NN [19], which is by nature adaptive as a local learning procedure is carried out, for which all older samples are taken as input.

For dealing with the on-line learning problem based on operator's feedback we applied an evolving clustering-based classifier [20], which is based on vector quantization and incorporates an on-line split-and-merge strategy for obtaining a more exact presentation of the cluster partition. It takes into account the class labels during the incremental clustering process for forming the classifier and is sufficiently flexible to integrate new operating conditions (such as new image types) and upcoming new fault classes into the structure of the classifier in sample-wise manner, without using any prior data. A timing of adaptation strategy is implemented which updates the classifier not always for each new sample, but only in the following cases: 1.) whenever the operator overrules a decision from the classifier: this increases the likelihood that the classifier will produce the correct decision when the same image is presented again, 2.) whenever the relative proportion between the classes is equally balanced: this always increases the classifier's classification accuracy and 3.) whenever the relative proportion of the samples belonging to the current class is lower than the relative proportion of samples to any other class: this enriches the classifier by balancing out the non-equal class distribution, which further increases the accuracy.

5   Ensemble Methods for Combining Classifiers

The idea of *classifier ensembles* is not to train a single classifier, but a set (ensemble) of classifiers and to combine their decisions in an appropriate way. Two necessary and sufficient conditions for an ensemble of classifiers to be more accurate than any of its individual members are that the individual classifiers are accurate and diverse [21]. Ensembles can be used either to combine the classifications of the classifiers, trained by the different operators (which may have some contradictory outputs), or to combine different classification algorithms which are trained for the same data set. In this sense, ensembles can be used either for resolving contradictions between different operators or for further improving the classification accuracy by exploiting the diversity of the different classifiers. In this paper, only the combination of classifiers which are trained by different operators, is considered. The diversity in the ensembles in this case comes from the different labels the operators will give for some of the inspected parts.

Table 1. Comparative classification accuracy % (CV-error) using aggregated data

Dataset	CART	C4.5	1NN	eVQ-Class (batch)
Artif01	87.9	87.8	78.9	80.6
Artif02	93.5	93.5	88.3	88.0
Artif03	94.3	94.4	89.1	89.9
Artif04	89.1	88.9	82.7	83.4
Artif05	91.2	90.9	86.5	86.3

There are generally two ways to combine the decisions of classifiers in ensembles: classifier selection and classifier fusion [22]. The assumption in *classifier selection* is that each classifier is "an expert" in some local area of the feature space. *Classifier fusion* assumes that all classifiers are trained over the whole feature space. For the application in this paper *classifier fusion* is considered, as the data for all the operators is spread over the entire space.

Several of the most effective classifier fusion methods (both fixed and trainable) are considered in this paper (for a detailed survey see e.g. [23]), such as *Voting, Algebraic connectives* such as *maximum, minimum, product, mean* and *median, Fuzzy Integral, Decision Templates*; *Dempster-Shafer combination,* and *Discounted Dempster-Shafer combination* (an extension of 5.) recently proposed in [24]). Also the *Oracle*, a *hypothetical* ensemble scheme that outputs the correct classification if at least one of the classifiers in the ensemble outputs the correct classification, was considered. Its accuracy can be seen as a "soft bound" on the accuracy which can be achieved by the classifiers and classifier fusion methods.

6   Evaluation Results

In this section we evaluate the whole classification framework with all its components on two different types of image sets, one artificially created and one from a real-world application. For both data sets, we will apply 10-fold cross-validation for eliciting the expected prediction accuracy, denoted as 'accuracy'. We begin by presenting results using only aggregate (image-level) data and then show how these are improved by the subsequent refinements available within our system.

The artificial data sets each consisted of 20000 different contrast images with a resolution of 128×128 pixels. A good/bad classification was assigned to the images by using 5 different sets of rules of increasing complexity. Table 1 shows the results obtained when different classifiers were trained using just the 17 image-level features. These results are some way short of the levels of accuracy necessary for industrial applications as significantly below 95% and sometimes even below 90%. It is clearly necessary to incorporate some information about individual objects in order to reach the levels of accuracy required. The first method implemented was to add some first-order statistics describing the distribution of values observed for each of the 57 object-level features. Initial experimentation revealed that the maximum value for each feature was the most useful. We

Table 2. Classification accuracy % and miss-detection rate using aggregated and extended data, data are labelled by different operators. Numbers in first column show the good/bad distribution in the data set. **eVQ** denotes the algorithm eVQ-Class.

Dataset Distribution	Measure	Aggregate				Aggregate+Object			
		CART	**C4.5**	**1NN**	**eVQ**	**CART**	**C4.5**	**1NN**	**eVQ**
Operator01 (370/1164)	Acc.	91.6	91.8	92.3	90.5	93.2	91.8	93.1	92.8
	Miss.	20.3	23.5	17.0	26.1	14.7	18.4	14.6	15.4
Operator02 (272/1262)	Acc.	95.5	95.5	95.1	95.2	95.6	95.4	95.5	96.1
	Miss.	15.1	17.6	14.7	21.1	17.7	14.7	15.4	12.3
Operator03 (304/1230)	Acc.	94.3	94.2	93.0	92.9	94.5	94.3	93.2	93.4
	Miss.	18.3	26.0	20.4	21.4	16.3	19.1	22.0	18.0
Operator04 (311/1223)	Acc.	94.9	94.1	93.5	92.9	94.9	95.2	94.7	94.6
	Miss.	13.5	20.9	18.3	25.5	13.4	14.1	16.4	14.5

then applied a combination of redundancy deletion and feature selection using a simple forward sequential selection algorithm to reduce the number of features, which typically gave 1-2% improvements compared with using all the features. The best results were obtained using one of the two decision tree methods, and were $\{93.0, 95.7, 94.8, 91.3, 92.0\}$ % for data sets 1-5 respectively, representing increases in accuracy of up to 5.1%. The data used for the next experiments was produced by re-labelling the aggregated feature vectors according to the set of pre-defined rules, thus removing intrinsic noise due to the image segmentation, with the added benefit of quantifying that noise. Applying C4.5 to the image level data gave improvements of 2.6% and 3.8% for data sets 1 and 2 respectively, but the error rates of 9.4% and 2.7% are still rather high. We next applied the rules to the individual objects and trained object level classifiers from this data whose outputs were incorporated into the image level classifiers by adding 2 features, one for the number of objects in each class on the image. The results here were excellent. Using the original image labels the errors are reduced to by 5.9% on data set 1 and 1% on data set 2, while using the "corrected" image labels 100% accuracy is achieved on both artificial data sets. This means that the C4.5 decision-tree approach is able to learn complex rules with 0 bias.

The classifier system was also evaluated on real world data of an application in the field of CD imprint inspection. There, the task is to detect faults due to weak colors, wrong palettes etc. during the on-line production process, which usually requires a detection frequency of about 1 Hz. The image data set collected during the on-line production process contains 1534 images, which were labelled by four different operators. Labelling was also performed at the object level, the objects being classified into 12 different classes. Table 2 shows the results obtained when different classifiers were trained using the image-level aggregate features (columns 3-7), and then the aggregate and maximum object features. The image-level results with respect to the over-all accuracy are acceptable for all operators, however the miss-detection rate is quite high. The main reason for this is the bad distribution of the good and bad samples (only between 15%

Table 3. Mean accuracy (in %) of different base classifiers and trainable ensembles for the CD data sets (agg.+object features), evaluated on the data provided by operator02

	eVQ	CART	C4.5	kNN
Operator01	90.65	91.76	92.16	91.31
Operator03	92.68	93.73	93.66	93.14
Operator04	94.18	93.66	94.38	94.58
Fuzzy Integral	93.86	94.71	95.56	94.84
Decision Templates	94.51	94.71	95.56	94.18
D-S Combination	94.51	94.71	95.56	94.58
Disc. D-S Combination	94.51	94.71	95.56	94.58
Oracle	97.78	98.63	99.22	97.84

Table 4. Performance of Incremental On-Line Classifiers vs. Batch Classifiers

Dataset	CART	eVQ-Class batch	eVQ-Class inc.
Operator01 Test Acc.	82.74	83.33	81.57
Operator02 Test Acc.	90.78	88.82	89.80
Operator03 Test Acc.	90.39	88.43	89.41
Operator04 Test Acc.	89.22	88.43	87.06

and 22% bad samples). As can be seen, adding the 57 object maximum features, improves the accuracies, and in particular the miss-detection rates.

By selecting the best-subset of features using tabu search (TS) [25], we obtained improvements of between 1.4% and 2.2% for the different operators. Results for this approach showed further improvements, with accuracies on the four data sets of 95.6, 98.1, 96.0 and 97.7% respectively. Similar improvements could be achieved when applying the fully supervised combination of object and image level classifier as also done for the artificial data.

As discussed in Section 5, different operators will train their individual classifiers as they think would be best. These classifiers are combined into the final decision using fixed classifier fusion methods or, if a "supervisor" labels the data, trainable classifier fusion methods can be used to better represent the supervisor's decisions. In our case, (base) classifiers were trained for three operators and the fourth operator was considered to be the supervisor. The results of the trainable ensembles, when considering the labels of Operator02 as supervisor, are demonstrated in Table 3. It can be realized that the classifier fusion methods (below the double horizontal line) can improve the results from the individual classifiers significantly (especially when using C4.5 as base classifier). Hence, the ensembles show their usefulness to combine the decisions of different operators. Note, however, that these results would probably not hold if the supervisor would systematically disagree with *all* the other operators, as it is very hard for the ensemble to output the correct decision if none of the classifiers does so.

We evaluate the on-line performance eVQ-Class in incremental mode (denoted as eVQ-Class inc.) on the two-level feature matrices. The simulation of on-line learning is carried out by dividing the feature matrices into a training data set and test data set, whereas the training data set is split into two halves: one for the purpose of initial off-line training, the other for further sample-wise adaptation simulating on-line learning mode, based on the label entries in the sample-wise loaded feature vectors (on-line adaptation), simulating the real operator's feedback during the on-line mode. Table 4 underlines the strength of eVQ-Class in its incremental version as it can come close to its batch version (in 2 cases even outperforms it) and also to the batch classifier CART [18].

7   Conclusion and Outlook

We have presented a flexible generic framework for image classification problems which is specifically designed to deal with important issues in modern image inspection applications, and shown how all of the components fit together synergistically. The results on both artificial and real-world data sets show the benefits of this approach. However, there still remain significant issues to tackle such as incorporation of confidence levels of class labels into the classifier's training process, further refinements of the incremental classifiers and ensembles, adaptive features, and a range of human-machine interaction issues.

Acknowledgements

This work was supported by the European Commission (project Contract No. STRP016429, acronym DynaVis). This publication reflects only the authors' views.

References

1. Demant, C., Streicher-Abel, B., Waszkewitz, P.: Industrielle Bildverarbeitung. Springer, Heidelberg (1998)
2. Hayes, B.: Fully automatic color print inspection by digital image processing systems. In: Becker, M., Daniel, R.W., Loffeld, O. (eds.) Proceedings SPIE, vol. 2247, pp. 235–244 (1994)
3. Silven, O., Niskanen, M.: Framework for industrial visual surface inspection In: Proc. 6th International Conference on Quality Control by Artificial Vision, pp. 1–6 (2003)
4. Kyong, I., Bowyer, K., Sivagurunath, M.: Evaluation of texture segmentation algorithms. In: IEEE Computer Society Conference on Computer Vision and Pattern Recognition (CVPR 1999), p. 1294 (1999)
5. Caleb-Solly, P., Smith, J.: Adaptive surface inspection via interactive evolution. Image and Vision Computing 25(7), 1058–1072 (2007)
6. Mikolajczyk, K., Schmid, K.: Scale and affine invariant interest point detectors. International Journal of Computer Vision 60(1), 63–86 (2004)

7. Gan, G., Ma, C., Wu, J.: Data Clustering: Theory, Algorithms, and Applications (Asa-Siam Series on Statistics and Applied Probability). In: Society for Industrial & Applied Mathematics, USA (2007)

8. Duda, R., Hart, P., Stork, D. (eds.): Pattern Classification - Second Edition, England. West Sussex PO 19 8SQ. Wiley-Interscience, Chichester (2000)

9. Kim, C., Koivo, A.: Hierarchical classification of surface defects on dusty wood boards. Pattern Recognition Letters 15, 712–713 (1994)

10. Stockman, G., Shapiro, L.: Computer Vision. Prentice-Hall, Englewood Cliffs (2001)

11. Jain, A., Dubes, R.: Algorithms for Clustering Data. Prentice-Hall, Englewood Cliffs (1988)

12. Chen, H., Liu, T., Fuh, C.: Probabilistic tracking with adaptive feature selection. In: Proc. of 17th International Conference on Pattern Recognition (ICPR 2004), vol. 2, pp. 736–739 (2004)

13. Guyon, I., Elisseeff, A.: An introduction to variable and feature selection. Journal of Machine Learning Research 3, 1157–1182 (2003)

14. Jain, A.K., Duin, R.P.W., Mao, J.: Statistical pattern recognition: A review. IEEE Transactions on Pattern Analysis and Machine Intelligence 22(1), 4–37 (2000)

15. Kudo, M., Sklansky, J.: Comparison of algorithms that select features for pattern classifiers. Pattern Recognition 33, 25–41 (2000)

16. Tahir, M.A., Kurugollu, A.B., F.: Simultaneous feature selection and feature weighting using hybrid tabu search/k-nearest neighbor classifier. Pattern Recognition Letters 28 (2007)

17. Quinlan, J.R.: C4.5: Programs for Machine Learning, USA. Morgan Kaufmann Publishers Inc, San Francisco (1993)

18. Breiman, L., Friedman, J., Stone, C., Olshen, R.: Classification and Regression Trees. Chapman and Hall, Boca Raton (1993)

19. Hastie, T., Tibshirani, R., Friedman, J.: The Elements of Statistical Learning: Data Mining, Inference and Prediction. Springer, Heidelberg (2001)

20. Lughofer, E.: Extensions of vector quantization for incremental clustering. In: Pattern Recognition (to appear, 2007), doi:10.1016/j.patcog.2007.07.19

21. Hansen, L., Salamon, P.: Neural network ensembles. IEEE Transactions on Patterns Analysis and Machine Intelligence 12, 993–1001 (1990)

22. Woods, K., Kegelmeyer, W.P., Bowyer, K.: Combination of multiple classifiers using local accuracy estimates. IEEE Transactions on Pattern Analysis and Machine Intelligence 19, 405–410 (1997)

23. Kuncheva, L.I.: Combining pattern classifiers: Methods and algorithms. Wiley, Chichester (2004)

24. Sannen, D., Van Brussel, H., Nuttin, M.: Classifier fusion using discounted dempster-shafer combination. In: Poster Proceedings of International Conferernce on Machine Learning and Data Mining, pp. 216–230 (2007)

25. Tahir, M.A., Smith, J.: Improving nearest neighbor classifier using tabu search and ensemble distance metrics. In: Proceedings of the Sixth International Conference on Data Mining (2006)

Communication-Aware Face Detection Using Noc Architecture

Hung-Chih Lai, Radu Marculescu, Marios Savvides, and Tsuhan Chen

Department of Electrical and Computer Engineering
Carnegie Mellon University, Pittsburgh, PA 15213, USA
{hlai,radum,marioss,tsuhan}@cmu.edu

Abstract. Face detection is an essential first step towards many advanced computer vision, biometrics recognition and multimedia applications, such as face tracking, face recognition, and video surveillance. In this paper, we proposed an FPGA hardware design with NoC (Network-on-Chip) architecture based on an AdaBoost face detection algorithm. The AdaBoost-based method is the state-of-the-art face detection algorithm in terms of speed and detection rates and the NoC provides high communication capability architecture. This design is verified on a Xilinx Virtex-II Pro FPGA platform. Simulation results show the improvement in speed 40 frames per second compared to software implementation. The NoC architecture provides scalability so that our proposed face detection method can be sped up by adding multiple classifier modules.

Keywords: Face detection, Hardware Architecture, Network-on-Chip.

1 Introduction

Face detection is the process of finding all possible faces in a given image or a video sequence. More precisely, face detection has to determine the locations and sizes of all possible human faces. It is a more complex case than face localization in which the number of faces is already known. On the other hand, face detection is the essential first step towards many advanced computer vision, biometrics recognition and multimedia applications, such as face tracking, face recognition, and video surveillance.

Due to scale, rotation, pose and illumination variation, face detection involves many research challenges. How to detect different scales of faces, how to be robust to illumination variation, how to achieve high detection rate with low false detection rates are only few of all issues a face detection algorithm needs to consider.

Face detection techniques have been researched for years and much progress has been proposed in literature. Most of the face detection methods focus on detecting frontal faces with good lighting conditions. According to Yang's survey [6], these methods can be categorized into four types: knowledge-based, feature invariant, template matching and appearance-based.

Knowledge-based methods use human-coded rules to model facial features, such as two symmetric eyes, a nose in the middle and a mouth underneath the nose [12]. Feature invariant methods try to find facial features which are invariant to pose,

A. Gasteratos, M. Vincze, and J.K. Tsotsos (Eds.): ICVS 2008, LNCS 5008, pp. 181–189, 2008.

lighting condition or rotation [10]. Skin colors, edges and shapes fall into this category. Template matching methods calculate the correlation between a test image and pre-selected facial templates [13]. The last category, appearance-based, adopts machine learning techniques to extract discriminative features from a pre-labeled training set. The Eigenface method [7] is the most fundamental method in this category. Recently proposed face detection algorithms such as support vector machines [11], neural networks [9], statistical classifiers [2,8] and AdaBoost-based face detection [1] also belong to this class.

Recently, appearance-based methods have achieved good results in terms of performance and speed. However, these methods are software-centric algorithms which do not take the hardware aspect into consideration. For instance, the state-of-the-art method in terms of speed and performance, AdaBoost-based face detection, requires inefficient memory space to store integral images (integral image will be discussed later). Besides, high demand of random data access of memory is necessary. For a 320x240 image, AdaBoost-based face detection needs 25 bits for one pixel, (a total of 1.92 Mbits), to store the whole integral image. Moreover, even the AdaBoost-based method uses a cascade architecture to reduce colloquial unnecessary operations; for an image of the same size, this method still requires accessing 25 bits of data over 21 million times for only the original scale and the first three classifier stages. (Assume that 41 features are in the first three stages, and each feature requires 8 points accessing)

In this paper, we adopt the AdaBoost-based face detection with NoC (Network-on-a-chip) architecture to satisfy the requirement of high data access rate. The NoC architecture [16, 17] is proposed with parallel and scalable links for communication within large VLSI implementation in a silicon chip. NoCs adopt the routing strategy from computer network to allow components to communicate data from source nodes through routers to destination nodes. There are many choices of mapping and routing methods which will not be discussed here. In this paper, we manually map the task and use the XY routing method.

2 Previous Work

2.1 Theory of AdaBoost Technique

The AdaBoost-based face detection method uses a set of simple rectangular features to detect faces. Three kinds of rectangles are used, a two-rectangle feature, a three-rectangle feature and a four-rectangle feature, as shown in Fig. 1.

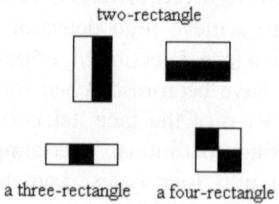

Fig. 1. Example of simple features

For a given feature, the sum of pixels in the white rectangles is subtracted from the sum of pixels in the black rectangles. Based on these simple features, the AdaBoost-based face detection method proposed three significant contributions which make face detection fast. The block diagram is shown in Fig. 2. First, by utilizing the integral image representation, the simple features can be rapidly computed in linear time. Second, a machine learning method, based on AdaBoost, trains an over-completed feature set and obtains a reduced set of critical features. Third, a cascade architecture of increasingly complex classifiers was proposed to quickly eliminate background windows and focus on more face-like windows.

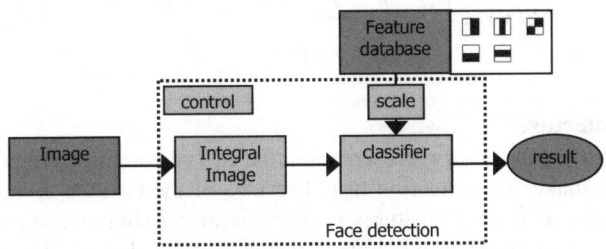

Fig. 2. Block diagram of AdaBoost-based face detection

Integral Image

An image is first converted into its corresponding integral image. The integral image at location (x, y) is the sum of all pixel values above and to the left of (x, y), inclusive [1].

$$ii(x, y) = \sum_{m=0}^{x} \sum_{n=0}^{y} i(m, n) \tag{1}$$

where ii is the integral image and i is the original image. Any rectangular sum can be computed efficiently by using integral images.

$$
\begin{aligned}
sum\,(\text{one rectangle}) \\
= ii(a) + ii(d) - ii(b) - ii(c)
\end{aligned}
\tag{2}
$$

Using the integral image, any rectangular sum can be computed in four-point access. Therefore, no matter what the size or the location of feature is, a two-rectangle feature, three-rectangle feature and four-rectangle feature can be computed in six, eight and nine data references, respectively.

AdaBoost Learning

AdaBoost is a machine learning technique that allows computers to learn based on known dataset. Recall that there are over 180,000 features in each sub-window. It is infeasible to compute the completed set of features, even if we can compute them very efficiently. According to the hypothesis that small number of features can be associated to form an effective classifier [1], the challenge now turns to be how to find these features. To achieve this goal, the AdaBoost algorithm is designed, for each iteration, to select the single rectangular feature among the 180,000 features available that best separates the positive samples from the negative examples, and determines the optimal threshold for this feature. A weak classifier $h_j(x)$ thus consists of a feature f, a threshold θ_j and a parity p_j indicating the direction of the inequality sign:

$$h_j(x) = \begin{cases} 1 & if \quad p_j f_j(x) < p_j \theta_j \\ 0 & otherwise \end{cases} \qquad (2)$$

The final strong classifier is shown in Eq. (4). Therefore, given a test sub-window x, the strong classifier classifies the sub-window as a face if the output is one.

$$h(x) = \begin{cases} 1, & if \quad \sum_{t=1}^{T} \alpha_t h_t(x) > \theta \\ 0, & otherwise \end{cases} \qquad (4)$$

Cascade Architecture

Along with the integral image representation, the cascade architecture is the important property which makes the detection fast. The idea of the cascade architecture is that simple classifiers, with fewer features (which require a shorter computational time) can reject many negative sub-windows while detecting almost all positive objects. The classifiers with more features (and more computational effort) then evaluate only the sub-windows that have passed the simple classifiers. Fig. 3 shows the cascade architecture consisting of n stages of classifiers. Generally, the later stages contain more features than the early ones.

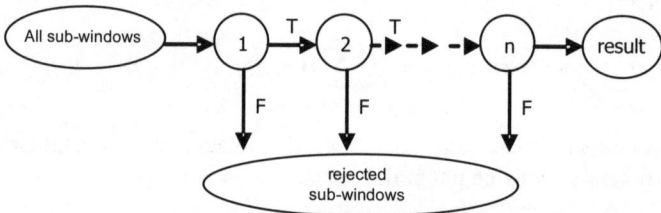

Fig. 3. Cascade architecture of classifier

2.2 Hardware Implementation of AdaBoost-Based Face Detection

Several studies have been proposed in hardware implementation for face detection. In one neural network implementation [14], high-frame-rate face detection is achieved. However, in this specific example, only 965 windows were evaluated for a 300x300 pixel image. In another hardware implementation, a good detection rate is achieved using a statistical classifier [13]. However, due to the large memory requirement, the hardware implementation needed to constraint the extracted features to a reduced model size.

There are fewer hardware studies involving AdaBoost-based face detection. However, most of the proposed solutions do not list the complete parameters that affect the detection speed. For example, the implementation using System Generator® and ISE® [3] does not mention the cost of accessing data. The other implementation on handheld camera [4] assumes the bandwidth and latency of bus and interface are guaranteed. Another parallel architecture [5] is proposed taking the advantage of parallel processing and can achieve 52 fps running at 500 MHz clock cycles. However, the size of the test images used to achieve 52 fps was not mentioned.

3 Architecture

Our NoC-based face detection framework consists of four parts: the image integrator, memory, the feature database, and the feature classifier. Each component is attached to an on-chip router to form the on-chip network, which is shown in Fig. 4. The main reason for choosing NoC as our architecture is that NoC is a scalable architecture which can allow us to work with higher resolution images and reach higher detection speeds by attaching several duplicated modules.

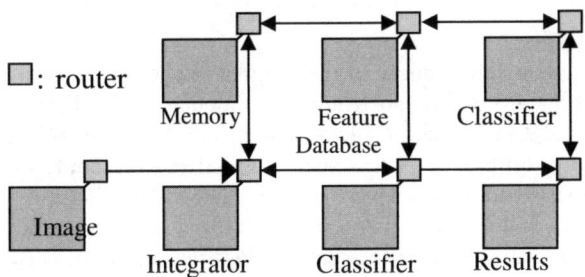

Fig. 4. NoC-based face detection framework

The Image Integrator
The target image resolution in this paper is 320 by 240 pixels. Therefore, we utilize one 320 length FIFO with 32-bit width to provide the integral data of the previous line. The accumulator performs the horizontal sum and stores it in the FIFO while the adder performs the vertical sum of the output of the accumulator and the FIFO. Fig. 5 shows the design of the integral image using System Generator®. The synthesis result of this implementation achieves a maximum frequency of 163.074 MHz and a total gate count of 8590 gates.

Memory
The size of integral images is large, and the minimum number of bits needed to store a pixel of an integral image varies greatly from the top-left pixel to the bottom-right pixel. As a result, we plan to use an external memory for integral image storage. The external memory will be accessed by a memory controller which is connected to the on-chip network through an on-chip router.

The Feature Database
This database includes a large set of features that characterize faces. Sub-windows in the original image that strongly respond to features in the database will be classified as faces. On the other hand, since faces in images may have different sizes, we also need to scale the features in order to identify various scales of faces.

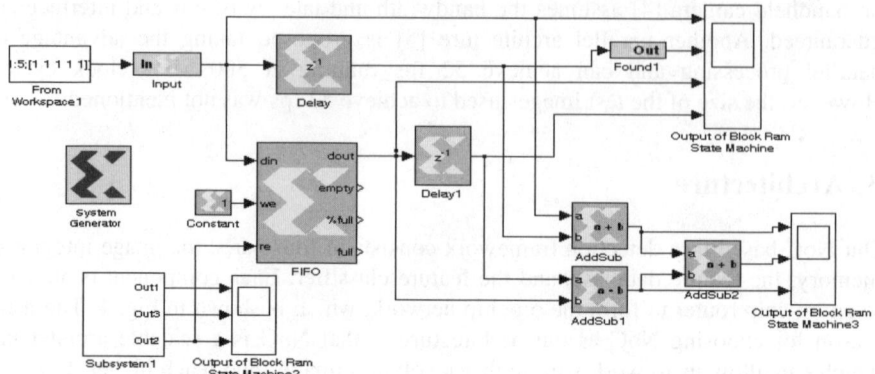

Fig. 5. Integral image design in System Generator

The Feature Classifier

Once we locate a target sub-window in the original image, the feature classifier will search for the best feature in this sub-window by calculating the difference between a feature and an equal-size searching block, which can be done by Equation (2) in constant time. If the difference is less than a specified threshold, we say that the pattern matches that feature. If a target pattern matches all features in the feature database, this pattern will be marked as a face. In order to exploit the advantage of the on-chip network, we can duplicate the feature classifier and each classifier searches for a sub-set of features in parallel.

We can also apply the cascade classification to split this procedure into several stages, with the fewer but more important features for the first stage and the other features for the last stage. Furthermore, several classifiers can be employed in the NoC architecture to achieve parallelism by processing several target patterns or detecting several features simultaneously.

4 On-Chip Router Architecture

We implemented the on-chip router by using System Generator®. However, we realize that using System Generator for the on-chip router is not that efficient because it consists of many control signals for the arbiter, crossbar switch, and channel controller.

The architectural overview of our on-chip router is shown in Fig. 6. Generally, each router has four pairs of input/output Routing Channels and one pair of input/output Local Channels, and each channel has its own Buffer. The Channel Controller extracts the source and destination addresses from an incoming packet, determines which output channel the packet should be delivered to, and sends the connection request to the Arbiter. The arbiter can decide which input channel has the right to send the packet through the Crossbar Switch, and then establish a link between the input channel and its corresponding output channel. In this NoC-based application, we will use deterministic XY routing and specify buffer length for each channel according to traffic congestion.

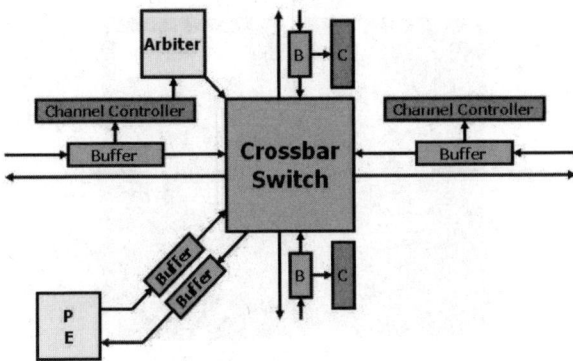

Fig. 6. Architectural overview of on-chip router

Fig. 7 shows our preliminary on-chip router design in the Xilinx System Generator. We used FIFOs as input and output buffers and implemented the crossbar switch by a set of MUXs. Channel controllers are accomplished by several control signals and the arbiter is implemented by writing a Matlab code in MCode block.

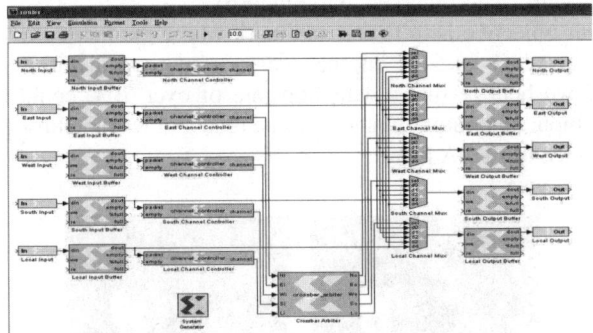

Fig. 7. On-chip router design in System Generator

5   Experimental Results

We modify the on-chip router and attach the router to the image integrator. In addition, a ROM which stores the original image and an internal memory which stores the integral image are also connected to on-chip network. More specifically, we can now read the original image from the ROM, calculate the corresponding integral image, and then store the integral image into memory. All these operations are achieved through on-chip network. These integrated components can be synthesized by Xilinx ISE and the synthesis result achieve a maximum frequency of 152.996 MHz.

Our proposed work is verified on a Xilinx Virtex-II Pro XC2VP30 FPGA on Xilinx® VirtexII Pro board, as shown in Fig. 8. This FPGA contains 200K equivalent

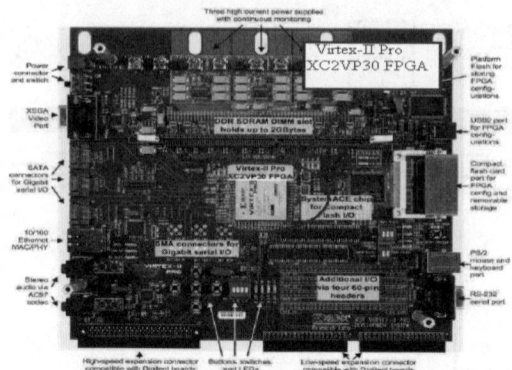

Fig. 8. Xilinx Virtex-II Pro system board

logic gates and 2.44Mb of on-chip memory. Using both Modelsim® simulation software and ISE® synthesize tool, a bitstream file is generated for FPGA verification. For more information about Xilinx FPGA, please refer to [15].

Input: Images with face(s), e.g. Fig. 9(a).
Output: Images with face(s) marked, e.g. Fig. 9(b)
Description: Our objective is to locate and mark where the faces are with acceptable accuracy. Right now, we take the internal memory into consideration and implement 44 features and we believe that a detection rate of over 70% could be achieved in normal images. Input and output images will be read and written through the Compact Flash (CF) interface of FPGA board.

(a)   (b)

Fig. 9. (a). An input image. (b). An output image

6 Conclusion

In this paper, we proposed an FPGA hardware implementation with NoC (Network-on-Chip) architecture based on the AdaBoost face detection algorithm. The AdaBoost method is the state-of-the-art face detection algorithm and the NoC provides high communication capability architecture. This design is verified on a Xilinx Virtex-II Pro FPGA platform. Our results achieve rates of 40 images per second for 320 by 240 resolution images which outperforms than current software implementation.

The evaluation of the performance in terms of detection rate, the optimization of logical circuit will be done in future work.

Acknowledgment

This research is supported by Carnegie Mellon CyLab. The authors would also like to thank Xilinx, Inc., for providing FPGA hardware and software tools by Xilinx University Program.

References

[1] Viola, P., Jones, M.J.: Rapid object detection using a boosted cascade of simple features. In: Proc. CVPR (2001)

[2] Schneiderman, H., Kanade, T.: Object detection using the statistic of parts. Int. J. Computer Vision (2004)

[3] Wei, Y., Bing, X., Chareonsak, C.: FPGA implementation of adaboost algorithm for detection of face biometrics. In: Int. Workshop on Biomedical Circuits & Systems (2004)

[4] Yang, M., Wu, Y., Crenshaw, J., Augustine, B., Mareachen, R.: Face detection for automatic exposure control in handheld camera. In: ICVS 2006 (2006)

[5] Theocharides, T., Vijaykrishnan, N., Irwin, M.J.: A parallel architecture for hardware face detection. In: Emerging VLSI Technologies and Architectures (2006)

[6] Yang, M.-H., Kriegman, D., Ahuja, N.: Detecting Faces in Images: A Survey. IEEE Trans. Pattern Analysis and Machine Intelligence 24(1), 34–58 (2001)

[7] Turk, M., Pentland, A.: Face recognition using eigenfaces. In: Proc. IEEE Conference on Computer Vision and Pattern Recognition, pp. 586–591

[8] Schneiderman, H., Kanade, T.: A Statistical Method for 3D Object Detection Applied to Faces and Cars. In: Proc. IEEE Conf. Computer Vision and Pattern Recognition, June 2000, pp. 746–751 (2000)

[9] Rowley, H.A., Baluja, S., Kanade, T.: Neural Network-Based Face Detection. IEEE Trans. Pattern Analysis and Machine Intelligence 20(1), 23–38 (1998)

[10] Sung, K.K., Poggio, T.: Example-Based Learning for View-Based Human Face Detection. IEEE Trans. Pattern Analysis and Machine Intelligence 20(1), 39–51 (1998)

[11] Kepenekci, B., Akar, G.B.: Face classification with support vector machine. In: Proc. IEEE Conf. Signal Processing and Communications Applications, April 2004, pp. 583–586 (2004)

[12] Yang, G., Huang, T.S.: Human Face Detection in Complex Background. Pattern Recognition 27(9), 712–735 (1997)

[13] Lanitis, A., Taylor, C.J., Cootes, T.F.: An automatic face identification System Using Flexible Appearance Models. Image and Vision Computing 13(5), 393–401 (1995)

[14] Theocharis, G., Theocharides, G.M., Link, V., Narayanan, M.J., Irwin, Wolf, W.: Embedded Hardware Face Detection. In: Procedings, VLSI Design 2004, IEEE Press, Los Alamitos (2004)

[15] http://www.xilinx.com/products/silicon_solutions/fpgas/virtex/virtex_ii_pro_fpgas/index.htm

[16] Jantsch, A., Tenhunen, H. (eds.): Networks on Chip. Kluwer Academic Publishers, Dordrecht (2003)

[17] Hu, J., Marculescu, R.: Energy-Aware Communication and Task Scheduling for Network-on-Chip Architectures under Real-Time Constraints. In: Proc. Design, Automation and Test in Europe Conf. Paris, France (February 2004)

Part IV

Calibration and Registration

A System for Geometrically Constrained Single View Reconstruction*

Manolis I.A. Lourakis

Institute of Computer Science - FORTH, N. Plastira 100, Heraklion 700 13, Greece
`lourakis@ics.forth.gr`

Abstract. This paper presents an overview of a system for recovering 3D models corresponding to scenes for which only a single perspective image is available. The system encompasses a versatile set of semi-automatic single view reconstruction techniques and couples them with limited interactive user input in order to reconstruct textured 3D graphical models corresponding to the imaged input scenes. Such 3D models can serve as the digital content for supporting interactive multimedia and virtual reality applications. Furthermore, they can support novel applications in areas such as video games, 3D photography, visual metrology, computer-assisted study of art and crime scene reconstruction, etc.

1 Introduction

Advances in 3D model rendering and visualization have resulted in an ever increasing demand for 3D digital content to be used for computer graphics, mixed reality and communication. This, in turn, has stimulated increased interest in techniques capable of producing digital 3D reconstructions corresponding to scenes and objects. A particularly attractive paradigm for generating photorealistic 3D models directly from a set of images is that of image-based modeling (IBM) [1]. This paper focuses on a particular class of IBM methods, namely those concerned with single view reconstruction (SVR), whose aim is to create 3D graphical models corresponding to scenes for which only a single perspective image is available. The need for SVR techniques arises when dealing with scenes such as those depicted in paintings, gravures, postcards or old photographs, for which multiple views are not available. SVR techniques are also applicable when reconstructing a scene from multiple images acquired from very disparate viewpoints, which are therefore hard to match automatically. Due to their limited amount of input data and in order to disambiguate among the infinitely many 3D reconstructions that are compatible with a given 2D image, SVR techniques call for a priori geometric scene knowledge that is supplied through user interaction.

To accomplish SVR, two key problems should be tackled. First, the input image has to be calibrated in order to determine the optical characteristics of the device that acquired it. Second, metric 3D properties regarding the imaged

---

* Supported in part by the EU COOP-CT-2005-017405 project RECOVER.

A. Gasteratos, M. Vincze, and J.K. Tsotsos (Eds.): ICVS 2008, LNCS 5008, pp. 193–205, 2008.

objects should be recovered. Single image calibration approaches are briefly reviewed in section 3, whereas approaches to recovering 3D properties are discussed next. The *tour into the picture* (TIP) technique of Horry et al. [2] is one of the earliest SVR methods proposed. Assuming images with one-point perspective, TIP roughly models a scene using an axis-aligned box. Foreground objects are manually modeled as "billboards" by separate polygons. A "spidery mesh" interface facilitates the interactive manipulation of the modeling box as well as its vanishing point, resulting in novel rendered views. The applicability of TIP is limited by the fact that the front and back faces of the employed box should be parallel to the image plane. When applicable, however, TIP produces visually convincing results. Two more flexible methods for SVR are proposed by Liebowitz et al. in [3]. The first is based on measuring the heights of points above a ground plane. To achieve this, the vertical projection on the ground plane of each point whose height is to be measured has to be visible in the image. Clearly, this requirement restricts the type of objects that can be reconstructed. The second method reconstructs planes sequentially and necessitates the computation of the vanishing line of each plane being reconstructed. As is the case with all sequential approaches, this second method may suffer from accumulated errors, unless the scene includes a reference ground plane that has visible intersections with all other planes being reconstructed.

Sturm and Maybank develop in [4] a method for reconstructing a piecewise planar scene from a single image. Their method relies on the availability of user-provided constraints regarding perpendicularity, parallelism and coplanarity that are used for camera calibration and 3D reconstruction. Compared to the methods of [3], that in [4] is capable of reconstructing planes with arbitrary orientations whose vanishing lines are not known, provided that they share at least three non-collinear points with already reconstructed planes. Therefore, [4] accepts a wider class of scenes that are amenable to SVR. On the other hand, perpendicularity and parallelism constraints are used only for camera calibration and not during reconstruction. Furthermore, coplanarity constraints are only approximately satisfied in the final reconstruction. User-provided geometric knowledge such as coplanarity, distance ratios, and plane angles is also employed by Grossman et al. [5], who describe an algebraic SVR method that employs this knowledge to disambiguate an imaged scene and obtain a unique reconstruction. Inspired by TIP [2], Hoiem et al. [6] propose an automatic method for SVR that models a scene as a collection of several planar billboards. Using statistical learning techniques, planar image regions are labeled into coarse categories depending on their orientation in the scene. Then, using simple assumptions on the relative orientation of regions from different categories, labels are used to derive a pop-up model by cutting and folding. Overall, and despite being limited to outdoor images with a ground plane and vertical planar structures, the method is interesting since it is the first attempt towards fully automatic SVR. All SVR methods briefly reviewed above are restricted to surfaces that are either planar or can be approximated by planes. The work of Zhang et al. [7] addresses the problem of reconstructing free-form curved surfaces by employing a sparse set of user-specified constraints on the local scene shape to formulate a constrained variational optimization problem whose solution yields a smooth 3D surface satisfying the constraints. Evidently, the resulting 3D surface is not necessarily geometrically accurate or even viable. Furthermore, owing to its assumption of an orthographic projection model, the method is applicable only to images with limited perspective distortion.

This paper describes our experiences in designing and developing a research prototype system for achieving SVR guided by geometric constraints. The system integrates techniques for a) single view intrinsic camera calibration from a variety of cues, b) geometrically constrained 3D reconstruction with minimal user interaction and c) texture mapping as well as manipulation. The developed techniques are accessible with the aid of a graphical user interface with an interaction model targeted to SVR. The design guidelines of the developed SVR system are presented in section 2 along with some background material. Our solutions to the problems of calibration and reconstruction are respectively presented in sections 3 and 4; sample results are in section 5.

2   Design Guidelines and Geometrical Background

Some of the fundamental choices made when designing the developed SVR system are presented next. Their impact will become clearer in subsequent sections, where the technical aspects of the system are discussed in more detail. It has already been mentioned that SVR inherently necessitates a certain amount of user intervention. In our case, the choice between what to obtain automatically and what to supply manually is guided by adopting the paradigm introduced in [1]: Tasks that are straightforward for a computer program to accomplish but not for a human user are delegated to the computer, whereas the user is responsible for tasks that are trivial for humans but nevertheless not easily obtainable from automatic processing. To this end, the system provides an interactive GUI component that facilitates the annotation of images with the primitives involved in the various aspects of SVR and their interrelations. A second important choice is to implement more than one technique for achieving the same result. In this manner, the system becomes more flexible as the user can choose the technique that seems the most natural or best suits a particular image. A third choice relates to modeling the surface of objects rather than their volume. Thus, we reconstruct planar faces as opposed to polyhedral primitive solids such as the prisms and pyramids employed in [1]. This is because solid primitives are often not fully visible in a single image due to occlusions and field of view limitations, therefore their reconstruction is not possible without considerable, arbitrary generalization. Furthermore, the intractability of recovering arbitrary curved surfaces from a single view, leads us to restrict our attention to mostly piecewise planar scenes.

In the rest of the paper, vectors and arrays appear in boldface and are represented using projective (homogeneous) coordinates [8]. Two concepts of foremost importance for SVR are those of *vanishing points* and planar *homographies*, arising from the geometry of perspective projection. Assuming an infinite 3D line that is imaged under perspective, a point on it that is infinitely far away from the camera projects to a finite image point known as the vanishing point that depends only on the 3D line's direction and not on its position. Thus, parallel 3D lines share the same vanishing points. Analogously, the vanishing points of sets of non-parallel, coplanar 3D lines lie on the same image line, which is known as the *vanishing line* of the underlying plane. Parallel planes share the same vanishing line. The transformation that maps a plane to another under perspective projection (e.g. a scene plane to image mapping) is a general plane-to-plane projective transformation that is known as a homography. A homography that maps an imaged plane to a frontoparallel one so that it removes the effects of perspective distortion, is referred to as a *metric rectification homography*. Such a homography allows metric properties of the imaged plane, such as angles, length and area ratios, to be directly measured from its perspective image. Typically, a metric rectification homography is estimated from a quadrilateral that is the image of a scene rectangle with known height over width (i.e. aspect) ratio. Alternatively, it can be estimated from the vanishing line of the underlying plane and at least two constraints involving known angles, equal angles, and/or known length ratios of line segment groups [9]. A third way to estimate a metric rectification homography is through the images of the *circular points* [8]. The latter are a pair of complex conjugate ideal points whose image projections are invariant to similarity transforms. The images of the circular points can be estimated either as the intersection points of two ellipses that are the images of two scene circles or from the intersection of an ellipse corresponding to an imaged circle with the vanishing line of the underlying plane [10].

The *intrinsic calibration matrix* $\mathbf{K}$ is a 3×3 matrix that depends on a camera's optical parameters and defines a mapping from normalized to pixel image coordinates. $\mathbf{K}$ is expressed analytically as [8]:

$$\mathbf{K} = \begin{bmatrix} f_u & s & u_0 \\ 0 & f_v & v_0 \\ 0 & 0 & 1 \end{bmatrix}. \tag{1}$$

The parameters f_u and f_v correspond to the focal length expressed in pixel units along the two axes of the image, s is the *skew* parameter and (u_0, v_0) are the coordinates of the image principal point in pixels. Parameter s is related to the angle between the two image axes and is zero for most cameras. Furthermore, the *aspect ratio* $r = \frac{f_v}{f_u}$ for a certain camera is fixed and equal to one in most cases. A camera with zero skew and unit aspect ratio is known as a *natural* one.

3   Camera Calibration

Camera calibration refers to the process of estimating the calibration matrix $\mathbf{K}$, thus upgrading a camera from a projective to a metric measuring device. Since relying on artificial calibration objects such as checkerboard grids is clearly not a viable option in SVR, a self-calibration approach relying on image properties has to be followed. A conic of purely imaginary points called the *absolute conic* (AC) is of central importance in this respect. This is due to the AC being invariant to Euclidean transformations. Hence, the *image of the absolute conic* (IAC) depends only on the intrinsic camera parameters. Since the IAC ω is related to $\mathbf{K}$ through $\omega = (\mathbf{K} \cdot \mathbf{K^T})^{-1}$, estimating $\mathbf{K}$ amounts to estimating ω, inverting it and finally computing its Cholesky decomposition.

Linear constraints on ω can arise from several geometric arrangements of image primitives. For instance, it has been shown in [11] that the vanishing points $\mathbf{v}_1$, $\mathbf{v}_2$ of two orthogonal directions yield one constraint on ω, namely $\mathbf{v}_1^T \cdot \omega \cdot \mathbf{v_2} = 0$. Another type of constraint is defined with the aid of a point and a line in a pole-polar relationship: If $\mathbf{l}$ is a plane's vanishing line and $\mathbf{v}$ is the vanishing point of the direction perpendicular to the plane, then $\mathbf{l} \times (\omega \cdot \mathbf{v}) = \mathbf{0}$ [12]. The last equation yields three linear constraints on ω (only two of which are linearly independent) and the line and point in it are called the horizon line and the apex, respectively. Yet another type of constraints on ω is defined by a metric rectification homography $\mathbf{H}$, specifically $\mathbf{h}_1^T \cdot \omega \cdot \mathbf{h_2} = 0$ and $\mathbf{h}_1^T \cdot \omega \cdot \mathbf{h_1} = \mathbf{h_2^T} \cdot \omega \cdot \mathbf{h_2}$, where $\mathbf{h}_i$ is the i-th column of $\mathbf{H}$; these are two linear constraints on ω.

To estimate all intrinsic parameters involved in a complete parametrization of ω, at least five linear constraints must be available. Four linear constraints suffice when skew is excluded from the set of intrinsic parameters to be estimated and three are enough when assuming a natural camera. In the absence of enough constraints, the calibration parameters can be further reduced by two, assuming that the principal point is fixed on the image center. Our system can combine all types of calibration constraints mentioned in the previous paragraph, whilst parametrizations of ω involving five down to one parameters are supported. Assuming that enough constraints for a chosen parametrization exist, ω is estimated in a manner similar to that outlined in [13] by solving the (possibly overdetermined) homogeneous linear system formed by all available calibration constraints. The estimated $\mathbf{K}$ can be further refined as proposed in [14]. Image line segments that are necessary for detecting vanishing points are defined manually by the user. This is facilitated by the image annotation tool that allows line segments to be drawn overlaid on the image and grouped according to their orientation in 3D. Maximum likelihood estimates (MLE) of the vanishing points corresponding to imaged parallel line segments are computed with the nonlinear technique suggested in [9], embedded in a robust estimation framework. Vanishing lines are estimated either via orthogonal line fitting on some of their vanishing points or from the image projections of at least three coplanar and equispaced parallel lines [15]. Metric rectification homographies can be estimated in any of the three manners mentioned in section 2, namely relying upon image quadrilaterals corresponding to scene rectangles, coplanar line segments with known 3D angles and/or length ratios or circular points defined with the aid of ellipses obtained through conic fitting. In all cases, it is the responsibility of the user to identify suitable calibration cues in an image and provide the system with the annotations necessary for exploiting them.

4   3D Reconstruction

Being one of the most flexible SVR methods proposed in the literature, the SVR method of Sturm and Maybank [4] was chosen as the basis of our approach to reconstruction. We build upon it by devising a refinement scheme that accepts a richer repertoire of user-supplied geometric constraints and ensures that the recovered model accurately satisfies all of them. An overview of [4] is given in subsection 4.1, whereas the refinement of the reconstructions it produces is described in 4.2. We next briefly turn our attention to the issue of representing the outline of a plane's image projection. The spatial extend of each plane to be reconstructed is captured by a closed polyline, i.e. a set of connected straight line segments whose endpoints correspond to image points. When defining a polyline, its endpoints should be specified in a consistent order (clockwise or counter clockwise). Polylines can be convex or concave and can even contain "holes" to exclude certain image regions. Using this representation, planes that intersect each other share line segments in their respective polylines. Polylines defining planes are supplied by the user using the system's image annotation tool.

4.1   Obtaining an Initial Reconstruction

The method of [4] aims to reconstruct points and planes. It assumes that vanishing lines of planes have been computed using user-supplied information concerning groups of parallel 3D lines and that the camera has been intrinsically calibrated. The origin of the 3D Euclidean coordinate system is taken to coincide with the camera's center of projection. 3D planes are represented in the so-called *Hessian normal form* $\mathbf{n}^T\mathbf{X} = -d$, where $\mathbf{n}$ is the unit normal vector and d is the distance of the plane from the origin. Consider now an image point $\mathbf{x}_i$ that is the projection of an unknown 3D point $\mathbf{X}_i$ that is to be reconstructed. The depth information of point $\mathbf{X}_i$ is lost after its projection on the image plane. Thus, $\mathbf{X}_i$ can lie anywhere along the ray defined by $\mathbf{x}_i$ and the center of projection. Knowledge of the camera calibration matrix $\mathbf{K}$ permits the definition of a parametric representation of this backprojected ray as $\lambda_i \mathbf{x}'_i$, where λ_i is a scalar that corresponds to the distance of a point on the ray from the optical center and $\mathbf{x}'_i = \mathcal{N}(\mathbf{K}^{-1}\mathbf{x}_i)$ with $\mathcal{N}(\cdot)$ denoting normalization to unit vector norm. In other words, to reconstruct a 3D point, it suffices to estimate a single parameter λ_i. Camera calibration also facilitates the estimation of a plane's normal $\mathbf{n}$ from its vanishing line $\mathbf{l}$ as [8]:

$$\mathbf{n} = \mathcal{N}(\mathbf{K}^T\mathbf{l}). \tag{2}$$

Thus, for the plane to be fully reconstructed, its only parameter that remains to be determined is its distance d from the origin.

The key observation behind the method of [4] is that the reconstruction of a certain plane permits the reconstruction of all points on it. Conversely, the reconstruction of at least one or three (depending on whether the normal vector has been estimated or not) points on a plane enables the reconstruction of the latter. Owing to the well-known depth/scale ambiguity, reconstruction from one or more images is possible only up to an unknown overall scale factor. For this reason, the position of the first plane to be reconstructed is determined arbitrarily by setting its parameter d to some value d_0. Having completed the estimation of the parameters of this plane, its intersections with the backprojected rays of all points lying on it allows these points to be reconstructed by determining their corresponding λ_i from $\lambda_i = -\frac{d}{\mathbf{n}^T \mathbf{x}_i}$. Then, the reconstructed points that belong to planes that have not yet been reconstructed facilitate the reconstruction of such planes, which in turn allows the recovery of more 3D points on them and so on. This scheme that alternates between reconstructing points and planes allows the reconstruction of points and planes that are "linked" together by means of common points. Despite them being essential for expanding a reconstruction, common points in the presence of noise cannot simultaneously satisfy the equations of all planes they belong to. This problem is dealt with in [4] by directly estimating a reconstruction which is such that minimizes the sum of squared distances from points to planes. More specifically, the signed Euclidean distance of point i on a backprojected ray from plane j is given by

$$D_{ij} = \mathbf{n}_j^T \mathbf{x}_i' \lambda_i + d_j. \tag{3}$$

Observing that Eq. (3) is linear in λ_i and d_j, all such distances can be concatenated together leading to a matrix expression of the form $\mathbf{M} \cdot \mathbf{r}$, where $\mathbf{M}$ depends on the plane normals $\mathbf{n}_j$ and image projections $\mathbf{x}_i'$ and the vector of unknowns $\mathbf{r}$ consists of the λ_i's and d_j's for all points and planes, respectively. Then, a reconstruction can be computed up to scale by minimizing $||\mathbf{M} \cdot \mathbf{r}||$ subject to $||\mathbf{r}|| = 1$. The solution to this minimization problem is the eigenvector of $\mathbf{M}^T \mathbf{M}$ corresponding to its smallest eigenvalue [8]. The complete reconstruction algorithm can be found in [4]. Our implementation of [4] extends it by employing geometric inference rules that are in come cases capable of deducing the orientations of planes whose vanishing lines have not been possible to estimate from image cues. Despite its elegance, the method of [4] has the major drawback that it cannot directly incorporate geometric constraints other than coplanarity. Recall, for instance, that the normals $\mathbf{n}_j$ of the various planes are kept fixed to the values computed from their vanishing lines with the aid of Eq. (2). Therefore, perpendicularity and parallelism constraints on planes might be employed for camera calibration but are impossible to enforce during reconstruction. Furthermore, no constraints such as length or area ratios, segment angles, etc, can be exploited for improving the accuracy of the reconstruction. Even the coplanarity constraints are eventually satisfied only approximately since the method minimizes the point to plane distances of Eq. (3) rather than demanding them to be exactly zero. All the above contribute to geometric inaccuracies in the reconstruction that manifest themselves as skewed planes and not perfectly parallel and/or perpendicular planes. Typically, such problems are most noticeable after mapping on skewed planes textures with regular patterns such as tiles. The following subsection suggests how these shortcomings can be remedied.

4.2 Refining the Initial 3D Reconstruction

Suppose that n image points and m 3D planes have been identified by the user and that an initial reconstruction of them has been obtained from a single view. Our SVR method of choice for this initial reconstruction is that of [4] presented in section 4.1. However, as it will soon become clear, our refinement technique is not tailored to it but can be used with any other SVR method producing a piecewise planar reconstruction. Assume further that the user has supplied her prior knowledge of the scene in the form of geometric constraints such as point coplanarity and known plane relative orientations (i.e., dihedral angles). Let $\mathbf{X}_i$, $i = 1 \ldots n$ be the reconstructed estimates of 3D points that project on image points $\mathbf{x}_i$, $i = 1 \ldots n$. Also, let Π_j, $j = 1 \ldots m$ denote the scene's planes whose initial parameter estimates are given by $\mathbf{n}_j, d_j, j = 1 \ldots m$ and let $\Pi = \{\Pi_j \,|\, j = 1 \ldots m\}$ be the set of all such planes. Finally, let $\mathsf{A} \subseteq \Pi \times \Pi$ be the set of unordered plane pairs (Π_i, Π_j) whose dihedral angles are a priori known and are equal to θ_{ij}. Notice that this set includes parallel and perpendicular plane pairs, whose dihedral angles are respectively $0°$ and $90°$. The rest of this section explains how can the available geometric constraints be imposed on the initial reconstruction.

The idea is to jointly refine the set of initial point and plane parameter estimates for finding the set of parameters that most accurately predict the locations of the observed n points on the image and, at the same time, satisfy the supplied geometric constraints. Formally, this can be expressed as minimizing the average *reprojection error* with respect to all point and plane parameters subject to the geometric constraints, specifically

$$\min_{\mathbf{X}_i, \mathbf{n}_j, d_j} \sum_{i=1}^{n} d(\mathbf{K} \cdot \mathbf{X}_i, \mathbf{x}_i)^2, \quad \text{subject to} \tag{4}$$

$$d_k = d_0,$$
$$\{\mathbf{n}_j^T \mathbf{X}_i + d_j = 0, \ \mathbf{X}_i \text{ on } \Pi_j\},$$
$$\{\|\mathbf{n}_j\| = 1, \ \Pi_j \in \Pi\},$$
$$\{\mathbf{n}_i^T \mathbf{n}_j = \cos(\theta_{ij}), \ (\Pi_i, \Pi_j) \in \mathsf{A} \},$$

where $\mathbf{K} \cdot \mathbf{X}_i$ is the predicted projection of point i on the image and $d(\mathbf{x}, \mathbf{y})$ denotes the reprojection error defined as the Euclidean distance between the image points represented by the homogeneous vectors $\mathbf{x}$ and $\mathbf{y}$. The first constraint in (4) specifies that the d parameter of some plane k is kept fixed to d_0 so that overall scale remains unchanged. Expressions in curly brackets of the form $\{C, P\}$ denote sets of constraints C defined by the geometric property P.

Clearly, (4) amounts to a non-linear least squares minimization problem under non-linear constraints. It involves 3 unknowns for each 3D point and 4 for each plane, which amount to a total of $3n + 4m$. Image projections are 2D, thus the total number of image measurements defining the average reprojection error equals $2n$. Regarding constraints, each plane introduces one constraint specifying that its normal vector should have unit norm. Furthermore, each point yields one constraint for each plane on which it lies and the known dihedral angles introduce |A| additional constraints. In practice, the planes to be reconstructed are "interconnected" with several common points, therefore the number of available constraints plus that of projected image point coordinates to be fitted well exceeds the total number of unknowns. Constraints in (4) model the prior geometric scene knowledge and being hard ones, force a constrained minimizer to exactly satisfy them. In addition, the criterion minimized is not an algebraic but rather a geometric one, therefore it is physically meaningful. Imposing all constraints simultaneously has the advantage of distributing the error to the whole reconstruction, avoiding the error build-up inherent in sequential reconstruction. It should also be noted that other types of geometric constraints such as known length ratios and angles can be incorporated into (4) in a straightforward manner. Finally, the set of minimization unknowns in (4) can be extended to include the parameters of $\mathbf{K}$, allowing intrinsic calibration to be refined as well.

The minimization in (4) is carried out numerically with the aid of the NLSCON constrained non-linear least squares routine [16], which implements a damped affine invariant Gauss-Newton algorithm. Bootstrapped with the initial reconstruction, NLSCON iteratively refines it until it converges to a local minimizer satisfying the specified constraints. Despite them being infeasible with respect to the constraints of (4), we have found experimentally that initial reconstructions computed as described in section 4.1 are sufficiently close to constrained minimizers, thus facilitating the convergence of the constrained minimization. The Jacobian of the objective function as well as that of the constraints in (4) with respect to the reconstruction parameters that are necessary for the nonlinear minimization, have been computed analytically with the aid of MAPLE's symbolic differentiation facilities.

The recovered reconstructions are saved in the VRML/X3D format, which is very convenient both for visualizing and for importing them into a wide variety of 3D graphics software for further use. To increase the realism of reconstructed 3D models, textures automatically extracted from their corresponding image regions are mapped on their surfaces. These textures are thus photorealistic and are saved in standard JPEG or PNG image formats after being compensated for perspective foreshortening effects using their corresponding rectification homographies. On the one hand, this choice renders easier the task of manipulating the extracted textures using ordinary image editing software and on the other, facilitates the generation of extended textures with the aid of texture synthesis or texture inpainting algorithms: One of the main shortcomings of SVR is its inherent inability to cope with occlusions that result in incompletenesses manifested as holes in the reconstruction. To fill in the missing information, our system incorporates hole filling techniques in the form of texture inpainting [17] and texture synthesis algorithms [18]. These techniques are in some cases capable of masking out certain image regions that correspond to unwanted objects or enlarging small patches by synthesizing stochastic textures based on their structural content.

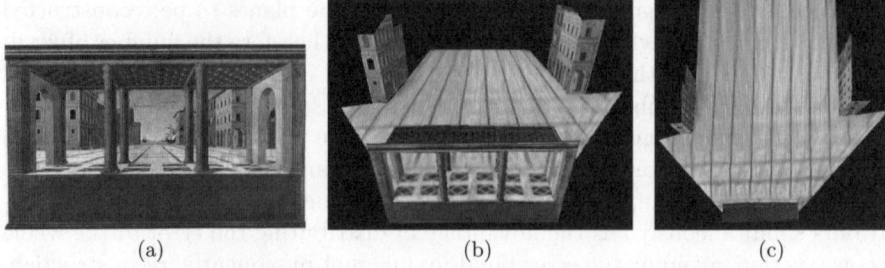

(a)   (b)   (c)

Fig. 1. (a) "Città Ideale", Francesco di Giorgio Martini, 1470s, (b), (c) side and top views of the reconstructed model. Notice the floor pattern revealed in (b) but not being clearly visible in the painting itself.

5   Experimental Results

Due to lack of space, only three of the reconstruction experiments performed with the presented system are reported here. More results can be found online[1]. The first experiment was carried out with the aid of the 674×400 image shown in Fig. 1(a). The image is a 15th century painting that illustrates a typical example of Renaissance architecture and urban planning. The painting was executed using one point perspective, under which the sides of buildings recede towards the vanishing point, while all vertical and horizontal lines are drawn face on. Camera calibration assumed a natural camera with a fixed principal point and was based on the homography of a three by two rectangle formed by floor tiles. The sole finite vanishing point was estimated from the intersection of inwards oriented parallel lines provided by the user and, since the vanishing line of the ground plane is horizontal, sufficed to estimate it. The outlines of planes to be reconstructed were then interactively marked on the painting and plane parallelism/perpendicularity relationships were specified by the user. Despite that the vanishing line corresponding to the vertical walls cannot be estimated from image primitives, walls can be reconstructed by constraining them to be perpendicular to the floor. Following this, the reconstruction was carried out fully automatically. Owing to occlusions by the pillars in the foreground of the painting, the texture automatically mapped to certain floor areas was erroneous. Nevertheless, the texture of the floor was corrected through a series of texture manipulation operations that exploited regularity. Two views of the final textured VRML model are illustrated in Figs. 1(b) and (c).

The second experiment concerns the reconstruction of another painting, shown in Fig.2(a). In this case, calibration of an assumed natural camera was performed with the aid of the floor's metric homography, which was estimated postulating square tiles, and the two orthogonal vanishing points corresponding to the tile edges. The primary difficulty in reconstructing this image stems from the fact

---

[1] See http://www.ics.forth.gr/recover/results.php

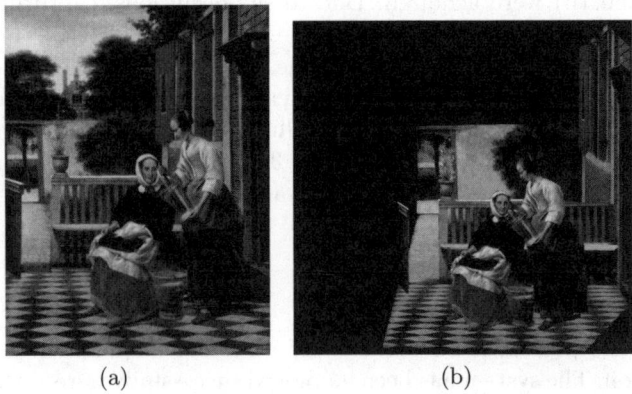

(a)   (b)

Fig. 2. (a) "A Mistress and Her Maid", Pieter de Hooch, 1660s, (b) view of the reconstructed 3D model. The red pyramid on the left corresponds to the painting's vantage point. The two humans and the flower pot on the background fence have been reconstructed as planar polygons with alpha textures saved in PNG format.

that it includes two human figures with complex shape, whose contours cannot be easily captured with polylines. To cope with such cases, alpha textures are employed. These are special texture maps, partly made up of normal color pixels and partly of transparent pixels. In the example at hand, human figures are reconstructed as planar billboards. The SVR system incorporates an interactive image cutout tool, which helps the user segment arbitrarily shaped regions by tracing their silhouettes using a small number of control points that are clicked with the mouse. Then, the texture of billboard regions that are outside the traced silhouette is made transparent, while those that are inside are made opaque and are textured normally. A view of the finished model is shown in Fig.2(b).

The third experiment is intended to demonstrate an atypical use of the developed system. More specifically, two disparate images of a building shown in

(a)   (b)   (c)

Fig. 3. (a), (b) Two views of the Adelaide House building, London. (c) top view of the 3D model reconstructed by stitching together the two partial models reconstructed from the images in (a) and (b). The left red pyramid corresponds to the estimated camera viewpoint for image (a) and the right for (b).

Figs. 3(a) and (b) were acquired. Due to self-occlusions, capturing the entire building with a single image is impossible, thus a complete 3D model cannot be reconstructed from a single image alone. However, partial 3D models reconstructed via SVR from individual images can be combined together, producing a more complete representation. This is illustrated in Fig. 3(c), where the two models obtained from the images of Figs. 3(a) and (b) have been merged after their difference in pose was estimated with an exterior orientation algorithm [19].

6   Conclusion

This paper has presented an overview of a system for interactive single view reconstruction. The system has been employed successfully to reconstruct several 3D models of diverse origins and types. After limited training, users have found it flexible and easy to use. From a technical viewpoint, the system's core calibration and reconstruction techniques have been implemented in ANSI C while its user interface has been developed as a plug-in for the Blender open-source 3D modeler using its native Python scripting.

References

1. Debevec, P., Taylor, C., Malik, J.: Modeling and Rendering Architecture from Photographs. In: Proc. of SIGGRAPH 1996, pp. 11–20 (1996)
2. Horry, Y., Anjyo, K., Arai, K.: Tour Into the Picture. In: Proc. of SIGGRAPH 1997, New York, USA, pp. 225–232 (1997)
3. Liebowitz, D., Criminisi, A., Zisserman, A.: Creating Architectural Models from Images. Computer Graphics Forum 18(3), 39–50 (1999)
4. Sturm, P., Maybank, S.: A Method for Interactive 3D Reconstruction of Piecewise Planar Objects from Single Images. In: Proc. of BMVC 1999, September 1999, pp. 265–274 (1999)
5. Grossmann, E., Ortin, D., Santos-Victor, J.: Single and multi-view reconstruction of structured scenes. In: Proc. of ACCV 2002, pp. 228–234 (2002)
6. Hoiem, D., Efros, A., Hebert, M.: Automatic Photo Pop-Up. In: Proc. of SIGGRAPH 2005, New York, USA, pp. 577–584 (2005)
7. Zhang, L., Dugas-Phocion, G., Samson, J., Seitz, S.: Single View Modeling of Free-Form Scenes. In: Proc. of CVPR 2001., vol. 1, pp. 990–997 (2001)
8. Hartley, R., Zisserman, A.: Multiple View Geometry in Computer Vision. Cambridge University Press, Cambridge (2000)
9. Liebowitz, D., Zisserman, A.: Metric Rectification for Perspective Images of Planes. In: Proc. of CVPR 1998, Santa Barbara, CA, June 1998, pp. 482–488 (1998)
10. Johnson, M., Farid, H.: Metric Measurements on a Plane from a Single Image. Technical Report 579, Dartmouth College (December 2006)
11. Caprile, B., Torre, V.: Using Vanishing Points for Camera Calibration. IJCV 4(2), 127–140 (1990)
12. Hartley, R.I., Kaucic, R.: Sensitivity of Calibration to Principal Point Position. In: Heyden, A., Sparr, G., Nielsen, M., Johansen, P. (eds.) ECCV 2002. LNCS, vol. 2351, pp. 433–446. Springer, Heidelberg (2002)

13. Liebowitz, D., Zisserman, A.: Combining Scene and Auto-calibration Constraints. In: Proc. of ICCV 1999, Kerkyra, Greece, September 1999, pp. 293–300 (1999)
14. Lourakis, M., Argyros, A.: Refining Single View Calibration With the Aid of Metric Scene Properties. WSCG Journal 15(1-3), 129–134 (2007)
15. Se, S.: Zebra-Crossing Detection for the Partially Sighted. In: Proc. of CVPR 2000, June 2000, pp. 211–217 (2000)
16. Nowak, U., Weimann, L.: A Family of Newton Codes for Systems of Highly Nonlinear Equations. Technical Report 91-10, ZIB Berlin (December 1991)
17. Criminisi, A., Perez, P., Toyama, K.: Region Filling and Object Removal by Exemplar-Based Image Inpainting. IEEE Trans. on IP 13(9), 1200–1212 (2004)
18. Efros, A., Freeman, W.: Image Quilting for Texture Synthesis and Transfer. In: Proc. of SIGGRAPH 2001, New York, NY, USA, pp. 341–346 (2001)
19. Horn, B.: Closed-Form Solution of Absolute Orientation Using Unit Quaternions. J. Optical Soc. Am. A 4(4), 629–642 (1987)

Monocular Omnidirectional Visual Odometry for Outdoor Ground Vehicles

Davide Scaramuzza and Roland Siegwart

Swiss Federal Institute of Technology Zurich (ETHZ)
Autonomous System Laboratory (ASL)
CH-8092, Zurich, Switzerland
{davide.scaramuzza,r.siegwart}@ieee.org
http://www.asl.ethz.ch

Abstract. This paper describes an algorithm for visually computing the ego-motion of a vehicle relative to the road under the assumption of planar motion. The algorithm uses only images taken by a single omnidirectional camera mounted on the roof of the vehicle. The front ends of the system are two different trackers. The first one is a homography-based tracker that detects and matches robust scale invariant features that most likely belong to the ground plane. The second one uses an appearance based approach and gives high resolution estimates of the rotation of the vehicle. This 2D pose estimation method has been successfully applied to videos from an automotive platform. We give an example of camera trajectory estimated purely from omnidirectional images over a distance of 400 meters. For performance evaluation, the estimated path is superimposed onto an aerial image. In the end, we use image mosaicing to obtain a textured 2D reconstruction of the estimated path.

Keywords: omnidirectional camera, visual odometry, vehicle ego-motion estimation, homography, SIFT features.

1   Introduction

Accurate estimation of the ego-motion of a vehicle relative to the road is a key component for autonomous driving and computer vision based driving assistance. Most of the work in estimating robot motion has been produced using stereo cameras and can be traced back to Moravec's work [1]. Similar work has been reported also elsewhere (see [2, 3]). Furthermore, stereo visual odometry has also been successfully used on Mars by the NASA rovers since early 2004 [4]. Nevertheless, visual odometry methods for outdoor applications have been also produced, which use a single camera alone. Very successful results have been obtained over long distances using either perspective or omnidirectional cameras (see [3,5]). In [3], the authors deal with the case of a stereo camera but they also provide a monocular solution implementing a structure from motion algorithm that takes advantage of the 5-point algorithm and RANSAC robust estimation [14]. In [5], the authors provide two approaches for monocular visual odometry

A. Gasteratos, M. Vincze, and J.K. Tsotsos (Eds.): ICVS 2008, LNCS 5008, pp. 206–215, 2008.

based on omnidirectional imagery. In the first approach, they use optical flow computation while in the second one structure from motion.

In our approach, we use a single calibrated omnidirectional camera mounted on the roof of the car (Fig. 3). We assume that the vehicle undergoes a purely two-dimensional motion over a predominant flat ground. Furthermore, because we want to perform visual odometry in city streets, flat terrains, as in well as in motorways where buildings or 3D structure are not always present, we estimate the motion of the vehicle by tracking the ground plane.

Ground plane tracking has been already exploited by the robotics community for indoor visual navigation and most works have been produced using standard perspective cameras ([6, 7, 8, 9]). In those works, the motion of the vehicle is estimated by using the property that the projection of the ground plane into two different camera views is related by a homography.

In this paper, we propose a similar approach for central omnidirectional cameras but our goal is to estimate the ego-motion of the vehicle in outdoor environments and over long distances. Thanks to the large field of view of the panoramic camera, SIFT keypoints [10] from the scene all around the car are extracted and matched between consecutive frames. After RANSAC based outlier removal [14], we use these features only to compute the translation in the heading direction. Conversely, to estimate the rotation angle of the vehicle we use an appearance based method. We show that by adding this second approach the result outperforms the pure feature based approach.

This paper is organized as follows. Section 2 describes our homography based ground plane navigation. Section 3 describes the appearance based method. Section 4 details the steps of the whole visual odometry algorithm. Finally, Section 5 is dedicated to the experimental results.

2   Homography Based Ground Plane Navigation

The motion information that can be extracted by tracking 2D features is central to our vehicle navigation system. Therefore, we briefly review here a method that uses planar constraints and point tracking to compute the motion parameters.

2.1   Homography and Planar Motion Parameters

Early work on exploiting coplanar relations has been presented by Tsai and Huang [11], Longuet-Higgins [12], and Faugeras and Lustman [13]. The coplanar relation between two different views of the same plane can be summarized as follows.

$$\lambda \mathbf{x_2} = \mathbf{K}(\mathbf{R} + \frac{\mathbf{Tn^T}}{h})\mathbf{K^{-1}x_1} = \mathbf{Hx_1} \tag{1}$$

where $\mathbf{R} \in SO(3)$ and $\mathbf{T} \in \mathbb{R}^3$ are the rotation and the translation matrices encoding the relative position of the two views; $\mathbf{n} \in \mathbb{R}^3$ is the plane normal and $h \in \mathbb{R}$ is the distance to the plane; $\mathbf{x_1}$, $\mathbf{x_2}$ are the images of the same scene points expressed in homogeneous coordinates ($[x, y, 1]^T$); $\mathbf{K}$ is a 3×3 matrix describing the camera intrinsic parameters; λ is a scalar; $\mathbf{H}$ is a 3×3 matrix called homography that relates the two camera projections of the same plane points. Note that matrix $\mathbf{K}$ in equation (1) is defined only for perspective cameras. However, in this paper we assume that our omnidirectional camera is already intrinsically calibrated and that the image points $\mathbf{x_1}$ and $\mathbf{x_2}$ are already normalized to have the third component equal to 1. This allows us to write $\mathbf{K} = \mathbf{I}$. If not stated otherwise, in the remainder of this paper we will assume that the image coordinates are always normalized. To calibrate our omnidirectional camera, we used the method proposed in [15].

In our experiments, we mounted the omnidirectional camera on the roof of the car (as in Fig. 3) with the z-axis of the mirror perpendicular to the ground plane (Fig. 4). By fixing the origin of our coordinate system in the center of projection of the omnidirectional camera (Fig. 4), we have that $\mathbf{n} = [0, 0, -1]^T$. The distance h of the origin to the ground plane can be manually measured.

2.2 Decomposing H

If a camera is internally calibrated, it is possible to recover $\mathbf{R}$, $\mathbf{T}$, and $\mathbf{n}$ from $\mathbf{H}$ up to at most a two-fold ambiguity. A linear method for decomposing $\mathbf{H}$ was originally developed by Wunderlich [17] and later reformulated by Triggs [18]. The algorithm of Triggs is based on the singular value decomposition of $\mathbf{H}$. The description of this method as well as its Matlab implementation can be found in [18]. This algorithm outputs two possible solutions for $\mathbf{R}$, $\mathbf{T}$, and $\mathbf{n}$ which are all internally self-consistent. In the general case, some false solutions can be eliminated by sign (visibility) tests or geometric constraints, while in our case we can disambiguate the solutions by choosing the one for which the computed plane normal $\mathbf{n}$ is closer to $[0, 0, -1]^T$. In the remainder of this paper, we will refer to this method as the "Triggs algorithm".

2.3 Non-linear Refinement

The solution given by the Triggs algorithm is obtained by a linear method that minimizes an algebraic distance which is not physically meaningful. We can refine it through maximum likelihood inference. The maximum likelihood estimate can be obtained by minimizing the following functional:

$$\min_{\theta, t_1, t_2} \sum_{i=1}^{n} \|\mathbf{x_1}^i - \hat{\mathbf{x}}_1^i(\mathbf{R}, \mathbf{T}, \mathbf{n})\|^2 + \|\mathbf{x_2}^i - \hat{\mathbf{x}}_2^i(\mathbf{R}, \mathbf{T}, \mathbf{n})\|^2, \qquad (2)$$

with $\hat{\mathbf{x}}_1 = \mathbf{H}^{-1}\mathbf{x_2}$ and $\hat{\mathbf{x}}_2 = \mathbf{H}\mathbf{x_1}$ according to equation (1). To minimize (2), we used the Levenberg-Marquadt algorithm. Furthermore, because we assume planar motion, we constraint the minimization so that the rotation is about the plane normal and the translation is parallel to the same plane.

2.4 Coplanarity Check

So far we have assumed that the corresponding image pairs x_1 and x_2 are correctly matched and that their correspondent scene points are coplanar. Even though in omnidirectional images taken from the roof of the car the ground plane is predominant, there are also many feature points that come from other objects than just the road, like cars, buildings, trees, guardrails, etc. Furthermore, there are also many unavoidable false matches that are more numerous than those usually output by SIFT on standard perspective images (about 20-30% according to [10]) because of the large distortion introduced by the mirror. To discard the outliers, we use the Random Sample Consensus paradigm (RANSAC) [14].

3 Visual Compass

In the previous session, we described how to use point features to compute the rotation and translation matrices. Unfortunately, when using features to estimate the motion, the resulting rotation is extremely sensitive to systematic errors due to the intrinsic calibration of the camera or the extrinsic calibration between the camera and the ground plane. This effect is even more accentuated with omnidirectional cameras due to the large distortion introduced by the mirror. In addition to this, integrating rotational information over the time has the major drawback of generally becoming less and less accurate as integration introduces additive errors at each step. An example of camera trajectory recovered using only the feature based approach described in Section 2 is depicted in Fig. 4.

To improve the accuracy of the rotation estimation, we use an appearance based approach. This approach was inspired by the work of Labrosse [16], which describes a method to use omnidirectional cameras as visual compass.

Directly using the appearance of the world as opposed to extracting features or structure of the world is attractive because methods can be devised that do not need precise calibration steps. Here, we describe how we implemented our visual compass.

For ease of processing, every omnidirectional image is unwrapped into cylindrical panoramas (Fig. 1). The unwrapping considers only the white region of the omnidirectional image that is depicted in Fig 2. We call these unwrapped versions "appearances". If the camera is perfectly vertical to the ground, then a pure rotation about its vertical axis will result in a simple column-wise shift of the appearance in the opposite direction. The exact rotation angle could then be retrieved by simply finding the best match between a reference image (before rotation) and a column-wise shift of the successive image (after rotation). The best shift is directly related to the rotation angle undertaken by the camera. In the general motion, translational information is also present. This general case will be discussed later.

The input to our rotation estimation scheme is thus made of appearances that need to be compared. To compare them, we use the Euclidean distance. The

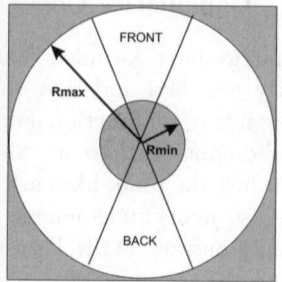

Fig. 1. Two unwrapped omnidirectional images taken at consecutive time stamps. For reasons of space, here only one half of the whole 360 *deg* is shown. The red line indicates the horizon.

Fig. 2. The cylindrical panorama is obtained by unwrapping the white region

Euclidean distance between two appearances I_i and I_j, with I_j being column-wise shifted (with column wrapping) by α pixels, is:

$$d(I_i, I_j, \alpha) = \sqrt{\sum_{k=1}^{h} \sum_{h=1}^{w} \sum_{l=1}^{c} |I_i(k, h, l) - I_j(k, h - \alpha, l)|^2} \tag{3}$$

where $h \times w$ is the image size, and c is the number of color components. In our experiments, we used the RGB color space, thus having three color components per pixel.

If α_m is the best shift that minimizes the distance between two appearances I_i and I_j, the rotation angle $\Delta\vartheta$ (in degrees) between I_i and I_j can be computed as:

$$\Delta\vartheta = \alpha_m \cdot \frac{360}{w} \tag{4}$$

The width w of the appearance is the width of the omnidirectional image after unwrapping and can be chosen arbitrarily. In our experiments, we used $w = 360$, that means the angular resolution was 1 pixel per degree. To increase the resolution to 0.1 *deg*, we used cubic spline interpolation with 0.1 pixel precision. We also tried larger image widths but we did not get any remarkable improvement in the final result. Thus, we used $w = 360$ as the unwrapping can be done in a negligible amount of time.

The distance minimization in (3) makes sense only when the camera undergoes a pure rotation about its vertical axis, as a rotation corresponds to a horizontal shift in the appearance. In the real case, the vehicle is moving and translational component is present. However, the "pure rotation" assumption still holds if the camera undergoes small displacements or the distance to the objects (buildings, tree, etc.) is big compared to the displacement. In the other cases, this assumption does not hold for the whole image but an improvement that can be done over the theoretical method is to only consider parts of the images, namely the front and back part (Fig. 2). Indeed, the contribution to the optical flow by the motion of the camera is not homogeneous in omnidirectional images; a forward/backward translation mostly contributes in the regions corresponding to the sides of the camera and very little in the parts corresponding to the front and back of the camera, while the rotation contributes equally everywhere.

Because we are interested in extracting the rotation information, only considering the regions of the images corresponding to the front and back of the camera allows us to reduce most of the problems introduced by the translation, in particular sudden changes in appearance (parallax).

According to the last considerations, in our experiments we use a reduced Field Of View (FOV) around the front and back of the camera (Fig. 2). A reduced field of view of about 30 *deg* around the front part is shown by the white window in Fig. 1. Observe that, besides reducing the FOV of the camera in the horizontal plane, we operate a reduction of the FOV also in the vertical plane, in particular under the horizon line. The objective is to reduce the influence of the changes in appearance of the road. The resulting vertical FOV is 50 *deg* above and 10 *deg* below the horizon line (the horizon line is indicated in red in Fig. 1).

4   Motion Estimation Algorithm

As we already mentioned, the appearance based approach provides rotation angle estimates that are more reliable and stable than those output by the pure feature based approach. Here, we describe how we combined the rotation angle estimates of Section 3 with the camera translation estimates of Section 2.

In our experiments, the speed of the vehicle ranged between 10 and 20 Km/h while the images were constantly captured at 10 Hz. This means that the distance covered between two consecutive frames ranged between 0.3 and 0.6 meters. For this short distance, the kinematic model of the camera configuration (x, y, θ), which contains its 2D position (x,y) and orientation θ, can be approximated in this way:

$$\begin{cases} x_{i+1} = x_i + \delta\rho_i \cos\theta \\ y_{i+1} = y_i + \delta\rho_i \sin\theta \\ \theta_{i+1} - \theta_i + \delta\theta_i \end{cases} \tag{5}$$

where we use $\delta\rho = |\mathbf{T}| \, h$ and $\delta\theta = \Delta\vartheta$. $|\mathbf{T}|$ is the length of the translation vector; h is the scale factor (i.e. in our case this is the height of the camera to the ground plane). The camera rotation angle $\Delta\vartheta$ is computed as in (4). Observe that we did not use at all the rotation estimates provided by the feature based method of Section 2.

Now, let us resume the steps of our motion estimation scheme, which have been detailed in Section 2 and 3. Our omnidirectional visual odometry operates as follows:

1. Acquire two consecutive frames. Consider only the region of the omnidirectional image, which is between *Rmin* and *Rmax* (Fig. 2).
2. Extract and match SIFT features between the two frames. Use the double consistency check to reduce the number of outliers. Then, use the calibrated camera model to normalize the feature coordinates.

3. Use RANSAC to reject points that are not coplanar (Section 2.4).
4. Apply the Triggs algorithm followed by non-linear refinement described in Section 2 to estimate $\mathbf{R}$ and $\mathbf{T}$ from the remaining inliers.
5. Unwrap the two images and compare them using the appearance method described in Section 3. In particular, minimize (3), with reduced field of view, to compute the column-wise shift α_m between the appearances and use (4) to compute the rotation angle $\Delta\vartheta$.
6. Use $\delta\rho = |\mathbf{T}|\,h$ and $\delta\theta = \Delta\vartheta$ and integrate the motion using (5).
7. Repeat from step 1.

5   Results

The approach proposed in this paper has been successfully tested on a real vehicle equipped with a central omnidirectional camera. A picture of our vehicle (a Smart) is shown in Fig 3.

Our omnidirectional camera, composed of a hyperbolic mirror (KAIDAN 360 One VR) and a digital color camera (SONY XCD-SX910, image size 640 × 480 pixels), was installed on the front part of the roof of the vehicle. The frames were grabbed at 10 Hz and the vehicle speed ranged between 10 and 20 Km/h.

The resulting path estimated by our visual odometry algorithm using a horizontal reduced FOV of 10 *deg* is shown in figures 4, 5, and 6. Our ground truth is a aerial image of the same test environment provided by Google Earth (Fig. 5). The units used in the three figures are in meters.

In this experiment, the vehicle was driven along a 400 meter long loop and returned to its starting position (pointed to by the yellow arrow in Fig. 5). The estimated path is indicated with red dots in Fig. 5 and is shown superimposed on the aerial image for comparison. The final error at the loop closure is about 6.5 meters. This error is due to the unavoidable visual odometry drift; however, observe that the trajectory is very well estimated until the third 90-degree turn.

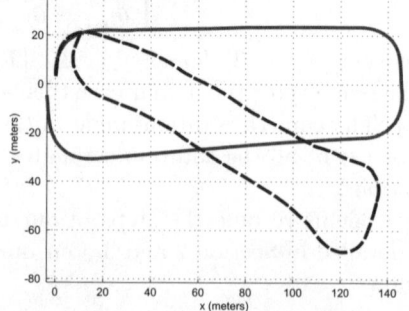

Fig. 3. Our vehicle with the omnidirectional camera (blue circle). The field of view is indicated by the red lines.

Fig. 4. Comparison between the standard feature based approach (dashed blue) and the approach combining features with visual compass proposed in this paper (red)

Fig. 5. The estimated path superimposed onto a Google Earth image of the test environment. The scale is shown at the lower left corner.

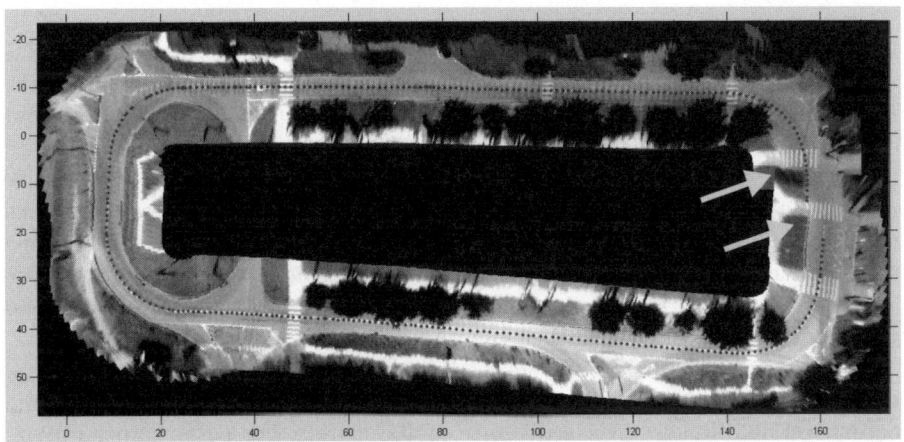

Fig. 6. Image mosaicing that shows a textured 2D reconstruction of the estimated path. The two arrows point out the final error at the loop closure (the pedestrian crossing pointed to by the cyan arrow should theoretically coincide with that pointed to by the yellow arrow).

After the third turn, the estimated path deviates smoothly from the expected path instead of continuing straight. After road inspection, we found that this deviation was due to three 0.3 meter tall road humps (pointed to by the cyan arrow in Fig. 5) that violate the planar motion assumption.

The content of Fig. 6 is very important as it allows us to evaluate the quality of motion estimation. In this figure, we show a textured top viewed 2D reconstruction of the whole path. Observe that this image is not an aerial image but is an image mosaicing. Every input image of this mosaic was obtained by an Inverse Perspective Mapping (IPM) of the original omnidirectional image onto an horizontal plane. After being undistorted through IPM, these images have been merged together using the 2D poses estimated by our visual odometry algorithm. The estimated trajectory of the camera is shown superimposed with red dots. If you visually and carefully compare the mosaic (Fig. 6) with the corresponding aerial image (Fig. 5), you will recognize in the mosaic the same elements that are present in the aerial image, that is, trees, white footpaths, pedestrian crossings, roads' placement, etc. Furthermore, you can verify that the location of these elements in the mosaic fits well the location of the same elements in the aerial image.

As we mentioned already in Section 3, the fact of reducing the field of view allows us to reduce most of the problems introduced by the translation, like sudden changes in parallax. We found that the best performance in terms of closeness to the ground truth is obtained when FOV=10 *deg*. This choice was a good compromise between accuracy and sensitivity to calibration errors.

6   Conclusion

In this paper, we described an algorithm for computing the ego-motion of a vehicle relative to the road under planar motion assumption. As only input, the algorithm uses images provided by a single omnidirectional camera. The front ends of the system are two different methods. The first one is a pure feature based method that implements the standard Triggs algorithm to compute the relative motion between two frames. The second one is an appearance based approach which gives high resolution estimates of the rotation angle of the vehicle. Using the first method to compute the vehicle displacement in the heading direction and the second one to compute the vehicle rotation proved to give very good visual odometry estimates against the pure feature based standard method.

The proposed algorithm was successfully applied to videos from an automotive platform. We gave an example of camera trajectory estimated purely from omnidirectional images over a distance of 400 meters. For performance evaluation, the estimated path was superimposed onto a aerial image of the same test environment and a textured 2D reconstruction of the path was done.

Acknowledgment

The research leading to these results has received funding from the European Commission Division FP6-IST Future and Emerging Technologies under the contract FP6-IST-027140 (BACS). The authors would also like to say thanks to Dr. Pierre Lamon and Luciano Spinello for their useful helps, suggestions, and discussions.

References

1. Moravec, H.: Obstacle Avoidance and Navigation in the Real World by a Seeing Robot Rover. PhD thesis, Stanford University (1980)
2. Jung, I., Lacroix, S.: Simultaneous localization and mapping with stereovision. In: Robotics Research: The 11th International Symposium (2005)
3. Nister, D., Naroditsky, O., Bergen, J.: Visual odometry for ground vehicle applications. Journal of Field Robotics (2006)
4. Maimone, M., Cheng, Y., Matthies, L.: Two years of visual odometry on the mars exploration rovers: Field reports. Journal of Field Robotics 24(3), 169–186 (2007)
5. Corke, P.I., Strelow, D., Singh, S.: Omnidirectional visual odometry for a planetary rover. In: IROS (2004)
6. Wang, H., Yuan, K., Zou, W., Zhou, Q.: Visual odometry based on locally planar ground assumption. In: IEEE International Conference on Information Acquisition, pp. 59–64 (2005)
7. Ke, Q., Kanade, T.: Transforming camera geometry to a virtual downward-looking camera: Robust ego-motion estimation and ground-layer detection. In: CVPR 2003 (June 2003)
8. Guerrero, J.J., Martinez-Cantin, R., Sagues, C.: Visual map-less navigation based on homographies. Journal of Robotic Systems 22(10), 569–581 (2005)
9. Liang, B., Pears, N.: Visual navigation using planar homographies. In: IEEE ICRA, pp. 205–210 (2002)
10. Lowe, D.: Distinctive image features from scale-invariant keypoints. International Journal of Computer Vision 20, 91–110 (2003)
11. Tsai, R., Huang, T.: Estimating three-dimensional motion parameters of a rigid planar patch. IEEE Trans. Acoustics, Speech and Signal Processing 29(6), 1147–1152 (1981)
12. Longuet-Higgins, H.C.: The reconstruction of a plane surface from two perspective projections. Royal Society London 277, 399–410 (1986)
13. Faugeras, O.D., Lustman, F.: Motion and structure from motion in a piecewise planar environment. International Journal of Pattern Recognition and Artificial Inteligence (3), 485–508 (1988)
14. Fischler, M.A., Bolles, R.C.: Random sample consensus: a paradigm for model fitting with applications to image analysis and automated cartography. Commun. ACM 24(6), 381–395 (1981)
15. Scaramuzza, D., Martinelli, A., Siegwart, R.: A flexible technique for accurate omnidirectional camera calibration and structure from motion. In: ICVS (january 2006)
16. Labrosse, F.: The visual compass: performance and limitations of an appearance-based method. Journal of Field Robotics 23(10), 913–941 (2006)
17. Wunderlich, W.: Rechnerische Rekonstruktion eines ebenen Objekts aus zwei Photographien. Mitteilungen der geodaetischen Institute, TU Graz 40, 365–377 (1982)
18. Triggs, B.: Autocalibration from planar scenes. In: Burkhardt, H.-J., Neumann, B. (eds.) ECCV 1998. LNCS, vol. 1406, pp. 89–105. Springer, Heidelberg (1998)

Eyes and Cameras Calibration for 3D World Gaze Detection

Stefano Marra and Fiora Pirri

Sapienza, University of Rome "Sapienza"
Dipartimento di Informatica e Sistemistica (DIS), via Ariosto 25, 00185, Roma

Abstract. Gaze tracking is a promising research area with application that goes from advanced human machine interaction systems, to human attention processes studying, modeling and use in cognitive vision fields. In this paper we propose a novel approach for the calibration and use of a head mounted dual eye gaze tracker. Key aspects are a robust pupil tracking algorithm based on prediction from infrared LED purkinje image position, and a new gaze localization method based on trifocal geometry considerations.

1 Introduction

Human gaze tracking has been used since a long time as a key tool to study human cognitive processes and mainly attention. Only in recent years, the development of non intrusive eye trackers, based on eye observation, through cameras, has made it accessible to a large range of applications in cognitive vision, such as human machine interaction or human behavior simulation by autonomous robots.

In this paper we propose a methodology for the detection and localization in space of human fixations, based on a head mounted three dimensional gaze tracker. This makes possible to study the human gaze in 3D space in full mode, that is, taking into account core aspects of visual search, such depth, directions, velocity and occlusion, just to mention few of them. Therefore the proposed system is very promising for cognitive vision.

Within the class of non invasive eye trackers, head mounted ones are more convenient than the remotely located ones (see [1] for a comparison), being more accurate and enabling gaze estimation with less constraints.

Eye gaze estimation systems are a combination of a pupil center detection algorithm and an homography or polynomial mapping between pupil positions and points on a screen observed by the user [2]. Since there is no real 3D gaze estimation, but just a bidimensional mapping, the user must stand still in front of the screen during the experiment. Recently this method was applied on a head mounted tracker [3] projecting the gaze direction on the image of a camera facing the scene. However the nature of the homography transformation makes an exact mapping possible only for points lying on the calibration plane (unless the optical center coincides with the camera projection center). Therefore there is an error, not taken into account in the mentioned work [3], proportional to the distance of the observed point from this plane. Other methods include pupil and corneal reflection tracking [4], dual Purkinje image tracking [5] or scleral coil searching [6].

A. Gasteratos, M. Vincze, and J.K. Tsotsos (Eds.): ICVS 2008, LNCS 5008, pp. 216–227, 2008.
© Springer-Verlag Berlin Heidelberg 2008

Three dimensional gaze direction estimation, instead, requires to determine the eye position with respect to the camera framing it. This process usually needs a preliminary calibration step where eye geometry is computed using a simplified eye model [7]. Majority of systems of this kind is composed of one or more cameras pointing to a subject looking to a screen, where fixation points are projected [8]. These methods, unlike bidimensional ones, allow the user to move, as long as the subject remains in the camera field of view. At every frame gaze vectors, and their intersection with the screen, are calculated in the camera reference system (using stereo camera, infrared led glint, Purkinje images, and the techniques mentioned for 2D case). Therefore other calibration tasks are often necessary in order to reckon up screen and leds position in the camera reference frame. The method proposed here, is an hybrid combination of bidimensional and threedimensional gaze trackers. It is based on a mapping between pupils position and user fixation coordinates on a camera pointing the scene, but allows the user to move in the world and move the gaze in every direction (not just at a fixated depth). The advantages, over the existing methods, are:

- Fixed position between cameras and user head, so all system parameters can be determined during the calibration stage (valid for all head mounted trackers).
- Easy calibration procedure that doesn't require the user to stand still, and look to a N-point known target.
- Novel pupil tracking method more robust to illumination changes.
- Problem reduction to a three views system, and application of standard trifocal geometry methods for its solution.

2   System Description

The system used in our experiments is composed of a helmet where two cameras, in stereo configuration for scene acquisition, and two CMOS eye-cameras for eye tracking (see Figure 1) are rigidly mounted. Each eye-camera provides two infrared LEDs, disposed along X and Y axes near the camera center (see [9] for details). All cameras were precalibrated using the well known Zhang camera calibration algorithm [10] for intrinsic parameters determination and lens distortion correction. Extrinsic and rectification parameters for stereo camera were computed, likewise standard stereo correlation and triangulation algorithms, used for scene depth estimation. An inertial sensor is attached to the system: in future development it will be used for accurate threedimensional localization, and to build a metric map of user fixations. Software for camera acquisition, image undistortion and depth estimation was written in C++ to allow real time logging of four simultaneous video streams. System acquires data at a frame rate of 15 Hz. Remaining software uses a mix of C++ and Matlab routines for calibration parameters computation and offline gaze estimation.

3   System Calibration

At the user level the calibration stage (preliminary to the acquisition) is composed of two consecutive phases: in the first one the user observe the two CMOS camera centre.

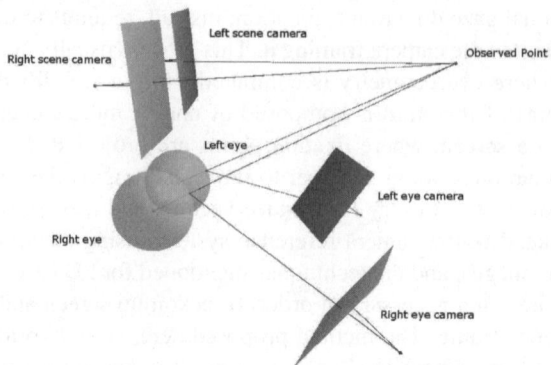

Fig. 1. Tracker camera configuration. Scene cameras are calibrated for stereo depth estimation. Eye cameras are CMOS camera with two LEDs each, for pupil tracking.

In the second one he is required to continuously observe a fixated punctiform target while moving. The entire process lasts about 15-20 seconds and afterwards starts the real acquisition (without break between calibration and acquisition stage).

This process allows both the initialization of kalman filtering for pupil tracking (see Section 4), and the determination of the parameters for the reprojection of the human gaze, on the scene cameras images (see next section).

3.1   Gaze Projection on Scene Camera

In this section we show how it is possible to consider the two eye-cameras and one of the scene camera, as a system of three cameras with a common field of view, and use trifocal geometry consideration to reproject user fixation on the scene camera image. In Figure 2 is given a bidimensional representation of a possible configuration of the eye-camera with respect to the user eye. In particular we show how we have obtained the model transforming the eye into the ideal image I_e.

Independently of the models considered for the corneal shape (see [11]) we shall consider the spherical surface S formed by the sequence of corneal vertices at the point of the line of sight (i.e. at the point corresponding to the pupil center p). Referring to Figure 2, the only information we have (as we'll see in next section) is the position of the pupil centre projection on the eye camera image (which we denote p_c, as it is referred to the distortion point d_c, see Figure 2). Our goal is the estimation of the point x_e, projection of the observed point X_w on the ideal camera image I_e. I_e is constructed taking the tangential plane to S, at the corneal vertex where the eye-camera observation axis coincides with the pupillary axis (see Section 4). Proceeding backwards x_e can be obtained from p_e through:

$$x_e = \frac{rp_e}{\sqrt{r^2 - p_e^2}} \, . \tag{1}$$

Here $p_e \simeq r \sin(\alpha)$.

The image I'_e is just a scaled version of image I_e (where the scale factor depends on the distance between the eye and eye-camera) and p'_e can be obtained from p_c knowing

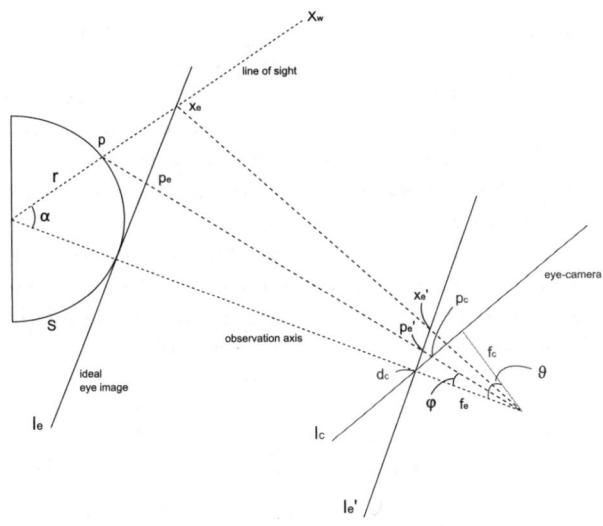

Fig. 2. Constrution of the ideal eye image I_e from the eye-camera image I_c

the focal length f_c of the eye-camera, and the angle θ between the observation axis and the eye-camera optical axis. Indeed p_c with respect to the distortion centre d_c (that is the position of the pupil centre on the eye-camera image when the user fixate the camera, acquired during the calibration sequence) has the sequent expression:

$$p_c = f_c \tan(\theta) - f_c \tan(\theta - \phi) \tag{2}$$

where $f_c \tan(\theta)$ is the distance between the eye-camera image centre and the distortion centre. Since $p'_e = f_e \tan(\phi) = \frac{f_c}{\cos(\theta)} \tan(\phi)$ after some trigonometric expansions we obtain the sequent expression for p'_e with respect to p_c:

$$p'_e = \frac{p_c}{\frac{1}{\cos(\theta)} - \frac{p_c}{f_c} \sin(\theta)} \cdot \tag{3}$$

So given the coordinate of the pupil centre in the eye-camera camera image we proceed thorough the following step for retrieving the projection of the observed point on the image I'_e of a ideal pinhole camera facing the scene:

-   Compute the coordinate p_c of the pupil centre with respect to the distortion center d_c.
-   Given f_c and θ calculate from p_c the position p'_e of p on camera perpendicular to the observation axis using (3).
-   Compute the corrected coordinate x'_e from p'_e applying (1) (but with r scaled).

Making these remarks for both eyes we can consider a system composed of three cameras, made up of the two virtual eye cameras (whose coordinates are computed from the ones of the eye-cameras, as just seen) and one world camera.

Goal of this calibration phase is the identification of a transformation that, given gaze projections on the eye virtual images, returns the corresponding point on the scene camera image. This task can be accomplished computing the trifocal tensor, an object that encapsulate all the geometric relations between three views. It consists of 27 elements generally expressed as a 3x3x3 cube of numbers. Considering slices on different direction of this cube allows to obtain parameters such the six epipoles or the three fundamental matrix between views [12].

Without using tensor notation (that would made this exposition dull reading, with no meaningfulness advantages), the trifocal tensor T can be expressed as a set of three 3x3 matrices $\{T_1, T_2, T_3\}$. A common way for its determination is considering corresponding points between the three images $\{I, I', I''\}$: each triple of points $\{x, x', x''\}$ must satisfy the following relation (called point-point-point trilinearity:

$$[x']_\times \left(\sum_i x_i T_i \right) [x'']_\times = 0_{3x3} \tag{4}$$

where $[\ ]_\times$ is the skew symmetric operator. This gives a total of nine equations (four independent), where the unknown quantities are the tensor elements. Therefore at least seven points correspondences are necessary for a direct numerical solution. Afterwards a better solution can be found ensuring that the trifocal tensor is geometrically valid. In our work we use the normalized linear algorithm and algebraic minimization algorithm exposed by Hartley and Zisserman in [13]. The determination of point correspondences for trifocal tensor computation is completely automated: for every frame of the calibration sequence pupil centers are extracted from the eye-camera images through the algorithm presented in next section, and observed point in the scene camera are extracted through tracking of the calibration target. The parameters for eye-camera coordinate correction (θ, f_c and r) are computed, from an initial estimate, through bundle adjustment, minimizing reprojection error, namely the distance between the points transferred through the trifocal tensor, and their ground truth corresponding to the positions of the calibration target on the scene camera image. Point with a high residual are discarded during this process to avoid that possible wrong correspondences (e.g. tracking failure), influence the result.

Once the trifocal tensor T has been obtained, it can be used to transfer points between views: given the line of sight projections $\{x, x'\}$ on the virtual eyes images, the corresponding point x'' on the world camera image can be found using the method outlined in [13] for point transfer using trifocal tensor. First, the fundamental matrix F_{21} between virtual views is found:

$$F_j = [e_2]_\times T_j e_3 \qquad \text{for } j = \{1..3\} \tag{5}$$

where e_2 and e_3 are the epipoles in second and third image corresponding to camera centre of first virtual view, also extracted from the trifocal tensor, and F_j is the j-th column of F_{21}. Then the epipolar line on I' corresponding to x, and the perpendicular to this line through x' are computed by:

$$l'_e = F_{21} x$$
$$l' = (l'_{e_2}, -l'_{e_1}, -x'_1 l'_{e_2} + x'_2 l'_{e_1}) \ .$$

Finally x'' is obtained resolving equations given by point-line-point trilinearity:

$$l'^T \left(\sum_i x_i T_i \right) [x'']_\times = \mathbf{0}^T \ . \tag{6}$$

We refer to [13] for a more detailed description.

Output of this process are the coordinates of the observed point in one of the scene camera image. By now depth estimation is demanded to stereo correlation algorithm. A possible extension could be the use of two trifocal tensor (one for the left scene camera and one for the right one) for coordinates determination on both scene images. More interesting could be the application of quadrifocal tensor [14], for the geometric modeling of all the four views in a unique consistent object.

4   Eye Auto-calibration

In this section we present a method for finding the pupils center automatically, hence it can be used on-line without any external intervention on the eye images. We only require that the subject at the beginning of the experiments, having worn the described machine (see Section 2), points the gaze for 3sec to the right eye-camera and then for 3sec to the left eye-camera. Because the images are acquired at 15Hz this gives approximately 90 frames to automatically estimate the eye region and the initial pupil centers. This step is sufficient to ensure to find the center of the pupil in each subsequent frame during the experiment. Note that eye rotations can reach a maximum of 60° in the direction of the nose and a maximum of 105° on the temporal side (see [15]). The eye needs only two parameters to be fully described, the value of the angle of torsion being fixed for given yaw and pitch (see Donder's law [16]).

To find the center of the pupil we use both the line of sight (joining the fixation point on the eye-camera center and the center of the entrance pupil, see Figure 3), through the visible pupil, and the pupillary axis which is made coincide with the observation axis (see [15]), that is, the eye-camera optical axis.

Because the eye is fixating the eye-camera, and the pupillary axis coincides with the observation axis (see [15]), the two *leds* at the x and y axes of the eye-camera project two Purkinje images on ideal x and y axes centered in the pupil center, see Figure 3. Let us define this reciprocal position of the pupil, and the origin of the Purkinje coordinates reflecting the *leds*, the *base* position C_b, as projected on the eye-image plane E.

During the mentioned 3sec at the beginning of the experiment the eye is fixating the eye-camera, still the pupil is subject to small movements and the detection of these movements make it possible to finding the center of the pupil, and hence to define a mask that includes the eye region discarding the background. More specifically, consider the 90 frames; given the Hessian matrix of the whole intensity image E and its determinant and trace, according to [17], we obtain an image U_t with the corners highlighted. Since the pupil is subject to slight movements, then $U_t - U_{t-1}$ will result in an image H_t which is everywhere zero but where the salient points, that is the pupil and the iris, have moved. Tracking the displacement of the salient pixels allows to both identify the center of the pupil and to determine when the pupil rotates to switch towards the left camera. Now, when the eyes fixate the right camera the left eye is completely rotated towards the nose, because the two eye-cameras are at a distance of less than 20cm and analogously when the eye are fixating the left camera the right eye is rotated in the nasal direction. From these positions, and the associated motion, it is possible to obtain both the center of the pupils and the maximal rotation in the nasal direction, which allows to define the mask for the eye region, centered in the center of the pupil in the *base* position C_b, i.e. looking at the camera lens.

This initial phase is followed by a phase in which the eyes are rotated purposefully towards a selected point, to calibrate the whole machine, this has been described in Section 3.

Because the subject can move and freely observe any spot in the real world the pupil is affected by light changes. Light is specularly reflected at the four major refracting surfaces of the eye (anterior and posterior cornea and anterior and posterior lens), forming images reflected by the pupil. For example, in the central image of Figure 3 it is possible to see the reflection of a window, and during outdoor experiments the light reflects on the pupil and the iris forming images. Therefore, when eye rotations have to be tracked to obtain the pupil center, in open space, the usual methods like the bright and dark eye, induced by the leds, cannot be taken into account. Moreover the first Purkinge image can be confused with other corneal reflections and cannot be considered as the brightest points appearing on the iris or pupil, as some authors claim. And because of the corneal asphericity, the first Purkinje image cannot be considered properly a convex mirror reflection as, in fact, the Purkinje image significantly rotates in the same direction of the eye, even from the same observation axis.

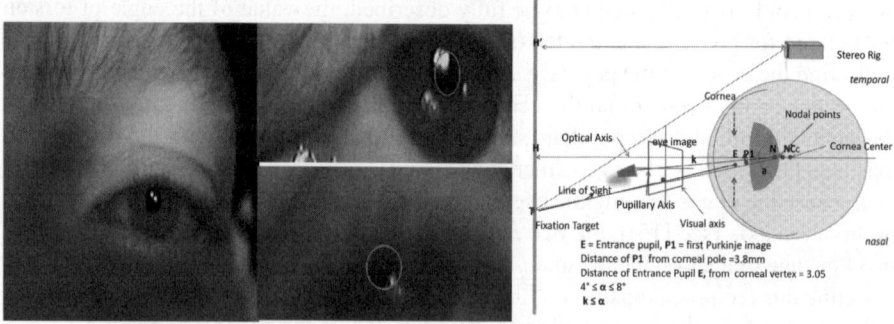

Fig. 3. The left image shows the collineation of the first Purkinje image with the observation axis (eye-camera optical axis) during geometric calibration. In the center the estimated pupil shape and the pupil center. On the right the eye-system schema.

4.1 Pupil Light Calibration and Tracking

In this section we discuss the steps we have taken for tracking the pupil center, and the results obtained, however many details will be omitted. In the initial phase, i.e. when the two first Purkinje images are seen in the image plane of the eye-camera in the center of the pupil (see the first image in Figure 3) with camera and pupillary axes coinciding, we have obtained the pupil center in base position $C_b(t_0)$ (the first 6sec are casted into t_0) and a mask $\mathbf{M} = E(C_{b_x} - m, C_{b_y} - k)$, $k < m$, E the image of the eye.

From experiments with eye-rotations computed in front of a calibration board of 81 squares projected on the wall and allowing for ample pitch and yaw eye rotations, it turns out that, the center of the pupil at time t can be estimated from the Purkinje positions at time t and $t-1$ and the previous pupil center. Let $PI(t) = [x_{pk}(t) \ y_{pk}(t)]$ and $PI(t-1)$ be the Purkinje positions on the image, at time step t ND $t-1$; let

$$c_{pup}(t-1) = [x_{pup}(t-1) \ y_{pup}(t-1)] \tag{7}$$

be the pupil center at time $t-1$ and

$$\theta = \tan^{-1}\left(\frac{\Delta y_{pk}(t)}{\Delta x_{pk}(t)}\right) \tag{8}$$

the angle formed by the the line through the points $PI(t)$ and $PI(t-1)$ and the x-axis whose ideal center is the pupil center in *base* position. Let $d_{cC}(t-1) = d(c(t-1), C_b(t_0))$, that is, the distance between the pupil center, on the image, at time $t-1$ and the center in base position C_b, at time t_0, and let $d_{PI}(t) = d(PI(t), PI(t-1))$, the distance between the Purkinje images at time t and $t-1$. On the basis of the mentioned experiments in with a projected board for calibrating eye-rotations, we define:

$$\mathbf{H} = \begin{pmatrix} 1.22 & 0.01 \\ 1.1 & 0.082 \end{pmatrix}$$

$$\mathbf{R} = \begin{pmatrix} \sin(\theta) & \cos(\theta) \\ 2\cos(\theta)\exp\left(-\frac{d_{cC}(t-1)}{d_{PI}(t)}\right) & \sin(\theta) \end{pmatrix} \tag{9}$$

$$\mathbf{D} = d_{PI}(t)\mathbf{I}_{2\times2}$$

Then

$$\begin{pmatrix} y_{pup}(t) \\ x_{pup}(t) \end{pmatrix} \approx \begin{pmatrix} y_{pup}(t-1) \\ x_{pup}(t-1) \end{pmatrix} + diag(\mathbf{HRD}) \tag{10}$$

The process is initialized at time t_0 with the pupil center coincident with the PI position, because the pupil is in *base* position, i.e. at C_b. The pupil center coordinates predicted according to the above equation, are affected by an error due to the different corneal asphericity of each subject. Let $f(c_{pup}(t-1), \mathbf{u}_{pk}(t-1))$ be the above function computing a plausible pupil center at time t and let $\mathbf{w}$ be the error due to corneal asphericity. The error is Gaussian with mean zero and covariance estimated during the first 6sec as $||\epsilon||^2/(n-2)$, with ϵ the distance between the pupil position and the PI, at frame i, and n the number of frames. Then:

$$c_{pup}(t) = f(c_{pup}(t-1), \mathbf{u}_{pk}(t-1)) + \mathbf{w} \tag{11}$$

Therefore at each time step a plausible pupil center $c_{pup}(t)$ is predicted as above. This hypothesis accounts for a region around $c_{pup}(t)$ to be extracted in order to re-estimate the center according to two criteria based on the image intensity, as specified below.

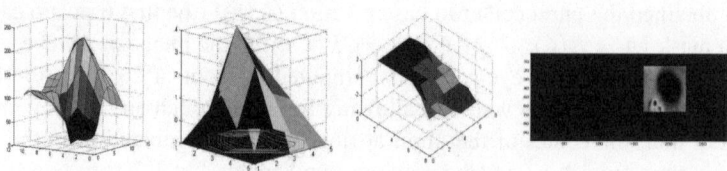

Fig. 4. Purkinje shape, first image, wavelet-like filter, second and third image and convolution of the eye image with the filter

We have noted above that specularly reflected light is image forming. However the Purkinje images (PI) generated by the leds positioned on the x and y axis of the eye-camera (see Section 2) are always visible, with varying intensity and at different positions, but when the eye is blinking. We have also noted that the PI are displaced in the same direction of the eye, because of corneal asphericity. However, the PI shape depends mostly on the led distance and the light conditions, but not on corneal asphericity. The shape of a PI is represented in Figure 4, where the third dimension is luminosity, the shape can be more or less elongated. Following the ideas of (Viola [18] and Leinhart et Al. [19]) we have defined a wavelet-like feature to extract these corneal reflections.

Given the center C_b obtained in *base* position and the mask $\mathbf{M} = E(C_{b_x} - m, C_{b_y} - k)$, $k < m$, obtained in the first phase (6sec), a Purkinje window 11×11 and a pupil window 21×21 are extracted. The two windows are re-sampled to obtain the smaller windows 5×5 and 11×11. Rescaling them with $W_k/max(W_k)$, $k \in \{5, 11\}$ and imposing for their functions $f_i^Q(.), Q \in \{pup, PI\}$ and the constraints functions $g_i(.)$:

$$g_i(W_k) = 1, \text{ and } \Delta(f_i^Q(W_k) + \lambda(g_i(W_k) - 1)) = 0$$

from each contour line i of the rescaled functions, with the z dimension, in f, given by the light, it is possible to obtain (but we do not describe here the method) the two wavelet-like filters represented in Figure 4. These features are used as follows. Given the estimated position of $PI(t - 1)$ the position of $PI(t)$ is estimated by the convolution $\mathbf{M} * f^{PI}(W_5)$, that maximizes the values of the corneal regions which have PI-like reflections. This, together with adequate constraints necessary to ascertain the distance and the angle between $PI(t - 1)$ and the discerned $PI(t)$, according to equation (11), obtain the estimated pupil center $c_{pup}(t)$. Given $c_{pup}(t)$ and the mask $\mathbf{M}$ the convolution $\mathbf{M} * f^{pup}(W_7)$ maximizes the values of the corneal regions having pupil like intensity. An ellipse is fitted in these regions with maximal values and the center of the ellipse is accounted for the new pupil center $c'_{pup}(t)$.

Since the pupil, in appropriate light conditions, is the darkest region of the image of the eye, it is rather useful to add a specific intensity criterion, which either returns the pupil region or nothing. The second intensity criterion is based on the mixture of probabilistic principal component analyzers (see [20]), which is a variant of the mixture of Gaussian. In $PPCA$ the covariance Σ_k of each k-th class is constrained as follows:

$$Q_k = H_k^\top H_k + \sigma_k^2 \mathbf{I}$$

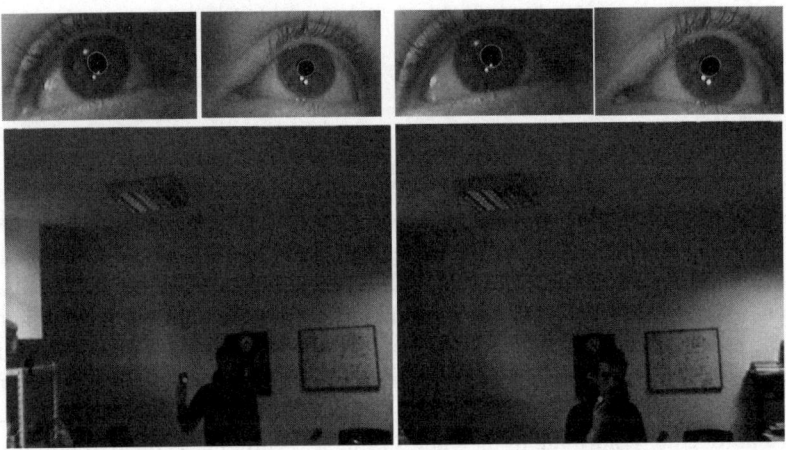

Fig. 5. Two snapshots of the sequence acquired in experiment two

Here, given a data matrix of q observations and n dimension, H_k is a matrix $d \times n$, whose columns are composed of the d eigenvectors corresponding to the d maximal eigenvalues $\lambda_1, .., \lambda_d$ of Σ_k, and $\sigma^2 \mathbf{I}$ is the noise, with:

$$\sigma_k^2 = \frac{1}{n-d} \sum_{m=d+1}^{n} \lambda_m \tag{12}$$

The estimation of the parameters is done only initially (t_0) on the region $\mathbf{M}$, which is certainly dark in the areas around the PI. The features considered are 4 rotations of $45°$ of $\mathbf{M}$ and the gradient. Then the pdf is evaluated on the region $\mathbf{M}$ and the highest values are back-projected as ones on an image of all zeroes, to identify the plausible regions. As above, an ellipse is fitted to the on-region and the ellipse center is returned as $c_{pup}''(t)$. Hence we have

$$cNew_{pup}(t) = h(c_{pup}''(t), c_{pup}'(t)|c_{pup}(t)) + \mathbf{v} \tag{13}$$

Here $h(c_{pup}''(t), c_{pup}'(t)|c_{pup}(t))$ is the function associated with the two criteria, given the estimated $c_{pup}(t)$, and $\mathbf{v}$ is the Gaussian noise with mean zero and variance estimated in t_0 by (12). These two equations (namely, 11,13) define the extended Kalman filter (EFK), in which both the conditional expectation and the covariance matrix are updated at each step, using a linear approximation of the measurement function. Each cycle of the EKF consists of a one step ahead and an update, which includes the update of the conditional expectation $E[c_{pup}(t+1)|Z(t)]$, of the current estimate given the measurements $Z(t)$, at time step t, and the update of conditional covariance matrix. At each step an approximation of the conditional mean is obtained, using a linear approximation of the measurement function f based on a second order Taylor expansion of both $f(.)$ and $h(.)$. Both the innovation matrix and the Kalman gain are computed using these approximations.

5 Results

A series of experimental acquisitions has been made in order to test the validity of the proposed algorithms. During these experiments the user was requested to fixate a known moving target, to make possible the evaluation of the error committed in gaze reprojection on the scene camera image. The results of three different experiments (with different users and light conditions) are summarised in table 1. The first column represents the mean reprojection error (in pixel), the second column the standard deviation and the third column the root mean square (RMS) of the error . All acquisition was made at a resolution of 640x480, at a frame rate of 15Hz. The three main sources of error (that together contribute to the values of table 1) are: occasionally pupil tracking algorithm failure, approximations made in section 3.1 for virtual eye camera modeling, little movements of the helmet on the user head, that produce a variation of the pupil coordinates on the eye-camera image. The last factor could be eliminated expressing the pupil coordinate with respect to a fixated reference (like the outer or inner canthus), or applying some kind of image stabilisation technique to the eye-cameras sequences.

Table 1. Results: mean, standard deviation and root mean square (RMS) of gaze reprojection error for three different test sequences

| | reprojection error in pixel | | |
	mean	standard deviation	RMS
first experiment	6.08	2.77	6.67
second experiment	7.21	3.93	8.21
third experiment	5.33	3.22	6.22

6 Conclusions

In this paper a new head mounted system for 3D human gaze estimation and tracking has been proposed. A unifying calibration framework has been presented that allows the subsequent execution of pupil tracking processes, and fixation point determination on scene camera image. In our experiments it has shown a good robustness under varying light conditions thanks to a prediction model of pupil position, based on glint detection and on analysis of previous frames. Virtual eye image construction permits at no cost, the determination of observed point on the scene camera image, through computation of the trifocal tensor linking the three views. Future developments includes the capability of the system to run in real time, jointly with a localization process (e.g. visual slam), allowing the building of a dynamic 3D metric map of user fixation. Moreover use of quadrifocal tensor for modeling of cameras geometry relations will be considered as outlined at the end of Section 3.1.

References

1. Morimoto, C.H., Mimica, M.R.M.: Eye gaze tracking techniques for interactive applications. Computer Vision Image Understing 98(1), 4–24 (2005)
2. Hansen, D.W., Pece, A.E.C.: Eye typing off the shelf. In: 2004 Conference on Computer Vision and Pattern Recognition (CVPR 2004), June 2004, pp. 159–164 (2004)
3. Li, D., Babcock, J., Parkhurst, D.J.: Openeyes: a low-cost head-mounted eye-tracking solution. In: ETRA 2006: Proceedings of the 2006 symposium on Eye tracking research & applications, pp. 95–100. ACM, New York (2006)
4. White, Jr., K,T.H., Carley, J.: Spatially dynamic calibration of an eye tracking system. IEEE Transaction on Systems, Man, and Cybernetics 23, 1162–1168 (1993)
5. Cornsweet, T.N., Crane, H.D.: Accurate two-dimensional eye tracker using first and fourth purkinje images. Journal of The Optical Society of America 68(8), 921–928 (1973)
6. Bour, L.: Dmi-search scleral coil. In: H2 214, Department of Neurology, Clinical Neurophysiology, Academic Medical Center, Amsterdam (1997)
7. Shih, S.W., Liu, J.: A novel approach to 3-d gaze tracking using stereo cameras. Systems, Man and Cybernetics, Part B, IEEE Transactions on 34(1), 234–245 (2004)
8. Ohno, T., Mukawa, N., Yoshikawa, A.: Freegaze: a gaze tracking system for everyday gaze interaction. In: ETRA 2002: Proceedings of the 2002 symposium on Eye tracking research & applications, pp. 125–132. ACM, New York (2002)
9. Belardinelli, A., Pirri, F., Carbone, A.: Bottom-up gaze shifts and fixations learning by imitation. IEEE Trans. Syst. Man and Cyb.B, 256–271 (2007)
10. Zhang, Z.: Flexible camera calibration by viewing a plane from unknown orientations. In: The Proceedings of the Seventh IEEE International Conference on Computer Vision, vol. 1, pp. 666–673 (1999)
11. Burek, H., Douthwaite, W.: Mathematical models of the general corneal surface. Ophthalmic and Physiological Optics 13(1), 68–72 (1993)
12. Ressl, C.: Geometry, Constraints and Computation of the Trifocal Tensor. PhD thesis, Technical University of Vienna (2003)
13. Hartley, R., Zisserman, A.: Multiple View Geometry in Computer Vision. Cambridge University Press, Cambridge (2000)
14. Shashua, A., Wolf, L.: On the structure and properties of the quadrifocal tensor. In: Vernon, D. (ed.) ECCV 2000. LNCS, vol. 1842, pp. 710–724. Springer, Heidelberg (2000)
15. Atchinson, D., Smith, G.: Optics of the Human Eye. Elsevier, Amsterdam (2002)
16. Carpenter, R.H.S.: Movements of the Eye, Pion, London (1977)
17. Harris, C., Stephens, M.: A Combined Corner and Edge Detector. In: 4th ALVEY Vision Conference, pp. 147–151 (1988)
18. Viola, P., Jones, M.: Rapid object detection using a boosted cascade of simple features. In: Proceedings of the IEEE Computer Society Conference on Computer Vision andPattern Recognition, vol. 1, pp. 511–518. IEEE Computer Society Press, Los Alamitos (2001)
19. Lienhart, R., Maydt, J.: An extended set of haar-like features for rapid object detection. In: Proceedings 2002 International Conference on Image Processing, 2002, vol. 1, pp. 900–903 (2002)
20. Tipping, M., Bishop, C.: Mixtures of principal component analyzers. NCRG 97/003, Neural Computing Research Group, Aston University, Birmingham, UK (1997)

Evaluating Multiview Reconstruction

Keir Mierle and W. James Maclean

University of Toronto, Toronto ON M5S 3G4, Canada
mierle@gmail.com, maclean@eecg.utoronto.ca

Abstract. We survey the state of evaluation in current multiview reconstruction algorithms, with a particular focus on uncalibrated reconstruction from video sequences. We introduce a new evaluation framework,
with high quality ground truth, as a vehicle for accelerating research in
the area. Our source code is also freely available under the GNU General
Public License, (GPL); a first for complete end-to-end reconstruction
systems.

Keywords: multiview, reconstruction, evaluation, open source.

1 Introduction

The proliferation of inexpensive digital cameras and cell phones with integrated
cameras has accelerated the rate at which images are produced. Yet, our ability
to automatically add relevant metadata has not grown at nearly the same rate.
One area, multiview geometry and reconstruction, has made large advances in
the last fifteen years, and is critical to our ability to annotate image sequences.

The general task in multiview geometry is as follows: Given a series of images
of a static scene (*e.g.* a building, a street, an office) estimate the orientation of
the camera that took each image, and also the 3D structure of the scene. While
estimating multiview geometry may not be as sophisticated as object recognition,
it is required for many tasks; examples include obtaining dense reconstructions,
measuring distances in images, robot navigation, and inserting special effects
into live-action video. Furthermore, the information acquired by a multiview
system may be used as input to a higher level recognition system.

In this paper we focus on the task of going from a set of images to a sparse
representation of the scene structure and camera orientations. There are several
papers in the literature describing such systems. What makes our system different, is that it is open source and designed to facilitate evaluation of a modular
reconstruction pipeline. In particular, our contributions are:

- An *end-to-end open source reconstruction system* designed to unite the community around a common, extensible, high-quality, reference codebase;
- Extensions to the open source modelling and rendering program Blender for
  producing *high-quality data sets with ground truth* for evaluation;
- Code for computing *metrics for reconstruction evaluation* using the ground
  truth to make *reproducible research results* simpler.

A. Gasteratos, M. Vincze, and J.K. Tsotsos (Eds.): ICVS 2008, LNCS 5008, pp. 228–237, 2008.
© Springer-Verlag Berlin Heidelberg 2008

To our knowledge, this system is the first end-to-end open source reconstruction system. Even with a toolbox of multiview algorithms such as those in VXL [1] and OpenCV [2], building a robust automatic reconstruction system is not trivial. By releasing our code and encouraging collaboration, we hope our platform will become the reconstruction framework of choice for research and evaluation.

Our system is a work-in-progress. The code is available now, directly from our source control repositories at `https://launchpad.net/libmv`, even though it is not mature. We are actively working with artists in the Blender community to create professional quality data sequences for evaluation. The data sequences coupled with the reconstruction system create a compelling platform for multiview research.

1.1 A Review of the Components in a Reconstruction Pipeline

There are many possible ways to go from a set of images to a final reconstruction. However, the various methods have much in common. Every reconstruction will go through most of the stages below, some more than once. For example, bundle adjustment may happen after reconstructing subsets, or perhaps only after the final metric upgrade.

- **Finding correspondences:** Before any multiview reconstruction can happen, correspondences must be found between the input images. For heterogeneous collections of photographs, this is usually accomplished by matching distinctive features across images, for example with SIFT [3]. For video sequences, sparse trackers such as the established KLT are typically used [4].
- **Correcting lens distortion:** Nonlinear distortions introduced by lens imperfections are usually corrected. It is unwise to ignore lens distortion, as it is particularly prevalent in inexpensive consumer digital cameras. The impact on the final reconstruction can be considerable if it is not accounted for [5]. When camera calibration information is available, it is straightforward to either unwarp the video before tracking, or unwarp the correspondences after tracking. If not, it can be incorporated into the final bundle adjustment.
- **Obtaining an initial projective reconstruction:** In stratified reconstruction methods, a projective reconstruction is obtained before upgrading to metric. This entails simultaneously estimating the cameras $P_j \in \mathbb{R}^{3 \times 4}$ and the structure $X_i \in \mathbb{R}^4$ given 2D image measurements and their correspondences, $x_{ij} \in \mathbb{R}^2$, such that $s_j x_{ij} = P_j X_i$, where s_j is an arbitrary scale factor. Recovering the initial projective reconstruction is the most challenging part of the reconstruction process, especially for longer sequences where no tracks live through the entire sequence. Even in [6], which is otherwise quite rigorous, Hartley & Zisserman say the area "is still to some extent a black art."
- **Bundle adjustment:** Minimizating reprojection error by modifying the camera and structure parameters with a least-squares minimizer is called bundle adjustment. It is usually implemented as a sparse Levenberg-Marquardt [7,8]

minimizer. Generally bundle adjustment is applied at several stages of reconstruction. For extended sequences, it is often necessary to run bundle adjustment in the middle of reconstruction, to prevent accumulated error from
breaking the reconstruction.
- **Metric upgrade** If the camera is uncalibrated, then some kind of constraints must be exploited to move from a projective reconstruction to a
metric one. This is a hard problem, and while working solutions exist, it is
not considered solved. There are many approaches in the literature [9,10,11].

For further details, see [6]. For a shorter overview, look online for [12].

1.2   Related Work

There are several pipelines either available commercially or described in the literature. Of particular note, because of the fairly detailed explanation of how
their pipeline works, is the pipeline developed by Marc Pollefeys [9]. Along with
Microsoft's Photosynth, it is alone in having an accessible description of how it
works. On the commercial side, there is 2d3's Boujou [13]. 2d3's Boujou was a
revolution when it was first released. It was developed by some of the same people who discovered many of the fundamental techniques used by all the described
pipelines. There are several other commercial players: PixelFarm's PFTrack [14],
SynthEyes [15], RealViz MatchMover [16], Science-D-Visions 3D-Equalizer [17].
There is a free alternative, which unfortunately has neither source code nor
papers describing its implementation: Voodoo Tracker [18]. Finally, there is Microsoft's Photosynth [19]. The project (formerly known as Phototourism from
University of Washington) is different than the other pipelines listed above; it
brings together large sets of photographs of the same location rather than working with video.

There are two open source toolkits, which have some multiview reconstruction
ability. First, there is Intel's OpenCV library [2]. It has functions for calibrating
a camera from views of a checkerboard, calculating fundamental matricies, and
multiple tracking algorithms, including an implementation of the KLT. At the
time this project was started, the author was not aware that further multi-view
capabilities were being developed (such as bundle adjustment and multifocal
tensor estimation), as they had to be found by examining the latest CVS versions source code. The authors are also not a fan of the C based API, which is
particularly cumbersome for matrix manipulation. The other toolkit, VXL [1],
was not chosen because it also has tremendous amounts of extra stuff in it, and
has its own implementation of most of the STL, and is difficult to compile. The
multiview capabilities were also not as evident, until after examining the source
code. Both VXL and OpenCV aim to be toolkits, rather than complete reconstruction pipelines. Furthermore, they are not exclusively focused on multiview
reconstruction. Hence, the desire for a clean C++ API with limited dependencies
led to the creation of a new framework.

Fig. 1. An example of the tracker working on two real sequences; the famous Blender monkey Suzanne has been inserted based on the reconstructed scene geometry. The top right shows the Blender setup.

2   The libmv Reconstruction System

In this section we provide an overview of the current state of the system, pointing out what is complete and what is still in progress. From an end user's point of view, the reconstruction system is a set of command line tools for performing reconstruction. There are commands for tracking from video sequences, finding keyframes, reconstructing subsets, upgrading projective reconstructions to metric ones, printing out statistics about reconstructions, exporting metric reconstructions to Blender, and more. Typically the user will run an included script on a .avi file, which will run through all the steps and finally produce a Blender export file. The script also saves the data from all the intermediate stages as it might be reused in the case of failure.

Ultimately, the goal is to support many different strategies for reconstruction. Right now, the system has only one automatic reconstruction strategy, which is as follows.

1. Export the sequence to a series of numbered .pgm files.
2. Run the KLT tracking program on the .pgm files, to track the sequence and obtain correspondences across images.
3. Unwarp the radial distortion from the tracks using camera calibration information (more on this later).
4. Find keyframes using an image-based bucketing heuristic. Tracks in the first frame are put into sixteen buckets formed from the image. If more than 10% of the buckets in any subsequent frame end up with less than a pre-set number of tracks, a keyframe is added and the process repeats.
5. Perform projective reconstruction from pairs of keyframes, using the three-frame reconstruction algorithm [20] where the third frame is taken as the frame in the middle of the two keyframes. We use a variant of MLESAC which estimates the noise in each candidate reconstruction, and then classifies inliers / outliers based on the Bayes-optimal decision boundary. It is a slightly different but independently discovered version of AMLESAC[21]. libmv also contains implementations of RANSAC, MLESAC[22], and LMedS.

6. Bundle adjust the subsets independently, using a robust Huber cost function instead of simple squared error, so as to prevent outliers from overtly skewing the results.
7. Merge the subsets together via structure pasting. By combining the robust technique used also for three frame reconstruction, the three-frame reconstructions can be robustly merged using the method described in [5]. Outliers are detected and removed, using the same robust fitting technique used during three-frame reconstruction.
8. Resection the remaining cameras, also using RANSAC as above to handle outliers.
9. Upgrade to a metric reconstruction by finding the plane at infinity, and transforming the cameras and structure by the rectifying homography [11]. Cameras which are only close to a Euclidean camera after the upgrade are forced to be Euclidean by taking the orthogonal polar complement.
10. Run a final bundle adjustment
11. (*optional*) For evaluation, there is robust point cloud alignment code to compare the obtained reconstruction to ground truth. See Figure 2.

Results of running the tracker on a real sequence can be seen in Figure 1. There, the resulting reconstructions were exported from our system into Blender via a Python script, and then rendered elements inserted on top. Readers who find the above explanation inadequate, as several details are omitted due to space, are referred to the source code.

2.1   Implementation Details

The implementation is completely open source, and licensed under the GPL. The core codebase is written in C++. There are unit tests for a fair amount of the code, which serve double duty for catching regressions as well as providing "working documentation." The only external dependencies are on the Boost headers for the matrix types, and LAPACK for SVD. OpenEXR, a library for loading and saving high-dynamic range images, is needed for loading ground truth data for evaluation. The plotting code for evaluation is written in Python with Matplotlib. Some of the derivations, in particular the metric upgrade code, used symbolic derivations done in Maxima. They are also provided, along with the Python script used to convert the symbolic output to C code for inclusion in the framework. The reconstruction data is stored in the JSON format. There are JSON reading / writing libraries for virtually every programming language, simplifying interoperation. The JSON library included (also written by us) is clean and suitable for use in other projects.

The system relies on a number of other libraries that are directly included in the source tree, and ported to the SCons build system. For bundle adjustment, sba [7] is included. levmar is also included for nonlinear minimization during projective alignment of reconstructions, and for reversing camera distortions. The public domain KLT implementation by Birchfield [23] is also included, for finding correspondences. The LAPACK wrappers for boost::numeric::ublas from Mimas (another computer vision toolkit) are also included.

2.2 Current Limitations

The system at time of writing (November 2007) is limited in a number of ways; most of which will be fixed in the next month or so. First, we do not have a reliable autocalibration system in place, despite using a stratified reconstruction approach. This means the user must calibrate their cameras prior to attempting reconstruction. Since we use the same camera distortion model as OpenCV, the user must download OpenCV and calibrate their camera. This is less of an issue for researchers and more an issue for artists wishing to use the package for tracking. Second, the system does not track uncertainty. This has a number of unfortunate consequences, leading to unacceptable tracking failure in hard cases, and even on some simple ones. The first step towards fixing this is to implement the unscented KLT algorithm [24]. Third, there is no explicit handling of degenerate cases. Fourth, no attempt has been made to optimize the code. In fact, it has never been compiled with any optimization, because this causes strange behaviour during debugging. Nevertheless, it is (at present) only two to three times slower than Voodoo Tracker. Finally, the code is slow to compile due to templates. This can be alleviated by careful code reorganization to reduce internal dependencies.

3 Evaluation

Evaluation of multiview reconstruction is challenging primarily because of the difficulty in obtaining ground truth for reconstructed sequences. This has led to varied quality of evaluations in the literature. Frequently, synthetic data is employed, where a point cloud is generated in 3D, projected into an image, then the points are perturbed by increasing amounts of noise, and the results examined; for example [10]. This is an entirely reasonable way to evaluate these algorithms in isolation.

However, it is also desirable to see how the algorithm performs on sequences where real tracking is used, to better show how tracking errors, which are not necessarily Gaussian, affect the final reconstruction. This applies to each of the algorithms which may be used in the stages described above.

The evaluation of autocalibration is particularly challenging, mainly because the only easy way to evaluate autocalibration is to compare obtained camera intrinsics to ground truth. Most autocalibration papers in the literature examine the relative error in estimated camera intrinsics obtained from their particular algorithm. In many practical applications, the accuracy of the camera intrinsics is not important; it is more important to have an accurate reconstruction. By not evaluating the quality of the final reconstruction, it is hard for a practitioner to decide which among the many autocalibration algorithms to choose. It is entirely possible that one autocalibration algorithm may appear much worse based on obtained parameters, but does only slightly worse in the final reconstruction. Or perhaps it is easier to implement.

In [25], Chandraker *et al.* evaluated many other algorithms, far more than in any other autocalibration paper that the authors are aware of, against their autocalibration work. However, the evaluation in [25] (and also [26,27]) is a subjective measure based on how 'distorted' the resulting reconstructions appear. The evaluation is quite impressive because of the sheer quantity of alternative algorithms investigated. However, with proper ground truth and a quantitative evaluation, the results of this paper could be made both more informative and compelling.

3.1 The Quest for Ground Truth, or, Graphics $=$ (vision)$^{-1}$

Computer graphics is, arguably, far ahead of computer vision if the two problems are considered inverses of each other. There are many real-world scenes which, in the hands of a moderately skilled artist, are reproducible such that renderings of the scene are indistinguishable from real life. Computer vision, however, is nowhere near being able to take a photo of the real world, and produce a complete understanding of the scene. The difficulty of the two problems is decidedly lopsided; but nevertheless the disparity exists.

In this disparity lies opportunity: by producing a high-quality detailed scene description (*'scene understanding'*) and rendering it with modern graphics techniques, we can then evaluate the performance of our vision algorithms using the scene description and the rendered 'photograph.'

There are advantages and disadvantages to using rendered images. The most obvious advantage is that ground truth is available. Another advantage is that it is possible to carefully control parameters such as exposure, noise, and distortion, yet have a resulting data set which is very representative of real sequences. This is especially true if skilled artists create the underlying scene, with help from computer vision researchers to make the most relevant scene.

We believe that for most purposes of comparison and evaluation, high-quality synthetic renderings are a powerful tool, especially with careful attention to detail to make the renderings approximate a real camera as much as possible. The details to incorporate include the following: CCD noise, lens distortion, blurriness, low-contrast, chromatic aberration ("dreaded purple fringing"), exposure variation, motion blur, and compression artifacts.

To produce such ground truth, an extension to Blender which exports camera data and world ground truth was developed. It works by exporting a new 'RenderPass' from the rendering system of Blender where each pixel location contains the 3D location of that pixel rather than a color. The RenderPass is then saved to an OpenEXR file. This can be seen in Figure 2. A generic metadata layer was also added to Blender's IMBuf class, and through that the camera data is exported to the resulting OpenEXR file. The extensions are slated for inclusion in Blender core, and will appear in the next release.

3.2 Results so Far

Our system is not complete, but nevertheless works reasonably well on real sequences, and has practical application for matchmoving (recovering camera movement of live footage for inserting special effects) with Blender. The hydrant

Fig. 2. *Left:* An example of the ground truth data produced by Blender with our patches. Each pixel contains the x, y, z coordinates of the corresponding scene point. *Center:* The corresponding image from the video sequence. *Right:* The Blender setup.

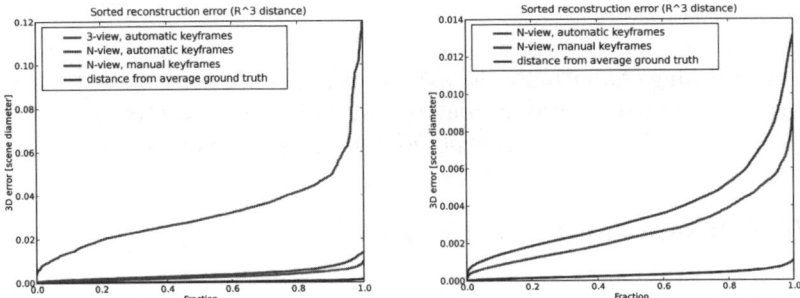

Fig. 3. This shows sorted 3D reconstruction error produced by three different reconstruction strategies, and 3D tracker error (a lower bound on reconstruction accuracy). The 'error' is computed as the 3D distance from the mean of each tracked point as computed from the ground truth. This shows that the reconstruction obtained from our system is within a few factors of the best possible reconstruction given tracking imprecision. The right is a zoom of the left omitting the 3-view results.

sequence shown in Figure 1 was tracked by running the tracking script on a `.avi` acquired by a handheld camera. After tracking, the metric reconstruction is exported to Blender as a point cloud and keyframed camera motion. The export is a Python script which instantiates the relevant items. The average residual reprojection error on the 640×480 hydrant sequence, which has 150 frames, is a bit less than a pixel. Ground truth is not available.

So far, the only ground truth scene we have made is a simple scene with textures specifically designed to track well. It is shown in Figure 2. The results when compared to ground truth from the 64 frame sequence are shown in Figure 3 and Figure 4. Figure 3 is the most informative, as it shows the structure error compared to tracking error. It also shows the results for N-view reconstruction rather than 3-view with resectioning; see [20]. Most reconstruction systems do not compare what the best-possible reconstruction given tracking error is, to the obtained reconstruction. The figure on the right shows that our system is approximately within a factor of five of the best possible reconstruction, given

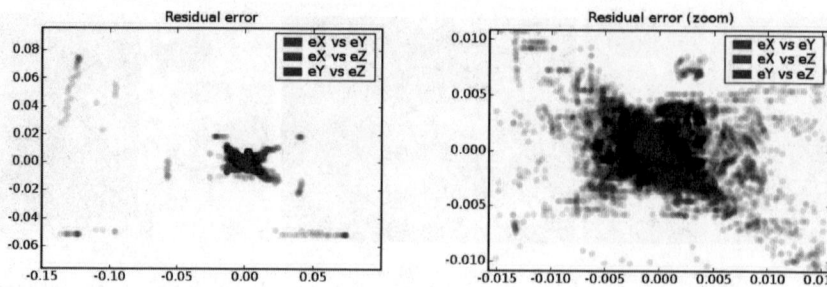

Fig. 4. Scatter plot of reconstruction errors in normalized x, y, z world coordinates (scene diameter=1.0) over all tracks, for one reconstruction. The errors are approximately 0.5% of the scene diameter.

imperfect tracking. Admittedly the data sequence is not hard. Nevertheless, the results are generated entirely automatically, such that it is straightforward to experiment with alternative strategies and meaningfully compare them.

4   Conclusions and Future Work

The presented open source reconstruction system is the first of its kind. It is not mature, yet it already has practical applications for camera matchmoving. The potential to facilitate further research is large, because now any researcher will be able to *start* with a full reconstruction system, rather than having to write one from scratch. The system is not finished, but will continue to evolve for the forseeable future.

References

1. VXL Community. VXL: (1999), http://vxl.sourceforge.net/
2. Intel. OpenCV (2000), http://opencvlibrary.sourceforge.net/
3. Lowe, D.G.: Distinctive image features from scale-invariant keypoints. Int. J. Comput. Vision 60(2), 91–110 (2004)
4. Lucas, B.D., Kanade, T.: An iterative image registration technique with an application to stereo vision. In: International Joint Conferences on Artificial Intelligence (IJCAI 1981), pp. 674–679 (1981)
5. Fitzgibbon, A., Zisserman, A.: Automatic camera tracking. In: Shah, M., Kumar, R. (eds.) Video Registration, ch. 2, pp. 18–35. Kluwer, Dordrecht (2003)
6. Hartley, R., Zisserman, A.: Multiple View Geometry in Computer Vision. Cambridge University Press, New York (2003)
7. Lourakis, M.I.A., Argyros, A.A.: The design and implementation of a generic sparse bundle adjustment software package based on the Levenberg-Marquardt algorithm. Technical Report 340, Institute of Computer Science - FORTH, Heraklion, Crete, Greece (August 2004), http://www.ics.forth.gr/~lourakis/sba

8. Triggs, B., McLauchlan, P.F., Hartley, R.I., Fitzgibbon, A.W.: Bundle adjustment - a modern synthesis. In: ICCV 1999: Proceedings of the International Workshop on Vision Algorithms, pp. 298–372. Springer, London (2000)

9. Pollefeys, M., Van Gool, L., Vergauwen, M., Verbiest, F., Cornelis, K., Tops, J., Koch, R.: Visual modeling with a hand-held camera. International Journal of Computer Vision 59(3), 207–232 (2004)

10. Thormählen, T., Broszio, H., Mikulastik, P.: Robust linear auto-calibration of a moving camera from image sequences. In: Narayanan, P.J., Nayar, S.K., Shum, H.-Y. (eds.) ACCV 2006. LNCS, vol. 3852, pp. 71–80. Springer, Heidelberg (2006)

11. Oliensis, J.: Linear stratified self-calibration and Euclidean reconstruction. In: NECI TR (2002)

12. Dang, T.K.: Technical report: A review of 3d reconstruction from video. Technical report, ISIS group, Universiteit van Amsterdam (2005)

13. 2d3. Boujou: http://www.2d3.com/

14. The Pixel Farm. PFTrack & PFMatch: http://www.thepixelfarm.co.uk/

15. Andersson Technologies. SynthEyes: http://www.ssontech.com/

16. MatchMover. RealViz: http://www.realviz.com/

17. Science-D-Visions. 3D-Equalizer v3: http://www.sci-d-vis.com/

18. digilab. Voodoo Tracker:
http://www.digilab.uni-hannover.de/docs/manual.html

19. Snavely, N., Seitz, S.M., Szeliski, R.: Photo tourism: Exploring photo collections in 3D. In: SIGGRAPH 2006: ACM SIGGRAPH 2006 papers, pp. 835–846. ACM Press, New York (2006)

20. Schaffalitzky, F., Zisserman, A., Hartley, R.I., Torr, P.: A six point solution for structure and motion. In: Vernon, D. (ed.) ECCV 2000. LNCS, vol. 1842, pp. 632–648. Springer, Heidelberg (2000)

21. Konouchine, A., Gaganov, V., Veznevets, V.: Amlesac: A new maximum likelihood robust estimator. In: Graphicon 2005 (2005)

22. Torr, P., Zisserman, A.: MLESAC: A new robust estimator with application to estimating image geometry. Computer Vision and Image Understanding 78, 138–156 (2000)

23. Birchfield, S.: KLT: An implementation of the Kanade-Lucas-Tomasi feature tracker (1997), http://www.ces.clemson.edu/~stb/klt/

24. Dorini, L.B., Goldenstein, S.K.: Unscented KLT: nonlinear feature and uncertainty tracking. In: SIBGRAPI, pp. 187–193. IEEE Computer Society Press, Los Alamitos (2006)

25. Chandraker, M.K., Agarwal, S., Kahl, F., Nistér, D., Kriegman, D.J.: Autocalibration via rank-constrained estimation of the absolute quadric. In: 2007 IEEE Computer Society Conference on Computer Vision and Pattern Recognition (CVPR 2007) (June 2007)

26. Nistér, D.: Untwisting a projective reconstruction. Int. J. Comput. Vision 60(2), 165–183 (2004)

27. Nistér, D.: Calibration with robust use of cheirality by quasi-affine reconstruction of the set of camera projection centres. In: ICCV 2001: Proceedings of the Seventh IEEE International Conference on Computer Vision, pp. 116–123 (2001)

Part V

Object Recognition and Tracking

Detecting and Recognizing Abandoned Objects in Crowded Environments

Roland Miezianko[1] and Dragoljub Pokrajac[2]

[1] Honeywell Labs, Minneapolis, MN 55418, USA
roland.miezianko@honeywell.com
[2] Delaware State University, Dover, DE 19901, USA
dpokrajac@desu.edu

Abstract. In this paper we present a framework for detecting and recognizing abandoned objects in crowded environments. The two main components of the framework include background change detection and object recognition. Moving blocks are detected using dynamic thresholding of spatiotemporal texture changes. The background change detection is based on analyzing wavelet transform coefficients of non-overlapping and non-moving 3D texture blocks. Detected changed background becomes the region of interest which is scanned to recognize various objects under surveillance such as abandoned luggage. The object recognition is based on model histogram ratios of image gradient magnitude patches. Supervised learning of the objects is performed by support vector machine. Experimental results are demonstrated using various benchmark video sequences (PETS, CAVIAR, i-Lids) and an object category dataset (CalTech256).

1 Introduction

Background modeling, background change detection, and object recognition have recently been active research areas. In background modeling, techniques have been developed to model background in order to extract foreground objects of interest. A more thorough examination of these techniques is presented in [1,2,3]. To adapt more quickly to changing environment, such as lighting changes and quasi-periodic motion, multi-modal background models were introduced. Some of the methods include foreground model analysis [4], eigenbackgrounds [5], and a more widespread model based on mixture of Gaussians [6]. A background change detection framework based on the recognition of known and unknown objects was presented in [7]. In this framework, a person detector recognizes people present in the scene, and all other objects detected that are different from the background are marked as unknown.

Object recognition and detection is also an active area in computer vision. Several recent approaches to detect objects in natural images [8,9] use an interest point detector to focus on small number of patches. The most widely accepted method is based on the DoG interest point detector. It extracts a 128 dimensional

A. Gasteratos, M. Vincze, and J.K. Tsotsos (Eds.): ICVS 2008, LNCS 5008, pp. 241–250, 2008.
© Springer-Verlag Berlin Heidelberg 2008

SIFT feature vector [8] as an object descriptor. Such feature descriptors are used in spatial pyramid matching techniques, where image is partitioned into smaller sub-regions and histograms of features are found for each sub-region [10].

In this paper, we address an abandoned object detection based on two novel techniques for background change detection and object recognition in videos. Our goal is to find an effective framework for detecting changed background in crowded environments (such as airports, train stations, etc.) and to recognize objects when multiple overlapping and registered cameras are not available.

The proposed system architecture is based on the two main components: background change detection and object recognition. Initially, each video frame is subdivided into non-overlapping blocks and each block is processed separately. Motion detection is performed and the non-moving blocks are collected to create a background texture map of each block. Wavelet coefficients are computed for small texture patches using a sliding window over the texture background map. The wavelet rough dissimilarity (WRD) matrix is generated from the coefficients and dynamic thresholding [11] is applied to the rows of the matrix to mark any detected background changes for each block location. Multiple marked background blocks are clustered to form the background regions of interest (ROIs). Sub-region model patches are generated for each ROI and model histogram ratios (MHR) are computed from these sub-region model patches. MHR are fed into a support vector machine (SVM), trained on a benchmark dataset [12], to detect objects under surveillance. The framework's main components are shown in Fig. 1.

Our approach is based on analyzing background texture blocks with wavelet coefficients as they offer texture localization in spatial frequency domain. Unlike global image sub-regions [10], our sub-region model pathes are local to predefined regions of the object. Computation of symmetric and dominant histogram ratios [13] is replaced in our approach by finding histogram ratios of localized subregions. Support vector machine with a linear kernel is our choice of a classifier. Its main advantages include less training time, and no parameters to tune except one constant.

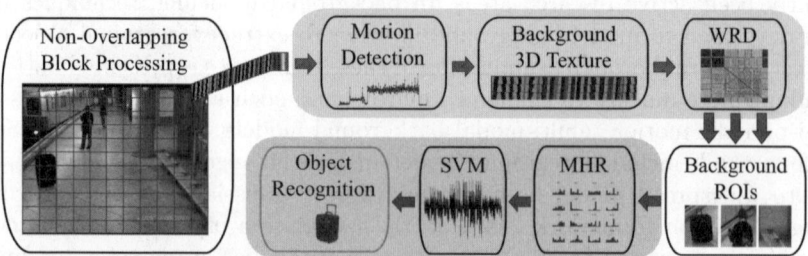

Fig. 1. The overall architecture is based on two main components: background change detection and object recognition. The background ROIs are generated from the detected dissimilarity of non-moving texture blocks. The SVM classifies the model histogram ratios obtained from background ROIs as either being an objects of interest or not.

2 Background Change Detection

We employ a motion detection method using spatiotemporal texture changes initially proposed in [11,14]. This method is based on performing incremental PCA decomposition over a sequence of non-overlapping texture blocks to detect motion. A block is defined as a 3D texture created at a specific spatial location from three consecutive frames. A largest eigenvalue of the projected texture blocks is dynamically thresholded to indicate if a block is moving at the given time. The end result of this method provides a binary vector for each of the spatial block location indicating whether the block is moving or non-moving. However, to detect background changes we are turning our attention to the non-moving blocks.

The 3D textures of non-moving blocks are concatenated and reshaped to form a 2D background texture map. Example of a reshaped 3D texture into 2D background texture map is shown in the *Background 3D Texture* box of Fig. 1. Each spatial block location (x, y) of the image has a corresponding background texture map $b_{x,y}$. A window around temporal location $b_{x,y,i}$ defines a small texture patch $\hat{b}_{x,y,i} = \langle b_{x,y,i-w}, \ldots, b_{x,y,i}, \ldots, b_{x,y,i+w} \rangle$, where $w = 3$. Haar wavelet transform of this texture patch yields corresponding wavelet coefficients $c_i(l), l = 1, \ldots, L$, where L is the number of wavelet coefficients. We define rough dissimilarity between wavelet coefficients of two texture patches $\hat{b}_{x,y,i}$ and $\hat{b}_{x,y,j}$ as

$$\zeta(\hat{b}_{x,y,i}, \hat{b}_{x,y,j}) = \left(\sum_{l=1}^{L} \left(c_i(l) - c_j(l) \right)^2 \right)^{1/2}. \tag{1}$$

The rough dissimilarity $\zeta(\hat{b}_{x,y,i}, \hat{b}_{x,y,j})$ is computed between all texture patches $\hat{b}_{x,y,i}$ generating a wavelet rough dissimilarity (WRD) matrix for each spatial block location (x, y). An example of this matrix in shown in the *WRD* box of Fig. 1. Dynamic thresholding method [11] is applied to each row of the WRD matrix to identify temporal location of changed background. Only continuously changed background lasting longer than a predefined threshold, such as 30 seconds, is finally marked as changed. This threshold was adopted from the PETS 2006 challenge [15] and is configurable.

Clustering of changed background between non-overlapping blocks is performed in the temporal domain. This basic block-neighborhood clustering [14] delimits the background regions of interest (ROIs) as shown in the *Background ROIs* box of Fig. 1. At this step, the processing of individual non-overlapping blocks stops and processing of extracted sub-images may begin.

An assumption is made that only spatial locations of the image with previously detected motion are analyzed to determine if background change has occurred. This eliminates processing of block locations with no detected motion. The motion detection algorithm handles gradual changes in illumination, such as illumination due to time of day changes. Such changes of the background appearance will not be considered significant, unless there is a drastic change in illumination especially in outdoor scenes. All the experiments were conducted on data collected under somewhat controlled indoor environments with minimal lighting and shadow effects.

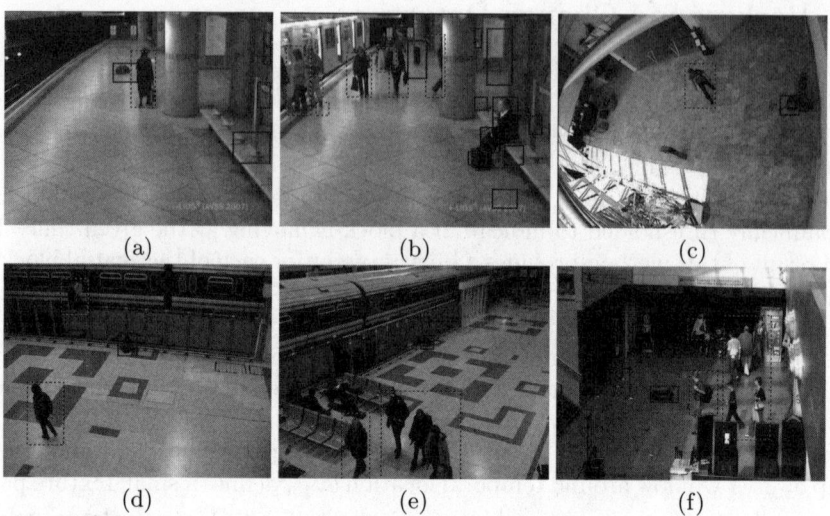

(a) (b) (c)

(d) (e) (f)

Fig. 2. Background change detection examples, where instantaneous motion regions are shown as dashed green rectangles and background regions of interest are shown as solid red rectangles for various datasets. Example frames from (a,b) i-Lids AVSS 2007, (c) CAVIAR, (d,e) PETS 2006, and (f) PETS 2007 datasets.

One of the challenging issues in detecting background ROIs is the camera location and continuous crowd motion within the area under observation. Areas with large motion volumes and small number of stationary objects as shown in Fig. 2(c,d,e) allow for near-perfect detection of changed background ROIs. Areas with large motion volumes and large number of slow-changing stationary objects will generate more background ROIs for our object recognition module to consider, Fig. 2(a,b,f). Additionally, any area of the image where an object was removed from the scene will also be marked as changed background. Both objects left behind and objects removed from the scene are detected with this method.

Multiple overlapping and registered cameras permit mapping the ground plane to detect abandoned objects as a function of distance from person to the abandoned object. Such scenarios are provided by the PETS 2006 & 2007 datasets. However, most of the other datasets and real surveillance configurations rarely provide such detail and sterile configurations. For this reason our method is based on single camera views to provide practical solutions to this important video analytics problem. The detected background ROIs are now continuously handed over to object recognition module to see if any of the background changes are due to known objects under surveillance.

3 Object Recognition

Construction of the feature vector used in object recognition requires several steps. In the first step, the edge detection is performed by convolving vertical and horizontal Sobel masks [13]. Let $G_x(x, y)$ and $G_y(x, y)$ represent the two gradients of an image I (of size $width \times height$) at point (x, y); then the magnitude G_m and orientation G_θ of the edge at point (x, y) is simply defined as follows

$$G_m(x, y) = \sqrt{G_x(x, y)^2 + G_y(x, y)^2} \tag{2}$$

$$G_\theta(x, y) = \arctan\left(\frac{G_y(x, y)}{G_x(x, y)}\right). \tag{3}$$

The orientation values are divided into N bins, where each bin n contains values in the range $\left[n\frac{\pi}{N}, (n+1)\frac{\pi}{N}\right)$. A new 3D image $\hat{I}$ of size $width \times height \times N$ is constructed. The value of $\hat{I}$ at any point (x, y, n) is the magnitude $G_m(x, y)$ if corresponding orientation belongs to the nth bin, or 0, otherwise. Therefore

$$\hat{I}(x, y, n) = \begin{cases} G_m(x, y) & \text{if } G_\theta(x, y) \in bin_n \\ 0 & \text{otherwise.} \end{cases} \tag{4}$$

This 3D image $\hat{I}$ is used to compute the histograms of any sub-image region of I by means of the *integral image* method introduced in [16]. An example of the combined magnitude image I is shown as second image from left in top row of Fig. 3 followed by of the *slices* of the image $\hat{I}$ created with $N = 9$ bins.

3.1   Model Patches

Features employed to encode the object are based on histogram ratios between patch windows (the generation of histogram ratios is described in the next section). Hence, before we can compute histogram ratios, we must first define the model patches. A set of model patches is constructed with fixed position relative to any scan window. We employ a set of model patches shown in the bottom left matrix of Fig. 3. This set of relative model patches may be applied recursively to any sub-window of the scan window retaining the relative position to the recursive sub-window. Model patches are specified as percentage of relative offset to the scan window. For example, $M2$ model patch width and height is defined as $0 \rightarrow 0.5 * S_x$ and $0 \rightarrow S_y$ respectively, where S_x and S_y are scan window sizes. First set of model patches created for the scan window become Level-1 model patches. Each of the Level-1 model patches becomes a new scan sub-window, and another set of Level-2 model patches is created. One example of Level-2 model patches created from Level 1 $M1$ is shown in Fig. 3. We use the following notation: Level-1 model patch Mk is the basis for generating Level-2 model patch set $\{M_i^k\}, i = 1 \ldots m$.

3.2   Model Histogram Ratios (MHR)

Let vector h_i^k be the gradient magnitude histogram of Level-2 model patch M_i^k. The gradient magnitude histogram h_i^k is computed as the sum of the magnitudes for each of the N bins, based on the model's position within the sub-window.

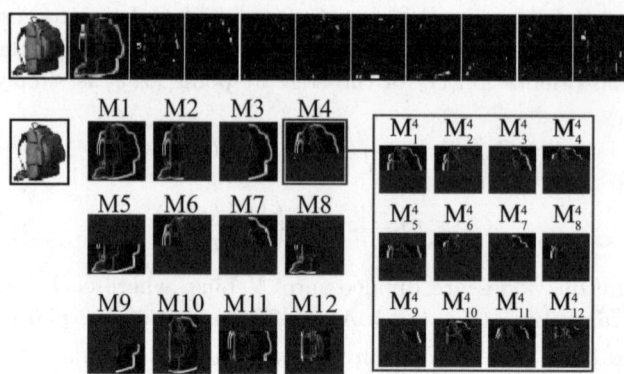

Fig. 3. Top row from left to right: training color image; combined gradient magnitude I from all bins; and gradient magnitudes of each of the nine bins of $\hat{I}$. Bottom matrix: relative position of Level-1 model patches $M1$ to $M12$. Relative position of Level-2 model patches M_1^4 to M_{12}^4 constructed from the model patch $M4$.

Computing the sum is done efficiently using integral images [16]. All histogram vectors belonging to k^{th} Level-2 set, $h^k = \{h_i^k\}, i = 1, \ldots, m$, are normalized using the $L2$-norm $h^k \rightarrow h^k/\sqrt{\|h^k\|_2^2 + \epsilon^2}$, where ϵ is a small constant. The model histogram ratio q between two Level-2 models M_i^k and M_j^k is defined as

$$q(k, i, j) = \ln\left(\frac{h_i^k + \epsilon}{h_j^k + \epsilon}\right), \tag{5}$$

where $k, i, j = 1, \ldots, m, i \neq j$.

Note that Level-1 model patches $M1$ to $M12$ are exactly the same as Level-2 model patches M_1^1 to M_{12}^1. Therefore, only Level-2 models are used in computing the model histogram ratios. The input vector to a support vector machine classifier is constructed by concatenating model histogram ratios $q(k, i, j)$. Observe that our model histogram ratios are different from edge orientation histogram features [13]. Namely, we compute the ratios of whole histograms between different scan windows and not ratios between individual histogram bin values of one histogram.

4 Experimental Results

Our experiments are based on publicly available video sequences and object category image datasets. First, we tested each component of the system (i.e., background detection and object recognition) and then we tested the system as a whole. The background change detection experiments were carried out on *PETS2006* [15], *PETS2007* [17], *AVSS i-Lids* [18], and *CAVIAR* [19] video sequences. Since the test video sequences did not consistently provide multi-camera views of the same scene, we used only single-camera view sequences. However, the use of multi-camera views (where available, e.g., for the *PETS* video sequences) could improve the accuracy of modeling, since in such cases a 2D ground model may be constructed allowing raising an alarm for objects left behind as a function of distance to the person leaving the object behind.

Figure 2 highlights background change detection results for all video datasets. In most abandoned luggage detection scenarios the luggage must be left behind for a predefined period of time. Hence, we set the time threshold to 30 seconds [15]. In each instance, the background change detection correctly labeled abandoned object ROIs. Other detected background ROIs are labeled since objects were removed from the scene. These objects were present during initialization of the motion detection module.

To distinguish objects of interest, we applied support vector machines (SVM) classifier. For simplicity, we used linear kernel SVM, that do not project data into non-linear feature space. To train the SVM, we collected over 1500 luggage images from the various internet sites. Our goal was to classify as positive 779 samples of objects of interest, including backpacks, daypacks, totes, and uprights. The images were cropped and rescaled to 50×50 pixel size. Top row of Fig. 4 shows examples of the positive training images. We bin the gradient orientation into $N = 9$ bins. The number of Level-1 models is $m = 12$, yielding 12 Level-2 sets of 12 sub-models M_i^k. The number of model histogram ratios $q(k, i, j)$ for each Level-2 set is $m(m - 1)/2 = 66$. The SVM input vector is constructed by concatenating all model histogram ratios $q(k, i, j)$ yielding a 7128 dimensional vector ($12 \times 66 \times 9$) per scan window.

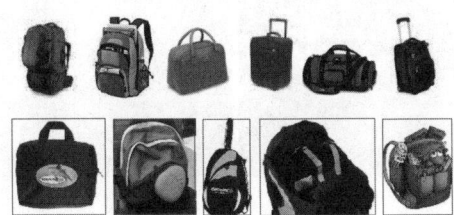

Fig. 4. Top row: Examples of training images include backpacks, daypacks, totes, and uprights. Bottom row: Examples of detected luggage from Caltech256 dataset, *003.backpack* category.

To test the object detection module of the proposed system, we used *003.backpack* and *257.clutter* categories of the CalTech256 object category dataset [12]. Overall, the detection rate of the proposed method for the entire *003.backpack* category was 64.2%. Examples of correctly identified objects are shown in Fig. 4. False positive rate of the *257.clutter* category was 0.0%. However, an example of a false positive response is shown in Fig. 6(b), where full image scan was performed. Both the background change detection and object recognition locate exactly the abandoned object.

Finally, we tested the whole system, on the *i-Lids* video sequences as shown in Fig. 5 and Fig. 6. Observe that computing the background change detection

(a)   (b)

Fig. 5. An example of a video frame from i-Lids AVSS Easy 2007 dataset. (a) Motion blocks are shown as green overlay and detected background regions of interest are shown as solid red rectangles. (b) Full image scan unclustered responses from the object detector are shown as blue centroids with bounding rectangles.

(a)   (b)

Fig. 6. An example of a video frame from i-Lids AVSS Medium 2007 dataset. (a) Motion blocks are shown as green overlay and detected background regions of interest are shown as solid red rectangles. (b) Full image scan clustered responses from the object detector are shown as blue rectangles. A false positive response does not match any background ROIs.

regions of interest limits the search space of the object recognition module. In Fig. 5 and Fig. 6 we show the detected changed background ROIs, and responses of the object recognition module when the whole frame is scanned, not just the background ROIs.

5   Conclusion

In this paper we presented a framework for detecting changed background regions of interest. The system can work in the presence of large moving and stationary crowds and can identify specific objects of interest within the background ROIs. The background change detection incorporates spatiotemporal motion detection and wavelet decomposition of the non-moving background texture maps. Object recognition module is based on model histogram ratios of second level model patches and utilizes linear kernel support vector machine for classification. While our object recognition achieved comparable results to current state of the art methods, there is still much room for improvement, e.g., in methods for feature generation. Also, the application of other classification techniques may lead to improvements of the recognition accuracy. In the future, we intend to incorporate people detection and tracking into the existing system, to extend the forensic analysis capabilities.

Acknowledgments

D. Pokrajac has been partially supported by NIH (grant #2 P20 RR016472-04), DoD/DoA (award 45395-MA-ISP) and NSF (awards # 0320991, #HRD-0630388). R. Miezianko performed this work at Temple University, Philadelphia.

References

1. Cheung, S.-C.S., Kamath, C.: Robust background subtraction with foreground validation for urban traffic video. EURASIP J. Appl. Signal Process. 2005(1), 2330–2340 (2005)
2. Hall, D., Nascimento, J., Ribeiro, P., Andrade, E., Moreno, P., Pesnel, S., List, T., Emonet, R., Fisher, R.B., Victor, J.S., Crowley, J.L.: Comparison of target detection algorithms using adaptive background models. In: ICCCN 2005: Proceedings of the 14th International Conference on Computer Communications and Networks, Washington, DC, USA, pp. 113–120. IEEE Computer Society Press, Los Alamitos (2005)
3. Piccardi, M.: Background subtraction techniques: a review. In: Proceedings of the IEEE International Conference on Systems, Man and Cybernetics, vol. 4, pp. 3099–3104 (2004)
4. Tian, Y.-L., Lu, M., Hampapur, A.: Robust and efficient foreground analysis for real-time video surveillance. In: Proc. IEEE Conf. on Computer Vision and Pattern Recognition, vol. 1, pp. 1182–1187 (2005)
5. Oliver, N.M., Rosario, B., Pentland, A.P.: A bayesian computer vision system for modeling human interactions. IEEE Trans. Pattern Anal. Mach. Intell. 22(8), 831–843 (2000)
6. Stauffer, C., Grimson, W.E.L.: Adaptive background mixture models for real-time tracking. In: Proc. IEEE Conf. on Computer Vision and Pattern Recognition, vol. 2, pp. 246–252 (1999)
7. Grabner, H., Roth, P.M., Grabner, M., Bischof, H.: Autonomous learning of a robust background model for change detection. In: Proceedings 9th IEEE International Workshop on PETS (2006)
8. Lowe, D.G.: Distinctive image features from scale-invariant keypoints. IJCV 60(2), 91–110 (2004)

9. Mikolajczyk, K., Schmid, C.: Scale and affine invariant interest point detectors. IJCV 60(1), 63–86 (2004)
10. Lazebnik, S., Schmid, C., Ponce, J.: Beyond bags of features: Spatial pyramid matching for recognizing natural scene categories. In: IEEE Conference on Computer Vision and Pattern Recognition, pp. 2169–2178 (2006)
11. Latecki, L.J., Miezianko, R., Pokrajac, D.: Motion detection based on local variation of spatiotemporal texture. In: 2004 Conference on Computer Vision and Pattern Recognition Workshop, vol. 8, pp. 135–141 (2004)
12. Griffin, G., Holub, A., Perona, P.: Caltech-256 object category dataset. Technical Report 7694, California Institute of Technology (2007)
13. Levi, K., Weiss, Y.: Learning object detection from a small number of examples: The importance of good features. In: IEEE Conference on Computer Vision and Pattern Recognition, pp. 53–60 (2004)
14. Latecki, L.J., Miezianko, R.: Object tracking with dynamic template update and occlusion detection. In: International Conference on Pattern Recognition, vol. 1, pp. 556–560 (2006)
15. PETS 2006: Performance Evaluation of Tracking and Surveillance 2006 Benchmark Data. http://www.cvg.rdg.ac.uk/PETS2006/
16. Viola, P., Jones, M.: Rapid object detection using a boosted cascade of simple features. In: CVPR, vol. 1, pp. 511–518 (2001)
17. PETS 2007: Performance Evaluation of Tracking and Surveillance 2007 Benchmark Data. http://www.cvg.rdg.ac.uk/PETS2007/
18. i Lids: i-Lids dataset for AVSS (2007), http://www.elec.qmul.ac.uk/staffinfo/an-drea/avss2007.html
19. CAVIAR: EC Funded CAVIAR project/IST 2001 37540. http://homepages.inf.ed.ac.uk/rbf/CAVIAR/

Diagnostic System for Intestinal Motility Disfunctions Using Video Capsule Endoscopy

Santi Seguí[1], Laura Igual[1], Fernando Vilariño[1], Petia Radeva[1,2],
Carolina Malagelada[3], Fernando Azpiroz[3], and Jordi Vitrià[1,2]

[1] Computer Vision Center, Universitat Autònoma de Barcelona, Bellaterra, Spain
[2] Departament de Matemàtica Aplicada i Anàlisis, Universitat de Barcelona,
Barcelona, Spain
[3] Digestive System Research Unit, University Hospital Vall d'Hebron; Ciberehd; and
Department of Medicine, Autonomous University of Barcelona, Barcelona, Spain

Abstract. Wireless Video Capsule Endoscopy is a clinical technique consisting of the analysis of images from the intestine which are provided by an ingestible device with a camera attached to it. In this paper we propose an automatic system to diagnose severe intestinal motility disfunctions using the video endoscopy data. The system is based on the application of computer vision techniques within a machine learning framework in order to obtain the characterization of diverse motility events from video sequences. We present experimental results that demonstrate the effectiveness of the proposed system and compare them with the ground-truth provided by the gastroenterologists.

1   Introduction

Medical image analysis is an important research topic in the field of computer vision. Nowadays, images are crucial in many clinical procedures such as laser surgery, endoscopy and ultra sound scan, only to cite a few [1]. Moreover, in the last years a considerable effort has been done in the development of new image acquisition techniques increasing image accuracy and getting more image modalities with different views of the human body. Miniaturization of hardware is used to design sophisticated techniques allowing the analysis of parts of organs of the human body unattainable before. Wireless Video Capsule Endoscopy (WVCE) [2] is a novel technique using an ingestible device which allows to access to the entire bowel without surgery. This device consists of a small capsule of $11mm$ diameter and $25mm$ length, equipped with four illuminating leds, a camera, a battery and a wireless system (see Figure 1). The capsule is swallowed by the patient and travels along the intestinal tract. The captured images are transmitted by the radio frequency communication channel to a data recorder providing a video with two frames per second and 256×256 pixels of resolution. The analysis of intestinal motility activity is an important source of information for gastroenterologists to assess the presence of certain intestinal disfunctions. So far, motility assessment has been mainly performed by using invasive techniques, such as intestinal manometry. In this specific scenario, WVCE represents a much

A. Gasteratos, M. Vincze, and J.K. Tsotsos (Eds.): ICVS 2008, LNCS 5008, pp. 251–260, 2008.

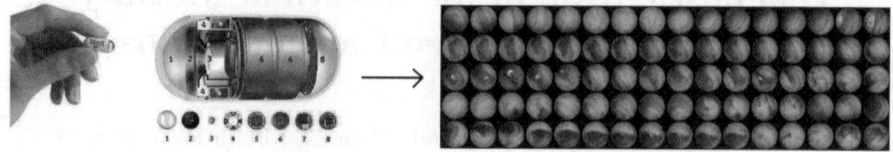

Fig. 1. Left: Wireless Video Capsule Endoscopy device: 1) Dome. 2) Lens holder. 3) Lens. 4) LEDs. 5) CMOS image sensor. 6) Battery. 7) ASIC transmitter. 8) Micro-antenna. Right: Example of capsule endoscopy video frames.

less invasive alternative, but it has the main drawback of the high amount of time needed for the off-line analysis by the expert, which is typically set around $4 - 6$ hours. This makes the visual analysis of WVCE unfeasible as a clinical routine. Novel approaches using video endoscopy data have been developed and successfully applied to detect some intestinal affections such as cancer, ulcers and bowel Crohn's disease [3,4,5,6,7,8]. However, up to our knowledge, automatic analysis based on WCVE has not yet been used to deal with intestinal motility diseases.

In this paper we manage this challenging open field of research by proposing an automatic system for the diagnosis of severe intestinal motility disfunctions using WVCE. Our proposal is based on the application of computer vision techniques within a machine learning framework in order to obtain the characterization of diverse motility events from video sequences. In particular, this study is focused on the automatic diagnosis of severe diseases by the analysis of video data from the portion of intestine comprised between the post-duodenum and cecum. In these sequences, the lumen, the gut wall and the intestinal contents can be distinguished. The lumen is the cavity where digested food goes through and can be recognized as a dark area, generally not centered in the image due to the free movement of the capsule within the gut. The intestinal wall is the visible part of the intestine and presents a range of colors spanning from orange to brown. The intestinal contents consist of remains of food in digestion and intestinal juices. The intestinal contractions are the result of muscular stimulation produced by the enteric nervous system. They appear as a closing of the intestinal lumen in a concentric way followed by an opening. Open lumen sequences are those sequences of frames in which the lumen appears static and opened for a long period of time when the intestine is relaxed, and there are not contractive movement. Sometimes, the camera has a null apparent motion and the visualized frames show the same image continuously. These frames belong to periods of repose in intestinal activity. In Figure 2 we display several examples of video frames. In the last years, machine learning has been applied to multiple medical image modalities in order to support clinical decisions. Support Vector Machines (SVM) [9] have become one of the state-of-the-art classification techniques due to their good performance and generalization power. Lately, different authors have shown the probabilistic version of SVM, namely Relevance Vector Machines (RVM) [10], to be useful in problems where an explicit outcome in

Fig. 2. Some examples of intestinal video images. From top to bottom: static sequence, turbid frames, tunnel sequence, occlusive contraction, non-occlusive contraction.

terms of the reliability of the classification result is important. Our system uses both SVM and RVM as essential parts of a global framework, in which multiple features are associated to the diverse motility events mentioned above.

This paper is organized as follows: Section 2 describes in detail the system architecture. In section 3 we present the experimental results and in Section 4 we expose the conclusions of this work.

2   System For Automatic Detection of Small Intestine Pathologies

Our system is developed in a modular way as is shown in the system architecture diagram displayed in Figure 3. It has two main blocks, namely: 1) the automatic capsule endoscopy video analysis, and 2) the characterization of pathologies. The first block is divided in three different modules which extract information of the video frames. These modules are referred to: *Intestinal Contents Analysis, Analysis of Idleness in Contractile Activity*, and, finally *Analysis of Manifest Contractile Activity*. In the second block, we use the extracted information in order to get new features with clinical relevance which describe the video in a higher level of interpretation. Then, we use them to learn and classify videos as belonging to patients and non-patients. Through the following paragraphs, we explain in more detail the system blocks.

2.1   Block 1: Automatic Capsule Endoscopy Video Analysis

1. Intestinal Contents Analysis Module: This module is in charge of finding all frames where intestinal contents are visualized. The intestinal contents can be present as intestinal juices, as well as food in digestion. The presence of the intestinal contents are characterized in terms of color, which usually ranges from brown to yellow, but mainly centered around green. Since the variability in color of the intestinal contents is very high and patient-specific, we propose a semi-automatic method for the detection of frames showing intestinal contents. Our approach consists of creating a non-supervised clustering with a Self-Organizing

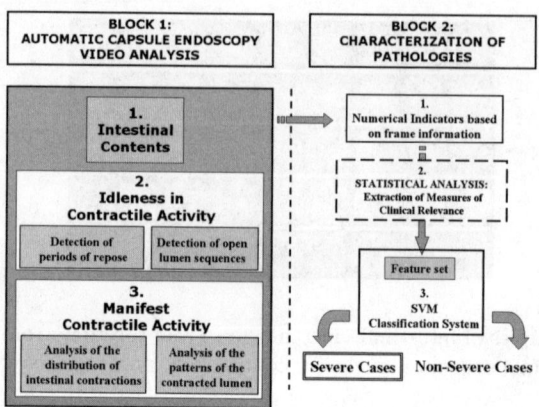

Fig. 3. System Architecture for automatic capsule endoscopy video analysis and pathology characterization

Map (SOM) method [11] with all video frames. To manage this, we first, convert each video image into the CIE-Lab [12] color space, then we compute the mean value of the components a and b of this color space for all video frames, and we clusterize the data using the SOM method. This process returns a set of cells which contains frames with similar color feature vector. Then, we manually select those cells of the SOM where intestinal contents can be appreciated (see Figure 4). We refer to these frames as *turbid frames*.

2. Analysis of Idleness in Contractile Activity: In this module we analyze the degree of quietness of the intestine from two different point of views: the movement of the camera and the movement of the intestine.

Detection of Periods of Repose: analyzes the quietness of the intestine from the point of view of the camera motion. We get three indicators for each image. (1) The *static degree* for each frame is computed by using the Earth Mover's Distance (EMD) method [13]. This method computes the distance between two distributions [13], which are represented by signatures. The signatures are sets of weighted features which capture the color distributions. The result is based on the minimal cost to transform a distribution into another. To compute the signatures of a color space, we first reduce the original RBG color space of the images into an RGB color space of 64 colors, resulting in a 64-bin histogram. For the computation of the EMD between two consecutive images, we use the Euclidian distance in this RGB color space. The output of the EMD method at the frame i represents the static degree, denoted SD_i. (2) Then, we define the *static label* of the frame i, denoted SL_i, as follows:

$$SL_i = \begin{cases} 1, \text{ if } \dfrac{1}{2n} \displaystyle\sum_{i-n<j<i+n} SD_j < \text{thr}_{\text{emd}} \\ 0, \text{ otherwise}, \end{cases}$$

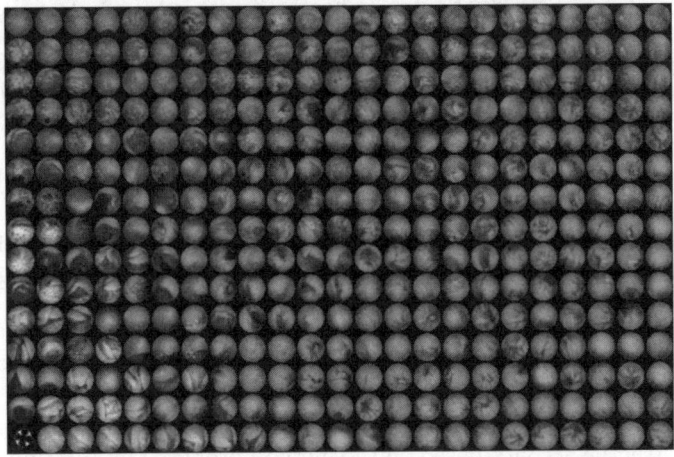

Fig. 4. Example of the cell prototypes of a SOM

where the threshold thr_{emd} and the value n were set to 0.01 and 40 respectively, after an empirical search. (3) Finally, in order to characterize static parts of the video, we consider the binary vector, $v = (SL_1, \ldots, SL_N)$ associated to a video sequence of size N and we perform a morphological closing to it with a structural element of size s (this value was fixed to 10 after several tests) to avoid small errors. A sequence with an associated vector v is defined as a *static sequences* if $\sum_{i=1,\ldots,N} SL_i \geq L$, where L was set to 60 experimentally. *Detection of open lumen sequences:* analyzes the quietness from the point of view of the intestinal lumen motion. Open lumen sequences are important cues to be studied, since they provide useful information about the degree of relaxation of the intestine. These sequences are described in terms of the lumen area along a sequence of nine frames. Nine is the number of frames usually involved in an contraction, since two is the rate of frames per second of the video and that the open-close-open cycle of a contraction takes between four to five seconds. In order to estimate the area of the lumen, denoted L_A, a Laplacian of Gaussian filter was applied (LoG)[14]. The LoG filter is a second order symmetric filter with a tunning parameter σ which plays the role of a scale parameter. The value of LoG is high when a dark hole is found in the image. The value of σ was fixed to 3, the minimum size of the lumen computed empirically. The system uses the following definition of the *tunnel label*:

$$TL_i = \begin{cases} 1, \text{if } \dfrac{1}{9} \sum_{i-4<j<i+4} L_{Aj} < \text{thr}_{\text{lumen}} \\ 0, \text{otherwise.} \end{cases}$$

In Figure fig:Tunnel we display some tunnel frames. Then, any sequence has a binary vector of this form $u = (TL_1, \ldots, TL_N)$ associated and it is called

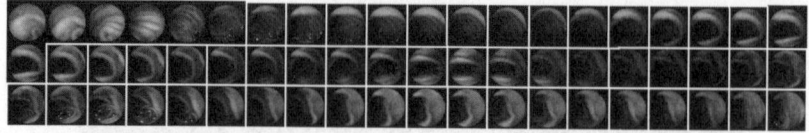

Fig. 5. Example of video frames. Frames with tunnel label are squared in white.

an *open lumen sequence* if after apply a morphological closing to u it verifies: $\sum_{i=1,\dots,N} TL_i \geq M$, where M is the minimum length (experimentally set to 60).

3. Analysis of Manifest Contractile Activity: This module analyzes the contractile activity of the intestine, and extracts the star-wise visual pattern that is present when the intestine is contracting.

Patterns of manifest contractile activity. In this module, we analyze the intestinal contractile activity based on the method proposed by Vilariño et al. [15], which is focused onto the detection of intestinal contractions. Each step of the system filters a different subset of video frames.

- **Step 1: Intestinal Contents Filter.** The aim of this step is to reject the frames where we cannot appreciate correctly whether there is contractile activity. This happens when the intestinal contents hinder the right visualization of the lumen. In particular, this step rejects the frames labelled as (*turbid frames*) in the module 1 *Intestinal Contents Analysis*.
- **Step 2: Periods of Repose Filter.** We focus on rejecting all those frames where the camera is apparently stopped. We explain this effect by the absence of the contractile activity. The frames previously labelled as static frames in the module 2 *Analysis of Idleness in Contractile Activity* are rejected here.
- **Step 3: SVM Classifier.** This last module performs the classification, which is based on SVM with a radial basis function kernel (the σ value was fixed by using cross-validation method). The feature vectors are built up by using the same 54 features proposed in the literature [15], which have shown to provide optimal results for the discrimination of contractile activity. The output of this last step gives us the distribution of the intestinal contractions.

In this module we also extract the *occlusive degree* of the frames with contractile activity. The area of the lumen is the principal feature to characterize this property, since generally, in non-occlusive contractions the lumen area in the central frame is bigger than in occlusive contractions. We compute the lumen area for each frame and its four previous and following neighbors. The resulting vector is used as feature vector for the classification. The result of the RVM Classifier is the occlusion degree of each frame.

Analysis of the contracted lumen. The star-wise pattern is an omnipresent characteristic of the contracted lumen. This pattern is characterized by strong edges of the folded intestinal wall, distributed in an approximately radial way around the intestinal lumen. In order to distinguish this pattern, an accurate wrinkle detector is essential. We follow the strategy proposed by Spyridonos et al.

[16]. First, the skeleton of the wrinkle pattern is extracted and the center of the intestinal lumen is detected. Finally, a set of descriptors are estimated taking into account the near radial organization of the wrinkle skeleton around the center of the intestinal lumen. At the end of this process 14 features are introduced and processed by a RVM Classifier.

2.2   Block 2: Feature Extraction and Classification

Feature Extraction. Once the important information at frame level is extracted we have to define a set of features at video level to characterize intestinal patients in motility disease. We used 19 features, which were selected by the physicians, provided their clinical relevance. Let us define all of them:

1. Related to *open lumen sequences feature*, we extract the percentage of open lumen sequences in the valid parts (valid parts are all frames except those where the intestinal contents do not allow a good visibility), the mean of the static values, computed by EMD, at all open lumen sequences frames and the mean length of the open lumen sequences.
2. From the *intestinal contents feature*, we extract the percentage of the video that are turbid, the percentage of turbid frames that are static, and the mean of static degree of all turbid frames.
3. From *static feature*, we extract the percentage of frames that are static from the set of valid frames and from all video frames, the mean of static degree from all video frames and the mean length of static sequences.
4. Related to *contractile activity*, we extract the number of detected contractions per minute in valid parts, as well as in the whole video, the percentage of contractions in which wrinkles are presented and the percentage of contractions that are non-occlusive.
5. Finally, related to *contracted lumen*, we extract the percentage of frames where the star-wise pattern can be observed, we get this feature considering all video frames, and only considering valid video frames. We also get the percentage of frames that has a low level of wrinkle presence, considering a low value 0.1, and the percentage of frames that have a high level of wrinkle presence, considering as all the frames that have a wrinkle level higher than 0.9. Additionally we get the mean length of wrinkle sequences.

Classification. The last stage of our approach consists of applying the SVM classifier to detect intestinal pathology from input capsule video. The output of the SVM consists of video data suggested by the specialist as the candidates for patients on motility diseases.

Semi-supervised learning. Medical field of work usually deals with imbalanced problems. It is common that the acquisition of labelled data is costly and not always possible, however, it is also usual to dispose of another data set of unlabelled examples. Standard classifiers only use labelled data, in contrast, the semi-supervised learning classifiers address the imbalanced problems by tacking profit of the available unlabelled data set. In our case, by using unlabelled data we pretend to increase the number of patient examples. We propose the algorithm displayed in Table 1. The basic idea is as follows: to create an initial training set with labelled data, and in each new iteration to add a new patient example from the unlabelled data set -this new example has to be the one classified as patient with the highest score-. This iterative loop will stop when no example within the unlabelled data set is classified as patient. Finally, all examples that were not classified as patient will be included in the healthy subjects set.

Table 1. Semi-supervised algorithm for imbalanced problem

---

1. Pick your favorite classification method.
2. Train a classifier f from (X_s, Y_s).
3. Use f to classify all unlabelled items $x \in X_u$.
4. Pick x^* such that $f(x^*) \in C_1$ (C_1: Patient class) and having the highest confidence, add $(x^*, f(x^*))$ to the labelled data.
5. Repeat until all samples are classified as C_2 (C_2: Non-Patient class).
6. Add the remaining $(x, f(x))$ to the labelled data.

---

3 Experimental Results

For our experiments, we considered a set 86 of videos obtained using the WVEC device developed and provided by Given Imaging, Ltd., Israel [17]. The capsule endoscopy interventions were conducted at Digestive Diseases Department of General Hospital "Vall d'Hebron" in Barcelona, Spain. The video data set is divided in three groups: control set of volunteers showing no apparent disease symptoms, patient set with pathological test manometry, and another set of subject with symptoms, but without pathological test manometry, and thus, without any diagnostics. Volunteers were randomly selected from a big pool of subjects without any apparent symptom. We considered these cases as *healthy* subjects without performing a manometry test, because the probability of them of being patient is too small. The final testing set was formed by 86 videos: 50 from healthy volunteers, 19 from patients with pathological manometry test and 17 from subjects with symptoms but without pathological manometry test. The first two groups, healthy volunteers and patients with pathological manometry test, were considered as *labelled data*. However, the data set composed by patients without pathological manometry test was considered as *unlabelled data*.

From a clinical point of view, the gastroenterologists are interested in assessing: a) *sensitivity*, b) *specificity*, c) system *precision*, and finally, d) the *False Alarm Ratio*. All these features are described in terms of true positives (TP), true negatives (TN), false positives (FP) and false negatives (FN). Table 2 summarizes these definitions.

Table 2. Validation Measures

Error	Sensitivity	Specificity	Precision	FAR
$FP + FN$	$\frac{TP}{TP+FN}$	$\frac{TN}{TN+FP}$	$\frac{TP}{TP+FP}$	$\frac{FP}{TP+FN}$

Classification results. A first test was performed with a data set formed only by the labelled data set. The first row of Table 3 shows the obtained results performing leave-one-out validation method [18] over this data set. As we can observe we get a 4.35% of error, 84.21% of sensitivity and 100.00% of specificity and precision. Three of the patients were considered as healthy subject and all of the healthy subjects were correctly classified.

The previous test presents an important drawback: the small size of the data set. In order to overcome this problem we perform a second test considering a new data set including the labelled and unlabelled data set after applying the algorithm proposed in Table 1. We perform a leave-one-out validation method with the new data set. Note that the obtained classification error is computed only by using labelled data, and the unlabelled data is only used in order to create the training data set. In the second row of Table 3 we display the obtained results to this test. The error decreased from 4.35% to 1.16% and the sensitivity increased from 84.21% to 94.74% without affecting to the specificity, precision and FAR.

Table 3. Classification Results

	Error	Sensitivity	Specificity	Precision	FAR
supervised learning	4.35%	84.21%	100.00%	100.00%	0.00%
semi-supervised learning	1.16%	94.74%	100.00%	100.00%	0.00%

4   Conclusions

In this paper we proposed an innovative automatic system for the diagnostic of intestinal motility disfunctions based on computer vision and machine learning techniques. This diagnostic process uses the WVCE data and is a promising alternative to the currently used invasive techniques, as the manometry. The proposed system, firstly, extract the important visual features which characterize phenomenons present in WVCE, secondly, define and analyze clinical patterns to characterize the pathologies and classify the video. This work entails a deep study of video frames and the definition of the most important physiological aspects leading to a new technical and medical terminology. Another important contribution is the application of the semi-supervised algorithm for overcoming the problem of the small quantity of patient examples. The obtained results show that this system represents a promising method for patient diagnostic in intestinal motility disfunctions. The principal strengths of this system test are the low level of invasion and that the monitorization of the clinical process by gastroenterologists is not necessary.

Acknowledgements

This work was supported in part by a research grant from Given Imaging Ltd., Yoqneam Israel, H. U. Vall d'Hebron, Barcelona, Spain, as well as the projects TIN2006-15308-C02 and FIS-PI061290.

References

1. Sonka, M., Fitzpatrick, J.M.: Handbook of Medical Imaging. SPIE Press (2000)
2. Iddan, G., Meron, G., et al.: Wireless capsule endoscopy. Nature 405, 417 (2000)
3. Tjoa, M.P., Krishnan, S.M.: Feature extraction for the analysis of colon status from the endoscopic images. Biomedical Engineering OnLine 2, 3–17 (2003)
4. Karkanis, S.A., Iakovidis, D.K., et al.: Computer aided tumor detection in endoscopic video using color wavelet features. IEEE Transactions on Information Technology in Biomedicine 7, 141–152 (2003)
5. Magoulas, G., Plagianakos, V., et al.: Neural network-based colonoscopic diagnosis using online learning and differential evolution. Applied Soft Computing 4, 369–379 (2004)
6. Zheng, M.M., Krishnan, S.M., Tjoa, P.: A fusion-based clinical support for disease diagnosis from endoscopic images. Computers in Biology and Medicine 35(3), 259–274 (2005)
7. Kodogiannis, V.S., Chowdrey, H.S.: Multi-network classification scheme for computer-aided diagnosis in clinical endoscopy. In: Proceedings of the International Conference on Medical Signal Processing (MEDISP), pp. 262–267 (2004)
8. Boulougoura, M., Wadge, V., et al.: Intelligent systems for computer-assisted clinical endoscopic image analysis. In: Proceedings of the 2nd IASTED Conference on Biomedical Engineering Innsbruck, pp. 405–408 (2005)
9. Vapnik, V.N.: An overview of statistical learning theory. IEEE Transactions on Neural Networks, 988–999 (1999)
10. Tipping, M.: The relevance vector machine. In: Advances in Neural Information Processing Systems, San Mateo, CA, Morgan Kaufmann, San Francisco (2000)
11. Kohonen, T.: Self-Organizing Maps. Springer, Heidelberg (1995)
12. CIE: Colorimetry - part 4: Cie 1976 l*a*b* colour spaces. Cie draft standard ds 014-4.2/e:2006 (2006)
13. Rubner, Y., Tomasi, C., Guibas, L.J.: The earth mover's distance as a metric for image retrieval. Int. J. Comput. Vision 40(2), 99–121 (2000)
14. Russ, J.C.: The Image Processing Handbook. CRC Press, Boca Raton (1999)
15. Vilariño, F., Spyridonos, P., Vitrià, J., de Iorio, F., Azpiroz, F., Radeva, P.: Intestinal motility assessment with video capsule endoscopy: Automatic annotation of intestinal contractions. IEEE Trans. on Medical Imaging (under revision) (2006)
16. Spyridonos, P., Vilariño, F., Vitrià, J., Radeva, P.: Anisotropic feature extraction from endoluminal images for detection of intestinal contractions. LNCS (in press, 2006)
17. Given Imaging, L. (2007), http://www.givenimaging.com
18. Stone, M.: Cross-validatory choice and assessment of statistical predictions (with discussion). Journal of the Royal Statistical Society B 36, 111–147 (1974)

An Approach for Tracking the 3D Object Pose Using Two Object Points

Sai Krishna Vuppala and Axel Gräser

Institute of Automation, University of Bremen,
M1040, NW1, Otto-Hahn-Allee 1, 28359 Bremen, Germany
{vuppala,ag}@iat.uni-bremen.de
http://www.iat.uni-bremen.de

Abstract. In this paper, a novel and simple approach for tracking the object pose, position and orientation, using two object points when the object is rotated about one of the axes of the reference coordinate system is presented. The object rotation angle can be tracked up to a range of 180° for object rotations around each axis of the reference coordinate system from an initial object situation. The considered two object points are arbitrary points of the object which can be uniquely identified in stereo images. Since the approach requires only two object points, it is advantageous for the robotic applications where very few feature points can be obtained because of lack of pattern information on the objects. The paper also presents the results for the pose estimation of a meal tray in a rehabilitation robotics environment.

Keywords: Tracking 3D Object Pose, Object Localization, 3D Reconstruction, Two Points Approach.

1 Introduction

Computer vision is an emerging field supporting the field of robotics with many vision based applications. In order robot manipulators to perform their actions autonomously, the 3D information about the environment is necessary. Among the various available sensors to retrieve the 3D environment information, stereo vision is occupying growing importance. This is because stereo vision provides the human like vision to the applications of robotics. Few such applications of stereo vision in robotics are, to find the pose of an object in 3D, reconstructing 3D environment for path planning, retrieving the geometry of a 3D object etc.

In robotic applications, in order robot manipulator to perform any object manipulation task different vision strategies are employed. Taxonomy of visual control systems is presented in [1] [2]. The two major classes of such systems are position-based and image-based systems. These systems have high accuracy since they are operated in a closed-loop manner. In a closed loop system the overall system error is minimized using the feedback information, where as in an open-loop system the error depends on the performance of the system in a single step. In a "look-and-move", an open loop approach the accuracy of the overall robotic system depends upon vision system output and the manipulator accuracy in

A. Gasteratos, M. Vincze, and J.K. Tsotsos (Eds.): ICVS 2008, LNCS 5008, pp. 261–270, 2008.

reaching the specified locations in the real world [3]. The algorithm proposed in this paper supports the "look-and-move" approach in object manipulation tasks. In a "look-and-move" approach, in order robot manipulator to manipulate an object, it is required to have 6-Degrees of Freedom (DoF) of object pose in robot base coordinate system assuming the transformation between the robot base and the gripper coordinate system is known to the tolerable precision. The 6-DoF of object pose consists of 3-DoF for the position of the object, and the rest 3-DoF for the orientation of the object in the reference coordinate system.

The orientation and position of the camera in the object space are traditionally called the camera extrinsic parameters [4] [5]. In other words, finding the 6DoF of an object pose with respect to the camera is same as finding the extrinsic camera parameters. The problem can also be described as a perspective n-point problem, since the pose of the object is estimated based on the known set of object points that are identified in the image. Typically the problem is solved using the least squares techniques [6] [7], where a large data set is needed in order to obtain a stable solution. Because of inherent computational complexity of such an approach it is often undesirable in the real-time robotic applications where the actions of the other components of the system depend on the stereo vision output. In order to overcome this problem certain number of researchers has tried to develop methods which require less number of points for the pose estimation. In addition to mentioning a solution for the pose estimation using 4 points, a summary of the available solutions for pose estimation starting from 3 points are given in [8].

The 3D pose of the object can also be tracked by reconstructing the object points in 3D. In [9], the 3D pose of the object is estimated by tracking and reconstructing the 3 distinguishable blobs as feature points of an industrial object. The geometry of the considered 3D points forms unique object coordinate system. The homogeneous transformation between the object and the reference coordinate system gives the 3D pose of the desired object. Limitation lies in considering the collinear points.

This paper explains an algorithm to track an object 3D pose using two object points which are identified uniquely in the images of the stereo vision system. The advantage of the algorithm is object pose can be tracked using only two points. Therefore it increases the possibility for estimating objects pose which have very less pattern information. Since the algorithm bases on the slope of a line in a plane, vector notation for these two points is not necessary. The constraints of the algorithm are:

☐ The transformation between the stereo vision system and the considered reference coordinate system is available and constant throughout the algorithm execution. In case it is changed, it is necessary to obtain this transformation using some initial setup.

☐ Objects are not allowed to rotate simultaneously about the multiple axes of the considered reference coordinate system in the environment.

☐ Objects are not allowed to rotate about the virtual line joining the considered two object points, or a parallel line to it in the reference coordinate system.

As mentioned, in "look-and-move" approach, basically the pose of the object with respect to the robot base has to be known. An example of such a robotic task which belongs to the field of service robotics is to fetch the object placed on the platform. I.e. a compound transformation between the robot base and the ultimate object to be manipulated has to be known. In a next abstraction level of the mentioned task, it can be divided into two sub tasks: one is to find the pose of the platform with respect to the robot base; the other is to find the pose of the object with respect to the platform. In the first sub task, the reference coordinate system belongs to the robot base, in the second sub task the reference coordinate system belongs to the platform. Satisfying the mentioned constraints, the pose of the platform with respect to the robot base and the pose of the object with respect to the platform can be obtained using the proposed algorithm. In the following, *Chapter 2* explains the proposed algorithm for tracking the pose of an object, *Chapter 3* presents the experimental results, and *Chapter 4* concludes the presented approach.

2   Tracking the 3D Object Pose Using Two Points

In this approach two object points are needed to track the object pose. Once the object pose is tracked, all the required object points are reconstructed in a reference coordinate system using the priory knowledge of these points in object coordinate system. The algorithm execution is done in the following steps:

☐ It is assumed that the pose of the reference coordinate system with respect to the stereo vision system is priory known.
☐ In the initial object situation, the considered two object points are reconstructed in 3D of the reference coordinate system using the calibrated stereo cameras [6].
☐ A virtual line joining the considered two 3D points makes an angle with each axis of the reference coordinate system. Using this line, the rotations of object around an axis of the reference coordinate system are tracked up to a span of 180° starting from the initial object situation in the reference coordinate system.

Fig. 1 shows the initial situation of the object in 3D. The line joining the 3D points P_1 and P_2 is considered for the algorithm explanation. The orthographic projection [10] of the line on the xy-plane forms a 2D line $P_1'P_2'$ which makes an angle α with x-axis. Similarly, the lines $P_1''P_2''$ and $P_1'''P_2'''$ formed in other planes make angles β and γ with y and z axes respectively.

$$\alpha = \arctan\left(dy'/dx'\right) \tag{1}$$

$$\beta = \arctan\left(dz''/dy''\right) \tag{2}$$

$$\gamma = \arctan\left(dx'''/dz'''\right) \tag{3}$$

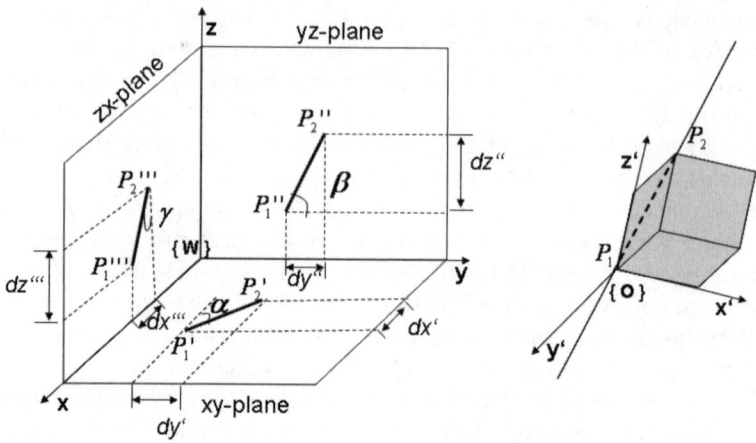

Fig. 1. Orthographic projections of the 3D line on each plane of the reference coordinate system correspond to the initial state of the object

where dx' and dy' are the lengths of the line $P_1'P_2'$ on the x and y axes respectively. Similarly dy'' and dz'' are the lengths of the line $P_1''P_2''$ on the y and z axes, and dx''' and dz''' are the lengths of the line $P_1'''P2'''$ on the x and z axes respectively. The ratios dy'/dx', dz''/dy'', and dx'''/dz''' are the slopes of the lines $P_1'P_2'$, $P_1''P_2''$, and $P_1'''P_2'''$ in xy, yz, and zx planes with respect to x, y, and z axes respectively.

2.1 Influence on Rotation Angles (α, β, and γ) When Object is Rotated Around an Axis of the Reference Coordinate System

When an object is rotated about an axis, the orthographic projections of the considered 3D line of the object are changed in all the planes of the reference coordinate system. Fig. 2 shows the orthographic projections of the considered object line on the 3 planes of the reference coordinate system when the object is rotated only about the z-axis of the reference coordinate system. In order to maintain the transparency, the point of rotation is shown at P_1 in fig. 2. The point of rotation can be any point in 3D. The new rotation angles are α^*, β^*, and γ^*.

Using this information one can deduce that the rotation of object around multiple axes of the reference coordinate system can not be tracked using two object points by considering slope of the line in reference planes. This is because when the object is rotated about multiple axes it has interlinked influence on rotation angles in all the planes.

2.2 Calculation of the Rotation Angle (θ) for Object Rotations Around an Axis In Range From $-90°$ Till $+90°$

Fig. 3 shows the rotations of a line l in xy-plane. The lines l_i and l_i' are the instances of the line l for different slopes, where $i = 1, 2$, and 3 . For each value

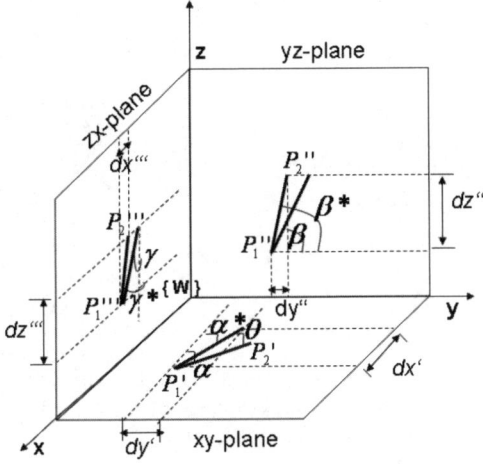

Fig. 2. Rotation of the object around z-axis of the reference coordinate system $\{W\}$

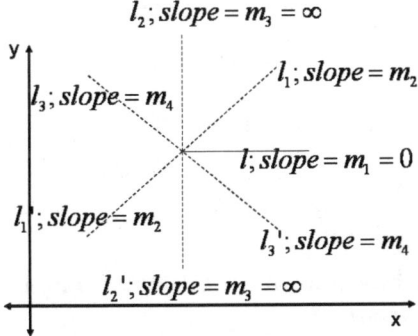

Fig. 3. Slope of the line l for its rotations in xy-plane

of i the slope of any line l_i is m_i, and is same for the line $l_i{}'$. This information reveals that the slope of the line is same for 180° of its rotation in a plane.

Relating this information for the rotations of object in 3D, using two object points object rotation angle around an axis of the reference coordinate system can be tracked uniquely up to a range of 180°. One can customize the range to be only positive or only negative or both positive and negative for object rotations from initial situation. Here, we have considered the object rotation angle (θ) is in a range between −90° and +90° from the object initial situation. In Fig. 4, the line l is the orthographic projection of the considered 3D object line in the xy-plane; it makes an angle α with the x-axis in its initial situation. Line l^* is the orthographic projection of the considered 3D object line when the object is rotated around the z-axis of the reference coordinate system for an angle θ.

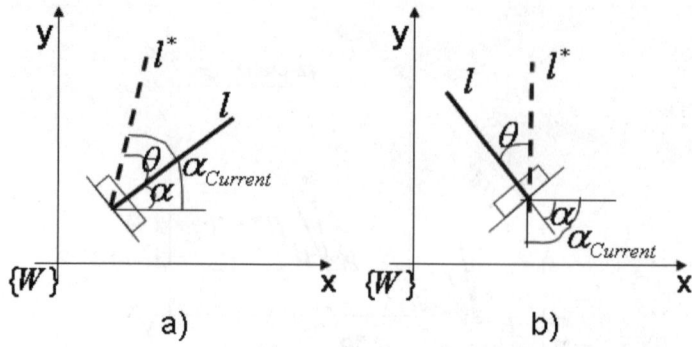

Fig. 4. Orthographic projection of considered 3D object line in the xy-plane; a) line l makes positive inclination ($\alpha \geq 0$) in the xy-plane with x-axis; b) line l makes negative inclination in the xy-plane ($\alpha < 0$)

The line l^* makes an angle $\alpha_{current}$ with the x-axis. The rotation angle θ can be calculated using the following formulae.

$$\text{if } \alpha \geq 0 = \begin{cases} \alpha_{Current} - \alpha, & \text{if } \alpha_{Current} \geq \alpha_{NegativeLimit} \\ \alpha_{Current} - \alpha + 180°, & \text{if } \alpha_{Current} < \alpha_{NegativeLimit} \end{cases} \quad (4)$$

$$\text{if } \alpha < 0 = \begin{cases} \alpha_{Current} - \alpha - 180°, & \text{if } \alpha_{Current} \geq \alpha_{PositiveLimit} \\ \alpha_{Current} - \alpha, & \text{if } \alpha_{Current} < \alpha_{PositiveLimit} \end{cases} \quad (5)$$

where, $\alpha_{NegativeLimit} = \alpha - 90°$, and $\alpha_{PositiveLimit} = \alpha + 90°$

2.3   Calculation of Position of an Object Point in the Reference Coordinate System

Fig. 5 shows the rotation of an object around z-axis of the reference coordinate system. The position of an object point P_3 which is initially known in object coordinate system is intended to be reconstructed in a reference coordinate system. According to the previous discussion, the line l joining the identified two points P_1 and P_2 tracks the object rotation angle around z-axis up to a range of 180° from object's initial situation. Though there are rotations introduced in the yz and zx planes for the projected lines, these rotations are kept constant in the calculated pose but are recorded to track further information for the object rotations around x and y axes of the reference coordinate system. When the object is rotated about z-axis of the reference coordinate system, the position of a point P3 is estimated in the reference coordinate system using the below mentioned formulae. The notations are according to [14].

$$^{W}_{P_3}p = {}^{W}_{O'}T \; {}^{O'}p_{P_3} \quad (6)$$

$$^{W}_{O'}T = \begin{bmatrix} rot(z,\theta) & {}^{W}p_{O'} \\ 0 & 1 \end{bmatrix} \quad (7)$$

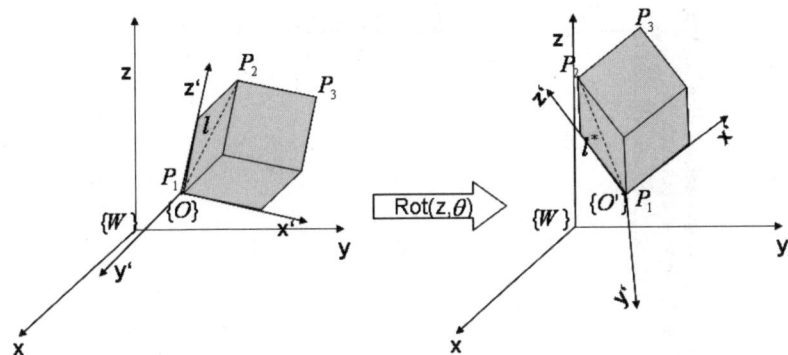

Fig. 5. Rotation of an object around z-axis of the reference coordinate system

where, $\theta = \angle(l, l^*)$ is obtained from stereo vision using equations 4 and 5. $\{O\}$ and $\{O'\}$ denote the object origins in initial situation and when the object is moved respectively. $\{W\}$ denotes the reference coordinate system. $^{O'}p_{P_i}$ is same as $^{O}p_{P_i}$, and denotes the priory known position of the object point P_i , where i = 1,2, and 3 in object coordinate system. $^{W}_{P_3}p$ denotes the position of the point P_3 in the reference coordinate system. $^{W}p_{O'}$ is the position of the new object origin in the reference coordinate system, and in the considered case it is same as $^{W}p_{P_1}$. And, $^{W}p_{P_1}$ denotes the position of the point P_1 in the reference coordinate system and is directly reconstructed using the stereo correspondences.

3   Experimental Results

Described algorithm is tested for the pose estimation of the meal tray in the environment of the rehabilitation robotic system FRIEND II (Functional Robot with dexterous arm and user-frIEndly interface for Disabled people) [11] [12]. The robotic system is intended to support the physically challenged people in their daily life activities. As one of the intelligent sensors, stereo vision system attached to the rehabilitation robotic system supports these tasks by providing the required environmental information. "Serving Meal" to the user is one of the considered tasks. Stereo vision system is intended to estimate the pose of the meal tray for the manipulation and obstacle avoidance purposes. In contrast to [9] where the objects in the environment are dynamic, the objects in the FRIEND II environment are static. The tests are performed offline on a Pentium 3GHz CPU with 1.99GB RAM. The images are retrieved from bumblebee stereo vision system developed by Point Grey Research group [13].

In order to test the algorithm accuracy two small blobs like features are used on the object. These blobs are artificially attached to the two ends of the meal tray handle. The centre points of these blobs are considered as the stereo feature points for the 3D reconstruction algorithm. The proposed algorithm is tested for the rotation of the meal tray around the z-axis of the reference coordinate

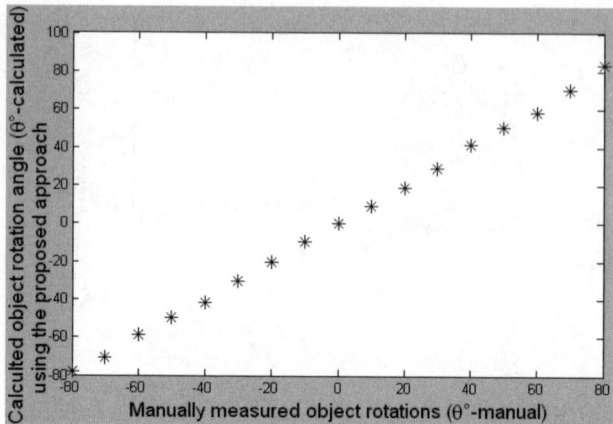

Fig. 6. Calculated rotation angle ($\theta°$-cal.) using proposed approach versus manually measured rotation angle ($\theta°$-man.) when meal tray is rotated around z-axis of reference coordinate system

system. The origin of the reference coordinate system is located about 90cm far from the middle point of the stereo vision system. The presented meal tray rotations are ranged "from $-80°$ till $80°$ in steps of $10°$" around z-axis in the reference coordinate system from the initial object situation. Since the object rotations are around the z-axis, the rotation angle is tracked in the xy-plane of the reference coordinate system with respect to the x-axis.

Fig. 6 shows the plot, calculated meal tray rotation angle using the proposed algorithm versus the manually measured rotation angle, when the meal tray is rotated about z-axis of the reference coordinate system. The Pearson correlation coefficient [15] is a measure of extent to which two samples are linearly related. The Pearson correlation coefficient for calculated rotation angle and the manually measured rotation angle is 0.999, which means that they are strongly and positively correlated.

Fig. 7 shows the results for the reconstruction of an object point P_3 in the reference coordinate system, the position of the considered point in object coordinate system is priory known. Horizontal axis shows reconstructed 3D point P_3 using direct stereo correspondences. Vertical axis shows the calculated 3D point using the proposed algorithm with equations 6 and 7. The Pearson correlation coefficients for the x and y values of the 3D point calculated using the proposed algorithm and reconstructed directly using stereo correspondences are 0.9992 and 0.9997 respectively, which clearly shows that they are strongly and positively correlated. Considering the Pearson correlation coefficient for the z-value is not meaningful since it is always pointed to a single value in the reference coordinate system for the considered case. Therefore the z-value is measured here with the standard deviation of the errors between the two methods, and is 0.005m.

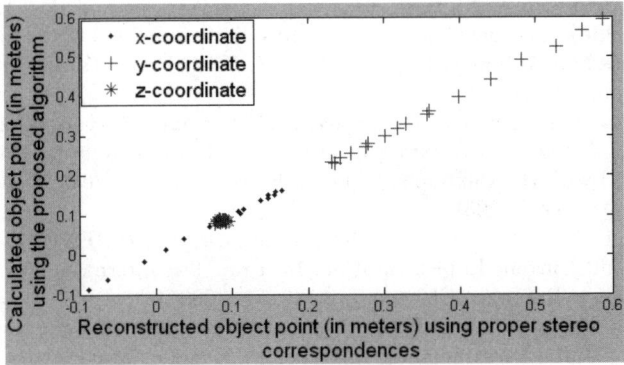

Fig. 7. Calculated 3D position of a point on the meal tray using the proposed algorithm versus reconstructed position of the same point using direct stereo correspondences

4   Conclusions

An algorithm for tracking the pose of the object when the object is rotated about an axis of the reference coordinate system is presented. The presented algorithm can track the rotations up to a range of 180°. The experimental results are presented for changing position and rotation of the meal tray around z-axis of the reference coordinate system. The observed error in estimating the rotation of an object around an axis of the reference coordinate system is minimal. Also, the error in estimated position of an object point using the presented algorithm and the 3D reconstruction of the same point using direct stereo correspondence is observed to be minimal.

References

1. Hutchinson, S., Hager, G., Corke, P.: A Tutorial on Visual Servo Control. IEEE. Trans. Robo. Auto. 12, 651–670 (1996)
2. Peter, I.C.: Visual Control of Robots. Research Studies Press Ltd, England (1996)
3. Garric, V., Devy, M.: Evaluation of the Calibration and Localization Methods for Visually Guided Grasping. In: International Conference on Intelligent Robots and Systems, pp. 387–393. IEEE Press, Pittsburgh (1995)
4. Yuan, J.S.C.: A General Photogrammetric Method for Determining Object Position and Orientation. IEEE. Robo. Auto. 5, 129–142 (1989)
5. A flexible New Technique for Camera Calibration. IEEE Trans. Pat. Anal. Mac Inte. 22, 1330–1334 (2000)
6. Hartley, R., Zisserman, A.: Multiple View Geometry in Computer Vision. Cambridge Univ. Press, Cambridge (2000)
7. Lowe, D.G.: Three-dimensional Object Recognition From Single Two-dimensional Images. Arti. Inte. 31, 355–395 (1987)
8. Horaud, R., Conio, B., Leboulleux, O., Lacolle, B.: An Analytic Solution for the Perspective 4-Point Problem. In: Computer Vision and Pattern Recognition, pp. 500–507. IEEE Press, San Diego (1989)

9. Yoon, Y., DeSouza, G.N., Kak, A.C.: Real-time Tracking and Pose Estimation for Industrial Objects using Geometric Features. In: Proceedings of the Int. Conference in Robotics and Automation, pp. 3473–3478. IEEE Press, Taiwan (2003)
10. Orthographic Projection,
    http://www.geneng.mtu.edu/courses/3000/current/07.spac.vis2.pdf
11. Ivlev, O., Martens, C., Graeser, A.: Rehabilitation Robots FRIEND-I and FRIEND-II with the Dexterous Lightweight Manipulator. Rest. Whee. Mobi. SCI. Reha. 17, 111–123 (2005)
12. Volosyak, I., Ivlev, O., Grser, A.: Rehabilitation Robot FRIEND II - The General Concept and Current Implementation. In: Proc. 9th International Conference on Rehabilitation Robotics, Chicago, pp. 540–544 (2005)
13. Point Grey Research, http://www.ptgrey.com/products/stereo.asp
14. Crane, C., Duffy, D., Kinematic Analysis, J.: of Robot Manipulators. Cambridge University Press, Cambridge (1998)
15. Pearson's Correlation Coefficient,
    http://hsc.uwe.ac.uk/dataanalysis/quantInfAssPear.asp

Adaptive Motion-Based Gesture Recognition Interface for Mobile Phones

Jari Hannuksela, Mark Barnard, Pekka Sangi, and Janne Heikkilä

Machine Vision Group, Infotech Oulu
Department of Electrical and Information Engineering
P.O. Box 4500, FIN-90014 University of Oulu, Finland
jari.hannuksela@ee.oulu.fi

Abstract. In this paper, we introduce a new vision based interaction technique for mobile phones. The user operates the interface by simply moving a finger in front of a camera. During these movements the finger is tracked using a method that embeds the Kalman filter and Expectation Maximization (EM) algorithms. Finger movements are interpreted as gestures using Hidden Markov Models (HMMs). This involves first creating a generic model of the gesture and then utilizing unsupervised Maximum a Posteriori (MAP) adaptation to improve the recognition rate for a specific user. Experiments conducted on a recognition task involving simple control commands clearly demonstrate the performance of our approach.

Keywords: human-computer interaction, handheld devices, finger tracking, motion estimation, MAP adaptation.

1 Introduction

Modern mobile communication devices with integrated multimedia functionalities offer advanced computational and media capabilities. However, mobile phones are designed to fulfil their primary tasks and therefore they have rather restricted user interfaces to access these resources. Various new techniques have been introduced to overcome the limitations of the current solutions with hand-held devices. Today, consumers can take advantage of features such as touch screens, voice recognition and motion sensors. Furthermore, the increasing availability of built-in video cameras has enabled the use of computer vision to improve interfaces toward more natural and convenient interaction.

Most of the previous work on vision based user interaction with mobile phones has utilized measured motion information for controlling purposes. In these systems the user can operate the phone through a series of hand movements whilst holding the phone. During these movements the ego-motion of the camera is recorded [1,2]. Recently, the motion input was also applied for more advanced interaction such as recognizing signs [3,4]. Another intuitive way to interact can be achieved by moving an object such as a finger in front of the camera and then recognizing observed gestures.

Vision based finger tracking and gesture recognition is a well studied problem with numerous applications [5]. Quek et al. [6] presented FingerMouse that utilizes color segmentation to detect the finger and track the fingertip. Their system allowed the user to make pointing gestures to control the cursor. O'Hagan et al. [7] used a single video

A. Gasteratos, M. Vincze, and J.K. Tsotsos (Eds.): ICVS 2008, LNCS 5008, pp. 271–280, 2008.

camera and dedicated hardware to track the motion of the user's finger. The location of the finger in the image was deterimined using a correlation measure. Information obtained was used to generate pointing and clicking gestures. Jin et al. [8] proposed a finger writing character recognition system. They used background subtraction to segment the finger from a cluttered background and detected fingertip based on feature matching. The recognition was performed using a dynamic time warping classifier. Dominguez et al. [9] presented a system for multimodal wearable computer interfacing using color information to segment skin-like regions, shape analysis to detect fingertip, and Kalman filtering for fingertip tracking. Starner et al. [10] developed a system for constrained environment where the user wears distinctly colored gloves. Hands are detected using color and shape analysis. Their gesture recognition is based on HMMs.

We propose a new gesture based interaction technique for camera-equipped mobile devices. The interface is operated through simple finger movements in front of the camera. During these movements the user's finger motion is recorded and trajectories obtained are then interpreted as commands. In order to track the finger, we have developed a method [11] that embeds the Kalman filter [12] and the EM [13] algorithms. Unlike other methods, such as background subtraction, developed for static cameras, our method is designed to detect true finger motion when the camera is also moving and the background is complex. Furthermore, existing techniques for finger tracking usually assume controlled lighting conditions. For example, skin color segmentation is unreliable when lighting conditions change constantly. Therefore, we detect a set of motion features for each frame in the image sequence. These features tolerate lighting changes and can be effectively used in tracking to distinguish finger motion from the background motion. Also, our method enables the replacement of the finger with some other object such as a pen since the method is solely based on motion information and we do not make any assumptions of the shape or color of the object.

In order to recognise the motion trajectories produced by finger tracking we are using HMMs. However, due to the diversity how people makes the gestures it may be difficult to create general models for each class that will perform well for many different users. In order to improve the model performance we propose using unsupervised MAP adaptation to tailor the general models for a specfic user. We address the problem of controlling unsupervised learning by proposing a method of selecting adaptation data using a combination of entropy and likelihood ratio. We demonstrate how this approach can significantly improve the performance in the task of finger gesture recognition.

2 Finger Tracking

The goal in our application is to estimate the motion of an object such as a finger which can then be used as a feature for recognising gestures. With hand-held devices also the camera is usually slightly moving. The problem is therefore formulated as a task of estimating two distinct motion components corresponding to the camera motion and the object motion. The object motion is then obtained by subtraction. For object tracking, we have developed an efficient method especially to be used in handheld mobile devices [11]. Our method combines the Kalman filtering [12] and the EM algorithm [13] to estimate the motion of interest.

We assume that the camera and the object motion can be approximated using a translational model. The state-space model of the camera ($j = 1$) and object ($j = 2$) motions is

$$x_j(k+1) = x_j(k) + \varepsilon_j(k), \tag{1}$$

where $x_j(k) = [u_j(k), v_j(k)]^T$ is the motion between the frames $k-1$ and k. $\varepsilon_j(k)$ is process noise, which is assumed to be Gaussian distributed with zero-mean and the covariance matrix $Q_j = \sigma_j^2 I$. As foreground motion contains both camera and object motion, it is reasonable to assume that $\sigma_2^2 > \sigma_1^2$.

The object tracking uses motion features extracted from the image as an input. We get a set of motion features $\mathcal{F}_i = (d_i, C_i)$ using a block matching method [14] to estimate displacement $d_i = [u_i, v_i]^T$ and related uncertainty information C_i as illustrated in Figure 1(a). Observed displacements of those features, d_i are modelled as

$$d_i(k) = \lambda_i x_1(k) + (1 - \lambda_i)x_2(k) + \eta_i(k), \tag{2}$$

where $\eta_i(k)$ is the observation noise, which is assumed to obey a Gaussian distribution with zero-mean and covariance R_i. λ_i is a hidden binary assignment variable with the value 1 for the camera and 0 for the object motion.

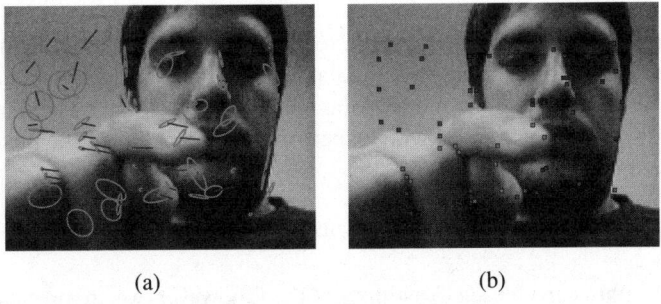

(a)   (b)

Fig. 1. (a) Motion features: feature block displacements (lines) and associated covariances (error ellipses). (b) Assignment of motion features to two components. Weightings are illustrated using colors (red=background ($w_{i,1}$ large), blue=foreground ($w_{i,2}$ large)).

To estimate the motions we use a technique where the Kalman filter [12] and the EM algorithm [13] are combined. Note that the Kalman filter could be used to directly estimate $x_j(k)$ if the assignments λ_i were known. As these assignments are unknown in practise, the predicted estimates of $x_j(k)$ and *a priori* probabilities of associating features to motion components are used to compute soft assignments $w_{i,j}$ in the range [0,1] using a Bayesian formulation. Figure 1(b) shows an example how the motion features are assigned. This step corresponds to the E step of the EM algorithm.

Soft assignments are then used in the computation of the Kalman gains which are needed to obtain the filtered estimates of $x_j(k)$. The principle is that the lower the value of $w_{i,j}$ is, the higher the observation noise R_i is. The weighting of the measurements corresponds to the M step of the EM algorithm.

The steps used to obtain the filtered estimate of the state $x_j(k)$ with $\hat{x}_j^+(k)$ at time instant $k+1$ are summarized in Algorithm 1. In our experimental tracker, 100 motion features are used, the block size is 5 by 5 pixels and the maximum displacement is 12 pixels. We assume that the majority of features are extracted from the background. Therefore, the initial probabilities π_1 and π_2 (See (5)) for the background and the finger motion was set to 0.7 and 0.3, respectively. The learning rate a in (10) was set to 0.95 that guarantees a decent change in the proportion of mixture components.

3   Gesture Recognition

In order to perform classification for the recorded finger movements an appropriate method of modelling the motion sequences should be selected. We are recognizing gestures using HMMs [15]. An HMM is a widely used statistical model capable of representing temporal relations in sequences of data [16,17,18]. However, it is usually difficult to create general models for each sequence that will perform well for many different users. Therefore, we propose using unsupervised MAP adaptation in order to improve recognition performance for a specific user.

3.1   Maximum a Posteriori Adaptation

When using statistical models for pattern recognition we must train the models based on a training set. If this training set is labelled then the *Maximum Likelihood* (ML) principle is used to update the model parameters during training. The likelihood of a training set X_{train} is maximised with respect to the parameters of the model θ. So we select the parameters θ^{ML} such that,

$$\theta^{ML} = \arg \max_{\theta} p(X_{train}|\theta). \tag{11}$$

The EM algorithm can be used to estimate (11). If, however, we are presented with un-labelled data to train the model then there is a chance that some of the training data will not correspond to the class we are training to recognise. Therefore we need some way of constraining the estimation of the model parameters to limit the effect of incorrect data. In MAP adaptation [19] a prior distribution over the parameters θ, $P(\theta)$, is used to constrain the updated parameters. The formulation for MAP estimation is similar to the formulation for ML estimation given in Equation 11. However, in MAP estimation it is assumed there is a prior distribution on the parameters to be estimated. The estimation of the parameters θ according to the MAP principle is given by

$$\theta_{MAP} = \arg \max_{\theta} P(\theta|X_{adapt}) \tag{12}$$

$$= \arg \max_{\theta} p(X_{adapt}|\theta)P(\theta), \tag{13}$$

where X_{adapt} is the data selected for adaptation. Again the EM algorithm can be used for MAP estimation. The next section will look at the use of MAP learning for adapting the parameters of HMMs.

Algorithm 1. The combined Kalman filter and EM algorithm to estimate the state using the given model.

Step 1. Predict estimate $\hat{x}_j^-(k+1)$ by applying dynamics (1)

$$\hat{x}_j^-(k+1) = \hat{x}_j^+(k) \tag{3}$$

and predict error covariance $P_j^-(k+1)$

$$P_j^-(k+1) = P_j^+(k) + Q_j. \tag{4}$$

Step 2. Compute the weights $w_{i,j}$ for each motion feature $\mathcal{F}_i(k+1) = (d_i(k+1), C_i(k+1))$ using a Bayesian formulation. Let $\pi_j(k) > 0$ be the *a priori* probability of associating a feature with the motion j ($\sum_j \pi_j(k) = 1$). The weight $w_{i,j}$ is the *a posteriori* probability given by ($\sum_j w_{i,j} = 1$)

$$w_{i,j} \propto p(\,d_i \mid \hat{x}_j^-(k+1), P_j^-(k+1) + C_i(k+1))\,\pi_j(k), \tag{5}$$

where the likelihood function $p(\cdot)$ is a Gaussian pdf, with mean $\hat{x}_j^-(k+1)$ and covariance $P_j^-(k+1)$.

Step 3. Use the weights $w_{i,j}$ to set the observation noise covariance matrices in (2) according to

$$R_{i,j} = C_i(w_{i,j} + \epsilon)^{-1}, \tag{6}$$

where ϵ is a small positive constant. Compute the Kalman gain

$$K_j(k+1) = P_j^-(k+1)H^T\left(HP_j^-(k+1)H^T + R_j\right)^{-1}, \tag{7}$$

where R_j is a block diagonal matrix composed of $R_{i,j}$, and $H = [I_2 I_2 ... I_2]^T$ is the corresponding $2N \times 2$ observation matrix. Note that if $w_{i,j}$ has a small value, corresponding measurement is effectively discarded by this formulation.

Step 4. Compute filtered estimates of the state

$$\hat{x}_j^+(k+1) = \hat{x}_j^-(k+1) + K_j(k+1)\left(z(k+1) - H\hat{x}_j^-(k+1)\right) \tag{8}$$

and compute the associated error covariance matrix

$$P_j^+(k+1) = (I - K_j(k+1)H)\,P_j^-(k+1), \tag{9}$$

where $z(k \mid 1) = [d_1(k+1)^T, d_2(k+1)^T, \ldots, d_N(k+1)^T]^T$.

Step 5. Update *a priori* probabilities for assignments with a recursive filter

$$\pi_j(k+1) = a\pi_j(k) + (1-a)\frac{1}{N}\sum_{i=1}^N w_{i,j}, \tag{10}$$

where $a < 1$ is a learning rate constant.

3.2 MAP Adaptation for Hidden Markov Models

In HMMs the data sequence is factorised over time by a series of hidden states and emissions from these states. The transition between states is probabilistic and depends only on the previous state. In our case the continuous emission probability from each state is modelled using *Gaussian Mixture Models* (GMMs) [15]. In a GMM the set of parameters θ for each mixture m is given by

$$\theta = \{W, \mu, \Sigma\}, \tag{14}$$

where $W = \{\omega_m\}$ is the set of scalar mixture weights, $\mu = \{\mu_m\}$ is the set of vector means and $\Sigma = \{\Sigma_m\}$ is the set of covariance matrices of the Gaussian mixture. This HMM is trained by updating the parameters of each Gaussian and also the transitions between each state. In MAP adaptation the estimation of the model parameters for each state is constrained by a prior distribution for these parameters, $\theta^{prior} = \{W^{prior}, \mu^{prior}, \Sigma^{prior}\}$. The updated parameters of a particular GMM mixture m, θ_m^{MAP}, can be estimated according to the following update equations:

$$w_m^{MAP} = \alpha \cdot w_m^{prior} + (1 - \alpha) \cdot w_m^{ML}, \tag{15}$$

$$\mu_m^{MAP} = \alpha \cdot \mu_m^{prior} + (1 - \alpha) \cdot \mu_m^{ML}, \tag{16}$$

$$\Sigma_m^{MAP} = \begin{array}{l} \alpha \cdot [\Sigma_m^{prior} + (\mu_m^{prior} - \mu_m^{MAP})(\mu_m^{prior} - \mu_m^{MAP})^T] \\ + (1 - \alpha) \cdot [\Sigma_m^{ML} + (\mu_m^{ML} - \mu_m^{MAP})(\mu_m^{ML} - \mu_m^{MAP})^T], \end{array} \tag{17}$$

where α is a weighting factor on the contributions of the prior parameters, θ^{prior}, and the current estimated parameters using ML, θ^{ML}.

3.3 Controlling Adaptation

A key point in unsupervised learning is control of the learning process or the data used for adaptation. One way to control unsupervised adaptation is to filter out any incorrectly classified sequences before they are used for adapting the model. In this case we propose the use of entropy and the log likelihood ratio as criteria for selecting sequences for adaptation. This is based on our previous work [4] where we demonstrated that a combination of log likelihood ratio and entropy can be used as a measure of the confidence in the recognition result for a sequence. To adapt the prior model to a user specific model, we first classify the sequences produced by the user using the general model. In our case the prior distribution is an HMM created using supervised ML learning with a labelled training set. We then apply the entropy and log likelihood ratio to attempt to filter incorrect sequences from these results. Finally sequences that pass the selection criteria are used to update the model for that class.

Likelihood ratio. If we have a set of classes $\{Cl_1, Cl_2, \ldots Cl_N\}$ and a sequence of data X then the class with the highest likelihood given X is denoted by Cl_a and the class with the second highest likelihood given X is denoted by Cl_b. The log-likelihood ratio δ for a particular sequence is given by

$$\delta = log(p(Cl_a|X)) - log(p(Cl_b|X)), \tag{18}$$

where $p(Cl|X)$ is the likelihood of the class Cl given the data sequence X. In our experiments any sequence that produces a value of δ below a certain threshold is not used for adaptation.

Entropy. Information Entropy is a measure of the randomness of a probability distribution of a random variable Y and is given by

$$H(Y) = -K \sum_{s=1}^{S} P(y_s) log_2 P(y_s), \tag{19}$$

where $P(y_s)$ is the probability of the sample value y_s, S is the number of samples and K is a constant. In our case we take the first derivative of the motion trajectory X, this gives us the velocity of the motion. This continuous velocity sequence is quantised into a histogram and we calculate the entropy of the entries in this histogram. A sequence with a larger entropy has a larger degree of randomness. Again, in previous work [4] we demonstrated how entropy could be used to distinguish random or poorly formed sequence. Our hypothesis was that well formed signs will have a more constant velocity, and so a lower entropy, than random or poorly formed signs. This hypothesis was supported by the results of our experiments. In this paper our hypothesis is that sequences with higher entropy are more likely to be incorrectly classified and that by setting a threshold on the entropy we can filter these potentially incorrect sequence from the data used for adaptation.

4 Experiments

In order to validate the technique described here a hypothetical control system of mobile phone functions was devised. In this system a series of simple control commands were proposed. The eight commands are shown in Figure 2. These command gestures are formed by the user drawing the sign in the air with an extended index finger in front of the mobile phone camera. So there are two challenges to overcome, first the tracking of the finger and secondly the classification of the sequences produced by this tracking.

Data and experimental procedure. The experimental data was collected from 10 subjects. Each subject was asked to draw each of the commands shown in Figure 2 four times using a standard camera equipped mobile phone, a Nokia N73. This formed the initial training and validation sets and also the baseline test set to measure the models performance before any adaptation. This was divided into a training set of four subjects (128 sequences), a validation set of two subjects (64 sequences) and a test set of four subjects (128 sequences). To form the training and test sets for adaptation two subjects from the test set were asked to draw each sign an additional 11 times. These sequences form an adaptation set and test set for each of the subjects. Seven sequences from each subject are used to create a model adapted to that specific subject and four sequences from each subject are used to test the performance of the adapted models.

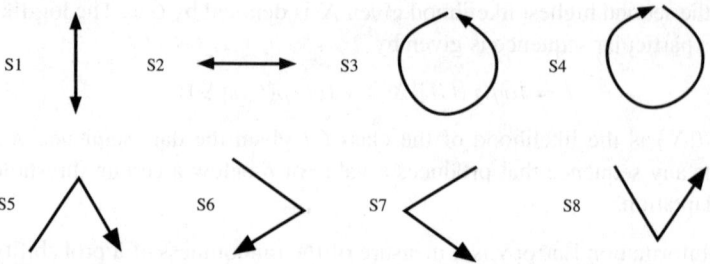

Fig. 2. The eight signs chosen to represent mobile phone commands. S1 and S2 are a single up and down and side to side movement respectively.

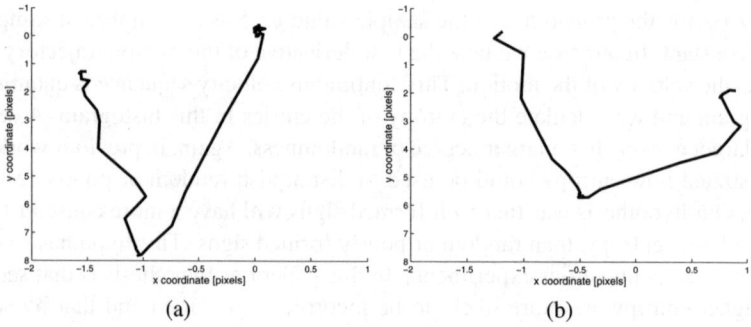

Fig. 3. The signs S1 (a) and S8 (b) performed by a single user

Table 1. Confusion matrix for the baseline recognition experiment using unadapted HMMs

Table 2. Confusion matrix for recognition experiment using HMMs adapted to the two subjects

	S1	S2	S3	S4	S5	S6	S7	S8
S1	6	0	0	0	0	0	0	0
S2	0	8	0	0	1	0	0	0
S3	2	2	15	0	0	1	1	0
S4	2	0	0	16	0	0	0	0
S5	0	0	0	0	15	0	0	0
S6	0	0	0	0	0	15	1	0
S7	0	6	0	0	0	0	14	0
S8	6	0	1	0	0	0	0	16

	S1	S2	S3	S4	S5	S6	S7	S8
S1	7	0	0	0	0	0	0	0
S2	0	8	0	0	0	0	0	0
S3	0	0	8	0	0	0	0	0
S4	1	0	0	8	0	2	0	0
S5	0	0	0	0	8	0	0	0
S6	0	0	0	0	0	4	0	0
S7	0	0	0	0	0	0	8	0
S8	0	0	0	0	0	2	0	8

Results and discussion. We first ran the baseline experiments using the training set of four subjects and the test set of four different subjects. This produced a sequence recognition rate of 82% on the test set. It can be seen from the confusion matrix in Table 1 that the errors show a distinct pattern of confusion between sign S1 and sign S8 and also between sign S2 and sign S7. These signs are quite similar to each other the only difference being a horizontal or vertical separation of the strokes in signs S8 and S7. Signs S1 and S8 are shown in Figure 3 clearly demonstrating the potential confusion between these signs. This may be due to the variability between different subjects when making the signs, so if a user in the training set does a particularly narrow S8 or S7 this may cause the model the incorrect classify S1 and S2 in the test set.

In the next experiments we tailored the general model to an individual user using unsupervised MAP adaptation. The results of these experiments are in Table 3, this shows that adapting with no constraints on all the data used for adaptation can produce an increased recognition rate. If, however, we filter the sequences used for adaptation by applying the likelihood ratio and entropy criteria we can significantly improve this result. This improvement can also been seen in the confusion matrix shown in Table 2.

Table 3. Results for the adaptation experiments. This shows the baseline percentage recognition rate, the recognition rate when adapting with no constraints and the recognition rate after adapting with entropy and likelihood ratio constraints.

	Baseline	Adapting with no constraints	Adapting with constraints
Subject 1	81.2	84.4	90.6
Subject 2	81.2	87.5	93.7

5 Conclusions

We have presented a new vision based interaction technique for mobile phones. The user operates the device through a series of finger movements. During these movements the motion of the finger is recorded using a tracker based on comination of Kalman filter and EM algorithms. Motion sequences obtained are recognized using HMMs. The performance of the system is improved by using unsupervised MAP adaptation to tailor the classification for a specific user. We demonstrated that the adaptation process could be controlled by filtering incorrect sequences from the adaptation data based on entropy and likelihood ratio. Experiments with a real motion sequences captured with a standard mobile phone clearly show the promising performance of our method.

Acknowledgments

The financial support of the Academy of Finland (project no. 110751) is gratefully acknowledged.

References

1. Hannuksela, J., Sangi, P., Heikkilä, J.: Vision-based motion estimation for interaction with mobile devices. Computer Vision and Image Understanding 108(1-2), 188–195 (2007)
2. Haro, A., Mori, K., Capin, T., Wilkinson, S.: Mobile camera-based user interaction. In: Proc. of IEEE Workshop on Human-Computer Interaction, pp. 79–89 (2005)

3. Wang, J., Zhai, S., Canny, J.: Camera phone based motion sensing: interaction techniques, applications and performance study. In: Proc. of the 19th annual ACM symposium on User interface software and technology, pp. 101–110 (2006)
4. Barnard, M., Hannuksela, J., Sangi, P., Heikkilä, J.: A vision based motion interface for mobile phones. In: The 5th International Conf. on Computer Vision Systems (2007)
5. Pavlovic, V.I., Sharma, R., Huang, T.S.: Visual interpretation of hand gestures for human-computer interaction: A review. IEEE Trans. on PAMI 19(7), 677–695 (1997)
6. Quek, F., Mysliwiec, T., Zhao, M.: Fingermouse: A freehand pointing interface. In: Proc. of International Workshop on Face and Gesture Recognition, pp. 372–377 (1995)
7. O'Hagan, R., Zelinsky, A.: Finger track - a robust and real-time gesture interface. In: Australian Joint Conference on Artificial Intelligence, pp. 475–484 (1997)
8. Jin, L., Yang, D., Zhen, L., Huang, J.: A novel vision based finger-writing character recognition system. In: Proc. of the 18th International Conf. on Pattern Recognition (2006)
9. Dominguez, S., Keaton, T., Sayed, A.: A robust finger tracking method for multimodal wearable computer interfacing. IEEE Transactions on Multimedia 8(5), 956–972 (2006)
10. Starner, T., Pentland, A.: Visual recognition of american sign language using hidden markov models. In: IEEE Workshop on Automatic Face and Gesture Recognition, pp. 189–194 (1995)
11. Hannuksela, J., Huttunen, S., Sangi, P., Heikkilä, J.: Motion-based finger tracking for user interaction with mobile devices. In: 4th European Conf. on Visual Media Production (2007)
12. Kalman, R.E.: A new approach to linear filtering and prediction problems. Trans. of the ASME-Journal of Basic Engineering Series D(82), 35–45 (1960)
13. Dempster, A., Laird, N., Rubin, D.: Maximum likelihood from incomplete data via the em algorithm. Journal of the Royal Statistical Society 39(1), 1–38 (1977)
14. Sangi, P., Hannuksela, J., Heikkilä, J.: Global motion estimation using block matching with uncertainty analysis. In: 15th European Signal Processing Conference (2007)
15. Rabiner, L.R.: A tutorial on Hidden Markov Models and selected applications in speech recognition. Proceedings of the IEEE 77(2), 257–286 (1989)
16. Jelinek, F.: Statistical methods for speech recognition. MIT Press, Cambridge (1997)
17. Hu, J., Brown, M.K., Turin, W.: Hmm based on-line handwriting recognition. IEEE Transactions on Pattern Analysis and Machine Intelligence 18(10), 1039–1045 (1996)
18. Barnard, M., Odobez, J.M., Bengio, S.: Multi-modal audio-visual event recognition for football analysis. In: Proceedings of IEEE Workshop on Neural Networks for Signal Processing (2003)
19. Gauvain, J.L., Lee, C.: Maximum a posteriori estimation for multivariate gaussian mixture observations of markov chains. IEEE Trans. Speech Audio Processing 2, 291–298 (1994)

Weighted Dissociated Dipoles: An Extended Visual Feature Set

Xavier Baró[1] and Jordi Vitrià[1,2]

[1] Computer Vision Center, Edifici O, Campus UAB, Bellaterra, Barcelona
[2] Dept. Matemàtica Aplicada i Anàlisi, UB, Gran Via 585, 08007 Barcelona, Spain
{xbaro,jordi}@cvc.uab.cat

Abstract. The complexity of any learning task depends on the learning method as on finding a good data representation. In the concrete case of object recognition in computer vision, the representation of the images is one of the most important decisions in the design step. As a starting point, in this work we use the representation based on Haar-like filters, a biological inspired feature set based on local intensity differences, which has been successfully applied to different object recognition tasks, such as pedestrian or face recognition problems. From this commonly used representation, we jump to the dissociated dipoles, another biological plausible representation which also includes non-local comparisons. After analyzing the benefits of both representations, we present a more general representation which brings together all the good properties of Haar-like and dissociated dipoles representations. Since these feature sets cannot be used with the classical Adaboost approach due computational limitations, an evolutionary learning algorithm is used to test them over different state of the art object recognition problems. Besides, an extended statistically study of these results is performed in order to verify the relevance of these huge feature spaces.

Keywords: Features selection, Object Recognition, Evolutive learning.

1 Introduction

The motivation for this work comes from a mobile mapping system named Geovan (see Fig. 1). In this project, a van equipped with a GPS/INS system and a set of digital cameras is used to take images from cities and roads. All the captured data must be analyzed to extract multiple information. In particular, one of the desired applications consists off the positioning of all the traffic signs in a cartographic database [1]. That traffic sign recognition problem was the seed of this work.

Object recognition is one of the most challenging problems in the computer vision field. Given an image, the goal is to determine whether or not the image contains an instance of an object category or not. In the literature there are two main approaches to deal with the object recognition problem: Holistic methods and heuristical local methods.

A. Gasteratos, M. Vincze, and J.K. Tsotsos (Eds.): ICVS 2008, LNCS 5008, pp. 281–290, 2008.

Fig. 1. Geovan mobile mapping system and a stereo-pair of images

Holistic methods use the whole image or a region of interest to perform object identification. These systems are typically based on Principal Component Analysis (PCA), Linear Discriminant Analysis (LDA) or on some form of artificial neural net. Although these methods have been used in a broad set of computer vision problems, there are still some problems that cannot be easily solved using this type of approaches. Complex backgrounds, partial object occlusions, severe lighting changes or changes in the scale and point of view represent a problem if they were to be faced under a holistic approach.

An alternative are the heuristic local appearance methods or feature based methods, which provide a richer description of the image. In contrast to holistic methods that are problem independent, in this case we should select the type of features which better adapts to the problem. We can choose from a wide variety of features, such as the fragments-based representation approach of Ullman [2], the gradient orientation based SIFT [3] or the Haar-like features used by Viola [4].

This paper is related to the feature based methods, namely, our starting point is the Haar-like feature model. Haar-like filters allow a powerful representation of an image using local contrast differences. This representation demonstrated to be a robust description to be applied over object recognition problems, specially in the case of face detection [4]. In addition, the evaluation of these filters using the integral image has a low computational cost, being potentially useful for real-time applications.

The Haar-like filters are local descriptors, in the sense that they only compare adjacent regions. In [5], Sinha presents the dissociated dipoles, a non-local representation based on region contrast differences. The evaluation is done in the same way that in the case of the previous ones, with the only difference that now the regions do not have the adjacency constraint. In fact, some type of Haar-like features can be represented via dissociated dipoles.

Comparing Haar-like filters and dissociated dipoles, we can see that they share some desired properties as the robustness in front of the noise (they are integral based features) and severe illumination changes (they use region differences, not directly the intensity value). On the other hand, the Haar-like have some filters to detect lines that the dipoles cannot simulate, and the dissociated dipoles have the non-local ability which Haar-like approach cannot perform.

In order to collect the good properties of both feature sets, a variant of dissociated dipoles is presented and evaluated. Using weights over the dissociated dipoles, we can represent most of the Haar-like features, obtaining a richer feature space that combines the benefits of both feature sets.

The evaluation of any of the above feature sets consists of the subtraction of the value of all the negative regions from the value of positive regions. Finally, the difference between the regions mean intensity is used to decide to which class a given image belongs.

At this point, two different approaches can be applied: Qualitative or quantitative. Although the most extended approach is the quantitative one used by Viola [4], which consists of finding the best threshold value to make a decision, recent works have demonstrated that qualitative approaches based only on the sign of the difference are more robust in front of noise and illumination changes [6].

All the previous feature sets have in common a high cardinality, which makes their application difficult for the classical learning methods. In the case of Haar-like approaches, it is solved by scaling the samples to a small training window where the number of possible features is computationally feasible. In the case of dissociated dipoles, the original image is repeatedly filtered and subsampled to create different levels of the image pyramid. Then, a point in the deeper levels of the pyramid corresponds to the mean value of a region in the upper levels of the pyramid. Thus, we can only consider the relation between points. In this work we use an evolutionary version of Adaboost that is able to work with huge feature spaces, such as the presented before.

This paper is organized as follows: Section 2 describes the three types of features and their properties. Section 3 introduces the qualitative approach to evaluate the features, and section 4 presents the learning strategy. Finally in section 5 we analyze and compare the behavior of each type of feature set using the evolutive approach.

2   Feature Set

Selecting a good feature set is crucial to design a robust object recognition system. In this work we use region based features, which consist of differences between the mean values of each region. These features are robust in front of the noise and severe light conditions. In addition, using the integral image (Fig. 2), the value of each region is calculated with just four accesses.

2.1   Haar-Like Features

This type of features is a discretized version of the Haar wavelets (see Fig. 3). Viola used this type of features in their real-time face detector [4] because they are easy to be computed by means of the integral image and in addition they are robust in front of noise and severe illumination changes. The original set of Haar-like features types was extended by Lienhart in [7], adding a rotated version of the original

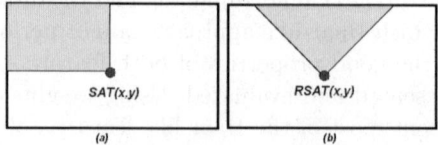

Fig. 2. Integral images. Each point contains the sum value of the gray region. *a)* Integral image *b)* 45° rotated integral image

types, and demonstrating that the performance of a classifier is related to the size of the feature space. The feature set is composed by all the possible configurations of position and scale inside a training window, therefore, learning a classifier using this feature set becomes unfeasible for large window sizes.

2.2   Dissociated Dipoles

The sticks or dissociated dipoles were defined by Shina in [5]. In their works, the authors perform a set of physical experiments to demonstrate that as in the case of Haar-like features, the dissociated dipoles are a biological plausible type of features. This is a more general feature set, which compares the mean illuminance values of two regions, the so called excitatory and the inhibitory dipoles (see Fig. 3). From a computational point of view, the evaluation of a dissociated dipole has the same cost as the evaluation of a Haar-like feature. They also share the robustness in front of noise and illuminance changes. In fact, the two regions Haar-like features can be represented by means of the dissociated dipoles. The feature set is composed by all the possible sizes and positions of each one of the two regions. Any exhaustive search (i.e Adaboost approach) over this feature set is unfeasible. An application based on scale-image approach can be found in [8].

2.3   Weighted Dissociated Dipoles

Weighted dissociated dipoles are a more general definition of the dissociated dipoles, where each region has an associated weight $W \in \{1, 2\}$. With this simple modification, we can represent all the edge, line and center-surrounding types of the Haar-like feature set. As in the case of the normal dissociated dipoles, the huge cardinality prevents the use of this type of features by classical approaches.

3   Ordinal Features

The term of ordinal features is related to the use of the sign instead of directly the value of the feature. In [6], a face detection approach is presented using only the sign of region intensity differences. They demonstrate that removing the magnitude of the difference, the model becomes more stable to illumination changes and image degradation.

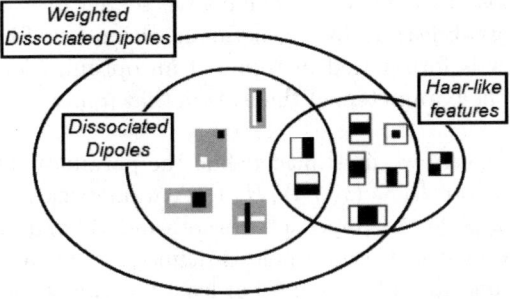

Fig. 3. Graphical comparison of all the presented feature sets

4 Evolutive Adaboost

The huge cardinality of all the explained feature sets is a problem for the classical learning approaches. In this work we use the system presented in [9], where an evolutive variation of the classical Adaboost used by Viola in [4] was presented.

Given: $(x_1, y_1), ..., (x_m, y_m)$ where $x_i \in X, y_i \in Y = \{-1, +1\}$
Initialize $D_1(i) = 1/m$
For $t = 1, .., T$:

Step 1. Use a genetic algorithm to minimize:

$$\epsilon_t = Pr_{i \sim D_t}[h_t(x_i) \neq y_i]$$

the given solution is taken as the hypothesis h_t

Step 2. Get weak hypothesis $h_t : X \mapsto \{-1, +1\}$ with error ϵ_t.

Step 3. Choose $\alpha_t = \frac{1}{2} \ln\left(\frac{1-\epsilon_t}{\epsilon_t}\right)$

Step 4. Update:

$$D_{t+1}(i) = \frac{D_t(i)}{Z_t} \times \begin{cases} e^{-\alpha_t} & if \ \ h_t(x_i) = y_i \\ e^{\alpha_t} & if \ \ h_t(x_i) \neq y_i \end{cases}$$

$$= \frac{D_t(i) \exp(-\alpha_t y_i h_t(x_i))}{Z_t}$$

where Z_t is a normalization factor (chosen so that D_{t+1} will be a distribution).

Step 5. Output the final hypothesis:

$$H(x) = sign\left(\sum_{t=1}^{T} \alpha_t h_t(x)\right)$$

Fig. 4. The evolutive Discrete Adaboost

The authors propose to change the exhaustive search over the feature space performed by the weak learner by a genetic algorithm (see Fig. 4). As a result, learning a classifier is formulated in terms of an optimization problem, where the goal is to find the parameters of the feature that minimizes the classification error.

To use that approach, we first must define the parametrization of each type of features. Let's denote $R_k = (x, y, W, H)$ the parametrization of the region R_k where the point (x, y) is the upper-left corner, and W and H the weight and height respectively. A dissociated dipole is defined by means of the excitatory and inhibitory regions, and thus we need at least 8 parameters. Analogously, the weighted dissociated dipoles, will be defined in the same way, but now we need to add two extra parameters $W^+ \in \{1, 2\}$ and $W^- \in \{1, 2\}$ which correspond to the weight of the excitatory and inhibitory regions. Thus, we need at least 10 parameters to describe the weighted dissociated dipoles. Finally, using the restrictions in position and size of the Haar-like features, with only one of the regions and the type of Haar-like feature we can describe all the feature set. Therefore, with just five parameters we can describe all the possible Haar-like features.

It is important to notice the differences in the descriptor vector, because high dimensions difficult the task of the evolutive algorithm, which must learn a large number of parameters.

5   Results

Once all the feature sets and the evolutive learning approach are exposed, we evaluate the performance of the classifier using the three types of features. To avoid the selection of too small regions, the area or the regions is restricted to be at least 9 pixels, and since the ordinal approach is used, no normalization is used. First, we describe the data and methodology used to evaluate the performance. Finally, a statistical study of the obtained results is performed in order to analyze the effect of using the different feature sets.

5.1   Performance Evaluation

We evaluate the performance of the classifiers over the following tasks:

Face detection: The first task is to learn a face detector. We use the MIT-CBCL face database [10] with a random selection of 1.000 face images and 3.000 non-face images, learning a classifier to distinguish between both classes.

Traffic sign detection: A traffic sign detector must be able to distinguish when a given image contains or not an instance of a traffic sign. The experiment is performed using real images acquired in the context of a mobile mapping project provided by the ICC[1]. The database consists on 1.000 images containing a traffic sign and 3.000 background images.

---

[1] Institut Cartogrfic de Catalunya. www.icc.es

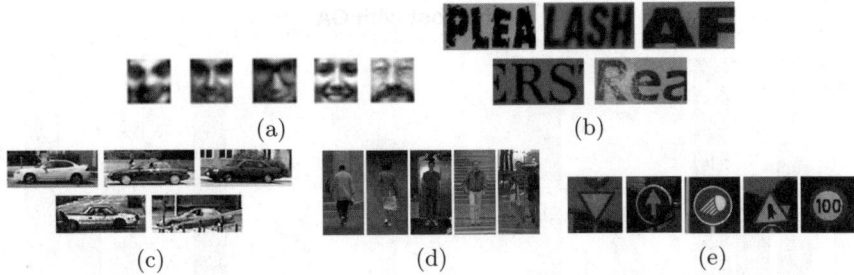

Fig. 5. Data set examples. *a)* Faces *b)* Text *c)* Cars *d)* Pedestrians *e)* Traffic signs

Pedestrian detection: In this case, a detector is trained to identify instances of pedestrians. We use the INRIA Person Dataset[2], with 2.924 images divided into 924 pedestrian instances and 2.000 background images.

Cars detection: This problem consists of detecting instances of a car in urban scenes. We use the UIUC cars database [11], with a total of 1.050 images containing 550 instances of lateral views of different cars and 500 of background images.

Text detection: This task consist on detect text regions in a given image. We use the text location dataset from the *7th International Conference on Document Analysis and Recognition (ICDAR03)*[3]. The images correspond to text regions over a wide set of surfaces and with several illumination changes. To obtain the training data, each text region has been split into overlapped subregions with the same size.

To perform the experiments we fix the maximum number of iterations in the Adaboost algorithm to 200, with a maximum of 50.000 evaluations for the genetic algorithm. The evaluation is carried out using a stratified 10-fold cross validation with a confidence interval at 95% (assuming normal distribution over the error), and the results are shown in Fig. 6.

The weighted dipoles outperform the other types of features in all the considered tasks, obtaining good performance rates in all of them. The next step is to check if the observed differences are statistically significant.

5.2   Statistical Analysis

In [12], Demšar performs a study of the validation schemes used in the works published in the International Conferences on Machine Learning between 1999 and 2003, pointing up the main validation errors and wrong assumptions. As a result of his work, Demšar describes a methodology to compare a set of methods over different data sets. In this section, we use that methodology to find out statistical significant differences between the use of the different feature sets used in the present paper. The techniques applied and the numerical results for the

---

[2] pascal.inrialpes.fr/data/human/
[3] algoval.essex.ac.uk/icdar/TextLocating.html

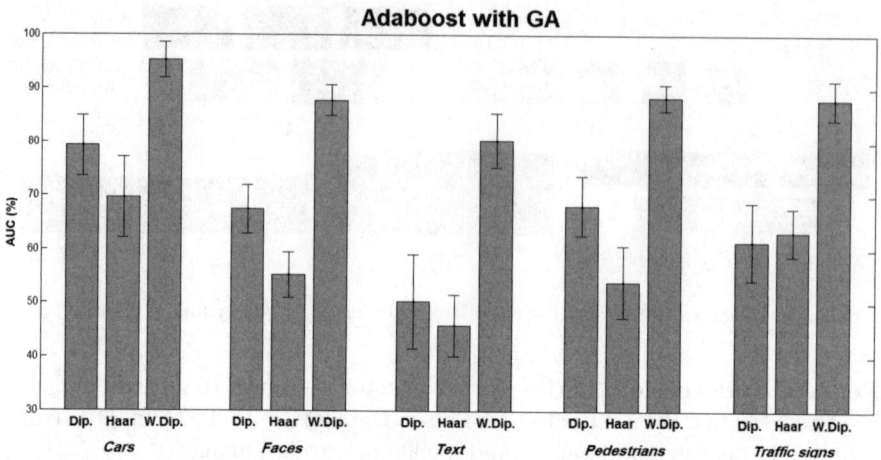

Fig. 6. Area under ROC curve (AUC) response and confidence intervals

statistical study are shown in table 1. In the following, we refer the combination of a feature set and the evolutive Adaboost as algorithm.

Let r_i^j be the rank of the j-th of k algorithms on the i-th of N data sets. The Friedman test compares the average ranks of algorithms, $R_j = \frac{1}{N}\sum_i r_i^j$. Under the null-hypothesis, which states that all the feature sets are equivalent, and so their average ranks R_j are equal, the Friedman statistic

$$\chi_F^2 = \frac{12N}{k(k+1)}\left[\sum_j R_j^2 - \frac{k(k+1)^2}{4}\right] = 8.4 \tag{1}$$

is distributed according to χ_F^2 with $k-1$ degrees of freedom when N and k are big enough. For a small number of algorithms and data sets, exact critical values have been computed. Iman and Davenport [13] showed that Friedmans χ_F^2 is undesirably conservative and derived a better statistic

$$F_F = \frac{(N-1)\chi_F^2}{N(k-1) - \chi_F^2} = \frac{4 \times \chi_F^2}{10 - \chi_F^2} = 21 \tag{2}$$

which is distributed according to the F-distribution with $k - 1 = 2$ and $(k-1)(N-1) = 2 \times 4 = 8$ degrees of freedom. The critical value of F(2,8) for $\alpha = 0.05$ is 4.4590, which is smaller than F_F, so we reject the null-hypothesis. To reject the null-hypothesis indicates that the algorithms are not statistically equivalent. As the null-hypothesis is rejected, we can proceed with a post-hoc test. In our case, as no algorithm is singled out for comparisons, we use the Nemenyi test for pairwise comparisons. The performance of the two classifiers is significantly different if the corresponding average ranks differ by at least the critical difference

$$CD = q_\alpha \sqrt{\frac{k(k+1)}{6N}} = 1.48 \tag{3}$$

where critical values q_α are based on the Studentized range statistic divided by $\sqrt{2}$. Using averaged ranks in table 1 we calculate all the pair-wise differences. Comparing those differences with the critical value, we can conclude that the Weighted dissociated dipoles are significantly better than the Haar-like features $(2.8 - 1.0 = 1.8 > 1.48)$ and Dissociated Dipoles $(2.6 - 1.0 = 1.6 > 1.48)$, but we can say nothing about the difference between dissociated dipoles and Haar-like features $(2.8 - 2.6 = 0.4 < 1.48)$.

The conclusion of this study is that we can affirm (with $\rho = 0.05$) that the Weighted dissociated dipoles are better than the Haar-like features and dissociated dipoles.

Table 1. Results obtained in the experiments and the obtained rank (AUC)

	Feature Set		
Data Set	**Dipoles**	**Haar-like**	**Weighted dipoles**
Face Det.	$67.47\% \pm 4.52(2.0)$	$55.22\% \pm 4.23(3.0)$	$87.74\% \pm 2.85(1.0)$
Traffic Signs Det.	$61.53\% \pm 7.17(3.0)$	$63.30\% \pm 4.41(2.0)$	$87.92\% \pm 3.61(1.0)$
Pedestrians Det.	$68.16\% \pm 5.57(2.0)$	$54.00\% \pm 6.68(3.0)$	$88.40\% \pm 2.40(1.0)$
Cars Det.	$79.27\% \pm 5.64(2.0)$	$69.65\% \pm 7.54(3.0)$	$95.21\% \pm 3.28(1.0)$
Text Det.	$50.33\% \pm 8.75(2.0)$	$45.84\% \pm 5.75(3.0)$	$80.35\% \pm 5.08(1.0)$
Average Rank	2.20	2.80	1.00

6   Conclusions and Future Work

Although the tests must be extended to a larger set of databases, the weighted dissociated dipoles demonstrated to perform good in combination with the evolutive strategy. As a feature work, we plan to extend the study to other evolutive strategies, as the Evolutive Algorithms based on Probabilistic Models (EAPM), which can better represent the relations between the parameters that configure the features. The proposed method has been successfully implanted in the target mobile mapping system, obtaining comparable performance to the manual inspection of the images, and drastically reducing the processing time.

Acknowledgments. This work has been developed in a project in collaboration with the *Institut Cartogràfic de Catalunya* under the supervision of Maria Pla. This work was partially supported by MEC grant TIC2006-15308-C02-01 and CONSOLIDER-INGENIO 2010 (CSD2007-00018).

References

1. Baró, X., Vitrià, J.: Fast traffic sign detection on greyscale images. In: Recent Advances in Artificial Intelligence Research and Development, October 2004, IOS Press, Amsterdam (2004)
2. Ullman, S., Sali, E.: Object classification using a fragment-based representation. In: BMVC 2000: Proceedings of the First IEEE International Workshop on Biologically Motivated Computer Vision, pp. 73–87. Springer, London (2000)

3. Lowe, D.G.: Object recognition from local scale-invariant features. In: Proc. of the International Conference on Computer Vision ICCV, Corfu. pp. 1150–1157 (1999)

4. Viola, P., Jones, M.: Rapid object detection using a boosted cascade of simple features. In: Proceedings of the 2001 IEEE Computer Society Conference on Computer Vision and Pattern Recognition, vol. 1, I–511–I–518 (2001)

5. Balas, B., Sinha, P.: Dissociated dipoles: Image representation via non-local comparisons, Sarasota, FL. Annual meeting of the Vision Sciences Society (2003)

6. Thoresz, K., Sinha, P.: Qualitative representations for recognition. Journal of Vision 1(3), 298–298 (2001)

7. Lienhart, R., Maydt, J.: An extended set of haar-like features for rapid object detection. In: Proceedings of the International Conference on Image Processing, Rochester, USA, September 2002, pp. 900–903. IEEE, Los Alamitos (2002)

8. Smeraldi, F.: Ranklets: orientation selective non-parametric features applied to face detection. In: Proceedings. 16th International Conference on Pattern Recognition, vol. 3, pp. 379–382 (2002)

9. Baró, X., Vitrià, J.: Real-time object detection using an evolutionary boosting strategy. In: Ninth International Conference of the Catalan Association for Artificial Intelligence (CCIA 2006), Perpinyà (France) (2006)

10. MIT-CBCL face database

11. Agarwal, S., Awan, A., Roth, D.: UIUC cars database

12. Demšar, J.: Statistical comparisons of classifiers over multiple data sets. JMLR 7 (January 2006)

13. Iman, R.L., Davenport, J.M.: Approximations of the critical region of the friedman statistic. Communications in Statistics, 571–595 (1980)

Scene Classification Based on Multi-resolution Orientation Histogram of Gabor Features

Kazuhiro Hotta

The University of Electro-Communications,
1-5-1 Chofugaoka, Chofu-shi, Tokyo 182-8585, Japan
hotta@ice.uec.ac.jp
http://www.htlab.ice.uec.ac.jp/~hotta/

Abstract. This paper presents a scene classification method based on multi-resolution orientation histogram. In recent years, some scene classification methods have been proposed because scene category information is used as the context for object detection and recognition. Recent studies uses the local parts without topological information. However, the middle size features with rough topological information are more effective for scene classification. For this purpose, we use orientation histogram with rough topological information. Since we do not the appropriate subregion size for computing orientation histogram, various subregion sizes are prepared, and multi-resolution orientation histogram is developed. Support Vector Machine is used to classify the scene category. To improve the accuracy, the similarity between orientation histogram on the same subregion is used effectively. The proposed method is evaluated with the same database and protocol as the recent studies. We confirm that the proposed method outperforms the recent scene classification methods.

1 Introduction

If the system can recognize the scene of an input image, it can estimate object candidates which are probably included in the scene. In addition, the size and position of objects may be estimated from the scene category [1]. Therefore, scene category is useful to speed up the object detection and improve the accuracy. It is also important as the first step of image understanding.

Szummer et al. proposed indoor and outdoor classification method [2]. In their method, color, texture and frequency features of local regions are used. Fei-Fei et al. proposed a scene classification method based on bag-of-keypoints [3]. Bosch et al. also proposed a scene classification method based on pLSA [4]. These methods used local patches without topological information. However, they [3,4] reported that accuracy is improved when local parts are selected from evenly sampled grid. The results show that rough information such as global appearance or relation between subregions with topological information are more effective for scene classification though they used only local parts without topological information. Torralba used the Principal Component Analysis (PCA) of multi-scale Gabor features as the context for object detection [1]. They used the local frequency and orientation information with topological information. In addition, global appearance features were also used by applying PCA. They combined

A. Gasteratos, M. Vincze, and J.K. Tsotsos (Eds.): ICVS 2008, LNCS 5008, pp. 291–301, 2008.

local information and global relations well. However, their approach depends heavily on the position of objects. In general, the positions of objects in the certain scene are not stable. Therefore, the robustness to small shift is required. Namely, rough topological information is better. In [5], the robustness to shift is introduced by averaging the outputs of steerable filters. However, the subregion size for computing the average outputs is fixed. The appropriate subregion size depends on the scene category.

In recent years, the effectiveness of orientation histogram [6,7,8,9] is shown in object categorization. The orientation histogram is robust to shift variations within the subregion in which orientation histogram is computed. In this paper, the idea of orientation histogram is used to extract the features with rough topological information for scene classification. We can not know the appropriate subregion sizes for orientation histogram. Therefore, various subregion sizes for computing orientation histogram are prepared. Orientation histograms are developed within all subregions. We obtain multi-resolution orientation histogram from an input image. In this paper, it is developed from multi-scale Gabor features because Gabor features which extract frequency and orientation information is better than the simple gradient. To classify the scene categories, Support Vector Machine (SVM) [10] is used. We use normalized polynomial kernel [11,12] in which the parameter dependency is low and comparable accuracy with Gaussian kernel is obtained. However, when one kernel is applied to the whole multi-resolution orientation histogram, each orientation histogram obtained at subregion is not used well. To avoid this problem, normalized polynomial kernel is applied to each orientation histogram. The outputs of kernels for all orientation histograms are integrated by summation [13,14]. By this kernel, the similarity between orientation histogram at the same subregion is used well, and the accuracy is improved. The proposed method may be similar to the spatial pyramid match kernel [9]. However, they measures the similarity of bag-of-keypoints within subregion. Local parts within subregion are used to compute the similarity. Since this method pays attention to the appearance of local parts, it is effective for object categorization rather than scene classification. On the other hand, the proposed method computes the similarity of orientation histogram within subregion. Only the orientation and frequency features within subregion are used. These rough information is effective for scene classification rather than object categorization. However, the summation kernel requires high computational cost because the number of kernel computation is large. To speed up and maintain the accuracy, the norm of each orientation histogram is normalized instead of applying normalized polynomial kernel to each orientation histogram. The inner product of multi-resolution orientation histogram after normalizing the norm of orientation histogram becomes the summation of correlation of each orientation histogram. Therefore, if one normalized polynomial kernel is applied to the whole features after normalizing the norm of orientation histogram, the similarity between the orientation histograms of the same subregion can be used. This gives the good accuracy with low computational cost.

The proposed method is evaluated using the database of 13 scene categories [15] which are used in recent studies [3,4]. The summation of normalized polynomial kernel gives better accuracy than standard normalized polynomial kernel because the similarity between orientation histogram on the same subregion is used effectively. We also

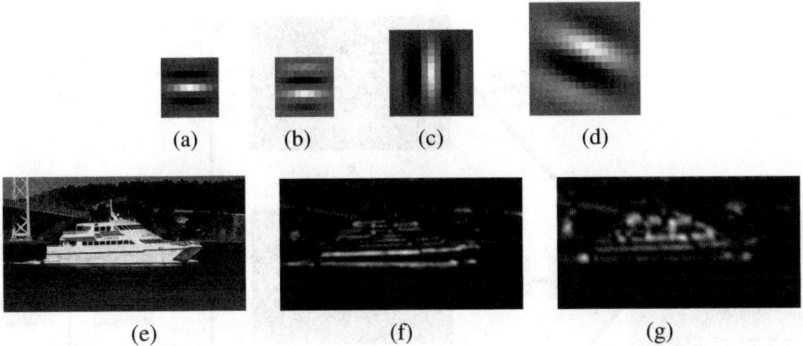

Fig. 1. Examples of Gabor filters and output images

evaluate that case in which standard normalized polynomial kernel is used after normalizing the norm of each orientation histogram. By normalizing the norm of each orientation histogram, nearly same accuracy as the summation kernel is obtained with low computational cost. The proposed method is compared with recent scene classification methods based on bag-of-keypoints [3,4] with the same protocol. We demonstrate that the proposed method outperforms recent scene classification methods.

This paper is organized as follows. In section 2, multi-resolution orientation histogram is explained. Section 3 explains the SVM and devices on kernel. Experimental results are shown in section 4. Effectiveness of the proposed method is demonstrated by the comparison with conventional methods. Finally, conclusions and future works are described.

2 Multi-resolution Orientation Histogram of Gabor Features

In recent years, the effectiveness of orientation histogram [8,9] for object recognition is reported. Therefore, we develop the orientation histogram from multi-scale Gabor features because Gabor features are better representation than simple gradient features.

First, we define Gabor filters. They are defined as

$$\psi_{\boldsymbol{k}}\left(\boldsymbol{x}\right) = \frac{k^2}{\sigma^2} \exp\left(\frac{-k^2 x^2}{2\sigma^2}\right) \left(\exp\left(i\boldsymbol{k}\boldsymbol{x}\right) - \exp\left(-\sigma^2/2\right)\right), \qquad (1)$$

where $\boldsymbol{x} = (x, y)^T$, $\boldsymbol{k} = k_\nu \exp\left(i\phi\right)$, $k_\nu = k_{max}/f^\nu$, $\phi = \mu \cdot \pi/8$, $f = \sqrt{2}$ and $\sigma = \pi$. In the following experiments, Gabor filters of 8 different orientations ($\mu = \{0, 1, 2, 3, 4, 5, 6, 7\}$) with 3 frequency levels ($\nu = \{0, 1, 2\}$) are used. The size of Gabor filters of 3 different frequency levels is set to 9×9, 13×13 and 17×17 pixels respectively.

Figure 1 shows the Gabor filters of various ν, μ and the output images. Figure 1 (a) and (b) show the real and imaginary parts of Gabor filter with $\nu = 0, \mu = 0$. Figure 1 (c) shows the real part of Gabor filter with $\nu = 1, \mu = 4$. Figure 1 (d) shows the imaginary part of Gabor filter with $\nu = 2, \mu = 7$. In the following experiments, the norm of real and imaginary part at each point is used as the output of a Gabor filter.

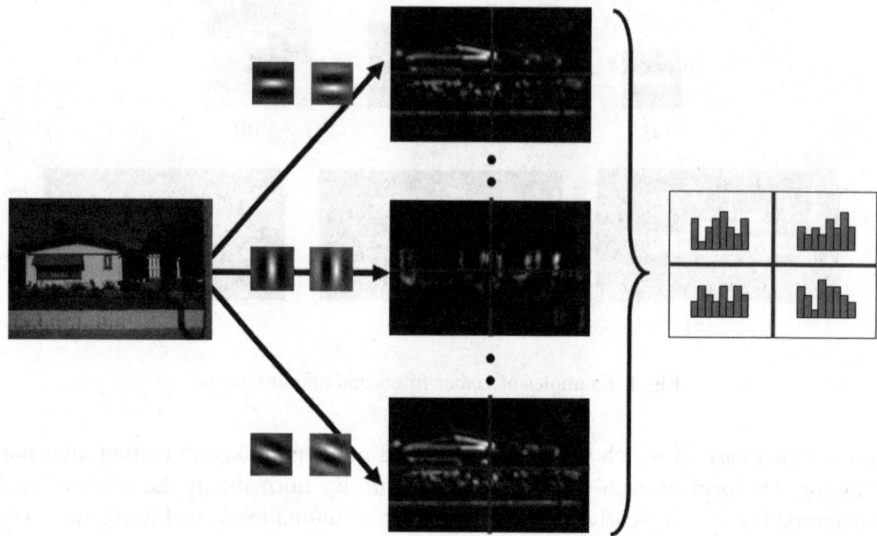

Fig. 2. How to develop orientation histogram from Gabor features

Figure 1 (f) is the Gabor output (norm of real and imaginary parts) when Gabor filters of $\nu = 0, \mu = 0$ are applied to Figure 1 (e). Figure 1 (g) is the output of Gabor filters of $\nu = 2, \mu = 7$. Since Gabor filter of small ν is sensitive to fine edges, the output image (f) is more clear than (g).

Next, we explain how to develop the orientation histogram from the output of Gabor filters. The orientation histogram is developed at each scale parameter independently. The orientation histogram of 8 orientation bins is developed within the unoverlapped subregion by voting the output value of the maximum orientation at each pixel to the orientation bin. How to develop the orientation histogram is shown in Figure 2. In this example, the input image is divided into 2×2 subregions. Note that this example shows the case of only one scale parameter[1]. First, Gabor features (real and imaginary parts) of 8 orientations are extracted from the input image. The norm of real and imaginary parts at each pixel is computed. Then the orientation histogram with 8 bins at each subregion is developed independently. This process is repeated at each scale parameter independently.

In this paper, we prepare various subregion sizes for computing the orientation histogram because we can not know the appropriate subregion size in advance. Concrete subregion sizes are shown in Figure 3. Since the fine subregion size depends heavily on the position, we use rough subregion sizes. The orientation histogram is developed at each subregion and scale parameter independently. Namely, the dimension of multi-resolution orientation histogram obtained from an input image is $2, 328$ (= 3 scales $\times$ 8 orientations $\times$ 97 subregions). We denote it as $x = (x_{1 \times 1}, x_{2 \times 2(1)}, \ldots, x_{2 \times 2(4)}, x_{4 \times 4(1)}, \ldots, x_{4 \times 4(16)}, \qquad x_{8 \times 8(1)}, \ldots, x_{8 \times 8(64)}, x_{1 \times 2(1)}, x_{1 \times 2(2)}, x_{1 \times 4(1)}, \ldots, x_{1 \times 4(4)}, x_{2 \times 1(1)}, x_{2 \times 1(2)}, x_{4 \times 1(1)}, \ldots, x_{4 \times 1(4)})$.

---

[1] In the following experiments, Gabor features of 3 scale parameters are used.

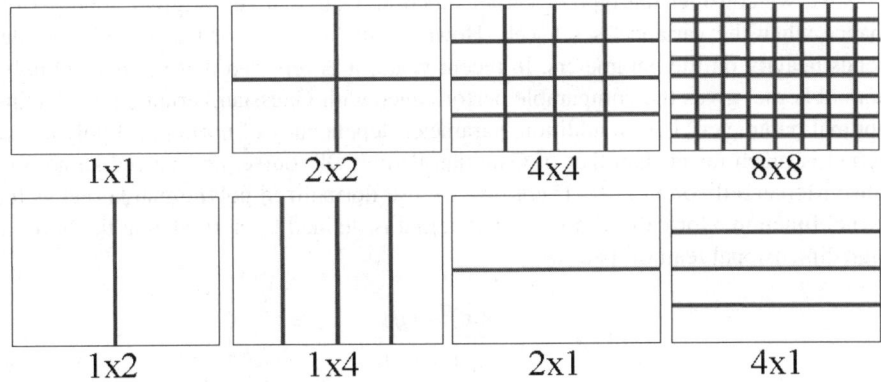

Fig. 3. Various subregion sizes for computing orientation histogram

3   Scene Classification by SVM with Normalized Polynomial Kernel

First, we explain the SVM [10,16] briefly. SVM determines the optimal hyperplane which maximizes the margin. The margin is the distance between hyperplane and nearest sample from it. When the training set (sample and its label) is denoted as $S = ((\boldsymbol{x}_i, y_i), \ldots, (\boldsymbol{x}_L, y_L))$, the optimal hyperplane is defined by

$$f(\boldsymbol{x}) = \sum_{i \in SV} \alpha_i y_i \boldsymbol{x}_i^T \boldsymbol{x} + b, \tag{2}$$

where SV is a set of support vectors, b is the threshold and α is the solutions of quadratic programming problem. The training samples with non-zero α are called support vectors.

This assumes the linearly separable case. In the linearly non-separable case, the non-linear transform $\phi(\boldsymbol{x})$ can be used. The training samples are mapped into high dimensional space by $\phi(\boldsymbol{x})$. By maximizing the margin in high dimensional space, non-linear classification can be done. If inner product $\phi(\boldsymbol{x})^T \phi(\boldsymbol{y})$ in high dimensional space is computed by kernel $K(\boldsymbol{x}, \boldsymbol{y})$, then training and classification can be done without mapping into high dimensional space. The optimal hyperplane using kernel is defined by

$$\begin{aligned} f(\boldsymbol{x}) &= \sum_{i \in SV} \alpha_i y_i \phi(\boldsymbol{x}_i)^T \phi(\boldsymbol{x}) + b, \\ &= \sum_{i \in SV} \alpha_i y_i K(\boldsymbol{x}_i, \boldsymbol{x}) + b. \end{aligned} \tag{3}$$

Mercer's theorem gives whether $K(\boldsymbol{x}, \boldsymbol{y})$ is the inner product in high dimensional space. The necessary and sufficient conditions are symmetry $K(\boldsymbol{x}, \boldsymbol{y}) = K(\boldsymbol{y}, \boldsymbol{x})$ and positive semi-definiteness of kernel matrix $\boldsymbol{K} = (K(\boldsymbol{x}_i, \boldsymbol{x}_j))_{i,j=1}^L$. If $\boldsymbol{\beta}^T \boldsymbol{K} \boldsymbol{\beta} \geq 0$ where $\beta \in \Re$ is satisfied, $\boldsymbol{K}$ is a positive semi-definite matrix. It is known that summation and production of kernels satisfies Mercer's theorem [16,17].

Next, we consider the type of kernel function. Gaussian kernel gives good performance when the variance is set well. However, the accuracy of Gaussian kernel depends heavily on the parameters. In recent years, it is reported that normalized polynomial kernel gives the comparable performance with Gaussian kernel after selecting optimal parameter [11]. In addition, parameter dependency of normalized polynomial kernel is much lower than that of Gaussian kernel. Of course, normalized kernel satisfies Mercer's theorem [12]. Therefore, we use normalized polynomial kernel as the kernel function. Normalized polynomial kernel is defined by normalizing the norm in high dimensional feature space as

$$
\begin{aligned}
K(\boldsymbol{x}, \boldsymbol{y}) &= \frac{\phi(\boldsymbol{x})^T \phi(\boldsymbol{y})}{\|\phi(\boldsymbol{x})\| \, \|\phi(\boldsymbol{y})\|}, \\
&= \frac{(1 + \boldsymbol{x}^T \boldsymbol{y})^d}{\sqrt{(1 + \boldsymbol{x}^T \boldsymbol{x})^d \, (1 + \boldsymbol{y}^T \boldsymbol{y})^d}},
\end{aligned}
\tag{4}
$$

where $\|\phi(\boldsymbol{x})\|$ is the norm in high dimensional feature space. By normalizing the output of standard polynomial kernel, the kernel value is between 0 and 1. In the following experiments, the optimal value of d is determined by the preliminary experiment.

The proposed multi-resolution orientation histogram consists of 291 (3 scales × 97 subregions) orientation histograms with 8 bins. We can apply one normalized polynomial kernel to whole features of 2,328 dimensions. However, the way may not use the effectiveness of each orientation histogram well. To use the orientation histogram of each subregion effectively, the similarity between orientation histogram at the same subregion should be used. Thus, normalized polynomial kernel is applied to each orientation histogram with 8 bins independently. They are integrated by summation [13,14].

The kernel applied to each orientation histogram is defined as

$$
K_p(\boldsymbol{x}, \boldsymbol{y}) = K(A_p^T \boldsymbol{x}, A_p^T \boldsymbol{y}) = \frac{(1 + \boldsymbol{x}^T A_p A_p^T \boldsymbol{y})^d}{\sqrt{(1 + \boldsymbol{x}^T A_p A_p^T \boldsymbol{x})^d \, (1 + \boldsymbol{y}^T A_p A_p^T \boldsymbol{y})^d}},
\tag{5}
$$

where A_p is the diagonal matrix and p is the p-th orientation histogram. We assign 1 to only diagonals which correspond to the orientation histogram used in the kernel. The other elements in A_p are 0. For example, only the first 8 diagonal elements of A_p on are 1 when kernel is applied to the orientation histogram of 1×1 subregion. Since one feature vector consists of 291 orientation histograms with 8 bins, 291 kernel outputs are obtained.

In this paper, 291 kernel outputs are integrated by summation. It is reported that the summation kernel is more robust to partial occlusion than the production kernel [18]. Therefore, it may be robust to the case that the similarities of some subregions become low. In general, the frequency and orientation of almost subregions of the same scene category are similar but some subregions may not be similar because the images in the same scene are not same. Therefore, this property is effective for scene classification. The summation kernel is defined as

$$
K_{sum}(\boldsymbol{x}, \boldsymbol{y}) = K_{1 \times 1}(\boldsymbol{x}_{1 \times 1}, \boldsymbol{y}_{1 \times 1}) + \cdots + K_{4 \times 1(4)}(\boldsymbol{x}_{4 \times 1(4)}, \boldsymbol{y}_{4 \times 1(4)}).
\tag{6}
$$

The proof that this kernel satisfies Mercer's theorem is easy [16]. When K_a and K_a satisfy Mercer's theorem, $\boldsymbol{\beta}^T \boldsymbol{K}_a \boldsymbol{\beta} \geq 0$ and $\boldsymbol{\beta}^T \boldsymbol{K}_b \boldsymbol{\beta} \geq 0$ where $\boldsymbol{K}_a$ is the kernel matrix of K_b, $\boldsymbol{K}_b$ is the kernel matrix of K_b and $\boldsymbol{\beta} \in \Re$. Therefore, the summation of them satisfies Mercer's theorem as follows.

$$\boldsymbol{\beta}^T (\boldsymbol{K}_a + \boldsymbol{K}_b)\boldsymbol{\beta} = \boldsymbol{\beta}^T \boldsymbol{K}_a \boldsymbol{\beta} + \boldsymbol{\beta}^T \boldsymbol{K}_b \boldsymbol{\beta} \geq 0. \tag{7}$$

The summation of normalized polynomial kernels improves the accuracy. However, the computational cost becomes high because the number of kernel computations is large. The essence of the use of summation kernel is to integrate the similarity between orientation histogram on the same subregion. If this hypothesis is correct, the accuracy will be improved by normalizing the norm of each orientation histogram with 8 bins instead of the summation kernel. We define the multi-resolution orientation histogram after normalizing the norm of orientation histogram as

$$x' = \left(\frac{\boldsymbol{x}_{1\times 1}}{||\boldsymbol{x}_{1\times 1}||}, \frac{\boldsymbol{x}_{2\times 2(1)}}{||\boldsymbol{x}_{2\times 2(1)}||}, \ldots, \frac{\boldsymbol{x}_{4\times 1(4)}}{||\boldsymbol{x}_{4\times 1(4)}||} \right). \tag{8}$$

When normalized polynomial kernel is applied to the whole multi-resolution orientation histogram after normalizing the norm of each orientation histogram, the inner product in the normalized polynomial kernel is computed as

$$x'^T y' = \left(\frac{\boldsymbol{x}_{1\times 1}^T \boldsymbol{y}_{1\times 1}}{||\boldsymbol{x}_{1\times 1}|| \, ||\boldsymbol{y}_{1\times 1}||} + \frac{\boldsymbol{x}_{2\times 2(1)}^T \boldsymbol{y}_{2\times 2(1)}}{||\boldsymbol{x}_{2\times 2(1)}|| \, ||\boldsymbol{y}_{2\times 2(1)}||} + \cdots + \frac{\boldsymbol{x}_{4\times 1(4)}^T \boldsymbol{y}_{4\times 1(4)}}{||\boldsymbol{x}_{4\times 1(4)}|| \, ||\boldsymbol{y}_{4\times 1(4)}||} \right) \tag{9}$$

This equation shows the inner product of normalized features becomes the summation of similarity between orientation histogram on the same subregion. If the norm of each orientation histogram is normalized in feature extraction step, the computational cost is as same as the standard normalized polynomial kernel. This is much faster than the summation of normalized polynomial kernels. Note that the similarity between orientation histogram of this approach is the correlation though the summation kernel measures the similarity by normalized polynomial kernel. We evaluate both kernels in section 4.

In this paper, the proposed method is applied to scene classification problem which is the multi-class classification problem. In order to use SVM for multi-class problem, there are two approaches; one-against-one and one-against-all [19,20,21]. It is reported that both approaches are comparable [21,22]. The maximum difference between two approaches is the number of SVMs required. The one-against-one approach needs to train $NC(NC - 1)/2$ SVMs for NC class classification problem. On the other hand, one-against-all approach requires only NC SVMs for classifying one class and remaining classes. Since we must classify 13 categories, one against-all approach is used. To classify an input, the input is fed into all NC SVMs, and it is classified to the class given maximum output.

4   Experiments

This section shows the experimental results. First, the image database used in this paper is explained in section 4.1. Next, evaluation results are shown in section 4.2. Comparison results with recent studies are also shown.

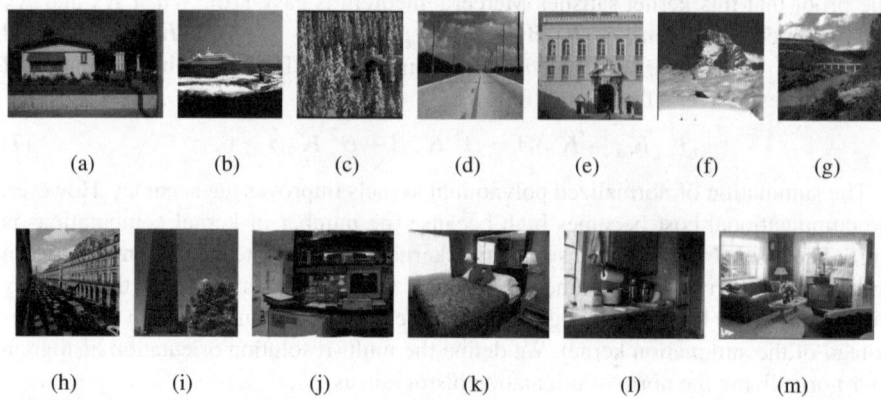

(a)   (b)   (c)   (d)   (e)   (f)   (g)

(h)   (i)   (j)   (k)   (l)   (m)

Fig. 4. Examples of 13 scene images. (a) suburb (b) coast (c) forest (d) highway (e) inside-city (f) mountain (g) open-country (h) street (i) tall-building (j) office (k) bedroom (l) kitchen (m) living-room.

4.1   Image Database

In this paper, we use the database of 13 scene categories [15] to compare with recent studies [3,4]. The database includes only gray-level images. The size of these images are not stable. Each scene category has the different number of images. Examples of 13 scene categories are shown in Figure 4. In the proposed method, Gabor features (3 scales × 8 orientations) are extracted, and multi-resolution orientation histogram of 2, 328 dimensions is developed from each image.

In this paper, the images of each scene category are divided into two sets; training and test sets. 100 images which are selected randomly are used as training set. The remaining images of each scene category are used as test set. This protocol is the same as the recent studies [3,4]. Each scene category has the different number of test images. To reduce the bias of the different number of test images, the mean of the classification rate of each scene category is used in evaluation. This evaluation is also the same as recent studies [3,4]. In this paper, this evaluation is repeated 5 times with different initial seed of random function. The mean classification rate of 5 runs is used as a final result for comparison.

4.2   Evaluation Results

First, we evaluate the case in which normalized polynomial kernel is applied to the whole 2, 328 dimensional multi-resolution orientation histogram. In this approach, the similarity between orientation histogram on the same subregion is not used well. The result is shown in Table 1. The classification rate shown in Table 1 is the average of 5 runs with different initial seeds. Next, in order to show the effectiveness of the summation of the similarity between each orientation histogram, normalized polynomial

Table 1. Comparison with conventional methods

Method	Classification rate
Proposed method (npoly)	71.66%
Proposed method (sum of npoly)	**76.12%**
Proposed method (npoly of normalized features)	76.01%
Fei-Fei (CVPR2005)	65.2%
Bosch (ECCV2006)	73.4%

kernel is applied to each orientation histogram with 8 bins, and they are integrated by summation. The training samples and evaluation method are the same in all experiments. The classification rate is also shown in Table 1. We understand that the accuracy is improved by applying the kernels to each orientation histogram. This kernel gives good accuracy but computational cost is high because the number of kernel computation is large. To speed up and maintain the accuracy, the norm of each orientation histogram is normalized before applying normalized polynomial kernel to the whole multi-resolution orientation histogram. In this approach, the summation of correlation between orientation histogram on the same subregions can be used. The classification rate is also shown in Table 1. The nearly same accuracy is obtained with low computational cost. This result shows the effectiveness of the integration of the similarity between orientation histogram on the same subregion.

Finally, the proposed method is compared with recent studies using the same database. The result of Fei-Fei's method based on bag-of-keypoints [3] is shown in Table 1. We understand that the proposed method gives much higher classification rate than the Fei-Fei's method. Next, we compare our method with Bosch's method based on pLSA [4]. The classification accuracy of their method is also shown in Table 1. The proposed method also outperforms the Bosch's method. These results demonstrate the effectiveness of the multi-resolution orientation histograms for scene classification and the integration of similarity between orientation histogram on the same subregion.

5   Conclusion

We proposed a scene classification method based on multi-resolution orientation histogram. Since the appropriate subregion sizes for computing orientation histogram, various subregion sizes are used. To use the similarity between orientation histogram on the same subregion, normalized polynomial kernels are applied to each orientation histogram. In addition, the norm of each orientation histogram is normalized to speed up the classification. By integrating the similarity of each orientation histogram, the accuracy is improved. This result shows that the effectiveness of integration of the similarity of each orientation histogram. The proposed method is compared with recent scene classification based on bag-of-keypoints. We show that our method outperforms those methods. These results demonstrate the effectiveness of multi-resolution orientation histogram.

In this paper, all orientation histograms are used in training and classification. However, effective orientation histogram depends on the scene category. To improve the accuracy further, the effective orientation histograms for each category should be selected from multi-resolution orientation histogram. For this purpose, Sequential Forward Selection [23] will be used. The margin of SVM can be used as selection criteria. This is a subject for future works.

References

1. Torralba, A.: Contextual priming for object detection. International Journal of Computer Vision 53(2), 169–191 (2003)
2. Szummer, M., Picard, R.W.: Indoor-outdoor image classification. In: Proc. IEEE International Workshop on Content-based Access of Image and Video Databases, pp. 42–51 (1998)
3. Fei-Fei, L., Perona, P.: A baysian hierarchical model for learning natural scene categories. In: Proc. IEEE Computer Society Conference on Computer Vision and Pattern Recognition, pp. 524–531 (2005)
4. Bosch, A., Zisserman, A., Munoz, X.: Scene classification via plsa. In: Proc. 9th European Conference on Computer Vision, pp. 517–530 (2006)
5. Torralba, A., Murphy, K.P., Freeman, W.T., Rubin, M.A.: Context-based vision system for place and object recognition. In: Proc. IEEE Conference on Computer Vision and Pattern Recognition, pp. 273–280 (2003)
6. Lowe, D.: Distinctive image features from scale-invariant keypoints. International Journal of Computer Vision 60(2), 91–110 (2004)
7. Dalal, N., Trigs, B.: Histogram of oriented gradients for human detection. In: Proc. IEEE Computer Society Conference on Computer Vision and Pattern Recognition, pp. 886–893 (2005)
8. Grauman, K., Darrell, T.: Discriminative classification with sets of image features. In: Proc. International Conference on Computer Vision, pp. 1458–1465 (2005)
9. Lazebnik, S., Schmid, C., Ponce, J.: Beyond bags of features: Spatial pyramid matching for recognizing natural scene categories. In: Proc. IEEE Computer Society Conference on Computer Vision and Pattern Recognition, pp. 2169–2178 (2006)
10. Vapnik, V.N.: Statistical Learning Theory. John Wiley, Chichester (1998)
11. Debnath, R., Takahashi, H.: Kernel selection for the support vector machine. IEICE Trans. Info. & Syst. E87-D(12), 2903–2904 (2004)
12. Shawe-Taylor, J., Cristianini, N.: Kernel Methods for Pattern Analysis. Cambridge University Press, Cambridge (2004)
13. Hotta, K.: Support vector machine with local summation kernel for robust face recognition. In: Proc. 17th International Conference on Pattern Recognition, pp. 482–485 (2004)
14. Hotta, K.: View independent face detection based on combination of local and global kernels. In: Proc. International Conference on Computer Vision Systems, pp. 1–10 (2007)
15. 13 Scene categories database,
    http://vision.cs.princeton.edu/Databsets/SceneClass13.rar
16. Cristianini, N., Shawe-Taylor, J.: An Introduction to Support Vector Machines. Cambridge University Press, Cambridge (2000)
17. Haussler, D.: Convolution kernels on discrete structures. Tech. Rep. UCSC-CRL-99-10 (1999)

18. Hotta, K.: A robust face detector under partial occlusion. In: Proc. IEEE International Conference on Image Processing, pp. 597–600 (2004)
19. Pontil, M., Verri, A.: Support vector machines for 3d object recognition. IEEE Trans. Pattern Analysis and Machine Intelligence 20(6), 637–646 (1998)
20. Schölkopf, B., Burges, C.J.C., Smola, A.: Advances in kernel methods: support vector learning. MIT Press, Cambridge (1998)
21. Hsu, C.-W., Lin, C.-J.: A comparison of methods for multiclass support vector machines. IEEE Trans. Neural Networks 13(2), 415–425 (2002)
22. Milgram, J., Cheriet, M., Sabourin, R.: One against one or one against all: Which one is better for handwriting recognition with svms? In: Proc. 10th International Workshop on Frontiers in Handwriting Recognition (2006)
23. Webb, A.: Statistical Pattern Recognition 2nd edition, Arnold (2002)

Automatic Object Detection on Aerial Images Using Local Descriptors and Image Synthesis

Xavier Perrotton[1,2], Marc Sturzel[1], and Michel Roux[2]

[1] EADS FRANCE Innovation Works, 12 rue Pasteur, BP 76, 92152 Suresnes, France
{xavier.perrotton,marc.sturzel}@eads.net
[2] Institut Télécom - Télécom ParisTech - LTCI UMR 5141 CNRS, 46 rue Barrault,
75013 Paris, France
michel.roux@telecom-paristech.fr

Abstract. The presented work aims at defining techniques for the detection and localisation of objects, such as aircrafts in clutter backgrounds, on aerial or satellite images. A boosting algorithm is used to select discriminating features and a descriptor robust to background and target texture variations is introduced. Several classical descriptors have been studied and compared to the new descriptor, the HDHR. It is based on the assumption that targets and backgrounds have different textures. Image synthesis is then used to generate large amounts of learning data: the Adaboost has thus access to sufficiently representative data to take into account the variability of real operational scenes. Observed results prove that a vision system can be trained on adapted simulated data and yet be efficient on real images.

Keywords: Object detection, statistical learning, histogram distance.

1 Introduction

Current and future observation systems provide a large amount of data which cannot be completely processed manually: therefore, automatic systems are required for image interpretation, for applications such as Automatic Target Recognition. ATR consists in detecting and classifying targets, potentially at low resolutions and with a high degree of variability in appearances. Defining Automatic Target Recognition algorithms is a challenging problem since precision, recall, robustness and computational efficiency are critical issues in operational contexts. More precisely, an operational ATD/ATR algorithm must be particularly robust to context changes and to varying scenes and conditions. No parameterization should occur, for the system may be used by non-experts. The final implementation should run in real-time on embedded (which means: constrained) systems; therefore, algorithmic choices are limited to realistic and reduced time-consuming solutions. The training time has no constraint. Both precision and recall must be optimized: targets cannot be missed and false alarms must be reduced to a very restrictive minimum. Difficulties start with complex backgrounds like urban areas, or highly textured scenes, such as suburban fields or painted tarmacs. Considered targets

A. Gasteratos, M. Vincze, and J.K. Tsotsos (Eds.): ICVS 2008, LNCS 5008, pp. 302–311, 2008.

are mobile man-made objects which can have various appearances and paintings, including camouflage. Moreover, statistical methods require a huge number of samples to generate appropriate and robust classification models. Unfortunately, large training databases with complete annotations are generally missing. This article presents a framework adapted to target detection and recognition robust to the texture variability of backgrounds and targets. The detection of planes in aerial and satellite images was chosen as an illustrative application. This paper is organized as follows. In section 2, the related work on target detection in aerial images and some more generic approaches are summarized. The suggested framework is presented in section 3. Several classical descriptors and the introduced HDHR are described in section 4. In section 5, the methodology to create training and test databases is detailed; results obtained on this basis and on some real images are then presented. Finally, concluding remarks are given in section 6.

2   Related Work

Many approaches published in the last decade on object recognition in satellite and aerial images rely on some a priori information, and generally reject statistical training because of insufficient annotated databases. Traditional recognition algorithms on such images are based on edge matching between an observation, the image, and a prediction, typically the projection of a 3D model [13,10]; some others process various shape characteristics, like Zernique moments, on a target segmentation [6] which can only be processed in some favourable cases. On real operational images, edge and gradient-based methods usually fail due to disturbances implied by highly textured surrounding areas. Therefore, segmentation must be avoided. A complementary approach exploits appearance characteristics. It can be achieved by using the object brightness and texture information [9]: characteristics of appearance can thus explain implicitly the various effects of sensors, textures, materials and segmentation. These methods based on machine learning algorithms suffer from a limited applicability when insufficient learning data is available. However, combined with invariant local descriptors, they have proven their relevance for specific object recognition tasks [9,7]. Besides, object detection is often considered as a two-class problem: target and background. For multi-class applications, a classifier is learnt for each class: this solution has been adopted in the present framework.

Two major approaches enable a classifier to be also chosen as detector: a voting scheme or a sliding window scheme. In the first case, several extracted points or blobs of interest at various positions and scales typically vote for potential target centroïds [2,3,8]. To achieve this, they are linked to clusters of local descriptors corresponding to similar appearances and to specific parts of the object. A statistical model is then defined to combine them and to introduce some geometric information. The second solution consists in training a classifier with several hundreds or even several thousands of positive and negative samples at a given scale [11,15], with a very cost-efficient algorithm. Once the classifier is trained, it can be applied to any window at the same scale as training images. The object detection is then achieved by sliding a window across the image (possibly at multiple scales), and by classifying each patch as detection or non-detection. This classification can be carried out by SVM [11] or by cascade of classifiers built by Adaboost [15].

3 Algorithm

3.1 Overview of the Approach

Target low resolutions and textured backgrounds generate instabilities in the extraction of points of interest on aerial images: a sliding window scheme has thus been chosen. Relevant and adapted local descriptions and classifiers must be defined: a comparative evaluation of several descriptors has been led and will be described in section 4. Boosted decision stumps are selected as classifiers [15], since they have been successfully applied on rigid object detection and are adapted to cascades of sub-classifiers, a common solution to reduce the computational cost for negative samples. The next section will briefly review the boosting algorithm for binary classification.

3.2 Adaboost

Adaboost [5] is a statistical learning method which combines the outputs of many "weak" classifiers to produce a powerful "committee" according to the process described in figure 1. Adaboost starts with a uniform distribution of weights over training samples. Iteratively, a weak classifier $h_j : X \rightarrow \{0,1\}$ is selected by the weak learning algorithm and the sample weights are modified: the weight of misclassified samples are increased, whereas other weights are decreased. At the end, all selected weak classifiers are combined through a weighted majority vote to produce the final prediction:

$$f(X) = \sum_{t=0}^{T} \alpha_t h_t(X) \tag{1}$$

where the α_t are the weights to give higher influence to the more accurate classifiers in the sequence.

3.3 Weak Classifier

The Adaboost performance mainly depends on the choice of an appropriate weak classifier. Theoretically speaking, a weak classifier only needs to be slightly better than random guessing. To recognize objects, a weak classifier derived from local descriptors is relevant. Adaboost also performs an efficient feature selection when each weak classifier is associated with a descriptor. Decision stumps based on local descriptors are simple, effective and fast weak classifiers. They are defined

Given observation images $(x_i, y_i)_{i=1,...,N}$, let T be the number of iterations.

1. Initialize the observation weights: $w_1^i = \frac{1}{N}$, $i = 1, ..., N$
2. For $t = 1, ..., T$
   (a) For each descriptor, j, train a classifier h_j to the data using weights w_t^i(see section 3.3)
   (b) Compute weighted error $\varepsilon_j = \sum_{i=1}^{N} w_t^i |h_j(x_i) - y_i|$ for each weak classifier h_j
   (c) Select the weak classifier, h_t, with the minimum weighted error ε_t
   (d) Compute confidence weight $\alpha_t = \frac{1}{2} ln(\frac{1-\varepsilon_t}{\varepsilon_t})$
   (e) Update observation weights:

$$w_{t+1}^i = \begin{cases} \frac{w_t^i}{2\varepsilon_t} & \text{if } h_t(x_i) \neq y_i \\ \frac{w_t^i}{2(1-\varepsilon_t)} & \text{else} \end{cases} \tag{2}$$

3. Final classifier is defined by:

$$f(X) = \begin{cases} 1 \text{ if } \sum_{t=1}^{T} \alpha_t h_t(X) > \frac{1}{2} \sum_{t=1}^{T} \alpha_t \\ 0 \text{ else} \end{cases} \tag{3}$$

Fig. 1. Adaboost algorithm

by a descriptor D_j, a threshold Θ_j, and a polarity p_j which indicates the direction of the inequality sign:

$$h_j(X) = \begin{cases} 1 \text{ if } p_j.D_j < p_j.\Theta_j \\ 0 \text{ else} \end{cases} \tag{4}$$

The threshold Θ_j and the polarity p_j are computed at each iteration of Adaboost: the weights of positive and negative samples are taken into account in order to minimize the number of missclassified examples. Next section describes several relevant descriptors for decision stumps.

4 Descriptors

4.1 Introduction

A whole set of descriptors has been studied and evaluated on the selected test database. Using gradient histograms or edges seems inappropriate due to highly variable textures for both targets and backgrounds. However, there are stable local oriented patterns in the image. Gabor filters and derivatives of Gaussian kernels, which are standard tools to reveal local oriented patterns, are potential solutions to learn them. Regions are another stable pattern: in particular, the distribution of gray levels generally differs between target and background. If this assumption is verified, the relative geometrical positions of the selected regions also constitute stable information for pattern recognition. Haar filters have already proven the relevance of such choices for face detection. They have been studied and a new descriptor has been introduced: it computes the distance between the Haar region histograms, instead of comparing mean values, in order to bring more robustness to the distance estimation between two different regions.

4.2   Classical Filters

Oriented image features are extracted with a set of Gabor filters [1]. A bank of 40 filters is considered: 8 orientations and 5 scales. A local descriptor is then defined as a filter response at a given pixel. Local descriptors are computed on an image sub-sampling grid whose step is fixed relatively to the filter scale. Derivatives of Gaussian filters are also tested, as they are effective filters for the detection of contours or dominant orientations. Moreover, steerable properties [4] may be used to synthesize responses at any orientation with only a limited base of filters, which reduces the computational cost. Local descriptors are devised the same way as for Gabor filters. Haar filters, introduced by Papageorgiu and al [11], are also evaluated and constitute a natural basis of functions to code the difference in intensity between two regions, corresponding areas and thresholds being computed during the learning. An integral image, introduced by [15], allows a very fast feature extraction at any location or scale.

4.3   Histogram Distance on Haar Regions(HDHR)

Haar filters measure local signed contrasts and are therefore well adapted for detection of darker or lighter regions. In order to differentiate in a more suitable way two adjacent regions, histograms provide more detailed information than classical Haar features. Furthermore, histograms can be computed linearly, which is a precious computational advantage. The HDHR descriptor computes a distance between histograms of Haar regions and is adapted to the assumption that target and background textures can be differentiated. The integral histogram [12], an extension of the integral image, takes advantage of the histogram transformation linearity to compute quickly and efficiently histograms for any given rectangular area. Let N be the number of bins of the histogram, and $q : \{0, ..., 256\} \rightarrow \{1, ..., N\}$ the function which associates the histogram bin index to a gray level. Then the integral histogram ih can be computed with only one pass on the image thanks to the following equations:

For $j \epsilon \{1, ..., N\}$,

$$sh(x, y, j) = \begin{cases} sh(x, y - 1, j) + 1 \text{ if } j = q(i(x, y)) \\ sh(x, y - 1, j) \quad\quad \text{else} \end{cases} \tag{5}$$

$$ih(x, y, j) = ih(x - 1, y, j) + sh(x, y, j) \tag{6}$$

where $sh(x, -1, j) = 0$ and $ih(-1, y, j) = 0$. A descriptor is defined by computing the distance D between histograms f and g associated to Haar regions:

$$D = \frac{\sum_{j=1}^{N} (f[j] - g[j])^2}{\sum_{j=1}^{N} (f[j]^2 + g[j]^2)} \tag{7}$$

This descriptor contains thus more information, while remaining simple and fast to process, despite a larger memory cost. It is easily extendable to colour images: colour histograms and an associated distance just need to be considered. More complex distances between histograms could be proposed. However, they suffer from a higher computational cost (which has a crucial impact on the global algorithm cost), whereas the proposed distance already provides a sufficiently rich information.

4.4   HDHR Discussion

The HDHR aims at evaluating the difference between two regions whereas many other descriptors, like the commonly used SIFT or HoG, code a local texture patch. It derives from the wanted robustness to potential texture changes on the target itself or on the background. Figure 2 shows some of the descriptors chosen during the learning process. As planned, the selected descriptors are comparing areas within and outside the target. The geometrical positions of those filters enable the algorithm to reject background samples. Based on the same idea, many other descriptors computing differences on region-based statistics could be suggested and implemented.

Fig. 2. Examples of selected descriptors

5   Experiments

Gathering amounts of learning data large enough to reflect reality and its variability is one of the major limitations of statistical training methods. Indeed, available and sufficiently representative annotated databases are hard to collect.The necessary amount of negative aerial images samples could be obtained without extensive manual labelling by following the method described in [14], but it requires 3D information which is rarely available and is still not adapted to annotate automatically the positive samples. The suggested solution relies on synthetic images, through a target simulator which avoids the intrinsic annotation difficulty. Next sections describe procedures to build training and test database, and present various obtained results.

5.1   Training and Test Databases

The adopted approach is hybrid and allows for a great flexibility. It combines the advantages of real acquisitions and those of synthesis. More precisely it combines real images and synthetic renderings of removable objects. Real high resolution pictures are used to constitute several backgrounds on which objects are incrusted. The target rendering is obtained from 3D models with appropriate or random textures. Target shadows are also simulated. Sensor effects are then modelled to increase realism, especially PSF (point-spread function) and noise, with various granularity and amplitudes. The image synthesis makes it possible to completely manage the position and appearances of the rendered targets, so that no manual annotation is needed. Training and test databases were generated with a high degree of complexity, due to random and non-coherent backgrounds, in order to select the most robust descriptors; this approach aims at acquiring higher generalization ability on real images. A real picture database with only background images has been divided into two sets: a training set and a test set. Each dataset has then been divided into positive and negative samples. On each positive sample, targets have been rendered and incrusted, but target textures, sensor parameters and illumination parameters were chosen randomly. The training and tests databases both contain 2000 targets and 2000 background images.

5.2   Results and Discussion

Comparative study of descriptors. To evaluate each selected descriptor, a specific Adaboost classifier made up of 100 weak classifiers has been trained on the same training database; the learned pictures are resized to 30 x 30 pixels. Figure 3 depicts the ROC curves for every tested descriptor on the same test database. These curves show that Gabor filters seem unadapted to efficiently distinguish targets from backgrounds, whereas derivatives of Gaussian filters and Haar filters give quite better results, while still having relatively similar performances. The new HDHR descriptor is tested for gray images and colours images, and obtains the best results. Colour images introduce a higher discriminative capacity, which is interesting since the colorimetric information is generally lost and unused with other descriptors. Besides, the HDHR descriptor could still be improved by considering more discriminative colour spaces than the RGB one (for instance the Lab space).

On the figure 4, the influence of histogram quantization on the descriptor performances has been evaluated. For images with 256 gray levels, 16 bins seem optimal in terms of compromise between recall and computational cost. Once again, the contribution of colour appears clearly.

Evaluation of sensor and resolution effects on HDHR performances can also profit from image synthesis. A training database of 200 targets and 800 background images without sensor effect has been generated. An Adaboost classifier made up of 100 weak classifiers based on the 16 bins colour quantified HDHR has been learnt. Five test databases with respectively no effects, low noise (Gaussian

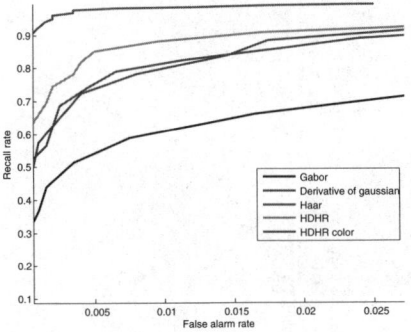

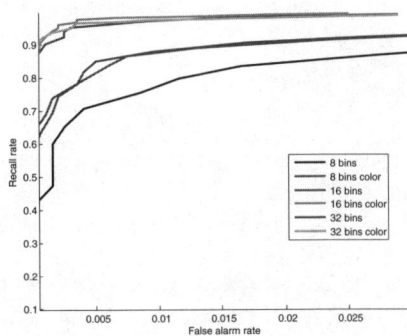

Fig. 3. Comparative performances of different descriptors

Fig. 4. Discretization effect on perfomances

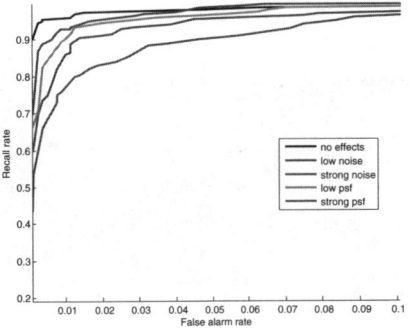

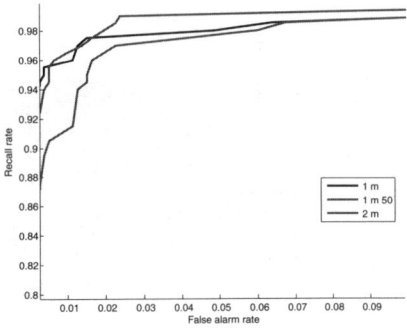

Fig. 5. Sensor effects on HDHR performances

Fig. 6. Resolution effect on HDHR performances

noise of standard deviation 2), strong noise (std: 5), low PSF (Gaussian kernel of radius 1) and strong PSF (radius: 3) were then produced. The classifier was evaluated on these five bases, so as to obtain the ROC curves depicted on figure 5. The descriptor is more sensitive to strong PSF than to noise. To study resolution effects, a classifier has been learned and tested on 3 training and test databases at resolution 1m, 1.50m and 2m. Figure 6 depicts ROC curves: an important loss of information is observed for 2m resolution.

Results. When applied to target detection on large images, boosted classifiers have to reject efficiently an overwhelming majority of negative tested subwindows while detecting almost all positive samples. To achieve this, a cascade of classifiers is employed to eliminate effectively and quickly large background areas. The cascade attempts to reject in the earliest stages as many negative patches as possible, which avoids to compute all descriptors. The implemented

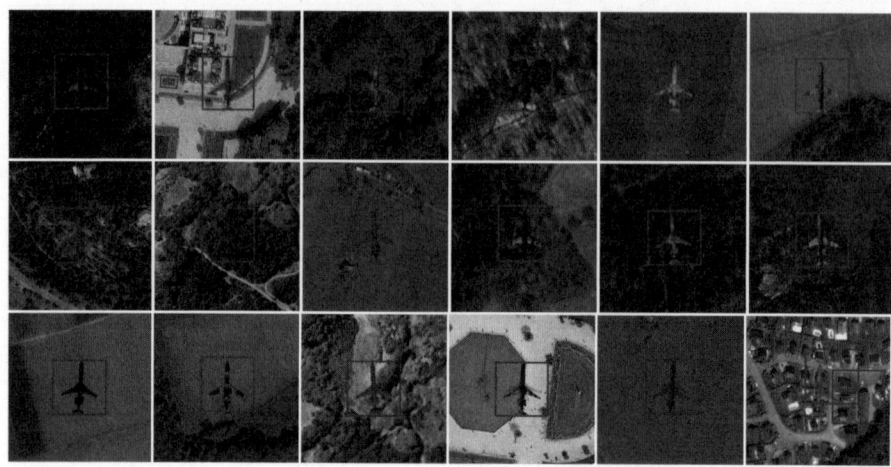

Fig. 7. Results on simulated test images

Fig. 8. Results on real images

Adaboost follows the structure developed by Viola and Jones [15], exploits however the 16 bins colour quantified HDHR. The cascade is applied at different image rotations in order to detect planes at various orientations. On the test database, the cascade obtains a 92% recall for a false alarm rate of $5e^{-3}$%. On figures 7, some detection samples are provided; on the bottom right, examples of an inaccurate detection and of a false detection are given. Despite background variability and target random textures, the algorithm proves to be very robust. Finally, with realistic simulated test databases (which means with more uniform textures), a light results improvement can be observed. It confirms the HDHR descriptor robustness to texture changes, for the textures appearing in the test databases were not used to generate the training database. Tests on real images show the effectiveness and relevance of simulation for the training. Indeed, on figure 8, detection results on real targets can be observed, although the classifier has been exclusively generated with simulated planes. Some planes are not detected due to the high threshold implemented to avoid false alarms. A good detection rate is achieved; the classifier seems to have learnt relatively generic plane shapes but does not make a clear distinction between different close classes of planes.

6   Conclusion

The proposed descriptor is effective and robust for target detection on aerial images. Moreover, it is simple and efficient thanks to the integral histogram. In particular, it resists to target and background texture changes. The inlay of synthesized targets in real images gives access to a great variability of appearances and to a complete control of both position and orientation of the target; it also generates annotations automatically. Such databases have proved their relevance for machine learning algorithms, with obtained classifiers being efficient on both synthetic and real images. The present analysis was limited to planes detection, with only two specific classes; current work consists in extending this approach to the multi-class and multi-view problematic.

References

1. Daugman, J.G.: Complete discrete 2-D Gabor transform by neural networks for image analysis and compression. IEEE Trans. on Acoustics, Speech and Signal Processing 36(7), 1169–1179 (1988)
2. Dorko, G., Schmid, C.: Selection of Scale-Invariant Parts for Object Class Recognition. In: Proc. ICCV, Nice, pp. 634–639 (2003)
3. Fergus, R., Perona, P., Zisserman, A.: Object Class Recognition by Unsupervised Scale-Invariant Learning. In: Proc. CVPR, Madison, vol. 2, pp. 264–271 (2003)
4. Freeman, W.T., Adelson, E.H.: The design and use of steerable filters. IEEE Trans. PAMI 13(9), 891–906 (1991)
5. Freund, Y., Schapire, R.E.: A decision-theoretic generalization of on-line learning and application to boosting. J. of Comp. And Sys. Sc. 55(1), 119–139 (1997)
6. Hsieh, J.-W., Chen, J.-M., Chuang, C.-H., Fan, K.-C.: Aircraft type recognition in satellite images. IEEE Proc.-Vis. Image Signal Process 152(3) (June 2005)
7. Lazebnik, S., Schmid, C., Ponce, J.: Affine invariant local descriptors and neighborhood statistics for texture recognition. In: Proc ICCV, Nice, vol. 2, pp. 914–921 (2003)
8. Leibe, B., Schiele, B.: Scale-Invariant Object Categorization using a Scale-Adaptive Mean-Shift Search, pp. 145–153. DAGM, Tübingen (2004)
9. Lowe, D.G.: Object recognition from local scale-invariant features. In: Proc. ICCV, Corfu. pp. 1150–1157 (1999)
10. Mostafa, M.G., Hemayed, E.E., Farag, A.A.: Target recognition via 3D object reconstruction from image sequence and contour matching. Pattern Recognition Letters 20, 1381–1387 (1999)
11. Constantine, P.: Papageorgiou, Michael Oren, and Tomaso Poggio, *A general framework for object detection*. In: Proc. ICCV, Bombay, pp. 555–562 (1998)
12. Porikli, F.M.: Integral histogram: A fast way to extract histograms in Cartesian spaces. In: Proc. CVPR, San Diego, pp. 829–836 (2005)
13. Ruch, O., Dufour, J.: Real-time automatic target recognition and identification of ground vehicles for airborne optronic systems. In: Proceedings of the SPIE, vol. 5909, pp. 11–20 (2005)
14. Stefan, K., Georg, P., Helmut, G., Horst, B., Joachim, B.: A 3D Teacher for Car Detection in Aerial Images. In: Proceedings of the Eleventh IEEE International Conference on Computer Vision, Workshop on 3D Representation for Recognition (3dRR-2007) (2007)
15. Viola, P., Jones, M.: Rapid object detection using a boosted cascade of simple features. In: Proc. CVPR, Hawaii, pp. 511–518 (2001)

CEDD: Color and Edge Directivity Descriptor:
A Compact Descriptor for Image Indexing and Retrieval

Savvas A. Chatzichristofis and Yiannis S. Boutalis

Department of Electrical and Computer Engineering
Democritus University of Thrace
12. Vas. Sofias, 67100 – Xanthi, Greece
{schatzic,ybout}@ee.duth.gr

Abstract. This paper deals with a new low level feature that is extracted from the images and can be used for indexing and retrieval. This feature is called "Color and Edge Directivity Descriptor" and incorporates color and texture information in a histogram. CEDD size is limited to 54 bytes per image, rendering this descriptor suitable for use in large image databases. One of the most important attribute of the CEDD is the low computational power needed for its extraction, in comparison with the needs of the most MPEG-7 descriptors. The objective measure called ANMRR is used to evaluate the performance of the proposed feature. An online demo that implements the proposed feature in an image retrieval system is available at: http://orpheus.ee.duth.gr/image_retrieval.

Keywords: Image Retrieval, Image Indexing, Compact Descriptors, Low Level Features, Color and Texture Histogram.

1 Introduction

The enormous growth observed in the multimedia applications, has led in the creation of large image databases. A characteristic example is the enormous number of images that "submerge" the internet after the growth of the Hyper Text Markup Language (HTML). In the past years a lot of systems were developed, which automatically are indexing and retrieving images, based on the low level features exported from them. This is widely known as content based image retrieval. CBIR undertakes the extraction of several features from each image, which, consequently, are used for the retrieval and the indexing procedure. These sorts of features are describing the content of the image and that is why they must be appropriately selected according to the occasion. The visual content of the images is mapped into a new space named feature space. The features have to be discriminative and sufficient for the description of the objects. Basically, the key to attain a successful retrieval system is to choose the right features that represent the images as "strong" and unique as possible. Regarding their type, CBIR systems can be classified in systems that use color features, those that use texture features and finally in systems that use shape features. It is very difficult to achieve satisfactory retrieval results by using only one of these feature categories. Many of the so far proposed retrieval techniques adopt methods, in which more than

A. Gasteratos, M. Vincze, and J.K. Tsotsos (Eds.): ICVS 2008, LNCS 5008, pp. 312–322, 2008.

one feature types are involved. For example, color and texture features are used in the QBIC [1], SIMPLIcity [2] and MIRROR [3] image retrieval systems. A question however, that emerged in the past years is how these features could become more compact. The characterization of an image with a high dimensional vector may have very good retrieval scores but it delays significantly the retrieval procedure.

The descriptors that were proposed by MPEG-7 [4] [5], for indexing and retrieval, maintain a balance between the size of the feature and the quality of the results. These descriptors appear to be able to describe satisfactorily the visual content of the image [3].

This paper deals with the extraction of a new low level feature that combines, in one histogram, color and texture information and its length does not exceed 54 bytes.

Firstly, the image is separated in a preset number of blocks.

In order to extract the color information, a set of fuzzy rules undertake the extraction of a Fuzzy-Linking histogram that was proposed in [6]. This histogram stems from the HSV color space. Twenty rules are applied to a three-input fuzzy system in order to generate eventually a 10-bin quantized histogram. Each bin corresponds to a preset color. The number of blocks assigned to each bin is stored in a feature vector. Then, 4 extra rules are applied to a two input fuzzy system, in order to change the 10-bins histogram into 24-bins histogram, importing thus information related to the hue of each color that is presented. The process is described in section 2.

Next, the 5 digital filters that were proposed in the MPEG-7 Edge Histogram Descriptor [7] are also used for exporting the information which is related to the texture of the image, classifying each image block in one or more of the 6 texture regions that has been fixed, shaping thus the 144 bins histogram. The process is described in section 3.

Section 4 describes the entire proposed method implementation.

With the use of the Gustafson Kessel fuzzy classifier [8] 8 regions are shaped, which are then used in order to quantize the values of the 144 CEDD factors in the interval {0-7}, limiting thus the length of the descriptor in 432 bits. The process is described in section 5.

Section 6 comprises the experimental results of an image retrieval system that uses the proposed feature and the MPEG-7 features. The objective measure called ANMRR (Averaged Normalized Modified Retrieval Rank) [5] is used in order to evaluate the system performance. Finally the conclusions are given in section 7.

2 Color Information

In [6], a fuzzy system was proposed to produce a fuzzy linking histogram, which takes the three channels of HSV as inputs, and forms a 10 bins histogram as an output. Each bin represents a preset color as follows: (0) Black, (1) Gray, (2) White, (3) Red, (4) Orange, (5) Yellow, (6) Green, (7) Cyan, (8) Blue and (9) Magenta. These colors were selected based on works that were presented in the past [9].

The method presented in [6] is further improved, by recalculating the input membership value limits and resulting in a better mapping on the 10 preset colors.

These new limit calculations are based on the position of the vertical edges of images that represent the channels H (Hue), S (Saturation) and V (Value). Figure 1 shows the vertical edges of the channel H, which were used for determining the position of

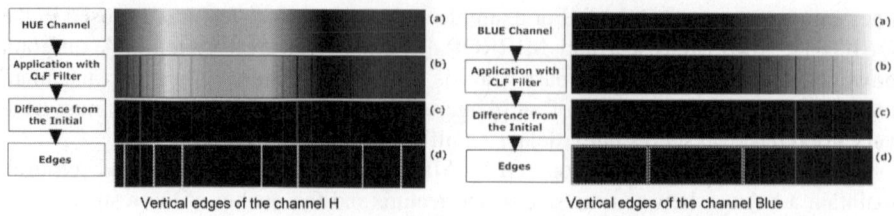

Vertical edges of the channel H   Vertical edges of the channel Blue

Fig. 1. Edges Extraction with CLF-AND Filter

membership values of Figure 2(a). The selected hue regions are stressed by dotted lines in figure 1(d). The membership limit values of S and V are identified with the same process.

The use of coordinate logic filters (CLF) [10] was found to be the most appropriate among other edge detection techniques for determining the fine differences and finally extracting these vertical edges. In the procedure followed, each pixel is replaced by the result of the coordinate logic filter "AND" operation on its 3x3 neighborhood. The result of this action, stresses the edges of the image. The total edges are exported by calculating the difference between the initial and the filtered image.

Based on these edges, the inputs of the system are analyzed as follows:

Hue is divided into 8 fuzzy areas. Their borders are shown in figure 2(a) and are defined as: (0) Red to Orange, (1) Orange, (2) Yellow, (3) Green, (4) Cyan, (5) Blue, (6) Magenta and (7) Blue to Red.

S is divided into 2 fuzzy regions as they appear in figure 2(b). This channel defines the shade of a color based on white. The first area, in combination with the position of the pixel in channel V, is used to define if the color is clear enough to be ranked in one of the categories which are described in H histogram, or if it is a shade of white or gray color.

The third input, channel V, is divided into 3 areas (Figure 2(c)). The first one is actually defining substantially when the pixel (block) will be black, independently from the values that the other inputs have. The second fuzzy area, in combination with the value of channel S gives the gray color.

A set of 20 TSK-like rules [11] with fuzzy antecedents and crisp consequents was used. The consequent part contains the variables that count the number of the original image pixels, which are mapped to each specific bin of the 10 bin histogram. Four of the rules depend on two only inputs (S and V). For these rules the decision is independent from the value of H. For the evaluation of the consequent variables two methods have been used. Initially LOM (Largest of Maximum) algorithm was used. This method assigns the input to the output bin which is defined from the rule that gives the greater value of activation. Next, Multi Participate algorithm was tried. This defuzzyfication method assigns the input to the output bins which are defined from all the rules that are being activated. More details about this algorithm are available in [6]. The experimental results show that the second algorithm performs better.

Next, a second system undertakes the task to separate each color in 3 hues. This system forms a 24 bins histogram as an output. Each bin represents a preset color as follows: (0) Black, (1) Grey, (2) White, (3) Dark Red, (4) Red, (5) Light Red, (6) Dark Orange, (7) Orange, (8) Light Orange, (9) Dark Yellow, (10) Yellow, (11) Light

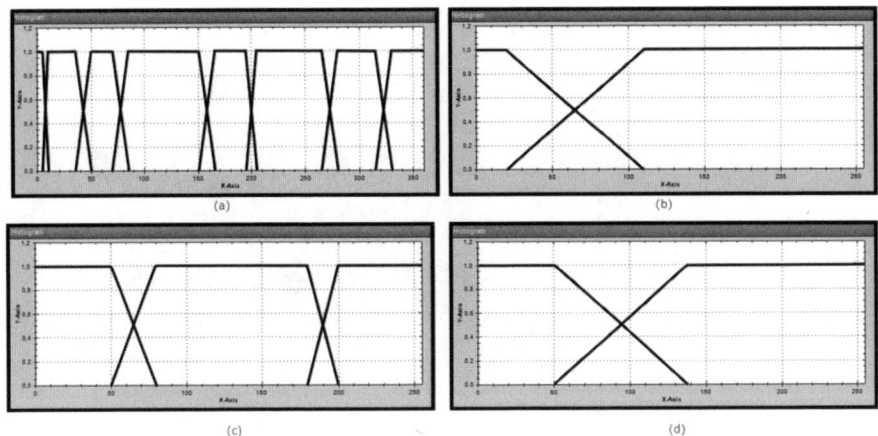

Fig. 2. Membership Functions for (a) Hue, (b) Saturation, (c) Value, (d) Saturation and Value for the expansion at 24-bins

Yellow, (12) Dark Green, (13) Green, (14) Light Green, (15) Dark Cyan, (16) Cyan, (17) Light Cyan, (18) Dark Blue, (19) Blue, (20) Light Blue, (21) Dark Magenta, (22) Magenta, (23) Light Magenta.

The design of a system that approaches these shades is based on the determinations of the subtle vertical edges appearing in images with smooth transition from the absolute white to the absolute black through a color. The use of the coordinate logic filter "AND" was found to be appropriate for determining these vertical edges too.

The values of S and V from each pixel as well as the value of the bin (or the bins) resulting from the fuzzy 10-bins unit constitute entries in the 24-bins Fuzzy Linking system.

So much the channels S as well as channel V are separated into 2 regions as they appear in figure 2(d).

This system actually undertakes to classify the input block in one (or more) from the 3 hue areas derived after the vertical edge extraction procedure described above. These hues are labeled as follows: Dark Color (as Color is used the color that attributed by the first 10-Bins system) - Color and Light Color.

In this system a set of 4 TSK-like rules [11] with fuzzy antecedents and crisp consequents were used. The Multi Participate algorithm was also employed for the evaluation of the consequent variables.

3   Texture Information

The 5 digital filters that were proposed by the MPEG-7 Edge Histogram Descriptor - EHD [7] [12], are shown in figure 3(A) [7]. These filters are used for the extraction of the texture's information. They are able to characterize the edges being present in their application region as one of the following types: vertical, horizontal, 45-degree diagonal, 135-degree diagonal and non-directional edges. The size of their application region will be described in section 4 and it is called henceforth *Image Block*.

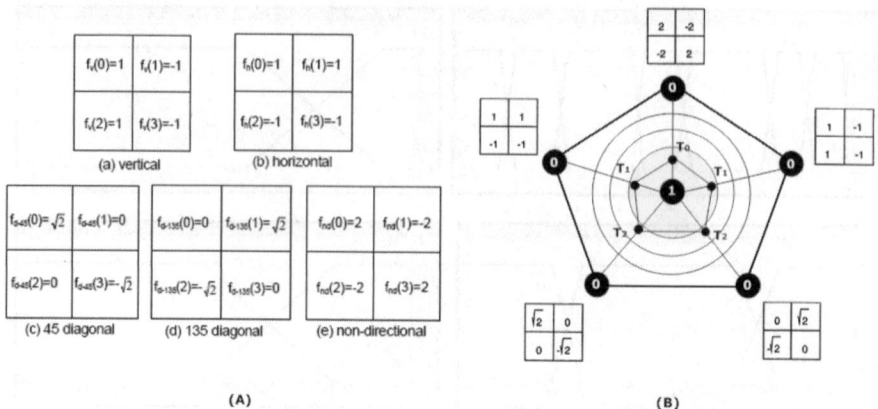

Fig. 3. (A) Filter coefficients for edge detection [7], (B) Edge Type Diagram

Each *Image Block* is constituted by 4 Sub Blocks. The average gray level of each Sub-Block at (i,j)th Image-Block is defined as $a_0(i,j)$, $a_1(i,j)$, $a_2(i,j)$, and $a_3(i,j)$. The filter coefficients for vertical, horizontal, 45-degree diagonal, 135-degree diagonal, and non-directional edges are labeled as $f_v(k), f_h(k), f_{d-45}(k), f_{d-135}(k)$, and $f_{nd}(k)$, respectively, where $k=0,...,3$ represents the location of the Sub Block. The respective edge magnitudes $m_v(i,j)$, $m_h(i,j)$, $m_{d-45}(i,j)$, $m_{d-135}(i,j)$, and $m_{nd}(i,j)$ for the (i,j)th Image Block can be obtained as follows:

$$m_v(i, j) = \left| \sum_{k=0}^{3} a_k(i, j) \times f_v(k) \right| \tag{1}$$

$$m_h(i, j) = \left| \sum_{k=0}^{3} a_k(i, j) \times f_h(k) \right| \tag{2}$$

$$m_{d-45}(i, j) = \left| \sum_{k=0}^{3} a_k(i, j) \times f_{d-45}(k) \right| \tag{3}$$

$$m_{d-135}(i, j) = \left| \sum_{k=0}^{3} a_k(i, j) \times f_{d-135}(k) \right| \tag{4}$$

$$m_{nd}(i, j) = \left| \sum_{k=0}^{3} a_k(i, j) \times f_{nd}(k) \right| \tag{5}$$

Then the max is calculated:

$$\max = MAX(m_v, m_h, m_{d-45}, m_{d-135}, m_{nd})$$ (6)

and normalize all **m.**

$$m_v' = \frac{m_v}{\max}, m_h' = \frac{m_h}{\max}, m_{d-45}' = \frac{m_{d-45}}{\max}, m_{d-135}' = \frac{m_{d-135}}{\max}, m_{nd}' = \frac{m_{nd}}{\max}$$ (7)

The output of the unit that exports texture's information from each Image Block is a 6 area histogram. Each area corresponds to a region as follows: EdgeHisto(0) Non Edge, EdgeHisto(1) Non Directional Edge, EdgeHisto(2) Horizontal Edge, Edge-Histo(3) Vertical Edge, EdgeHisto(4) 45-Degree Diagonal and EdgeHisto(5) 135-Degree Diagonal. The way that the system classifies the Image Block in an area is the following: Initially, the system checks if the *max* value is greater than a given threshold. This threshold defines when the Image Block can be classified as Texture Block or Non Texture Block (Linear).

If the Image Block is classified as Texture Block, all the m' values are placed in the heuristic pentagon diagram of figure 3(B). Each m' value is placed in the line that determines the digital filter from which it was emanated. The diagram centre corresponds in value 1 while the utmost corresponds in value 0. If m' value is greater than the threshold in the line in which it participates, the Image Block is classified in the particular type of edge. Thus the Image Block can participate in more than one type of edges. The source code that follows describes the process.

```
program SetEdgeType(max, m_nd, m_h, m_v, m_d_45, m_d_135)
{
        if (max < TEdge) then EdgeHisto(0)++
        else
            {
            if  (m_nd   >   T0)         then   EdgeHisto(1)++
            if  (m_h    >   T1)         then   EdgeHisto(2)++
            if  (m_v    >   T1)         then   EdgeHisto(3)++
            if  (m_d_45     >   T2)     then   EdgeHisto(4)++
            if  (m_d_135    >   T2)     then   EdgeHisto(5)++
            }
        endif
return(EdgeHisto)
}
```

Threshold values were selected to be: $T_{Edge}=14$, $T_0=0.68$, $T_1=T_2=0.98$.

4   CEDD Implementation

The configuration of CEDD is resolved as follows:

The unit associated with the extraction of color information is called Color Unit. Similarly, the Texture Unit is the unit associated with the extraction of texture information. The CEDD histogram is constituted by 6 regions, determined by the Texture Unit. Each region is constituted by 24 individual regions, emanating from the Color

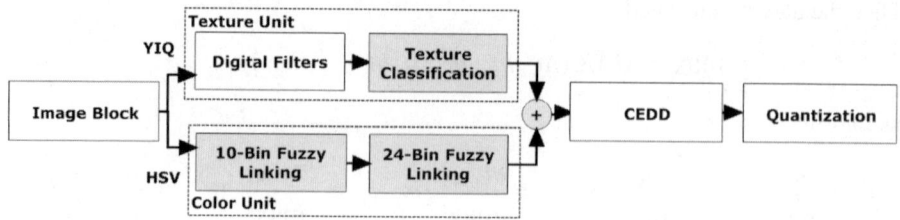

Fig. 4. CEDD Flowchart

Unit. Overall, the final histogram includes $6 \times 24 = 144$ regions. In order to shape the histogram, firstly we separate the image in 1600 Image Blocks. This number was chosen in order to compromise between the image detail and the computational power. Each Image Block feeds successively all the units. If we define the bin that results from the Texture Unit as N and as M the bin that results from the Color Unit, then the Image Block is placed in the output histogram position: $N \times 24 + M$.

In the Texture Unit, the Image Block is separated into 4 regions, the Sub Blocks. The value of each Sub Block is the mean value of the luminosity of the pixels that participate in it. The luminosity values are derived from the transformation througth the YIQ color space. Each Image Block is then filtered with the 5 digital filters that were described in section 3, and with the use of the pentagon's diagram it is classified in one or more texture catogories. Assume that the classification resulted in the second bin, which defines NDE (Non Directional Edge).

In the Color Unit, every Image Block is transported in the HSV color space. The mean values of H, S and V are calculated and they constitute the inputs of the fuzzy system that shapes the fuzzy 10-bins histogram. Assume that the classification resulted in the fourth bin, which dictates that the color is red. Then, the second fuzzy system (24- Bin Fuzzy Linking), using the mean values of S and V as well as the value of the bin (or bins) expense from the previous system, calculates the hue of the color and shapes the fuzzy 24-bins histogram. Assume again that the system classifies this block in the fourth bin which dictates that color is the dark red. The combination of the 3 fuzzy systems finally will classify the block in the 27 bin ($1 \times 24 + 3$). The process is repeated for all the blocks of the image. At the completion of the process, the histogram is normalized in the interval $\{0\text{-}1\}$. Each histogram value is then quantized in 3 bits. The quantization process is described in section 5.

5 CEDD Quantization

For the restriction of the CEDD length, a 3bits/bin quantization was used, limiting thus its total length in $144 \times 3 = 432$ bits. A sample of 10000 images was used to calculate the quantization table. Initially, CEDD vectors were calculated for the total of images. The crowd of 10000×144 elements constitutes the entry of the fuzzy Gustafson Kessel classifier [8], which separates the volume of the samples in 8 regions. Basically this classification maps the bin values from the decimal area $\{0\text{-}1\}$ to the integer area $\{0\text{-}7\}$.

Table 1. Quantization Table

Bin: 0-23							
0.00018	0.02373	0.06145	0.11391	0.17912	0.26098	0.34179	0.55472
Bin: 24-47							
0.00020	0.02249	0.06025	0.12070	0.18112	0.23413	0.32566	0.52070
Bin: 48-95							
0.00040	0.00487	0.01088	0.01816	0.02704	0.03812	0.05267	0.07955
Bin: 96-143							
0.00096	0.01075	0.02416	0.04155	0.06289	0.09306	0.13697	0.26289

Gustafson Kessel parameters were selected to be: Clusters: 8, Repetitions: 2000, e=0.002, m=2. The resulting quantization is given in Table 1. The entries of the table have the following meaning: The values of the histogram appearing in bins 0-23 are assigned to one of the values {0-7} according to the minimum distance of each bin value from one of the eight entries in the first row of the table. The same procedure is followed for the entries of bins 24-47, 48-95 and 96-143 where in this case the eight entries of the second, the third and the fourth row respectively are used.

6 Experimental Results

The proposed low level feature has been integrated in the retrieval software system img(Rummager), which has been developed in the "Automatic Control Systems & Robotics" laboratory of "Democritus University of Thrace - Greece". Initially, experiments were performed in the database of 1000 images that was used by James Wang [2] [13]. CEDD was used in the retrieval procedure and the results are compared with the corresponding results of the following MPEG-7 [4] [5] descriptors:

Color Descriptors: Dominant Color Descriptor (DCD), Scalable Color Descriptor (SCD), Color Layout Descriptor (CLD), Color Structure Descriptor (CSD).

Texture Descriptors: Edge Histogram Descriptor (EHD), Homogeneous Texture Descriptor (HTD).

For the measurement of the distance of CEDD between the images, Tanimoto coefficient [14] was used.

$$T_{ij} = t(x_i, x_j) = \frac{x_i^T x_j}{x_i^T x_i + x_j^T x_j - x_i^T x_j} \qquad (8)$$

Where x^T is the transpose vector of x. In the absolute congruence of the vectors the Tanimoto coefficient takes the value 1, while in the maximum deviation the coefficient tends to zero.

The objective measure called ANMRR (Averaged Normalized Modified Retrieval Rank) [5] is used in order to evaluate the performance of the image retrieval system. The average rank $AVR(q)$ for query q is:

$$AVR(q) = \sum_{k=1}^{NG(q)} \frac{Rank(k)}{NG(q)} \qquad (9)$$

Where

- *NG (q)* is the number of ground truth images for query *q*. As ground truth we define a set of visually similar images.
- $K = min (2 \times NG (q), 2 \times GMT)$ *where GTM = max {NG (q)}.*
- Consider a query . Assume that as a result of the retrieval, the kth ground truth image for this query *q* is found at a position *R*. If this image is in the first *K* retrievals then *Rank (k)=R* else *Rank (k) = (K+1)*.
- *Rank (k)* is the retrieval rank of the ground truth image.

The modified retrieval rank is:

$$MRR(q) = AVR(q) + 0.5 - 0.5 * NG(q) \tag{10}$$

Note that *MRR* is 0 in case of perfect retrieval.

The normalized modified retrieval rank is computed as follows:

$$NMRR(q) = \frac{MRR(q)}{K + 0.5 - 0.5 * NG(q)} \tag{11}$$

Finally average of *NMRR* over all queries defined as:

$$ANMRR(q) = \frac{1}{Q} \sum_{q=1}^{Q} NMRR(q) \tag{12}$$

The ANMRR is always in range of 0 to 1 and the smaller the value of this measure is, the better the matching quality of the query is. ANMRR is the evaluation criterion used in all of the MPEG-7 color core experiments. Evidence was shown that the ANMRR measure approximately coincides linearly, with the results of subjective evaluation about retrieval accuracy of search engines. A set of ground truth images that are most relevant to query were identified.

In particular experiments we used as ground truth, the groups of images proposed in the MIRROR image retrieval system [3]. MIRROR separates the Wang's database in 20 queries. In table 2 that follows certain indicative results appear, while in table 3 the values of ANMRR for the total of the 20 queries have been calculated. An online demo of the application is available at [15] and the NMRR values for the MPEG-7 descriptors in Wang's database are available at [16].

For every query, the average NMRR value of the MPEG-7 descriptors is calculated. Figure 5(a) illustrates these values in juxtaposition with the CEDD results.

Table 2. Query (Image Number) / NMRR Values for the Descriptors

	DCD	SCD	CLD	CSD	EHD	HTD	CEDD
600	0.5273	0.0828	0.4543	0.0658	0.2771	0.4451	**0.04798**
327	0.3363	0.4063	0.5419	0.3477	0.3172	0.5944	**0.12015**
102	0.3893	0.5668	0.3697	0.4923	0.4684	0.9355	**0.27547**
204	0.4039	0.4417	0.6164	0.3228	0.7817	0.8867	**0.29035**
522	0.6018	0.5077	0.4544	0.5263	0.6904	0.7343	**0.34489**

Table 3. ANMRR Results for the Descriptors (Wang's Database)

	DCD	SCD	CLD	CSD	EHD	HTD	CEDD
ANMRR	0.4959	0.3566	0.3999	0.3162	0.5088	0.7054	**0.2431**

Table 4. Descriptors Results in img(Rummager) Database

	DCD	SCD	EHD	CLD	CEDD
ANMRR	0.5111	0.3214	0.5987	0.3645	**0.2333**

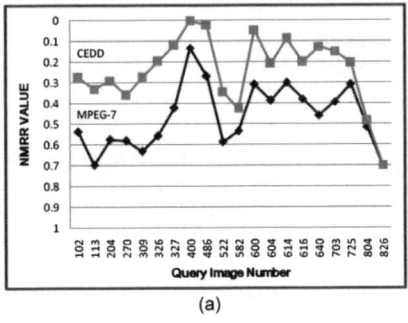 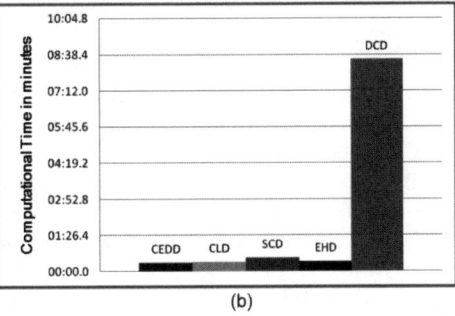

(a)   (b)

Fig. 5. (a) CEDD and MPEG-7 Average NMRR Values in Wang's Database, **(b)** Descriptor Extraction Computational Time in Wang's Image Database

Experiments have also been performed on the database that is incorporated in the application img(Rummager). This database has 15000+ images, coming from several retrieval systems and images from private collection. Table 4 presents the descriptors' results in the Img (Rummager) database. The experiments concern 102 queries.

Note that DCD, SCD, EHD and CLD implementation in img(Rummager) application match the XM implementation [18].

One of the most important attribute of the proposed feature is the low computational power needed for its extraction, in comparison with the needs of the most MPEG-7 descriptors. Figure 5(b) illustrates the CEDD computational time in the Wang's database (1000 images) in juxtaposition with the CLD, SCD, EHD and DCD descriptors. Extraction time was measured in the img(Rummager) application.

7 Conclusions

This paper presents the extraction of a new low level feature that contains, in one histogram, color and texture information. This element is intended for use in image retrieval and image indexing systems. Experimental results show that the proposed feature can contribute in accurate image retrieval. Its main functionality is image-to-image matching and its intended use is for still-image retrieval, where an image may consist of either a single rectangular frame or arbitrarily shaped, possibly disconnected, regions.

References

1. Flickner, M., Sawhney, H., Niblack, W., Ashley, J., Huang, Q., Dom, B., Gorkani, M., Hafner, J., Lee, D., Petkovic, D., Steele, D.: Query by image and video content: the QBIC system. Computer 28(9), 23–32 (1995)
2. Wang, J.Z., Li, J., Wiederhold, G.: SIMPLIcity: Semantics-Sensitive Integrate, Matching for Picture Libraries. IEEE transactions on pattern analysis and machine intelligence 23(9) (2001)
3. Wong, K.-M., Cheung, K.-W., Po, L.-M.: MIRROR: an interactive content based image retrieval system. In: Proceedings of IEEE International Symposium on Circuit and Systems 2005, Japan, vol. 2, pp. 1541–1544 (2005)
4. Martinez, J.M.: http://www.chiariglione.org/mpeg/standards/mpeg-7
5. Manjunath, B.S., Ohm, J.-R., Vasudevan, V.V., Yamada, A.: Color and Texture Descriptors. IEEE Transactions on Circuits and Systems for Video Technology 11(6), 703–715 (2001)
6. Chatzichristofis, S., Boutalis, Y.: A Hybrid Scheme for Fast and Accurate Image Retrieval Based on Color Descriptors. In: De Mallorca, P. (ed.) IASTED International Conference on Artificial Intelligence and Soft Computing (ASC 2007), Spain (2007)
7. Won, C.S., Park, D.K., Park, S.-J.: Efficient Use of MPEG-7 Edge Histogram Descriptor. ETRI Journal 24 (2002)
8. Gustafson, E.E., Kessel, W.C.: Fuzzy Clustering with a Fuzzy Covariance Matrix. In: IEEE CDC, San Diego, California, pp. 761–766 (1979)
9. Konstantinidis, K., Gasteratos, A., Andreadis, I.: Image Retrieval Based on Fuzzy Color Histogram Processing. Optics Communications 248(4-6), 15, 375–386 (2005)
10. Mertzios, B., Tsirikolias, K.: Coordinate Logic Filters: Theory and Applications Nonlinear Image Processing. In: Mitra, S., Sicuranza, G. (eds.), ch. 11, Academic Press, London (2004), ISBN: 0125004516
11. Zimmerman, H.J.: Fuzzy Sets, Decision Making and Expert Systems. Kluwer Academic Publ. Boston (1987)
12. ISO/IEC/JTC1/SC29/WG11: MPEG-7 XM Document: MPE- G-7 Visual Part Experimentation Model Version 10.0, MPEG Document N4063, Singapore (2001)
13. Li, J., Wang, J.Z.: Automatic linguistic indexing of pictures by a statistical modeling approach. IEEE Transactions on Pattern Analysis and Machine Intelligence 25(9), 1075–1088 (2003)
14. Chi, Z., Yan, H., Pham, T.: Fuzzy Algorithms: With Applications to image processing and pattern recognition. In: Advance in fuzzy systems – Applications and theory, vol. Volume 10, World Scientific, Singapore (1996)
15. img(Rummager) on line demo, http://orpheus.ee.duth.gr/image_retrieval/
16. MIRROR v2 on line demo, http://abacus.ee.cityu.edu.hk/~corel1k/
17. ISO/IEC/JTC1/SC29/WG11: Description of Core Experiments for MPEG-7 Color/Texture Descriptors, MPEG document N2929, Melbourne (1999)

Ranking Corner Points by the Angular Difference between Dominant Edges

Rafael Lemuz-López and Miguel Arias Estrada

Instituto Nacional de Astrofísica Óptica y Electrónica
Luis Enrique Erro 1 Puebla, Mexico. A.P 216 C.P 72000
{rlemuz,ariasmo}@inaoep.mx

Abstract. In this paper a variant of the Harris corner point detector is introduced. The new algorithm use a covariance operator to compute the angular difference between dominant edges. Then, a new cornerness strength function is proposed by weighting the log Harris cornerness function by the angular difference between dominant edges. An important advantage of the proposed corner detector algorithm is its ability to reduce false corner responses in image regions where partial derivatives have similar values. In addition, we show qualitatively that ranking corner points with the new cornerness strength function better agrees with the intuitive notion of a corner than the original Harris function. To demonstrate the performance of the new algorithm, the new approach is applied on synthetic and real images. The results show that the proposed algorithm rank better the meaningful detected features and at the same time reduces false positive features detected when compared to the original Harris algorithm.

1 Introduction

Detection of corner points on images is a fundamental stage for many computer vision algorithms such as object recognition, tracking, motion detection, motion segmentation, and recently much attention has been received since salient points detection is the first step for self calibrated reconstruction. The selection of distinguishable features is important in self calibrated reconstruction since, from the entire set of features available in a pair of images, the minimum set of salient points by which the geometric constraints can be robustly estimated must be selected. By improving the ranking of corner points the minimal set of feature points could be selected using less trials in a robust RANSAC framework [1]. Furthermore, general matching algorithms can establish better correspondences between putative match candidates in corner like points [2]. In this work we address the problem of ranking corner points with more meaning from a human expert point of view. By explicitly computing dominant edge direction using a covariance operator a new cornerness function is proposed. The proposed algorithm has the purpose of solving a specific problem of the original Harris feature point detection algorithm: to reduce false corner responses on image regions where partial derivatives have similar values giving rise to false corner responses.

A. Gasteratos, M. Vincze, and J.K. Tsotsos (Eds.): ICVS 2008, LNCS 5008, pp. 323–332, 2008.
© Springer-Verlag Berlin Heidelberg 2008

Fig. 1. Up: Original image. Middle: Partial Ix derivative Down: Partial Iy Derivative. Note that partial derivatives in diagonal regions have overlapping gradient regions.

To find corner points on images a preprocessing step computes partial derivatives in the horizontal and vertical direction using convolutional filters. Ideally the results of applying these derivatives filters should have non overlapping edge regions. But due to the discretized filter version and image artifacts the partial gradient response usually present overlapping areas which can be observed in diagonal edge image regions (see Fig. 1). Then, since only the gradient magnitude is considered to find corner points in previous approaches those algorithms produce false corner responses on overlapping partial derivative areas. Our hypothesis is that considering angular gradient information the number of false corner points can be greatly reduced and at the same time it can provide a better corner significance metric.

2   Related Work

The initial interest point detector approaches work on a single image scale [3]. By computing a cornerness function on an image window patch where the cornerness function reach a local maximum are selected as interest points. In [4] the Harris detector is introduced based on the second moment matrix, also called the auto-correlation matrix, which is often used for feature detection of corner like regions. This matrix describes the gradient distribution in a local region around a point:

$$M = (\mu, \sigma_I, \sigma_D) = \sigma_D g(\sigma_I)$$
$$= \begin{bmatrix} I_x^2(x, \sigma_D) & I_x I_y(x, \sigma_D) \\ I_x I_y(x, \sigma_D) & I_y^2(x, \sigma_D) \end{bmatrix} \tag{1}$$

Local image derivatives I_x, I_y are computed with Gaussian kernels of scale σ_D (differentiation scale). Then, the squared derivatives I_x^2, I_y^2 are smoothed with a Gaussian window of scale σ_I (integration scale). The eigenvalues of this matrix (λ_1, λ_2)represent two principal signal changes in a neighborhood of the point. This property enables the extraction of points, for which the magnitude of both orthogonal directional gradients is high. Various methods including KLT [5] and, Förstner [6] consider a similar idea by evaluating the cornerness strength of each point by analyzing the eigenvalues of the auto-correlation matrix explicitly or using the determinant and the trace of the second moment matrix. Table 1 shows similar corner quality functions proposed by pioneer corner detection algorithms based on covariance matrix computation and the threshold values suggested by corresponding authors.

Table 1. Cornerness strength function for similar corner detectors

Feature Detector	Cornerness Strength Function
Harris	$C_{str} = det(M) - ktrace(M)^2$ $0.04 \leq k \leq 0.06$
KLT	$C_{str} = \lambda_2 > Threshold$ $value$
Fortsner	$C_{str} = det(M)/trace(M) > th$ $th \geq 0.5$

A similar approach to detect salient regions computes the Hessian of an image with second order partial derivatives. Derivatives encode the shape information by providing the description of blob like regions derived from the shape of the hessian filter. Second derivative salient region detectors are based on the determinant and the trace of this matrix similar to the first derivative salient detectors. Examples of Hessian local feature extractors are the proposed by Beaudet [7], Kitchen and Rosenfeld [8]. The trace of matrix denotes the Laplacian filter, which is often used for isotropic edge detection [9].

Others alternatives for feature detection were proposed by Sojka, Smith and Brady [10,11] to detect junction regions. A recent study [13] of the corner stability and corner localization properties of the features extracted by different algorithms suggest that Hessian based salient region detectors are more stable under different image data sets.

Recent progress in the development of feature detectors have looked for the extraction of salient regions invariants to image scale, rotation and partially robust to projective distortion due to change in viewpoint and illumination variations.

Automatic scale selection has been studied by Lindeberg [12]. The idea is to select the characteristic scale, for which a given feature detector has its maximum response over scales. The size of the region can be selected independently of image resolution for each salient region. The Laplacian operator is used for scale selection since it gives the best results in the experimental comparison in [13].

Examples of viewpoint invariant corner detectors are the proposed in [14], which maximize the entropy within the region. Harris-Laplace and Harris-Affine detectors proposed by Mikolajczyk and Schmid [15], are extensions of the Harris corner detector, and the edge-based regions proposed by Tuytelaars and Van Gool [16], which exploits Harris corners and nearby edges. Focusing on speed, [17] proposed to approximate the Laplacian of Gaussians (LoG) by a Difference of Gaussians (DoG) filter. An excellent review of the state of the art feature detectors can be consulted in [18,13].

An important advantage of pioneer corner detection algorithm when compared to scale space methods is that they provide better localization on real corner regions since the blurring effect on higher scales tend to displace edges and then the detected salient regions are biased. We limit our work to Harris point corner detection because the application we are targeting is concerned with self calibrated reconstruction and having corner regions on intuitive real regions improve the qualitative visual results [19].

The idea of using angular information for corner detection has been explored in [20,21] using a polar mapping to find the subtend angle of dominant edges. One important drawback of those approaches is that the polar mapping reduce the angular resolution to some discrete values. The key difference of our work is that we estimate the dominant orientation directly from the covariance matrix of the image gradient which provide a higher angular resolution for each dominant edge.

2.1   Edge Direction Estimation by a Covariance Operator

Given probable corner points and its associated image region I and partial derivatives $I_m = \{I_x, I_y\}$ (see figure 2 for an example). We estimate the individual covariance matrices $Cov_{u=x,y}$ for each partial derivative.

Covariance Operator. We introduce the circular covariance operator for dominant edge orientation estimation.

Given a partial derivative from I_m we convolve the image with kernels C_x, C_y and compute the summatory over the resulting convolved region. We obtain a Covariance matrix for each partial derivative.

$$Cov_{u=x,y} = \begin{bmatrix} \Sigma(I_m C_x)^2 & (I_m C_x C_y) \\ \Sigma(I_m C_x C_y) & (I_m C_y)^2 \end{bmatrix} \qquad (2)$$

The covariance matrix defines an ellipse where the maximum variance correspond to the major axis of the ellipse which represent the dominant edge direction for the associated partial derivative.

By analyzing individually covariance matrices we can obtain the orientation of the two most dominant edges in a region window, with one edge for each partial derivative.

Let $c_{i=1,2}$ be the column vectors of the covariance matrix. Then, the column with greater norm represent the most dominant edge with large gradient variations. The angle between the canonical vectors and the dominant edge can be estimated directly and its given by:

$$\theta_m = \begin{cases} \cos^{-1}(c_1/c_2) & \text{if } norm(c_1) >= norm(c_2) \\ \cos^{-1}(c_1/c_2) & \text{if } norm(c_1) < norm(c_2) \end{cases} \qquad (3)$$

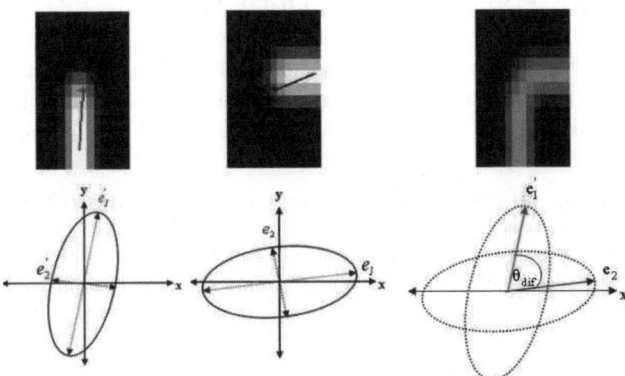

Fig. 2. Top: Example of partial derivatives for a probable corner point and the gradient magnitude. Bottom: The covariance regions for each partial derivative and the angular difference between dominant edges.

$C_{X=}$

0	-1	0	1	0
-2	-1	0	1	2
-2	-2	0	1	2
-2	-1	0	1	2
0	-1	0	1	0

$C_{Y=}$

0	2	2	2	0
1	1	1	1	1
0	0	0	0	0
-1	-1	-1	-1	-2
0	-2	-2	-2	0

Fig. 3. 5x5 circular Convolution Mask for Covariance operator. Observe that $C_y = C_x^T$.

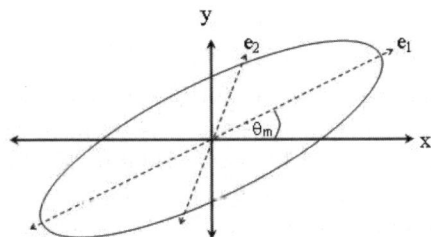

Fig. 4. An example of a ellipse defined for the Iy partial derivative of the putative corner point in Figure 2

Then, the angular difference between dominant edges are directly computed from θ_m. By estimating the angular difference between dominant edges in this way a broader angular resolution is obtained.

$$\theta_{Dif}(\theta_x, \theta_y) = min \begin{cases} \theta_x - \theta_y \\ \theta_x - (\theta_y + 180) \end{cases} \quad (4)$$

3   Improving Harris Corner Detection

For every putative corner point arising from the original Harris corner detector with standard $k = .04$ threshold value empirically obtained in [4], the new algorithm adds directional gradient information to rank corner points as follow.

3.1   Computing the Angular Difference of Dominant Edges

The proposed algorithm computes the angular difference between dominant edges for every putative corner point selected by the Harris function (eq: 1) as follow:

1. For each discrete partial derivative a weighted covariance matrix is estimated (eq: 2).
2. The dominant edge direction is computed (eq: 3).
3. The difference between dominant edges is found using (eq: 4).

3.2   Proposed Cornerness Function for Ranking Feature Points

Intuitively corners are better defined as the angular difference between dominant edges approximates to 90 degrees. This important fact is not considered by previous corner point detectors in the cornerness strength functions. We show that by adding a weighting factor corresponding to the difference in edge directions the corresponding Harris function allows the ranking of corner like points better than the original function. In addition, the proposed cornerness function can remove false corner regions due to discrete derivative artifacts.

$$C_{str} = log(det(M) - k \ \ trace(M)^2) * \theta_{Dif}(\theta_x, \theta_y) \tag{5}$$

Proper threshold setting is key for finding coherent corner points. When false corner responses arise due to image noise this problem can partially be solved by over-smoothing the images at the cost of loosing localization accuracy. However, when the partial derivatives present overlapping responses it is specially difficult to set up a appropriate threshold value since setting a high value will discard corner regions having average gradient responses while a lower threshold parameter will bring up corner points in noisy regions.

To solve this problem we first apply the log function to the original Harris, this has the effect of normalizing the corner response to avoid large variations. Then, the $log(Harris)$ strength function is weighted by the angular difference between dominant edges $\theta_{Dif}(\theta_x, \theta_y)$ which yield stronger corner responses as the putative corner regions define L shape junctions corners.

4   Results on Salient Points Detection

This section shows the comparative results of the proposed salient point detection algorithm against the original Harris method.

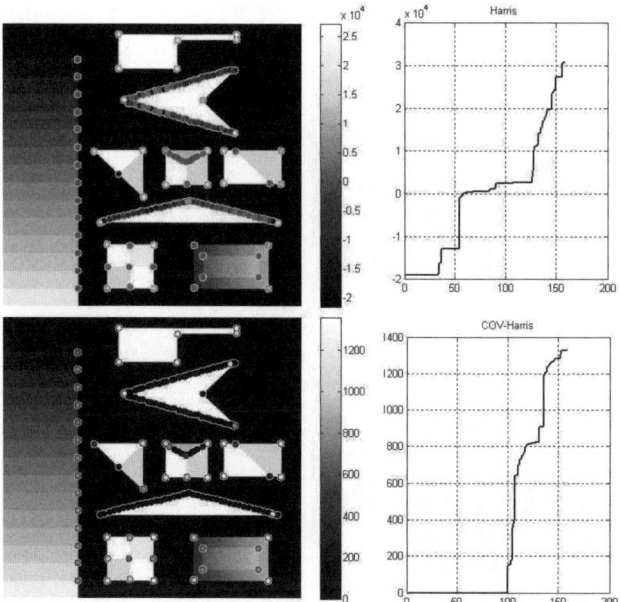

Fig. 5. Corners ranked by the original Harris (Top) and the proposed algorithm (Bottom) in the Artificial Synthetic image

The detected corners are displayed with its associated strength corner value using a color scale, a lighter salient point location is related with a higher cornerness value and viceversa. Moreover, on the left each image displays corner's strength value in ascendent order. Figure 5 top shows the corners found by the original Harris function. Observe that there are several putative corner points with hight cornerness strength response in diagonal edges. In figure 5 bottom shows the results of the proposed algorithm.

Observe how the proposed corner response function assigns lower cornerness strength values in image regions where partial derivatives define similar dominant edge directions in both partial derivatives and at the same time highlight subjective truly corner regions on the left side of the images.

In figures 6 we use the House images to evaluate the performance of the new algorithm. Again, the detected corner points are shown sorted according to the corresponding corner response function using color scale. On the left Harris function is computed and on the right when corners are ranked using the proposed function (in section 4.3.2) highlighting truly corner points.

$$C_{str} = log(det(M) - ktrace(M)^2) * \theta_{Dif}(\theta_1, \theta_2) \qquad (6)$$

Observe that when using Harris cornerness function many corners points on diagonal edge regions have a high significance value. While using the proposed cornerness

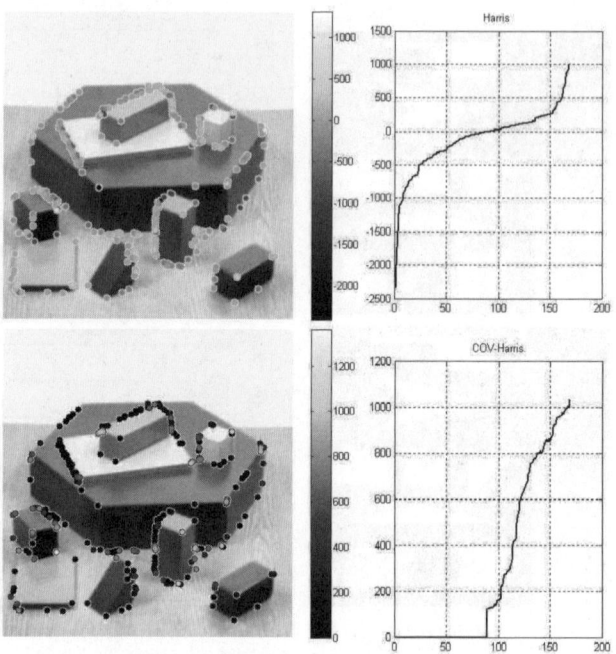

Fig. 6. Corners ranked by the original Harris (Top) and the proposed algorithm (Bottom) in the Blocks image

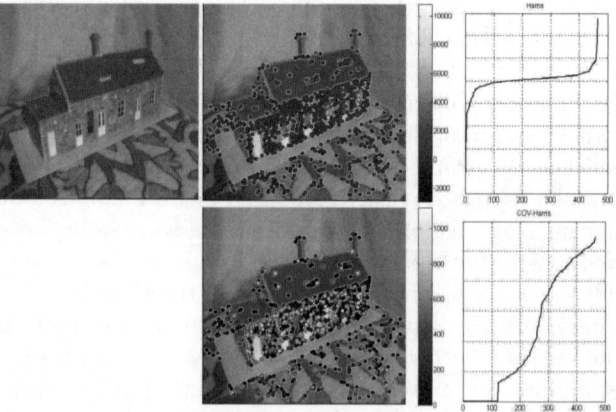

Fig. 7. Corners ranked by the original Harris (Top) and the proposed algorithm (Bottom) in the House image

function the majority of these false corners are associated with a low strength value since the difference between dominant edge direction tends to zero.

5   Conclusions

The majority of previous approaches on salient point detection have employed the gradient magnitude of partial derivatives to compute a measure of salient point strength. However, edges are not fully described by the edge magnitude. Additional edge features as edge direction and gradient normal have been scarcely considered for salient point detection.

In this work a new algorithm for corner point detection was introduced. The angular difference between dominant edges was used to improve the Harris corner detection. Dominant edges are directly identified by estimating the covariance matrix of individual partial derivatives. Then, from each covariance matrix the principal edge direction is analytically computed to estimate the angular difference between dominant edges. An important advantage of the proposed algorithm is that directional edge information is estimated with a broader angular resolution when compared to previously developed polar mapping methods.

Adding angular information was shown under experimental tests to reduce false corner responses in image regions where the slope of partial derivatives have similar ratio change and to rank corners with more meaning from a human expert point of view.

An important advantage of the proposed ranking corner function is that common indoor/outdoor images have hundreds and even thousands of corner like points. Then, having features well sorted by the corner strength function can avoid the construction of complex descriptors in false corner regions and at the same time reducing significantly the computational cost of solving the subsequent matching stage. The evaluation of the proposed COV-Harris interest point detector in tracking application is part of our current work.

Acknowledgment

This work was done with the help of CONACYT scholarship support 184921.

References

1. Fischler, M.A., Bolles, R.C.: Random sample consensus: A paradigm for model fitting with applications to image analysis and automated cartography. Commun. ACM 24(6), 381–395 (1981)
2. Shi, J., Tomasi, C.: Good features to track. In: IEEE Conference on Computer Vision and Pattern Recognition (CVPR 1994), pp. 593–600 (1994)
3. Moravec, H.P.: Visual mapping by a robot rover. In: International Joint Conference on Artificial Intelligence, vol. 1, pp. 598–600 (1979)
4. Harris, C., Stephens, M.: A combined corner and edge detector. In: Matthews, M.M. (ed.) Proc. Of the 4th ALVEY vision conference, vol. 27, pp. 147–151 (1988)
5. Kanade, T., Tomasi, C.: Detection and tracking of point features. CMU Technical Report CMU–CS–91–132 1, 91–132 (1991)
6. Förstner, W., Gülch, E.: A fast operator for detection and precise location of distinct points, corners and centres of circular features. Intercommission Conference on Fast Processing of Photogrammetric Data 1, 281–305 (1996)

7. Beaudet, P.: Rotationally invariant image operators. In: Proceedings of the 4th International Joint Conference on Pattern Recognition, vol. 1, pp. 579–583 (1978)
8. Kitchen, L., Rosenfeld, A.: Gray–level corner detection. Pattern Recognition Letters 1, 95–102 (1982)
9. Torre, V., Poggio, T.A.: On edge detection. IEEE Transactions on Pattern Analysis and Machine Intelligence 8, 147–163 (1986)
10. Sojka, E.: A new approach to detecting the corners in digital images. In: Proc. IEEE Int. Conf. on Image Processing, vol. 2, pp. 445–448 (2003)
11. Smith, S.M., Brady, J.M.: Susan – a new approach to low level image processing. International Journal of Computer Vision 23, 45–78 (1997)
12. Lindeberg, T.: Feature detection with automatic scale selection. International Journal of Computer Vision 30, 79–116 (1998)
13. Mikolajczyk, K., Schmid, C.: A comparison of affine region detectors. International Journal of Computer Vision, 43–72 (2005)
14. Kadir, T., Brady, M.: Scale, saliency and image description. International Journal of Computer Vision 45, 83–105 (2001)
15. Mikolajczyk, K., Schmid, C.: An affine invariant interest point detector. In: Proc. of 7th ECCV, vol. 1, pp. 128–142 (2002)
16. Tuytelaars, T., Van Gool, L.: Matching widely separated views based on affine invariant regions. International Journal of Computer Vision 59, 61–85 (2004)
17. Lowe, D.: Object recognition from local scale-invariant features. In: International Conference on Computer Vision, vol. 1, pp. 1150–1157 (1999)
18. Mikolajczyk, K., Schmid, C.: Scale and affine invariant interest point detectors. Int. Journal Computer Vision 60, 63–86 (2004)
19. Lemuz-López, R., Arias-Estrada, M.: A domain reduction algorithm for incremental projective reconstruction. In: ISVC (2), pp. 564–575 (2006)
20. Rosin, P.L.: Augmenting corner descriptors. Graphical Models and Image Processing 58, 286–294 (1996)
21. Zitova, B., Kautsky, J., Peters, G., Flusser, J.: Robust detection of significant points in multiframe images. Pattern Recognition Letters 20, 2, 199–206 (1999)

Skeletonization Based on Metrical Neighborhood Sequences

Attila Fazekas[1], Kálmán Palágyi[2], György Kovács[1], and Gábor Németh[2]

[1] University of Debrecen, Hungary
{attila.fazekas, gykovacs}@inf.unideb.hu
[2] University of Szeged, Hungary
{palagyi,gnemeth}@inf.u-szeged.hu

Abstract. Skeleton is a shape descriptor which summarizes the general form of objects. It can be expressed in terms of the fundamental morphological operations. The limitation of that characterization is that its construction based on digital disks such that cannot provide good approximation to the Euclidean disks. In this paper we define a new type of skeleton based on neighborhood sequences that is much closer to the Euclidean skeleton. A novel method for quantitative comparison of skeletonization algorithms is also proposed.

Keywords: shape representation, skeletonization, neighborhood sequences, mathematical morphology.

1 Introduction

Skeleton is a region-based shape descriptor which summarizes the general form of objects/shapes [2]. There are three major definitions for the skeleton of an Euclidean set/object:

1. **Medial Axis Transformation (MAT).** For each point in an object, we find the closest border point. If a point has more than one such closest point, then it is said to belong to the skeleton of that object.
2. **Prairie-fire analogy or wavefront propagation.** The object boundary is set on fire and the skeleton is formed by the loci where the isotropic fire fronts meet and extinguish each other.
3. **Maximal inscribed disks/hyperspheres.** The centers of all maximal inscribed disks/hyperspheres comprise the skeleton. (A disk/hypersphere is maximal inscribed in an object if there exists no other disk/hypersphere within that object properly containing it.)

The extensions of those definitions to discrete sets lead to various skeletons and skeletonization methods [8].

Mathematical morphology is a powerful tool for image processing and image analysis [7]. Its operators can extract relevant topological and geometrical information from binary (and grey-scale) images by using structuring elements

A. Gasteratos, M. Vincze, and J.K. Tsotsos (Eds.): ICVS 2008, LNCS 5008, pp. 333–342, 2008.

with various sizes and shapes. The discrete skeletons can be characterized morphologically: the homotopic wavefront propagation can be defined in terms of morphological hit-or-miss transforms and the centers of all maximal inscribed disks/hyperspheres can be expressed in terms of erosions and dilations.

In their classical paper, Rosenfeld and Pfaltz [6] investigated two types of motions in the two-dimensional digital space. The cityblock motion allows horizontal and vertical movements only, while in the case of chessboard motion one can diagonal movements, as well. The octagonal distances can be obtained by the mixed use of these motions.

This concept has been investigated and extended by many authors, in several directions. Here for the general history and the basic properties of these and related concepts of digital topology, we only refer to the survey paper [5] and the book [9].

Das, Chakrabarti and Chatterji [4] considered arbitrary periodic sequences of cityblock and chessboard motions, called periodic neighborhood sequences, and also their corresponding generalizations in $\mathbb{Z}^n$. Moreover, they established a formula for calculating the distance $d(p, q; A)$ of any two points $p, q \in \mathbb{Z}^n$, determined by such a neighborhood sequence A. Th ey introduced a natural partial ordering relation for periodic neighborhood sequences: if for two periodic neighborhood sequences A, B we have $d(p, q; A) \leq d(p, q; B)$ for all $p, q \in \mathbb{Z}^n$ then A is "faster" than B. Das [3] investigated the lattice properties of the set of periodic neighborhood sequences and some of its subsets under this relation, in 2D. He obtained some positive, but also some negative results. Note that similar results were obtained in 3D case [10].

Later, the investigation were extended to arbitrary, not necessarily periodic neighborhood sequences (see [11]). Such sequences have important applications. For example, it turns out that neighborhood sequences which provide the best approximations to the Euclidean distance in $\mathbb{Z}^2$ in some sense, are not periodic (see [13]).

Those neighborhood sequences which generate metrics on the digital space $\mathbb{Z}^n$ naturally play a special role in several problems, for example in skeletonization. Hence it is important to analyze the structural properties of these sequences. Such an investigation was performed in [12]. It turns out that in 2D the set of such sequences has a nice algebraic structure under the above mentioned natural partial ordering relation.

The structure of this paper is the following. After the Introduction to skeletonization and neighborhood sequences, we summarize the most inportant definitions about neighbourhood sequences (Section 2), and morphological skeleton (Section 3). We define a new type of skeleton based on neighborhood sequences in Section 4.The novel method for quantitative comparison of skeletons can be found in Section 5. In the last section we report our first experimental results.

2   Neighborhood Sequences

In this section we introduce some standard notation concerning neighborhood sequences.

Let $n, m \in \mathbb{N}$ with $m \le n$. The points $p = (p_1, \ldots, p_n)$ and $q = (q_1, \ldots, q_n)$ in $\mathbb{Z}^n$ are m-neighbors, if the following two conditions hold:

- $|p_i - q_i| \le 1 \quad (1 \le i \le n)$,
- $\sum_{i=1}^{n} |p_i - q_i| \le m$.

The sequence $A = (A(i))_{i=1}^{\infty}$, where $A(i) \in \{1, \ldots, n\}$ for all $i \in \mathbb{N}$, is called an n-dimensional (shortly nD) neighborhood sequence. If for some $l \in \mathbb{N}$ we have $A(i + l) = A(i)$ for $i \in \mathbb{N}$ then A is called periodic with period l. The set of the nD-neighborhood sequences will be denoted by S_n, while the set of periodic ones by P_n.

Let $p, q \in \mathbb{Z}^n$ and $A \in S_n$. The point sequence $p = p_0, p_1, \ldots, p_t = q$, where p_{i-1} and p_i are $A(i)$-neighbors in $\mathbb{Z}^n$ $(1 \le i \le t)$, is called an A-path from p to q of length t. The A-distance $d(p, q; A)$ of p and q is defined as the length of the shortest A-path(s) between them. As a brief notation, we also use $d(A)$ for the A-distance.

3   Morphological Skeleton

When using a morphological approach, skeleton is related to the set of centres of all the maximal insribed disks which can be expressed in terms of erosions and dilations [7]. Fist, some concepts of mathematical morphology will be given below.

The *dilation* of set $X \subseteq \mathbb{Z}^n$ by *structuring element* $Y \subseteq \mathbb{Z}^n$ is defined by

$$X \oplus Y = \{ \, p \mid (\hat{Y})_p \cap X \ne \emptyset \, \} \,,$$

where $\hat{Y}$ denotes the *reflection* of set Y defined as $\hat{Y} = \{ \, -y \mid y \in Y \, \}$, and $(Y)_p$ denotes the translation of set Y by point $p \in \mathbb{Z}^n$ defined as $(Y)_p = \{ \, y + p \mid y \in Y \, \}$.

The *erosion* of X by structuring element Y is defined by

$$X \ominus Y = \{ \, p \mid (Y)_p \subseteq X \, \} = (X^c \oplus \hat{Y})^c \,,$$

where $(X)^c$ denotes the set-theoretic complement of X.

The *morphological skeleton* of set X by structuring element Y is defined by

$$S(X, Y) = \bigcup_{k=0}^{K} S_k(X, Y) = \bigcup_{k=0}^{K} (X \ominus Y^k) - ((X \ominus Y^{k+1}) \oplus Y) \,,$$

where

$$Y^k = \begin{cases} \{\mathcal{O}\} \text{ (simply the origin)} & \text{if } k = 0 \\ \{\mathcal{O}\} \oplus Y = Y & \text{if } k = 1 \\ Y^{k-1} \oplus Y & \text{otherwise} \end{cases} \,,$$

and K is the last step before X is eroded completely:

$$K = \max\{ \ k \mid X \ominus Y^k \neq \emptyset \ \}.$$

The formulation states that $S(X,Y)$ is obtained as the union of the *skeletal subsets* $S_k(X,Y)$. It can be readily be seen that the set $S_k(X,Y)$ contains all points $p \in X$ such that x is the center of a maximal "disk" included in X. Note that the limitation of the morphological skeleton is that its construction is based on "disks" of the form Y^k. Hence the morphological skeleton does not provides a good approximation to the Euclidean skeleton.

4   Sequence Skeleton

In order to cut the shortage of the morphological skeleton, we propose a new type of skeleton that is based on neighborhood sequences.

Let $A = (A(i))_{i=1}^{\infty}$ be an nD neighborhood sequence and let $\mathcal{Y} = (Y(i))_{i=1}^{\infty}$ be the sequence of structuring elements in which $Y(i)$ corresponds to $A(i)$ $(i = 1, 2, \ldots)$. For example, if $n = 2$ and $A(i) = 1$, then

$$Y(i) = \{(0,0), (-1,0), (1,0), (0,-1), (0,1)\} \ .$$

The *sequence skeleton* of set X by sequence of structuring elements $\mathcal{Y}$ is defined by

$$\mathcal{S}(X,\mathcal{Y}) = \bigcup_{k=0}^{K} (X \ominus \mathcal{Y}^k) - ((X \ominus \mathcal{Y}^{k+1}) \oplus Y(k+1)) \ ,$$

where

$$\mathcal{Y}^k = \begin{cases} \{\mathcal{O}\} & \text{if } k = 0 \\ \{\mathcal{O}\} \oplus Y(1) = Y(1) & \text{if } k = 1 \\ \mathcal{Y}^{k-1} \oplus Y(k) & \text{otherwise} \end{cases}$$

and

$$K = \max\{ \ k \mid X \ominus \mathcal{Y}^k \neq \emptyset \ \}.$$

It is easy to see that

$$\mathcal{S}(X,\mathcal{Y}) = S(X,Y)$$

if $\mathcal{Y} = (Y, Y, \ldots)$. Hence the conventional morphological skeleton is a special case of sequence skeletons.

5   Quantitative Comparison of Skeletons

In this Section, a new and fairly general method is presented for quantitative comparison of different skeletonization algorithms/methods.

The proposed method consists of the following steps for each selected base (binary) image BI:

1. Reference skeleton RS is extracted from BI by a topologically correct skeletonization algorithm.
2. Euclidean distance map DM_{BI} is calculated from object boundary in base image BI [1].
3. Reference image RI is created by replacing each skeletal point p in RS by an Euclidean disk with radius $DM_{BI}(p)$.

   In this way we get a reference image from a base image with its known, connected, and exact reference skeleton. A base image, its reference skeleton, its distance map, and the reference image (as union of Euclidean disks) are shown in Fig. 1.
4. Euclidean distance map DM_{RS} is computed from reference skeleton RS.
5. A skeleton S is extracted from reference image RI by an arbitrary skeletonization algorithm.

   Fig. 2 presents some illustrative examples for sequence skeletons extracted from a reference image.
6. Euclidean distance map DM_S is computed from skeleton S.

   Examples of skeletal distance maps are presented in Fig. 3
7. $d(RS, DM_S)$ is determined, where

$$d(X, Y) = \sum_{p \in X, X(p)=1} Y(p).$$

   In other words, $d(X.Y)$ is the sum of distances in the distance map Y at each skeletal points (having value 1) in sekelton X. It is obvious that $d(RS, DM_{RS}) = 0$.
8. $d(S, DM_{RS})$ is calculated as well.

   We use $d(RS, DM_S)$ and $d(S, DM_{RS})$ to measure the goodness of the investigated skeleton S.

6   Experiments

We made an experiment, using 10 different binary images with different complexity (number of components, shape of components, size). We generated the sequence skeletons of the images using the classical $d_4 = (4)_1^\infty$, $d_8 = (8)_1^\infty$ neighborhood sequences that consist of only one kind of neighborhood examination repeatedly. Furthermore we generated the sequence skeletons with the $d_{\{84\}} = (84)_1^\infty$, called octogonal neighborhood sequence, (which is verified to give a finer approximation of the Euclidean distance then the d_4 or d_8 [3]), and the $d_{opt} = (844484844844)_1^\infty$ sequence, which consists of the prenex of the best 2 dimensional Euclidean distance approximating non-periodical neighborhood sequence [13]. The length of this prenex is related to the image content, it is about half of the diameter of the objects on most image. There can be several sequences approximating the Euclidean distance well, but the infinite neighborhood sequence described in [13] is theoretically prooved to give the best approximation.

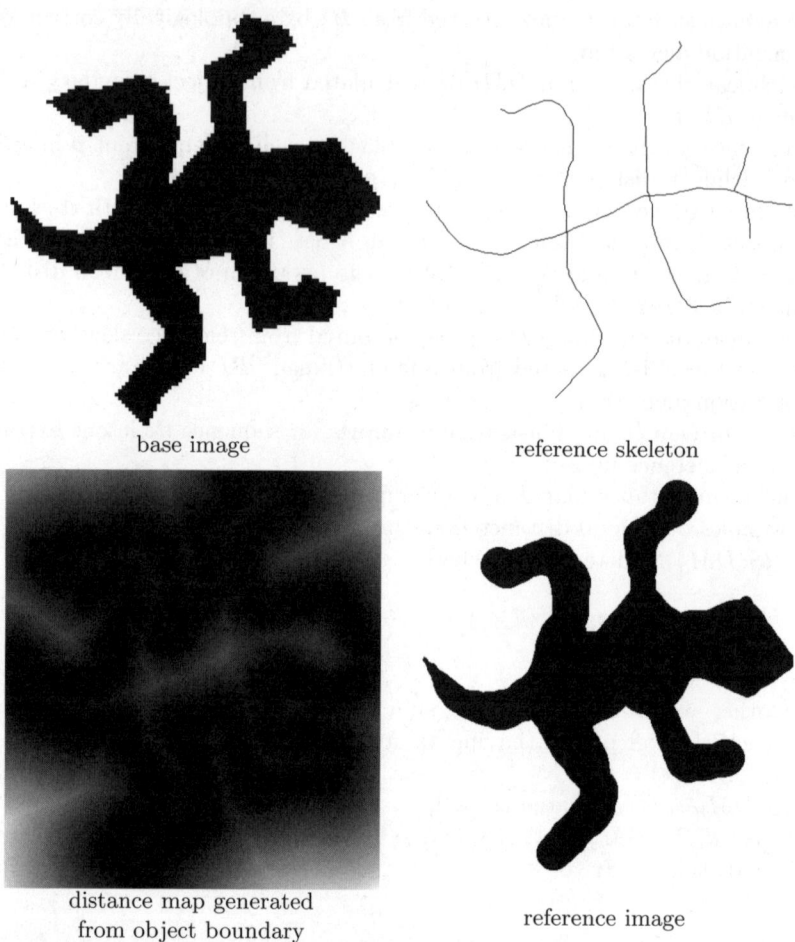

base image   reference skeleton

distance map generated   reference image
from object boundary

Fig. 1. Base image #1 (of size 428×462), its reference skeleton, its Euclidean distance maps, and the derived reference image #1

According to the comparison method above to measure the goodness of a skeleton the $D1 = d(S, DM_{RS})$ and the $D2 = d(RS, DM_S)$ values have been computed. We computed the following four measures:

$$MAX = max\{D1, D2\} \ ,$$
$$AVG = (D1 + D2)/2 \ ,$$
$$|D1| = 100 * D1/(number\ of\ pixels\ in\ S) \ ,$$
$$|D2| = 100 * D2/(number\ of\ pixels\ in\ RS) \ .$$

In Table 1, for all measures the smaller value means the better similarity of the sequence skeleton and the reference skeleton.

Table 1. Comparison for the 10 base images

Image	Size	Goodness	d_4	d_8	$d_{\{84\}}$	d_{opt}
		D1	2039	3653	1802	1481
		D2	4061	2523	1469	1471
	428×464	MAX	4061	3653	1802	1481
		AVG	3050	3088	1635	1476
		|D1|	184	231	126	114
		|D2|	320	199	116	116
		D1	131	293	240	165
		D2	3820	3772	2348	2129
	118×135	MAX	3820	3772	2348	2129
		AVG	1975	2032	1294	1147
		|D1|	66	129	94	73
		|D2|	529	523	325	295
		D1	131	293	240	165
		D1	200	261	198	173
		D2	164	236	150	142
	160×183	MAX	200	261	198	173
		AVG	182	248	174	157
		|D1|	50	62	48	44
		|D2|	45	65	41	39
		D1	1902	3831	2356	1825
		D2	7332	8943	4560	4006
	586×425	MAX	7332	8943	4560	4006
		AVG	4617	6387	2458	2915
		|D1|	189	349	200	160
		|D2|	484	591	301	265
		D1	3636	8985	5152	3894
		D2	10049	13416	5920	4834
	696×731	MAX	10049	13416	5920	4834
		AVG	6842	11200	4036	4364
		|D1|	126	255	142	110
		|D2|	245	363	160	131
		D1	184	441	335	229
		D2	1101	1148	709	620
	174×224	MAX	1101	1148	709	620
		AVG	642	794	522	424
		|D1|	45	87	62	49
		|D2|	198	206	127	111
		D1	129	488	371	237
		D2	1015	1316	646	556
	160×224	MAX	1015	1316	646	556
		AVG	572	902	508	396
		|D1|	47	147	107	72
		|D2|	230	298	146	126
		D1	765	2924	1551	967
		D2	3217	5151	1863	1601
	512×512	MAX	3217	5151	1863	1601
		AVG	1991	4037	1707	1284
		|D1|	59	187	102	70
		|D2|	191	306	111	95
		D1	846	3157	1754	1046
		D2	3444	5269	2204	1857
	512×512	MAX	3444	5269	2204	1857
		AVG	2145	4213	1979	1451
		|D1|	64	197	109	74
		|D2|	203	310	130	110
		D1	1792	2358	1588	1270
		D2	4462	4530	2610	2692
	512×512	MAX	4462	4530	2610	2692
		AVG	3127	3444	2099	1981
		|D1|	137	146	94	84
		|D2|	253	257	148	153

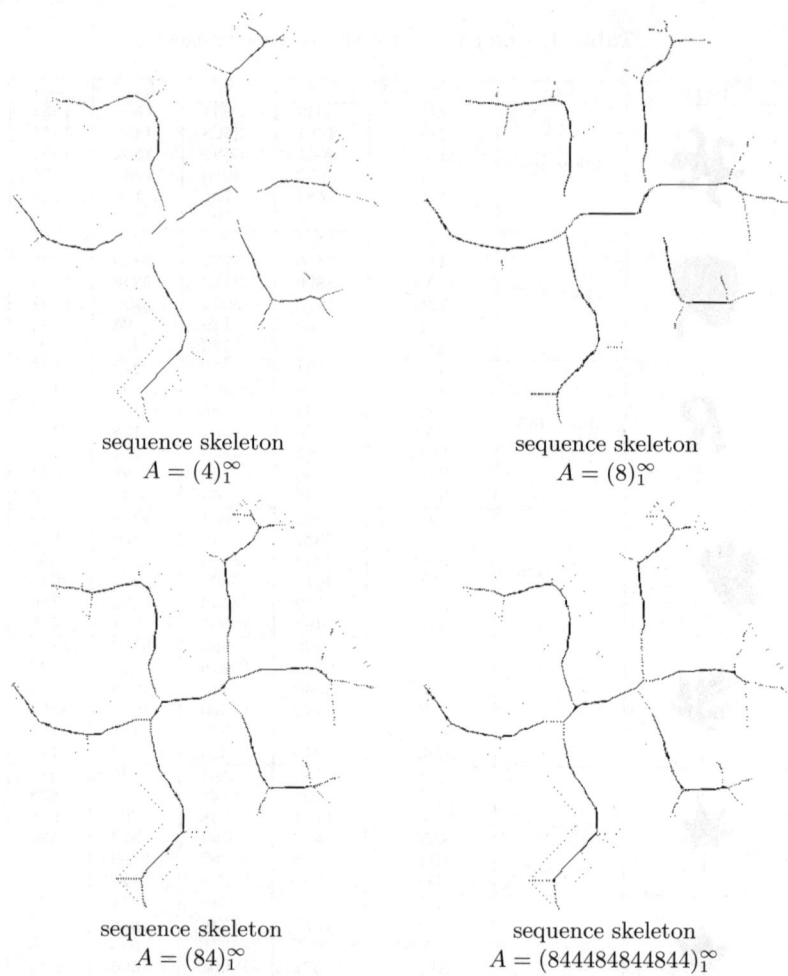

sequence skeleton
$A = (4)_1^\infty$

sequence skeleton
$A = (8)_1^\infty$

sequence skeleton
$A = (84)_1^\infty$

sequence skeleton
$A = (844484844844)_1^\infty$

Fig. 2. Examples of sequence skeletons of reference image #1

Considering the $D1$, $D2$ and MAX measures we can state, that in most cases the sequence skeleton generated by the d_{opt} neighborhood sequence is the best one, and the sequence skeleton by $d_{\{84\}}$ is the second best one of the four sequence skeletons. That matches the theoretical expectations and the observations can be made comparing the sequence skeletons visually in Fig. 2.

In some cases, when the input image contains thin components, the d_4 can give better results for $D1$ then d_{opt}. In these cases the $D2$ of d_4 is worse then $D2$ of d_{opt}. The reason of this is the torn sequence skeleton (and so the small number of skeleton pixels) of thin objects using d_4. Computing $D1$, fewer values from the distance map will be added resulting smaller sum (higher similarity). On the contrary, due to the torn sequence skeleton, in the distance map of S in the positions of RS pixels are not zeros, but positive numbers, meaning how far

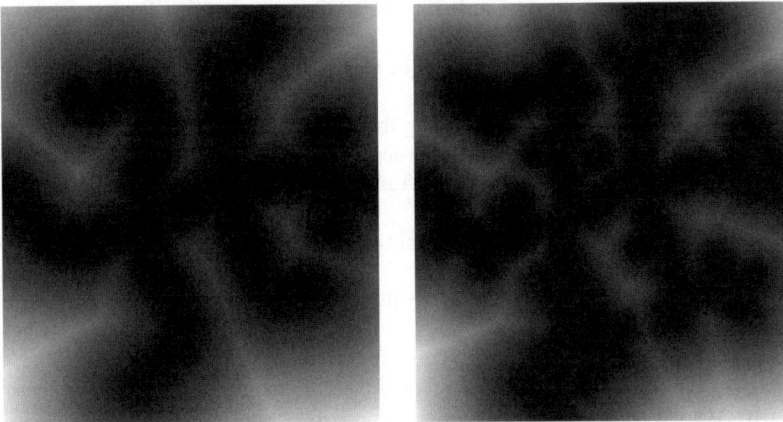

Fig. 3. Distance maps generated from the reference skeleton #1 (left) and the sequence skeleton $A = (4)$ extracted from reference image #1 (right)

the closest skeleton pixel is. That is why the $D2$ sum will be greater and giving worse results in the same time. To solve this problem, we introduced the average of $D1$ and $D2$ to measure the similarity of S to the RS. The results of AVG fit the expectations in all cases.

We introduced two more measures, the $|D1|$ and $|D2|$ are in order the $D1$ and $D2$ normalized by the number of skeleton pixels in the S and RS, respectively. These values are free from the error due to the different number of skeleton pixels in S and RS, but still contain the error originated from the torns in the sequence skeletons.

In this experiment we found the d_{opt} neighborhood sequence to result the best approximation of the RS. Also the $d_{\{84\}}$ sequence gives a better approximation (according to the 6 measures we introduced) of the RS, then the d_4 or d_8 sequences. That matches the theoretical expectations and the visual observations which can be made on the images.

The comparison algorithm for skeletonization methods gave also the expected results, the derived measures are robust, the best one (AVG) gave the theoretical results in all cases. In virtue of these, the comparison algorithm described and applied above can be used to compare skeletoniztation algorithms.

That was the first experiment we have made. To draw stronger conclusions, we make a more exhaustive experiment on a greater set containing binary images of various size and complexity. Another aim is to do similar examination of the sequence based skeletonization algorithm in 3 dimensions.

References

1. Borgefors, G.: Distance transformations in arbitrary dimensions. Computer Vision, Graphics, and Image Processing 27, 321–345 (1984)
2. Blum, H.: A transformation for extracting new descriptors of shape. In: Wathen-Dunn, W. (ed.) Models for the Perception of Speech and Visual Form, pp. 362–380. MIT Press, Cambridge (1967)

3. Das, P.P.: Lattice of octagonal distances in digital geometry. Pattern Recognition Lett. 11, 663–667 (1990)
4. Das, P.P., Chakrabarti, P.P., Chatterji, B.N.: Distance functions in digital geometry. Inform. Sci. 42, 113–136 (1987)
5. Kong, T.Y., Rosenfeld, A.: Survey. Digital topology: Introduction and survey. Computer Vision, Graphics, and Image Processing 48, 357–393 (1987)
6. Rosenfeld, A., Pfaltz, J.L.: Distance functions on digital pictures. Pattern Recognition 1, 33–61 (1968)
7. Serra, J.: Image analysis and mathematical morphology. Academic Press, London (1982)
8. Soille, P.: Morphological image analysis - Principles and applications. Springer, Berlin (1998)
9. Voss, K.: Discrete images, objects, and functions in $\mathbb{Z}^n$. Springer, Berlin (1991)
10. Fazekas, A.: Lattice of distances based on 3D-neighbourhood sequences. Acta Math. Acad. Paedagog. Nyházi (N.S.) 15, 55–60 (1999)
11. Fazekas, A., Hajdu, A., Hajdu, L.: Lattice of generalized neighborhood sequences in nD and ∞D. Publ. Math. Debrecen 60, 405–427 (2002)
12. Fazekas, A., Hajdu, A., Hajdu, L.: Metrical neighborhood sequences in $\mathbb{Z}^n$. Pattern Recognition Lett. 26, 2022–2032 (2005)
13. Hajdu, A., Hajdu, L.: Approximating the Euclidean distance by digital metrics. Discrete Math. 283, 101–111 (2004)

Bottom-Up and Top-Down Object Matching Using Asynchronous Agents and *a Contrario* Principles

Nicolas Burrus[1,2], Thierry M. Bernard[1], and Jean-Michel Jolion[2]

[1] ENSTA - UEI, 32 Boulevard Victor, 75015 Paris, France
[2] Université de Lyon, F-69361 Lyon
INSA de Lyon, F-69621, Villeurbanne
CNRS, LIRIS, UMR5205

Abstract. We experiment a vision architecture for object matching based
on a hierarchy of independent agents running asynchronously in parallel.
Agents communicate through bidirectional signals, enabling the mix of top-
down and bottom-up influences. Following the so-called *a contrario* principle, each signal is given a strength according to the statistical relevance
of its associated visual data. By handling most important signals first, the
system focuses on most promising hypotheses and provides relevant results
as soon as possible. Compared to an equivalent feed-forward and sequential
algorithm, our architecture is shown capable of handling more visual data
and thus reach higher detection rates in less time.

Keywords: object matching, top-down and bottom-up, *a contrario* reasoning, parallel vision.

1 Introduction

We consider the task of 2d object matching: given a database of pictures of
objects, we want to detect these objects in new images. Numerous methods
have been proposed to solve this task, and most of them are either purely top-
down or purely bottom-up. Top-down methods are generally based on template
matching and their main limitation is their computational cost when object poses
are not constrained in the image and when the database of objects is big. On
the other hand, purely bottom-up methods are generally feature-based. Local
invariant features are extracted from the image under analysis and matched
to the features of database objects. Then concordant features are grouped to
make object pose hypotheses. These approaches are much more efficient, but
often have less discriminative power. Moreover, to save computation time, weak
feature matches may need to be discarded at an early stage, and features actually
belonging to an object can be wrongly ignored, thereby reducing detection rates.
This motivates a joint use of top-down and bottom-up processing, as done in
some recent works [1,2,3,4].

In order to break sequentiality in detection algorithms, we use parallelism
between processing levels. Then, it becomes possible for strong hypotheses to

A. Gasteratos, M. Vincze, and J.K. Tsotsos (Eds.): ICVS 2008, LNCS 5008, pp. 343–352, 2008.

reach high level analysis and give the first detection results early, much before the complete termination of low level processing. In addition to biological motivations [5], there are several practical interests. First, applications waiting for detection results can be triggered earlier, and the detection process can be constrained to run in a predefined time, and still return useful information (e.g. most contrasted and easy to discriminate objects). Second, since high level steps can be reached before the complete termination of lower level steps, they can influence low level processing at the light of current evidence and accelerate the detection process. Finally, more visual data can be analyzed and thus higher detection rates can be obtained without degrading too much the average detection delays, since promising hypotheses can be handled first.

Enabling a mixed use of top-down and bottom-up processing within a parallel architecture is a difficult algorithmic task. Some systems have already exploited these principles, for example at a very low level in [6,7] or using complex scheduling strategies in [8,9]. In this paper, we experiment an original object matching architecture that keeps things simple by using high level independent agents running in parallel without explicit synchronization nor scheduling.

2   Breaking the Feed-Forward and Sequential Model

Our starting point is the object matching approach presented in [10]. It will be referred as LBU (Lowe Bottom-Up) in the rest of this paper. It is feed-forward and bottom-up. First, and offline, all the SIFT points of the objects in the database are extracted from their 2d picture and stored. Then, when an image is given for analysis, the following algorithm is applied:

1. Extract the SIFT points of the image.
2. Match each SIFT point of the image to the closest point in the object database. Discard matches whose distance is too high.
3. For the remaining matches, thanks to the location, rotation and scale information embedded in SIFT points, each match results into a full object pose hypothesis. Matches leading to compatible poses are clustered with a Hough transform. Clusters with less than 3 matches are discarded.
4. For the remaining clusters, a probability of object presence is computed and then thresholded to make decisions.

Each step takes decisions using only partial information, and thus can discard relevant hypotheses. We observed that more than 30% of good matches may be lost in step 2 if the object database is quite large and contains rather similar objects. These early decisions also prevent the use of further top-down processing to discriminate weak hypotheses.

We propose to break this sequentiality by using a hierarchy of simple and independent agents. The proposed system is ruled by the following principles:

1. Parallelism. Agents run in parallel and asynchronously in that they run as soon as and as long as they have data to proceed. This allows high level

processing to start without waiting for the complete termination of low level processing. For example, it becomes possible to reach step 4 of LBU for some salient hypotheses even if step 2 is not fully completed. To take an even greater advantage of hardware with several processing units, we also enable spatial parallelism by associating a receptive field to each agent.

2. Systematic evaluation of visual data relevance. To handle most promising hypotheses first, we evaluate visual data relevance not only at the final decision level, but also at lower levels when only partial information is available.

3. Bidirectional and asynchronous communications between agents. When an agent has processed its data, it creates a signal holding the result, and sends it to its parent (bottom-up) or to its children (top-down). Each agent keeps a buffer of signals to process so that agents never have to wait for each others. The signal system allows top-down and bottom-up influences to navigate freely through the hierarchy of agents. To ensure that signals containing strong evidence are handled first, principle 2 is used to assign a strength to every signal, and agents process their signal buffer by strength order.

Let us now apply these principles to create a functional object matching system.

3   Object Matching with a Hierarchy of Agents

3.1   Overview

The overall architecture is presented on Figure 1. It is composed of two parts. The first one is based on SIFT matching, and is a pyramid of agents whose levels roughly correspond to LBU's steps. The second one analyzes gray level histogram similarities and contains only one agent. Finally, the architecture has six different kinds of agents.

The bottom-up workflow in the SIFT part is similar to LBU. The detection system starts with the SiftPointComputer agents, which extract SIFT points in the image under analysis and send one signal to their SiftMatcher parent for each point. These SiftMatcher agents then look for the best SIFT match in the object database and send one signal to their SiftMain parent for each match. The SiftMain agent clusters SIFT matches that vote for similar object poses. When a cluster is updated, the associated pose hypothesis is embedded into a signal and sent to the Main agent.

Top-down signals are sent by the SiftMain and Main agents. According to current hypotheses, the SiftMain agent makes SIFT point predictions in order to accelerate the process. These predictions are then handled by the SiftPointComputer agents. The Main agent also emits top-down signals for the IntensityHistogramComparator agent to request histogram difference analyzes.

3.2   Evaluating Visual Data Relevance

To evaluate the relevance of visual data w.r.t. the object matching task and make decisions, a unified scheme is highly desirable. We propose to rely on so-called a

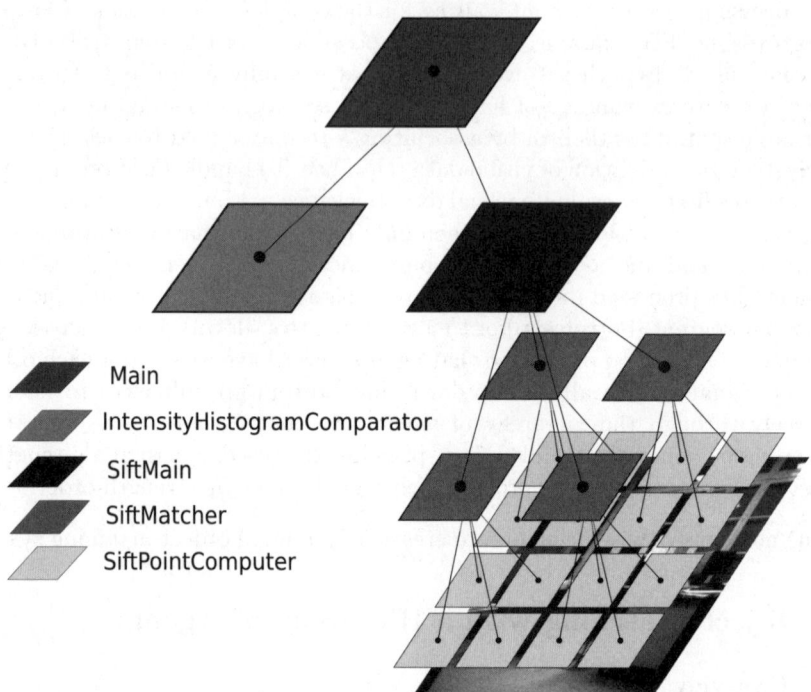

Fig. 1. Our architecture for object matching. At the lowest level, 16 SiftPointComputer agents extract SIFT points from the image and send them to their SiftMatcher parent. SiftMatcher agents then look for the closest SIFT point in the object database. SIFT matches are then handled by the SiftMain agent, which clusters them into compatible object pose hypotheses and send top-down predictions for future SIFT matches. The Main agent gathers SIFT evidence for an object presence, requests top-down histogram analyses from the IntensityHistogramComparator agent, and finally takes decisions.

contrario statistical methods [11]. They measure the significance of an event from its probability of occurrence under a model of chance. In our application, chance means that no object of the database is present. Thus, the lower the probability of occurrence of an event under the chance model, the higher the confidence that it is associated to an object of the database. The main interest of this approach is that it is generally much easier to estimate accurate probabilities when no object is present, than the contrary. Let w be the visual data associated to a signal. We propose the following procedure to assign a strength to the signal holding w:

1. Determine a discriminative random variable X, such that $X(w_1) < X(w_2)$ implies that the visual data w_1 is *less* likely to be explained by chance than w_2.
2. Compute the cumulative distribution function $P_c(X \leq x)$ under the chance model. Analytical computations are often intractable, but it is possible to

get empirical estimations by observing X values obtained on background images without any object of the database, which are simple to collect.

3. The lower $P_c(X \leq X(w))$, the higher the confidence that w is not due to chance. To get a signal strength proportional to the importance of the data, we take the inverse of this probability and set the strength of the signal associated to w to:

$$S(w) = \frac{1}{P_c(X \leq X(w))}$$

This statistical procedure also enables adaptive behaviors. Estimations of P_c are done on images which do not contain the objects to detect. These estimations will depend on the choice of these images: outdoor, indoor, highly textured, etc. If there is an *a priori* on the environment, it can be included here. It is also possible to incrementally update these estimations online in a video or robot navigation context.

Thanks to its genericity, this procedure can be used everywhere in the system, including the object presence decision step. Now, the discriminative random variables remain to be defined for each kind of visual data. This is detailed in the next Sections, where agent behaviors are described more precisely.

3.3   SiftPointComputer Agents

These agents create one bottom-up signal for each SIFT point within their receptive field on the image under analysis. At this step, only a priori information can be used to evaluate the relevance of SIFT points. We exploit saliency estimates from the saliency maps of [12]. This attentional bias is particularly interesting for outdoor scenes, as will be shown in Section 4. For these signals, the discriminative random variable X_p associated to a SIFT point p is the opposite value of the normalized saliency map at the location of p. This way, the lower $X_p(p)$, the higher the saliency, and the higher the probability that there is an object of interest.

SiftPointComputer agents are also influenced by top-down predictions emitted by the SiftMain agent. A prediction specifies an object pose hypothesis and a SIFT point of the object for which a corresponding point should be found in the image. One can deduce from the candidate object pose the theoretical location, scale and orientation of the object SIFT point in the image, if the object is present. Thus, SiftPointComputer agents will look for the closest image SIFT point which is compatible with the object pose. Details on the notion of compatibility between poses is given in Section 3.5. A bottom-up signal is created if a compatible point is found. Let $P_\Delta(p, \delta)$ be the probability that a SIFT point p in the image is compatible with pose δ by chance. Definition of P_Δ can be found in [13]. For predictions, we define the discriminative random variable X_{pp} for a point p as the joint probability of having p compatible with the candidate pose and such a high saliency, if there were no object:

$$X_{pp}(p) = P_\Delta(p, \delta) \times P_c(X_p \leq X_p(p))$$

3.4   SiftPointMatcher Agents

Given a signal containing an image SIFT point, these agents find its closest match in the object database. They generate one bottom-up signal for each match. In [10], it was shown that the ratio between the distance to the closest point and to the second closest point in the database is very good at discarding false matches. The smaller the ratio, the stronger the match. We also take into account that an object with many SIFT points is more likely to accidentally hold the closest SIFT point than an object with a few SIFT points. Let $D(m)$ be the distance ratio for a SIFT match m and O the object to which the matched point belongs, we define the following discriminative variable for match signals:

$$X_m(m) = P_c(D \leq D(m)) \times \frac{\text{number of SIFT points in } O}{\text{number of SIFT points in the database}}$$

3.5   The SiftMain Agent

It receives bottom-up signals emitted by SiftPointMatcher agents containing SIFT point matches. It identifies groups of matches leading to compatible poses using the same Hough-based procedure as in [10].

When it receives a new match, the SiftMain agent either adds it to an already existing hypothesis with the same pose, or creates a new hypothesis. Then it builds a bottom-up signal containing the updated hypothesis. The discriminative random variable for these signals is defined as follows. Let us suppose that we get k matches voting for a pose hypothesis h. Let n be the number of potential matches one can get for h, i.e. the number of SIFT points lying in the expected bounds of the candidate object in the image under analysis. Let $\{m_1, m_2, \ldots, m_k\}$ denote the set of k SIFT matches, ordered such that: $X_m(m_1) \leq X_m(m_2) \leq \ldots \leq X_m(m_k)$. To measure how unlikely a set of matches is to be accidental, we could evaluate the probability of observing a group of k matches among n voting for the same hypothesis with so low discriminative variables X_m. However this probability is difficult to compute, and following [11], we rely here on an estimation of the expectation of the number of groups of k matches having as low X_m values as h. This expectation acts as a bound on the previous probability, thanks to Markov inequality, and provides our discriminative variable X_s for an hypothesis h:

$$X_s(h) = \binom{n}{k} \times \prod_{i=1}^{k} P_c(X_m \leq X_m(m_k))$$

The SiftMain agent also emits top-down predictions for futures SIFT matches. These predictions contain the current object pose hypothesis and a SIFT point which has not yet been matched. To look for most reliable SIFT points first, a score is given to each SIFT point during an offline learning phase. Each object is artificially added to background images, with various affine transformations and degrees of noise. We then apply our object matching algorithm on theses images, and whenever a SIFT point is correctly matched the distance ratio is added to its score. It is easy to know when a SIFT match is correct since we generated the training images. Then, to make predictions, the SiftMain agent starts with points having the highest scores and thus the highest probability to be present and discriminative.

3.6   The IntensityHistogramComparator Agent

The Main agent can send top-down requests for histogram analysis for a given object pose hypothesis. The IntensityHistogramComparator agent computes the difference between the normalized histogram of the candidate object with the normalized histogram of the projected candidate zone in the image and creates a bottom-up signal holding the result . The difference between the two histograms is measured using the χ^2 distance, and this directly gives the discriminative variable for histogram signals X_h.

3.7   The Main Agent

It receives bottom-up object pose hypothesis signals from the SiftMain and the IntensityHistogramComparator agents. When histogram information is not available for an hypothesis, it sends a top-down request, which will be handled by the IntensityHistogramComparator agent. Once all the information is collected for an hypothesis h, it decides whether h is due to chance or not, according to the accumulated evidence. The latter is given by the joint probability of having so many SIFT matches voting for h and having such a low histogram difference when there is no object:

$$X_a(h) = P_c(X_s \leq X_s(h)) \times P_c(X_h \leq X_h(h))$$

X_a then has to be thresholded to take decisions. To get robust and adapted decision thresholds, we follow [11] and compute the expectation of the number of hypothesis with such evidence in the image under analysis, if there were no object. Since only a few matches get clustered when the database is quite big, the number of analyzed hypothesis in an image can be approximated by the number of SIFT points N_s in the image. Thus, we get:

$$\mathrm{NFA}(h) = N_s \times P(X_a \leq X_a(h))$$

If NFA(h) is very low, then the candidate object is certainly present. A threshold on this value has a physical interpretation: if only hypotheses h such that NFA$(h) < \varepsilon$ are accepted, then it is guaranteed that in average, less than ε false detections will be made in an image.

4   Results

We evaluated our approach using the COIL-100 database [14] with a procedure similar to [15] to generate two difficult test sets of cluttered images. Test images

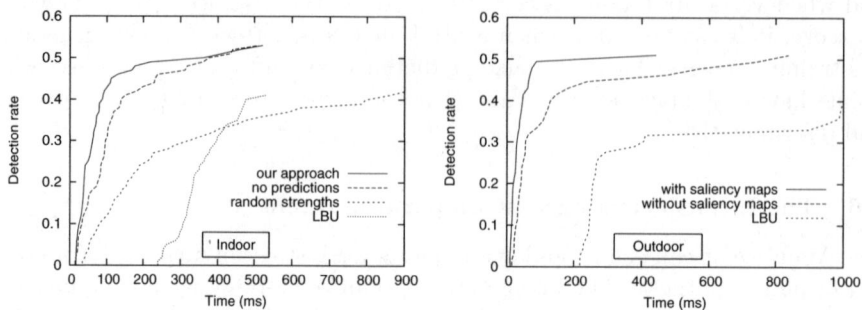

Fig. 2. For each time limit, the detection rate of different algorithms are shown. Decision thresholds were chosen to get no false alarms. The left figure is obtained on a test set with complex indoor images. In this case, the saliency maps in SiftComputer agents were not used. Our approach clearly outperforms LBU both in terms of detection rates and processing time. Since we have much more data to process, prioritization is essential: execution times obtained with random signal strengths are very poor (the curve continues and will reach the optimal detection rate in about 2 seconds). Top-down SIFT point predictions also brings a significant gain on execution time. The right figure is obtained on an outdoor test set and shows the possible speed improvements when using saliency maps in SiftComputer agents.

were obtained by embedding each of the 100 objects on 640x480 background images. One test set contained only indoor background images, and the other one only outdoor background images. A contrario probability distributions were learned separately for each test set using 10 additional indoor and outdoor background images. Each object was inserted with a planar rotation of 30 degrees, a shear of 0.1, and a scale factor of 0.7. Finally, 5% of noise was added to the final images. Since many objects of COIL-100 are not very textured, this detection task is rather difficult. Processing times were measured on a 2.4 Ghz dual-core processor. It should be noted that since our focus is not on absolute time, no particular optimizations were implemented. In particular, no kd-tree is used for SIFT point matching.

The performance gain of our approach is summarized in Figure 2. These performance profiles show the obtained detection rates as a function of running time. The decision thresholds were chosen so that there were no false alarms on the test set. This figure clearly shows that parallelism, prioritization and top-down processing significantly increase detection rates while drastically reducing execution times. LBU detection times only depend upon the number of SIFT points in the analyzed image, whereas execution times also depend on objects saliency for our system. On indoor images, some of the most salient and textured objects can be detected in less than 20ms, and the maximal detection rate of LBU can be obtained in less than 90ms instead of 500ms.

On outdoor images, saliency maps are very good at predicting object locations, and thus detection times are even more reduced when saliency values are used to set signal strengths in SiftComputer agents. In this case, LBU's maximal detection rate can be achieved in about 40ms.

5   Conclusion

We have experimented an architecture for object matching based on a hierarchy of agents running in parallel. This architecture allows a mixed use of top-down and bottom-up processing. Bottom-up analysis efficiently proposes object pose hypotheses using local feature matching, while top-down influences accelerate the process by predicting future matches and increase detection rates with histogram analysis. To further improve detection rates, early bottom-up thresholds were replaced by a systematic evaluation of the statistical relevance of visual data. Then at any time, the system focuses on most promising hypotheses, and thanks to asynchronism, detection times can be greatly reduced. The system can also be constrained to run in a pre-defined time, in which case only the most salient and textured objects will be detected.

These results are encouraging and motivate further work. The concepts behind our architecture are not limited to object matching, and we are currently investigating the application of the same approach to object class detection. Very good top-down generative models have been proposed for this vision task, and we expect their combination with bottom-up analysis to be fruitful. Moreover, object matching and object class recognition are not incompatible applications, and since our architecture is modular and uses a unified statistical scheme, they could be used jointly and compete to provide the best image interpretation.

References

1. Kokkinos, I., Maragos, P., Yuille, A.: Bottom-Up & Top-down Object Detection using Primal Sketch Features and Graphical Models. In: Proceedings of the 2006 IEEE Computer Society Conference on Computer Vision and Pattern Recognition, vol. 2, pp. 1893–1900 (2006)
2. Ulusoy, I., Bishop, C.M.: Generative versus discriminative methods for object recognition. Proc. CVPR 2, 258–265 (2005)
3. Lampinen, J.: Sequential Monte Carlo for Bayesian Matching of Objects with Occlusions. IEEE Transactions on Pattern Analysis and Machine Intelligence 28(6), 930–941 (2006)
4. Tu, Z., Chen, X., Yuille, A.L., Zhu, S.: Image parsing: Unifying segmentation, detection, and recognition. International Journal of Computer Vision 63(2), 113–140 (2005)
5. Delorme, A., Rousselet, G.A., Mace, M.J., Fabre-Thorpe, M.: Interaction of top-down and bottom-up processing in the fast visual analysis of natural scenes. Technical report, Cognitive Brain Research 19 (2004)
6. Tsotsos, J.: Toward a computational model of visual attention. Early vision and beyond, 207–218 (1995)
7. Borowy, M., Jolion, J.: A pyramidal framework for fast feature detection. In: Proc. of 4th Int. Workshop on Parellel Image Analysis, pp. 193–202 (1995)
8. Draper, B., Collins, R., Brolio, J., Hanson, A., Riseman, E.: The schema system. International Journal of Computer Vision 2(3), 209–250 (1989)
9. Guhl, P., Shanahan, P.: Machine Perception using a Blackboard Architecture . In: The 5th International Conference on Computer Vision Systems Conference Paper (2007)

10. Lowe, D.G.: Distinctive Image Features from Scale-Invariant Keypoints. International Journal of Computer Vision 60(2), 91–110 (2004)
11. Desolneux, A., Moisan, L., Morel, J.-M.: Maximal meaningful events and applications to image analysis. Annals of Statistics 31(6), 1822–1851 (2003)
12. Itti, L., Koch, C., E.,, Niebur, o.: A model of saliency-based visual attention for rapid scene analysis. IEEE Transactions on Pattern Analysis and Machine Intelligence 20(11), 1254–1259 (1998)
13. Lowe, D.: Object recognition from local scale-invariant features. International Conference on Computer Vision 2 (1999)
14. Nene, S., Nayar, S., Murase, H.: Columbia Object Image Library (COIL-100). Techn. Rep. No. CUCS-006-96, dept. Comp. Science, Columbia University (1996)
15. Stein, A., Hebert, M.: Incorporating Background Invariance into Feature-Based Object Recognition. In: Seventh IEEE Workshop on Applications of Computer Vision (WACV) (2005)

A Tale of Two Object Recognition Methods for Mobile Robots

Arnau Ramisa[1], Shrihari Vasudevan[2], Davide Scaramuzza[2],
Ramón López de Mántaras[1], and Roland Siegwart[2]

[1] Artificial Intelligence Research Institute (IIIA-CSIC), Campus UAB, 08193
Bellaterra, Spain
[2] Autonomous Systems Lab, ETH Zurich, Switzerland

Abstract. Object recognition is a key feature for building robots capable of moving and performing tasks in human environments. However, current object recognition research largely ignores the problems that the mobile robots context introduces. This work addresses the problem of applying these techniques to mobile robotics in a typical household scenario. We select two state-of-the-art object recognition methods, which are suitable to be adapted to mobile robots, and we evaluate them on a challenging dataset of typical household objects that caters to these requirements. The different advantages and drawbacks found for each method are highlighted, and some ideas for extending them are proposed. Evaluation is done comparing the number of detected objects and false positives for both approaches.

1 Introduction

Robots like the Sony Aibo or the Robox are ready to enter our homes, but they lack a lightweight object perception method that allows them to interact with the environment. In order to make robots useful assistants for our everyday life, the ability to learn and recognize objects is of essential importance. For example, in [1] the authors investigate underlying representations of spatial cognition for autonomous robots. Although not specifically addressed in that work, object perception is an essential component that the authors reported to be the most limiting factor. Object recognition in real scenes is one of the most challenging problems in computer vision, as it is necessary to deal with difficulties such as viewpoint changes, occlusions, illumination variations, background clutter or sensor noise. Furthermore, in a mobile robotics scenario a new challenge is added to the list: computational complexity. In a dynamic world, information about the objects in the scene can become obsolete even before it is ready to be used if the recognition algorithm is not fast enough. All these complications make object recognition in real scenes a hard problem, that will demand significant effort in the years to come.

Numerous methods for object recognition have been developed over the last decades, but few of them actually scale to the demands posed by a mobile robotics scenario. Furthermore, most of them concentrate on specific cases, like

A. Gasteratos, M. Vincze, and J.K. Tsotsos (Eds.): ICVS 2008, LNCS 5008, pp. 353–362, 2008.

faces or pedestrians. This paper moves towards object recognition for mobile robots comparing two very popular object recognition techniques suitable to be used in this context. The work itself is aimed at the bigger goal of developing a robust yet lightweight object perception system that can actually be used by mobile robots and meet their hard constraints. Two recent and successful general object recognition approaches include: the constellation method proposed by Lowe together with its interest point detector and descriptor SIFT [2] and a *bag of features* approach, the one developed by Nistér and Stewénius [3]. The authors of both approaches have specifically addressed the issue of computational complexity and claim that proper implementations of their algorithms can recognise a significant number of objects in real time. An object training dataset with different types of object was acquired. Three different categories of objects occurring in typical household environments are considered: textured, untextured and with repetitive textures. Each object has approximately 20 training images and every category consists of three different objects. To evaluate the methods, a test dataset with the same objects was acquired. The test dataset includes occlusions, illumination changes, blur and other typical nuisances that will be encountered while navigating with a mobile robot. Both datasets (training and testing) are available for download[1].

The rest of this work is organized as follows: in Section 2 the methods evaluated are outlined. In order to perform our tests, some modifications had to be done to the bag of features method, they are explained in Section 3. In Section 4 the image dataset and the experiments performed are detailed. Finally, in Section 5 we conclude the article with our findings.

2   Methods

To make this work more self-contained, the two evaluated methods are briefly reviewed in this section. For further information on the object recognition methods used, the reader is referred to [2] for the Lowe method and [3] for the Nistér and Stewénius bag of features approach.

2.1   Lowe Constellation Method

Lowe's object recognition approach is a single view object detection and recognition system with some interesting characteristics for mobile robots, most significant of which is the ability to detect and recognize objects at the same time in an unsegmented image. Another interesting features is the Best-Bin-First algorithm used for approximate fast matching, which reduces the search time by two orders of magnitude for a database of 100,000 keypoints for a 5% loss in the number of correct matches. The first stage of the approach consists on matching individually the SIFT descriptors of the features detected in a test image to the ones stored in the object database using the Euclidean distance. False matches are rejected if the distance of the first nearest neighbor is not distinctive enough when

---

[1] http://www.asl.ethz.ch/research/asl/cogniron

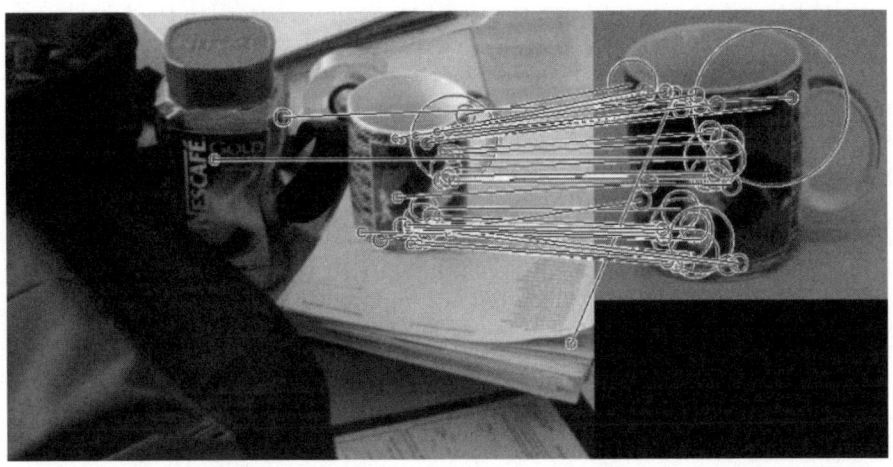

Fig. 1. Matching stage in the Lowe object recognition method

compared with that of the second. In Figure 1, the matching features between a test and model images can be seen. The presence of some outliers can also be observed. Once a set of matches is found, the generalized Hough transform is used to cluster each match of every database image depending on its particular transformation (translation, rotation and scale change). Although imprecise, this step generates a number of initial coherent hypotheses and removes a notable portion of the outliers that could potentially confuse more precise but also more sensitive methods. All clusters with at least three matches for a particular image are accepted, and fed to the next stage: the Iterative Reweighed Least Squares is used to improve the estimation of the affine transformation between the model and the test images.

2.2 Bag of Features Method

The bag of features (or bag of words) approach to object classification comes from the text categorization domain, where the occurrence of certain words in documents is recorded and used to train classifiers that can later recognize the subject of new texts. This technique has been adapted to visual object classification substituting the words with local descriptors such as SIFT [4]. In order to make the local descriptors robust to changes in point of view and scale, local feature detectors are often used to select the image patches that will be used [5], although some authors point that using bigger numbers of randomly selected patches gives better results than a limited number of regions defined around local features [6]. A histogram of descriptor occurrences is built to characterize an image. In order to limit the size of the histogram, a code-book or vocabulary computed applying a clustering method to the training descriptors is used. This code-book should be general enough to distinguish between different descriptor types but specific enough to be insensitive to small variations in the local patch. Next a multi-class classifier is trained with the histograms of local descriptor counts. In the approach used in this work, the problem of recognizing a large number of objects in an efficient way is addressed. A hierarchical vocabulary tree is used, as it allows to code a larger number of visual features and simultaneously reduce the look-up time to logarithmic in the number of leaves. The vocabulary tree is built using hierarchical k-means clustering, where the parameter k defines the branch factor of the tree instead of the final number of clusters. The signature of an image is a histogram with a length equal to the number of nodes of the tree. For each node i, a histogram bin is computed in the following way:

$$q_i = n_i\omega_i, \tag{1}$$

where n_i is the number of descriptor vectors of the image that have a path through node i of the vocabulary tree, and ω_i is the weight assigned to this node. To improve retrieval performance a measure based in entropy is used for the weights:

$$\omega_i = ln(\frac{N}{N_i}), \tag{2}$$

where N is the number of images in the database, and N_i is the number of images in the database with at least one descriptor vector path through node i. To compare a new query image with a database image, the following score function is used:

$$s(q, d) = \|\frac{q}{\|q\|} - \frac{d}{\|d\|}\| \tag{3}$$

where q and d are the signatures of the query and database image. The normalization can be in any desired norm, but L1-norm was found to perform better. The class of the object in the query image is determined as the dominant in the k nearest neighbors from the database. Two interesting aspects of this approach are that a fast method to compute the scoring of new query histograms using inverted files is proposed in the article, and new images can be added to the database in real-time, which makes this method suitable for incremental learning.

3   Modifications

For the tests, we have used our own implementation of the Lowe schema and a modified version of Andrea Vedaldi's implementation of the Nistér and Stewénius bag of features method[2].

Because of the necessarily broad clusters of the Hough transform, some erroneous matches can still be present and need to be removed. In order to do so a RANSAC step is added to the Lowe approach. RANSAC labels non-coherent

---

[2] http://vision.ucla.edu/~vedaldi/code/bag/bag.html

matches as outliers and, additionally, estimates the most probable affine transformation for every hypothesis given its initial set of matches. Hypotheses that
lose matches below three are discarded. The hypotheses that remain after the
RANSAC step are reasonable outlier-free and a more accurate model fitting algorithm like IRLS can be used. One of the drawbacks of the bag of features
method is that, in contrast to Lowe's constellation method, is designed to work
with pre-segmented images. If one image contains more background than a certain threshold, the probability of miss-classification increases. Furthermore, if
a particular image contains two objects, there is no way to recognize both. A
straightforward solution is to define a grid of overlapping windows with different
sizes and shapes covering the whole image. This can be done in an efficient way
using a technique similar to that of integral images with the keypoint counts. As
most windows from the grid will be selecting areas without any object known by
the robot, some technique to reject the false positives is required. In this work
we have tested two strategies to this end. The first one consists in introducing a
background category to which windows selecting no object can be matched, and
the second one consists in imposing some constraints to accept the result of a
window as a true positive. Among the advantages of the background category
method we have that no additional parameters are introduced, and the current
schema can be used as is. The drawbacks are that the background category
should be general enough to cover all the possible negative windows but specific enough to avoid losing important windows due to changes in point of view
or small amounts of background clutter in a good window. Regarding the constraints method, an advantage is that the object database will remain smaller,
but some new parameters will be introduced and, if not adjusted wisely, the
number of correctly detected objects can decrease as miss-classifications remain
at a similar level. To determine the significance of the k nearest neighbors, we
have weighted the votes in the following way:

$$D = [\, d_1 \; d_2 \; d_3 \; ... \; d_k\,] \qquad (4)$$

$$W = [\, w_i \;=\; 1 - \frac{d_i}{max(D)} \;\mid\; \forall d_i \in D\,], \qquad (5)$$

being D the set of distances of the k nearest neighbors and W the set of weights
applied to each vote. In our experiments we have used a grid of approximately
60,000 rectangular windows, with side sizes that range from 100 to 500 pixels
with steps of 50 pixels, placed every 30 pixels both in vertical and horizontal
axis. For the window rejection method we have used the following constraints:

- We are only interested in windows that clearly stand for a category. If the
  score of the second classified object category is more than λ times the votes
  of the first object category the window is discarded. In our experiments λ
  has been set to 0.8.

– Keypoint occurrence statistics can be used to reject windows. A window is only accepted if:

$$N(\tilde{x}_i + 2\sigma_i) > s \qquad (6)$$
$$N(\tilde{x}_i - 2\sigma_i) < s \qquad (7)$$

for a window labeled as class i, where N is the number of pixels of the window, $\tilde{x}_i$ is the mean number of keypoints per pixel of the class i, σ_i is the standard deviation of the number of keypoints per pixel of class i and s is the number of keypoints found in the current window.

An alternative to the grid of windows is to use a segmentation technique over the image. This strategy has been applied in [7] where the authors report notable improvement in the results. The segmentation technique can be based in pixel intensity or color and also, if stereo images are available, disparity can be used to improve the segmentation. An obvious benefit of using a segmentation technique is a relief in the computational effort of the object recognition step, as the number of considered regions will be much smaller than in the grid of windows approach. More meaningful regions will be used, and therefore the probability of a correct classification will be much higher. The main drawback of using a segmentation technique is that the performance of the object recognition step relies on the quality of the segmentation, and the computational cost of the segmentation step must be added.

4   Experimental Results

To evaluate the performance of the two methods the following experiments were carried out: first, to validate the suitability of the bag of features method for our purposes, a preliminary test with a dataset of cropped images of objects from our lab has been done. Next, we evaluated both methods using the nine household objects dataset.

4.1   Preliminary Test

The dataset used consists of a hundred training and approximately 125 testing images for each of five categories: cupboard, mug, laptops, screens and background. On-line processing means that images acquired by a mobile robot hardly have a resolution greater than one megapixel, and the object to be detected will probably only occupy the image partially. Additionally, movement often implies blurred images. The capacity to maintain good performance under these circumstances is of key importance for an object recognition system intended to be used in a mobile robot. To test the strength of the bag of features method under these difficulties the test images have been acquired in low resolution and a significant portion of them are blurred.

In this test we compared the performance of three region detectors: Harris Affine (from now haraff), Hessian Affine (hesaff) and a combination of Harris

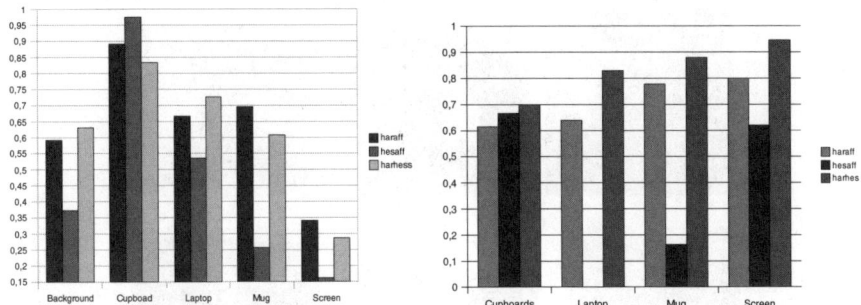

(a) Ratio of correct classifications with cropped images

(b) Ratio of false negatives among errors

Fig. 2. Results of bag of features test with manually cropped images

Laplace and Hessian Laplace without rotation invariance (harhes). All these region detectors are described in [5] and are known to produce regions with a hyphenate repeatability rate. In Figure 2(a), it can be observed that the ratio of correct classifications is over 60% for all classes except for the screens category. Furthermore, as can be seen in Figure 2(b), the majority of the errors where false negatives (objects confused with background). On average, haraff classified correctly 63.8% of the test images, harhes 61.7% and hesaff only 45.4%. Based on these results it was decided to use Harris Affine in the subsequent experiments. Taking into account the characteristics of the test images used, the results obtained are good enough to take the method into consideration.

4.2 Comparison of Methods

The main purpose of this work is to evaluate two candidate object recognition algorithms to be used in an indoor mobile robot. To this end, we have created an image dataset of nine typical household objects. These objects are divided in three categories (three objects per category): textured, untextured and textured but with repetitive patterns. In Figure 4.2 one training object from each category can be seen. Additionally, 36 test stereo pairs were acquired with the robot cameras, a STHMDCS2VAR/C stereo head by Videre design. Each test image contains one or more instances of objects from the dataset, some of them with illumination changes or partial occlusions. The training images have been taken with a standard digital camera at an original resolution of 2 megapixels, although the region of interest has been cropped for every image. The test images where acquired at 1.2 megapixels, the maximum resolution allowed by the stereo head. In this experiment we are not testing neither for viewpoint invariance nor for intraclass variation as the Lowe constellation approach does not effectively handle these kinds of transformations. For comparison purposes, two versions of the training images have been considered: a rectangular cropped version of the object, that inevitably includes some background texture, and a precise

Fig. 3. Images from the dataset. First column corresponds to objects with repetitive texture, second to textured objects and third to non-textured objects.

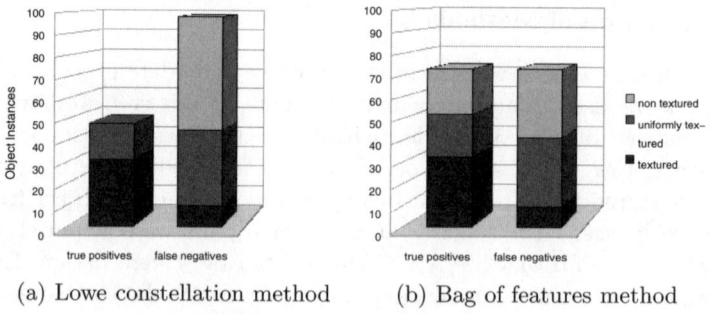

(a) Lowe constellation method   (b) Bag of features method

Fig. 4. Results of the comparison

segmentation of the object boundaries. Using the Lowe approach, the method that worked best is the rectangular cropped version of the training images. Almost all of the textured object occurrences and some instances of the uniformly textured book have been detected (Figure 4(a)). However none of the non-textured objects were recognized. The best performance of the bag of features approach has been achieved using the window rejection method (Figure 4(b)).

Table 1. Results for the two bag of words approaches evaluated. False positives and miss-classifications are combined.

	Considered Windows	True Positives	False Positives	False Negatives	True Negatives
Background category	43228	3.76%	17.02%	32.1%	47.12%
Window filtering	18825	12.79%	87.21%	–	–

As can be seen, the number of detected objects, especially for the categories of uniformly textured and non-textured, has increased using this approach.

As expected, the main drawbacks of the bag of features approach using the grid of windows is the amount of false positives, suggesting that posterior verification stages based, for example, in feature geometry inside the considered window should be introduced. In the background category approach, the best results were obtained with the manually segmented training dataset, while in the window filtering approach the cropped training images produced better results. The percentage of true positive and false positive windows for both approaches can be seen in Table 1. At a posterior stage, overlapping windows must be combined to yield object hypotheses. In spite of being more effective than the Lowe method in objects without texture, the bag of features has some drawbacks that need to be properly addressed. Its main problem is the pre-segmentation of the image that is required to recognize objects. Regarding computational complexity, our C++ implementation of the Lowe method takes approximately one second per image while the matlab implementation of the bag of features method complexity varies hugely upon scene content, and can take from 38 to 7 minutes. All tests where done in a P3 with 1Ghz of memory running a Linux operating system.

5   Conclusions

In this work we have addressed the problem of object recognition applied to mobile robots. Two state-of the-art object recognition approaches are compared. A dataset of nine typical household objects is used for the tests. The dataset incorporates typical problems that would be experienced by object recognition systems being deployed in home environments. This includes lack of texture and repetitive patterns. Further, the test images were acquired with the vision system of our robot instead of a good quality digital camera. The experiments presented in this report conclude that the bag of features method combined with a grid of windows over the image is able to detect poorly textured objects in low quality images typical of a mobile robot scenario. However, this method still lacks a fast yet robust way to reject false positives and a technique to reliably fuse multiple overlapping windows, each representing one potential hypothesis of the object occurring in the image, towards a single occurrence of the particular object. As an alternative to the computationally expensive windowing strategies, an image segmentation strategy is proposed. This method could improve results by reducing background clutter. However, this is a "two-edged sword" in that the object recognition quality is greatly influenced by that of the image segmentation. A verification stage based on feature geometry is proposed as a method to reject unlikely hypothesis.

Future work includes evaluating different strategies for improving the grid of windows method as well as testing different image segmentation strategies. A fast implementation of the bag-of-features approach that includes efficient scoring methods (such as those employed in [3]) is being developed. Future work would also test the robustness of the bag of features method to intra-class variation and viewpoint change in this context.

Acknowledgements

This work has been partially funded by the FI grant and the BE grant from the AGAUR, the European Social Fund, the 2005/SGR/00093 project, supported by the Generalitat de Catalunya, the MIDCBR project grant TIN 200615140C0301, TIN 200615308C0202 and FEDER funds. The authors would also like to thank Andrea Vedaldi for making available his implementation of the Nistr and Stewnius bag of words algorithm.

References

1. Vasudevan, S., Gachter, S., Nguyen, V., Siegwart, R.: Cognitive maps for mobile robots - an object based approach. In: Robotics and Autonomous Systems, May 31, 2007. From Sensors to Human Spatial Concepts, vol. 55(5), pp. 359–371 (2007)
2. Lowe, D.G.: Distinctive image features from scale-invariant keypoints. Interantional Journal of Computer Vision 60(2), 91–110 (2004)
3. Nister, D., Stewenius, H.: Scalable recognition with a vocabulary tree. Conf. Computer Vision and Pattern Recognition 2, 2161–2168
4. Csurka, G., Bray, C., Dance, C., Fan, L.: Visual categorization with bags of keypoints. In: Workshop on Statistical Learning in Computer Vision, ECCV, pp. 1–22 (2004)
5. Mikolajczyk, K., Tuytelaars, T., Schmid, C., Zisserman, A., Matas, J., Schaffalitzky, F., Kadir, T., Van Gool, L.: A comparison of affine region detectors. International Journal of Computer Vision 65(1/2), 43–72 (2005)
6. Nowak, E., Jurie, F., Triggs, B.: Sampling Strategies for Bag-of-Features Image Classification. In: Leonardis, A., Bischof, H., Pinz, A. (eds.) ECCV 2006. LNCS, vol. 3954, pp. 490–503. Springer, Heidelberg (2006)
7. Rabinovich, A., Vedaldi, A., Galleguillos, C., Wiewiora, E., Belongie, S.: Objects in context. In: Proceedings of the International Conference on Computer Vision (ICCV) (2007)

A Segmentation Approach in Novel Real Time 3D Plant Recognition System

Dejan Šeatović

Zurich University of Applied Sciences
IMS Institute of Mechatronic Systems
P.O. Box 805, 8401 Winterthur, Switzerland
dejan.seatovic@zhaw.ch
http://www.zhaw.ch/~sede/

Abstract. One of the most invasive and persistent kind of weed in agriculture is Rumex Obtusifolius L. also called "Broad-leaved Dock". The origin of the plant is Europe and northern Asia, but it has also been reported that this plant occurs in wide parts of Northern America. Eradication of this plant is labour-intensive and hence there is an interest in automatic weed control devices. Some vision systems were proposed that allow to localize and map plants in the meadow. However, these systems were designed and implemented for off-line processing. This paper presents a segmentation approach that allows for real-time recognition and application of herbicides onto the plant leaves. Instead of processing the gray-scale or colour images, our approach relays on 3D point cloud analysis and processing. 3D data processing has several advantages over 2D image processing approaches when it comes to extraction and recognition of plants in their natural environment.

Keywords: Precision Farming, Plant Recognition, Segmentation, Real-Time Systems.

1 Introduction

Segmentation is a crucial part of data analysis. It ranges from simple binarisaton of images to complex analysis of multispectral images, multidimensional data, etc. Real time data analysis challenges lay in reliable and fast segmentation of raw data. An initial step of the segmentation is edge extraction. In machine vision literature there is a variety of algorithms published and evaluated. One of the most comprehensive evaluations was published by [1], which compares different edge detection algorithms and proposes a novel evaluation method to compare edge detection algorithms on gray-scale images. Possibilities of transferring 2D image-processing approaches to 3D data are rather limited, however one interesting proposal can be found in [2]. Finally, real-time edge extraction solutions are described in [3,4,5,6]. One context free approach is shown in [7]. Interesting watershed segmentation on triangle meshes are shown in [8] and [9]. The system described in these papers show that 3D segmentation in real time is an effective way to analyze plants in their biotope. The focus in this paper is on processing 3D type of data concerning real-time constraints.

A. Gasteratos, M. Vincze, and J.K. Tsotsos (Eds.): ICVS 2008, LNCS 5008, pp. 363–372, 2008.
© Springer-Verlag Berlin Heidelberg 2008

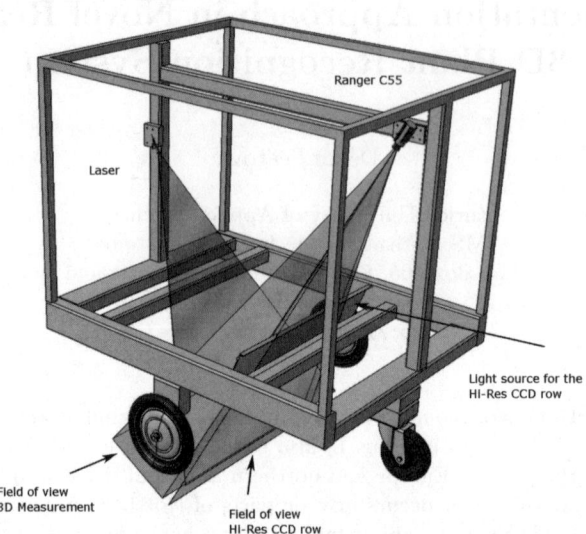

Fig. 1. Vehicle prototype with mounted components of the measurement system

2   Project Requirements and System Description

In this section we would like to explain the motivation for using a 3D based segmentation approach. In [10,11,12] was described a 2D Rumex Obtusifolius recognition system that requires powerful computing resources for a segmentation of high resolution images. The main benefit of using the third dimension is: with the help of height information to actually be able to segment plant leaves in very cluttered and complex scenes such as can be found in overgrown fields. The prototype of the vehicle is in shown in Fig. 1. It contains the following components:

- Sick Ranger C55 with near infra red laser (780nm).
- Two encoder: Baumer Electric, MDFK 08T7105/N16, mounted on the wheels.
- Carrier (vehicle) with security box and supporting devices.

The speed of vehicle during the recognition and treatment is $1\,ms^{-1}$. The data collection is continuous and the system extracts the plant leaves out of collected data in real time. In a subsequent step the coordinates of the particular leaves or leave parts are computed and passed to the treatment device that applies herbicide on the plants. The system has roughly 0.6 seconds time to process $1\,m^2$ of meadow. Some data facts are as follows:

1. On $1\,m^2$ of meadow system measures $1536 \times 1000 = 1\,536\,000$ points.
2. Every measurement point has single word (16 bit) precision.
3. High-Res gray-scale row of C55 produces $3072 \times 1000 = 3\,072\,000$ 8-bit pixels per $1\,m^2$.

Thus, the processing unit must process $2.9\,MBs^{-1}$ of 3D data and the same amount of gray-scale textures within one second. Under these conditions it is crucial to have fast and reliable segmentation algorithms, if possible already on raw data. The highly efficient segmentation procedure is required during first phase of the project.

3   Data Model

For better understanding of the data processing procedure, the nature of the data will be described in this section. The measurement principle of the 3D-Engine is a laser triangulation [13], where the smart camera Ranger C55 extracts the laser line projected on the ground and stores it in an array:

$$a_{raw\,i} = \{a_0, a_1, \ldots, a_{n-1}\}, n = 1536, a_n \epsilon \begin{cases} \{1, 2, \ldots, 1024\} = valid \\ \{0\} = invalid \end{cases} \tag{1}$$

The system produces arrays $a_{raw\,0} \ldots a_{raw\,i}$, $i \in N$ in the required resolution. In the following text every array $a_{raw\,i}$ will be called a *profile*. To achieve the best possible results and acquire optimally the ground truth, to achieve the optimal results, a less than 1mm resolution in the object area was chosen. The frame rate, better called "profile" rate, is 1kHz. The system must be calibrated for each measurement session. After a measurement session is finished, control calibration is done to insure that the whole measurement system was not altered or damaged. The following parameters are computed during the measurement system calibration:

- Camera interior parameters: c, $S = \{s_{x'}, s_{y'}\}$, $\tilde{r}$
- Camera exterior parameters: $T = \{x_C, y_C, z_C\}$, $R = \{\omega, \rho, \kappa\}$
- Position of camera and its orientation to the laser plane:
  $\overrightarrow{N_L} = \frac{x_0 - x_C}{\overrightarrow{N_X}} = \frac{y_0 - y_C}{\overrightarrow{N_Y}} = \frac{z_0 - z_C}{\overrightarrow{N_Z}}$

In a first step, pinhole-camera's intrisic and extrinsic parameters are computed using the Tsai calibration method [14]. Additional procedure was added to the calibration process to compute the position and orientation of the laser plane. For this purpose a special calibration body was designed which is also suitable for field usage.

4   Recognition Approach and Segmentation

Currently there are several plant recognition and classification approaches published. The most recent and comprehensive one was already mentioned [12] earlier in this paper. However, vision systems, and especially passive systems, can fail when the environmental conditions change during the data acquisition process. Also a failure can be caused by deficient contrast in a given input image, so additional image processing steps are necessary in order to extract the objects from the scene. Further recognition results depend strongly on the angle between the object and the optical axis of the camera. In extreme cases there is no possibility to distinguish between the blades of grass and broad leaves. All these problems are partly resolved if the acquired data is three dimensional. The other side of the coin is that processing algorithms increase their complexity by order of magnitude. One possible solution is parallelizing procedures to maximal possible extent. Roughly our system is divided in seven temporally independent processes see Tab. 1.

Table 1. Processes of the recognition engine

Time	Edge(I,II)	CCL	Extraction	Shape	Surface	Texture
t_0	e_0	$\emptyset$	$\emptyset$	$\emptyset$	$\emptyset$	$\emptyset$
t_1	e_1	ccl_0	$\emptyset$	$\emptyset$	$\emptyset$	$\emptyset$
t_2	e_2	ccl_1	$extr_0$	$\emptyset$	$\emptyset$	$\emptyset$
t_3	e_3	ccl_2	$extr_1$	sh_0	su_0	tx_0
$\vdots$	$\vdots$	$\vdots$	$\vdots$	$\vdots$	$\vdots$	$\vdots$
t_n	e_n	ccl_{n-1}	$extr_{n-2}$	sh_{n-3}	su_{n-3}	tx_{n-3}

The segmentation contains three tasks: edge detection *Edge(I,II)*, 3D connected components labeling *CCL* and extraction of the objects *Extraction*. Subtasks of the recognition tast are three analyzers: *Shape, Surface, Texture* that process their parts respectively. Parameters for all three tasks are computed out of the calibration of the measurement system, so the algorithms operate on the raw data. Most important issue: The time. The time difference between the data arrival and finishing recognition-localization task must be less than 0.6 seconds if the vehicle speed is $1\,ms^{-1}$ and giving the system some processing-time buffer.

$$\Delta t = t_{n+4} - t_n \leq 0.6\,seconds \tag{2}$$

The tight time constrain in Eq. (2) forces a simple, efficient and parallel edge detection algorithm as a base for the following segmentation. Though edge detection in 3D is still more difficult as analyzed, described and researched as its relative in 2D. Due to the high data quality of the Sick Ranger C55 no noise reduction and smoothing of the raw data is necessary. The analysis takes place in 3×3 point neighborhood .

$$B = \begin{matrix} b_0 & b_1 & b_2 \\ \nwarrow & \uparrow & \nearrow \\ b_7 \longleftarrow & P_i & \longrightarrow b_3 \\ \swarrow & \downarrow & \searrow \\ b_6 & b_5 & b_4 \end{matrix} \tag{3}$$

Point P_i builds a surface patch with its neighbors b_j, $j \epsilon \{0, 1, \ldots, 7\}$:

$$n_j = (P_i^j - P_i) \times (P_i^k - P_i), \; j + 1 = k \, mod(8) \tag{4}$$

$$n'_j = (P_i^j - P_i) \times (P_i^k - P_i), \; j + 2 = k \, mod(8) \tag{5}$$

Point P_i is a edge point when the following conditions are satisfied:

$$edge(P_i) = \begin{cases} \exists j, & P_i^j = 0 \\ sin\varphi_{jk} > T_\alpha \, \exists j, k, \varphi_{jk} \angle (n_j, n_k), \; j + 1 = k \, mod(8) \\ sin\varphi_{jk} > T_\alpha \, \exists j, k, \varphi_{jk} \angle (n_j, n_k), \; j + 2 = k \, mod(8) \\ \exists n_i, & \frac{|n_i|}{\sum_{j=0, j \neq i}^{7} |n_j|} < T_s, \; j \epsilon \{0, 1, \ldots, 7\} \end{cases} \tag{6}$$

I Image, 3D points cloud:
n Normal vectors on subsequent $\triangle (b_j, P_i, b_{j+1})$, $j + 1 = j \, mod(8)$
n' Normal vectors on subsequent $\triangle (b_j, P_i, b_{j+2})$, $j + 2 = j \, mod(8)$.
B Vector of neighborhood points see Eq: (3).
T_α Angle threshold.
T_S Surface threshold.

Description of segmentation procedure

Check neighborhood of P_i using conditions described in (6), condition one.
one b_i is 0, then mark P_i as an edge, otherwise go for full computation.
    Full computation:
        compute All **n** and **n'**.
        compute All $\angle$ between **n** and **n'**.
        analyze All computed $\angle$. Conditions two and three in (6).
        analyze $\triangle$ in neighborhood of P_i, compute ratios between $\frac{\triangle_i}{\sum \triangle_j - \triangle_i}$,
            condition four in (6).
        mark P_i ass an edge if any of conditions met.
Run 3D connected component labeling:
    compute Labels and mark objects.
Notify Object extraction process that data is ready.
    filter Objects according to the size limitation.
    remove Small objects.
    copy Accepted objects.
Notify Recognition task.

Without explaining the implementation details, the algorithm shown above describes the most important steps in the segmentation procedure. As mentioned in the Section 1, we have a RT system that moves continuously over the meadow. Continuous computation (segmentation, extraction, recognition and localization) must be guaranteed. The processing engine has following architecture:

- All algorithms are grouped into processes.
- Every process has its own data buffer. One process contains algorithms that are dependent on each other.
- To increase performance of the tasks the algorithms are parallelized where ever it is reasonable.
- After a task finishes its part of computation, it passes the processed data to the next task via an efficient communication pipe.

The edge detection I, edge detection II and connected component labelling are segmentation preparation tasks. The object extraction stage contains the segmentation logic and is the last step before recognition. From Eq. (6) follows immediately that for every point at least one and maximally eight neighbors have to be be analyzed.

5   Results

First tests of the segmentation procedure have shown that our chain of operations performs well. The algorithms we described in this paper were not optimized beyond the regular compiler optimization. The whole hardware part of the system was described in detail in a previous publication in [15]. The appraisal of the segmentation algorithm is divided in two steps:

1. Tests on synthetic data causing worst case scenarios.
2. Field test where the whole system was tested.

The synthetic data contains squares of various sizes. The objects are tightly packed, without interspace. This presents the worst case for the system. Test data set encloses $2.9 \times 1.2\,m$ surface. Other properties are shown in Table 2. Automatic testing on data sets are repeated 100 times. The standard deviation of the values is 0.01 seconds, caused by the timer itself. Results are presented in Fig. 2 and Tab. 3. Edge extractors and connected component labeling change only slightly by the increasing number of objects in the data. However, the

Table 2. Test data properties

Objects count (width)	Size of square [px]	Surface [cm²]	Count (height)	Total number of objects	Number of edges
5	307.20	37.75	9.44	50	200
10	153.60	9.44	18.88	190	760
15	102.40	4.19	28.32	435	1740
20	76.80	2.36	37.76	760	3040
25	61.44	1.51	47.20	1200	4800
30	51.20	1.05	56.64	1710	6840
50	30.72	0.38	94.40	4750	19000
100	15.36	0.09	188.80	18900	75600

Table 3. Execution time of different tasks

Object count (width)	Edge det. I [s]	Edge det. II [s]	CCL [s]	Extraction [s]
5	0.000	3.059	1.314	4.470
10	0.000	2.920	1.235	4.871
15	0.000	3.408	1.235	5.828
20	0.000	2.998	1.130	6.406
25	0.000	2.940	1.249	6.856
30	0.000	2.893	1.234	7.627
50	0.000	3.218	1.361	12.233
100	0.000	3.371	1.500	28.876

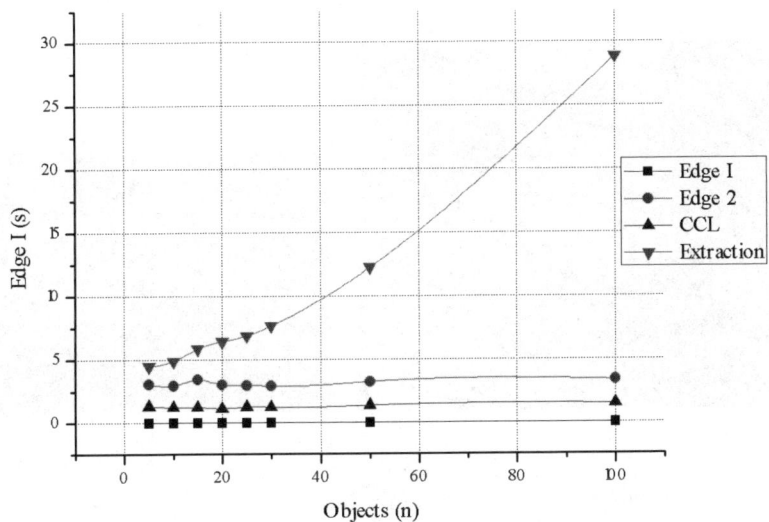

Fig. 2. Synthetic tests

time needed to extract objects for the recognition increases exponentially. This part of segmentation is still in optimization. The aim was to reduce algorithm behavior to a linear one. In the worst case the whole system fails to fulfill the requirements in current development state. Still there is room for improvements because average pre-processing time is about 4.38 seconds which exceeds the required 2.9 seconds by 50%. Hence, further optimization is necessary. In the field the situation is different. In Fig. 3 a typical meadow slices are shown. Following rules are applied during the treatement on the meadow:

- No surface smaller than 16 cm^2 will be extracted.
- Only Broad Leaved Dock that has wide and big leaves, which exceed 16 cm^2, are processed.
- The measurement system delivers not more than 15-20 sparse leaves per square meter. For higher densities such a recognition system is expendable, because herbicides will be applied on the whole meadow patch.

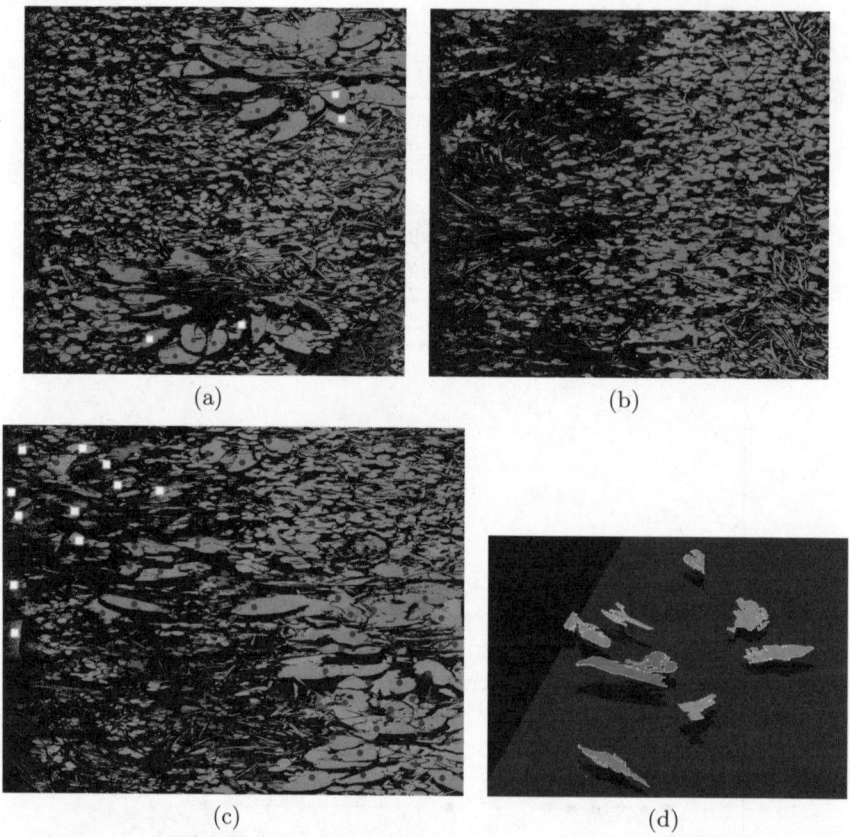

Fig. 3. 3D data samples are shown in figures (a), (b) and (c). Height is color coded, warmer colors imply higher points. Scene in figure (a) represents successful example of segmentation. Red dots mark surfaces that are passed to the recognition task, while white rectangles represent missed leaves that should have been marked for further processing. This is a 1.5 m long slice out of 26 × 1.2 m *natural* meadow patch. The scene in (b) shows the worst case situation for the algorithm: any small objects, in this case clover leaves, gather to the one surface due to thin leaves. This wrongly computed large surface is passed to the recognition task as one suitable object for deep analysis. Scene in (c) in the upper left corner are eleven leaves that have been missed during the segmentation marked by white rectangles. The leaves are fragmented in small surface patches. The fragmentation is caused by inhomogeneous laser light distribution through the prism mounted in front of the laser source [15]. (d) Shows extracted leaves rendered in 3D scene.

Field tests have shown that the recognition vehicle in this development state can localize and extract large surfaces in the required time frame. The experiments enclose 100 m natural meadow, no artificial grassland was processed! Manual control has shown that 62-91% of the large surfaces were localized and marked for treatment. However also up to 25% of objects were missed, caused by:

1. Weak laser signal, see Fig. 3(c).
2. Too complex or extremely fragmented scenes in overgrown areas.

In this stage of the project position accuracy is as low as 10 cm. The treatment system has twelve nozzles. They spray a spot within a 10 cm radius, so only a few recognized leaves per plant are needed to successfully apply the herbicide.

6 Conclusion

The solution demonstrated in this paper shows that a 3D segmentation procedure has greater potential when compared to 2D approaches that have been described in the literature. Thee robustness and speed of edge detection and object extraction are main benefits out of third dimension. This approach shows that processing 3D data is faster between 30% and 50% compared to the 2D solutions. However the procedure is still to be refined and there is room for improvement. Object extraction is inefficient and under the worst-case conditions; it is ten times slower than required for reliable real time processing. Next step in the project is implementation of analysis algorithms for the extracted surfaces in the recognition task. The classification of objects makes the final decision if the extracted surface is leave of Broad Leaved Dock or not. For this purpose shape analysis in 3D space will be combined with texture analysis algorithms like one described in [12].

Acknowledgement. Thanks to the *Gerbert Rüf Stiftung* who sponsors our project and supports us beyond financial matters. Further thanks belongs to the Swiss Federal Department of Economic Affairs, Agroscope who is our partner and advisor in the precision farming field. Further, my personal thanks to Beat Fasel, Paul Alves and Joachim Wirth, who always help and guide me in the field of scientific work.

References

1. Heath, M.D., Sarkar, S., Sanocki, T., Bowyer, K.W.: A robust visual method for assessing the relative performance of edge-detection algorithms. In: IEEE Transactions, December 1997. IEEE Transactions on Pattern Analysis and Machine Intelligence, vol. 12, pp. 1338–1359. IEEE, Los Alamitos (1997)
2. Dorkowski, A.: Modellierung von Oberflächen mit Diskontinuitäten. PhD thesis, Fakultät für Forst-, Geo- und Hydrowissenschaften der Technischen Universität Dresden, Deutsche Geodätische Kommission, Marstallplatz 8, D-80539 München (2004)
3. Basano, L., Caprile, B., De Micheli, E., Geminiani, A., Ottonello, P.: Edge-detection schemes highly suitable for hardware implementation. J. Opt. Soc. Am. A 5(7), 1170–1175 (1988)
4. Sarkar, S., Boyer, K.: Optimal, efficient, recursive edge detection filters. In: Proceedings, 10th International Conference on Pattern Recognition, 1990, vol. 1, pp. 931–936 (1990)

5. Wunderlich, W., Linderer, T., Backs, B., Fischer, F., Noering, J., Schroeder, R.: Optimizing edge detection in quantitative coronary arteriography: problems and proposals. In: Proceedings of Computers in Cardiology 1993, pp. 583–586 (1993)

6. Hsiao, P.-Y., Li, L.-T., Chen, C.-H., Chen, S.-W., Chen, S.-J.: An fpga architecture design of parameter-adaptive real-time image processing system for edge detection. In: Emerging Information Technology Conference, 2005., p. 3 (2005)

7. Giannarou, S., Stathaki, T.: Edge detection using quantitative combination of multiple operators. In: IEEE Workshop on Signal Processing Systems Design and Implementation, 2005, pp. 359–364 (2005)

8. Sun, Y., Page, D., Paik, J., Koschan, A., Abidi, M.: Triangle mesh-based edge detection and its application to surface segmentation and adaptive surface smoothing. In: Proceedings of 2002 International Conference on Image Processing. 2002, vol. 3, pp. 825–828 (2002)

9. Mangan, A.P., Whitaker, R.T.: Partitioning 3d surface meshes using watershed segmentation. In: IEEE Transactions. IEEE Transactions on Visualization and Computer Graphics, vol. 4, pp. 308–322. IEEE, Los Alamitos (1999)

10. Gebhardt, S., Schellberg, J., Lock, R., Kühbauch, W.: Identification of broad-leaved dock (rumex obtusifolius l.) on grassland by means of digital image processing. In: Precision Farming, University of Bonn, Katzenburgweg, July 2006. Precision Agriculture, Institute of Crop Science and Resource Management -Crop Science and Plant Breeding, vol. 3(5), pp. 165–178. Springer, Netherlands (2006), D-53115 Bonn

11. Gebhardt, S.: Automatic classification of grassland herbs in close-range sensed digital colour images. PhD thesis, Mathematisch-Naturwissenschaftliche Fakultät, University Bonn (2007)

12. Gebhardt, S., Kühbauch, W.: A new algorithm for automatic rumex obtusifolius detection in digital images using colour and texture features and the influence of image resolution. In: Precision Farming, University of Bonn, Katzenburgweg. Precision Agriculture, Institute of Crop Science and Resource Management-Crop Science and Plant Breeding, vol. 1-2(5), pp. 1–13. Springer, Netherlands (2007), D-53115 Bonn

13. Sick: Sick ag official web site (2008), http://www.sick.com/

14. Tsai, R.: A versatile camera calibration technique for high-accuracy 3d machine vision metrology using off-the-shelf tv cameras and lenses. In: IEEE Proceedings. Number 4 in Robotics and Automation, IEEE Journal of [legacy, pre -,], IBM T. J. Watson Research Center, Yorktown Heights, NY,USA, IEEE, Los Alamitos(1987) 323–344 (1988)

15. Seatovic, D., Grüninger, R.: Smartweeder: Novel approach in 3d object recognition, localization and treatement of broad dock in its natural environment. In: RAAD 2007: Programme and Book of Abstracts, RAAD 2007 (2007)

Face Recognition Using a Color PCA Framework

M. Thomas[1], S. Kumar[2], and C. Kambhamettu[1]

[1] Video/Image Modeling and Synthesis Lab,
University of Delaware, Newark, DE 19711
[2] Bell Laboratories, Lucent Technologies,
600 Mountain Avenue, Murray Hill, NJ 07974

Abstract. This paper delves into the problem of face recognition using color as an important cue in improving recognition accuracy. To perform recognition of color images, we use the characteristics of a 3D color tensor to generate a subspace, which in turn can be used to recognize a new probe image. To test the accuracy of our methodology, we computed the recognition rate across two color face databases and also compared our results against a multi-class neural network model. We observe that the use of the color subspace improved recognition accuracy over the standard gray scale 2D-PCA approach [17] and the 2-layer feed forward neural network model with 15 hidden nodes. Additionally, due to the computational efficiency of this algorithm, the entire system can be deployed with a considerably short turn around time between the training and testing stages.

1 Introduction

With the surge of security and surveillance activities, biometric research has become one of the important research topics in computer vision. From the results of the Face Recognition Vendor Test (FRVT 2006) [10], it is obvious that the current face recognition algorithms can achieve a very high accuracy in recognition. In some cases the tests indicate that some algorithms are superior to the human recognition rates. This high recognition accuracy occurs in the faces observed under very high resolution cameras where the average separation between the eye centers is ~350 pixels.

The current state of imaging technology does not indicate a linear relationship between the price and quality of a camera, with a slight increase in quality imposing significant increase in camera cost. With this in mind, it is essential that the robustness of any vision algorithm can be tested against images from the lower end of the quality spectrum. This is especially true in typical low end commodity cameras (e.g. web cameras), where the presence of noise and the limited pixel resolution would provide an acid test to the workings of the algorithm. The other issue which is usually not given it due importance is the computational efficiency of the vision algorithm. The requirement for an algorithm to strike a balance between the computational cost and the estimation accuracy would define two of the important aspects for any vision algorithm.

A. Gasteratos, M. Vincze, and J.K. Tsotsos (Eds.): ICVS 2008, LNCS 5008, pp. 373–382, 2008.
© Springer-Verlag Berlin Heidelberg 2008

The above requirements is especially true for the problem of face recognition using web cameras where the typical image quality is low while the efficiency requirements are high. In order to satisfy such a need, we propose a face recognition algorithm, where we use color to improve the recognition accuracy over the 2D-PCA approach [17]. The organization of the paper is as follows. In the next section, we describe some of the important works that defined our study. This is followed by a description of the algorithm that we implemented and the results obtained from the face databases. Finally, we conclude our work with possible future directions.

2   Background Studies

Visual developments in infants rapidly move from poor fixation ability and a limited ability to discriminate color to a mature visual acuity in 3 years. It is of interest to note that the color is one of the primary recognition cues for an infant much before it begins to observe shapes and structures (`www.ski.org/Vision/infanttimeline.html`). We believe that, it is essential to utilize this very important stimulus when attempting to identify and recognize faces.

Typical face recognition algorithms is composed of two sequential stages, the detection step followed by the recognition step [19]. In this work, we assume that the faces have already been located, either as a cropped face database or as the output from an external face detection algorithm. For the face detection section of our work, we have used the face detection algorithm proposed by Lienhart and Maydt [9], which identifies faces using ada-boost of Haar-like features. Readers are directed to the works by Lienhart and Maydt [9] and Barreto et al. [1] for a detailed overview of this algorithm.

The research in face recognition has burgeoned over the past few years and it would be impossible to list all the currently ongoing works. The readers can get a better picture of the current state of the art in face recognition algorithms at `http://www.face-rec.org/`. The graphs in `http://www.face-rec.org/interesting-papers/` shows the rate at which research in face recognition is currently progressing. Therefore, in lieu of the current research question, we would like to review some significant previous works that were influential to our research.

One of the earliest contributions to the field of recognition via subspace decomposition was by Sirovich and Kirby [13] and Turk and Pentland [15]. The principal component analysis (PCA) of the face space or the "Eigenfaces" approach was seminal. It has since then given rise to many variants and reformulations that attempt to tackle the difficulties present in its original formulation. A different subspace decomposition strategy was proposed by Belhumeur et al. [2] based on the Fisher's linear discriminant analysis (LDA). This was shown to be superior to the original PCA formulation but required an increased computational requirement. The "Eigenfaces" and the "Fisherfaces" approaches can be considered the two main subspace decomposition work that has been improved upon by other researchers. Comparative studies by Ruiz-del-Solar and Navarrete

[4], Delac et al. [5] and G. Shakhnarovich and Moghaddam [11] to name but a few, might direct interested readers to the available subspace techniques.

The use of 3D Principal Component Analysis was first proposed by Tucker [14] who used it to analyze a 3-way psychometric dataset. A multi-linear generalization to the 3-way data analysis was subsequently proved by Lathauwer et al. [8], which has been the primary analysis of the mathematical aspects of the Higher Order Singular Value Decomposition (HOSVD).

Higher order SVD has been applied in different contexts. Costantini et al. [3] recently developed a dynamic texture synthesis algorithm by applying linear updates to the HOSVD of the spatio-temporal tensor. In the field of face recognition, the earliest application of HOSVD was by Vasilescu and Terzopoulos [16] who described a "tensorfaces" framework to handle aspects such as scene structure, illumination and viewpoint. Recently, Yu and Bennamoun [18] used these generalization in performing face recognition using 3D face data. However, according to these authors, the biggest problem in performing HOSVD lay in its computational complexity

3   Tensor Concepts

For the sake of completeness, we shall briefly describe the concept of a tensor from multi-linear algebra. A tensor is a multi-linear mapping over a set of vector spaces, $\mathcal{D} \in \mathrm{R}^{I_1 \times I_2 \times \cdots \times I_N}$ and can be seen as generalizations of vectors (1st order tensor) and matrices (2nd order tensor). Given a tensor, $\mathcal{D}$ we can unfold it along any of its $n \leq N$ dimensions to obtained a mode-n matrix version of the tensor. Figure 1 shows the 3 possible unfoldings along each of its highlighted dimensions and mode-n unfolding can be visualized along similar lines.

The mode-n product of a tensor, $\mathcal{D} \in \mathrm{R}^{I_1 \times I_2 \times \cdots \times I_n \times \cdots \times I_N}$ with a matrix $\mathbf{U} \in \mathrm{R}^{J_n \times I_n}$ is computed by unfolding $\mathcal{D}$ along I_n, performing matrix multiplication and then folding the result back into the tensorial form ($\mathcal{D} \times_n \mathbf{U}$). Having thus defined the mode-n multiplication, the HOSVD for $\mathcal{D}$ can be defined as

$$\mathcal{D} = S \times_1 \mathbf{U}^{(1)} \times_2 \cdots \times_N \mathbf{U}^{(N)}, \tag{1}$$

where $\mathbf{U}^{(n)}$ is a unitary matrix of size $I_n \times I_n$ and S is an all-orthogonal core tensor, which is analogous to the eigenvectors and eigenvalues in the SVD formulation, respectively. The unitary matrices, $\mathbf{U}^{(n)}$ can be obtained by unfolding $\mathcal{D}$ to obtain the mode-n matrix and performing the regular SVD on the unfolded matrix.

4   Algorithm

Yang et al. [17] showed the superiority of the 2D-PCA over the 1D-PCA (Eigenfaces) approach, in terms of accuracy and efficiency. One of the possible reasons for the improvement in accuracy might be due to the pixel coherence that exists within any finite neighborhood when images are observed as 2D matrices.

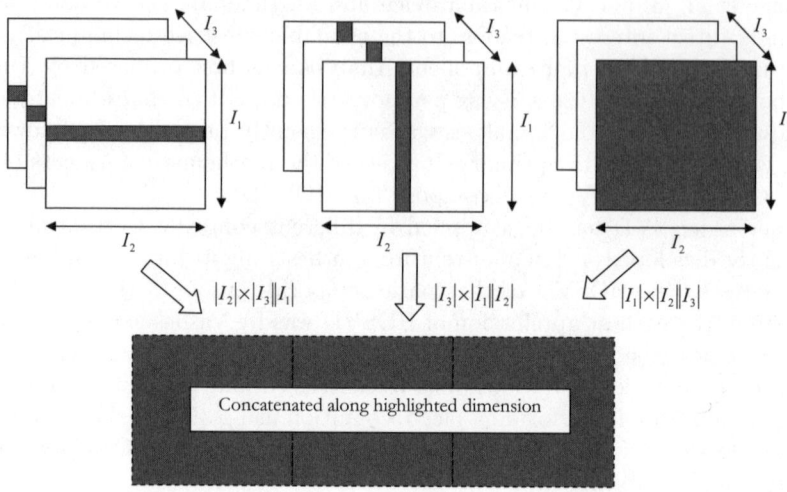

Fig. 1. Mode-1, mode-2 and mode-3 unfolding of a 3rd order tensor ($|\cdot|$ denotes the size of the dimension)

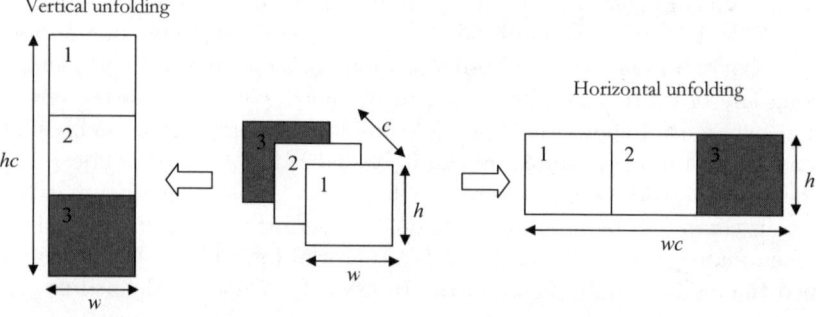

Fig. 2. Horizontal and vertical mode-3 unfolding of the 3D color tensor

Typically, skin pixels would occur in close proximity to other skin pixels, except of course at boundaries. In the 1D-PCA approach, this coherence is disturbed due to the vectorization of the image pixels, while the 2D-PCA maintains the neighborhood coherence thereby achieving higher recognition accuracy.

We can observe that the mode-3 unfolding of the 3D color tensor best maintains the coherence between local pixel neighborhoods and thus we use this unfolding for our experiments. Another observation we can make is that the mode-3 unfolding can be performed along two directions, the horizontal direction and the vertical direction. The two types of mode-3 unfolding is shown in figure 2, where h is the image height, w is the image width and c is the number of channels in the image (in our case $c = 3$).

Given M training images, we compute the vertical and horizontal mode-3 unfolding for each of the images. The image covariance (scatter) matrix, Φ over the M training samples can then be computed as

$$\Phi = \frac{1}{M} \sum_{i=1}^{M} (\Gamma_i - \Psi)^T (\Gamma_i - \Psi) \qquad \Psi = \frac{1}{M} \sum_{i=1}^{M} \Gamma_i \qquad (2)$$

where Γ_i is the ith training image. In the case of a vertical unfolding $\Gamma_i, \Psi \in R^{hc \times w}$ and $\Phi \in R^{w \times w}$ while for the horizontal unfolding case, $\Gamma_i, \Psi \in R^{h \times wc}$ and $\Phi \in R^{wc \times wc}$.

The optimal projection axes that maximizes the variance of the M images correspond to the top d eigenvector-eigenvalue pairs of Φ [17]. These ortho-normal eigenvectors span the required 2D color subspace. Once the color subspace is computed, each of the training images can be projected into the subspace and their projection vector can be stored in the face database. In the recognition stage, an input test sample is unfolded and projected into this subspace. The minimum Euclidean distance between the projected test vector and all the stored projections are computed and the class of the closest projection can be used for the test image.

5   Results and Analysis

For quantitative comparisons, we have performed our analysis on two face databases. The first one was the Georgia Tech (GATech) face database (www.anefian.com/face_reco.htm) and the second was a pruned version of the California Institute of Technology (CalTech) face database (www.vision.caltech.edu/html-files/archive.html).

The GATech images (figure 3(a)) were cropped low resolution ($\sim$200 $\times$ $\sim$150 pixels) color images of 50 individuals with 15 views per individual, with no specific order in their viewing direction. The pruned Caltech database (figure 3(b)) was composed of 19 individuals with 20 views per image. The original database was composed of 450 face images of 27 individuals, but we pruned out individuals who had lesser than 20 views to maintain uniformity within the database. Unlike

(a)   (b)

Fig. 3. Sample images from the two face databases (a) GATech (b) CalTech

the GATech database, these images were compressed jpeg images captured at a higher resolution ($\sim$450 × $\sim$300 pixels), which might indicate the differences in recognition accuracy.

5.1   Error Analysis Against Face Databases

For comparing our algorithm against the face databases, we computed the recognition rate in a K-fold cross validation scheme [7] where K varied from 1 (leave-one-out) to one less than the total number of training images. Thus for the each K, we randomly selected K views of each individual for training and used the remaining $N - K$ images ($N = 15$ for GATech and $N = 20$ for CalTech) for testing. We averaged the recognition accuracy for each value of K to obtain an average rate of identification. The results below are the output from the best K-fold cross validation scheme. To compare various possible measurements we have conducted the following experiments:

Unfolding Direction. In this experiment, we tested the unfolding direction and its contribution to the recognition rate. From the test cases, we observed that unfolding the 3D color tensor along the vertical direction was better than unfolding along the horizontal direction for most color spaces. Figure 4 shows the results from the RGB and HSV color space where we can see that the vertical unfolding provided a better recognition rate over the horizontally unfolded version for both the color spaces.

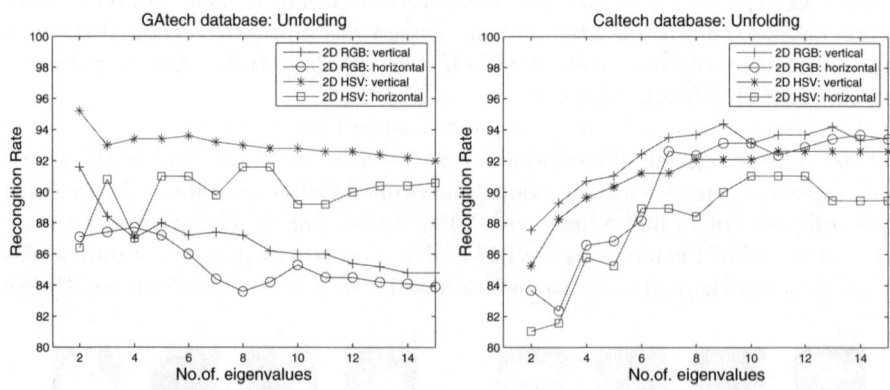

Fig. 4. Variations in the direction of unfolding of the 3D color tensor

1D/2D Variations. Here, we tried to observe the improvement of the color space 2D-PCA approach in face-recognition over the traditional 1D-PCA and grayscale 2D-PCA. For comparative purposes, we experimented with 1D grayscale (original eigenface approach [15]), 1D RGB (original eigenface approach using color components), 2D grayscale (2D-PCA based face recognition [17]) and 2D RGB (color space based PCA). For the 2D RGB case, we used the horizontal unfolding of the

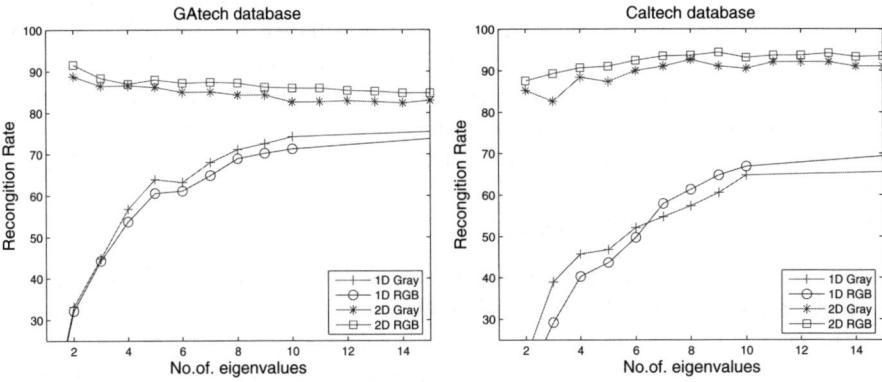

Fig. 5. Variations in using 1D vectors or their 2D counterparts (comparison between gray scale and RGB color)

3D color tensor to compute the subspace. Figure 5 shows the recognition rates with the use of 1D/2D data. From the figure it is observable that the 2D oriented approach is better than the 1D-PCA, despite the use of color components in the 1D analysis. Between the gray scale and the color based 2D approaches, using the color space improved recognition rate by around 2∼3% in the case of both the databases.

Color Space Variations. To understand the variability of the algorithms towards color space, we analyzed the recognition rate with 4 color spaces, RGB, HSV, YUV and YIQ [6]. From the previous two experiments, we observed that vertical unfolding of the 2D face images was better than the others. Here we only show the results across the 4 color spaces with the vertical mode-3 unfolding. The

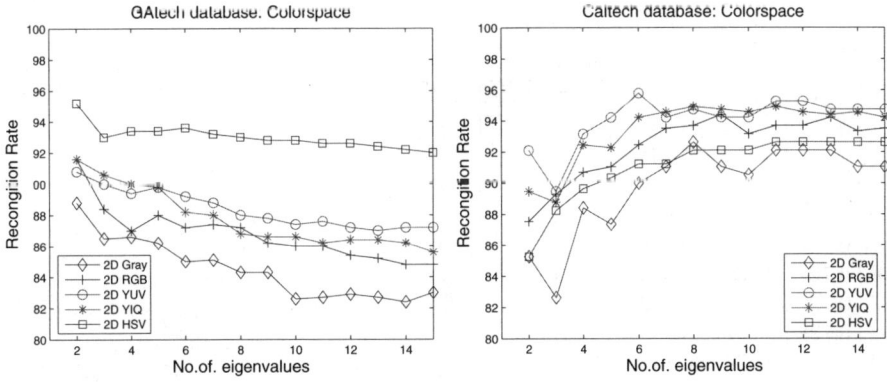

Fig. 6. Variations in using different color spaces for analysis (with vertical unfolding)

conspicuous finding that can be observed immediately from the figure 6 is that any color space performs better than the grayscale 2D-PCA approach. In fact the performance of the 2D HSV is significantly better for the GATech database (an improvement from 86% to 94%). Unfortunately, we could not achieve any conclusive evidence to the superiority of one color space over the other since the results from the two databases indicate superiority of different color spaces.

5.2   Recognition Performance

Among the many existing techniques, neural network models have been used in the past to perform reasonably accurate identification. Typically, facial features like the eyes, nose and mouth are extracted, vectorized and used in the training process. For our experiments, we used a holistic face recognition neural network model instead of a feature oriented approach so as to provide a uniform basis for comparison against the subspace techniques we implemented. The 2-layer feed forward neural network model that we used was adapted from the ANN toolbox developed by S. Sigurdsson et al. [12]. The weights in the network was computed using the BFGS optimization algorithm using soft line search to determine step lengths. The readers are directed to the code (http://isp.imm.dtu.dk/toolbox/ann/) and the references therein for additional information.

For a reasonable computational effort, we used 15 individuals from the GATech database and generated the classification error rates with two neural network models, one that used 15 hidden layer nodes and the other that used 7 hidden layer nodes. To reduce the dimensions of the face space, we first converted the color images into grayscale and then projected the 1D grayscale faces images into their eigenspace so as to retain $\leq 75\%$ of their cumulative variance. Using the leave-one-out cross validation [7], we repeated our measurements by training a new network for every simulation step and used the trained network to perform the recognition.

Table 1. Performance comparison against the multi-class neural network classifier (a) Time required to perform training (b) recognition rate for the corresponding technique

Training time in seconds				
λ_i	1D-Gr	2D-Gr	2D-HSV	NN-7	NN-15
1	0.705	0.253	0.800		
2	0.716	0.256	0.805		
3	0.719	0.257	0.809		
4	0.719	0.259	0.815		
5	0.723	0.271	0.821	97.18	357.4
6	0.721	0.265	0.826		
7	0.727	0.278	0.832		
8	0.728	0.267	0.838		
9	0.729	0.272	0.842		
10	0.730	0.273	0.848		

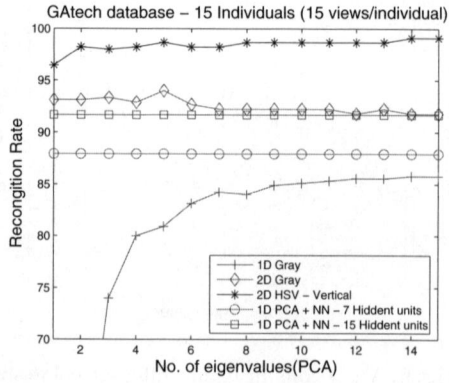

The table 1 and the adjacent figure, shows the recognition accuracy and computational requirements of using our PCA oriented approach and the neural network model. Increasing the number of hidden nodes improved the recognition rate but required a higher computational cost. Table 1(a) shows the time in seconds that were required for various algorithms that were compared. It is important to observe that the training time for a PCA oriented algorithm was dependent on the number of eigenvalues that were used to represent the eigenspace and is depicted in the first column of table 1(a). The neural network models produced improved recognition rates, but it came at the cost of computational efficiency. On the contrary, our approach showed a better recognition accuracy at a significantly lower computational cost.

6 Conclusions

In this paper, we have shown that the utilization of color cues would improve the accuracy of a face recognition algorithm. Instead of computing a full HOSVD, we compute a partial mode-n unfolding of the original tensor and apply 2D-PCA on the unfolded color tensor. From the quantitative experiments, we have observed that a color space oriented approach can improve recognition accuracy when compared to the grayscale 2D-PCA approach. Differences between the various color spaces has not been conclusively established and further research is needed to see which color space performs better. Another important observation is that the vertical unfolding of the color tensor improves recognition rate as against the horizontal unfolding. This is observed to occur independent of the color space that is used and we are currently trying to understand the reason for this improvement. With the availability of cameras that provide color information by default, color based recognition would provide means to improve the recognition accuracy by utilizing all the available information.

References

1. Barreto, J., Menezes, P., Dias, J.: Human-robot interaction based on haar-like features and eigenfaces. In: Proceedings of the IEEE International Conference on Robotics and Automation, 2004 (ICRA 2004), vol. 2, pp. 1888–1893 (2004)
2. Belhumeur, P.N., Hespanha, J., Kriegman, D.J.: Eigenfaces vs. fisherfaces: Recognition using class specific linear projection. IEEE Transactions on Pattern Analysis and Machine Intelligence 19(7), 711–720 (1997)
3. Costantini, R., Sbaiz, L., Süsstrunk, S.: Higher Order SVD Analysis for Dynamic Texture Synthesis. IEEE Transactions on Image Processing (2007)
4. del Solar, J.R., Navarrete, P.: Eigenspace-based face recognition: a comparative study of different approaches. IEEE Transactions on Systems, Man and Cybernetics - Part C: Applications and Reviews 35(3), 315–325 (2005)
5. Delac, K., Grgic, M., Grgic, S.: Independent comparative study of PCA, ICA, and LDA on the FERET data set. IJIST 15(5), 252–260 (2005)
6. Ford, A., Roberts, A.: Colour space conversions (August 1998)

7. Kohavi, R.: A study of cross-validation and bootstrap for accuracy estimation and model selection. In: IJCAI, pp. 1137–1145 (1995)
8. Lathauwer, L.D., Moor, B.D., Vandewalle, J.: A multilinear singular value decomposition. SIAM Journal on Matrix Analysis and Applications 21(4), 1253–1278 (2000)
9. Lienhart, R., Maydt, J.: An extended set of haar-like features for rapid object detection. In: Proceedings of the International Conference on Image Processing, September 2002, pp. 900–903 (2002)
10. Phillips, P.J., Scruggs, W.T., O'Toole, A.J., Flynn, P.J., Bowyer, K.W., Schott, C.L., Sharpe, M.: FRVT 2006 and ICE 2006 Large-Scale Results. Technical Report NISTIR 7408, National Institute of Standards and Technology (March 2007)
11. Shakhnarovich, G., Moghaddam, B.: Handbook of Face Recognition, chapter Face Recognition in Subspaces. Springer, Heidelberg (2004)
12. Sigurdsson, S., Larsen, J., Hansen, L., Philpsen, P., Wulf, H.: Outlier estimation and detection: Application to Skin Lesion Classification. In: Proceedings of the Int. Conf. on Acoustics, Speech and Signal Processing, pp. 1049–1052 (2002)
13. Sirovich, L., Kirby, M.: Low-dimensional procedure for the characterization of human faces. Journal of the Optical Society of America A(4), 519–524 (1987)
14. Tucker, R.L.: Some mathematical notes on the three-mode factor analysis. Psychometrika 31, 279–311 (1966)
15. Turk, M.A., Pentland, A.P.: Eigenfaces for recognition. Journal of Cognitive Neuroscience 3(1), 71–86 (1991)
16. Vasilescu, M.A.O., Terzopoulos, D.: Multilinear image analysis for facial recognition. In: In Proceedings of the International Conference of Pattern Recognition (ICPR 2002), vol. 2, pp. 511–514 (2002)
17. Yang, J., Zhang, D., Frangi, A.F., Yang, J.: Two-dimensional PCA: A new approach to appearance-based face representation and recognition. IEEE Transactions on Pattern Analysis and Machine Intelligence 26(1), 131–137 (2004)
18. Yu, H., Bennamoun, M.: 1D-PCA, 2D-PCA to nD-PCA. In: Proceedings of the International Conference of Pattern Recognition (ICPR2006), vol. IV, pp. 181–184 (2006)
19. Zhao, W., Chellappa, R., Phillips, P.J., Rosenfeld, A.: Face recognition: A literature survey. ACM Comput. Surv. 35(4), 399–458 (2003)

Online Learning for Bootstrapping of Object Recognition and Localization in a Biologically Motivated Architecture

Heiko Wersing[1], Stephan Kirstein[3], Bernd Schneiders[2],
Ute Bauer-Wersing[4], and Edgar Körner[1]

[1] Honda Research Institute Europe GmbH,
Carl-Legien-Str. 30, 63073 Offenbach/Main, Germany
[2] University of Applied Sciences Trier, P.O. Box 1380, 55761 Birkenfeld, Germany
[3] Technical University of Ilmenau, 98693 Ilmenau, Germany
[4] Univ. of Applied Sciences Frankfurt, Nibelungenplatz 1, 60318 Frankfurt, Germany

Abstract. We present a modular architecture for recognition and localization of objects in a scene that is motivated from coupling the ventral ("what") and dorsal ("where") pathways of human visual processing. Our main target is to demonstrate how online learning can be used to bootstrap the representation from nonspecific cues like stereo depth towards object-specific representations for recognition and detection. We show the realization of the system learning objects in a complex real-world environment and investigate its performance.

1 Introduction

The human visual system enables us to easily perform tasks like navigation, collision avoidance or searching. Understanding the internal processes that lead to these perceptual powers is a major goal of cognitive neuroscience and has high relevance for computer vision. One interesting question is the degree of modularity observable in the human visual system. It has been argued that the visual system consists of a number of interacting but still autonomously functioning subsystems processing different cues like shape, color and motion [1]. Another example are the ventral and dorsal pathways of visual perception, also called "what" and "where" streams due to their role in recognition and localization of objects. This viewpoint is challenged by findings that emphasize the rich interactions between these pathways [2]. Within such a network, subsystems can serve as mutual partners for learning to bootstrap their representations, combining sensory input and output of other modules. In this contribution we investigate an online learning model for this bootstrapping process.

Approaches to online learning have recently gained interest due to their importance for intelligent cognitive systems interacting with dynamically changing environments [3,4]. Nevertheless this topic is still in its infancy, compared to the large effort done on object recognition and detection methods using offline learning on large image databases. Along one line of research, online learning

A. Gasteratos, M. Vincze, and J.K. Tsotsos (Eds.): ICVS 2008, LNCS 5008, pp. 383–392, 2008.
© Springer-Verlag Berlin Heidelberg 2008

of representations for larger object ensembles was investigated using segmentation methods during training and recognition, and employing either dimension reduction methods [5,6] or high-dimensional sparse feature map representations motivated from the ventral pathway [7]. Another research direction is the focus on cross-modal interactive learning of visual and auditory stimulus concepts [8], where generally only simple visual object attributes like color and global shape are considered. Localization and detection of objects has also frequently been considered for attentional processes in visual search [9]. Here the main focus was so far on attenuating low-level features like color, intensity and orientation contrasts to facilitate top-down attention towards target objects [10,11].

In this contribution we propose a modular online learning architecture using interactions of the "what" and "where" pathways, based on concurrent adaptation of representations. The target is a visual system that is capable of bootstrapping its visual object representations from unspecific (e.g. depth) towards more object-specific cues like shape. The situation that we consider is the learning of object detection and localization using shape and color cues only, where bootstrapping is based on stereo depth information. In analogy to related response properties of neurons in the ventral pathway, the model uses topographic population code representations of visual object information for recognition and localization and adapts these online using simple linear learning models. We thus extend prior work on online learning using segmentation towards segmentation-free detection of arbitrary objects within a scene.

In Section 2 we first present the biological background of our model and then introduce in Section 3 the system architecture. In Section 4 we give some results for our approach on benchmark data for offline learning and then discuss the system performance for online training and testing scenarios.

2   Biological Background

Although ventral and dorsal pathways have long been considered as dissociate in their processing of "what" and "where" [1], recent biological evidence has emphasized similarities that could ease interactions between the anatomically segregated modules. In the ventral pathway, neurons in higher areas like the inferotemporal (IT) cortex are increasingly selective to particular objects and parts, with larger spatial invariance. It has been shown, that selectivity to position shows a Gaussian tuning curve within the receptive field for many object specific IT neurons [12] and also size-specific tuning can be observed [13]. This provides a population code based representation that could be used to obtain estimates of object position and size. The superior temporal sulcus (STS) in the superior temporal cortex has been considered as such an area combining information from both ventral and dorsal pathways, and is strongly involved in spatial search and attention to objects [2].

There has been an increasing effort in the recent years to provide models of the hierarchical processing in the ventral pathway leading to so-called view-tuned-units with response properties similar to IT neurons [14,15,16]. Online learning

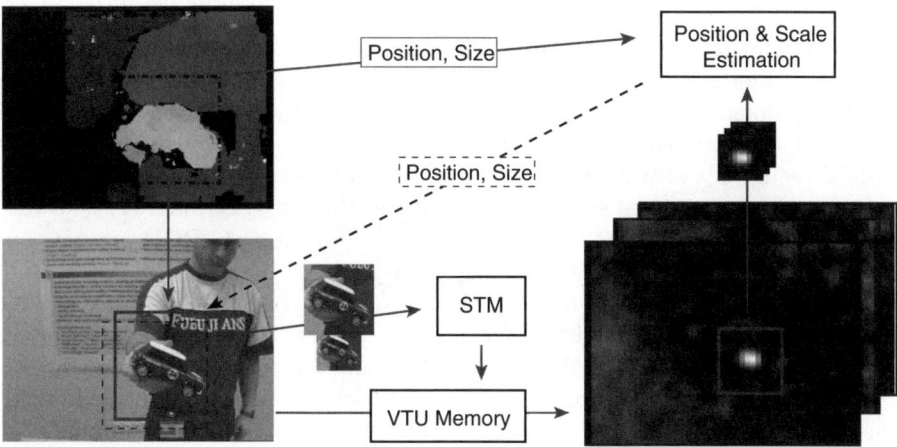

Fig. 1. Architecture overview. A stereo-based position and size estimation is used to bootstrap learning of these properties from a view-tuned unit (VTU) object-specific feature map. Learning of VTUs at multiple scales using attention and an appearance-based short-term memory is done synchronously with position and scale learning.

of object representations using these models was demonstrated by [7] and shown to scale well also for larger object ensembles.

3   System Architecture

The visual input for the system is given by the output of a stereo camera head mounted on a pan-tilt unit and delivering two RGB images. The architecture (see Fig. 1) consists of the following main components:

- A stereo-based attention system determines a near object in the peripersonal space [17], points the camera gaze towards it, and delivers a size and position estimate for the object blob hypothesis as a region of interest (ROI).
- A short-term memory (STM) collects several views of the current object in the focus of attention, using a hierarchical sparse feature map representation. Views are stored at multiple resolutions and online learning of view-tuned units (VTUs) is performed for several object classes.
- Based on the trained VTUs, a map of object selective VTU responses is computed on the scene image and can be used for object localization
- An integration component independently estimates object identity, position and scale, based on maximum selection and the local activation in the VTU map. If an object is in the depth-based attended ROI, the component is trained with the current local VTU response map as input and the ROI parameters as output.

In the following we describe the system components in more detail:

Attention and Gaze Selection. The attention system is based on the gaze control system presented by Goerick et al. [17] for online learning of object representations. Using a stereo-based depth map, connected pixels lying within a defined depth range (also called peripersonal space) are clustered, and the frontal region is taken as an initial object hypothesis. The focus of attention and gaze direction of the system is centered on the center of mass (x, y) of this region. The size s (in pixels) of a square region of interest (ROI) around this point is scaled according to the distance estimate using the depth map. The ROI size s in pixels is computed as $s = 144 \cdot 0.6/d$, i.e. an object at distance $d = 60$ cm gives a ROI of $s = 144$ pixels. The attended ROI is rescaled to a set of input RGB patches $\mathbf{I}^{\{1,2,3\}}$ of fixed sizes 144, 128, and 96, which are passed to the short-term-memory for learning. This induces size normalization in each of the three scales. In addition to setting the focus of attention we use the parameters of the attended ROI $\mathbf{r} = (x, y, s)$ to train the position and scale estimation module that is capable of localizing objects, when no stereo-based attention is available. This is the case, when the objects are not separable within the scene based on stereo alone. Unspecific object size and position within the peripersonal space is an example of an action-related representation that is typically localized in the dorsal pathway of human visual processing.

Short-term Memory for Online Training of VTUs. The short-term memory module collects object views, when an object is in the focus of attention. Using a concept of sensory memory as proposed in [7], views are buffered until a label is given by speech input, after which the views in the sensory buffer are assigned to the object in the current context. Representation in the STM is based on the output of a hierarchical feature detection model of the ventral visual pathway as described in [16]. For each input RGB patch $\mathbf{I}^{\{1,2,3\}}$, the output of the feature hierarchy is computed as $\mathbf{x}^k(\mathbf{I}^k) = (\mathbf{c}_1^k, \ldots, \mathbf{c}_{50}^k, \hat{\mathbf{I}}_R^k, \hat{\mathbf{I}}_B^k, \hat{\mathbf{I}}_G^k)$, where $\mathbf{c}_i^k$ is the output of the topographic combination feature detection map of feature i, and $\hat{\mathbf{I}}_R^k, \hat{\mathbf{I}}_B^k, \hat{\mathbf{I}}_G^k$ are downsampled coarse images of the RGB image channels. Due to the spatial convergence the size of each map is 8 times reduced compared to the input patch size, (i.e. 18x18, 16x16, 12x12). The collection is incremental, if a new view is sufficiently dissimilar to existing view representatives based on Euclidean distance, it is added to the STM. From this STM, training views are concurrently randomly drawn and used to train VTUs as linear discriminating units with a one-against-all classification output vector [16]. Here we perform online gradient descent in the quadratic error between output and target value from supervised learning. To increase the rejection capability we also add a set of clutter views, based on a collection of arbitrary images from the internet, which are trained as a rejection class. We also performed experiments using clutter from our real scene setting, but observed no consistent improvement. Note that unlike previous work by [7] we do not perform segmentation during learning, since this is also not available for object detection in the scene.

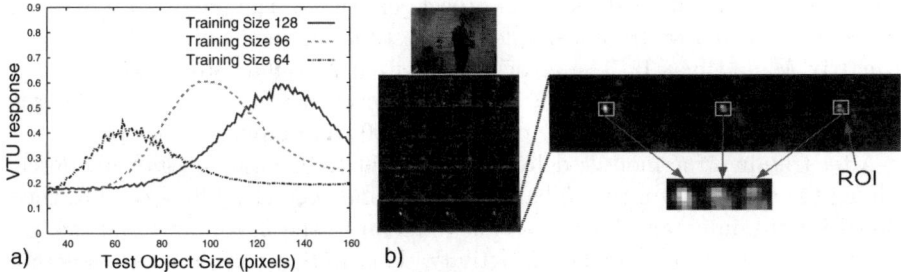

Fig. 2. a)VTU size tuning. Average response of VTUs trained at particular object sizes, using the COIL17 object data. b) Selection of training data from VTU maps for localization. For training, the map activity of the current object is taken at different scales around the maximum within the attended ROI.

Object-specific VTU Maps for Detection and Localization. The VTUs are trained for each object class in three scales using the STM. Formally, a VTU is a linear discriminator, which is trained to respond on a receptive field of shape feature and coarse color input. As a result of the spatial integration in the feature hierarchy, these VTUs exhibit a rather regular Gaussian tuning with respect to spatial displacement and size change of the object within the receptive field (see Fig. 2a). This tuning behaviour is similar to the sensitivities in the IT cortex [12,13]. Due to the topographic arrangement of the feature map input the VTU was trained for, we can setup a complete map of VTUs for each object and scale, covering the complete input scene (600x450 pixels) at 8 times reduced resolution. From the population code of the map response with displaced receptive fields and multiple scales we can train a model to read out the precise localization and scale information.

Position and Scale Estimation. This component learns the mapping from the local VTU map population response to the local position and size for objects, without being specific to single objects. Functionally, this could be realized in the STS area of the human visual pathway, combining convergent inputs from ventral and dorsal pathways, and important for object-based search and spatial attention processes [2]. If an object is present in the depth-based focus of attention, the ROI parameters $\mathbf{r}$ are computed based on the depth blob and used as a training target. The training input pattern is obtained from combining the local VTU map responses in a neighbourhood of the maximal response within the attended region. Due to the topographic representation, the ROI from the original image can be easily remapped to the VTU maps by division by 8.

Around the maximum we cut out within each scale map of the current object a local patch $\mathbf{p}^{\{1,2,3\}}$ of 7x7 VTU output responses (see Fig. 2b). It turns out that it is recommendable to restrict the training to appropriate patches, i.e. for which a proper localization is principally possible. Therefore we reject all cases, when the global maximum in the VTU maps for the currently attended object is not inside the attended ROI. Consequently, the learning begins only after the

VTU learning has reached a certain object selectivity. The patches are written into a vector $\mathbf{v}$ and we train a simple linear estimation model $\mathbf{r}^* = M\mathbf{v} + \mathbf{b}$ with a matrix M and bias $\mathbf{b}$. The error is minimized by online stochastic gradient descent in the summed quadratic differences between $\mathbf{r}$ and $\mathbf{r}^*$. The training is based on a local memory history of the past 500 valid input patches $\mathbf{p}$.

After training, the module delivers new target ROIs based on globally determining the maximum in the global VTU map, and then using its locally learned model for obtaining an object position (relative to the maximum) and size estimate from the local population activity. This ROI can be used to generate a new focus of attention, even if no stereo-driven hypothesis is available. In a preliminary study [18] we also investigated alternative models for the position and scale estimation using only offline learning and artificial data and compared

- just taking the maximum position and scale in the map and compute corresponding position by multiplying by 8
- computing the center of gravity around the local maximum in the map
- training a radial-basis-function (RBF) network with the VTU map input and the target outputs using different numbers of hidden nodes
- using a linear model mapping the local VTU activity pattern to the target values like in this contribution

The first two simple models exhibited roughly a double position and scale error compared to the trained models, due to the lack of robust interpolation from the population code output. The RBF networks delivered best performance, but the linear model was only slightly worse. Since the linear approach is best suited for an online setting we therefore chose this one for our combined architecture.

System Implementation. The whole system runs in a component environment for the large-scale real-time simulation of intelligent systems [19]. The STM learning runs at a frame rate of about 5 Hz, while the computation of the VTU maps on the whole image runs at 1-2 Hz. Computation hardware is a 2.4 GHz Quadcore Intel processor.

4   Results

We first state some results for comparison to other computer vision detection approaches using offline learning on a benchmark problem. We then show the temporal learning curves for the online learning system in interaction with a user and evaluate the performance for different scenarios.

4.1   Benchmark Comparison for Offline Learning Detection Task

The task of object detection in complex cluttered scenes has been intensively studied using several different computer vision approaches. To assess the detection and discrimination capabilities of the VTU map model, we performed a benchmark comparison on the UIUC single scale car detection task [20]. This is a single-class detection problem for side views of cars, based on a training

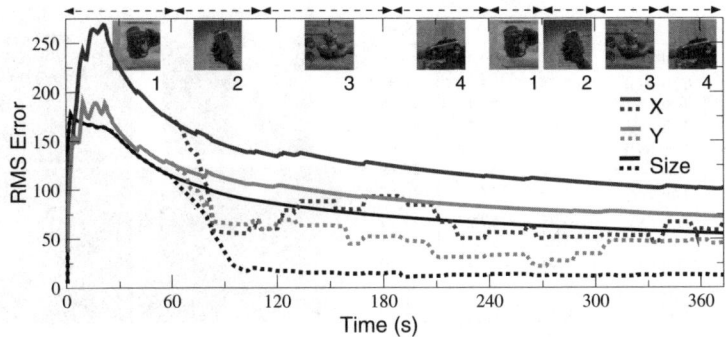

Fig. 3. Temporal dynamics of online learning RMS error for x, y, and size of object ROI. The solid lines give the total average error, while the dashed lines are local averages over the last 70 steps. At the top the shown object is visualized, we first train 4 objects and then test them from 240s on. Learning begins to successfully reduce errors, when the VTU response is getting more tuned. New objects first increase the local errors, and then require some time until error converges again.

ensemble of 500 car and 500 clutter views. The test ensemble consists of 170 test images with varying difficulty, where one or several cars have to be detected. With the introduction of the database, Agarwal et al. achieved 76.5% equal error detection rate using a parts-based approach. This was improved by Leibe et al. [21] to 97.5% using a parts-based implicit shape model, and recently Mutch & Lowe [15] achieved 99.9% using a biologically motivated feature hierarchy similar to our approach. We train a single VTU sensitive to the car training views and then take the local maxima in the VTU map output as target detection. Using this, we obtain an equal error rate of 97%. One advantage of our model is that it is based on only 50 shape features obtained from sparse coding [16], compared to large libraries of up to 1000 local features as in [21,15]. This causes a 50 − 100 times faster implementation and makes online learning possible.

4.2   Online Learning Scenario and Evaluation

We present the objects to be learned in an office environment, where the gaze control system is responsible for keeping the objects within camera view (compare Fig. 4b). Starting from an empty object memory we can train a number of objects and interactively watch the progress both in learning of object representations and the position and size estimation. Figure 3 shows an example for a learning curve recorded during a typical training session for 4 objects.

For a more comprehensive evaluation of the architecture we selected one artificial scenario with perfect ground truth, and three online scenarios of varying difficulty. For the latter we considered the training of the position estimation after convergence of VTU training, to leave out the transient phase. The test error is computed on data from a disjoint sequence, performed by another subject. The four scenarios are:

		X	Y	Size
COIL17	Training	4.92	4.59	6.76
	Test ROI	5.75	5.53	8.44
	Test scene	52.83	56.12	12.58
Single Pose	Training	8.02	6.27	12.04
	Test ROI	11.60	8.68	14.64
	Test Scene	69.37	58.58	16.69
Multi Pose	Training	17.16	14.77	16.69
	Test ROI	20.92	17.23	17.24
	Test scene	158.32	96.65	22.11
Single Pose ++Size Var	Training	15.94	15.13	19.74
	Test ROI	21.08	19.30	22.33
	Test scene	130.71	92.45	24.50

a) Position and size errors (pixels)   b) Artifical and real views

Fig. 4. a) Results of position and size estimation RMS error for 4 scenarios. b) One artificial image and three images showing view-point variation during online interaction.

1. We select 17 objects from the COIL20 [22] database, where we removed similar objects (2 cars and one pillbox) from the same category, since we are here not interested in detailed identification of single objects. Objects are segmented and placed at random positions and scale variations from 64-128 pixels visible size onto a set of clutter images of size 320x320, cropped from images collected from the internet. All the images are greyscale only.
2. We train 10 objects in an interactive fashion, where the pose variance is limited to a single pose with a variation of about 10-30 degree rotation around all axes. Object distance varies from 40-80 cm, while position in space is strongly varied (compare Fig. 4b).
3. Like 2. but allowing full rotation with multiple poses
4. Like 2. but distance varying from 40-120 cm

The table in Fig. 4a summarizes the performance of the position and scale estimation component. The training error is the root mean square (RMS) error of the position x, y and ROI size s. The test error is computed by either restricting the maximum search in the VTU maps to the attended target ROI or allowing free search in the whole scene. The first error allows to asses the performance of the local population code estimation from the VTU map, while the second is also heavily influenced by globally wrong responses of VTUs to clutter.

The results show that the COIL17 scenario is easiest, although it contains full rotation in depth along a single axis and no color. Within the test ROI, test position and scale error is only slightly larger than training error. The test position error in the complete scene corresponds to about half the maximal object size. For the online learning scenario, the single pose is easiest, with the increased depth interval raising difficulty and the multi-pose setting as the hardest task. This is consistent across all errors. As is evident from the large discrepancy between errors in ROI and scene settings, false maxima determine here most of the position error. The larger errors in x than in y position are induced by the larger x dimension of the scene images.

Table 1. Equal error rates (%) for object detection in the test scenarios

Single Pose	0.4	4.7	2.4	0.9	1.2	3.2	1.5	2.1	4.0	1.2
Multi Pose	15.0	26.9	25.2	47.1	22.5	27.2	21.8	39.9	29.5	7.4
S. Pos+Dpth	6.6	23.1	18.4	12.4	15.8	28.3	17.9	30.9	25.0	19.0

We also performed an evaluation of the detection performance regardless of position, independently for each object. For each test frame containing a test object, the maximum activity is computed within each object set of VTU maps. Based on the vector of confidences, we can compute an ROC curve, where each frame is counted as a true positive for the object contained in the frame and a possible false positive for other objects. The results are listed for each object in Table 1. Across all objects, the detection of a single pose with limited size variation is substantially easier with much less false positive detections. Especially for the multi-pose setting the integration of changing object appearance information over the whole viewing sphere reduces the VTU selectivity considerably.

5 Discussion

We proposed an online learning framework for cross-modal bootstrapping of object-specific representations from unspecific cues like stereo depth. This extends prior work on object online learning from segmentation-based methods to the case of object detection in a scene. An immediate application of this approach could be the search for a recently trained object by a mobile robot, e.g. building on methods as presented in [9]. For the single pose case, detection can be achieved without substantial false positives. For multiple poses, the performance figures show that the model could still serve as an object-specific attention delivering candidate ROIs for objects, that are then inspected by a fovealized more precise recognition method. This allows to combine more selective shape feature channels, than simpler models using only orientation and contrast.

We believe that the concept of modular subsystems that are learning in interaction is of high relevance both for biological vision systems and their computer vision counterparts. Our example illustrated that this can be achieved using the biological principles of sparse and topographic representations and population coding in combination with linear learning methods. We consider the extension of this concept to more complex visual architectures as a promising future research direction.

Acknowledgments. We thank A. Ceravola, B. Bolder, J. Eggert, C. Goerick, M. Dunn, and M. Stein for providing the processing infrastructure.

References

1. Zeki, S.: Localization and globalization in conscious vision. Annual Review Neuroscience 24, 57–86 (2001)
2. Karnath, H.O.: New insights into the functions of the superior temporal cortex. Nature Reviews Neuroscience 2, 568–576 (2001)
3. Crowley, J.L., Hall, D., Emonet, R.: Autonomic computer vision systems. In: Proc. ICVS, Bielefeld (2007)
4. Steil, J.J., Wersing, H.: Recent trends in online learning for cognitive robotics. In: Verleysen, M. (ed.) Proc. European Symp. on Neural Networks, pp. 77–88 (2006)
5. Bekel, H., Bax, I., Heidemann, G., Ritter, H.: Adaptive computer vision: Online learning for object recognition. In: Proc. DAGM, Tuebingen, pp. 447–454 (2004)
6. Roth, P.M., Donoser, M., Bischof, H.: On-line learning of unknown hand held objects via tracking. In: Proc. Second Int. Cognitive Vision Workshop (2006)
7. Wersing, H., Kirstein, S., Götting, M., Brandl, H., Dunn, M., Mikhailova, I., Goerick, C., Steil, J., Ritter, H., Körner, E.: Online learning of objects and faces in an integrated biologically motivated architecture. In: Proc. ICVS, Bielefeld (2007)
8. Skokaj, D., Berginc, G., Ridge, B., Stimec, A., Jogan, M., Vanek, O., Leonardis, A., Hutter, M., Hawes, N.: A system for continuous learning of visual percepts. In: Proc. ICVS, Bielefeld (2007)
9. Tsotsos, J., Shubina, K.: Attention and visual search: Active robotic vision systems that search. In: Proc. ICVS, Bielefeld (2007)
10. Hamker, F.H.: The emergence of attention by population-based inference and its role in distributed processing and cognitive control of vision. Computer Vision and Image Understanding 100(1-2), 64–106 (2005)
11. Navalpakkam, V., Itti, L.: An integrated model of top-down and bottom-up attention for optimizing detection speed. In: Proc.CVPR (2006) II, pp. 2049–2056 (2006)
12. Beeck, H.O.D., Vogels, R.: Spatial sensitivity of macaque inferior temporal neurons. Journal Comparative Neurology 426(4), 505–518 (2000)
13. Ito, M., Tamura, H., Fujita, I., Tanaka, K.: Size and position invariance of neuronal responses in monkey inferotemporal cortex. J. Neurophysiol 73(1), 218–226 (1995)
14. Serre, T., Wolf, L., Bileschi, S., Riesenhuber, M., Poggio, T.: Robust object recognition with cortex-like mechanisms. IEEE PAMI 29(3), 411–426 (2007)
15. Mutch, J., Lowe, D.G.: Multiclass object recognition with sparse, localized features. In: CVPR, New York, pp. 11–18 (2006)
16. Wersing, H., Körner, E.: Learning optimized features for hierarchical models of invariant recognition. Neural Computation 15(7), 1559–1588 (2003)
17. Goerick, C., Wersing, H., Mikhailova, I., Dunn, M.: Peripersonal space and object recognition for humanoids. In: Proc. Humanoids, Tsukuba (2005)
18. Hegde, A.: Object position and size estimation from output activations of a hierarchical invariant object recognition framework. Master's thesis, Univ. Applied Sciences Frankfurt (2006)
19. Ceravola, A., Joublin, F., Dunn, M., Eggert, J., Goerick, C.: Integrated research and development environment for real-time distributed embodied intelligent systems. In: Proc. IROS, IEEE Press, Bejing (2006)
20. Agarwal, S., Awan, A., Roth, D.: Learning to detect objects in images via a sparse, part-based representation. IEEE PAMI 26(11), 1475–1490 (2004)
21. Leibe, B., Leonardis, A., Schiele, B.: Combined object categorization and segmentation with an implicit shape model. In: Pajdla, T., Matas, J(G.) (eds.) ECCV 2004. LNCS, vol. 3021, pp. 17–32. Springer, Heidelberg (2004)
22. Nayar, S.K., Nene, S.A., Murase, H.: Real-time 100 object recognition system. In: Proc. of ARPA Image Understanding Workshop, Palm Springs (1996)

Vein Segmentation in Infrared Images Using Compound Enhancing and Crisp Clustering

Marios Vlachos and Evangelos Dermatas

Department of Electrical Engineering & Computer Technology
University of Patras, Patras, Greece
{mvlachos,dermatas}@george.wcl2.ee.upatras.gr

Abstract. In this paper an efficient fully automatic method for finger vein pattern extraction is presented using the second order local structure of infrared images. In a sequence of processes, the veins structure is normalized and enhanced, eliminating also the fingerprint lines using wavelet decomposition methods. A compound filter which handles the second order local structure and exploits the multidirectional matching filter response in the direction of the smallest curvature is used in order to enrich the vein patterns. Edge suppression decreases the misclassified edges as veins in the forthcoming crisp clustering step. In a postprocessing module, a morphological majority filter is applied in the segmented image to smooth the contours and to remove some small isolated regions and a reconstruction process reduces the outliers in the finger vein pattern. The proposed method was evaluated in a small database of infrared images giving excellent detection accuracy of vein patterns.

Keywords: finger vein, 2D DWT, local intensity normalization, compound filter, Hessian matrix, matched filter, edge suppression, morphological postprocessing.

1 Introduction

Recently, the problem of finger vein extraction is studied in biometric and biomedical applications. In a few number of studies, due to the recent scientific interest in this area, vein enhancement methods in infrared images have been presented [1-10]. The main advantage of the human verification and recognition using infrared images over the other conventional verification methods such as keys, passwords and PIN numbers is that veins pattern verification does not suffer from thefts, loss and reliance on the user's memory because the vein patterns are inside the human body. Vein or vessel extraction is also very useful in biomedical imaging, vascular pathology, improving diagnosis and follow-up of angiogenesis in the human body. Inspection of the retinal vasculature may reveal hypertension, diabetes, arteriosclerosis, cardiovascular disease, stroke, and glaucoma, the second commonest cause of blindness in West countries and the commonest cause of blindness world wide.

Typically, the infrared images suffer from extremely low contrast due to light scattering effect. Moreover, differences in the tissue structure, the presence of skeleton and skin, the blood circulation introduce strong distortion in the acquired infrared

A. Gasteratos, M. Vincze, and J.K. Tsotsos (Eds.): ICVS 2008, LNCS 5008, pp. 393–402, 2008.

images. An application specific processor for vein pattern extraction, and its application to a biometric identification system, is proposed in [1], consists of three sequential processes, finger detection in the original infrared image, image enhancement, and veins detection. The last two processes are the most time consuming parts of the complete method. The image enhancement consists of a Gaussian low-pass filter, a high-pass filter, and a modified median filter. Consequently, low-pass spatial filtering is used for noise removal, and high-pass spatial filtering for emphasizing vascular patterns, followed by thresholding [1-2, 4].

An improved vein pattern extracting method is proposed in [3], compensating the loss of vein patterns in the edge area, producing more reliable vein pattern information, giving better performance than similar methods. The problem, arising from the iterative nature of the image enhancement filters, is solved by designing a robust one-pass filtering method, giving fast extraction of vein patterns, reducing significant the required computational resources. The false acceptance rate in verification experiments was five times lower than existing algorithm and the processing speed is measured to be 100 ms/image.

In [5], a vascular pattern extraction algorithm, based on the directional information of vascular patterns, is implemented using two filters: a row-pattern filter for abscissa vascular pattern extraction and a column-pattern filter for effective extraction of the ordinate vascular patterns. The combined output produces the vascular patterns in hand images. Unlike the conventional hand vascular pattern extraction algorithm, the directional extraction approach prevents loss of the vascular pattern connectivity. In [6-7], a method for personal identification, based on finger vein patterns, is presented and evaluated using line tracking starting at various positions. Local dark lines are identified and a pixel based line tracking algorithm is executed by moving along the lines.

A method for finger vein pattern extraction in infrared images is proposed in [8]. Using image enhancement and kernel filtering methods, the vein patterns in low contrast images are detected. Further improvement is achieved by a two level morphological process: a majority filter smoothes the contours and removes some of the misclassified isolated pixels, followed by a reconstruction procedure used to remove the remaining misclassified regions.

In [9], a certification system is proposed comparing vein images for low cost, high speed and high precision certification. The recognition algorithm is based on phase correlation and template matching. Several noise reduction filters, sharpness filters and histogram manipulations are tested, giving a high certification ratio.

The theoretical foundation and difficulties of hand vein recognition are introduced and threshold segmentation and line thinning method in hand vein images are studied in [10]. As a result, a new segmentation method and an improved conditional thinning method are proposed, followed by a feature extraction method based on end points and crossing points. In human verification experiments using distance measures a 99.1% pass ratio is achieved.

2 Finger Vein Segmentation

The proposed algorithm performs image enhancement of the finger vein patterns using the second order local structure (Hessian) and the multidirectional response of a

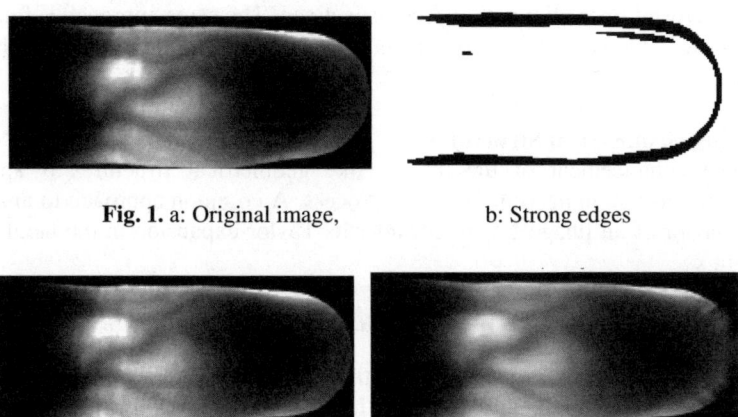

Fig. 1. a: Original image,   b: Strong edges

Fig. 2. a: Original image after local intensity normalization, b: Image after fingerprint lines elimination

matching filter. After edge suppression, robust segmentation is achieved using crisp clustering based on the Kmeans algorithm, detecting the vein patterns from tissue areas. Two pre-processing steps, intensity normalization and fingerprint lines elimination and a postprocessing step including mathematical morphology operators in binary images are applied to extract accurate vein patterns.

Intensity Normalization
The preprocessing module enhances the low contrast infrared images correcting also the non-uniform illumination or shading artifacts. The proposed local linear normalization process adapts the image brightness, taking into account the statistical properties of the neighbor pixels. The local normalization is applied in small windows as follows:

$$g(x, y) = \frac{f(x, y) - m_f(x, y)}{\sigma_f(x, y)},\tag{1}$$

where $f(.)$ is the original image, $m_f(.)$ is an estimation of the brightness local mean of $f(.)$, $\sigma_f(.)$ is an estimation of the local standard deviation, and $g(.)$ is the normalized image. The estimation of the local mean and standard deviation is performed through spatial smoothing. The original image after local intensity normalization is shown in Fig. 2a.

Fingerprint Lines Elimination
Although, after local normalization the image has satisfactory contrast, the fingerprint lines are still visible and in some cases are enhanced also. In typical human fingers, the fingerprint lines are perpendicular to vein lines. Extended experiments at different decomposition levels of the discrete wavelet transform from one to five have shown that the presence of fingerprint lines can be separated and therefore can be eliminated with a very low influence to the tissue and vein patterns. In [8], a detailed presentation

of the fingerprint lines elimination process is given. The same approach is followed in the proposed method. Fig. 2b shows the normalized image after fingerprint elimination.

Enhancing Geometrical Structures

Additional enhancement of the tubular like geometrical structures is applied to facilitate the forthcoming vein detection process. A common approach to analyze the local behavior of an image L is to consider its Taylor expansion in the neighborhood of a point x_0

$$L(x_0 + \delta x_0, s) \approx L(x_0, s) + \delta x_0^T \nabla_{0,s} + \delta x_0^T \cdot H_{0,s} \cdot \delta x_0, \tag{2}$$

This expansion approximates the structure of the image up to second order. $\nabla_{0,s}$ and $H_{0,s}$, are the gradient vector and Hessian matrix of the image, computed in x_0 at scale s. The computations of differential operators are achieved using the linear scale space theory [11-12]. In this framework, differentiation is defined as a convolution with derivatives of Gaussian:

$$\frac{\partial}{\partial x} L(x, s) = s^\gamma \cdot L(x) * \frac{\partial}{\partial x} \frac{1}{\sqrt{(2 \cdot \pi \cdot s^2)}^D} \cdot e^{-\frac{\|x\|^2}{2 \cdot s^2}}, \tag{3}$$

where D is the Gaussian dimensionality. The parameter γ was introduced by Lindeberg [13] to define a family of normalized derivatives. This normalization is particularly important for a fair comparison of the differential operators response at multiple scales. In the absence of multiscale analysis, γ should be set to unity. Uniscale analysis is required in infrared finger images, because the diameter of the finger veins does not vary significantly along the image.

The Hessian matrix has an intuitive justification in the context of vein detection. The second derivative of Gaussian kernel at scale s generates a probe kernel that measures the contrast between the regions inside and outside the range $(-s,s)$ in the direction of the derivative. The eigenvalue analysis of the Hessian extracts the principal directions of the local second order structure of the image. Since the pair of eigenvalues and eigenvectors defines the direction of smallest curvature, i.e. along the vein, the accurate principal component analysis can be used to replace similar approaches such as directional filters. This latter approach is computationally more expensive and requires a discretization of the orientation space. Let $\lambda_{s,k}$ denote the eigenvalue corresponding to the kth normalized eigenvector $u_{s,k}$ of the Hessian $H_{0,s}$, computed at scale s. The eigenvalue decomposition extracts three orthonormal directions (two in the 2D case) which are invariant up to a scaling factor when mapped by the Hessian matrix. In the remainder of this paper the eigenvalues are sorted according to their subscript value, i.e $|\lambda_1| \leq |\lambda_2|$. Under this assumption Table 1 summarizes the relations that must hold between the eigenvalues of the Hessian matrix for the detection of different geometrical structures. In particular, a pixel belonging to a vein has small λ_1 and large positive λ_2. The respective eigenvectors point out singular directions: u_1 indicates the direction along the vein (minimum intensity variation).

Table 1. Geometrical structures in 2D, as a function of the ordered eigenvalues λ_k (H=high, L=low, N=noisy, usually small, +/- indicate the sign of the eigenvalue)

2D		Pattern orientation
λ_1	λ_2	
N	N	Noisy
L	H-	Tubular structure (bright)
L	H+	Tubular structure (dark)
H-	H-	Blob-like structure (bright)
H+	H+	Blob-like structure (dark)

Both eigenvalues play an important role in the discrimination of the local orientation pattern. In the proposed tubular enhancement filter, the eigenvalues ratio R_B is adopted, which is insufficient along to distinguish between a line and a plate like pattern:

$$R_B(x, y) = \frac{|\lambda_1(x, y)|}{|\lambda_2(x, y)|}. \tag{4}$$

The ratio attains its maximum for a blob like structure and is gray level invariant i.e. contains only the geometrical information of the scene. In addition, information about the background pixels is incorporated to the filtering process producing the desired filter response. The derivatives magnitude of the background pixels and consequently the corresponding eigenvalues are small. The Hessian matrix is real and symmetric and therefore, the simpler expression of the Frobenius matrix is used to estimate the second order geometrical structure (SoGS):

$$S(x, y) = \left\| H(x, y) \right\|_F = \sqrt{\lambda_1^2(x, y) + \lambda_2^2(x, y)}. \tag{5}$$

The SoGS measure is smaller in the background pixels, where the scene does not contain any geometrical structure, and the eigenvalues are small for the lack of contrast. In regions with high contrast, compared to the background, the SoGS become greater since at least one of the eigenvalues has been increased. Taking into account the behavior of both measures in geometrical structures, the following combined function is defined to construct the Hessian filter:

$$H(x, y) = \begin{cases} \exp\left(-\dfrac{R_B^2(x, y)}{2 \cdot \beta^2} \right) \cdot \left(1 - \exp\left(-\dfrac{S^2(x, y)}{2 \cdot c^2} \right) \right), & \lambda_2 \geq 0 \\ 0, & \lambda_2 < 0 \end{cases}, \tag{6}$$

where β and c are constants used to control the sensitivity of the line filter to the measures $R_B(.)$, $S(.)$.

The idea behind this expression is to unify the features properties in a unique function, capable to derive pixels belonging to a vein. The response of this Hessian based filter is shown in Fig. 3a. The combined measures use the product operation to

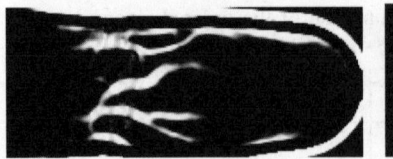

Fig. 3. a: The response of the Hessian based filter, b: Multidirectional matched filter response in the direction of the smallest curvature

ensure that the response of the filter is maximum only if both criteria belong to the neighbor of independent maximum values. In typical infrared images, an experimentally derived value for the parameter β is 0.5. The selection of parameter c depends on the grayscale range, and an adequate value is the half of the maximum value of the Hessian norm.

If the veins diameter varies significantly in the same image, multiscale analysis must be applied [14]. In this case, the maximum response of the above filters is selected, which approximately matches the filter scale and the vessel size to be detected. Therefore, the combined filter response is estimated along different scales as the maximum value of the independent filters' responses at those scales.

Filtering in the Direction of the Smallest Curvature

The proposed combined function cannot distinguish edges from veins effectively as matched filters, due to the fact that it uses local information, while the matched filters use wider area of neighbour pixels in the veins cross section. Therefore, an additional filtering process is applied by convolving the image with a matched filter in the direction of the smallest curvature, i.e. along the vein.

The filter is designed to represent a cross sectional profile using a symmetrical filter kernel with odd number of coefficients. The centre element has the minimum negative value and the value of the adjacent elements is incrementing consequently by one until the two terminal elements are met. The filter coefficients are normalized to ensure that the corresponding sum is zero. The number of the negative elements represents the width of the cross sectional profile. In order to detect veins with large diameter, a greater number of negative elements must be selected, and vice versa. All the rows of the kernel are identical, orientating the filter at a unique direction, detecting veins that have darker pixel values than the background.

The kernel size varies, depends on the acquisition specifications. In our image database the kernel size is 11x11 pixels, because the average vein diameter has almost six pixels width and does not vary too much along image. However, if we want to detect finer veins, we must decrease the filter kernel size accordingly. Recently, the filter kernel [8] was applied to the whole image by convolution in six different directions from 0 to 180 degrees (0, 30, ..., 150) to detect finger veins. This is accomplished by rotating sequentially the filter kernel by the appropriate amount of degrees. In this paper, instead of computing the above filter responses in six directions and compute its maximum, a computational efficient and more accurate approach is followed: the filter response is estimated in the direction of the smallest curvature.

Thus, the response of the compound filter, which can be written as

$$C(x, y) = H(x, y) \cdot M(x, y) \tag{7}$$

where $C(.)$ is the produced image, $H(.)$ is the response of the Hessian based filter, and $M(.)$ is the image created after directional filtering. Fig. 3b shows the response of the multidirectional matched filter in the direction of the smallest curvature, while Fig. 4a shows the response of the compound filter.

Edge Suppression

In several infrared images, the sequence of previous processes overemphasizes edge and vein patterns. Thus, selectively edge suppression is performed, using the global thresholding Otsu's method [15], to avoid erroneous classification of irrelevant tissue structures as veins. The suppression of strong edges is achieved by multiplying the response of the compound filter with the complement of the strong edge response image. In the regions with strong edges, the filter response is near to zero and in all other regions the response of the previous compound filter remained almost unchanged. Fig. 1b shows the strongest edges in black, whereas Fig. 4b shows the response of the compound filter after edge suppression.

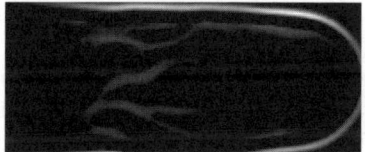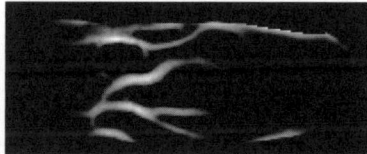

Fig. 4. a: The response of the Compound filter, b: Compound filter response after edge suppression

Crisp Clustering

A critical point in any segmentation problem is the pixels classification process. In the proposed method, the image segmentation is exploited the well known capabilities of the Kmeans algorithm in clustering data into individual classes. Fig. 5a shows the result of the Kmeans clustering.

Morphological Postprocessing

Although the classification gives satisfactory results, in some isolated regions erroneous veins can be derived. These regions must be removed from the binary image for more accurate finger pattern extraction. The proposed postprocessing transformations are based on morphological filtering in the segmented binary image [16]. The majority filter removes small misclassified regions and smoothes the contours by setting each pixel to 1, if five or more pixels in its 3-by-3 neighbour pixels have the value 1, otherwise sets the pixel to 0. The filtering process is applied iteratively until the output image remains the same in two successive transformations.

Morphological reconstruction is a type of binary transformation involving two images and a structuring element. One image, the marker, is the starting point of the transformation. The other image, the mask, constrains the transformation. The

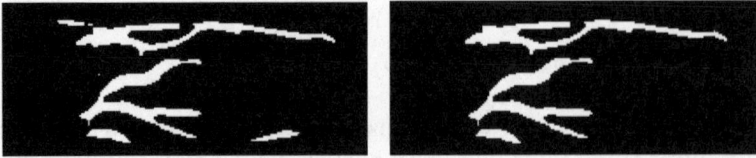

Fig. 5. a: Kmeans clustering in fig.4.b image, b: the finger veins after morphological postprocessing

structuring element used contains the connectivity information. In the proposed method a fast hybrid reconstruction algorithm is adopted, which described in detail elsewhere [17]. The mask image is the output of the majority filter and as marker, the morphological opening of majority filter output is used. The structuring element is a disk with radius of 2, in order to eliminate all the remaining isolated misclassified blob-like structures that have radius smaller than 2 pixels. The binary image after the postprocessing stage should be an outlier free finger vein pattern, which was the aim of the proposed system. Fig. 5b shows the extracted finger vein pattern after the application of the two stage morphological postprocessing module.

3 Experimental Results

The hardware used to acquire the infrared images consists of an array of five infrared leds at 940nm with adjustable illumination, an inexpensive CCD camera, and a low cost frame grabber as shown in Fig. 6. The finger was placed between the camera and the light source. The leds' intensity is controlled by a voltage regulator to produce the appropriate illumination, taking into account the exposure time, the finger thickness, and the colour of the skin. Excellent illumination conditions facilitate the forthcoming digital processing methods, but the accuracy of the vein extraction process remains robust to small variations in the illumination conditions, as the experimental results show. Due to the fact that haemoglobin has strong absorption in the infrared wavelengths than the other parts of the human body i.e. tissue, the veins are reached in the darker areas.

In this section we present the results of the execution of our algorithm in the original image shown in Fig. 1a. We present results from all the steps of our algorithm.

Fig. 3a shows the output of the Hessian based filter. As it is obvious the filter cannot effectively distinguish between veins and edges. Fig. 3b shows the response of the multidirectional matching filter. Fig. 4a shows the output of the compound filter. Fig. 1b shows the complement of the image obtained after the edge enhancement step and the retaining of the strongest edges, while Fig. 4b shows the output of the compound filter after the edge suppression process.

In the latter image, shown in Fig. 4b, the veins are dramatically enhanced, comparing with the original image shown in Fig. 1a. So, the application of a trivial crisp clustering algorithm such as Kmeans is the appropriate choice in order to segment the veins from the surrounding tissue. Fig. 5a shows the results of the Kmeans classification.

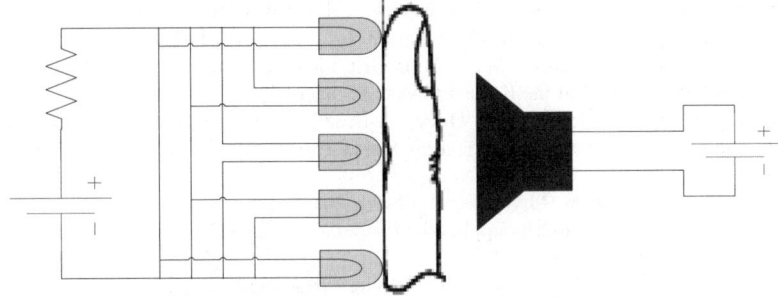

Fig. 6. The experimental device

The final result of the proposed algorithm is shown in Fig. 5b, which is the binary image produced by the morphological filters. This result is achieved by postprocessing the enhanced images, giving robust segmentation of finger in two regions (vein and no vein).

4   Conclusions

In this paper an efficient method for extraction of finger vein patterns is presented. The algorithm is based on the application of a compound filter which enhance vein like structures. The response of this filter is the product of two individual responses, a Hessian matrix exploiting the second order local structure of the image and a specially designed matching filter. An edge suppression step is also employed in order to avoid the erroneous classification of strong edges as veins. The preliminary segmentation result was unsatisfactory, due to the presence of some outliers in the form of small blobs. A final morphological postprocessing step is required to remove misclassifications and to produce a robust finger vein pattern.

The extraction is robust enough against noise and shading. Future work includes improvements in hardware devices in order to acquire images with less shading and noise artefacts, specifications that will guarantee the successful application of our algorithm in the majority of infrared images.

Acknowledgements

This work is partially supported by grant KARATHEODORIS of the University of Patras.

References

[1] Park, G.T., Im, S.K., Choi, H.S.: A Person Identification Algorithm Utilizing Hand Vein Pattern. In: Proc. of Korea Signal Processing Conf. vol.10(1), pp. 1107-1110 (1997)
[2] Hong, D.U., Im, S.K., Choi, H.S.: Implementation of Real Time System for Personal Identification Algorithm Utilizing Hand Vein Pattern. In: Proc. of IEEK Fall Conf. vol. 22(2), pp. 560-563 (1999)

[3] Im, S.K., Park, H.M., Kim, S.W., Chung, C.K., Choi, H.S.: Improved Vein Pattern Extracting Algorithm and its Implementation. In: Proc. of IEEE ICCE, pp. 2-3 (2000)

[4] Im, S.K., Park, H.M., Kim, S.W.: A Biometric Identification System by Extracting Hand Vein Patterns. Journal of the Korean Physical Society 38(3), 268-272 (2001)

[5] Im, S.K., Choi, H.S., Kim, S.-W.: Direction-Based Vascular Pattern Extraction Algorithm for Hand Vascular Pattern Verification Korea University, Seoul, Korea. ETRI Journal 25(2) (April 2003)

[6] Miura, N., Nagasaka, A., Miyatake, T.: Feature extraction of finger-vein patterns based on repeated line tracking and its application to personal identification. Machine Vision and Applications 15, 194-203 (2004)

[7] Miura, N., Nagasaka, A., Miyatake, T.: Feature extraction of finger-vein patterns based on iterative line tracking and its application to personal identification. Systems and Computers in Japan 35(7) (2004)

[8] Vlachos, M., Dermatas, E.: A finger vein pattern extraction algorithm based on filtering in multiple directions. In: 5th European Symposium on Biomedical Engineering (July 2006)

[9] Tanaka, T., Kubo, N.: Biometric Authentication by Hand Vein Patterns. In: SICE Annual Conference in Sapporo (August 2004)

[10] Ding, Y., Zhuang, D., Wang, K.: A Study of Hand Vein Recognition Method. In: Proceedings of the IEEE International Conference on Mechatronics \& Automation, Niagara Falls, Canada (July 2005)

[11] Florack, L.M.J., et al.: Scale and the differential structure of images. Imag. And Vis. Comp. 10(6), 376-388 (1992)

[12] Koenderink, J.J.: The structure of images. Biol. Cybern. 50, 363-370 (1984)

[13] Lindeberg, T.: Edge detection and ridge detection with automatic scale selection. In: Proc. Conf. on Comp. Vis. And Pat. Recog. San Francisco, pp. 465-470 (1996)

[14] Frangi, A.F., et al.: Multiscale vessel enhancement filtering

[15] Otsu, N.: A threshold selection method from grey-level histograms. IEEE Trans. Syst. Man. Cybern SMC-9, 62-66 (1979)

[16] Gonzalez, R., Woods, R., Eddins, S.: Digital image processing using matlab. Prentice Hall, Englewood Cliffs

[17] Vincent, L.: Morphological grayscale reconstruction in image analysis: Applications and efficient algorithms. IEEE Trans.Pattern Anal. Machine Intell. 13(6), 583-598 (1993)

Multiscale Laplacian Operators for Feature Extraction on Irregularly Distributed 3-D Range Data

Shanmugalingam Suganthan[1], Sonya Coleman[1], and Bryan Scotney[2]

[1] School of Computing and Intelligent Systems, University of Ulster, Northern Ireland
[2] School of Computing and Information Engineering, University of Ulster, Northern Ireland
{S.Suganthan,SA.Coleman,BW.Scotney}@ulster.ac.uk

Abstract. Multiscale feature extraction in image data has been investigated for many years. More recently the problem of processing images containing irregularly distribution data has became prominent. We present a multiscale Laplacian approach that can be applied directly to irregularly distributed data and in particular we focus on irregularly distributed 3D range data. Our results illustrate that the approach works well over a range of irregular distributed and that the use of Laplacian operators on range data is much less susceptive to noise than the equivalent operators used on intensity data.

Keywords: 3D Range data, Feature extraction, Laplacian Operators.

1 Introduction

In the field of computer vision, images are normally considered as regular lattices of two-dimensional samples, however images containing irregularly distributed data can result from motion or disparity compensation, such as in motion-compensated video coding, motion compensated video interpolation or disparity-compensated interpolation in stereoscopic images [1]. Irregularly distributed image data also occur frequently in areas such as remote sensing [2], medical imaging, oceanography and human retinal perception, [3, 4]. For example, in human retinal perception, human photoreceptors are not regularly distributed but in fact have a personal signature denoted by the random positioning of cells and hence to be able to replicate human retinal perception, use of irregular image data needs to be supported.

In this paper we focus on the use of irregularly distributed range data and the application of standard image processing algorithms to such irregularly data often results in unreliable results due to fact that many such algorithms require the availability of complete, and regularly sampled, image data. This means that such algorithms are often applied to complete images that have been reconstructed from irregularly distributed, and noisy data without a priori knowledge of the image content using either computationally expensive techniques such as those in [1, 5, 6] or simpler techniques, such as image interpolation, that are usually not adequate to support subsequent reliable image processing. Therefore some means of considering the direct use of irregularly sampled images needs to be considered and [7] also suggests that such a mathematical approach would be advantageous.

A. Gasteratos, M. Vincze, and J.K. Tsotsos (Eds.): ICVS 2008, LNCS 5008, pp. 403–412, 2008.

Multiscale boundary detection in range images has proven to be effective at dealing with discontinuities occurring at a variety of spatial scales. Gunsel *et al.* [8] followed this approach by considering the boundary detection process as a fusion of *n* different sensory processing modules, each corresponding to a specific scale. The output of each module was modelled to be dependent on all other outputs by being part of a joint *a posteriori* probability distribution. Boundary detection was then achieved by maximising this probability function using the Bayesian approach. A multiscale approach is also necessary to achieve good localisation and reliability for extracting low-frequency discontinuities, such as a smooth crease, along with relatively high frequency events, such as jump edges. One example of a multiscale approach is that of [9] who fitted Legendre polynomials to one-dimensional windows of range data and varied the kernel size of the polynomial. Zero-crossings of the second derivative were used to detect edges: when a small kernel size was used, many zero-crossings, including noise, were detected, and when a large kernel size was used, the quality of edge localisation decreased.

The problem of feature detection when using range images is significantly different from that when using intensity images, not only do we consider the locational distribution of the data but consideration must also be given to what defines an edge in a range image. This paper presents the design of the multi-scale Laplacian operators for feature extraction from range images. Such operators can naturally alter they shape in accordance with the local data distribution, enabling them to be applied directly on irregularly distributed range data, without any pre-processing requirements, over a range of scales. An overview of the range image representation is presented accompanied by the finite element framework employed. We demonstrate how the output differs from that achieved using an intensity image and hence illustrate how to determine features in range images using Laplacian operators. The main problem encountered when using outputs of second order derivative operators is that the feature map is very susceptible to noise, as every zero-crossing in the output is used to represent a feature point. However, comparative results using the Laplacian operators are presented and these demonstrate that a Laplacian approach to feature extraction in range images is not as susceptible to noise as the tradition approaches used on intensity data.

2   Edges in Range Images

In intensity images, edges are generally defined by significant changes in grey level values and hence may be modelled as steps or ramps. This is not so in the case of range image data, where there are three categories of edges to be extracted: jump edges, crease edges and smooth edges. Jump edges are found where range values are discontinuous, such as when one object occludes another. Crease edges occur where two surfaces meet; these can be two surfaces of positive gradient, two surfaces of negative gradient, or when a special instance of a crease edge (known as a roof edge) occurs at a local extremum. Crease edges prove difficult to detect as they do not correspond to large range variation and therefore are inclined to be suppressed along with noise [10]. A third edge type found in range images is the smooth edge, which is identified by continuity of the surface but discontinuity of the curvature. This particular type of edge is most difficult to detect, as, like the roof edge, it does not correspond to rapid range variation. Most edge detection techniques for range image data do not attempt to extract smooth edges; with the exception of [11] most other known techniques distinguish only between jump and crease edges. Although the main aim of edge detection is to accurately detect edges at the correct location, it is also desirable to classify the edges into edge types, and this paper aims to do so by differentiating between jump and crease edges and then characterising the crease edges into convex roof, concave roof, convex non-roof, and concave non-roof edges. Each of the edge subtypes considered is illustrated in Fig 1 where the range images depth values, z are defined as two planes, $S_1(x, y) = a_1 x + b_1 y + c_1$ and $S_2(x, y) = a_2 x + b_2 y + c_2$. Such plane equations are subsequently used to create a regularly distributed range image for each edge type.

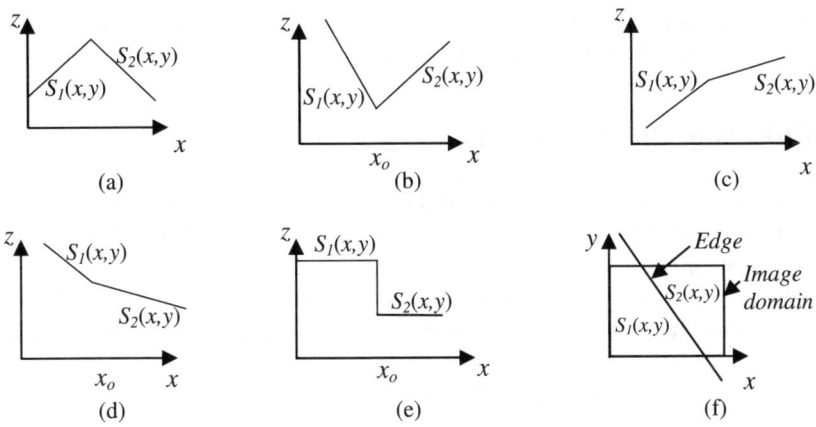

Fig. 1. Edge model: (a)-(e) edge model in x-z plane (a) Convex roof edge (b) Concave roof edge (c) Convex crease edge (d) concave crease edge (e) Jump edge (f) edge model in x-y plane

3 Range Data Representation

We consider a range image to be represented by a spatially irregular sample of values of a continuous function $u(x, y)$ of the depth value on a domain Ω. Our operator design is then based on the use of a quadrilateral mesh as illustrated in Fig 2 in which the nodes are the sample points. With each node i in the mesh is associated a piecewise bilinear basis function $\phi_i(x, y)$ which has the properties $\phi_i(x_j, y_j) = 1$ if $i - j$ and $\phi_i(x_j, y_j) = 0$ if $i \neq j$, where (x_j, y_j) are the co-ordinate of the nodal point j in the mesh. Thus $\phi_i(x, y)$ is a "tent-shaped" function with support restricted to a small neighbourhood centred on node I consisting of only those elements that have node i as a vertex. We then approximately represent the range image function u by a function $U(x, y) = \sum_{j=1}^{N} U_j \phi_j(x, y)$ in which the parameters $\{U_1, ..., U_N\}$ are mapped from the range image pixel value at the N irregularly located nodal points. Therefore,

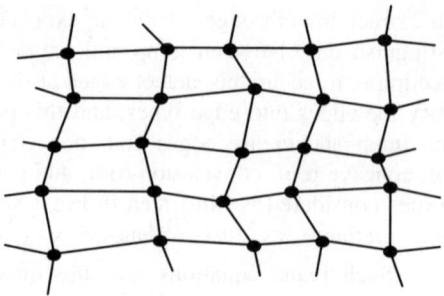

Fig. 2. Sample of the irregularly distributed range image

approximate image representation takes the form of a simple function (typically a low order polynomial) on each element and has the sampled range value U_j at node j.

4 Multiscale Operator Design

We describe the operator framework for the construction of the multiscale Laplacian operators as example of an 5×5 operator is illustrated in Fig 3. We create image operators that correspond to weak forms in the finite element method [12], in a similar manner as described in [13]. Corresponding to a second directional derivative $-\underline{\nabla} \cdot (\mathbf{B}\underline{\nabla}u)$, we may use test function $v \in H^1(\Omega)$ to define the weak form

$$Z(u) = -\int_\Omega \underline{\nabla} \cdot (\mathbf{B}\underline{\nabla}u)v\,d\Omega \tag{1}$$

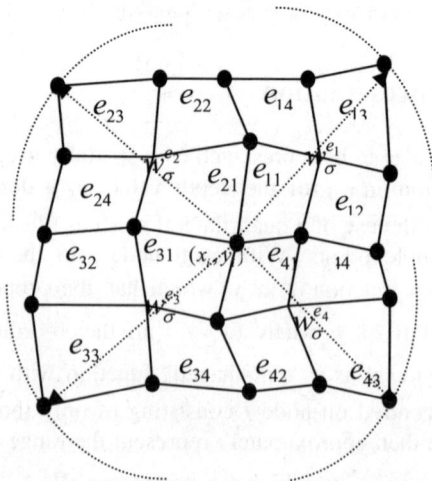

Fig. 3. Local 5×5 operator neighbourhood

However, as we are interested only in the isotropic form of the second order derivative, namely the Laplacian $-\underline{\nabla} \cdot (\underline{\nabla} u)$, this is equivalent to the general form in which the matrix $\mathbf{B}$ is the identity matrix $\mathbf{I}$.

Since we are focusing on the development of operators that can explicitly embrace the concept of size and shape variability, our design procedure uses a finite-dimensional test space size that explicitly embodies a size parameter σ that is determined by the local data distribution. Using such test functions, the Laplacian functional is defined as:

$$Z_i^\sigma (U) = - \int\limits_{\Omega_i^\sigma} \underline{\nabla} U \cdot \underline{\nabla} \psi_i^\sigma \, d\Omega_i \qquad (2)$$

This generalization allows sets of test functions $\psi_i^\sigma(x, y)$, $i = 1, \ldots, N$, to be used when defining irregular derivative based operators and the chosen test function is a Gaussian basis function. Hence, we embody scaling parameter that supports the development of scalable operators, and also naturally builds in Gaussian smoothing. Within any local neighbourhood, a different scale parameter is computed for each quadrant of the neighbourhood, enabling the Gaussian test function to adapt to the local area more accurately. As illustrated in Fig 3, $W_\sigma^{e_m}$ is chosen as the diagonal of the neighbourhood from the operator centre (x_i, y_i), and in each case the quadrant scale parameter $\sigma_m = W_\sigma^{e_m} / 1.96$ ensures that the diagonal of the quadrant through (x_i, y_i) encompasses 95% of the cross-section of the Gaussian.

The Laplacian operators: substituting the image representation from Section 3 $U(x, y) = \sum\limits_{j=1}^{N} U_j \phi_j(x, y)$ into the weak form $Z_i^\sigma (U) = - \int\limits_{\Omega_i^\sigma} \underline{\nabla} U \cdot \underline{\nabla} \psi_i^\sigma \, d\Omega_i$ gives

$$Z_i^\sigma (U) = -\sum_{j=1}^{N} K_{ij}^\sigma U_j - \sum_{j=1}^{N} L_{ij}^\sigma U_j \qquad (3)$$

Where K_{ij}^σ and L_{ij}^σ are given as

$$K_{ij}^\sigma = \int\limits_{\Omega_i^\sigma} \frac{\partial \phi_j}{\partial x} \frac{\partial \psi_i^\sigma}{\partial x} dxdy \quad \text{and} \quad L_{ij}^\sigma = \int\limits_{\Omega_i^\sigma} \frac{\partial \phi_j}{\partial y} \frac{\partial \psi_i^\sigma}{\partial y} dxdy \qquad (4)$$

These integrals need be computed only over the neighbourhood Ω_i^σ, rather than the entire image domain Ω, since ψ_i^σ has support restricted to Ω_i^σ. The integration is readily perform by mapping an irregular element to the standard square element $\hat{e}$ in order to facilitate the integration of the Gaussian test functions using simple quadrature rules. Fig 4 shows a typical quadrilateral element in which the nodes have locations in the x, y co-ordinates.

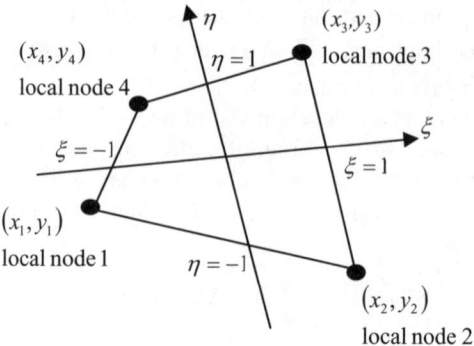

Fig. 4. 3×3 Operator, Quadrilateral Coordinates and Iso-parametric Mappings

The local (x, y) co-ordinate reference system for element e_m is mapped to a co-ordinate system (ξ, η) with $-1 \leq \xi \leq 1$ and $-1 \leq \eta \leq 1$ where (ξ, η) is a rectangular co-ordinate system in the standard element $\hat{e}$. The co-ordinate transformation is defined as

$$x = \frac{1}{4}(x_1(1-\xi)(1-\eta) + x_2(1+\xi)(1-\eta) + x_3(1+\xi)(1+\eta) + x_4(1-\xi)(1+\eta)) \quad (5)$$

$$y = \frac{1}{4}(y_1(1-\xi)(1-\eta) + y_2(1+\xi)(1-\eta) + y_3(1+\xi)(1+\eta) + y_4(1-\xi)(1+\eta)) \quad (6)$$

5 Laplacian Output

We demonstrate how the Laplacian output when using a range image differs from that when an intensity image is used. Given the 1D signal in Fig 5(a), if this represented a ramp edge in an intensity image, the edge is distinguished in the Laplacian output as a zero-crossing as illustrated in Fig 5(b). However, if the 1D signal in Fig 5(a) corresponds to a section of a range image, each line segment in the signal is equivalent to an object surface. Therefore, each of the peaks in the Laplacian output, as illustrated in Fig 5(b), represents an edge in a range image. Hence, features in range images can be found readily by computing the absolute value of the Laplacian output together with simple thresholding to ensure that only the most significant peaks are representative of edges. Thus the use of Laplacian operators for feature extraction in range images is less susceptible to noise than in intensity images [14].

For completeness, we present comparative edges maps for our proposed technique and for the scan-line approach in Fig 7. We present results for our 3×3, 5×5 and 7×7 irregular operators illustrating that the 3×3 operator finds the fine image detail and the larger operators find coarse details. It should be noted that our proposed technique automatically finds all features whereas the technique in [15] does not automatically find the object boundary via the scan-line approximation but instead, in all cases, assumes the boundary at the transition between data and no data in the range image.

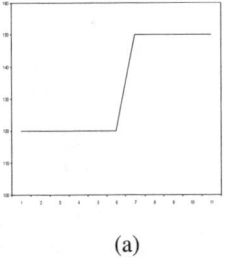   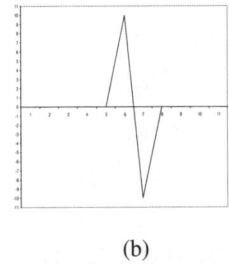

(a)   (b)

Fig. 5. (a) 1D signal; (b) Laplacian response

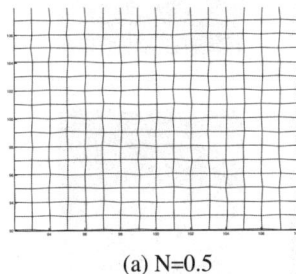   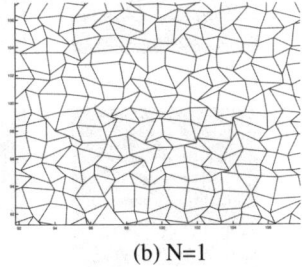

(a) N=0.5   (b) N=1

Fig. 6. Examples of irregular meshes

Typically, when Laplacian operators are applied to intensity images, the resulting edge maps are quite noisy. However the approach used here for the detection of features in 3D range data does not result in noisy feature maps, in fact the use of the built-in Gaussian function in the operator design works well as a noise suppressant.

In order to demonstrate the flexibility of the proposed multi-scale Laplacian operators for the purpose of 3D feature extraction over a range of irregularly distributed range images, we generate a set of synthetic test images for each edge type. We concern ourselves with two main edge types: jump and crease. Crease edges can be further defined as convex roof, concave roof, convex crease, and concave crease edges. To generate the images with irregularly distributed data, we create a regularly distributed image and add varying degrees of random values to the x and y co-ordinates such that $x = x + r_x$, $y = y + r_y$ where $N \geq r_x \geq 0$ and $N \geq r_y \geq 0$ and N defines the degree of irregularity; examples of such image representation is illustrated in Fig 6.

For evaluation purposes, we use the Figure of Merit measure [17] and compare our proposed technique with that of the well-known scan-line approximation algorithm [15]. In Fig 8 we show results using the Figure of Merit evaluation technique for a vertical edge within a range image using varying degrees of irregularity and no noise. In each case the threshold value used provides the best Figure of Merit; in addition, it is computed over all possible parameter combinations for the scan-line approach and again the optimal value selected. The results are computed on five randomly generated meshes, comprising five of each range edge type: Jump, convex roof, concave roof, convex crease, concave crease, and the Figure of Merit value is

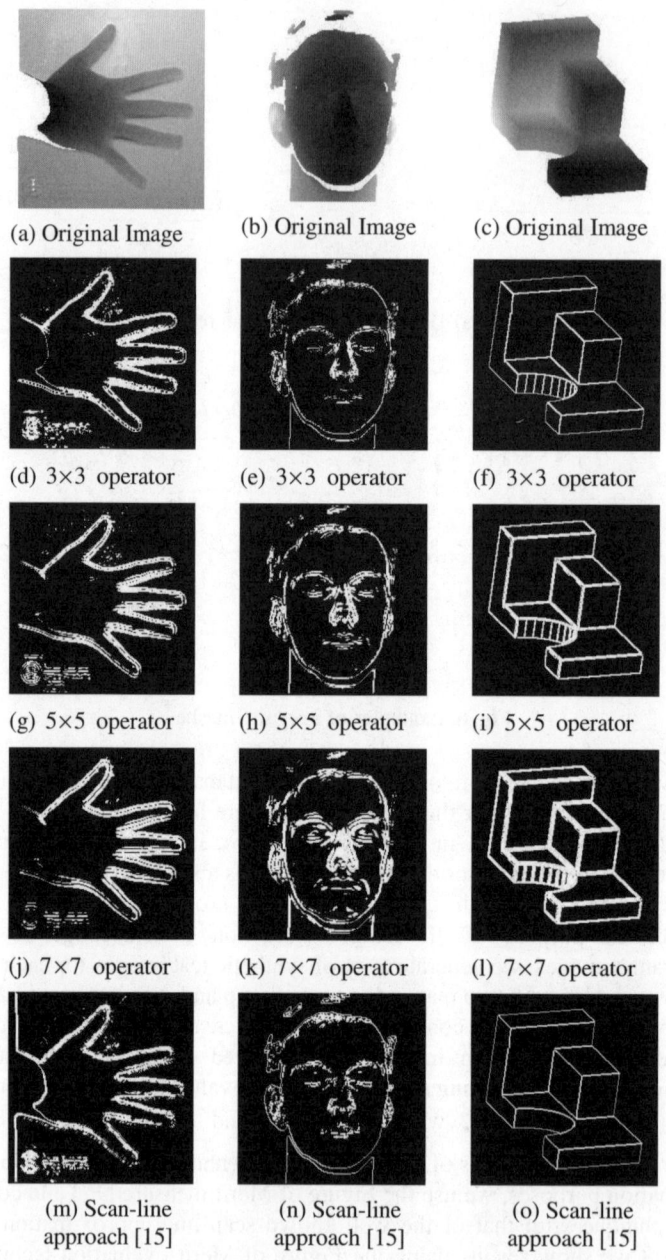

(a) Original Image　　(b) Original Image　　(c) Original Image

(d) 3×3 operator　　(e) 3×3 operator　　(f) 3×3 operator

(g) 5×5 operator　　(h) 5×5 operator　　(i) 5×5 operator

(j) 7×7 operator　　(k) 7×7 operator　　(l) 7×7 operator

(m) Scan-line　　(n) Scan-line　　(o) Scan-line
approach [15]　　approach [15]　　approach [15]

Fig. 7. Original range images from [16] and corresponding edge maps

averaged for each. The multiscale operators and the scan-line technique behaviour is a similar manner, however the larger scale operator clearly perform better than the other techniques in the case where the range data is very irregular in nature.

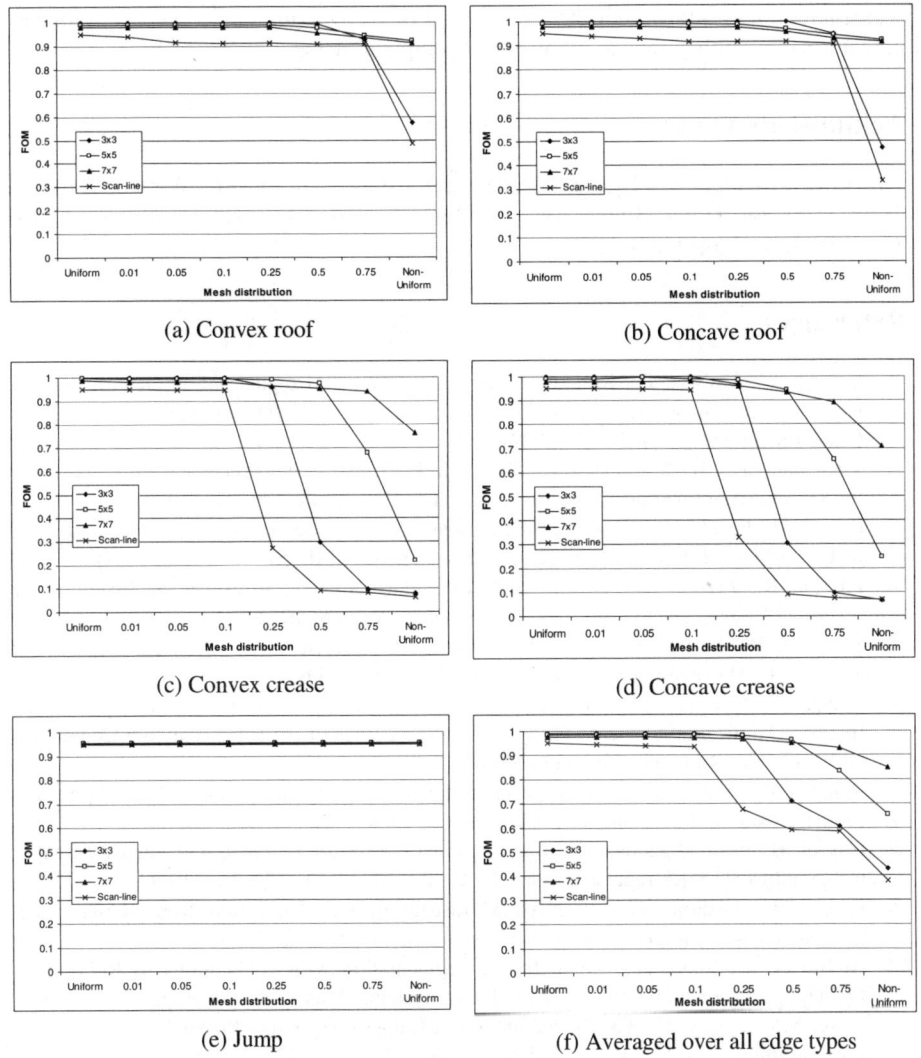

(a) Convex roof

(b) Concave roof

(c) Convex crease

(d) Concave crease

(e) Jump

(f) Averaged over all edge types

Fig. 8. Figure of Merit results for different edge types over a range of data irregularity

6 Summary and Future Work

We have presented a design procedure within the finite element framework for the development of shape-adaptive multiscale Laplacian operators that can be used directly on irregularly distributed 3D range data without the need for any image pre-processing. Through the use of the Figure of Merit evaluation measure, we have illustrated that our adaptive approach can accurately detect each edge sub-type over a varying degrees of data irregularity. We have compared performance with the scan-line approach of Jiang et al. [15] and found that the proposed approach is superior as the irregularity of the data increases. Future work will be evaluated with respect to existing edge based segmentation algorithms with the overall goal of recognizing objects in range images in real time for applications in robotics and computer vision.

Acknowledgments

This work was supported by the U.K Research Council via EPSRC. We would like to thank Professor Horst Bunke for providing us with the code for the scan line approximation algorithm in [15].

References

1. Vazquz, C., Dubois, E., Konrad, J.: Reconstruction of Irregularly-Sampled Images by Regularization in Spline Spaces. In: Proceedings of IEEE International Conference on Image Processing, pp. 405–408 (2002)
2. Yegnanarayana, B., Mariadassou, C.P., Saini, P.: Signal Reconstruction from Partial Data for Sensor Array Imaging applications. Signal Processing 19, 139–149 (1990)
3. Petrou, M., Piroddi, R., Chandra, S.: Irregularly Sampled Scenes. In: Proceedings of SPIE Image and Signal Processing for Remote Sensing, vol. SPIE5573 (2004)
4. Piroddi, R., Petrou, M.: Dealing with Irregular Samples, Advances in Imaging and Electron Physics, vol. 132, pp. 109–165. Elsevier, Amsterdam (2004)
5. Stasinski, R., Konrad, J.: POCS-Based Image Reconstruction from Irregularly-Spaced Samples. In: Proceedings of IEEE ICIP, pp. 315–318 (2000)
6. Vazquz, C., Konrad, J., Dubois, E.: Wavelet-Based Reconstruction of Irregularly-Sampled Images : Application to Stereo Imaging. In: Proceedings of IEEE International Conference on Image Processing, pp. 319–322 (2000)
7. Ramponi, G., Carrato, S.: An Adaptive Irregular Sampling Algorithm and its Application to Image Coding. Image and Vision Computing 19, 451–460 (2001)
8. Gunsel, B., et al.: Reconstruction and boundary detection of range and intensity images using multiscale MRF representations. In: CVIU, vol. 63, pp. 353–366 (1996)
9. Parvin, B., Medioni, G.: Adaptive Multiscale Feature Extraction from Range Data, Computer Vision Graphics. Image Understanding 45, 346–356 (1989)
10. Al-Hujazi, E., Sood, A.: Range Image Segmentation with applications to Robot Bin-Picking Using Vacuum Gripper. IEEE Trans. Systems, Man, and Cybernetics 20(6) (1990)
11. Jiang, X.Y., Bunke, H.: Fast Segmentation of Range Images into Planar Regions by Scan Line Grouping. Machine Vision and Applications 7(2), 115–122 (1994)
12. Becker, E.B., Carey, G.F., Oden, J.T.: Finite Elements: An Introduction. Prentice Hall, London (1981)
13. Coleman, S.A., Suganthan, S., Scotney, B.W.: Laplacian Operators for Direct Processing of Range Data. In: Proceeding of IEEE International Conference on Image Processing, San Antonio, Texas, pp. 261–264 (2007)
14. Ali, M., Clausi, D.: Using the Canny Edge Detector for Feature Extraction and Enhancement of Remote Sensing Images. In: Proceeding of IEEE Geoscience and Remote Sensing Symposium, Sydney, NSW, Australia, vol. 5, pp. 2298–2300 (2001)
15. Jiang, X.Y., Bunke, H.: Edge detection in range image based on scan line approximation. Computer Vision ad Image Understanding 73(2), 183–199 (1999)
16. http://sampl.eng.ohio-state.edu/~sampl/data/3DDB/RID/-index.htm
17. Abdou, I.E., Pratt, W.K.: Quantitative Design and Evaluation of Enhancement/ Threshold Edge Detectors. In: Proceedings of the IEEE, vol. 67(5) (1979)

Part VI

Learning

A System That Learns to Tag Videos by Watching Youtube

Adrian Ulges[1,2], Christian Schulze[2], Daniel Keysers[2], and Thomas M. Breuel[1,2]

[1] Department of Computer Science, Technical University of Kaiserslautern
{a_ulges,tmb}@informatik.uni-kl.de
[2] Image Understanding and Pattern Recognition Group
German Research Center for Artificial Intelligence (DFKI), Kaiserslautern
{schulze,keysers}@iupr.dfki.de

Abstract. We present a system that automatically tags videos, i.e. detects high-level semantic concepts like objects or actions in them. To do so, our system does not rely on datasets manually annotated for research purposes. Instead, we propose to use videos from online portals like youtube.com as a novel source of training data, whereas tags provided by users during upload serve as ground truth annotations. This allows our system to learn autonomously by automatically downloading its training set.

The key contribution of this work is a number of large-scale quantitative experiments on real-world online videos, in which we investigate the influence of the individual system components, and how well our tagger generalizes to novel content. Our key results are: (1) Fair tagging results can be obtained by a late fusion of several kinds of visual features. (2) Using more than one keyframe per shot is helpful. (3) To generalize to different video content (e.g., another video portal), the system can be adapted by expanding its training set.

Keywords: content-based video retrieval, automatic video annotation, online videos.

1 Introduction

During the last years, online video has evolved as a source of information and entertainment for users world-wide. For an efficient access to this video data, most commercial providers rely on text-based search via user-generated tags – an indexing that requires manual work and is thus time-consuming and incomplete.

In parallel, content-based techniques have been developed that try to use the content of a video to infer its semantics. To achieve such "tagging", i.e. an automatic annotation of videos with high-level concepts like objects, locations, or actions, systems are usually trained on a set of labeled videos. Acquiring such ground truth information manually is costly and poses a key limitation for the practical use of automatic annotation systems.

In this paper, we introduce a system that learns to tag videos from a different kind of training data, namely by watching video clips downloaded from online

A. Gasteratos, M. Vincze, and J.K. Tsotsos (Eds.): ICVS 2008, LNCS 5008, pp. 415–424, 2008.

(a)   (b)   (c)   (d)   (e)

Fig. 1. Some sample keyframes extracted from videos with the tag desert. Tagging such material is made difficult by the visual diversity of the concept (a,b,c), shots not directly visually linked to to the tag (d), and low production quality (e).

video portals like youtube.com. Thereby, tags provided by users when uploading content serve as ground truth annotations. Our work is thus targeted at online video (1) as an *application* (our system proposes adequate tags for videos and can thus support users with tagging or keyword search), and (2) as a *data source* for visual learning: online videos are publicly available and come in a quantity that is unmatched by datasets annotated for research purposes. We envision this data to complement (or even replace) existing training sets.

Despite the enormous diversity of online video content and the fact that it shows lots of irrelevant scenes (as is illustrated in Figure 1), we present a prototype that shows how visual learning of semantic concepts from online video is possible (a demo can be found at http://demo.iupr.org/videotagging). Compared to our previous workshop publication [17], we present several novel quantitative experiments with our prototype on large-scale datasets of real-world online videos. Our key results are the following: (1) A fusion of multiple feature modalities is essential for a successful tagging. (2) Using more than a single keyframe per shot improves tagging performance. (3) The system adapts well to different video data if expanding its training set.

2   Related Work

An area strongly related to our work via the use of keyframes is automatic image annotation, which has been dealt with by modeling latent visual concepts in images [3] or joint occurrences of local descriptors and tags [10]. Also, multiple instance learning methods have been used to detect local features associated with a concept [19]. Image annotation is also performed at a large scale (see the 'Automatic Linguistic Indexing of Pictures - Real Time' [ALIPR] server [6]). Closest to ours, however, is the work by Fergus et al. [2], who introduced the idea of learning from low-quality online data for the domain of images.

If dealing with video content, the detection of semantic concepts often follows a keyframe extraction for efficiency reasons, leading to an image retrieval problem (e.g., [10,18]). A valuable source of information beyond such static image content is *motion*, which has for example been employed in form of motion descriptors [8].

As far as video annotation is concerned, a lot of related work has been done as part of TRECVID[1], an annual video retrieval contest that hosts quantitative

---

[1] http://www-nlpir.nist.gov/projects/t01v/

evaluations on an extensive corpus of news video. In its "high-level features" task, the automatic tagging of shots is addressed. To boost standardization and comparability of results, groups share large sets of manual annotations [12], low-level features, and baseline results [15].

When dealing with online video content, several characteristics need to be respected: First, online video comes in a greater diversity, ranging from home video to commercial TV productions. Second, annotations in TRECVID are done on shot level, while we are interested in tagging whole videos. To the best of our knowledge, no prior research with the focus on online video tagging exists.

3   Our Approach

Given a video X and a semantic concept t (in the following referred to as a "tag"), the problem of automatic annotation is to return a "score" $P(t|X)$, i.e. the probability that the tag is present in the video.

Figure 2 gives an overview of our system architecture: we represent a video X by a set of representative keyframes $X_1, .., X_n$. Each keyframe X_i is fed to several "feature pipelines" $F_1, .., F_k$, each using visual features of a certain type to return a score $P_{F_j}(t|X_i)$. These pieces of evidence are first fused over all keyframes of a video, obtaining feature-specific scores $P_{F_j}(t|X)$. Second, those are again fused over all feature pipelines in a late-fusion step, obtaining the final score $P(t|X)$. In the following, the system components are described in the order of processing.

3.1   Keyframe Extraction

A standard way to extract a set of representative keyframes for each video is to segment the video into shots and use one frame per shot as a keyframe. This causes considerable information loss for long shots containing strong camera motion and scene activity, which is why an adaptive approach providing multiple keyframes per shot seems more adequate for online videos.

We use a divide-and-conquer approach that delivers multiple keyframes per shot in two steps: first, shot boundary detection is applied, for which reliable standard techniques exist [7]. Second, for each of the resulting shots, a clustering approach is applied similar to [11]: we extract MPEG-7 color layout descriptors [9] for all frames in a shot and then fit a Gaussian mixture model to

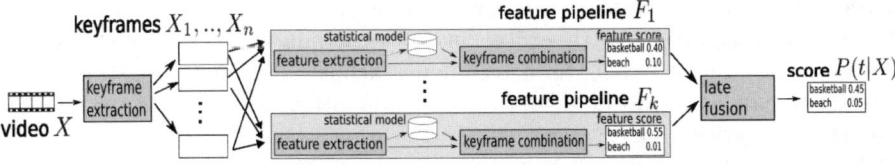

Fig. 2. An overview of our tagging system: a video X is represented by keyframes $X_1, .., X_n$. Each of them is fed to feature pipelines $F_1, .., F_k$, in which visual features are extracted and give scores $P_{F_j}(X_i)$ for each keyframe. These posteriors are fused over all keyframes, and finally over all features, to obtain the result $P(t|X)$.

the resulting feature set using k-means. For each mixture component, the frame next to the center is extracted as a keyframe. The number of components is determined using the Bayesian Information Criterion (BIC) [13].

3.2 Feature Pipelines

A key aspect of our tagging system is the combination of several visual features. We organize these in "feature pipelines" $F_1, .., F_k$, each of which represents a type of visual feature (e.g., color histograms) and gives a feature-specific score $P_{F_j}(t|X_i)$ for a keyframe X_i. We use three feature pipelines outlined in the following. Note, however, that more pipelines can be integrated easily.

Pipeline 1 - Color and Texture: This feature pipeline uses frame-level descriptors based on color (RGB color histograms with $8 \times 8 \times 8$ bins) and texture (Tamura features [16]). Both features are combined by early fusion (i.e. concatenated) to obtain a joint feature vector $F_1(X_i)$.

As a statistical model, we use nearest neighbor matching as illustrated in Figure 3: given a training set of tagged keyframes Y, we find the nearest neighbor $x' := \arg\min_{y \in Y} ||F_1(y) - F_1(X_i)||_2$, and the score for a tag t is a vote for the tag of this neighbor:

$$P_{F_1}(t|X_i) := \delta(t, t(x')) \tag{1}$$

Pipeline 2 - Motion: Some semantic concepts (e.g., `interview`) can be characterized better by a discriminative motion pattern than by color or texture. To do so, we use a simple compressed domain feature of block motion vectors extracted by the MPEG-4 codec XViD[2] to describe *what* motion occurs as well as *where* in the frames it occurs.

For this purpose, the spatial domain is divided into 4×3 regular tiles, and for each tile a two-dimensional 7×7 histogram over the 2D components of all motion vectors in a shot is stored (vectors are clipped to $[-20, 20] \times [-20, 20]$). By concatenating all those histograms, a 588-dimensional descriptor is extracted on shot level, i.e. it is the same for all keyframes in a shot.

Like for color and texture, nearest neighbor matching is used to model the keyframe score.

Pipeline 3 - Visual Words: Modern recognition systems have been successful by representing images with collections of local image regions (or "patches", respectively). These patch-based techniques achieve excellent robustness with respect to partial occlusion, deformations, and clutter, which is why we adapt a similar approach for our system.

More precisely, we use a "bag-of-visual-words" representation [1,2,14]. This model clusters visual features according to their appearance into patch categories referred to as "visual words". Histograms over these visual words indicate the

---

[2] www.xvid.org

Fig. 3. Left: In nearest neighbor matching, a test frame (top row) votes for the tag of its nearest neighbor in the training set (bottom row). **Right:** The maximum entropy model learns these sample patches as discriminative for the tag `eiffeltower`.

frequency with which all kinds of features appear in a frame, an analogy to the "bag-of-words" model from textual information retrieval.

A vocabulary of 500 visual words was learned by sampling patches of size 32×32 pixels at regular steps of 16 pixels and clustering them using k-means. Patches are described by low-frequency discrete cosine transform (DCT) coefficients in YUV space. We extract 36 coefficients for the intensity, and 21 for each chroma component in a zigzag pattern, obtaining a 78-dimensional patch descriptor.

As a statistical model for the resulting 500-bin histograms, we adapt a discriminative approach based on the maximum-entropy principle, which has successfully been applied to object recognition before [1]. The posterior is modeled in a log-linear fashion:

$$P_{F_3}(t|X_i) \propto \exp\left(\alpha_t + \sum_{c=1}^{500} \lambda_{tc} h_i^c\right), \tag{2}$$

where h_i^c is entry number c in the visual word histogram for frame X_i. The parameters $\{\alpha_t, \lambda_{tc}\}$ are estimated from a training set of tagged frames using an iterative scaling algorithm [1].

3.3 Fusion

From several keyframes of the input video and from several feature pipelines, we obtain many weak pieces of evidence in form of scores indicating the presence of semantic concepts. These are fused in two steps to obtain a global score.

Keyframe Fusion: For a fusion over the keyframes $X_1, .., X_n$ of a video X, we use the well-known *sum rule* from classifier combination:

$$P_{F_j}(t|X) = \frac{1}{n} \sum_{i=1}^{n} P_{F_j}(t|X_i) \tag{3}$$

Late Fusion: To combine scores obtained from several feature pipelines, several standard measures from classifier combination can be applied (like the sum rule, product rule, etc.). We present a small study in the following experimental section (Figure 5), in which we evaluate several combination strategies.

4 Experiments

We present quantitative experiments on real-world online videos to study (1) how the single components of the system influence its overall performance, and (2) how the system can be adapted to different kinds of video data.

Most of our experiments are done on a database of real-world online videos we downloaded from the video portal youtube.com. We selected 22 tags manually, including activities (e.g., riot, sailing), objects (e.g., cat, helicopter), and locations (e.g., desert, beach). For the complete list of tags, please visit our website http://demo.iupr.org/videotagging/tagging-description.html.

We used the youtube API to download 100 videos per tag (total database: 2200 videos / 194 hrs.). The whole set was separated into a training set (50 videos per tag), a validation set, and a test set (both 25 videos per tag). To avoid training on the testing data, the test set was only used for the final evaluation.

A problem for the evaluation are duplicate or slightly edited videos uploaded multiple times by different users. We identify and remove (near-)duplicates in two steps: First, exact duplicates are detected automatically using a signature matching similar to [4]. Second, near-duplicates are removed by a manual check of videos that gave suspiciously good results in our tagging experiments.

4.1 Feature Modalities

Figure 4 illustrates the influence of several feature pipelines on the performance on the system (all fusion of features was done using the sum rule): when starting only with color and texture (feature pipeline 1), a mean average precision (MAP) of 25.4% is achieved. Though motion (feature pipeline 2) alone does not improve performance, it supports the system when combined with color and texture (MAP 27.1%). An in-depth analysis reveals the strongest improvements for motion-affine concepts like videoblog (from 17 to 37%) and riot (from 14 to 23%).

Visual words by themselves (feature pipeline 3) give an even better performance, particularly for objects like eiffeltower (here, the MAP was improved

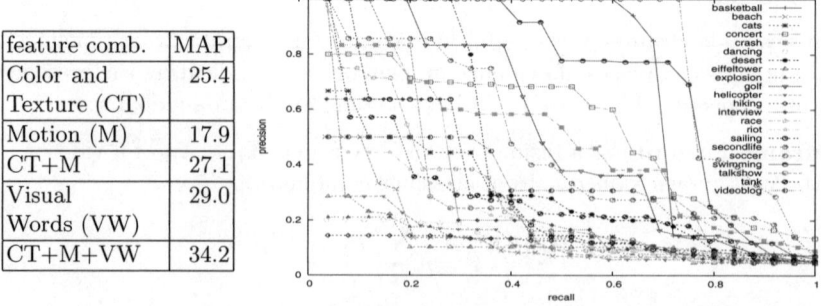

feature comb.	MAP
Color and Texture (CT)	25.4
Motion (M)	17.9
CT+M	27.1
Visual Words (VW)	29.0
CT+M+VW	34.2

Fig. 4. Left: Experimental results for several feature combinations in terms of mean average precision (MAP). **Right:** The recall-precision curves when fusing all features. The average precision per concept varies between 81% (soccer) and 11% (hiking).

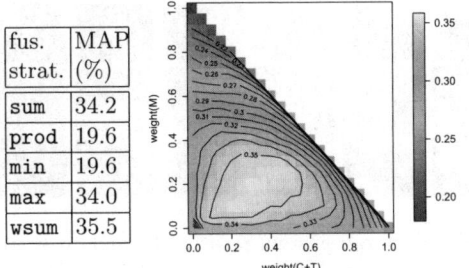

fus. strat.	MAP (%)
sum	34.2
prod	19.6
min	19.6
max	34.0
wsum	35.5

feature combination	MAP (%)		
	adapt	first	reg
Color and Texture (CT)	25.4	16.8	29.4
Motion (M)	17.9	16.6	16.2
CT+M	27.1	21.7	24.7
Visual Words (VW)	29.0	25.4	28.2
CT+M+VW	34.2	31.6	34.8

Fig. 5. Left: Tagging performance when using several combination strategies. **Center:** The MAP on the test set plotted against the weights for color+texture and motion. The sum rule $(0.33, 0.33)$ and the weights learned from the validation set $(0.45, 0.2)$ are both near to the optimal peak $(0.3, 0.2)$. **Right:** Comparing our keyframe extraction (adapt) with two baselines.

from 7.3% to 70.6%). This is because the maximum-entropy model associates patches with a weight and thus emphasizes discriminative features of an object, as is illustrated in Figure 3. Finally, a sum rule fusion of all features achieves the best overall performance.

We also compared the sum rule fusion to several other classifier combination strategies. (Figure 5, left). The sum rule performs superior to other methods, which agrees with earlier results [5] that claim good robustness properties against noise in the weak (in our case, keyframe) estimates. Our results confirm that this robustness is crucial in our context, since many keyframes may not be visually related to the true tag and thus give misleading scores.

We also tested a more general approach, namely a *weighted sum*:

$$P(t|X) = \sum_{j=1}^{3} w_j P_{F_j}(t|X),\qquad(4)$$

where the feature weights $(w_1, w_2, w_3) = (0.45, 0.2, 0.35)$ are learned from the validation set (i.e. color and texture are given the highest weight, and motion the lowest). The left Table in Figure 5 indicates that by learning feature weights from the validation set, we obtain a slightly better performance with 35.5%.

An in-depth view of the performance for all 22 tags is given in form of recall-precision curves in Figure 4. Obviously, a successful tagging strongly depends on the concept: Sports like soccer and swimming are easy to tag due to their restricted color layout and low diversity in appearance, while concepts with a high visual diversity are difficult, like explosion or dancing.

4.2 Keyframe Extraction

In this experiment, we compare our keyframe extraction (Section 3.1) with two baseline methods to investigate whether our adaptive approach is in fact essential for a successful tagging. The first baseline named first uses only the first frame

Fig. 6. Shots from a TV news dataset for which our system returns the highest scores, for the concepts `interview`(top), `swimming`(center), and `riot`(bottom). True positives are highlighted in green, false positives in red.

of a shot as a keyframe (which is often done in practice). It generates only 56% keyframes compared to ours (ca. 97.000). The right table in Figure 5 shows that the use of additional keyframes leads to performance increases between 2 and 9% – i.e., tagging is improved by using multiple keyframes per shot.

Note that our clustering approach adapts to the activity of a shot, i.e. it produces more keyframes if the content of a shot varies. To answer whether this adaptivity is essential for tagging, we compare our approach to a second baseline (`regular`) that regularly samples keyframes at an interval of about 7 seconds. This baseline generates more keyframes than our approach (8.2%), and does not adapt to the content of a shot. The table shows about the same performance as for our adaptive method. This result indicates that the use of adaptive keyframes plays a negligible role.

4.3   Generalization to Different Video Data

Obviously, our system makes use of redundancy in youtube videos, which may occur due to duplicate shots or series sharing common production styles and locations. While we explicitly eliminate the former, our system still implicitly uses the latter, weaker type as is illustrated by the rightmost match in Figure 3 (left). While this helps the system to tag videos from the online portal trained on, it is unclear how the system generalizes to different content. This is why we tested our system trained on `youtube` on two other data sources.

TV News Data: This test set contains 5.5 hours of unlabeled German news video (ca. 4.000 keyframes). Given a tag, our system (all three feature pipelines, sum rule fusion) returns the TV shots sorted by their scores. In Figure 6, we illustrate the shots with top scores for three tags we expect to occur in news video. For `interview`, the system gives a near-perfect result (only 2 false positives). For `swimming`, many false positives can be observed, since the system is attracted by blue background that has not been present in the training set. Finally, we obtain four hits for the concept `riot`.

Though – due to the lack of ground truth – no quantitative results can be presented. , this result generally indicates that tagging of TV data can be learned from online video data.

training	test set	
set	youtube	revver
youtube	37.0	11.1
revver	15.7	31.4
both	33.6	26.4

Fig. 7. Left: Sample frames for the concept `crash` from `youtube` (top) and `revver` (bottom). While `youtube` videos show mostly car and motorbike crashes, `revver` contains also skiing and biking accidents. **Right:** Our results show that a joint tagger for multiple video portals (here, `youtube` and `revver`) can be successful if trained on all data sources.

Revver Video Portal: For this experiment, we use videos from the portal `revver.com`. We created a dataset similar to the `youtube` one. Two concepts were left out, and for four other concepts less than 100 videos were found. We used the system setup that gave the best results on the `youtube` data (all features, sum rule fusion). Since no further parameter tuning was done, we split the `revver` data into a $\frac{2}{3}$ training set and $\frac{1}{3}$ test set.

Figure 7 illustrates that the system generalizes poorly if trained on one portal and applied to the other. An explanation for this is illustrated in Figure 7 for the example of the concept `crash`: `youtube` videos (top row) contain lots of TV material showing car and motorbike races, while `revver` videos show significantly more home video content (here, skiing or biking). Obviously, a system that is not trained on this novel content cannot correctly tag such data.

Therefore, we studied if a generalized tagger can be created by training the system on *both* data sources. We obtain a system that performs comparable (about 4% worse) to the specialized systems trained for the single portals. This demonstrates how a general tagger can be created by adapting the training set.

5 Conclusions

In this paper, we have introduced a system that learns to detect semantic concepts in videos by watching content from online video portals. Our experimental results show that fair tagging results can be obtained when combining several visual feature modalities, namely color, texture, motion, and a patch-based approach.

However, two key aspects of learning from online videos have been neglected so far: (1) Can training be adapted better for certain concept types (e.g., objects vs. locations)? (2) Can the system be made robust to shots in a video that are irrelevant for a concept? So far, our answer to both questions has been the integration of multiple feature modalities using a robust sum rule fusion. We expect a better tagging by addressing these problems using explicit models, and therefore envision our system to be a baseline for future work.

Acknowledgements

This work was supported in part by the Stiftung Rheinland-Pfalz für Innovation, project InViRe (961-386261/791).

References

1. Deselaers, T., Keysers, D., Ney, H.: Discriminative Training for Object Recognition Using Image Patches. In: CVPR, Washington, DC, pp. 157–162 (2005)
2. Fergus, R., Fei-Fei, L., Perona, P., Zisserman, A.: Learning Object Categories from Google's Image Search. Computer Vision 2, 1816–1823 (2005)
3. Barnard, K., Duygulu, P., Forsyth, D., de Freitas, N., Bleib, D., Jordan, M.: Matching Words and Pictures. J. Mach. Learn. Res. 3, 1107–1135 (2003)
4. Hoad, T.C., Zobel, J.: Detection of Video Sequences using Compact Signatures. ACM Trans. Inf. Systems 24(1), 1–50 (2006)
5. Kittler, J., Hatef, M., Duin, R., Matas, J.: On Combining Classifiers. IEEE Trans. Pattern Anal. Mach. Intell. 20(3), 226–239 (1998)
6. Li, J., Wang, J.: Real-time Computerized Annotation of Pictures. In: Intern. Conf. on Multimedia, Santa Barbara, CA, pp. 911–920 (2006)
7. Lienhart, R.: Reliable Transition Detection in Videos: A Survey and Practitioner's Guide. Int. J. of Image and Graphics 1(3), 286–469 (2001)
8. Ma, Y.-F., Zhang, H.-J.: Motion Pattern-based Video Classification and Retrieval. EURASIP J. Appl. Signal Proc. 1, 199–208 (2003)
9. Manjunath, B.S., Ohm, J.-R., Vasudevan, V.V., Yamada, A.: Color and Texture Descriptors. IEEE Trans. on Circuits Syst. for Video Techn. 11(6), 703–715 (2001)
10. Feng, S.L., Manmatha, R., Lavrenko, V.: Multiple Bernoulli Relevance Models for Image and Video Annotation. In: CVPR, Washington, DC, pp. 1002–1009 (2004)
11. Hammoud, R., Mohr, R.: A Probabilistic Framework of Selecting Effective Key Frames for Video Browsing and Indexing. In: Intern. Worksh. on Real-Time Img. Seq. Anal., Oulu, Finland, pp. 79–88 (2000)
12. Naphade, M., Smith, J., Tesic, J., Chang, S.-F., Hsu, W., Kennedy, L., Hauptmann, A., Curtis, J.: Large-Scale Concept Ontology for Multimedia. IEEE Multimedia 3(13), 86–91 (2006)
13. Schwarz, G.: Estimating the Dimension of a Model. Ann. of Stat. 6(2), 461–464 (2003)
14. Sivic, J., Zisserman, A.: Video Google: A Text Retrieval Approach to Object Matching in Videos. In: ICCV, Washington, DC, pp. 1470–1477 (2003)
15. Snoek, C., et al.: The MediaMill TRECVID 2006 Semantic Video Search Engine. TRECVID Workshop, Gaithersburg, MD (2006) (unreviewed workshop paper)
16. Tamura, H., Mori, S., Yamawaki, T.: Textural Features Corresponding to Visual Perception. IEEE Trans. on Sys., Man, Cybern. 8(6), 460–472 (1978)
17. Ulges, A., Schulze, C., Keysers, D., Breuel, T.: Content-based Video Tagging for Online Video Portals. In: MUSCLE/ImageCLEF Workshop, Budapest (2007)
18. Snoek, C., Worring, M., van Gemert, J., Geusebroek, J.-M., Smeulders, A.: The Challenge Problem for Automated Detection of 101 Semantic Concepts in Multimedia. In: Intern. Conf. on Multimedia, Santa Barbara, CA, pp. 421–430 (2006)
19. Yang, C., Lozano-Perez, T.: Image Database Retrieval with Multiple-Instance Learning Techniques. In: Int. Conf. on Data Eng., San Diego, CA, pp. 233–243 (2000)

Geo-located Image Grouping Using Latent Descriptions

Marco Cristani, Alessandro Perina, and Vittorio Murino

Computer Science Department, Università degli studi di Verona,
Strada le Grazie 15, 37134 Verona, Italy

Abstract. Image categorization is undoubtedly one of the most challenging problems faced in Computer Vision. The related literature is plenty of methods dedicated to specific classes of images; further, commercial systems are also going to be advertised in the market. Nowadays, additional data can also be associated to the images, enriching its semantic interpretation beyond the pure appearance. This is the case of *geo-location data*, that contain information about the geographical place where an image has been captured. This data allow, if not require, a different management of the images, for instance, to the purpose of easy retrieval and visualization from a geo-referenced image repository. This paper constitutes a first step in this sense, presenting a method for geo-referenced image categorization. The solution presented here places in the wide literature on the statistical latent descriptions, where the probabilistic Latent Semantic Analysis (pLSA) is one of the most known representative. In particular, we extend the pLSA paradigm, introducing a latent variable modelling the geographical area in which an image has been captured. In this way, we are able to describe the entire image data-set grouping effectively proximal images with similar appearance. Experiments on categorization have been carried out, employing a well-known geographical image repository: results are actually very promising, opening new interesting challenges and applications in this research field.

1 Introduction

Categorizing pictures in an automatic and meaningful way is the root challenge in all the retrieval-by-content systems [1]. Nowadays, the common working hypothesis upon which most categorization algorithms are built is that images are located in a single repository, and described with features vectors which summarize their visual properties. Recently, this classical framework has been improved with the use of textual labels or *tags*, associated to the images. Textual labels are usually given by a human user and constrain the number of ways an automatic system can categorize an image.

Very recently, this framework has been further updated with the introduction on the market of several cheap GPS devices, mounted on cameras. Such devices automatically assign tags to the captured pictures, indicating the geographical position (latitude, longitude) of the shot. This capability charmed

A. Gasteratos, M. Vincze, and J.K. Tsotsos (Eds.): ICVS 2008, LNCS 5008, pp. 425–434, 2008.
© Springer-Verlag Berlin Heidelberg 2008

researchers and web designers, which understood the potential scenario of a novel and more advanced way of sharing pictures, succeeding and outperforming the "non-spatial" public image databases. This yielded to the creation of global repositories for the *geo-located* images, as in Panoramio[1], and the addition of novel functionalities for the display of geo-located images in Google Earth[2] and Flickr[3].

In this new framework, novel *geo-located image categorization* algorithms can be developed, taking into account the geographic locations of the images, other than their visual aspect. The underlying idea is to put in the same category images which are visually similar and geographically proximal. Therefore, particular geographical areas can be described as geo-visual categories by means of the (visually similar) pictures which have been taken within by the human users.

In this way, the geo-located categorization eases the analysis of the geo-located databases. Nowadays, the exploration of a geo-located image database occurs by zooming on a map in a desired location and visualizing a set of randomly sampled images lying in the related neighborhood. This layout becomes very unattractive and uncomfortable in presence of a massive number of images, as it is currently in all the databases considered. With a geo-located categorization policy, the exploration of a geo-located database can be strongly improved. Grouping the images for similarity and proximity in *geo-categories* permits to consider and visualize a small number of representative (member) images per category. In this way, a better global visualization scheme can be exploited, in which each depicted picture represents a different geographical pattern; in other words, each different zone depicted on the map can be visualized by means of few good representatives.

In this paper, we propose a novel statistical framework aimed at the geo-located image categorization, based on a *latent* representation. Latent or topic models, such as the ones built through probabilistic Latent Semantic Analysis (pLSA)[2], were originally used in the text understanding community for unsupervised topic discovery in a corpus of documents. In Computer Vision, topic models have been used to discover scene classes, or visual topics, from a collection of unlabeled images. Here the input data are the 'bags of visterms', i.e. histograms of local visual aspects extracted from the images. Co-occurrences of visterms in the images form the topics, which can be considered as higher level descriptions of the images. As a result, images can be categorized according to the topics they contain.

Here, we take inspiration by the pLSA framework, extending it, introducing in addition to the (visual) topic a *geo-topic*. The geo-topic is associated to the visual topic information, via a conditional dependency relation: in practice, each geo-topic describes visually a geographical area, by means of a distribution on the visual topics. We called this paradigm *Geographic-pLSA* (G-pLSA).

---

[1] http://www.panoramio.com

[2] http://earth.google.com/

[3] http://www.flickr.com/

In the following, we will detail how the G-pLSA performs when applied to a consistent database, built from the Panoramio repository, providing also comparative tests of categorization. Then, we explain how the visualization of a geo-located image database can be eased by means of G-pLSA.

The rest of the paper is organized as follows. In Sec. 2, background notions on pLSA are given. Then, in Sec. 3, the outline of our system for geo-categorization is detailed. Sec.4 illustrates the experiments carried out to validate our framework, and concludes the paper. A conclusion section is omitted here due to the lack of space.

2 Probabilistic Latent Semantic Analysis

In this section, we briefly review the probabilistic Latent Semantic Analysis (pLSA), in its adaption to visual data, adopting the notation of [2]. The input is a dataset of N documents (images) $d_i, i = 1, \ldots, N$, each containing local regions found by interest operators, whose appearance has been quantized into M visual words $w_j, j = 1, \ldots, M$ [3]. Therefore, the dataset is encoded by a co-occurrence matrix of size $M \times N$, where the location $< w_j, d_i >$ indicates the number of (visual) words w_j in the document d_i. The model incorporates a single latent topic variable, z, that links the occurrence of word w_j to document d_i. In formulae:

$$P(w_j, d_i) = \sum_{k=1}^{Z} P(w_j|z_k)P(z_k|d_i)P(d_i) \tag{1}$$

As a result, we have obtained a decomposition of a $M \times N$ matrix into a $M \times Z$ matrix and a $Z \times N$ one. Each image is modeled as a probability distribution over the topics, i.e., $P(z_k|d_i)$; the distribution $P(w_j|z_k)$ encodes the topic z_k as a probabilistic co-occurrence of words. The graphical model of this approach is depicted in Fig.1a. The distributions of the model, $P(w_j|z_k)$ and $P(z_k|d_i)$, are learned using Expectation Maximization (EM) [4]. The E-step computes the posterior over the topic, $P(z_k|w_j, d_i)$ and then the M-step updates the distributions; this maximizes the likelihood L of the model over the data

$$L = \prod_{i=1}^{N} \prod_{j=1}^{M} P(w_j, d_i)^{n(w_j, d_i)} \tag{2}$$

where $n(w_j, d_i)$ indicates the number of occurrences of word w_j in the document d_i. For a deeper review of pLSA, see [2]; for an application on scene recognition, see [5].

3 The Proposed Method: G-pLSA

In G-pLSA, we have N geo-located images $\{l_i\}, i = 1, \ldots, N$, indexed as couples of latitude and longitude coordinate values. Associated to each i-th couple, we have a $M \times 1$ counting array $n(w, l_i)$ of visual words, for a total of n_i words. Our

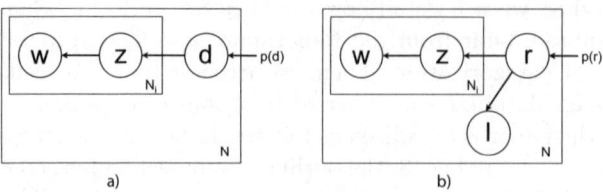

Fig. 1. Graphical models: a) pLSA; b) G-pLSA. N is the number of images, N_i the number of visual words in the $i-$th image.

purpose is to simultaneously extract *two* different kinds of latent classes underlying the observed data: the *visual* topic and the *geo*-topic classes. The visual topic class z encodes, as in the original pLSA framework, probabilistic co-occurrences of visual words. The geo-topic class $r \in R = \{r_1, ..., r_R\}$ serves to partition the entire geographic area spanned by the geo-located images into regions, each one characterized by a specific set of visual topics. The joint distribution over visual words and geo-located images can be factorized as follows:

$$P(w_j, l_i) = \sum_{k=1}^{Z} P(w_j|z_k) \sum_{c=1}^{R} P(z_k|r_c) p(r_c|l_i) P(l_i) \tag{3}$$

In the formula above, we have Z and R visual and geo-topic instances, respectively. The meaning of $P(w|z)$ is the same as in the original pLSA; the distribution $P(z|r)$ is a $Z \times R$ matrix, where each entry $<z_k, r_c>$ represents the probability that visual topic z_k is present in the region r_c. The density $p(r|l)$ is encoded as a $R \times N$ matrix, and models the likelihood of being in a particular region r_c, given the geo-located image l_i. Finally, $P(l)$ functions as the classical document-distribution $P(d)$ of pLSA.

An alternative consistent factorization of the model can be obtained by applying the Bayes theorem to $p(r|l)p(l)$, as done in a similar way in the classical pLSA in [2], obtaining the joint probability

$$P(w_j, l_i) = \sum_{k=1}^{Z} P(w_j|z_k) \sum_{c=1}^{R} P(z_k|r_c) p(l_i|r_c) p(r_c) \tag{4}$$

which permits to characterize geo-topics in both visual sense by means of $P(z_k|r_c)$, and under a topological aspect through $p(l_i|r_c)$. The correspondent graphical model is depicted in Fig.1b. In this paper, we assume a Gaussian form for $p(l|r)$, *i.e.*,

$$p(l_i|r_c) = \mathcal{N}(l_i; \mu_{r_c}, \Sigma_{r_c}) \tag{5}$$

where the parameters μ_{r_c}, Σ_{r_c} indicate the mean location of the r_c-th region and the associated spread, respectively. Finally, $p(r_c)$ is a discrete distribution over the region variable.

As compared to pLSA, the biggest difference is that G-pLSA introduces a conditional independence relation between the visual topic z_k and the geo-located image l_i, given the geo-topic value r_c. This means that here the visual topic is evaluated as a global characteristic that influences *all* the images that lie within a region.

3.1 Model Fitting with the EM Algorithm

Given a set of training data, our model is learned by maximizing the data log-likelihood

$$LL = \sum_{i=1}^{N} \sum_{j=1}^{M} n(w_j, l_i) \log P(w_j, l_i) \tag{6}$$

where the joint probability is factorized as in Eq.4. The learning equations can be straightforwardly derived from those of pLSA, permitting a fast training via exact EM. In the E-step, the Bayes formula is applied in the parameterization of Eq.4, obtaining the posterior[4]

$$P(z, r|w, l) = \frac{P(w|z)P(z|r)p(l|r)p(r)}{\sum_{z,r} P(w|z)P(z|r)p(l|r)p(r)} \tag{7}$$

In the M-step, the expected complete data likelihood has to be maximized, which is

$$E[L] = \sum_{w,d} n(w, d) \sum_{z,r} P(z, r|w, l)$$
$$\cdot [\log P(w|z)P(z|r)p(l|r)p(r)] \tag{8}$$

The maximization of $E[L]$ can be derived straightforwardly for the parameters describing $P(w_j|z_k)$, $P(z_k|r_c)$, $P(r_c)$ and $p(l_i|r_c)$, employing Lagrange multipliers where necessary. The M-step re-estimation equations are thus:

$$P(w|z) = \frac{\sum_l n(w, l) \sum_r P(z, r|w, l)}{\sum_{w,l} n(w, l) \sum_r P(z, r|w, l)} \tag{9}$$

$$P(z|r) = \frac{\sum_{l,w} n(w, l) P(z, r|w, l)}{\sum_{w,l} n(w, l) \sum_z P(z, r|w, l)} \tag{10}$$

$$P(r) = \frac{\sum_{l,w} n(w, l) \sum_z P(z, r|w, l)}{\sum_{w,l} n(w, l)} \tag{11}$$

$$\mu_r = \frac{\sum_{w,l} n(w, l) \sum_z P(z, r|w, l) l}{\sum^{w,l} n(w, l) \sum_z P(z, r|w, l)} \tag{12}$$

$$\Sigma_r = \frac{\sum_{w,l} n(w, l) \sum_z P(z, r|w, l)(l - \mu_r)(l - \mu_r)^\mathsf{T}}{\sum_{w,l} n(w, l) \sum_z P(z, r|w, l)} \tag{13}$$

---

[4] In the following, we omit the pedices for clarity in the reading, resorting them only when necessary.

The E-step and the M-step equations are alternated until a convergence criteria is met.

The geo-topic membership label of an image can be estimated in a Maximum Likelihood framework: starting from the image likelihood $\sum_w n(w, l_i) \log p(w, l_i)$, we build the geo-topic class conditional, calculating then the geo-topic index $R(l_i) \in 1, ..., R$ that maximizes it. In formulae

$$R(l_i) = \arg\max_c \sum_w n(w, l_i) \log p(w, l_i | r_c)$$

$$= \arg\max_c \sum_w n(w, l_i) \log \sum_z P(w|z) P(z|r_c) p(l_i|r_c) \qquad (14)$$

4   Experiments

To analyze our framework, we built a geo-located database considering the southern part of France. The database is composed by 1013 geo-located pictures downloaded from Panoramio (whose details regarding the photo owners can be found at http://profs.sci.univr.it/ cristanm/Publications_files/GR2.html). We choose France because of its large variety of natural scenes, ranging from mountains to sea, with middleage, industrial or costal cities, fields and villages, so as to deal with a difficult setting.

Given our set of geo-located images, affine elliptical regions are estimated for each image, converted in grey scale, constructed by elliptical shape adaptation about an interest point [6]. Each region is mapped to a circle by appropriate scaling along its principal axis and a 128-dim SIFT descriptor is built. Then, descriptors are quantized into visual words via K-means, and histogram word representations are built for each image.

We perform G-pLSA setting the number of topic $Z = 16$, considering that each topic models a particular semantic concept, such as *sky,water,grass* etc. being present an outdoor scene, and applying the same considerations on the number of such concepts illustrated in [7]. Then, we set the number of regions $R = 16$. The choice of this parameter depends on the level of detail that an user wants to achieve in analyzing a particular geographical area. The model selection issue has been not explored in this paper, but will be subject of future research in this context.

We run the EM algorithm, that takes approximately 30 minutes to converge on a 1.98 Ghz Xeon with a Matlab implementation. After the learning, we obtain a set of Gaussian geo/topics, from here called simply *regions*, each one of them described by a distribution over visual topics $P(z|r_c)$, where the topics are co-occurrences of visual words, described by $P(w|z_k)$.

The Gaussian regions are depicted in Fig.2b, and the image locations, labeled as described in Eq.14, are shown in Fig.2c. For each region, in Fig.2 on the right, we show some of the member pictures, ordered in decreasing order of $P(l_i|r_c)$, from left to right; the last column shows images with very low $P(l_i|r_c)$. It is

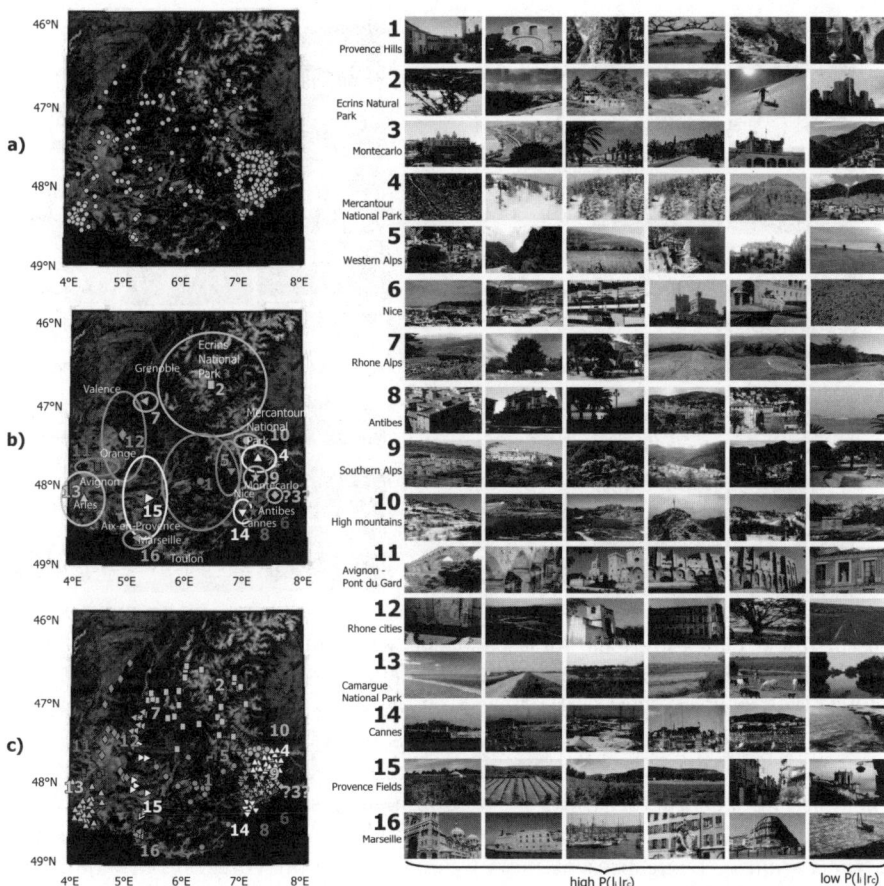

Fig. 2. Categorization results; a) image locations; b) Gaussian regions discovered by G-pLSA; c) class labeling of the image locations. On the right, for each region (numbered in b)) a set of 6 member images: 5 belong to the region with high probability, while the sixth has lower membership probability (photos are courtesy of www.panoramio.com: the photos are under the copyright of their owners).

easy to see how each one of the regions discovered represents a different group of images which are geographically proximal and visually related. It is worth to note how each region is meaningful, in the sense that exhibits a particular visual motif, such as cities (cat. 3,6,8,11,14,16), fields (cat. 15), mountains (cat. 2,4,5,10), mountain villages (cat.9), coastal areas (cat.13).

For a deeper understanding of our technique, we evaluate, for each word w_j, the topic for which $P(w_j|z_k), k = 1, \ldots, Z$ is the highest, linking thus each topic with the visual words that best represent it. Then, for some member images of all the geo-categories, we highlight those words that encode the visual topic that best represent that region (see Fig.3), *i.e.*, for a given region r_c, we extract the

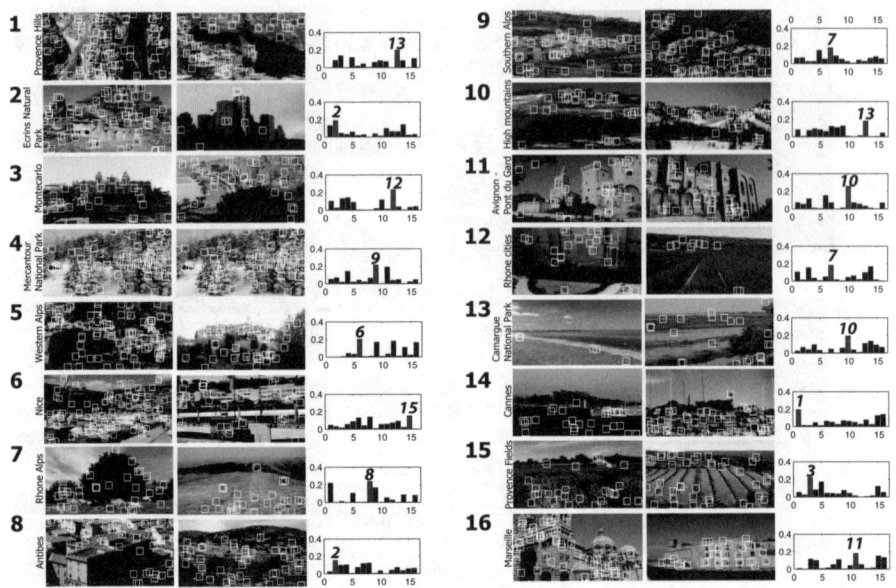

Fig. 3. Topic representations: for each region we highlight the most characterizing visual topic (numbered on the respective histograms). The visual words that best characterize that topic are show on the images on the left.

index k for which $P(z_k|r_c)$ is maximal. As visible, for each region there is a topic which strongly characterizes its most prominent visual aspect. For example, in the region 3, visual words are located on buildings, and not on the vegetation. In the region 5, being present mostly small mountain villages, both buildings and vegetation are considered. Region 2 is formed mostly by mountains, thus the visual word representation discards the buildings. In the region 15, visual words are located on the vegetation, while the few fields of the region 12, being not characteristic, are not captured by any visual word.

Another method to highlight the ability of G-pLSA in the creation of peculiar descriptions of each region via $p(z|r)$ distribution, we build the confusion matrix among the region descriptions. As a inter-region similarity measure between two generic regions i and i' we employ the Kullback-Leibler divergence KL, building the following symmetrized measure $s(\cdot, \cdot)$:

$$s(c, c') = \frac{KL(i, i') + KL(i', i)}{2} \qquad (15)$$

The confusion matrix, depicted in Fig.4a, shows how cities as Marseille, Antibes, Cannes and Nice and Montecarlo are more similar among themselves instead of the regions characterizing the mountains; the same applies for the viceversa.

As further analysis to examine the region descriptions, we consider a particular test image, and we show the visual words related to different visual topics, other than the most characteristic for the region of the test. As visible in Fig.4, the

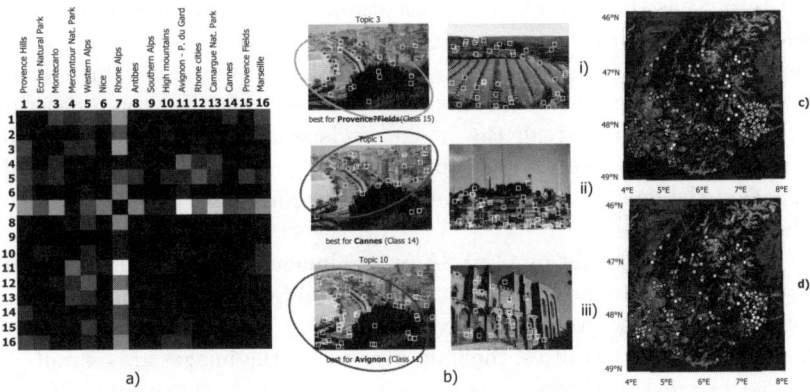

Fig. 4. Categorization analysis: a) confusion matrix among the topic distributions related to each region. b) On the left, different visual words of the test image related to three different topics. The three topics are the most characterizing for three regions, whose member images are depicted on the right, with the associated visual words; c-d) clustering results -c) considering only image location information -d) considering only topic information.

test image comes from the region 3 (Montecarlo). Then we visualize the words representing the topic 3, which is the most characteristic for the region 15 (Rhone fields, see an example image in Fig.4i). As visible, here the visual words are mostly located on vegetation patterns. Another example is shown in Fig.4ii; here the topic 1, characteristic for region 14 (Cannes) is visualized. As visible, here the vegetation is discarded, and the visual words are mostly located on the building. This confirms the high similarity shown in the confusion matrix of Fig.4a between the two regions. Finally, in Fig.4iii, the visualization of the visual words related to the topic most representative of region 11 (Avignon) is displayed. As visible, words are located quite uniformly in the image, with particular emphasis on curve elements present on the bottom-left corner. This agrees with what is visible in Fig.4iii on the left, and, in general, with most the images characterizing the region of Avignon, in which the Popes' Palace and the famous bridge are portrayed; both abound actually of curve architectural features, captured in the visual topic more characteristic for Avignon.

In order to compare the ability of our framework to perform geo-segmentation, we create two alternative clustering strategies: 1) perform gaussian clustering via EM, considering only the location information; 2) perform classic pLSA with $T = 16$ topics on all the images, obtaining as feature vectors the distributions $p(z|d)$, that give a different latent description to each image d. Perform gaussian clustering via EM using such features vectors. This policy does not take in account the location information.

In the clustering performed by considering only the location information, groups of photos related to visually different geographical zones are fused together, as occurred for clusters 4 and 8, and clusters 6 and 3 (see Fig. 4c-d)). In the clustering based only on topic information, the non-informative clusters are sparse and spread out over the entire map.

The reason for the high difference between the clustering obtained with the second policy and our method is that, in the first case, the topic description $P(w|z)$ is built evaluating all the images independently in the same fashion, while in our case the visual topic representation is mediated by the geo-topics, which weight the images that have to be taken into account, with the $P(z, r|w, l)$ distribution.

The advantages brought by G-pLSA on the image categorization can be fruitful for the image database visualization and could be ease the interaction of a user with the database. Actually, conversely to what happens with all the current geo-located image repositories, the map over which the images are exhibited can be divided in areas, each one of them being a geo-topic. Then, only few, characterizing images can be visualized on the map. Moreover, the user could select only a region over which analyze images, diminishing the feeling of dispersion typical of the geo-located image database interfaces. A prototype of interface built on top of the G-pLSA description is currently under development.

References

1. Smeulders, A., Worring, M., Santini, S., Gupta, A., Jain, R.: Content-based image retrieval at the end of the early years. IEEE Trans. Pattern Anal. Mach. Intell. 22(12), 1349–1380 (2000)
2. Hofmann, T.: Unsupervised learning by probabilistic latent semantic analysis. Mach. Learn 42(1/2), 177–196 (2001)
3. Lowe, D.: Object recognition from local scale-invariant features. In: Proceedings of the Seventh IEEE International Conference on Computer Vision, vol. 2, pp. 1150–1157 (1999)
4. Dempster, A., Laird, N., Rubin, D.: Maximum likelihood from incomplete data via the EM algorithm. J. Roy. Statist. Soc. B 39, 1–38 (1977)
5. Bosch, A., Zisserman, A., Muoz, X.: Scene classification via plsa. In: Proceedings of European Conference on Computer Vision 2006, vol. 4, pp. 517–530 (2006)
6. Mikolajczyk, K., Schmid, C.: An affine invariant interest point detector. In: ECCV, vol. 1, pp. 128–142 (2002)
7. Vogel, J., Schiele, B.: A semantic typicality measure for natural scene categorization. In: DAGM-Symposium, pp. 195–203 (2004)

Functional Object Class Detection Based on Learned Affordance Cues

Michael Stark[1], Philipp Lies[1], Michael Zillich[2],
Jeremy Wyatt[2], and Bernt Schiele[1]

[1] Computer Science Department, TU Darmstadt, Germany
{stark,lies,schiele}@informatik.tu-darmstadt.de
[2] School of Computer Science, University of Birmingham, United Kingdom
{mxz,jlw}@cs.bham.ac.uk

Abstract. Current approaches to visual object class detection mainly focus on the recognition of basic level categories, such as cars, motorbikes, mugs and bottles. Although these approaches have demonstrated impressive performance in terms of recognition, their restriction to these categories seems inadequate in the context of embodied, cognitive agents. Here, distinguishing objects according to functional aspects based on object affordances is important in order to enable manipulation of and interaction between physical objects and cognitive agent.

In this paper, we propose a system for the detection of functional object classes, based on a representation of visually distinct hints on object affordances (*affordance cues*). It spans the complete range from tutor-driven acquisition of affordance cues, learning of corresponding object models, and detecting novel instances of functional object classes in real images.

Keywords: Functional object categories, object affordances, object category detection, object recognition.

1 Introduction and Related Work

In recent years, computer vision has made tremendous progress in the field of object category detection. Diverse approaches based on local features, such as simple bag-of-words methods [2] have shown impressive results for the detection of a variety of different objects. More recently, adding spatial information has resulted in a boost in performance [10], and combining different cues has even further pushed the limits. One of the driving forces behind object category detection is a widely-adopted collection of publicly available data sets [3,7], which is considered an important instrument for measuring and comparing the detection performance of different methods. The basis for comparison is given by a set of rather abstract, basic level categories [15]. These categories are grounded in cognitive psychology, and category instances typically share characteristic visual properties.

In the context of embodied cognitive agents, however, different criteria for the formation of categories seem more appropriate. Ideally, an embodied, cognitive

A. Gasteratos, M. Vincze, and J.K. Tsotsos (Eds.): ICVS 2008, LNCS 5008, pp. 435–444, 2008.
© Springer-Verlag Berlin Heidelberg 2008

Fig. 1. Basic level (left) vs functional (right) object categories

agent (an autonomous robot, *e.g.*), would be capable of categorizing and detecting objects according to potential uses, and *w.r.t.* their utility in performing a certain task. This *functional* definition of object categories is related to the notion of *affordances* pioneered by [6].

Fig. 1 exemplifies the differentiation between functional and basic level categories, and highlights the following two key properties: 1) functional categories may generalize across and beyond basic level categories (both a mug and a watering-can are *handle-graspable*, and so is a hammer), and 2) basic level categories can be recovered as *composite* functional categories (a mug is both *handle-graspable*, *sidewall-graspable*, and can be *poured* from).

Attempts to detect objects according to functional categories date back to the early days of computer vision. [21] was among the first to suggest functional characterizations of objects as consequences of basic geometric properties. [17] pioneered a body of work on functional categorization of CAD-inspired face-vertex object descriptions by geometric reasoning, and was later extended by visual input for recognizing primitive shapes from range images of idealistic scenes [18]. [14] introduced an explicit mapping between geometric and corresponding functional primitives and relations, again restricted to a small class of parametric shapes. [1] added force feedback for distinguishing among different tools that afford piercing other objects. Only recently, [16] stepped into the direction of more realistic settings, recognizing previously unseen, real world objects, but specifically tailored towards grasp point prediction. The approach is based on training a logistic regression model on annotated synthetic images, combining 2D filter responses with 3D range data in a dense, multi-scale image representation.

In this paper, we approach the challenge of functional object categorization from a completely different angle. First, we build our system on robust and well-established grounds in the field of object recognition, applicable to real-world images of cluttered scenes. We explore the capabilities of a widely adopted detection framework, based on a suitable geometric local feature representation. Second, we choose to acquire functional category representations by observing few prototypical human-object interactions rather than explicitly modeling physical object properties. Naturally, the set of functional categories that our local feature-based vision system will be able to represent is restricted to those that are characterized by distinct visual features. As an example, consider the bent shape of a mug handle, which suggests to grasp the mug in a specific way. We call such distinct visual features *affordance cues*, and base our system for functional object category detection on the recognition of these cues. In particular, our paper makes the following contributions:

1. We present an integrated system for the acquisition, learning and detection of functional object categories based on affordance cues.
2. The system is based on a state-of-the-art object category detection framework, and acquires affordance cues from observing few prototypical human-object interactions.
3. We report first results for the detection of two functional object categories learned by our system, and demonstrate their generalization capabilities across and beyond basic level categories. We show that our system supports the interpretation of these categories as composite functional ones.

The rest of this paper is organized as follows: Sec. 2 describes tutor-driven affordance cue acquisition. Sec. 3 presents the integration of affordance cues into a state-of-the-art object recognition framework. We give experimental results in Sec. 4, showing that promising detection performance can be achieved even for learning from as few as a single image, and conclude with a perspective on future work in Sec. 5.

2   Affordance Cue Acquisition

Given an observed human-object interaction featuring a single affordance cue (a video sequence plus tutor guidance), the purpose of the affordance cue acquisition sub-system is to obtain a visual feature-based representation of that cue. It proceeds by first estimating an accurate per-pixel segmentation of the *interaction region* (the region where tutor and object pixels overlap during interaction), and then extracting features in a local neighborhood around that region. Tutor guidance informs the system about the beginning and the end of an interaction. Fig. 2 gives an overview of affordance cue acquisition, which is detailed in the following.

2.1   Foreground/Background Segmentation and Skin Labeling

We employ the *Background Cut* [20] algorithm originally proposed in the context of video conferencing for foreground/background segmentation. It combines

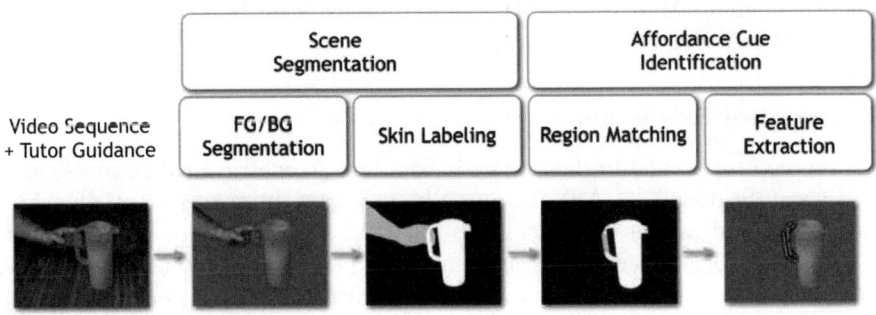

Fig. 2. Affordance cue acquisition overview

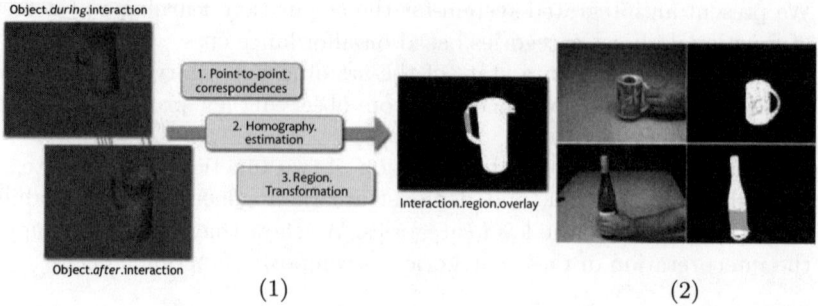

Fig. 3. (1) Region matching overview, (2) examples, interaction regions given in gray

global and local Gaussian mixture color models with a data-dependent discontinuity penalty in a Conditional Random Field model [9], and provides accurate segmentations in near real-time.

In order to distinguish human tutor and manipulated object, we apply a likelihood ratio test on all pixels labeled as foreground by foreground/background segmentation. We build the ratio between the likelihood of a pixel originating from object color and the corresponding likelihood for skin color, using a pre-trained skin color model [8]. Fig. 2 includes an example labeling (black denotes *background*, white *object*, and gray *skin*).

2.2 Region Matching

We determine the interaction region as the set of object pixels that has been occluded by the human tutor in the course of an interaction. We identify those pixels by choosing two frames from the interaction sequence, i) one during the interaction, and ii) one after (but with the object still visible). Then, the set of occluded object pixels is computed as the intersection of all skin-labeled pixels of frame i) with all object-labeled pixels of frame ii), transformed in order to equalize object pose differences between the two frames. The transformation is obtained by estimating the homography between frames i) and ii), using RANSAC. Initial point-to-point correspondences are established by Robust Nearest-Neighbor Matching of SIFT descriptors [12] on Harris-Laplace interest points [13] (see Fig. 3 for an example).

2.3 Feature Extraction

Our representation of affordance cues is based on geometric local features called k-Adjacent Segments (k-AS) [5], initially proposed in the context of shape-matching line drawings to real images [4]. k-AS detect distinct edge segments in an image, form groups of k such segments, and then encode their relative geometric layout in a low dimensional, scale-invariant shape descriptor. In our experiments, we consistently use $k = 2$, since 2-AS features have shown a good discrimination/repeatability tradeoff [19]. We augment the groups returned by the 2-AS detector by additional pairs of edge segments according to perceptual grouping criteria in the spirit of [22]. By indexing the space of detected edge segments by histogramming orientations, we maintain linear grouping complexity. We transfer the per-pixel segmentation into 2-AS features by growing the interaction region, and including edge segments with sufficient overlap.

3 Affordance Cue-Based Object Detection

A variant of the Implicit Shape Model (ISM) [11] serves as the basis for our functional object category detection system, using the affordance cue representation of Sec. 2. We extend the original model in order to allow for independent training of several different affordance cues, and flexible combination for detecting composite functional categories. Fig. 4 gives an overview of the ISM.

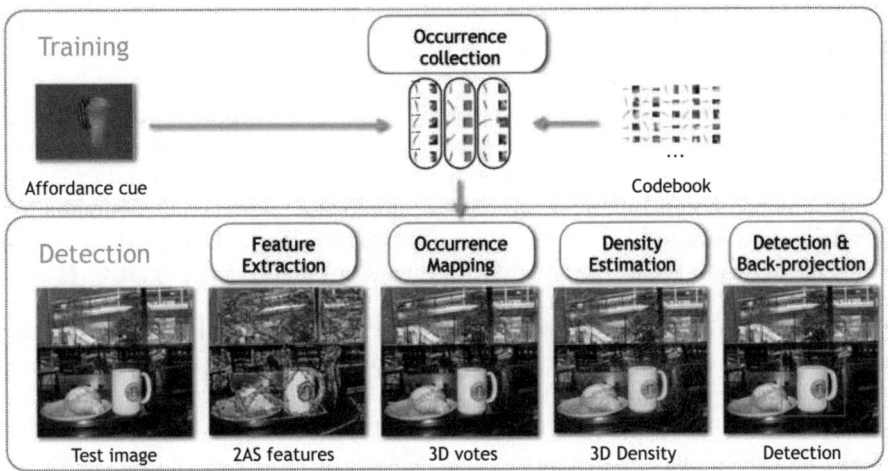

Fig. 4. Implicit Shape Model Overview

Training. Training an ISM for an affordance cue amounts to matching acquired affordance cue features to a previously built codebook, and storing the relative position (x, y) and size $(scale)$ of the object $w.r.t.$ the feature occurrence along with matched codebook entries. Position and scale can be easily obtained from a bounding box surrounding all object-labeled pixels from the acquisition stage.

Detection. For detecting an affordance cue in a previously unseen image, all features in a test image are again matched to the codebook. For every matched codebook entry, each stored feature occurrence probabilistically votes for a hypothesized object position in a generalized three-dimensional Hough voting space $(x, y, scale)$. The probabilistic vote is a function of its distance to the codebook entry in feature space, the edge-strength of the corresponding image feature, and the amount of overlap between the stored feature occurrence and the interaction region of the originating training affordance cue.

We estimate modes in the distribution of votes by standard kernel density estimation techniques, and accept modes as detections according to a confidence threshold. Since we are interested in a precise estimate of where exactly an affordance cue is located in an image, we proceed by back-projecting those features into the image, which contribute significantly to either of the modes, by selecting a fixed volume of probability mass around each mode. Fig. 7 shows example detections, where highlighted edges correspond to back-projected 2-AS features.

Combining Multiple Affordance Cues. One of the reasons for choosing an ISM for our approach is its extendibility to multiple affordance cues. Having trained multiple affordance cue models separately, these models can be joined for detecting *composite functional categories* by combining votes of all models in a single Hough voting space, and estimating modes of the joint distribution.

4   Experimental Results

For all experiments, we build generic codebooks by hierarchical agglomerative clustering of 2-AS features from a set of randomly selected real images, augmented by additional pairs of edge segments according to perceptual grouping criteria, as presented in Sec. 2. We report qualitative results for the detection performance of our system on a subset of the ETHZ Shape Classes data set [4], and a series of images from the environment of our embodied, cognitive agent.

The *handle-graspable* category. We begin by giving results for the *handle-graspable* functional category (rows (a) to (c) of Fig. 7), learned from affordance cue features of single images given in column (1). We observe that the models learned from either of the three mugs perform comparably well in detecting handle-like structures in the given test images, despite apparent appearance differences between the objects used for training and testing, and considerable background clutter. The affordance cue features learned from mugs (1)(a) and (1)(c) achieve slightly more accurate localization of handle-like features in the test images, apparently due to their symmetry *w.r.t.* the horizontal axis, resulting in increased repeatability.

Row (d) highlights the generalization of a *handle-graspable* model learned from mug (1)(c) over other object categories such as *coffee pot, vase*, and *electric water jug*. Image (5)(d) indicates the limitations of our approach. While the detector mistakenly fires on a circular sign in the background (false positive), it misses an obvious *handle-graspable* affordance cue on the white Thermos bottle (false negative). While the false positive can be explained by the limited information encoded by the 2-AS features, the false negative may be attributed to predominant background structures.

Affordance cues for feature selection. An interesting question is how the performance of object detection based on affordance cues compares to the

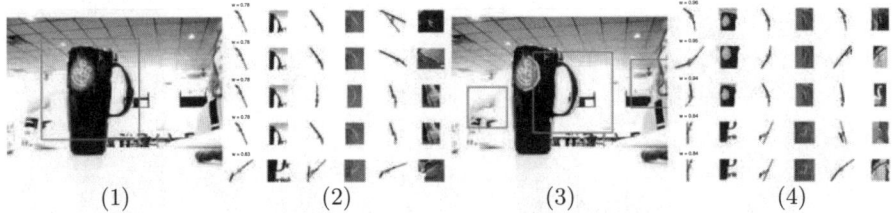

(1)   (2)   (3)   (4)

Fig. 5. Comparison of affordance cue-based (*handle-graspable*) *vs.* whole-object training. (1) and (3) depict detections, (2) and (4) the corresponding top-five *2*-AS features, stored codebook occurrences, and matched codebook entries (from left to right).

Left camera   Right camera   Grasping attempt

Fig. 6. Binocular affordance cue acquisition and resulting grasping attempt

performance of a system that has been trained without being directed towards these cues. Fig. 5 contrasts detections of an ISM trained on *handle-graspable* affordance cue features (1) *vs.* an ISM trained on *all* features of a mug (3). In fact, the latter provides less accurate localization of the mug in the test image; none of the shown three bounding boxes in (3) (the three most significant modes) comes as close to the true position of the mug as the single one in (1). Fig. 5 (2) and (4) pinpoint the difference, by listing the respective top-five features contributing to the most significant mode, together with the corresponding stored codebook occurrences and matched codebook entries. While the *handle-graspable* detector correctly relates handle features from training and test image, the *all*-detector matches mostly texture features between the two, misleading its prediction of object center and scale.

One possible approach to overcoming the weak discriminative power of the employed features is the exploitation of additional affordance cues in a joint, composite functional category model, as will be demonstrated in the following.

The *sidewall-graspable* category. Rows (e) and (f) of Fig. 7 show the detection results for a second category, *sidewall-graspable*, again learned from single images. In row (e), a model has been learned from a bottle, and from a mug in row (f). The *sidewall-graspable* detector exhibits remarkable performance in the detection of sidewall-like structures in cluttered images, although it is slightly more susceptible to false positives than the *handle-graspable* detector, again due to the limitations of the employed features (see (e)(5)).

442   M. Stark et al.

Fig. 7. Example detections. Each row corresponds to a single experiment, unless otherwise stated. For each row (a) to (g), columns (2) to (5) give example detections for a system that has been trained solely on the highlighted affordance cue features in column (1). Line segments are plotted in yellow, and pairs selected as 2-AS feature are connected by a blue line. Row (d) continues example detections of row (c), and row (g) depicts detections from a system trained on affordance cue features (1)(a) *and* (1)(f). Back-projected edges from the *handle-graspable* detector are plotted in yellow, those from the *sidewall-graspable* detector in red.

The *handle-graspable / sidewall-graspable* category. We now combine both *handle-graspable* and *sidewall-graspable* affordance cues by training two independent ISM models, one for each cue, and joining their predictions for detection. In fact, the combination of both cues improves the detection performance of our system (example detections are given in row (g)). In particular, the *sidewall-graspable* affordance cue compensates for inaccuracies in the localization of *handle-graspable* features. By back-projecting features, the joint detector is able to to distinguish and accurately localize both of the two affordance cues, shown in yellow (*handle-graspable*) and red (*sidewall-graspable*).

Grasping. Fig. 6 depicts an attempt to grasp a jug at its handle by a robot arm mounted onto our agent, after the system has acquired the corresponding affordance cue. Although actual grasping fails due to limited visual servoing capabilities, the agent manages to touch the jug at the correct position. We applied affordance cue acquisition independently for two cameras of a calibrated stereo rig, and obtained 3D coordinates by triangulation.

5   Conclusions and Future Work

In this paper, we have approached the challenge of functional object categories from the perspective of state-of-the-art object detection, and presented a system for the tutor-driven acquisition, learning, and recognition of affordance cues in real-world, cluttered images. Clearly, our system is limited by the 2D nature of the used local features, but exhibits promising detection performance in our experiments even for one-shot learning. We plan to explore the benefit of added 3D information, and to extend the set of recognized affordance cues by incorporating a larger quantity of training examples.

Acknowledgements. This work has been funded, in part, by the EU project CoSy (IST-2002-004250).

References

1. Bogoni, L., Bajcsy, R.: Interactive recognition and representation of functionality. In: CVIU, vol. 62(2), pp. 194–214 (1995)
2. Csurka, G., Dance, C.R., Fan, L., Willarnowski, J., Bray, C.: Visual categorization with bags of keypoints. In: SLCV (2004)
3. Everingham, M., Van Gool, L., Williams, C.K.I., Winn, J., Zisserman, A.: The PASCAL Visual Object Classes Challenge 2007 (VOC2007) Results.
4. Ferrari, V., Tuytelaars, T., Van Gool, L.J.: Object detection by contour segment networks. In: ECCV (2006)
5. Ferrari, V., Fevrier, L., Jurie, F., Schmid, C.: Groups of adjacent contour segments for object detection. Rapport De Recherche Inria (2006)
6. Gibson, J.J.: The theory of affordance. In: Percieving, Acting, and Knowing, Lawrence Erlbaum Associates, Hillsdale, NJ (1977)

7. Griffin, G., Holub, A., Perona, P.: Caltech-256 object category dataset. Technical Report 7694, California Institute of Technology (2007)
8. Jones, M.J., Rehg, J.M.: Statistical color models with application to skin detection. In: CVPR, pp. 1274–1280. IEEE Computer Society, Los Alamitos (1999)
9. Lafferty, J., McCallum, A., Pereira, F.: Conditional random fields: Probabilistic models for segmenting and labeling sequence data. In: ICML 2001 (2001)
10. Lazebnik, S., Schmid, C., Ponce, J.: Beyond bags of features: Spatial pyramid matching for recognizing natural scene categories. In: CVPR 2006 (2006)
11. Leibe, B., Leonardis, A., Schiele, B.: An implicit shape model for combined object categorization and segmentation. In: Toward Category-Level Object Recognition, Springer, Heidelberg (2006)
12. Lowe, D.G.: Distinctive image features from scale-invariant keypoints. IJCV 60(2), 91–110 (2004)
13. Mikolajczyk, K., Tuytelaars, T., Schmid, C., Zisserman, A., Matas, J., Schaffal-itzky, F., Kadir, T., Van Gool, L.J.: A comparison of affine region detectors. In: IJCV 2005 (2005)
14. Rivlin, E., Dickinson, S.J., Rosenfeld, A.: Recognition by functional parts. Computer Vision and Image Understanding: CVIU 62(2), 164–176 (1995)
15. Rosch, E., Mervis, C.B., Gray, W.D., Johnson, D.M., Braem, P.B.: Basic objects in natural categories. Cognitive Psychology (1976)
16. Saxena, A., Driemeyer, J., Ng, A.Y.: Robotic grasping of novel objects using vision. In: IJRR (2007)
17. Stark, L., Bowyer, K.: Achieving generalized object recognition through reasoning about association of function to structure. PAMI 13(10), 1097–1104 (1991)
18. Stark, L., Hoover, A.W., Goldgof, D.B., Bowyer, K.W.: Function-based recognition from incomplete knowledge of shape. In: WQV 1993, pp. 11–22 (1993)
19. Stark, M., Schiele, B.: How good are local features for classes of geometric objects. In: ICCV (October 2007)
20. Sun, J., Zhang, W.W., Tang, X., Shum, H.Y.: Background cut. In: ECCV II, pp. 628–641 (2006)
21. Winston, P.H., Katz, B., Binford, T.O., Lowry, M.R.: Learning physical descriptions from functional definitions, examples, and precedents. In: AAAI 1983 (1983)
22. Zillich, M.: Incremental Indexing for Parameter-Free Perceptual Grouping. In: 31st Workshop of the Austrian Association for Pattern Recognition (2007)

Increasing Classification Robustness with Adaptive Features[*]

Christian Eitzinger[1], Manfred Gmainer[1], Wolfgang Heidl[1], and Edwin Lughofer[2]

[1] Profactor GmbH, Im Stadtgut A2, 4407 Steyr, Austria
[2] Department of Knowledge-Based Mathematical Systems, Johannes Kepler University, Altenbergerstrasse 69, 4040 Linz, Austria

Abstract. In machine vision features are the basis for almost any kind of high-level postprocessing such as classification. A new method is developed that uses the inherent flexibility of feature calculation to optimize the features for a certain classification task. By tuning the parameters of the feature calculation the accuracy of a subsequent classification can be significantly improved and the decision boundaries can be simplified. The focus of the methods is on surface inspection problems and the features and classifiers used for these applications.

Keywords: feature adaptation, classification, surface inspection.

1 Introduction

In many industrial inspection systems and particular in those for surface inspection, there are three processing steps: image segmentation to extract interesting objects, feature calculation to determine the properties of the objects and classification to decide whether the object is a fault. While an appropriate classifier is usually found using machine learning methods - probably following a feature selection process - the features themselves are usually considered to be given, application-specific quantities. Typical features for surface inspection tasks are the total area of an object, shape descriptors such as compactness or texture-based features that analyze the inner structure of the object. Many of the algorithms for feature calculation use parameters that are to be set by the image processing expert. Such parameters are e.g. thresholds that determine which pixels belong to the object to calculate the total area. However, the selection of these thresholds and parameters is not always straightforward. One might e.g. want to select the parameters in such a way that the upstream classification task becomes easier, e.g. by selecting the parameters so as to maximize the separation between the "fault" and "no fault" class. We thus want to develop methods that adapt parameters of features in order to increase the accuracy and robustness of a classification task. We will demonstrate the basic idea on a simple, but illustrative test case and also present results on more complicated problems.

---

[*] This work was funded by the EC under grant no. 016429, project DynaVis. It reflects only the authors views.

A. Gasteratos, M. Vincze, and J.K. Tsotsos (Eds.): ICVS 2008, LNCS 5008, pp. 445–453, 2008.

2   State of the Art

In order to find a good and small set of features for a classification task the strategy is to select the relevant features from a large set of pre-existing features [5]. This can either be done by a filter approach, where the subset is selected based on a measure (distance, information, dependency, consistency) [1], [2], [3] or by a so-called wrapper [4] approach that minimizes the error rate of the classifier. For both approaches the aim is to reduce the number of features while maintaining a high classification accuracy. The inner core of the problem is a subset selection task, which has a runtime of $O(2^N)$ for exhaustive search and $O(N^2)$ for most heuristic methods. A wide range of algorithms has been developed, such as RELIEF [7],[8], decision tree method [9], or branch & bound [15]. Recent surveys [10],[6] list 42 different algorithms and we refer the interested reader to the literature cited there.

Adaptivity of the features has been considered in the literature mainly by adapting the feature selection process. This is particularly important for tracking, where the relevance of features may change depending on the angle of view. Some recent results can be found in [11] and [12]. An adaptive feature transformation is described in [14], where the feature vector is post-processed by an adaptive transformation matrix that is used to make the features invariant to environmental changes. The joint optimization of classifiers and features is investigated in [13], but also in this case the optimization of features is done by a selection process rather than by adapting parameters inside the feature calculation.

Some classification methods, such as linear discriminant analysis, have an inbuilt feature selection process. In those cases it is most often a projection that reduces the high-dimensional features space and tries to maximize the distance between the classes. By interpreting the projection as a weighting operation, this may also be considered a feature selection process. However, also in these classifiers the focus is on using predefined features rather than modifying the feature calculation itself.

3   Our Approach

In machine vision applications features are based on functions or algorithms that map a high-dimensional input (the gray values of the image) to a single real number (the feature). Feature calculation usually depends on a set of parameters that needs to be chosen for each application. A very illustrative example is a "size"-feature that calculates the number of connected pixels that are above a certain gray-level threshold. The actual value of the feature depends on how the threshold is chosen and for a typical application we may change that threshold in a range of ± 20. While the feature will still be considered as being the size of that object it will yield different values for each selection of the threshold. Another example would be a histogram feature that calculates the relative amount of pixels in a range of gray values. Again the start and end point of the interval may be chosen within a certain range and the feature will still yield similar results. However, some choices of thresholds or intervals will perform better on the classification task than others.

Theoretically, it would be possible to consider various instances of the same feature, each with a different parameter setting, and then perform feature selection. But the number of features would thus increase dramatically making selection an infeasible approach.

In order to state the basic concept in a more formal way, consider a classification problem with two classes $X_0 = \{x_{0,1}, x_{0,2}, ..., x_{0,n_0}\}$ and $X_1 = \{x_{1,1}, x_{1,2}, ..., x_{1,n_1}\}$ that each contain images $x_{i,j}, i = \{0, 1\}, j = 1..n$. For each image we calculate a feature $F(x, p)$, that also depends on a set of parameters p. The goal is to find a parameter setting p so as to make the classification task easier for the upstream classifier. For the optimality criterion we may build upon the ideas that have proven to be useful for feature selection. One possible and efficient approach is the distance measure that minimizes the within-class scatter s_W in relation to the between-class scatter s_B.

$$s_W(p) = \frac{1}{n_0} \sum_{j=1..n_0} (F(x_{0,j}, p) - m_0)^2 \tag{1}$$

$$+ \frac{1}{n_1} \sum_{j=1..n_1} (F(x_{1,j}, p) - m_1)^2$$

$$s_B(p) = (m_0 - m_1)^2$$

with m_0 and m_1 being the average of the feature values for class 0 and class 1. The optimization problem would thus be

$$\min_p J(p) \text{ with } J(p) = \frac{s_W(p)}{s_B(p)}. \tag{2}$$

Another option would be to use a correlation-based optimality criterion. If we use the indicator function $c(x) = 0$ whenever $x \in \{x_{0,j}\}$ and $c(x) = 1$ otherwise, then we may search for

$$\max_p J(p) \text{ with } J(p) = \rho(F(x_i, p), c(x_i)),$$

where ρ is the linear correlation coefficient.

It should be noted that this optimization problem usually has some specific properties that limit the choice of optimization algorithms. The relation between F and p may be complicated and derivatives might not exist. Numerical differentiation may be required for gradient descent methods, discontinuities and non-smoothness [18] need to be taken care of. Genetic algorithms or heuristic methods are other options that can more easily deal with these problems. Sometimes p can only be chosen from a set of discrete values, e.g. gray values are usually limited to a range of 0 to 255. If the search space is not too large, an exhaustive search will also be an option. Additionally, the time for computing the feature F for the whole test set may be high and one might want to use an optimization method that only requires few evaluations of F. The specific choice of the optimization method is thus application-dependent, relevant algorithms are found in [16] or [17].

4   Optimizing Multiple Features

For the joint optimization of a set of features $F_i, i = 1..m$, which we collect in a feature vector $\mathbf{F} \in \mathbb{R}^m$, the upstream classifier needs to be considered. Feature adaptation should lead to a decision boundary that can be easily reproduced by the classifier at hand and that maximizes the distance between the classes perpendicular to the decision boundary. We will discuss this for three commonly used types of classifiers: nearest neighbor classifiers, linear classifiers and decision trees.

In its most general form nearest neighbor classifiers use a distance measure $\|.\|$ to determine the distance of a feature vector to the class center. Classification performance will improve, if the feature parameters are adapted to maximize the distance between the classes with respect to this distance measure. The target function for the optimization will thus be very similar to (2), with

$$s_W(\mathbf{p}) = \frac{1}{n_0} \sum_{j=1..n_0} \|\mathbf{F}(x_{0,j}, \mathbf{p}) - \mathbf{m}_0\|^2 \qquad (3)$$

$$+ \frac{1}{n_1} \sum_{j=1..n_1} \|\mathbf{F}(x_{1,j}, \mathbf{p}) - \mathbf{m}_1\|^2$$

$$s_B(\mathbf{p}) = \|\mathbf{m}_0 - \mathbf{m}_1\|^2 .$$

Note that $\mathbf{F}$ is now a vector of features, depending on a vector of parameters $\mathbf{p}$.

In the case of linear classifiers the decision boundary is a hyperplane in feature space. Features should be adapted to maximize the distance between the classes in a direction perpendicular to the separating hyperplane. We choose a vector $\mathbf{c}$ to describe this direction and the optimization criterion (2) turns into

$$J(\mathbf{c}, \mathbf{p}) = \frac{s_W(\mathbf{c}, \mathbf{p})}{s_B(\mathbf{c}, \mathbf{p})} \qquad (4)$$

with

$$s_W(\mathbf{c}, \mathbf{p}) = \frac{1}{n_0} \sum_{j=1..n_0} \left(\mathbf{c}^T (\mathbf{F}(x_{0,j}, \mathbf{p}) - \mathbf{m}_0) \right)^2 \qquad (5)$$

$$+ \frac{1}{n_1} \sum_{j=1..n_1} \left(\mathbf{c}^T (\mathbf{F}(x_{1,j}, \mathbf{p}) - \mathbf{m}_1) \right)^2 ,$$

$$s_B(\mathbf{c}, \mathbf{p}) = \left(\mathbf{c}^T (\mathbf{m}_0 - \mathbf{m}_1) \right)^2$$

The vector $\mathbf{c} \in \mathbb{R}^m$ is not known beforehand and thus has to be considered as being an additional parameter in the optimization process. Once the optimization is solved, we will thus not only have a set of parameters for the feature calculation, but also the classifier $\mathbf{c}$ itself.

Finally, for decision trees we need to keep in mind that decision trees can best reproduce decision boundaries that are parallel to the axes of the feature space. If we think of a decision tree as a sequential application of a number of linear classifiers with **c** being the unit vectors $\mathbf{e}_i$ then we find based on (4) and (5) that

$$J(\mathbf{p}) = \sum_{i=1..m} J(\mathbf{e}_i, \mathbf{p}) = \sum_{i=1..m} \frac{s_W(\mathbf{e}_i, \mathbf{p})}{s_B(\mathbf{e}_i, \mathbf{p})}, \tag{6}$$

which decomposes into a sequential application of equations (1) and (2) to each feature F_i. The optimization problem can thus be split into m smaller problems, each dealing with a single feature. The optimization problems (2), (4), or (6) are usually non-smooth and - considering the discrete nature of the threshold - even discontinuous. For the simple example of the next section, an exhaustive search was possible. For more complicated data sets we found that gradient descent methods with a simple numerical estimation of the gradient work well. As usual only a local minimum can be guaranteed in this case.

We would like to point out that in all of the equations above, we assume that minimizing the within-class scatter in relation to the between-class scatter is an appropriate optimization criterion. We thus make certain assumptions about the feature statistics and if more is known about how the features are distributed in feature space, other measures of optimality may also be good and valid choices for the target function.

5 Evaluation

5.1 A Simple Example

We will now demonstrate the basic idea on a simple but illustrative example. We would like to stress the fact, that we are not trying to solve this particular problem, but to demonstrate how the distribution of patterns in the feature space will change if the features are optimized for certain classifiers.

The task is to distinguish between two different types of functions, a Gaussian and a triangular shaped function g as show in figure 1.

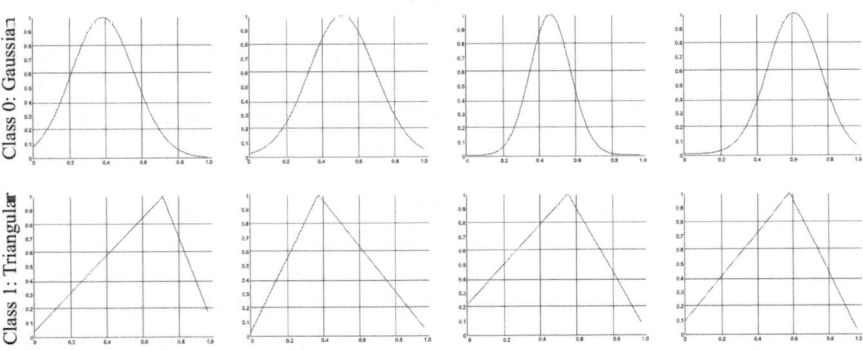

Fig. 1. Typical members of the classes

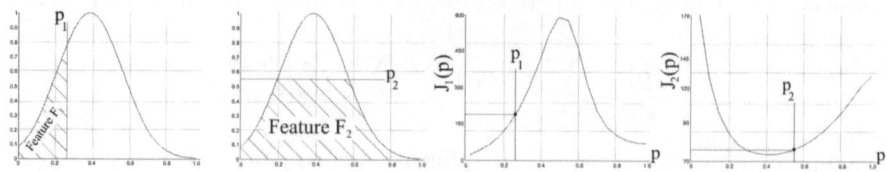

Fig. 2. The features F_1, F_2 and their parameters p_1, p_2 (left). The target function for both features (right). The optimal values are at $p_1 = 0.1$ and $p_2 = 0.45$.

For this task we want to use two features F_1 and F_2, which are calculated in the following way

$$F_1 = \int_0^p g(x)dx \quad \text{and} \quad F_2 = \int \min(g(x), p)dx,$$

which is shown on the left in figure 2. The target functions $J_{1,2}(p)$ based on equation (2) for features F_1 and F_2 are shown on the right hand side of this figure. It is obvious that even in this simple case the target function is not necessarily convex. However, it seems to be sufficiently smooth to allow a gradient descent method.

For an initial selection of $p_1 = 0.5$ and $p_2 = 0.9$ the patterns are located in the feature space as shown in graph (a) of figure 3. Graphs (b) to (d) show the results after feature adaptation based on the target functions (2), (4), and (6) respectively. The distributions of data points in feature space differ substantially depending on which target function is used. Aside from the fact that both of the classes have much less overlap, the distributions also show how selecting an optimal set of parameters for the features may support or simplify the design of a classifier. This is particularly obvious for the linear classifier (c) and the decision tree (d). Decision boundaries are drawn into the graphs as dotted lines.

5.2   Application to Surface Inspection

The following example demonstrates the capabilities of adaptive features on a surface inspection problem. The data set consists of about 10.000 images labelled as "fault" or "no fault" by a human quality expert. The images are preprocessed such that the background is removed. Typical examples of such images are shown in figure 4.

The goal is to classify the image as "fault" or "no fault" corresponding to the human expert's decision. The decision is made based upon a rule system predefined by the quality control instructions, but includes a significant subjective element that depends on the experience of the human expert. A set of 14 features was chosen, such as the area (number of pixels) covered by the object, its position in the image, its compactness and a range of other shape descriptors. These features proved to be relevant for the classification task in earlier experiments. Each of the features had one parameter, which in the case of the surface inspection problem was a grey

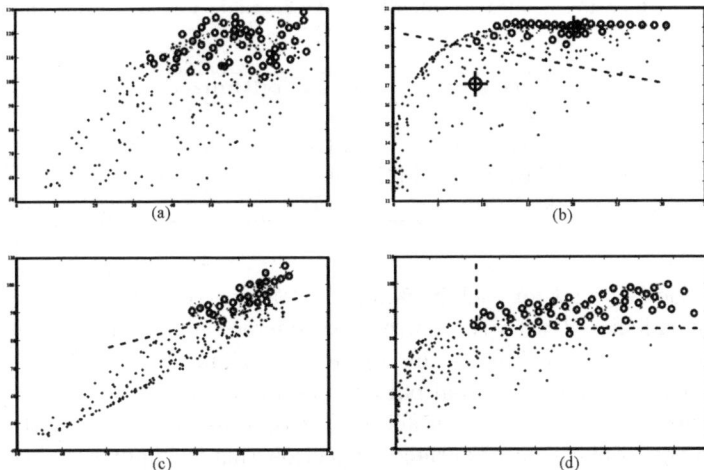

Fig. 3. (a) The original distribution of the data points in feature space. (b-d) Distributions of data points after feature adaptation with different target functions. Decision boundaries are shown as dotted lines. (b) features optimized for nearest-neighbor classifiers; class centers are shown; (c) features optimized for linear classifier; (d) features optimized for decision tree classifiers.

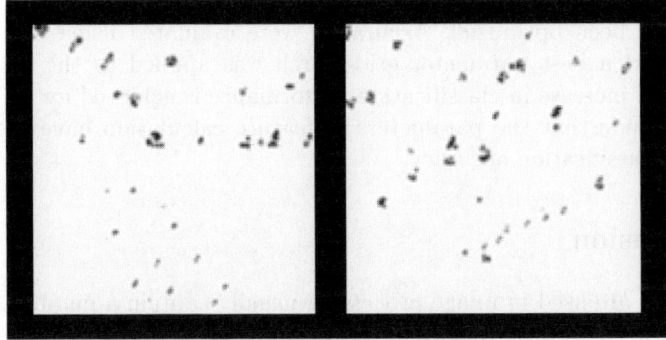

Fig. 4. Two typical images of the surface inspection problem. The background is removed only possible faults remain visible as grey spots.

level threshold. If the pixel was above the threshold, it would be considered as belonging to the fault, and otherwise as belonging to the background. A reasonable range for the threshold was between 0 and 128. For the sake of optimization this was scaled to an interval of 0..1. The goal was to adapt these thresholds in such a way that the classification accuracy is improved and that the decision boundary can be easily reproduced by the classifier.

Regarding the computational complexity it should be noted that the computational effort of optimizing the feature parameters can be significant. This is

Table 1. Classification accuracies for different classifiers for the initial and the optimized features

Classifier	initial	optimized
C4.5 [22]	74.2%	85.7%
CART[19]	73.8%	90.0%
Cluster based [21]	74.0%	78.1%
kNN [20]	68.7%	87.8%

caused by the fact that for each iteration the features of all objects in all images need to be calculated with the current parameter settings. Depending on the size and number of the images this optimization may take several hours. On the other hand, once the optimal parameters are found, the feature calculation and classification takes the same amount of time as any other method. With respect to the application of surface inspection this is important, because the "online" processing of the images, which has usually tight constraints on computing time, is not affected. It is just the "offline" training process that becomes quite time-consuming.

We have chosen four different classifiers that performed well on this and similar tasks and used target function (6) for optimization. Even though this required the repeated processing of 10.000 images an exhaustive search was performed in order to be sure that the global optimum is found.

Table 1 shows the accuracies for different classifiers before and after the features have been optimized. Accuracies were evaluated using ten-fold cross validation and a best parameter grid-search was applied to the decision-tree classifiers. An increase in classification performance is achieved for all classifiers and we conclude that the parameters of feature calculation have a significant impact on classification accuracy.

6   Conclusion

Features that are used in image processing usually contain a number of parameters that can be chosen within a certain range and offer significant potential for optimization. Adapting the feature calculation has a potential of decreasing the error rate of a classifier by 50%. It may also simplify the structure of the classifier if the target function is chosen specifically for this classifier. We have demonstrated that by tuning the parameters of 14 features in a surface inspection problem with 10.000 images as test data.

References

1. Rao, C.R.: Linear statistical inference and its applications. John Wiley & Sons, Inc. New York (1965)
2. Hand, D.J.: Discrimination and classification. Wiley Series in Probability and Mathematical Statistics. Wiley, Chichester (1981)

3. Costanza, C.M., Afifi, A.A.: Comparison of stopping rules in forward stepwise discriminant analysis. J. Amer. Statist. Assoc. 74, 777–785 (1979)
4. Kohavi, R., John, G.: Wrappers for feature subset selection. Artificial Intelligence 97, 273–324 (1997)
5. Dash, M., Liu, H.: Feature selection for classification. International Journal of Intelligent Data Analysis 1, 131–156 (1997)
6. Guyon, I., Elisseeff, A.: An introduction to variable and feature selection. Journal of Machine Learning Research 3, 1157–1182 (2003)
7. Kononenko, I.: Estimating attributes: Analysis and extensions of relief. In: Bergadano, F., De Raedt, L. (eds.) ECML 1994. LNCS, vol. 784, Springer, Heidelberg (1994)
8. Reisert, M., Burkhardt, H.: Feature Selection for Retrieval Purposes. In: Campilho, A., Kamel, M. (eds.) ICIAR 2006. LNCS, vol. 4141, pp. 661–672. Springer, Heidelberg (2006)
9. Cardie, C.: Using decision trees to improve case-based learning. In: Proceedings of 10th International Conference on Machine Learning, pp. 25–32 (1993)
10. Molina, L.C., Belanche, L., Nebot, A.: Feature Selection Algorithms: A Survey and Experimental Evaluation. In: ICDM 2002: Proceedings of the 2002 IEEE International Conference on Data Mining, p. 306 (2002)
11. Chen, H.T., Liu, T.L., Fuh, C.S.: Probabilistic Tracking with Adaptive Feature Selection, icpr. In: 17th International Conference on Pattern Recognition (ICPR 2004), vol. 2, pp. 736–739 (2004)
12. Collins, R., Liu, Y.: On-line selection of discriminative tracking features. In: Proceedings of the 2003 International Conference of Computer Vision ICCV 2003 (October 2003)
13. Krishnapuram, B., Hartemink, A.J., Carin, L., Figueiredo, M.A.T.: A Bayesian Approach to Joint Feature Selection and Classifier Design. In: IEEE Transactions on PAMI, September 2004, vol. 26(9), pp. 1105–1111 (2004)
14. Yao, D., Azimi-Sadjadi, M.R., Dobeck, G.J.: Adaptive feature mapping for underwater target classification. IJCNN 1999. International Joint Conference on Neural Networks 5, 3221–3224 (1999)
15. Narendra, P., Fukunaga, K.: A Branch and Bound Algorithm for Feature Subset Selection. IEEE Transactions on Computer C26(9), 917–922 (1977)
16. Boros, E., Hammer, L.P.: Discrete Optimization, February 2003. JAI Press (2003)
17. Dennis, J.E., Schnabel, R.S.: Numerical Methods for Unconstrained Optimization and Nonlinear Equations (Classics in Applied Mathematics. SIAM (1987)
18. Eitzinger, C., Plach, H.: A New Approach to Perceptron Training. IEEE Transactions on Neural Networks 14(1), 216–221 (2003)
19. Breiman, L., Friedman, J., Stone, C.J., Olshen, R.A.: Classification and Regression Trees. Chapman and Hall, Boca Raton (1993)
20. Hastie, T., Tibshirani, R., Friedman, J.: The Elements of Statistical Learning: Data Mining, Inference and Prediction. Springer, New York, Berlin, Heidelberg, Germany (2001)
21. Lughofer, E.: Extensions of vector quantization for incremental clustering. Pattern Recognition 41(3), 995–1011 (2008)
22. Quinlan, J.R.: C4.5: Programs for Machine Learning. Morgan Kaufmann Publishers Inc., U.S.A (1993)

Learning Visual Quality Inspection from Multiple Humans Using Ensembles of Classifiers

Davy Sannen, Hendrik Van Brussel, and Marnix Nuttin

Katholieke Universiteit Leuven, Department of Mechanical Engineering,
Celestijnenlaan 300B, B-3001 Heverlee (Leuven), Belgium
{davy.sannen,hendrik.vanbrussel,marnix.nuttin}@mech.kuleuven.be

Abstract. Visual quality inspection systems nowadays require the highest possible flexibility. Therefore, the reality that multiple human operators may be training the system has to be taken into account. This paper provides an analysis of this problem and presents a framework which is able to learn from multiple humans. This approach has important advantages over systems which are unable to do so, such as a consistent level of quality of the products, the ability to give operator-specific feedback, the ability to capture the knowledge of every operator separately and an easier training of the system.

The level of contradiction between the decisions of the operators is assessed for data obtained from a real-world industrial system for visual quality inspection of the printing of labels on CDs, which was labelled separately by five different operators. The results of the experiments show that the system is able to resolve many of the contradictions which are present in the data. Furthermore, it is shown that in several cases the system even performs better than a classifier which is trained on the data provided by the supervisor itself.

Keywords: Visual quality inspection, image classification, input from multiple humans, contradictory training data, ensembles of classifiers.

1   Introduction

The most effective and flexible way to reproduce the human cognitive abilities needed to automate visual quality inspection is by learning this task from human experts [1]. Traditionally, this is done using supervised learning, the data for which is provided by one selected person. The learning system is trained on this single set of data items, each of which has a unique label assigned to it. There may be some minor inconsistencies within the data, but these are usually considered as being random and each label is considered to be the ground truth.

However, production processes nowadays require the highest possible flexibility (due to e.g. changing customer demands, slight changes in the production line, new products to be inspected, etc.) [2]. This requires the human quality inspection operators to be able to directly train and adapt the system without too much intervention from their supervisors. A typical situation is that there are three shifts and one operator per shift is doing the quality inspection. Their

A. Gasteratos, M. Vincze, and J.K. Tsotsos (Eds.): ICVS 2008, LNCS 5008, pp. 454–463, 2008.

supervisors would like to be in control of their decisions as much as possible, but do not perform the inspection themselves. The decisions the operators make will inevitably be different for some of the products to be inspected. Therefore, a system is needed which can deal with these contradictions and inconsistencies in a systematic way. Two levels of contradiction can be distinguished. The *inter-operator contradictions* are the *systematic* contradictions between the decisions of different operators. They can be caused e.g. by different levels of experience, training, skill, etc. The *intra-operator contradictions* are the contradictions an operator makes with decisions he has made himself. They can be caused by personal factors (such as the level of fatigue, attention, stress and boredom), environmental factors (such as recent complaints of customers), etc. (see e.g. [3]).

The standard solution to this problem would be to gather training data from all of the operators who work on the system, put the data in one data set and use this to train the system. There are several problems with this approach, however. If the different operators provide their labels for the same set of data items, there will be data items in the set which have different labels. If there are too many inter-operator contradictions it will be difficult to train some classifiers properly (consider e.g. the Nearest Neighbour classifier [4]). The system would also not be transparent to the operators anymore: if one operator teaches something to the system, another operator might unlearn this behaviour, making it difficult to train the system. The feedback from the system to the operators would also turn problematic: it is impossible to determine what has been taught to the system by which operator.

To deal with this issue, in this paper an architecture to learn visual quality inspection from several different human operators is proposed in Section 2. Suitable ensemble methods, which are at the basis of this architecture, are discussed in detail in Section 3. The experiments that were performed are detailed in Section 4 and the corresponding results for a real-world inspection problem are discussed in Section 5. A conclusion is formulated in Section 6.

2   Architecture

In Figure 1 a generic framework for learning visual quality inspection from multiple human operators is shown. Starting from the original image of the product which is to be inspected (left-hand side of the figure), a so called "contrast image" is calculated. The grey-level value of each pixel in this image correlates to the degree of deviation from the "optimal" image of the product. Usually the im age is mostly black, with the potentially defective parts highlighted by non-black pixels. The contrast image is used to eliminate application-specific elements from subsequent processing steps. From the contrast image Regions Of Interest (ROIs) are extracted. Essentially this is a grouping of the non-black pixels in the image into one or more distinct groups (called "objects"), each of which is a potential defect. The features of each object are calculated and can be complemented by three additional data sources: information about the ROIs, information about the status of the production process and aggregate features, characterising the

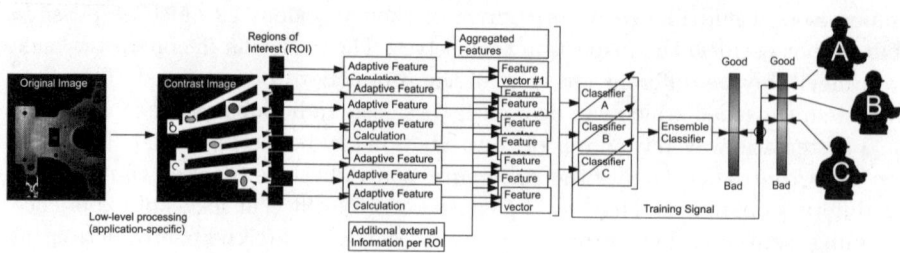

Fig. 1. General classification framework for visual quality inspection which can be trained by different human operators

images as a whole (information about all objects together). The feature vectors are processed by a trainable classifier which generates a good/bad decision for the entire image. This result is compared to the input of the human quality operators and a feedback loop adapts the classification system. The intra-operator contradictions, which are basically random, are dealt with by the classifier itself. Several learning techniques can naturally handle noisy data (see e.g. [4]).

Each operator will train his own classifier as he thinks would be best according to his experience and expertise. These operators will inevitably contradict each other (the inter-operator contradictions) for some of the images – and thus their personal classifiers will also produce different classifications. These contradicting decisions are resolved using ensemble methods. This combination can be done using fixed rules or, if a supervisor labels the data as well, trainable ensemble methods, to better represent the decisions of the supervisor (a detailed discussion can be found in Section 3). The decision the ensemble makes is the final decision of the classification system.

This architecture has several important advantages over other architectures which cannot deal with training input from several different human operators:

- If all training data is used together and there are too many inter-operator contradictions, it will be difficult to train some learning techniques properly (consider e.g. the Nearest Neighbour classifier [4]). By separating the training data provided by the operators this problem can be overcome: only the (basically random) intra-operator contradictions need to be dealt with by the classifiers; the inter-operator contradictions are handled by the ensemble.
- It can be clearly distinguished what has been taught by which operator, enabling the system to give operator-specific feedback. This can help the users to better understand the system. This enables them to give more appropriate input to the system, so the system can be trained in a more effective way.
- The knowledge of *each* of the operators can be captured in the system. This is considered to be very valuable information, as it usually takes a long time before the operators are experienced enough to make proper decisions about the quality of the produced products.
- Inconsistent quality of the delivered goods is considered to be a major problem by companies. The combining ensembles will keep the quality of the

products on the same level, regardless of which operator is currently working with the system.
– The classifiers will be easier to train, as they only need to take into account the (non-systematic) intra-operator contradictions. The inter-operator contradictions are dealt with by the ensembles.

3 Ensemble Methods to Combine the Operators' Decisions

3.1 Overview

The idea of *ensembles* of classifiers is not to train a single classifier, but a set (ensemble) of classifiers to do classifications. Most research has considered the case where there is a single data set to be classified. In this paper ensemble methods are used in a different context: the different operators train their individual classifiers as they think would be best and the contradictions among these operators are resolved using the ensemble methods. Additionally, if a supervisor labels the data, the ensemble methods can be used to learn to best represent the decisions of the supervisor, given only the decisions of the operators.

Ensemble methods can be divided into two classes: generative and non-generative [5]. *Generative* ensemble methods generate sets of classifiers by acting on the learning algorithm or on the structure of the data set, trying to actively improve the diversity and accuracy of the classifiers. In contrast, *non-generative* ensemble methods do not actively generate new classifiers but try to combine a set of different existing classifiers in a suitable way (e.g. by combining different types of classifiers). Clearly the non-generative approach is necessary for the application in this paper: the operators train their own classifiers in the way they think is the best and there is no way for the system to intervene in this process.

There are generally two ways to combine the decisions of classifiers in ensembles: classifier selection and classifier fusion [6]. The assumption in *classifier selection* is that each classifier is "an expert" in some local area of the feature space. In contrast, *classifier fusion* assumes that all classifiers are trained over the entire feature space. For the application which is described here *classifier fusion* is considered. The operators train the system with the data which is provided by the vision system and this data is spread over the entire data space; the classifiers trained by the operators are thus no "local experts".

Classifier fusion techniques are briefly discussed in Section 3.2; *Grading*, an ensemble method closely related to classifier fusion (as it also does not assume the classifiers to be local experts either), is discussed briefly in Section 3.3.

3.2 Classifier Fusion

The fusion of the outputs of the individual classifiers can be done using fixed or trainable combination rules. Several of the most effective classifier fusion methods are considered in this paper and will be shortly discussed in this section. For overviews and detailed discussions, see e.g. [7,8,9].

To produce their final decision, classifier fusion methods take as their inputs the outputs (classifications) of the classifiers in the ensemble. This fusion can be done using fixed rules such as *Voting* [10] or algebraic functions (*maximum, minimum, product, mean* and *median*) [11]. For the fixed classifier fusion methods the output is solely based on the outputs of the classifiers in the ensemble.

To optimise the performance of the classifier fusion techniques, a training process can be applied, taking as its input the outputs of the classifiers for the training set or their accuracies, estimated for the training set. The trainable classifier fusion methods considered here, which have shown their good performance for classification tasks, are *Fuzzy Integral* [12], *Decision Templates* [8], *Dempster-Shafer combination* [13] and *Discounted Dempster-Shafer combination* [9].

For comparison, also the performance of the *Oracle* are also included in the results in Section 5. This is a *hypothetical* ensemble scheme, which outputs the correct classification if at least one of the classifiers in the ensemble outputs the correct classification [8]. This can be seen as a "soft bound" on the accuracy we can expect from the ensembles, as it will be hard for the ensemble to output the correct classification if none of its members outputs the correct classification.

3.3   Grading

In the *Grading Classifiers* ensemble technique [14], for each of the classifiers in the ensemble a so-called "Grading classifier" is trained (on the *original* feature set) to estimate whether or not the classifier will output the correct decision or not. When a new data point is to be classified, only the classifiers in the ensemble which are estimated to be correct by their corresponding Grading classifiers are considered. The Majority Vote from these classifiers is taken as the final output of the Grading ensemble. One major difference with respect to the classifier fusion methods discussed in Section 3.2 is that the original feature space is considered instead of the space of the classifier outputs. Note that the classifiers are not assumed to be "local experts" in certain regions of the feature space (similar to classifier fusion methods), so this technique can also be applied within the framework presented in this work.

4   Experimental Setup

As discussed in Section 2, the proposed architecture for teaching the quality inspection to the system by the decisions of multiple operators clearly has many advantages. By only taking into account the data provided by the operators, we want to model the decisions of the supervisor. Of course, the accuracy of this system should not drop compared to a simple system which would only be trained on the data provided by the supervisor. The way this was assessed is described in this section; the corresponding results are discussed in Section 5.

For the experiments in this paper a data set, obtained from an industrial visual inspection system used for checking the quality of the labels printed on CDs and DVDs, is used. This data set contains 1534 samples and was independently labelled by 5 different operators (hence, there are actually 5 different data sets). As discussed in Section 2, from the images obtained from the vision system 57 general features (such as the area of the object, the maximum grey-level of the object, etc.) are calculated for every ROI. These features vectors for each object in an image are aggregated into an "aggregated" feature vector, describing all the objects in one image together. The aggregated feature vector contains 17 features, such as the number of object that were detected, the size of the largest object, the maximal grey-level of the image, the total area of the objects, etc. In the experiments that were performed the aggregated feature vector was used; so exactly one feature vector with 17 features was derived for each of the images.

To evaluate the performance of the ensembles when combining the decisions of multiple operators and trying to model the supervisor as well as possible, each of the operators is in turn considered as the supervisor. The supervisor's decisions were considered as being the "ground truth". So the experiments were repeated 5 times, every time considering another operator as the supervisor.

For the data sets provided by each of the operators a CART classifier [4] was trained. The accuracy of these classifiers was determined on the data set provided by the operator who is considered to be the supervisor in the experiment at hand (using the average over 100 random 90% train / 10% test splits). The outputs of the classifiers trained for the operators were then used for training the ensemble methods to better model the decisions of the supervisor: the decisions of the classifiers trained for the operators (evaluated on the training set) were used as input to the ensemble and the labels the supervisor has given were used as the targets. This is of course only possible in case a trainable classifier fusion method or Grading is used as the ensemble; if a fixed ensemble is used no training is possible. The results of these experiments can be found in Section 5.

As the experiments are performed in a general framework (see Section 2), the results presented in Section 5 should carry over to other visual inspection tasks involving multiple operators as well. The presented methodology is even not restricted to visual inspection problems. The ensembles combine the decisions of the classifiers (for which general techniques are used) that are trained by the different operators. This provides an abstraction of the actual task the operators perform. The most important factor in the performance of the system is the amount of systematic differences between the different operators. Random errors (such as the ones caused by e.g. fatigue) do not play a significant role in these results: they influence the learning process of the classifiers (fine-tuning the classifiers' representation of the decisions of the operators), but not so much the one of the ensembles (learning the *systematic* differences between the operators and the supervisor).

5   Results and Discussion

In this section the use of ensemble methods to combine the decisions of different operators will be evaluated (as explained in Section 4). For the data provided by each of the operators a CART classifier [4] was trained using an optimal pruning strategy. These classifiers were evaluated on the data provided by each

Table 1. Mean accuracy (in %) of CART classifiers for the CD data sets. Each row denotes a different training set (labelling provided by a particular operator) and each columns denotes a different evaluation set (labelling provided a particular operator).

Classifier trained on data provided by	Evaluation on data provided by				
	Operator01	Operator02	Operator03	Operator04	Operator05
Operator01	90.57	89.27	85.33	88.94	71.42
Operator02	88.83	95.38	91.88	93.10	69.42
Operator03	86.50	93.42	93.90	92.68	70.59
Operator04	88.82	93.67	92.08	94.38	71.91
Operator05	72.42	71.64	71.73	73.58	91.25

of the operators (as each operator was in turn considered to be the supervisor and hence the labels he provided are considered to be the "ground truth").

The results of this evaluation can be found in Table 1. Each row in this table denotes a different training set (labelling provided by a particular operator) and each columns denotes a different evaluation set (labelling provided a particular operator). Note that the values on the "diagonal" of the table refer to evaluating the classifiers on the test part of the data set they were trained for (hence these values are the highest for each of the columns). From this table we can see that the classifiers are well trained. If the classifiers are evaluated on the data set they were trained for, their mean accuracies range from 90.57% to 95.38%. By looking at the evaluation of the classifiers on the data provided by the other operators, we can see that Operators02, 03 and 04 make similar decisions; Operator01 differs slightly from these three; and Operator05 labelled the data in a way very different from the other operators. In fact, about 20% of the labels provided by Operator05 were contradicting *each* of the other four operators. This can also be seen in the table: evaluation of the classifier trained on the data provided by Operator05 (last row of the table) on the data provided by the other operators resulted in mean accuracies ranging from 71.64% to 73.58%; evaluation of the classifiers trained on the data provided by the operators on the data provided by Operator05 resulted in mean accuracies ranging from 69.42% to 71.91%. From these results we can conclude that there are systematic contradictions between the operators, which need to be resolved.

A question now is on which of the data provided by the operators the final classification should be based. If this would be Operator05, a classifier trained on the data provided by another operator would be not very accurate. Usually in a company there is a supervisor who is in charge of the quality inspection, but usually does not operate the quality inspection systems himself. By having this supervisor label some data samples as well, we can train the ensembles to better model the decisions of the supervisor.

To this extent, the use of ensemble methods was investigated. Each of the operators was in turn considered to be the supervisor, and the decisions of the other operators are combined in such a way to represent the supervisor's decisions

Table 2. Mean accuracy (in %) of the different ensemble methods (different rows) for the CD data sets. Different operators are considered to be the supervisor (different columns); training input for the ensembles is provided by the other operators.

Ensembles to combine the classifiers trained for the operators	Evaluation on data provided by (considered the supervisor)				
	Operator01	Operator02	Operator03	Operator04	Operator05
Voting	88.35	92.31	90.22	92.72	70.33
Algebraic Mean	88.19	89.86	88.28	91.56	71.74
Fuzzy Integral	88.50	94.42	91.61	93.69	71.25
Decision Templates	88.19	94.42	89.16	91.59	74.75
D-S Combination	88.19	94.42	91.82	92.07	71.75
Disc. D-S Combination	88.31	94.42	92.24	93.54	71.75
Grading	91.19	96.05	93.57	94.61	74.69
Oracle	95.83	98.89	97.07	98.60	78.90

as well as possible. The labels of the supervisor for the training part of the data set were taken as the "ground truth" to train the trainable ensembles.

In Table 2 the results can be found of this evaluation. Each column in the table relates to a different operator being considered the supervisor; each row contains the results for a particular ensemble method, combining the decisions of the other operators. In the table we can see that the performance of the fixed classifier fusion methods is worse than the other methods, the accuracies being about 1% to 5% lower than the other methods. From the trainable classifier fusion methods the Fuzzy Integral and especially the Discounted Dempster-Shafer Combination were in general the most successful. However, if Operator05 was considered to be the supervisor (making decisions significantly different from all other operators), the Decision Templates performed better than the other trainable classifier fusion methods. The most notable improvement came from the Grading ensemble, however (using CART [4] as Grading classifier): it outperformed all other classifier fusion methods. The improvements in accuracy over the *best* classifier fusion method range from about 1% to 3%. Only in the case that Operator05 was considered to be the supervisor it performed slightly worse than the Decision Templates method (0.06% less accuracy). Also the results of the hypothetical Oracle are shown, providing a soft limit on the maximum accuracy for the ensembles (and classifiers).

If we compare the results in Table 1 and Table 2, we see that the results of the trainable ensemble methods are better than the results of the classifiers trained on data which is not the supervisor's. This, of course, could be expected as the ensembles are in fact trained to combine the decisions of the operators to resemble those of the supervisor. What is does show is the robustness of the ensemble methods with respect to badly performing classifiers, as the ensembles learn to assign a low importance to the classifier trained by Operator05 (significantly different from the other operators). Another important observation is the increase in accuracy of the Grading ensemble when compared to the classifiers which were actually trained for the supervisor himself (the values on the "diagonal" of Table 1), ranging up to 0.67%. This means that the ensembles, which are trained to combine the decisions of the different operators (not including the supervisor), can perform better than a classifier which is specifically trained to classify the data set provided by the supervisor. However, if Operator05 is considered to be the supervisor the Grading ensemble fails to do so. In this case the performance is significantly lower than a classifier trained for this data set. This is due to the fact that this operator differs so much from the other operators (hence even the hypothetical Oracle performs at a comparable level).

6   Conclusions

When applying Machine Learning technology to real-world applications, such as visual quality inspection, several practical issues need to be taken care of. One problem is posed by the reality that usually there are multiple human operators doing the inspection. Additionally, their supervisor would like to be in control of the operators' decisions as much as possible, without doing the inspection himself. The operators might be contradicting each other as well as the supervisor, making it very difficult to properly train the system.

In this paper a novel framework for dealing with this problem was proposed. This framework explicitly takes into account that multiple operators may be training the visual quality inspection system. Within the framework each operator trains his own classifier. These classifiers are combined using ensemble methods, which are trained to resolve the contradictory input provided by the operators and to model the decisions of their supervisor as well as possible, based on the outputs of these classifiers. This gives the system important advantages over systems which are unable to do so, such as a consistent level of quality of the products, the ability to give operator-specific feedback, the ability to capture the knowledge of every operator separately and an easier training of the system.

Evaluation of data obtained from a real-world industrial system to do visual quality inspection of the printing of labels on CDs, which was labelled separately by 5 different operators, showed that there are systematic contradictions between the decisions of the operators. To resolve these contradictions, the performances of 7 different ensemble methods are compared against each other as well as to the classifiers which are trained by the operators. It is shown that the system is able to resolve many of the contradictions which are present in the data. Furthermore, it is shown that in several cases the system even performs better than a classifier which is trained on the data provided by the supervisor itself. Particularly the Grading ensemble was successful in the experiments, compared to the 6 classifier fusion techniques considered in this paper.

Acknowledgements

This work was supported by the European Commission (project Contract No. STRP016429, acronym DynaVis). This publication reflects only the authors' views.

References

1. Castillo, E., Alvarez, E.: Expert Systems: Uncertainty and Learning. Springer Verlag, New York (2007)
2. Malamas, E., Petrakis, E., Zervakis, M., Petit, L., Legat, J.D.: A survey on industrial vision systems, applications and tools. Image and Vision Computing 21 (2003)
3. Govindaraju, M., Pennathur, A., Mital, A.: Quality improvement in manufacturing through human performance enhancement. Integrated Manufacturing Systems 12(5) (2001)
4. Duda, R., Hart, P., Stork, D.: Pattern Classification, 2nd edn. John Wiley & Sons, New York (2000)
5. Valentini, G., Masulli, F.: Ensembles of learning machines. In: Marinaro, M., Tagliaferri, R. (eds.) WIRN 2002. LNCS, vol. 2486, pp. 3–22. Springer, Heidelberg (2002)
6. Woods, K., Kegelmeyer, W., Bowyer, K.: Combination of multiple classifiers using local accuracy estimates. IEEE Transactions on Pattern Analysis and Machine Intelligence 19(4), 405–410 (1997)
7. Kuncheva, L.I.: Combining Pattern Classifiers: Methods and Algorithms. Wiley, Chichester (2004)
8. Kuncheva, L., Bezdek, J., Duin, R.: Decision templates for multiple classifier fusion: An experimental comparison. Pattern Recognition 34(2), 299–314 (2001)
9. Sannen, D., Van Brussel, H., Nuttin, M.: Classifier fusion using Discounted Dempster-Shafer combination. In: Poster Proceedings of the 5th International Conference on Machine Learning and Data Mining, pp. 216–230 (2007)
10. Kuncheva, L., Whitaker, C., Shipp, C., Duin, R.: Limits on the majority vote accuracy in classifier fusion. Pattern Analysis & Applications 6(1), 22–31 (2003)
11. Kittler, J., Hatef, M., Duin, R., Matas, J.: On combining classifiers. IEEE Transactions on Pattern Analysis and Machine Intelligence 20(3), 226–239 (1998)
12. Cho, S., Kim, J.: Combining multiple neural networks by fuzzy integral for robust classification. IEEE Transactions on Systems, Man, and Cybernetics 25(2), 380–384 (1995)
13. Rogova, G.: Combining the results of several neural network classifiers. Neural Networks 7(5), 777–781 (1994)
14. Seewald, A., Fürnkranz, J.: An evaluation of grading classifiers. In: Hoffmann, F., Adams, N., Fisher, D., Guimarães, G., Hand, D.J. (eds.) IDA 2001. LNCS, vol. 2189, pp. 115–124. Springer, Heidelberg (2001)

Learning Contextual Variations for Video Segmentation

Vincent Martin and Monique Thonnat

INRIA Sophia Antipolis, PULSAR project-team
2004 route des lucioles, BP 93
F-06902 Sophia Antipolis
{Vincent.R.Martin, Monique.Thonnat}@sophia.inria.fr,
http://www-sop.inria.fr/pulsar/

Abstract. This paper deals with video segmentation in vision systems. We focus on the maintenance of background models in long-term videos of changing environment which is still a real challenge in video surveillance. We propose an original weakly supervised method for learning contextual variations in videos. Our approach uses a clustering algorithm to automatically identify different contexts based on image content analysis. Then, state-of-the-art video segmentation algorithms (e.g. codebook, MoG) are trained on each cluster. The goal is to achieve a dynamic selection of background models. We have experimented our approach on a long video sequence (24 hours). The presented results show the segmentation improvement of our approach compared to codebook and MoG.

Keywords: video segmentation, weakly supervised learning, context awareness, video surveillance, cognitive vision.

1 Introduction

Figure-ground segmentation consists in separating the foreground pixels of the background pixels. In video applications, the variability of the two classes makes the detection of foreground pixels fairly impossible to predict without motion information. A widely used method to tackle this problem is to model the background in order to detect only moving pixels. In this paper, we consider the problem of the figure-ground segmentation task in video surveillance applications where both quick-illumination changes and long term changes are present. In this situation, the major difficulty at the segmentation level is to deliver robust results whatever lighting changes occur in the scene. These lighting effects can be due to weather conditions changes in outdoor scenes, to the switching of an artificial lighting source in indoor scenes, or to a combination of changes of different natures. The consequences at the pixel level are variations of intensity, color saturation, or inter-pixel contrast. At the image level, these changes can affect just a local area or the whole image. Another source of problems arises from the presence of non-static objects in the background as swaying trees or mobile objects as chairs.

A. Gasteratos, M. Vincze, and J.K. Tsotsos (Eds.): ICVS 2008, LNCS 5008, pp. 464–473, 2008.

Our objective is to cope with all these issues with a cognitive vision approach by endowing video segmentation methods with learning and adaptation faculties. To this end, we first relate some work dealing with these issues then present our learning-based approach for dynamic selection of background model. Finally, we show the effectiveness of our approach on a difficult video sequence.

2   Related Work

A basic approach to estimate the motion is to compute the difference between a background image, called the reference image, and the current frame. The result is then thresholded to get a binary image of moving pixels. The result is obviously very sensitive to the threshold. Most of the time, the user must tune this threshold in a trial-and-error process. One difficulty arises when the background pixels are varying along the time. In this case, more elaborated approaches build a background model for each pixel based on the pixel's recent history by using, for instance a chronological average or median of the n previous frames [1]. Parametric models as Mixture of Gaussian (MoG) [2], Kernel Density Estimator (KDE) [3], and codebooks [4] have been proposed to cope with multiple modal background distributions. These algorithms are based on a training stage to estimate the Gaussian parameters (for MoG), to compute the probability density functions (for KDE), or to construct the codebooks. The training data are composed of background samples, i.e. a set of frames without any moving objects of interest. The training stage of the Mog model consists in estimating k Gaussian parameters set (ω, μ, Σ) for each pixel using an expectation-minimization algorithm, where k is the number of gaussians in the mixture. For the codebook model, the learning stage consists in constructing the set of codewords (i.e. a codebook) for each pixel. A codework is composed of a vector of mean RGB values and of a five-tuple vector containing intensity (brightness) minimum and maximum values, the frequency with which the codeword has occurred with its first and last access time. Each of these techniques can provide acceptable accuracy in specific applications: MoG are adapted to multi-modal background distributions but fail to provide sensitive detection when background has fast variations. KDE overcomes this problem but are limited to short-term videos due mostly to memory constraints. Codebooks alleviate this computation limitation by constructing a highly compressed background model but produce too wide background models when the environment is highly variable as in long-term videos. We propose to add to these algorithms a learning-based layer. We will compare the performance of our approach with codebooks and MoG.

3   Proposed Approach

Our approach is based on a preliminary (off-line) weakly supervised learning module (see Figure 1) during which the knowledge of the context variations is acquired. In our approach we suppose that: (1) the video camera is fixed and

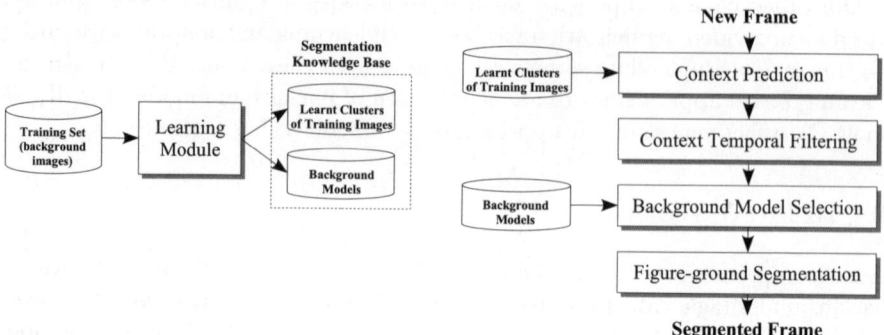

Fig. 1. The learning module in video segmentation task

Fig. 2. Adaptive figure-ground segmentation schema based on context identification and background model selection

(2) background images are available as training samples. We define the context of an image as the numerical representation of its local and global characteristics. We call this approach weakly supervised because the role of the user is restricted to establish a training image set composed of background samples that point out context variations, e.g. the different illuminations changes that could be encountered in real-time use. In a practical point of view, the collection can be achieved by a manual selection of frame sequences. These assumptions fit quite good with the targeted applications where videos can be acquired continuously, typically 24 hours per day and seven days per week. The quick availability of data allows to build huge training image set.

We tackle the context modelling problem by performing an unsupervised clustering of the training images. The goal is to make the background modelling problem more reliable by restricting the model parameter space. This approach is particularly interesting for motion segmentation algorithms relying on a training stage of models as mixture of Gaussian [2] or codebook [4]. The clustering is based on the analysis of global image characteristics like color variations. At the end of the clustering process, each cluster gathers training images sharing similar global features, i.e. images of the same context.

3.1   Context Analysis by Image Sequence Clustering

The fixed field of view of the video camera allows to analyze the image variations both globally and locally. To this end, a straightforward approach consists in a global histograming of pixel intensity as in [5]. However, this technique is not fully adapted. Actually, classic histograms lack spatial information, and images with different appearances can have similar histograms. To overcome this limitation, we use an histogram-based method that incorporates spatial information [6]. This approach consists in building a coherent color histogram based

Fig. 3. Four frames representative of the illumination changes at different times of the day

on pixel membership to large similarly-colored regions. For instance, an image presenting red pixels forming a single coherent region will have a color coherence histogram with a peak at the level of red color. An image with the same quantity of red pixels but widely scattered, will not have this peak. This is particularly significant for outdoor scene with changing lighting conditions due to the sun rotation, as in Figure 3.

In our experiment, we have used a Density-Based Spatial clustering algorithm called DBScan [7] to identify the image clusters. This algorithm is well-adapted for clustering noisy data of arbitrary shape in high-dimensional space as histograms. Starting from one point of the data set, the algorithm searches for similar points in its neighborhood based on a density criteria to manage noisy data. Non clustered points are considered as 'noise' points. The runtime of the algorithm is of the order $O(n \log n)$ with n the dimension of the input space. DBScan requires only one critical input parameter, the *Eps*-neighborhood, and supports the user in determining an appropriate value for it. A low value will raise to many small clusters and may also classify a lot of points as noisy points, a high value prevents from noisy point detection but produces few clusters. A good value would be the density of the least dense cluster. However, it is very hard to get this information on advance. Normally one does not know the distribution of the points in the space. If no cluster is found, all points are marked as noise. In our approach, we set this parameter so as to have at the most 15% of the training images classified as 'noise' data.

Then, for each identified cluster, the corresponding training frames are put together and used to train a background model (the codebooks for instance). Internal knowledge of the DBScan algorithm as the tree nodes and elements are also stored for further classifications of new images. So, to each cluster of training image corresponds a trained background model. The next step is the real-time adaptive segmentation of the video using a dynamic selection of trained background models.

3.2 Real-Time Adaptive Figure-Ground Segmentation

We denote κ a cluster of training images belonging to the same context θ. The set of the n clusters is noted $\mathcal{K} = \{\kappa_1, \ldots, \kappa_n\}$ and the corresponding context set

$\Theta = \{\theta_1, \ldots, \theta_n\}$. For a new incoming image I not belonging to the training set, a global feature vector $\mathbf{v}(I)$, here a coherent color histogram in the HSV color space, is extracted and classified into a cluster. The classification is based on the minimization of the L2 distance between the feature vector and the cluster set $\{\kappa_i\}$ as follows:

$$I \in \theta_i \Leftrightarrow \mathbf{v}(I) \in \kappa_i \mid i = \arg \min_{i \in [1,n]} dist\,(\mathbf{v}(I), \kappa_i) \qquad (1)$$

The background model associated with the detected context θ_i, is returned.

We also use a temporal filtering step to reduce the instability of the clustering algorithm when a foreground object appears. Indeed, in this case, a noise context is detected most of the time. So, it is important to smooth the analysis by balancing the current result with respect to previous ones. Our temporal filtering criterion is defined as follows. Let us define θ the context cluster identifier (the buffered context), θ_I the cluster identifier for the incoming image I, and μ_θ the mean of cluster probability computed on a temporal window. To decide if θ_I is the adequate cluster for an incoming image I, we compare it with θ as in Algorithm 1. In this algorithm, three cases are investigated. If θ_I is equal to θ or to 0 (noise context), μ_θ is averaged based on the last context probability $p(\theta_I)$ and θ remains unchanged. In the third case, (θ_I differs from θ and 0), θ is updated and μ_θ is updated according to $p(\theta_I)$.

When the context is identified, the corresponding background model is selected and the figure-ground segmentation of I is performed, as sketched in Figure 2.

Algorithm 1. Context Temporal Filtering Algorithm

Input: I
Output: θ

    $\theta \leftarrow 0$ {set buffered context identifier to 'noise' (for the first frame only)}
    $\mu_\theta \leftarrow 0$ {set θ probability to 0 (for the first frame only)}

    $[\theta_I, p(\theta_I)] \leftarrow ContextAnalysis\{I\}$ {θ_I = context ident. of I}
    if $\theta = \theta_I$ *or* $\theta = 0$ **then**
        $\mu_\theta \leftarrow \frac{\mu_\theta + p(\theta_I)}{2}$ {μ_θ averaging}
    else
        $\theta \leftarrow \theta_I$ {θ updating}
        if $p(\theta_I) \geq \mu_\theta$ **then**
            $\mu_\theta \leftarrow p(\theta_I)$ {μ_θ updating}
        else
            $\mu_\theta \leftarrow \frac{\mu_\theta + p(\theta_I)}{2}$ {μ_θ averaging}
        end if
    end if
return θ

---

4   Experimental Results

4.1   Experiment

The experimental conditions are the followings: the video data are taken during a period of 24 hours, at eight frames per second, from a video surveillance camera fixed above an outdoor cash desk of a car park. The video camera parameters are set in automatic mode. The size of the images is 352×288 pixels and are stored in JPEG format. For the experiment, we have taken one frame on five which correspond to 138000 frames in total. Four samples picked from the image set are shown in Figure 3. They have been chosen to illustrate the background modelling problem. In the learning stage, we have manually defined a training image set I composed of 5962 background frames (i.e. without foreground objects) along the sequence. This corresponds to pick one frame every 15 seconds in mean and represents 4.3% of the whole image set. Figure 4 gives a quick overview of the global feature distribution along the sequence. In this figure, each X-Z slice is an histogram which represents the percentage of the number of pixels (Z axis) belonging to a given color coherent feature (X axis). The coherent color feature scale has been divided into 3 intervals for the three HSV channels. The Y axis represents the time in the course of a day. Several clusters of histograms can be easily visually discriminated as notified for cluster number 1, 10 and 2. Other clusters, not represented here, are intermediate ones and mainly correspond to transitions states between the three main clusters. Sixteen clusters are found (see Figure 5 for context class distribution). Three major clusters can be identified (number 1, 2 and 10). The order of class representation does not necessary

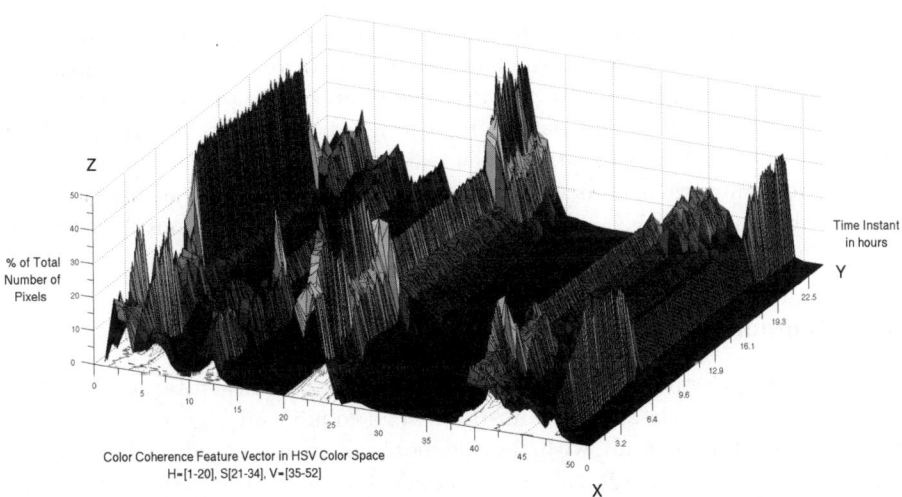

Fig. 4. 3-D histogram of the training image set used for the clustering (see Figure 3 for samples)

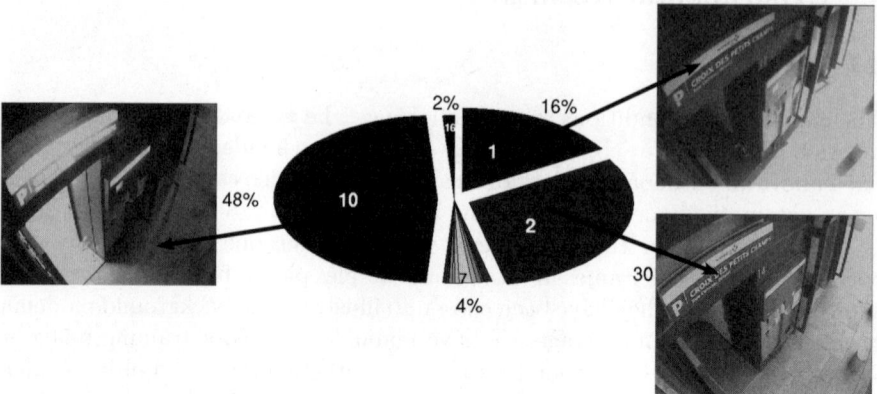

Fig. 5. Pie chart of the context distribution. The three most represented image clusters are shown corresponding to night, sunny, and cloudy contexts.

correspond to consecutive time instants. Cluster 1 corresponds to noon (sunny context), cluster 2 corresponds to the morning (lower contrast) and cluster 14 to the night. We compare the results obtained with different segmentation settings (with or without the context adaption, etc.) at different times of the day and in several difficult situations.

4.2   Model Selection Effects

In this section, we show three examples (three columns) in Figure 6 where the selection of the background model helps to improve the segmentation. Boundaries of the detected regions (in green) have been dilated for a better visualization. `context ID` is the identifier of the detected context and `prob` is the estimate probability of the identified context. In this figure, the first row corresponds to the direct codebook segmentation when trained on the whole training image set. The second row corresponds to our context-based codebook segmentation. We can see that our approach achieves a better detection rate without adding false detection.

4.3   Temporal Filtering Effects

In this section, we present some situations where the temporal filtering algorithm can help to correct classification mistakes. The columns of Figure 7 correspond to the segmentation result with the codebook algorithm based on respectively one background model (left column), dynamic selection of the background model (middle column), and dynamic selection of the background plus temporal filtering (right column). The presence of a person modifies the pixel distribution of the scene and then disturbs the context classification. Consequentely, a 'noise' context (`ID:0`) is often detected as shown in Figure 7 (second row middle column).

Fig. 6. Comparison of direct search codebook segmentation (first row) with our context-based codebook segmentation (second row) for three different contexts

Fig. 7. Illustration of the temporal filtering effect on the context analysis. Columns are, from left to right: without context adaptation, with context adaptation, with filtered context adaptation. Rows are frame at time t and $t+1.87$".

The temporal filtering algorithm smooths the context analysis by integrating the results of the previous frames, and then helps in keeping a correct context classification in such cases. We can also see on the second row that the man's shadow is not detected. In fact, context ID:1 gathers frames from sunny and shaded illumination conditions of this scene part. The corresponding background model has thus integrated these values during the training.

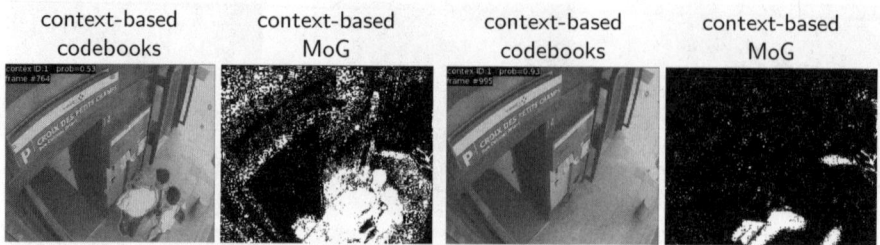

| context-based codebooks | context-based MoG | context-based codebooks | context-based MoG |

Fig. 8. Comparison between the proposed approach applied to the codebook model [4] and the MoG model [2] for two frames at time t and $t+2'24"$

4.4 Comparison with Mixture of Gaussian

In this section, we compare our approach with the MoG approach. We use an implementation of the algorithm proposed in [2]. We use the default parameter setting[1]. A MoG background model is trained for each identified cluster then dynamically selected during the real-time segmentation. Figure 8 shows the high sensitivity of Mog to global changes (first frame) and the effects of a too large learning rate (second frame): foreground pixels from the first frame still remain 231 frames later (ghost formations).

5   Conclusion

In this paper, we have presented an original weakly supervised learning approach for the dynamic selection of background model. This approach, consisting in generating sub-goals and training learning-based algorithms on each sub-goal is similar to a meta-learning approach. Our main contribution is thus at the context modelling level: based on local and global image information, different contextual situations are automatically identified and learned thanks to a clustering algorithm. This approach is particularly interesting for very long video sequences (several hours) where both quick and long-term image variations do not allow to maintain robustly a background model.

Promising results are presented on a very long-term video surveillance application (outdoor car park entrance surveillance) where both gradual and sudden changes occur. In a weakly supervised learning stage, the user collects background samples of the different situations. The clustering algorithm has successfully identified meaningful clusters of training images like sunny context, night context, or dawn context. For each identified image cluster, a background model has been trained using the codebooks [4] and the MoG [2]. In real-time figure-ground segmentation, the different contexts are successfully retrieved thanks to the temporal filtering algorithm. The codebook model has shown to be well-adapted to deal with background model splitting and real-time constraints.

---

[1] Number of gaussians = 3, Learning rate = 0.05, μ and σ Update rate = 0.005.

Comparisons with the MoG model reveal its robustness in different situations as quick illuminations changes variations or shadows removal.

However, some problems remain in the context adaptation especially when unforeseen changes occur. We plan to cope with these problems by applying incremental clustering techniques. Moreover, a quantitative evaluation study remains to be done to objectively assess our approach against other algorithms. We are currently investigating video databases with ground truth data.

References

[1] Prati, A., Mikic, I., Trivedi, M., Cucchiara, R.: Detecting moving shadows: algorithms and evaluation. IEEE Transactions on Pattern Analysis and Machine Intelligence 25(7), 918–923 (2003)

[2] Stauffer, C., Grimson, W.: Adaptive background mixture models for real-time tracking. In: Proc. of IEEE Conf. on Computer Vision and Pattern Recognition, pp. 246–252 (1999)

[3] Elgammal, A.M., Harwood, D., Davis, L.S.: Non-parametric model for background subtraction. In: Vernon, D. (ed.) ECCV 2000. LNCS, vol. 1843, pp. 751–767. Springer, Heidelberg (2000)

[4] Kim, K., Chalidabhongse, T.H., Harwood, D., Davis, L.: Real-time foreground-background segmentation using codebook model. Real-Time Imaging 11(3), 172–185 (2005)

[5] Georis, B., Bremond, F., Thonnat, M.: Real-time control of video surveillance systems with program supervision techniques. Machine Vision and Applications 18(3-4), 189–205 (2007)

[6] Pass, G., Zabih, R., Miller, J.: Comparing images using color coherence vectors. In: ACM International Conference on Multimedia, pp. 65–73. ACM Press, New York, USA (1997)

[7] Ester, M., Kriegel, H.P., Sander, J., Xu, X.: A density-based algorithm for discovering clusters in large spatial databases with noise. In: Proc. 2nd Int. Conf. on Knowledge Discovery and Data Mining, Portland, pp. 226–231 (1996)

Learning to Detect Aircraft at Low Resolutions

Stavros Petridis[*], Christopher Geyer, and Sanjiv Singh

Robotics Institute, Carnegie Mellon University,
Pittsburgh, PA, USA
sp104@doc.ic.ac.uk, {cgeyer,ssingh}@cs.cmu.edu

Abstract. An application of the Viola and Jones object detector to the problem of aircraft detection is presented. This approach is based on machine learning rather than morphological filtering which was mainly used in previous works. Aircraft detection using computer vision methods is a challenging problem since target aircraft can vary from subpixels to a few pixels in size and the background can be heavily cluttered. Such a system can be a part of a collision avoidance system to warn the pilots of potential collisions. Initial results suggest that this (static) approach on a frame to frame basis achieves a detection rate of about 80% and a false positive rate which is comparable with other approaches that use morphological filtering followed by a tracking stage. The system was evaluated on over 15000 frames which were extracted from real video sequences recorded by NASA and has the potential of real time performance.

Keywords: automatic target detection, aircraft detection, collision avoidance, obstacle detection, computer vision applications.

1 Introduction

The use of computer vision for detecting obstacles in the flight path of an aircraft is investigated in this paper. Such a system can be used to warn the pilots for potential collisions and would also be useful aboard unmanned aerial vehicles (UAVs). Any aircraft detection technique should provide high detection rate, low false alarm rate and early detection. The main challenges in this problem are the presence of image noise, the almost stationary nature of the target on collision course, the possible presence of heavily cluttered background, and the extremely small size of the obstacles that can vary from subpixels to a few pixels. In addition, the algorithm should be able to run in real time imposing severe constraints on execution time.

Obstacle detection in the flight path of an aircraft is a key component of a collision avoidance system. That also includes a collision risk estimation component together with a component that performs appropriate avoidance maneuvers in order to maintain minimum separation distances. Such an approach must demonstrate a level of performance which meets or exceeds that of a human pilot as stated in FAA order 7610.4 [1].

---

[*] This work was done while the author was visiting the Robotics Institute at Carnegie Mellon University. He is currently with the Department Of Computing, Imperial College London.

A. Gasteratos, M. Vincze, and J.K. Tsotsos (Eds.): ICVS 2008, LNCS 5008, pp. 474–483, 2008.
© Springer-Verlag Berlin Heidelberg 2008

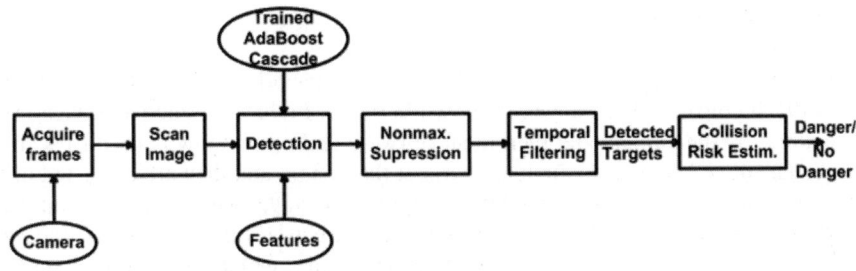

Fig. 1. The proposed architecture for collision detection

There are several different approaches which address the problem of obstacle detection in the framework of collision avoidance including morphological filtering [2], dynamic programming [3], and recursive max filter [4]. McCandless [5] proposed an optical flow method which is suitable only for moving objects. Gandhi [6] proposed a two stage approach, an image processing stage followed by a tracking stage. The image processing stage isolates potential features using morphological filtering and the tracking stage tracks these features to distinguish the real targets from background clutter using the rate of translation and expansion. Carnie [7] implemented a similar approach using morphological filtering followed by a dynamic programming algorithm to enhance detection.

The use of morphological filtering is popular on computer vision based collision avoidance systems [2], [6], [7]. However, this approach generates a significant number of false positives and requires tracking of the features over a large number of frames as reported in [7], [8].

In this paper we present a machine learning approach based on AdaBoost to detect aircraft. We report results on the application of a modified version of the Viola and Jones object detector [9], which has been used successfully in face detection, on the aircraft detection problem. Initial experiments show that it achieves a high detection rate (around 80%) whereas the number of false positives generated by the static classifier, i.e. no tracking is used, is comparable with that obtained by systems based on morphological filtering and tracking. The system was evaluated on over 15000 frames taken from real video sequences which is a much higher number than the typical number of test frames used by the majority of the existing aircraft detectors (less than 1000). An attractive property of this detector is that it has the potential to run on or close to real time. The original Viola and Jones classifier tries to detect faces from their internal structure whereas our classifier tries to separate the target from the background since targets which are far away do not have any structure; they appear as a row or a rectangle of few pixels.

The paper is organized as follows: section 2 gives an overview of the proposed system, section 3 describes the data we used, section 4 discusses the results of two different scenarios (collision course and crossing) and section 5 concludes the paper.

2 System Overview

The system we propose here is based on the framework introduced by Viola and Jones [9]. It consists of six stages as shown in Fig. 1. In the first stage an image frame is acquired by the camera and then in stage two a sliding window is used to scan the frame. The next 3 stages are the main parts of the system and they are consisted of the detector followed by a non-maximal suppression stage which is followed by a temporal filtering stage. Then all the detected targets (both real targets and false positives) are passed to the final stage which determines which targets pose a threat to the aircraft. The main focus of this paper was the development of stage 3 but some simple temporal filtering approaches were evaluated. The system shown in Fig. 1 should work in real time. However, the detector should be trained off – line and when the training process ends then it can be used on line as well.

2.1 Cascade Training

A cascade is a structure which consists of a series of classifiers as shown in Fig. 2. When a pattern is fed into the cascade then it is labeled as positive if it successfully passes all stages whereas there are multiple exits for the patterns which fail at some point and those are labeled as negative.

In the third stage, a cascade classifier is applied to all subwindows of each frame. The key point is that within any single frame the vast majority of subwindows are negative so the cascade attempts to reject as many negatives as possible at the earliest stage possible. So the first stages consist of simple and fast classifiers which reject most of the negative subwindows while keeping almost all of the positive subwindows whereas subsequent stages eliminate additional negatives but they are more complex. Stages in the cascade are constructed by training classifiers using AdaBoost as in [9]. However we do not use the original cascade where each classifier outputs "Yes" or "No" but we follow the boosting chain approach [10] where each classifier outputs a real value which is added to the sum of the outputs of all the previous classifiers. If the new sum is greater than the stage's threshold then the pattern is fed into the next classifier, otherwise it is discarded. So the cascade's function can be summarized in the following three steps

1.   Given an input pattern initialize $s = 0$
2.   For all stages ($i = 1\ldots K$)
        $s = s +$ stage output (c_i)
        if $s <$ stage threshold (r_i) then exit with negative response
3.   Exit with positive response

The output value of the i-th stage is c_i and the corresponding rejection threshold is r_i (see Fig. 2). A real example of how the cascade works is shown in Fig. 2 (right). The X-axis represents the stages of the cascade and the Y-axis represents the cumulative sum of the stage outputs. Similarly to [11] we can define a rejection trace (black trace) which represents the thresholds of each stage. So as long as the partial sums are greater than the rejection trace then the pattern is kept. Blue lines represent aircraft (targets) and red lines represent negative patterns. So the red lines that are above the rejection threshold until the final stage are false positives. The red dashed lines

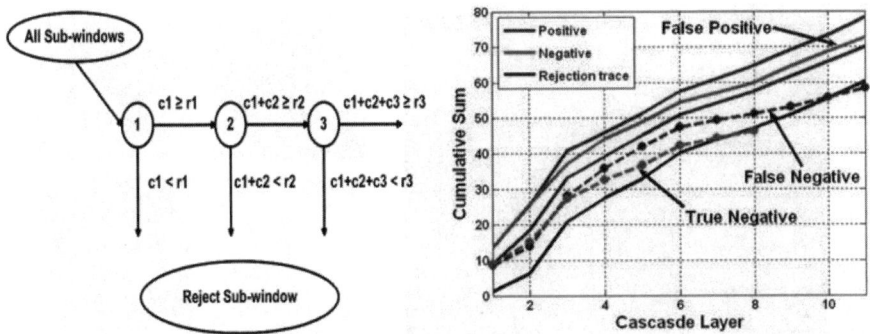

Fig. 2. Left: The cascade structure used in this paper, Right: An example of how the cascade works

represent rejected negative subwindows whereas the blue dashed-lines represent false negatives. Using this approach the performance of a pattern in the prior stages is taken into account and also a pattern may fail one or more stages but as long as it stays above the rejection threshold it can be correctly classified.

2.2 Features

The 4 types of Haar features from which the training system will extract the best features are shown in Fig. 4 Apart from the two commonly used filters, two more filters were introduced to take into account the nature of the problem. A target in a large distance is expected to have greater width than height as shown in Fig. 3 (right). Since we can not detect the aircraft from its structure (as in the case of face detection) but we want to distinguish the target from the background then the inclusion of these filters helps towards this goal (Fig 4, top row, columns 3-4). The features are used in all locations and scales that fit in the detector. The output of each feature is the sum of the pixels which lie within the white rectangle subtracted from the sum of the pixels which lie in the black rectangle.

The four best features selected by AdaBoost are shown in the bottom of Fig 4. It is obvious that all of them measure the difference in intensity between the target (mainly rows 6 and 7) and the background. The best feature is of type 3 and the second best feature is of type 4. This fact also justifies the introduction of the new features.

2.3 Non-maximal Suppression and Temporal Filtering

In the fourth stage, non-maximal suppression is performed to the output of the classifier to get a single detection in a 13 x 13 neighborhood. The cascade classifier is insensitive to small changes in translation so multiple detections usually occur near each positively detected pixel.

In the fifth stage, a simple temporal filtering is used. For each detection in frame k we check a 5 x 5 neighborhood around the target in frame $k-1$. If a detection exists in that neighborhood in the previous frame then the detection in frame k is kept, otherwise it is discarded. We consider the n previous frames for every detection and if

Fig. 3. Left: a heavily cluttered scene from our data, Right: Examples of positive training images

there are at least $m < n$ detections in those n frames then this detection is identified as a target. We chose a 5 x 5 neighborhood since a target on collision course is expected to be almost stationary.

3 Data Collection and Training

We had access to about 4 hours of video that was captured during test flights conducted at NASA Langley Research Center in 1997 [5]. We did not have access either to the navigational data or to the distance between the target and the host aircraft for each frame. In total, there are 15 sequences with aircraft and 3 different classes of maneuvers. There are 4 sequences where the target aircraft is on collision course (~110 sec), i.e. it flies towards the host aircraft, 5 where the target aircraft flies perpendicular to the host aircraft (~22 sec) and 6 where the target aircraft flies directly away from the host aircraft (~ 480 sec). A frame from our data is shown in Fig. 3. We manually extracted all the 15 sequences that contain aircraft (total ~10min). In 8 sequences there is low clutter in the background whereas in the rest the background is heavily cluttered, including clouds, ground and sea regions.

In order to train the cascade we used 1266 positives patterns from 2 of the crossing object maneuvers. For each pattern also its mirror image and its left and right translation by a few pixels were included in the training set in order to generate a less biased training set [12]. All the patterns were contained in a 12 x 12 window. Some examples of the training images are shown in Fig. . Training was performed in exactly the same way as the original cascade detector proposed in [9]. The final detector is an 11 layer cascade of classifiers which includes 335 features. The number of features used by each classifier is: 8, 12, 16, 22, 32, 33, 34, 36, 44, 48 and 50.

The top row of Fig. 3 shows two aircraft which fly perpendicular to the host aircraft and the bottom row shows two aircraft on collision course. Since the appearance of the aircraft in these two cases is quite similar we used the same classifier in both cases.

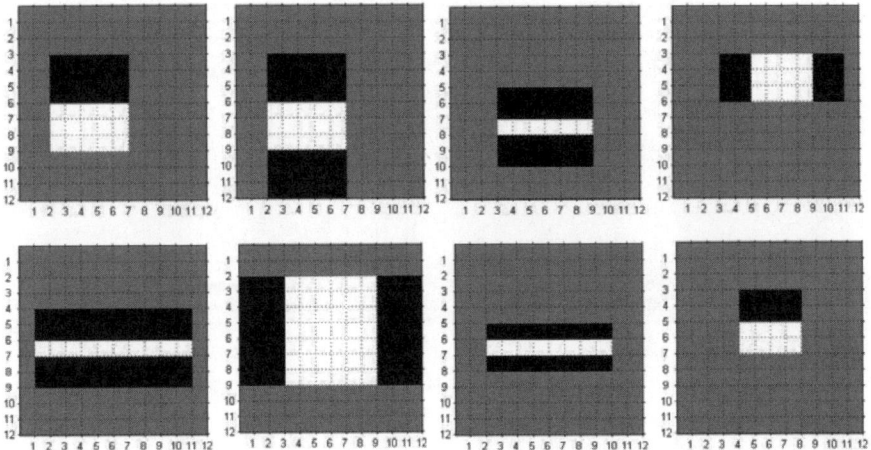

Fig. 4. Top row: The 4 types of features used, Bottom row: The 4 best features selected by AdaBoost for the first classifier

4   Results

4.1   Collision Course Scenario

We tested the trained classifier on the collision course maneuvers and the results are shown in Table 1, and Fig. 5. The background of sequence 1 and 3 is smooth whereas the background of sequences 2 and 4 is heavily cluttered. Fig. 4 (right) shows a frame from sequence 2 together with the classifier's output (squares). So in this frame we see that the plane is correctly detected (top right) but there are also four false positives.

We tested the classifier from the point that the target occupies at least 3-4 pixels since the performance of the classifier for targets less than 4-5 pixels is poor. Fig. 5 shows the ROC curves for the second and fourth sequence respectively. In the first case (sequence 2) the classifier ran for the part of the sequence between 25 seconds to collision and 10 seconds to collision whereas in the second case (sequence 4) the classifier ran for the part of the sequence between 20 seconds to collision and 5 seconds to collision. . The operating point shown in the ROC curves corresponds to the default classifier trained by AdaBoost. Both sequences 2 and 4 are heavily cluttered so the use of the static classifier generates a significant number of false positives per frame, 7.9 and 14.67 respectively. However, the detection rate is very good 84.3% and 89.14% respectively

The use of the temporal filtering approach has a positive effect on the system's performance. After trying a series of different values for m and n we found that the set of values $m = 25$, $n = 50$ result in satisfactory performance. For example, $m = 25$, $n = 50$ means that in order to consider one detection as valid then at least 25 detections should occur in the current detection neighborhood in the last 50 frames. In order to better demonstrate the effect of this temporal filtering approach we removed two

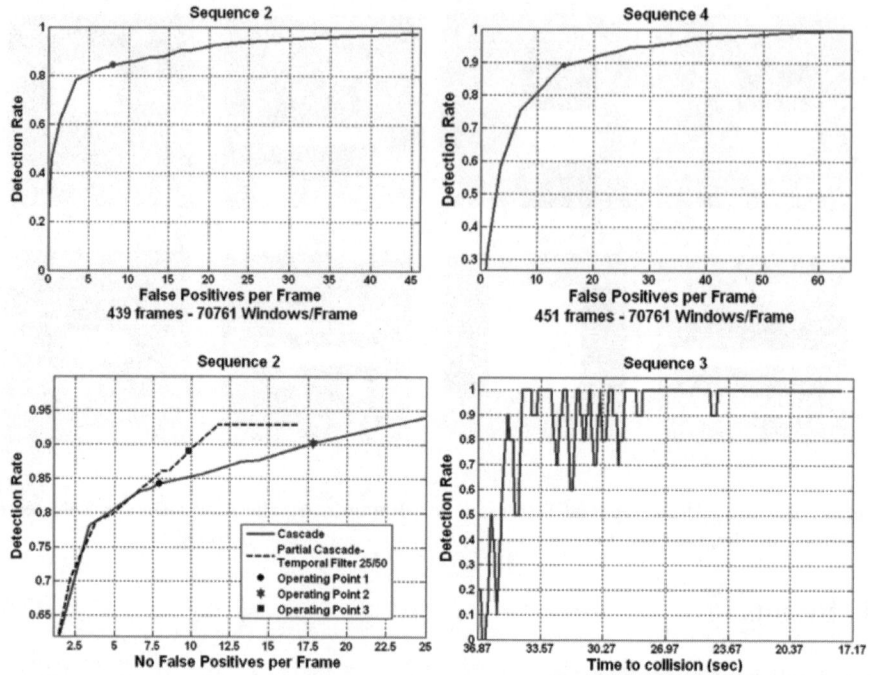

Fig. 5. Top Left: ROC curve for sequence 4, Top Right: ROC curve for sequence 2, Bottom Left: ROC curve for sequence 2 using temporal filtering, Bottom Right: Detection rate as a function of time to collision

layers of the cascade (so 9 classifiers in this case) so a much higher number of false positive detections is generated. The second operating point in Fig. 5 corresponds to the 9-layer cascade and the third operating point corresponds to the 9-layer cascade after the above mentioned temporal filter is applied. It is obvious from Fig. 5 that the application of this simple temporal filtering results in a significant reduction of the number of false positives, about 7.5 false positives per frame.

From Fig. 5 we see that a relatively high number of false positives detections is generated per frame for sequences 2 and 4. Although this is not acceptable for a real world application it is an excellent result from a machine learning point of view. In each frame the classifier checks more than 70000 windows and only 7-15 windows are identified as false positives. This is expected since the classifier detects target-like objects so high cluttered background increases the probability of regions with the same pixel distribution as a real target. The performance of the classifier in the all sequences is shown in Table 1.

Apart from the four collision course sequences there were also six sequences where the target aircraft is flying directly away from the host aircraft. If we play those sequences backwards then it seems that the target aircraft is on collision course. The main drawback of this approach is that the time to collision does not correspond to a real collision course scenario. In such a scenario the relative velocity between the two

Table 1. Detection rate and false positives (FP) for all sequences

	Detection Rate / FP per frame	Frames
Sequence 1	81.68% / 0.005	606
Sequence 2	84.3 % / 7.9	439
Sequence 3	96.38% / 0.003	1107
Sequence 4	89.14 % / 14.67	451
Average	87.88 % / 3.88	-

Table 2. Detection rate and number of FP for the sequences that the target aircraft is flying directly away from the host aircraft

	Detection rate / Total No of FP	Total No of frames
Sequence 5	83.15% / 0	902
Sequence 6	90% / 264	1181
Sequence 7	92.28% / 0	1400
Sequence 8	88.47 % / 115	1301
Sequence 9	87.44% / 0	1401
Sequence 10	85.98% / 663	1270
Average	87.89%	-

Table 3. Detection rate and number of FP for the crossing target maneuvers

	Detection rate / Total number of FP	Frames with planes
Sequence 1C	98.45% / 2	129
Sequence 2C	97.65% / 6	213
Sequence 3C	97.09% / 20	103
Sequence 4C	99.34% / 3	151
Sequence 5C	100% / 0	41
Average	98.506%	-

aircraft is the sum of their velocities. On the other hand, when the aircraft flies directly away then the relative velocity is the difference between the two velocities (in both cases the velocities are collinear). So when we play that video sequence backwards the target aircraft approaches the host aircraft with a much lower speed. This results in an increased time to collision and this is obvious from Table 2 in which the number of frames used is much higher than the number of frames used in the real collision course sequences.

Fig. 5 (bottom right) shows the detection rate as a function of the time to collision. The third sequence from the collision course results section was used in this experiment. In order to get a single point in the curve we average ten consecutive frames. We see that in the beginning the detection rate is low and as the target approaches the host aircraft (time to collision decreases) the detection rate increases. We should also note that the detection rate for about 6-7 seconds is high but the detections are not consistent as shown from the fluctuation around 80%. After a point

Fig. 6. Left: An aircraft on a crossing maneuver, Right: An aircraft on collision course (top) together with four false positives

the target is detected consistently and consequently the detection rate becomes constant. The background of this sequence is smooth and that so it is reasonable to consider the detection rate obtained as upper limit. In a heavily cluttered sequence or in a sequence with low contrast it is expected that the detection rate will be worse.

4.2 Crossing Scenario

We also tested the trained classifier on the crossing target maneuvers and the results are shown in Table 3. Sequences 1C and 4C were used for training and sequence 2C was used for validation so it is expected a high detection rate and a low false positive rate for those sequences. Fig. (left) shows a frame from sequence 2 in which the plane is successfully detected and there are no false positives.

The remaining sequences (3C and 5C) were used for testing. The background of sequence 5C is almost uniform and that is why the target is detected in all frames with zero false positive alarms. Sequence 3C is heavily cluttered but the performance of the classifier is very good. This may be the result of the similar background and lighting conditions with sequence 4C. We should note here that most of the missed detections occur when the target enters or leaves the scene and therefore the classifier fails to detect a partial target.

5   Conclusions

In this paper a different approach to the problem of aircraft detection was presented. Instead of using an image processing method we used a learning method to learn the targets from real data. The system described here is a very popular method in the area of face detection and with few modifications was successfully used in the problem of target detection in video sequences. The advantage of this method is that it detects the targets on a frame to frame basis with a high detection rate, usually around 80%, and lower false positive rate than the commonly used morphological filtering which is susceptible to false positives. The described approach achieves a false positive rate which usually lies between 1 and 5 false positives per frame, and in some cases up to

10, without further processing and this is an encouraging result. The above results were obtained using over 15000 test frames which is a much higher number than the typical number of frames used by the majority of the detection systems. The described system has also the potential of real time execution.

We were mostly focused on the detection part and developed a detection framework that works on a frame to frame basis. In this work we used very simple temporal filters so future work includes the use of more complicated temporal filters or tracking algorithms which are expected to further enhance the system's performance. The consistent detection of targets which occupy less than 5 pixels is something that has to be addressed too.. Finally the development of a reliable system to estimate the collision risk is an important issue that should be addressed in order to have a final collision avoidance system.

Acknowledgments. We would like to thank Dr J. W. McCandless from NASA Ames Research Center for providing us with the data.

References

1. Federal Aviation Administration, ch. 12, Section 9, Remotely Operated Aircraft, in Order 7610.4: Special Military Operations, US Gov. Printing Office
2. Casasent, D., Ye, A.: Detection filters and algorithm fusion for ATR. IEEE Trans. On Image Processing 6(1), 114–125 (1997)
3. Barniv, Y.: Dynamic programming solution for detecting dim moving targets. IEEE Trans. On Aerospace and Electronic Systems 21(1), 144–156 (1985)
4. Nishiguchi, K., Kobayashi, M., Ichikawa, A.: Small target detection from image sequences using recursive max filter. In: Proc. Of SPIE, pp. 153–166 (1995)
5. McCandless, J.W.: Detection of aircraft in video sequences using a predictive optical flow algorithm. Optical Engineering 3(3), 523–530 (1999)
6. Gandhi, T., Yang, M.T., Kasturi, R., Camps, O., Coraor, L., McCandless, J.: Detection of obstacles in the flight path of an aircraft. IEEE Trans. On Aerospace and Electronic Systems 39(1) (2003)
7. Carnie, R., Walker, R., Corke, P.: Image processing algorithms for UAV Sense and Avoid. In: Proc. ICRA, pp. 2848–2853 (2006)
8. Gandhi, T., Yang, M.T., Kasturi, R., Camps, O., Coraor, L., McCandless, J.: Performance Characterization of the Dynamic Programming Obstacle Detection Algorithm. IEEE Trans. On Image Proces. 15(5), 1202–1214 (2006)
9. Viola, P., Jones, M.: Rapid object detection using a boosted cascade of simple features. In: Proc. CVPR 2001, pp. 511–518 (2001)
10. Xiao, R., Zhu, L., Zhang, H.J.: Boosting chain learning for object detection. In: Proc. ICCV, pp. 709–715 (2003)
11. Bourdev, L., Brandt, J.: Robust object detection via soft cascade. In: Proc. CVPR 2005, pp. 236–243 (2005)
12. Sung, K., Poggio, T.: Example-based learning for view-based human face detection. IEEE Trans. On PAMI 20(1), 39–51 (1998)

A Novel Feature Selection Based
Semi-supervised Method for Image Classification

M.A. Tahir, J.E. Smith, and P. Caleb-Solly

School of Computer Science
University of the West of England
Bristol, BS161QY, UK
{muhammad.tahir,james.smith,praminda.caleb-solly}@uwe.ac.uk

Abstract. Automated surface inspection of products as part of a manufacturing quality control process involves the applications of image processing routines to segment regions of interest (ROI) or objects which
correspond to potential defects on the product or part. In these type of
applications, it is not known in advance how many ROIs may be segmented from images, and so classification algorithms mainly make use of
only image-level features, ignoring important object-level information.
In this paper, we will investigate how to preprocess high-dimensional
object-level features through a unsupervised learning system and present
the outputs of that system as additional image-level features to the supervised learning system. Novel semi-supervised approaches based on K-
Means/Tabu Search(TS) and SOM/Genetic Algorithm (GA) with C4.5
as supervised classifier have been proposed in this paper. The proposed
algorithms are then applied on real-world CD/DVD inspection system.
Results have indicated an increase in the performance in terms of classification accuracy when compared with various existing approaches.

1 Introduction

Automated surface inspection of products as part of a manufacturing quality
control process involves the application of image processing routines to segment
regions of interest (ROI) or objects which correspond to potential defects on the
product or part. A range of features are then calculated which describe each
ROI in terms of morphology, location within the image and position relative to
other ROI. For most automated surface inspections applications, a database of
example images is captured, the ROI features are extracted and the images are
annotated (part "ok or "defective") by a domain expert and this information
is then used to train a classifier. The domain expert's decision regarding the
annotation can depend on the occurrence of one or more physical artefacts of a
certain type on the same image. The importance of a single artefact may depend
not just on its shape etc, but on its position in the image. Additionally not
all physical artefacts will on their own result in the part being considered as
defective. It is possible that a decision of an image being defective is based on
the co-incidence of a number of individually acceptable artefacts. Although, even

A. Gasteratos, M. Vincze, and J.K. Tsotsos (Eds.): ICVS 2008, LNCS 5008, pp. 484–493, 2008.

the presence of a number of artefacts may not be enough to make a decision as their spatial distribution might be important - for example whether they are clustered tightly (and so more noticeable) or widely scattered.

Annotation of each individual ROI identified by the segmentation routine in an image is a time intensive task and in itself can be a problematic due to the geometry of the defects being specified by vague terms and attributes resulting in variations in labelling by experts due to lack of objective criteria [1] or may simply be infeasible on-line due to the speed of production. Also the reality of production environments and physical image capture systems can often mean that variations in lighting etc. can cause the segmentation routines to identify spurious ROI which do not correspond to physical artefacts on the part therefore adding complexity to the task of annotating each ROI separately. As a result the annotation is usually on a per image basis as opposed to a per ROI basis. From the perspective of training a machine learning algorithm, this constitutes a lack of crucial information regarding the individual ROI which could potentially improve the defect recognition rate, which might be lowered due to the apparent noise in the data resulting from the variability of possible manifestations of defects on the surface of the product being inspected.

All of these issues can on their own make the problem more challenging from a Machine Learning perspective. However there is one major issue which impacts in the whole decision of a classification system: it cannot be known in advance how many regions of interests may be segmented from images occurring in the future, and yet most classification algorithms assume a fixed-size input data space. Initial analysis reveals a number of possible approaches to solve this issue:

Approach 1: Presenting the object feature vectors sequentially into the classifier and utilising approaches from fields such as time-series forecasting.

Approach 2: Defining a set of aggregate (image-level) features which include some descriptors of the objects e.g. their total number.

Approach 3: Considering the distribution of values for each of the object-level features for a given image. Descriptors of these distributions may be added to the aggregate data; for example the mean, minimum, maximum, or standard deviation of the values for each object-level feature.

Approach 4: Preprocessing the object feature vectors through a supervised learning system if object-level labels are present, and then presenting the outputs of that system as an additional image-level information. For example, if the data is labelled at the object-level, then supervised object-level classifiers can be built [2].

Approach 5: Preprocessing the object feature vectors through a unsupervised learning system if object labels are not available, and then presenting the outputs of that system as an additional image-level. Unsupervised clustering methods can be used to reduce the dimensionality [3].

Of these possible approaches, the first is deemed unsuitable since it increases the problem of having sparse data in a high-dimensional space - for example if there are n objects present, they could be presented to the system in any of $n!$ ways, and the system has to learn that these are identical. The second and third approaches are of course highly feasible and will be investigated here. Note that for time-critical high-throughput applications the second approach may be considered preferable since it requires significantly less processing. It also presents a much lower dimension space to the classifiers which will often be beneficial. In contrast to this, the third approach creates the problem of knowing what type of techniques should be used for data modelling. First order techniques treat each object feature independently - for example the mean/maximum size or brightness of objects. Second order techniques might be more useful ("size of brightest object ...") but incur the curse of dimensionality. The fourth and fifth approaches avoid some of the problems of the third, but comes with some of its own. Supervised learning methods are highly useful if the training images contain labels for each object, but obtaining this information requires significant operator input which may not be available off-line, or may simply be infeasible on-line due to the speed of production. In contrast unsupervised methods do not require operator input but are highly reliant on the choice of input features, whether to clustering algorithms such as k-means [5,6] or to unsupervised neural methods such as Self-Organizing Maps (SOM) [4].

The aim of this paper is to examine last four options in more detail, in particular focussing on the two-level approach and looking at semi-supervised learning. This paper presents two novel semi-supervised approaches based on KMeans/C4.5/TS [5,7,8,9] and SOM/C4.5/GA [4,15] to deal with a similar problem as described above where only image level expert annotation is available and more reliable classification of defects can be achieved by utilising additional information regarding the individual ROI generated by the use of unsupervised learning methods.

The rest of this paper is organized as follows. Section 2 provides a brief review on related work. Section 3 describes proposed Semi-Supervised Classification algorithm followed by a brief discussion of the application and results in section 4. Section 5 concludes the paper.

2   Related Work

Many methods for analyzing region-of-interests (ROIs) or objects within an image have been proposed but by fixing the number of ROIs within an image [14]. To deal with this type of image classification problem in which each image consists of varying number of objects or ROIs, some methods use first-order statistics such as maximum, minimum, average etc as described in Section 1. However, these methods of aggregation can result in loss of information. An alternative method for dealing with varying numbers of ROI is to use a two-level approach of unsupervised object level classification feeding into supervised image-level classifiers. The significance of clustering ROI in an image using unsupervised learning has been highlighted in [2] particularly in cases where there are several categories of sub-classes of defects corresponding to severity and physical manifestation. Operator supplied image level labels often do not reflect individual characteristics of the objects in the image. Unsupervised clustering algorithms such as k-means and SOM are sensitive to irrelevant features and therefore feature selection (FS) can improve the performance as shown in [15]. A genetic-based K-means algorithm is proposed by [12] for selection of the k value and selection of feature variables by minimizing an associated objective function. Their algorithm combines the advantage of genetic algorithm(GA) and K-means to search the subspace thoroughly. Recently, a supervised/unsupervised approach is proposed by Gaddam et al. [13] for network intrusion problem. In their work, a novel method is proposed to cascade k-Means clustering and the ID3 decision tree learning methods for classifying anomalous and normal activities in a computer network. The k-Means clustering method first partitions the training instances into k clusters using Euclidean distance similarity and on each cluster, decision tree is then built. In this paper, we have combined the basic ideas proposed in [15,13,12]. TS and GA are used to remove irrelevant object features and to provide good quality clusters using K-Means/SOM respectively while C4.5 is used as a supervised learning algorithm working on the output from the unsupervised clustering algorithms and the image level features.

3   Proposed Methodology

In this section, we will discuss the proposed semi supervised classification algorithm using K-Means/C4.5 and FS using TS. Figure 1 shows the the training phase of the proposed algorithm. In this approach, we first run k-means clustering algorithm on the object feature vectors from all images in the training set in order to obtain k cluster centroid. Then, for each image, a new feature vector with k attributes is obtained by counting the number of hits for each of the k cluster centroid. For example, if number of objects in an image i are 6 and the number of clusters k are 2; then one possible new feature vector is $\{2,4\}$ i.e. 2 objects belong to cluster A while 4 objects belong to cluster B. These new

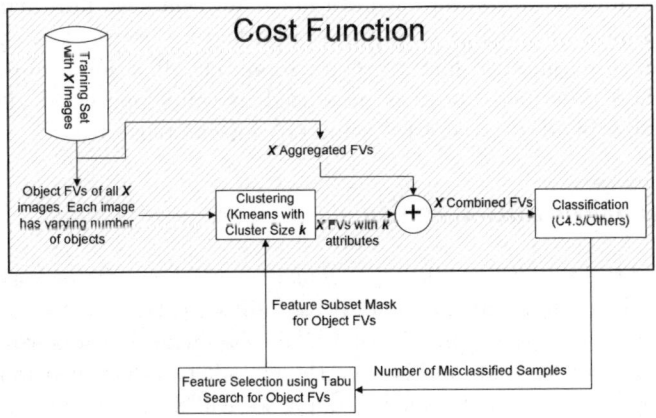

Fig. 1. Training Phase of proposed Semi-Supervised Classification Algorithm

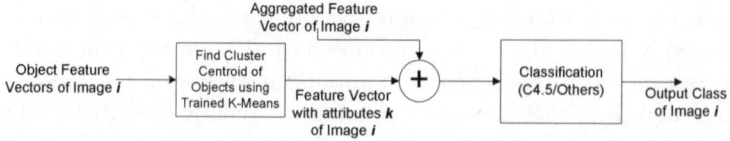

Fig. 2. Testing Phase of proposed Semi-Supervised Classification Algorithm

Image Number	F1	F2	F3
1	f_{11}	f_{12}	f_{13}
1	f_{21}	f_{22}	f_{23}
2	f_{31}	f_{32}	f_{33}
2	f_{41}	f_{42}	f_{43}
3	f_{51}	f_{52}	f_{53}

K-Means ⟹

Image Number	C1	C2
1	1	-
1	-	1
2	1	-
2	1	-
3	-	1

Feature Vector ⟹

Image Number	F1	F2
1	1	1
2	2	0
3	0	1

Fig. 3. An example of getting Feature Vector from Object data using K-Means

features are then added into image-level aggregated features. This is done for all of the images in both the training and testing sets. Decision tree classifier (C4.5) is then built from the labelled images in the training set. The feedback from C4.5 classifier allows the TS to iteratively search for feature subset mask of object feature vectors that improves the classification accuracy. In the testing phase, only K-Means/C4.5 is used as shown in Figure 2.

Figure 3 shows an example showing how feature vector is obtained from images when each image consists of varying number of objects. This example consists of 3 images with varying number of objects. K-Means clustering algorithm is used on each object to determine its cluster type. Feature vector is then obtained by counting the number of hits for each of the cluster centroid. This feature vector is then combined with image-level aggregated feature vector. C4.5 classifier is then used on this combined feature vector to get classification accuracy.

The method described above is also used as semi-supervised classification algorithm using SOM/C4.5 and FS using GA for comparison.

4   Application and Results

Our proposed technique is applied to "DynaVis" which is a framework being developed for self-reconfigurable and adaptive fault detection used in manufacturing quality control as shown in Figure 4. This classification framework classifies each image as good or bad, and adapts the classifier on-line in response to the operator's feedback. The particular example we will demonstrate here concerns inspecting the printing of images and text onto CDs and DVDs, the objective being to detect faults due to weak colours, incorrect palettes etc. For this print

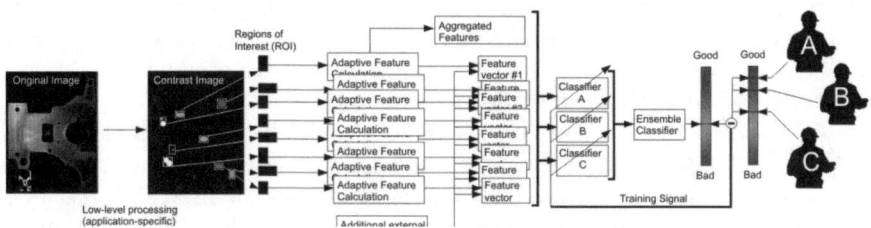

Fig. 4. Classification Framework for classifying images into good or bad. This is a general framework and the machine part shown here as input is CD/DVD imprints in this paper.

Fig. 5. An image showing ROIs of different shapes, sizes and densities

application, a "master" image is available and the approach taken is to subtract this from the image of each produced part so as to generate "contrast" images. In the contrast image, the gray value of each pixel correlates to the deviation from the normal appearance of the surface. Thus the image is mostly black, with potential faults highlighted by non-zero gray values. From these contrast image, ROIs (objects) are extracted. Figure 5 shows a deviated image showing ROIs of different shapes, sizes and densities.

One aspect of the DynaVis system is the recognition of the fact that not only factors such as fatigue cause inconsistencies in the labels applied by individual operators, but there will also be systematic differences in the decisions made by different operators arising from factors such as inexperience and different roles in the organisation. In order to cope with this the system has been designed to build a model of each operator and use a weighted voting technique to combine these - a true "mixture of experts". Therefore it is necessary to create classifiers which model the decisions made by each operator as closely as possible. It is also necessary for the technique used to combine these classifiers to take account of the fact that, since each operators may display different levels of inconsistency, the classifier(s) modelling them will have different levels of predicted accuracy.

The data set consists of 1534 images, each labeled by 4 different operators. There are total 4500 objects for all these images. For each image, 17 aggregated features are extracted and for each object, 57 object features are extracted. These features describe the distribution, density, shape etc. of the ROI (objects)

in the images. In all data sets, N fold stratified cross validation has been used to
estimate error rates [10,11]. For N-fold cross validation, each data set is divided
into N blocks using $(N-1)$ blocks as a training set and the remaining block as a
test set. Therefore, each block is used exactly once as a test set.

Table 1 shows the classification accuracy when only a supervised classifier
(C4.5) is used. The results in brackets indicates standard deviation. Three different feature vectors (FVs) are used for the analysis. The first FV consists of
image-level aggregated features (the second approach discussed in Section 1).
The second FV consists of both image-level aggregated features and object-level
aggregated features(first order statistics on objects as per the third approach
discussed in Section 1). In particular, after initial experiments, we consider the
maximum value of all objects in an image. For third FV, we take the fourth
approach again identified in Section 1 and assume the existence of object-level
labels. Supervised learning is then used to build a (C4.5) object classifier, and
the outputs of that system in the form of hit-counts for each object class are
presented as an additional image-level information. It is clear from Table 1 that
the best classification accuracy is achieved when object classifier output is used
as an additional image-level information. In this case, we could use two-level
supervised learning if object-level labels were present. Of course in general this
will not be the case, so we also examine an unsupervised variant of the fifth
(two-level) approach as outlined in the Section 3.

Table 1. Classification Accuracy (%) using Supervised Classifier only (C4.5). KM =
K-Means. F_T = Total Number of Features.

Data Set Good/Bad	C4.5 (Agg.) $F_T = 17$	C4.5 (Agg+AggObject) $F_T = (17+57)=74$	C4.5 (Agg & Object Classifier) $F_T = (17+13)=30$
Operator1 1164/370	91.8 (2.1)	91.8 (1.9)	**93.1** (2.1)
Operator2 1262/272	95.5 (1.7)	95.4 (1.7)	**96.7** (1.0)
Operator3 1230/304	94.2 (1.4)	94.3 (1.1)	**96.9** (1.0)
Operator4 1223/311	94.1 (1.1)	95.2 (1.6)	**95.6** (1.7)

Table 2 shows the classification accuracy using proposed semi-supervised approach but without any FS. The results clearly indicates that no significant
improvement is achieved when object data extracted from K-Means clustering
algorithm is used along with image-level data. This is because the presence of
irrelevant features among the 57 descriptors for each object "confuses" k-means.
Table 3 shows the classification accuracy using proposed approach and FS using TS. [1] and with different k value. The results clearly indicates a significant
improvement in classification accuracy since irrelevant features from Object feature vectors are removed by TS and thus K-Means able to find clusters of good

---

[1] In this paper; standard parameters are used for Tabu Search (TS). $N = T = \sqrt{F}$
where N is the number of neighbourhood solutions, T is the Tabu List size and F
is the number of features.

Table 2. Classification Accuracy (%) without FS and using semi-supervised approach (K-Means/C4.5). KM = K-Means.

Data Set	Good/Bad	KM/C4.5 (k=2)	KM/C4.5 (k=4)	KM/C4.5 (k=8)	KM/C4.5 (k=12)
Operator1	1164/370	91.6 (1.2)	**92.2** (1.4)	91.9 (1.9)	91.5 (1.3)
Operator2	1262/272	95.3 (1.7)	95.6 (1.7)	95.2 (1.6)	**95.8** (1.6)
Operator3	1230/304	94.1 (1.6)	94.1 (1.2)	94.0 (1.7)	**94.2** (1.4)
Operator4	1223/311	94.1 (1.6)	94.0 (1.8)	94.5 (1.8)	**95.5** (1.1)

Table 3. Classification Accuracy (%) with FS and using proposed semi-Supervised approach. KM = K-Means.

Data Set	Good/Bad	KM/C4.5/TS (k=2)	KM/C4.5/TS (k=4)	KM/C4.5/TS (k=8)	KM/C4.5/TS (k=12)
Operator1	1164/370	93.2 (0.70)	93.7 (1.6)	94.1 (1.2)	**94.5** (1.6)
Operator2	1262/272	96.6 (1.4)	97.1 (1.3)	97.4 (1.6)	**97.4** (1.3)
Operator3	1230/304	95.3 (1.9)	95.7 (1.8)	**96.2** (1.5)	96.2 (2.4)
Operator4	1223/311	95.2 (1.6)	96.2 (1.2)	**96.8** (1.1)	**96.8** (1.1)

Table 4. Total number of features using KMeans/C4.5/TS. F_T = Total number of features

Data Set	Good/Bad	F_T	F (k=2)	F (k=4)	F (k=8)	F (k=12)
Operator1	1164/370	57	20	29	29	27
Operator2	1262/272	57	31	28	39	31
Operator3	1230/304	57	29	21	24	27
Operator4	1223/311	57	27	26	20	22

quality that results in increase in classification accuracy. The best classification accuracy is achieved for $k = 12$. Future work consists of investigating k as a parameter in encoding solution of TS.

As can be seen the results from this approach are in fact even better than when using supervised learning at the object level except for operator3, which suggests that the clustering approach may be able to better represent the actual distribution of data than the supervised approach which "forces" the results into a set of 13 pre-determined classes which may reflect users preconceptions and may not be supported without external process data.

Table 4 shows the number of features used by proposed TS semi-supervised algorithm for different data sets for Object Feature Vectors. Thus, our proposed method not only has the ability to find good clusters that result in higher classification accuracy but also has the ability to reduce the size of the object feature vector and thus reducing the cost of extracting these features.

Table 5. Classification Accuracy (%) with FS and using SOM/C4.5/GA. $N =$ Number of Nodes

Data Set Good/Bad	SOM/C4.5/GA ($N = 12$)	SOM/C4.5/GA ($N = 15$)
Operator1 1164/370	91.7(1.2)	92.0 (1.7)
Operator2 1262/272	95.7 (0.7)	95.7 (1.9)
Operator3 1230/304	94.4 (1.7)	93.6 (2.0)
Operator4 1223/311	96.7 (2.0)	94.5 (1.5)

4.1   Comparison with Other Semi-supervised Algorithm (SOM/C4.5/GA)

An alternative semi-supervised strategy was used in order to compare the results obtained using the Kmeans/C4.5/TS. Here feature selection on the object data was conducted using a SOM/GA wrapper approach [16] and hits count data from SOMs created using the best feature sets together with image level features were classified using C4.5. The results shown in Table 5 are comparable to those obtained using KMeans/C4.5/TS which demonstrates the efficacy of the approach of using an unsupervised learning algorithm to obtain good quality object feature based clusters, followed by supervised learning algorithm using the object cluster information and image level features.

5   Conclusion

Within the field of Machine Vision, there are broad range of problems where the task is to classify an image or scene according to the presence (or otherwise) of a number of objects within that image. However there is one major issue which impacts in the whole decision of a classification system: it cannot be known in advance how many regions of interests may be segmented from images occurring in the future, and yet most classification algorithms assume a fixed-size input data space. A new semi-supervised algorithm is proposed in this paper to address the above mentioned issue which results from unlabelled objects in images and each object consisting of high-dimensional FV. Feature selection is used to remove irrelevant object features and thus enabling clustering algorithms to find good quality clusters. C4.5 is then used as supervised learning algorithms working on the output from KMeans/SOM respectively and the image level features. Results have indicated an increase in the performance in terms of classification accuracy when compared with existing approaches that ignores important object-level information.

Acknowledgements. This work was supported by the European Commission (project Contract No. STRP016429, acronym DynaVis). This publication reflects only the authors' views.

References

1. Eichor, A., Girimonte, D., Klose, A., Kruse, R.: Soft Computing for automated surface quality analysis of exterior car body panels. Applied Soft Computing 5, 301–313 (2005)
2. Caleb-Solly, P., Steuer, M.: Classification of surface defects on hot rolled steel using adaptive learning methods. In: Proc. of the 4th IEEE International Conference on Knowledge-Based Intelligent Engineering Systems and Allied Technologies (2000)
3. Caleb-Solly, P., Smith, J.E.: Adaptive Surface Inspection via Interactive Evolution. Image and Vision Computing 25(7), 1058–1072 (2007)
4. Kohonen, T.: Self-Organizing Maps, 2nd extended edn. Springer, Heidelberg (1995)
5. MacQueen, J.B.: Some Methods for classification and Analysis of Multivariate Observations. In: Proceedings of 5th Berkeley Symposium on Mathematical Statistics and Probability, vol. 1, pp. 281–297. University of California Press, Berkeley (1967)
6. Jain, A.K., Duin, R.P.W., Mao, J.: Statistical Pattern Recognition: A Review. IEEE Transactions on Pattern Analysis and Machine Intelligence 22(1), 4–37 (2000)
7. Quinlan, J.R.: C4.5: Programs for Machine Learning. Morgan Kaufmann Publishers Inc., San Francisco (1993)
8. Glover, F.: Tabu search I. ORSA Journal on Computing 1(3), 190–206 (1989)
9. Tahir, M.A., Smith, J.: Improving Nearest Neighbor Classifier using Tabu Search and Ensemble Distance Metrics. In: Proceedings of the IEEE International Conference on Data Mining (ICDM) (2006)
10. Kohavi, R.: A study of cross-validation and bootstrap for accuracy estimation and model selection. In: Proceedings of the Fourteenth International Joint Conference on Artificial Intelligence, vol. 2 (12), pp. 1137–1143. Morgan Kaufmann, San Mateo (1995)
11. Raudys, S., Jain, A.: Small Sample Effects in Statistical Pattern Recognition: Recommendations for Practitioners. IEEE Transactions on Pattern Analysis and Machine Intelligence 13(3), 252–264 (1991)
12. Yu, Z., Wong, H.: Genetic-based K-means algorithm for selection of feature variables. In: Proceedings of the 18th International Conference on Pattern Recognition, pp. 744–747 (2006)
13. Gaddam, S.R., Phoha, V.V., Balagani, K.S.: K-Means+ID3: A Novel Method for Supervised Anomaly Detection by Cascading K-Means Clustering and ID3 Decision Tree Learning Methods. IEEE Transactions on Knowledge and Data Engineering 19(3) (2007)
14. Poon, C., Wong, D.C.M., Shen, H.C.: A New Method in Locating and Segmenting Palmprint into Region-of-Interest. In: Proceedings of the 17th International Conference on Pattern Recognition (2004)
15. Smith, J.E., Fogarty, T.C., Johnson, I.R.: Genetic Feature selection for clustering and classification. IEE Colloquium on Genetic Algorithms in Image Processing & Vision, IEE Digest 193 (1994)
16. Kohavi, R., John, G.: The Wrapper Approach. In: Liu, H., Motoda, H. (eds.) Feature Selection for Knowledge Discovery and Data Mining, pp. 33–50. Kluwer Academic Publishers, Dordrecht (1998)

Sub-class Error-Correcting Output Codes

Sergio Escalera, Oriol Pujol, and Petia Radeva

Computer Vision Center, Campus UAB, Edifici O, 08193, Bellaterra, Spain
Dept. Matemàtica Aplicada i Anàlisi, Universitat de Barcelona,
Gran Via 585, 08007, Barcelona, Spain

Abstract. A common way to model multi-class classification problems is by means of Error-Correcting Output Codes (ECOC). One of the main requirements of the ECOC design is that the base classifier is capable of splitting each sub-group of classes from each binary problem. In this paper, we present a novel strategy to model multi-class classification problems using sub-class information in the ECOC framework. Complex problems are solved by splitting the original set of classes into sub-classes, and embedding the binary problems in a problem-dependent ECOC design. Experimental results over a set of UCI data sets and on a real multi-class traffic sign categorization problem show that the proposed splitting procedure yields a better performance when the class overlap or the distribution of the training objects conceil the decision boundaries for the base classifier.

1 Introduction

In the literature, one can find several powerful binary classifiers. However, when one needs to deal with multi-class classification problems, many learning techniques fail to manage this information. Instead, it is common to construct the classifiers to distinguish between just two classes, and to combine them in some way. In this sense, Error Correcting Output Codes were born as a general framework to combine binary problems to address the multi-class problem [3].

The ECOC technique can be broken down into two distinct stages: encoding and decoding. Given a set of classes, the coding stage designs a codeword[1] for each class based on different binary problems, that are combined in a coding matrix M. The decoding stage makes a classification decision for a given test sample based on the value of the output code.

It was when Allwein et al. [8] introduced a third symbol (the zero symbol) in the coding process when the coding step received special attention. This symbol increases the number of partitions of classes to be considered in a ternary ECOC framework by allowing some classes to be ignored. Then, the ternary coding matrix becomes $M \in \{-1, 0, 1\}^{N \times n}$, for N number of classes and n number of binary problems. In this case, the symbol zero means that a particular class is not considered by a certain binary classifier. Recently, new improvements in the

---

[1] The codeword is a sequence of bits of a code representing each class, where each bit identifies the membership of the class for a given binary classifier.

A. Gasteratos, M. Vincze, and J.K. Tsotsos (Eds.): ICVS 2008, LNCS 5008, pp. 494–504, 2008.
© Springer-Verlag Berlin Heidelberg 2008

ternary ECOC coding demonstrate the suitability of the ECOC methodology to deal with multi-class classification problems [6][7]. These recent designs use the knowledge of the problem-domain to learn relevant binary problems from ternary codes. The basic idea of these methods is to use the training data to guide the training process, and thus, to construct the coding matrix M focusing on the binary problems that better fit the decision boundaries of a given data set. However, the final accuracy is still based on the ability of the base classifier to learn each individual problem. Difficult problems, those which the base classifier is not able to find a solution for, require the use of complex classifiers, such as Support Vector Machines with Radial Basis Function kernel [1], and expensive parameter optimizations. Look at the example of fig. 1(a). A linear classifier is used to split two classes. In this case, the base classifier is not able to find a convex solution. On the other hand, in fig. 1(b), one of the previous classes has been split into two sub-sets, that we call *sub-classes*. Then, the original problem is solved using two linear classifiers, and the two new sub-classes have the same original class label. Some studies in the literature tried to form sub-classes using the labels information, which is called Supervised Clustering [10]. In these types of systems, clusters are usually formed without taking into account the behavior of the base classifier that learns the data. In a recent work [11], the authors use the class labels to form the sub-classes that improve the performance of particular Discriminant Analysis algorithms.

In this paper, we present a problem-dependent ECOC design where classes are partitioned into sub-classes using a clustering approach for the cases that the base classifier is not capable to distinguish the classes. Sub-groups of problems are split into more simple ones until the base classifier is able to learn the original problem. In this way, multi-class problems which can not be modelled by using the original set of classes are modelled without the need of using more complex classifiers. The final ECOC design is obtained by combining the sub-problems. The novel Sub-class ECOC design is compared with the state-of-art ECOC designs over a set of UCI Machine Learning Repository data sets and on a real multi-class traffic sign categorization problem using different base classifiers. The results show that in most cases the sub-class strategy is able to obtain significant performance improvements.

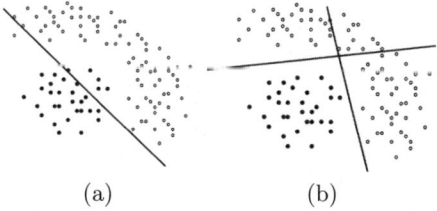

(a)   (b)

Fig. 1. (a) Decision boundary of a linear classifier of a 2-class problem. (b) Decision boundaries of a linear classifier splitting the problem of (a) into two more simple tasks.

2   Problem-Dependent ECOC Sub-class

From an initial set of classes C of a given multi-class problem, the objective of the Sub-class ECOC strategy is to define a new set of classes C', where $|C'| > |C|$, so that the new set of binary problems is easier to learn for a given base classifier. For this purpose, we use a guided procedure that, in a problem-dependent way, groups classes and splits them into sub-sets if necessary.

Recently, the authors of [6] proposed a ternary problem-dependent design of ECOC, called DECOC. The method is based on the embedding of discriminant tree structures derived from the problem domain. The binary trees are built by looking for the partition that maximizes the mutual information (MI) between the data and their respective class labels. Look at the 3-class problem shown on the top of fig. 2(a). The DECOC algorithm considers the whole set of classes to split it into two sub-sets of classes $\wp^+$ and $\wp^-$ maximizing the MI criterion on a sequential forward floating search procedure ($SFFS$). In the example, the first sub-sets found correspond to $\wp^+ = \{C_1, C_2\}$ and $\wp^- = \{C_3\}$. Then, a base classifier is used to train its corresponding dichotomizer h_1. This classifier is shown in the node h_1 of the tree structure shown in fig. 2(d). The procedure is repeated until all classes are split into separate sub-sets $\wp$. In the example, the second classifier is trained to split the sub-sets of classes $\wp^+ = C_1$ from $\wp^- = C_2$ because the classes C_1 and C_2 were still contained in a single sub-set after the first step. This second classifier is codified by the node h_2 of fig. 2(d). When the tree is constructed, the coding matrix M is obtained by codifying each internal node of the tree as a column of the coding matrix (see fig. 2(c)).

In our case, sequential forward floating search ($SFFS$) is also applied to look for the sub-sets $\wp^+$ and $\wp^-$ that maximizes the mutual information between the data and their respective class labels [6]. The $SFFS$ algorithm used is the one proposed in [12], and the implementation details of the fast quadratic mutual information can be found in [6]. To illustrate our procedure, let us to return to the example of the top of fig. 2(a). On the first iteration of the sub-class ECOC algorithm, $SFFS$ finds the sub-set $\wp^+ = \{C_1, C_2\}$ against $\wp^- = \{C_3\}$. The encoding of this problem is shown in the first matrix of fig. 2(c). The positions of the column corresponding to the classes of the first partition are coded by $+1$ and the classes corresponding to the second partition to -1, respectively. In our procedure, the base classifier is used to test if the performance obtained by the trained dichotomizers is sufficient. Observe the decision boundaries of the picture next to the first column of the matrix in fig. 2(b). One can see that the base classifier finds a good solution for this first problem.

Then, the second classifier is trained to split $\wp^+ = C_1$ against $\wp^- = C_2$, and its performance is computed. To separate the current sub-sets is not a trivial problem, and the classification performance is poor. Therefore, our procedure tries to split the data $J_{\wp^+}$ and $J_{\wp^-}$ from the current sub-sets $\wp^+$ and $\wp^-$ into more simple sub-sets. Applying a splitting criteria SC over the two sub-sets, two clusters are found for $\wp^+ = C_1$ and for $\wp^- = C_2$. We select the split that maximizes the distance between the means of the clusters. And then, the original encoding of the problem C_1 vs C_2 is transformed to two more simple problems $\{C_{11}\}$

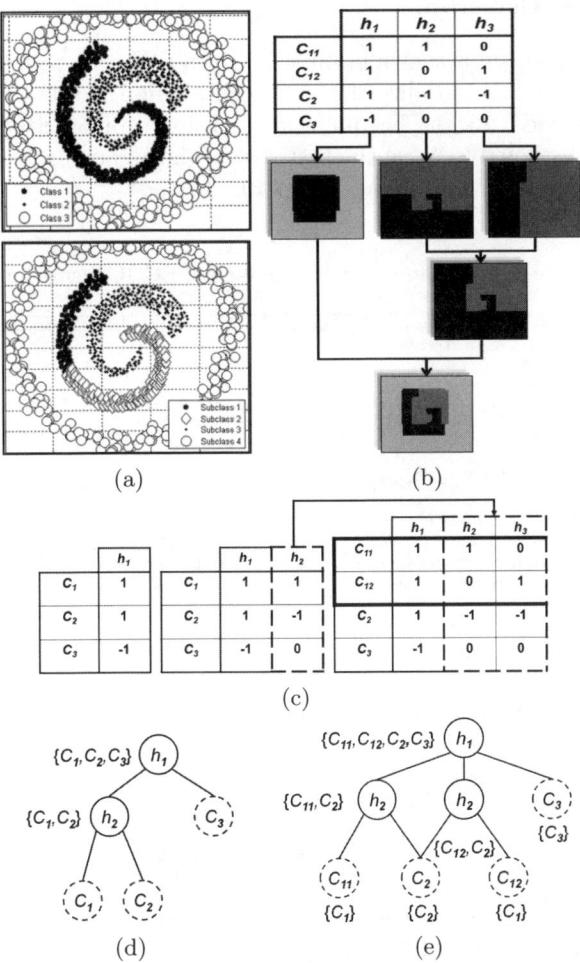

Fig. 2. (a) Top: Original 3-class problem. Bottom: 4 sub-classes found. (b) Sub-class ECOC encoding using the four sub-classes using Discrete Adaboost with 40 runs of Decision Stumps. (c) Learning evolution of the sub-class matrix M. (d) Original tree structure without applying sub-class. (e) New tree-based configuration using sub-classes.

against $\{C_2\}$ and $\{C_{12}\}$ against $\{C_2\}$. It implies that the class C_1 is split into two sub-classes (look at the bottom of fig. 2(a)), and the original 3-class problem $C = \{C_1, C_2, C_3\}$ becomes the 4-sub-class problem $C' = \{C_{11}, C_{12}, C_2, C_3\}$. As the class C_1 has been decomposed by the splitting of the second problem, previous dichotomizers that take this class into account need to be updated. The dichotomizer h_1 considers the sub-sets $\wp_1^+ = \{C_1, C_2\}$ and $\wp_1^- = \{C_3\}$. Then, those positions containing class C_1 are replaced with C_{11} and C_{12}. Now, the original tree encoding of the DECOC design shown in fig. 2(d) can be represented by the tree structure of fig. 2(e), where the original class associated to each sub-class is shown in the leaves.

2.1   Sub-class Algorithm

The encoding algorithm is shown in table 1. Given a N-class problem, the whole set of classes is used to initialize the set L containing the sets of labels for the classes to be learned. At the beginning of each iteration k (**Step 1**), the first element of L is assigned to S_k in the first step of the algorithm, and the optimal binary partition BP of S_k is found (**Step 2**).

Table 1. Problem-dependent Sub-class ECOC algorithm

Inputs: $J, C, \theta = \{\theta_{size}, \theta_{perf}, \theta_{impr}\}$ //Thresholds for the number of samples, performance, and improvement between iterations
Outputs: $C', J', \wp', M$
[Initialization:]

   Create the trivial partition $\{\wp_0^+, \wp_0^-\}$ of the set of classes $\{C_i\}$: $\{\wp_0^+, \wp_0^-\} = \{\{\emptyset\}, \{C_1, C_2, ..., C_N\}\}$
   $L_0 = \{\wp_0^-\}; J' = J; C' = C; \wp' = \emptyset; M = \emptyset; k = 1$
Step 1 S_k is the first element of L_{k-1}
   $L'_k = L_{k-1} \backslash \{S_k\}$
Step 2 Find the optimal binary partition $BP(S_k)$:
   $\{\wp_k^+, \wp_k^-\} = argmax_{BP(S_k)}(I(\mathbf{x}, d(BP(S_k))))$
   where I is the mutual information criterion, $\mathbf{x}$ is the random variable associated to the features and d is the discrete random variable of the dichotomy labels[a], defined in the following terms,
   $d = d(\mathbf{x}, BP(S_k)) = \begin{cases} 1 & \text{if } \mathbf{x} \in C_i | C_i \in \wp_k^+ \\ -1 & \text{if } \mathbf{x} \in C_i | C_i \in \wp_k^- \end{cases}$
Step 3 // Look for sub-classes
   $\{C', J', \wp'\} = SPLIT(J_{\wp_k^+}, J_{\wp_k^-}, C', J', J, \wp', \theta)$[b]
Step 4 $L_k = \{L'_k \cup \wp_k^i\}$ if $|\wp_k^i| > 1 \; \forall i \in \{+, -\}$
Step 5 If $|L_k| \neq 0$
   $k = k + 1$ **go to Step 1**
Step 6 Codify the coding matrix M using each partition $\{\wp_i^+, \wp_i^-\}$ of $\wp', i \in [1, .., |\wp'|]$ and each class $C_r \in \wp_i = \{\wp_i^+ \cup \wp_i^-\}$ as follows:
$$M(C_r, i) = \begin{cases} 0 & \text{if } C_r \notin \wp_i \\ +1 & \text{if } C_r \in \wp_i^+ \\ -1 & \text{if } C_r \in \wp_i^- \end{cases} \qquad (1)$$

---

[a] Use $SFFS$ of [12] as the maximization procedure and MI of [6] to estimate I
[b] Using the splitting algorithm of table 2.

   At **Step 3** of the algorithm, the splitting criteria SC takes as input a data set $J_{\wp^+}$ or $J_{\wp^-}$ from a sub-set $\wp^+$ or $\wp^-$, and splits it into two sub-sets $J_{\wp^+}^+$ and $J_{\wp^+}^-$ or $J_{\wp^-}^+$ and $J_{\wp^-}^-$. The splitting algorithm is shown in table 2.

   When two data sub-sets $\{J_{\wp^+}^+, J_{\wp^+}^-\}$ and $\{J_{\wp^-}^+, J_{\wp^-}^-\}$ are obtained, we select the sub-sets that have the highest distance between the means of each cluster. Suppose that the distance between $J_{\wp^+}^+$ and $J_{\wp^-}^-$ is larger than between $J_{\wp^+}^+$ and $J_{\wp^+}^-$. Then, only $J_{\wp^+}, J_{\wp^-}^+$, and $J_{\wp^-}^-$ are used. If the new sub-sets improve the classification performance, new sub-classes are formed, and the process is repeated.

   The function $TEST\_PARAMETERS$ in table 2 is responsible for testing the constraints based on the parameters $\{\theta_{size}, \theta_{perf}, \theta_{impr}\}$. If the constraints are satisfied, the new sub-sets are selected and used to recursively call the splitting function (**Step 3** of the algorithm in table 2). The constraints of the function

Table 2. Sub-class *SPLIT* algorithm

Inputs: $J_{\wp 1}, J_{\wp 2}, C', J', J, \wp', \theta$ // C' is the final set of classes, J' the data for the final set of classes, and $\wp'$ is the labels for all the partitions of classes of the final set.

Outputs: $C', J', \wp'$

Step 1 Split problems:
$$\{J^+_{\wp+}, J^-_{\wp+}\} = SC(J_{\wp+})^a$$
$$\{J^+_{\wp-}, J^-_{\wp-}\} = SC(J_{\wp-})$$

Step 2 Select sub-classes:
  if $|\overline{J^+_{\wp+}, J^-_{\wp+}}| > |\overline{J^+_{\wp-}, J^-_{\wp-}}|$ // find the largest distance between the means of each sub-set.
$$\{J^+_+, J^-_+\} = \{J^+_{\wp+}, J_{\wp-}\}; \{J^+_-, J^-_-\} = \{J^-_{\wp+}, J_{\wp-}\}$$
  else
$$\{J^+_+, J^-_+\} = \{J^+_{\wp-}, J_{\wp+}\}; \{J^+_-, J^-_-\} = \{J^-_{\wp-}, J_{\wp+}\}$$
  end

Step 3 Test parameters to continue splitting:
  if $TEST\_PARAMETERS(J_{\wp 1}, J_{\wp 2}, J^1_1, J^2_1, J^1_2, J^2_2, \theta)$// call the function with the new subsets
$$\{C', J', \wp'\} = SPLIT(J^1_1, J^2_1, C', J', J, \wp', \theta)$$
$$\{C', J', \wp'\} = SPLIT(J^1_2, J^2_2, C', J', J, \wp', \theta)$$
  end

Step 4 Save the current partition:
  Update the data for the new sub-classes and previous sub-classes if intersections exists J'.
  Update the final number of sub-classes C'.
  Create $\wp_c = \{\wp_c 1, \wp_c 2\}$ the set of labels of the current partition.
  Update the labels of the previous partitions $\wp$.
  Update the set of partitions labels with the new partition $\wp' = \wp' \cup \wp_c$.

---

^{a} SC corresponds to the splitting method of the input data into two main clusters.

$TEST\_PARAMETERS$ are fixed as: 1) The number of objects in $J_{\wp+}$ has to be larger than θ_{size}, 2) The number of objects in $J_{\wp-}$ has to be larger than θ_{size}, 3) The error $\xi(h(J_{\wp-}, J_{\wp+}))$ obtained from the dichomomizer h using a particular base classifier applied on the sets $\{\wp^+, \wp^-\}$ has to be larger than θ_{perf}, and 4) The sum of the well-classified new objects (based on the confusion matrices) divided by the total number of objects has to be greater than $1 - \theta_{impr}$.

θ_{size} corresponds to the minimum number of object samples that has to be in a sub-set, θ_{perf} is the threshold for the performance of the current binary problem, and θ_{impr} looks for the performance improvements of the split groups in relation with the previous one.

When a new sub-class is formed, we need to save the information of the current sub-sets $\{\wp^+, \wp^-\}$ and the previous sub-sets affected by the new splitting (**Step 4** of the splitting algorithm). When the final set of binary problems is obtained, its respective set of labels $\wp'$ is used to create the coding matrix M (eq. (1)).

Finally, to decode the new sub-class problem-dependent design of ECOC, we take advantage of the recently proposed Loss-Weighted decoding design [9]. The decoding strategy uses a set of normalized probabilities based on the performance of the base classifier and the ternary ECOC constraints [9].

3   Experimental Results

In order to evaluate the methodology, we discuss the data, compared methods, experiments, and performance evaluation.

• *Data*: The data used for the experiments consists of eight arbitrary multi-class data sets from the UCI Machine Learning Repository [4] and one real 9-class traffic sign classification problem from the Geomobil project of [5]. The characteristics of the UCI data sets are shown in table 3.

Table 3. UCI Machine Learning Repository data sets characteristics

Problem	#Train	#Attributes	#Classes	Problem	#Train	#Attributes	#Classes
Iris	150	4	3	Thyroid	215	5	3
Ecoli	336	8	8	Vowel	990	10	11
Wine	178	13	3	Balance	625	4	3
Glass	214	9	7	Yeast	1484	8	10

• *Compared methods*: We compare our method with the state-of-the-art ECOC coding designs: one-versus-one, one-versus-all, dense random, sparse random [8], and DECOC [6]. Each strategy uses the previously mentioned Linear Loss-weighted decoding to evaluate their performances at identical conditions. Five different base classifiers are applied over each ECOC configuration: Nearest Mean Classifier (NMC) with the classification decision using the Euclidean distance between the mean of the classes, Discrete Adaboost with 40 iterations of Decision Stumps [2], Linear Discriminant Analysis, Linear Support Vector Machines with the regularization parameter C set to 1 [1], and Support Vector Machines with Radial Basis Function kernel with the default values of the regularization parameter C and the gamma parameter set to 1 [1][2].

• *Experiments*: First, we illustrate the effect of the sub-class algorithm over toy problems. Second, we classify the set of UCI Machine Learning Repository data sets with the ECOC designs and the different base classifiers. Finally, a real multi-class traffic sign recognition problem is evaluated.

• *Performance evaluation*: To evaluate the performance of the different experiments, we apply stratified ten-fold cross-validation and test for the confidence interval at 95% with a two-tailed t-test.

3.1   Illustration Over Toy Problems

To show the effect of the Sub-class ECOC strategy for different base classifiers, we used the previous toy problem of the top of fig. 2(a). Using the previously commented base classifiers on the toy problem, the original DECOC strategy with the Loss-Weighted algorithm obtains the decision boundaries shown on the top row of fig. 3. The new learned boundaries are shown on the bottom row of fig. 3 for fixed parameters θ. Depending on the flexibility of the base classifier more sub-classes are required, and thus, more binary problems. Observe that all base classifiers are able to find a solution for the problem, although with different types of decision boundaries.

---

[2] We selected this parameter after a preliminary set of experiments.

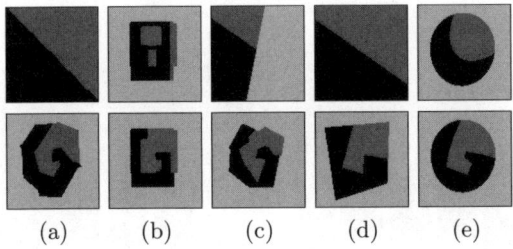

Fig. 3. Sub-class ECOC without sub-classes (top) and including sub-classes (bottom): for *FLDA* (a), Discrete Adaboost (b), *NMC* (c), Linear *SVM* (d), and *RBF SVM* (e).

Table 4. Rank positions of the classification strategies for the UCI experiments

	one-versus-one	one-versus-all	dense	sparse	DECOC	Sub-class ECOC
Discrete Adaboost	2.2	3.2	2.6	3.5	2.2	**1.3**
NMC	2.2	4.7	5.0	5.2	2.6	**1.1**
FLDA	1.6	3.8	3.1	3.8	2.1	**1.3**
Linear SVM	2.1	3.5	3.3	3.2	1.8	**1.0**
RBF SVM	2.3	4.2	2.6	4.3	2.6	**1.2**
Global rank	2.1	3.9	3.3	4.0	2.3	**1.2**

3.2   UCI Machine Learning Repository

Using the UCI data sets of table 3, the five base classifiers, and the six ECOC designs, we have performed a total of 240 ten-fold tests. The set of parameters of the sub-class approach $\theta = \{\theta_{size}, \theta_{perf}, \theta_{impr}\}$ has been fixed to $\theta_{size} = \frac{|J|}{50}$ minimum number of objects to apply sub-class (thus, 2% of the samples of each particular problem), $\theta_{perf} = 0$ to split classes if the binary problem does not learn properly the training objects, and $\theta_{impr} = 0.95$, that means that the split problems must improve at least a 5% of the performance of the problem without splitting. The last measure is simply estimated by dividing the sum of the well-classified objects from the two sub-problems the total number of objects by looking at the confusion matrices. For simplicity and fast computation, the used splitting criterion is k-means with $k=2$.[3] The results of some UCI data sets for *NMC* are shown graphically in fig. 4. One can see that the results of the sub-class approach are significantly better for most of the cases because of the failure of *NMC* to model the problems by only using the original set of classes. The mean rank of each ECOC design for each base classifier and for the whole set of UCI problems are numerically shown in table 4[4]. The ranks are obtained estimating each particular rank r_i^j for each problem i and each ECOC design j, and then, computing the mean rank R for each design as $R_j = \frac{1}{P} \sum_i r_i^j$, being P the number of experiments. Observing the ranks of each ECOC design for

---

[3] It is important to save the history of splits to re-use the sub-groups if they are required again. It speeds up the method and also reduces the variation in the results induced by different random initializations of k-means.

[4] We realize that averaging over data sets has a very limited meaning as it entirely depends on the selected set of problems.

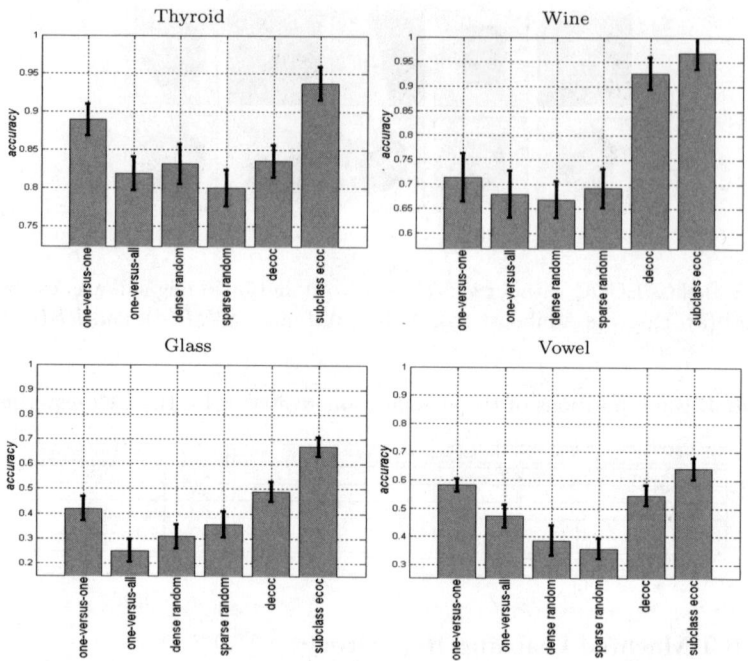

Fig. 4. UCI experiments for *NMC*

each base classifier and the global rank, one can see that the Sub-class approach attains the best position, and thus, performance, in all cases.

3.3   Traffic Sign Categorization

For this experiment, we use the video sequences obtained from the Mobile Mapping System [5] to test a real traffic sign categorization problem. We choose the speed data set since the low resolution of the image, the non-controlled conditions, and the high similarity among classes make the categorization a difficult task. In this system, the position and orientation of the different traffic signs are measured with fixed video cameras in a moving vehicle [5]. Fig. 5 shows several samples of the speed data set used for the experiments. The data set contains a total of 2500 samples divided into nine classes. Each sample is composed by 1200 pixel-based features after smoothing the image and applying a histogram equalization. From this original feature space, about 150 features are derived using a *PCA* that retained 90% of the total variance.

The performance and the estimated ranks using the different ECOC strategies for the different base classifiers are shown in table 5. One can see that in this particular problem, the sub-class is only required for Discrete Adaboost and *NMC*, while the rest of base classifiers are able to find a solution for the training set without the need for sub-classes. In this case, *RBF SVM* obtains low

Fig. 5. Speed data set samples

Table 5. Rank positions of the classification strategies for the Speed data set

	one-versus-one	one-versus-all	dense	sparse	DECOC	Sub-class ECOC
D. Adaboost	66.1(3.1)	56.6(3.1)	55.2(2.8)	52.3(3.6)	58.6(3.2)	60.8(3.1)
NMC	60.7(3.2)	50.65(3.7)	47.4(3.8)	45.1(3.8)	51.9(3.2)	62.8(3.1)
FLDA	74.7(2.8)	71.4(2.9)	74.9(2.6)	72.7(2.5)	72.6(2.8)	76.2(3.0)
Linear SVM	74.9(2.7)	72.3(2.1)	71.8(2.1)	68.2(2.9)	78.9(2.1)	78.9(1.9)
RBF SVM	45.0(0.9)	45.0(0.9)	45.0(0.9)	44.0(0.9)	45.0(0.9)	45.0(0.9)
Global rank	1.8	3.6	3.4	4.6	2.6	1.2

performances, and parameter optimization should be applied to improve these results. Nevertheless, it is out of the scope of this paper. Finally, though the results do not significantly differ between the strategies, the Sub-class ECOC approach attains a better position in the global rank of table 5.

4   Conclusions

The Sub-class ECOC strategy presents a novel way to model complex multi-class classification problems. The method is based on embedding dichotomizers in a problem-dependent ECOC design by considering sub-sets of the original set of classes. In particular, difficult problems where the given base classifier is not flexible enough to distinguish the classes benefit from the sub-class strategy. Sequential Forward Floating Search based on maximizing the Mutual Information is used to generate sub-groups of problems that are split until the desired performance is achieved. The experimental results over a set of UCI data sets and on a real multi-class traffic sign categorization problems for different base classifiers over the state-of-the-art ECOC configurations show the utility of the present methodology.

References

1. OSU-SVM-TOOLBOX, http://svm.sourceforge.net
2. Friedman, J., Hastie, T., Tibshirani, R.: Additive logistic regression: a statistical view of boosting. The annals of statistics 38, 337–374 (1998)
3. Dietterich, T., Bakiri, G.: Solving multiclass learning problems via error-correcting output codes. JAIR 2, 263–286 (1995)
4. Asuncion, A., Newman, D.J.: UCI Machine Learning Repository, University of California, Irvine, School of Information and Computer Sciences (2007)
5. Casacuberta, J., Miranda, J., Pla, M., Sanchez, S., Serra, A., Talaya, J.: On the accuracy and performance of the geomobil system. International Society for Photogrammetry and Remote Sensing (2004)

6. Pujol, O., Radeva, P., Vitrià, J.: Discriminant ECOC: A heuristic method for application dependent design of error correcting output codes. Trans. on PAMI 28, 1001–1007 (2006)
7. Pujol, O., Escalera, S., Radeva, P.: An Incremental Node Embedding Technique for Error Correcting Output Codes. Pattern Recognition (to appear)
8. Allwein, E., Schapire, R., Singer, Y.: Reducing multiclass to binary: A unifying approach for margin classifiers. JMLR 1, 113–141 (2002)
9. Escalera, S., Pujol, O., Radeva, P.: Loss-Weighted Decoding for Error-Correcting Output Codes. In: CVCRD, pp. 77–82 (October 2007)
10. Daume, H., Marcu, D.: A Bayesian Model for Supervised Clustering with the Dirichlet Process Prior. JMLR 6, 1551–1577 (2005)
11. Zhu, M., Martinez, A.M.: Subclass Discriminant Analysis. IEEE Transactions on Pattern Analysis and Machine Intelligence 28(8), 1274–1286 (2006)
12. Pudil, P., Ferri, F., Novovicova, J., Kittler, J.: Floating Search Methods for Feature Selection with Nonmonotonic Criterion Functions. In: Proc. Int. Conf. Pattern Recognition, pp. 279–283 (1994)

Part VII

Human Machine Interaction

Spatio-temporal 3D Pose Estimation of Objects in Stereo Images

Björn Barrois and Christian Wöhler

Daimler AG, Group Research, P.O. Box 2360, D-89013 Ulm, Germany

Abstract. In this contribution we describe a vision system for model-based 3D detection and spatio-temporal pose estimation of objects in cluttered scenes. As low-level features, our approach requires 3D depth points along with information about their motion and the direction of the local intensity gradient. We extract these features by spacetime stereo based on local image intensity modelling. After applying a graph-based clustering approach to obtain an initial separation between the background and the object, a 3D model is adapted to the 3D point cloud based on an ICP-like optimisation technique, yielding the translational, rotational, and internal degrees of freedom of the object. We introduce an extended constraint line approach which allows to estimate the temporal derivatives of the translational and rotational pose parameters directly from the spacetime stereo data. Our system is evaluated in the scenario of person-independent "tracking by detection" of the hand-forearm limb moving in a non-uniform manner through a cluttered scene. The temporal derivatives of the current pose parameters are used for initialisation in the subsequent image. Typical accuracies of the estimation of pose differences between subsequent images are 1–3 mm for the translational motion, which is comparable to the pixel resolution, and 1–3 degrees for the rotational motion.

Keywords: 3D scene segmentation; 3D pose estimation; spacetime stereo; temporal pose derivatives; tracking by detection.

1 Introduction

The interaction between humans and robots requires reliable vision methods for 3D pose estimation of human body parts based on 3D scene analysis. A classical approach to the model-based segmentation of point clouds and pose estimation is the iterative closest point (ICP) algorithm [1,16]. An approach to model-based 3D human body tracking based on the ICP algorithm is presented in [9]. Normal optical flow is used in [3] to predict the location of a moving object in a "tracking by detection" framework. Translational and rotational components of camera motion are estimated in [5] based on a combined analysis of stereo correspondences and optical flow. Moving objects are detected in complex scenes in [14] by segmenting a 3D point cloud with motion attributes, where multi-hypothesis tracking of the objects is performed based on a particle filter framework. A model-based 3D human body tracking system with 21 degrees of freedom has

A. Gasteratos, M. Vincze, and J.K. Tsotsos (Eds.): ICVS 2008, LNCS 5008, pp. 507–516, 2008.

recently been introduced in [13], where pose estimation relies on silhouettes extracted based on level set functions. A high metric accuracy is achieved in the absence of cluttered background. Model-based 3D tracking of the hand-forearm limb based on the multiocular contracting curve density algorithm is described in [6]. This method yields a high metric accuracy in the presence of cluttered background but requires a good initial pose. A detailed overview about the large field of human motion capture is given in [11].

In this study we present a method for model-based spatio-temporal 3D pose estimation, i. e. determination of 3D pose and its temporal derivative, from a 3D point cloud with motion attributes extracted from stereo image pairs. In contrast to most approaches mentioned above, no initial pose needs to be known a-priori and no temporal filtering (e. g. Kalman filtering) is used. An extended constraint line approach inspired by [7,15] is introduced to infer the translational and rotational motion components of the objects based on the low-level motion information provided by spacetime stereo data.

2   Spatio-temporal 3D Pose Estimation

2.1   Spacetime Stereo Image Analysis

In our system, the acquired sequence of stereo image pairs is analysed by spacetime stereo based on local intensity modelling, a technique introduced in [14]. The cameras are calibrated and the images are rectified to standard stereo geometry with epipolar lines parallel to the image rows [10]. A correspondence search is performed for each interest pixel in the left image for which a sufficiently high vertical intensity gradient is observed. To the local spatio-temporal neighbourhood of each interest pixel a parameterised function $h(\boldsymbol{P}, u, v, t)$ is adapted, where u and v denote the pixel coordinates, t the time coordinate, and $\boldsymbol{P}$ the vector of function parameters. The greyvalues around an interest pixel are modelled by a combined sigmoid-polynomial approach (cf. [14] for details):

$$h(\boldsymbol{P}, u, v, t) = p_1(v, t) \tanh\left[p_2(v, t)u + p_3(v, t)\right] + p_4(v, t). \tag{1}$$

The terms $p_1(v, t)$, $p_2(v, t)$, $p_3(v, t)$, and $p_4(v, t)$ denote polynomials in v and t. The polynomial $p_1(v, t)$ describes the amplitude and $p_2(v, t)$ the steepness of the sigmoid function, while $p_3(v, t)$ accounts for the row-dependent position of the model boundary. The polynomial $p_4(v, t)$ is a spatially variable offset which models local intensity variations across the object and in the background. Interest pixels for which no parametric model of adequate quality is obtained are rejected if the residual of the fit exceeds a given threshold. In this study, we will directly fit the model function (1) to the spatio-temporal pixel neighbourhoods, using the Levenberg-Marquardt algorithm. An approximate but faster linearised approach is described in [14].

The maximum value of the intensity gradient in horizontal direction is obtained at the root $u_e(v, t) = -p_3(v, t)/p_2(v, t)$ of the hyperbolic tangent. The horizontal position of the intensity gradient at the current time step for the epipolar line on which the interest pixel is located is given by the value $u_e(v_c, t_c)$, where the index c denotes the centre of the local neighbourhood of the interest pixel. The direction δ of the intensity gradient and the velocity μ of the intensity gradient along the epipolar line are given by $\delta = \partial u_e/\partial v|_{v_c,t_c}$ and $\mu = \partial u_e/\partial t|_{v_c,t_c}$. For correspondence analysis, the sum-of-squared-differences similarity measure is adapted to our algorithm by comparing the fitted functions $h(\boldsymbol{P}_l, u, v, t)$ and $h(\boldsymbol{P}_r, u, v, t)$ according to

$$S = \int \left[h(\boldsymbol{P}_l, u - u_e^l(v_c, t_c), v, t) - h(\boldsymbol{P}_r, u - u_e^r(v_c, t_c), v, t) \right]^2 du\ dv\ dt, \quad (2)$$

where u, v, and t traverse the local spatio-temporal neighbourhood of the interest pixel in the left (index l) and the right (index r) image, respectively. Once a correspondence between two interest pixels on the same epipolar line has been established by searching for the best similarity measure, the disparity d corresponds to $d = \left[u_i^l + u_e^l(v_c, t_c) \right] - \left[u_i^r + u_e^r(v_c, t_c) \right]$ with u_i^l and u_i^r as the integer-valued horizontal pixel coordinates of the left and the right interest pixel, respectively. For a stereo system in standard geometry with a baseline b and identical camera constants f, the depth z is given by $z = (bf)/(d_p\,d)$ [8], where d_p denotes the size of a pixel on the sensor. The epipolar velocity $\partial x/\partial t$ and the velocity $\partial z/\partial t$ along the z axis can then be computed in metric units according to $U = \partial x/\partial t = \left[b \left(\mu^l + \mu^r \right) \right]/(2d)$ and $W = \partial z/\partial t = - \left[bf \left(\mu^l - \mu^r \right) \right]/(d_p\,d^2)$. The vertical velocity component $V = \partial y/\partial t$ cannot be inferred pointwise from the spacetime stereo data due to the aperture problem. For a typical example scene, Fig. 1a displays the pixels for which stereo correspondences are established as well as the values determined for the epipolar velocity $\partial x/\partial t$. For each pair of corresponding image points, the described spacetime stereo approach directly yields the 3D coordinates, the velocity components parallel to the epipolar lines and parallel to the z axis, and the direction of the local intensity gradient – these features are needed for the subsequent processing stages of our system. Alternatively, a separate estimation of horizontal optical flow and local intensity gradient combined with traditional stereo analysis [8] or the stereo system introduced in [4] might be employed to derive this information.

2.2 Scene Clustering and Model-Based Pose Estimation

An initial segmentation of the attributed 3D point cloud extracted with the spacetime stereo technique is obtained by means of a graph-based unsupervised clustering technique [2] in a four dimensional space spanned by the spatial coordinates and the epipolar velocity of the 3D points. This clustering stage generates a scene-dependent number of clusters, essentially separating the moving object from the (stationary or differently moving) background. For the first image of a sequence, the approximate position and orientation of the object are estimated based on a principal component analysis of the corresponding cluster points and used as initial values for the model adaptation procedure. For the subsequent images, the initial pose parameters are inferred for the current time step from the previous spatio-temporal pose estimation result as described in Section 2.3.

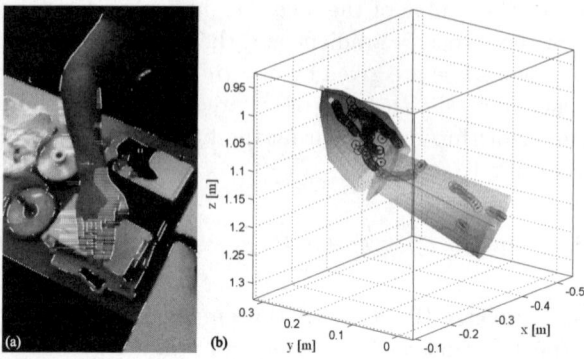

Fig. 1. (a) Image from the first test sequence (cf. Section 3). Interest pixels for which stereo correspondences are established are shown as yellow dots. Epipolar velocities are indicated as white lines. (b) 3D model adapted to the 3D point cloud.

A classical method to assign a point cloud to a geometric object model is the iterative closest point (ICP) algorithm introduced in [1]. Given an initial estimate of the object pose, the pose parameters are updated by minimising the mean squared distance between the scene points and the model. This procedure is applied in an iterative manner. As a result, the algorithm yields the three-dimensional object pose. In [1], this method is applied to the registration of point sets, curves, and surfaces. Since this approach can only be used in situations where all scene points belong to the object, it is a pose estimation rather than a scene segmentation technique. In the ICP algorithm proposed in [16], the scene points and the object model are represented as sets of chained points. During each iteration step the pose parameters are updated while at the same time some scene points are assigned to the object model and others are rejected, based on the distance to the object and the similarity of the tangent directions of the scene and model curves. Thus, outliers in the 3D point cloud are automatically rejected, and the algorithm is robust with respect to disappearing and re-appearing object parts as well as partial occlusions. As a result, the subset of scene points belonging to the object, i. e. a scene segmentation, is inferred along with the 3D object pose.

In this study we follow the approach according to [16] in order to fit a 3D model of the hand-forearm limb (which does not necessarily represent the object at high accuracy) to the 3D points determined to belong to the moving foreground object by the preceding clustering stage. We utilise the hand-forearm model introduced in [6], made up by a kinematic chain connecting the two rigid elements forearm and hand. The model consists of five truncated cones and one complete cone (cf. Fig. 1b). The cone radii corresponding to the hand and the upper end of the forearm are both set to 60 mm, and the lengths of the forearm and the hand are fixed to 220 mm and 180 mm, respectively. The other radii are inferred from human anatomy according to [6]. For each of the two rotationally symmetric model parts, the 5-dimensional vector $\boldsymbol{\Phi}$ of translational and rotational pose

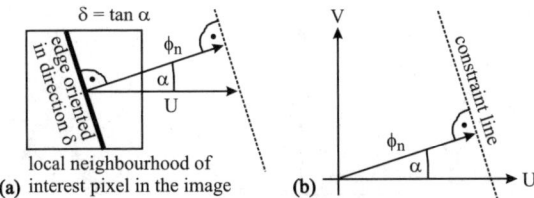

Fig. 2. (a) Relation between edge direction δ and normal velocity ϕ_n. (b) Definition of the constraint line in UV space representing the configurations (U, V) which are consistent with the observed normal velocity ϕ_n.

parameters is determined. The relative orientation between forearm and hand is described by two angles, which are included into the model as internal degrees of freedom. In the course of the adaptation process, 3D points not previously determined to belong to the object may be added to it while others may be rejected, resulting in a robust behaviour with respect to errors of the preceding clustering stage. The optimisation procedure is implemented as an M-estimator [12] with the "fair" weighting function.

2.3   Estimation of the Temporal Pose Derivatives

Both motion components of a scene point parallel to the image plane can only be recovered from the corresponding local pixel neighbourhood if the intensity distribution around the pixel is corner-like. Edge-like intensity distributions only allow the determination of one velocity component, such as the component parallel to the epipolar lines computed by the spacetime stereo algorithm (cf. Section 2.1). This ambiguity is a consequence of the well-known aperture problem [8]. Restricting the stereo and motion analysis to corner-like image features [4] may result in fairly sparse depth maps. If edge-like image features are evaluated, as it is the case in all image sequences regarded in this study, projecting the determined velocity component onto a line orthogonal to the local edge direction yields the normal velocity ϕ_n as depicted in Fig. 2a. The angle α between the direction of the horizontal epipolar lines and the direction of the normal velocity is given by $\delta = \tan \alpha$ with δ as defined in Section 2.1.

In the following, the translational velocity components of the object parallel to the x, y, and z axis are denoted by U_{obj}, V_{obj}, and W_{obj}, respectively, and expressed in metres per second. Given the observed normal velocity ϕ_n, all consistent configurations (U, V) are represented by the corresponding constraint line in UV space as defined in [7,15] (cf. Fig. 2b). For an object performing a purely translational motion parallel to the image plane, all constraint lines belonging to pixels on the object intersect in a single point in UV space. Both components of the translational motion are thus uniquely recovered. For objects with a rotational motion component in the image plane, a case which is not addressed in [7,15], the intersection points between constraint lines are distributed across an extended region in UV space. This situation is illustrated in Fig. 3a for an

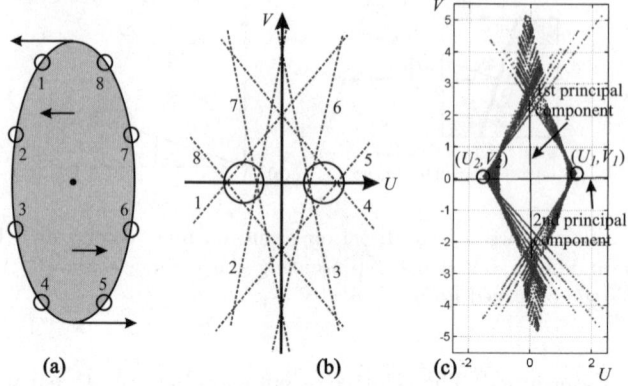

Fig. 3. (a) Rotating ellipse with reference points marked on its boundary. (b) Constraint lines resulting from the rotation of the ellipse. (c) Typical distribution of constraint line intersections in UV space for a real-world image from the first test sequence (cf. Fig. 1). The mean of the distribution has been subtracted from all points, the principal components are drawn as solid black lines.

ellipse rotating counterclockwise. The constraint lines belonging to the indicated contour points are shown in Fig. 3b. In this example, the U coordinates of the constraint line intersection points are a measure for the mean horizontal velocities of the corresponding pairs of image points. The V coordinates have no such physical meaning. The distribution of intersection points is elongated in vertical direction due to the fact that a vertical edge detector is used for interest pixel extraction and because only image points with associated values of $|\delta| < \delta_{max}$ with δ_{max} typically chosen between 1 and 2 (cf. Section 3) are selected by the spacetime stereo approach. Hence, constraint lines running at small angles to the x axis do not exist.

Fig. 3c shows a distribution of constraint line intersection points obtained from the scene shown in Fig. 1a, being typical of a rotationally symmetric and elongated object like the forearm partial model used in this study. The points in UV space are weighted according to the spatial density of the corresponding 3D points along the longitudinal object axis. The mean (U_{obj}, V_{obj}) of the intersection point distribution, corresponding to the translational motion component of the object, has already been subtracted from the intersection points in Fig. 3c. The translational motion component W_{obj} parallel to the z axis is given by the median of the (fairly noisy) values of $\partial z/\partial t$ for all 3D points assigned to the object or object part.

In the example regarded in Fig. 3c, scene points near the wrist are moving faster in the image plane than scene points near the elbow. The resulting intersection points are strongly concentrated near the points (U_1, V_1) and (U_2, V_2) depicted in Fig. 3c, which represent the motion of the scene points near the elbow and near the wrist. In this scenario, two circular markers attached to the upper and the lower end of the forearm, respectively, would yield two narrow clusters of intersection points in UV space at (U_1, V_1) and (U_2, V_2). Regarding scene points at arbitrary positions on the forearm instead of well-localised markers yields a distribution which is largely symmetric with respect to the line connecting the points (U_1, V_1) and (U_2, V_2). The information about the rotational motion of the object is thus contained in the range Δv covered by the projections of the intersection points on the principal component of the distribution which is oriented perpendicular to the longitudinal axis of the object (the second principal component in Fig. 3c). The value of Δv then corresponds to the velocity dispersion across the object caused by rotational motion in the image plane. In our system, we robustly estimate Δv based on the 10% and 90% quantiles of the distribution of the projection values. The angular velocity ω_p of the object rotation parallel to the image plane is then obtained by $\omega_p = \Delta v / \Delta l$ with Δl as the length interval parallel to the longitudinal object axis covered by the assigned 3D points.

The rotation orthogonal to the image plane is determined based on the values of $\partial z / \partial t$ determined in Section 2.1 for the extracted 3D points. For each model part, the projections $p^{(i)}$ of the assigned 3D points on the longitudinal object axis are computed, and a regression line is fitted to the $(p^{(i)}, \partial z / \partial t^{(i)})$ data points. The slope of the regression line directly yields the velocity dispersion Δw in z direction and thus the angular velocity ω_o of the object rotation orthogonal to the image plane. Due to the rotational symmetry of the object models regarded in this study, the rotational motion of the object is already fully determined by the two components ω_p and ω_o of the angular velocity.

The technique described in this section allows to extend the determination of the vector $\boldsymbol{\Phi}$ of pose parameters by a direct estimation of the temporal pose derivative $\dot{\boldsymbol{\Phi}}$ without the need for an object tracking stage.

3   Experimental Investigations and Evaluation

The described method is evaluated by analysing three realistic image sequences displaying a hand-forearm limb moving at non-uniform speed in front of complex cluttered background (cf. Figs. 1 and 4). The distance of the hand-forearm limb to the camera amounts to 0.85–1.75 m, the image resolution to 2–3 mm per pixel. For acquisition of stereo image pairs a PointGrey Digiclops CCD camera system is used. The time step between subsequent image pairs amounts to $\Delta t = 50$ ms. Spacetime stereo information according to Section 2.1 is determined based on triples of subsequent stereo image pairs, where we have set $\delta_{\max} = 2$. Ground truth information has been determined based on three markers attached to points located on the upper forearm $(\boldsymbol{P}_1)$, the wrist $(\boldsymbol{P}_2)$, and the front of the hand $(\boldsymbol{P}_3)$. The 3D coordinates of the markers were determined by bundle adjustment.

For each of the two parts of the hand-forearm model, the corresponding 5 translational and rotational pose parameters (denoted by the vector $\boldsymbol{\Phi}$) are determined independently. For the evaluation, our method is employed as a "tracking by detection" system, i. e. the pose $\boldsymbol{\Phi}(t)$ and the pose derivative $\dot{\boldsymbol{\Phi}}(t)$ are used to compute a pose $\boldsymbol{\Phi}_{\mathrm{init}}(t + n\Delta t) = \boldsymbol{\Phi}(t) + \dot{\boldsymbol{\Phi}}(t) \cdot (n\,\Delta t)$ for the next time step $t + n\Delta t$ at which a model adaptation is performed. The pose $\boldsymbol{\Phi}_{\mathrm{init}}(t + n\,\Delta t)$ is used as

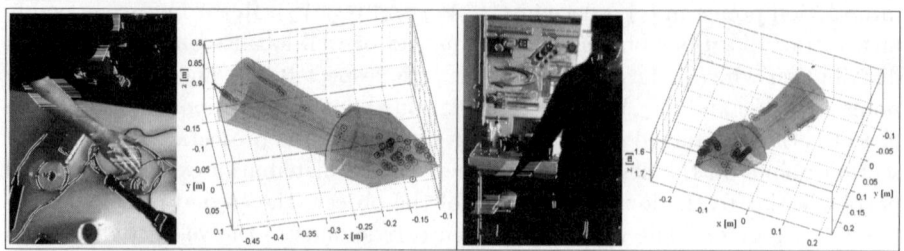

Fig. 4. Spacetime stereo and model adaptation results for example images from the second (left) and the third (right) test sequence

an initialisation for the model adaption procedure described in Section 2.2. The temporal derivatives of the pose parameters are determined independently for each model part, where the translational motion is constrained such that the two model parts are connected with each other at the point P_2.

For each sequence, the evaluation is performed for different values of n. As a measure for the accuracy of the estimated pose, the mean Euclidean distances in the scene between the estimated and the ground truth positions are shown for P_1 (circles), P_2 (squares), and P_3 (diamonds) columnwise for the three test sequences in the first row of Fig. 5. The second row shows the mean errors and standard deviations of the translational motion components U_{obj} (circles), V_{obj} (squares), and W_{obj} (diamonds) per time step. For each value of n, the left triple of points denotes the forearm and the right triple the hand. The third row displays the mean errors and standard deviations of the rotational motion components ω_p (circles) and ω_o (squares). For each value of n, the left pair of points denotes the forearm and the right pair the hand.

The Euclidean distances between the estimated and true reference points typically amount to 40–80 mm and become as large as 150 mm in the third sequence, which displays a pointing gesture (cf. Fig. 4). Being independent of n, the values are comparable to those reported in [6]. Furthermore, the deviations measured for our system are comparable to the translational accuracy of about 70 mm achieved by the stereo-based upper body tracking system described in [17]. These discrepancies are to some extent caused by a shift of the model along the longitudinal object axis but also by the fact that the lengths of the partial models of the forearm and the hand are fixed to 220 and 180 mm, respectively. For the three sequences, the true lengths correspond to 190, 190, and 217 mm for the forearm and to 203, 193, and 128 mm for the hand. Especially in the third sequence the hand posture is poorly represented by the model, as the hand forms a fist with the index finger pointing. However, this does not affect the robustness of the system. Our evaluation furthermore shows that the motion between two subsequent images is estimated at a typical translational accuracy of 1–3 mm, which is comparable to the pixel resolution of the images, and a typical rotational accuracy of 1–3 degrees. Due to its roundish shape, the rotational motion of the hand is estimated less accurately than that of the more elongated forearm (the

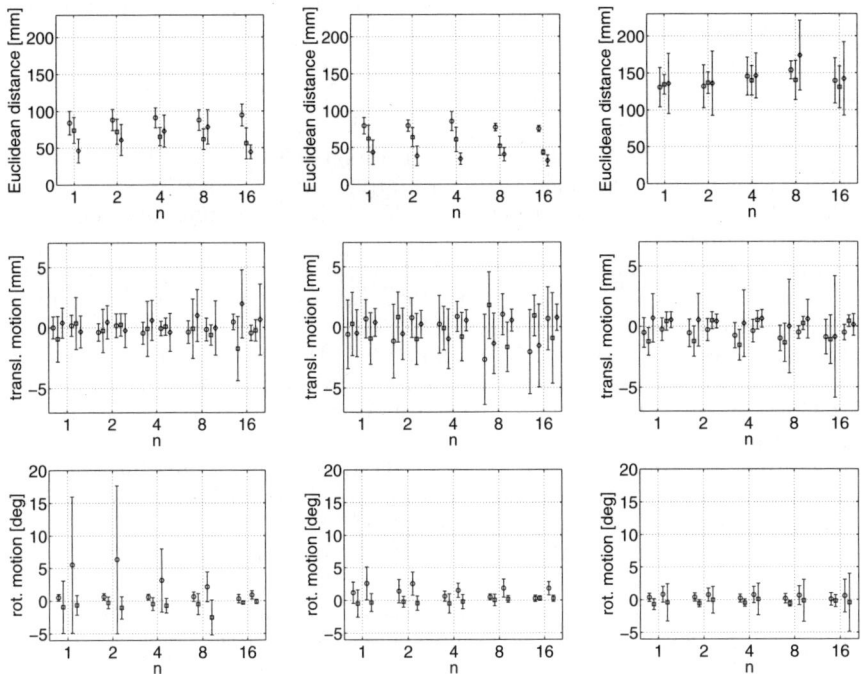

Fig. 5. Evaluation results, columnwise displayed for the three test sequences. "Motion" refers to the pose variation between subsequent images. For details cf. Section 3.

very large errors observed for ω_p in the first sequence are due to sporadically occurring outliers). A robust detection and pose estimation of the hand-forearm limb is achieved for time intervals between subsequent model adaptations as long as 800 ms ($n = 16$). The accuracy of the estimated pose and its temporal derivative is largely independent of n.

4 Summary and Conclusion

In this study we have presented a method for model-based spatio-temporal 3D pose estimation from a 3D point cloud with motion attributes extracted from stereo image pairs. Our evaluation in a "tracking by detection" framework has demonstrated that a robust and accurate estimation of the 3D object pose and its temporal derivative is achieved in the presence of cluttered background without requiring an initial pose. A new extended constraint line approach has been introduced to directly infer the translational and rotational motion components of the objects based on the low-level spacetime stereo information.

Future work may involve an extension of the proposed constraint line method to arbitrary objects not being rotationally symmetric, involving a detailed mapping of intersection points in UV space on pairs of 3D points in the scene to estimate ω_p, as well as a determination of two angular velocity components orthogonal to the image plane.

References

1. Besl, P.J., McKay, N.D.: A method for registration of 3-D shapes. IEEE Trans. on Pattern Analysis and Machine Intelligence 14(2), 239–256 (1992)
2. Bock, H.H.: Automatische Klassifikation, Vandenhoeck & Ruprecht, Göttingen, Germany (1974)
3. Duric, Z., Li, F., Sun, Y., Wechsler, H.: Using Normal Flow for Detection and Tracking of Limbs in Color Images. In: Proc. Int. Conf. on Pattern Recognition, Quebec City, Canada, vol. 4, pp. 268–271 (2002)
4. Franke, U., Rabe, C., Badino, H., Gehrig, S.K.: 6D-Vision: Fusion of Stereo and Motion for Robust Environment Perception. In: Kropatsch, W.G., Sablatnig, R., Hanbury, A. (eds.) DAGM 2005. LNCS, vol. 3663, pp. 216–223. Springer, Heidelberg (2005)
5. Gonçalves, N., Araújo, H.: Estimation of 3D Motion from Stereo Images – Differential and Discrete Formulations. In: Proc. Int. Conf. on Pattern Recognition, Quebec City, Canada, vol. 1, pp. 335–338 (2002)
6. Hahn, M., Krüger, L., Wöhler, C., Groß, H.-M.: Tracking of Human Body Parts using the Multiocular Contracting Curve Density Algorithm. In: Proc. Int. Conf. on 3-D Digital Imaging and Modeling, Montréal, Canada (2007)
7. Horn, B.K.P., Schunck, B.G.: Determining optical flow. Artificial Intelligence 17(1–3), 185–203 (1981)
8. Horn, B.K.P.: Robot Vision. MIT Press, Cambridge (1986)
9. Knoop, S., Vacek, S., Dillmann, R.: Modeling Joint Constraints for an Articulated 3D Human Body Model with Artificial Correspondences in ICP. In: Proc. Int. Conf. on Humanoid Robots, Tsukuba, Japan (2005)
10. Krüger, L., Wöhler, C., Würz-Wessel, A., Stein, F.: In-factory calibration of multiocular camera systems. In: Proc. SPIE Photonics Europe (Optical Metrology in Production Engineering), Strasbourg, pp. 126–137 (2004)
11. Moeslund, T.B., Hilton, A., Krüger, V.: A survey of advances in vision-based human motion capture and analysis. Computer Vision and Image Understanding 104(2), 90–126 (2006)
12. Rey, W.J.J.: Introduction to Robust and Quasi-Robust Statistical Methods. Springer, Heidelberg (1983)
13. Rosenhahn, B., Kersting, U., Smith, A., Gurney, J., Brox, T., Klette, R.: A system for marker-less human motion estimation. In: Kropatsch, W.G., Sablatnig, R., Hanbury, A. (eds.) DAGM 2005. LNCS, vol. 3663, pp. 230–237. Springer, Heidelberg (2005)
14. Schmidt, J., Wöhler, C., Krüger, L., Gövert, T., Hermes, C.: 3D Scene Segmentation and Object Tracking in Multiocular Image Sequences. In: Proc. Int. Conf. on Computer Vision Systems, Bielefeld, Germany (2007)
15. Schunck, B.G.: Image Flow Segmentation and Estimation by Constraint Line Clustering. IEEE Trans. on Pattern Analysis and Machine Intelligence 11(10), 1010–1027 (1989)
16. Zhang, Z.: Iterative point matching for registration of free-form curves. Technical report no. 1658, Institut National de Recherche en Informatique et en Automatique (INRIA) Sophia Antipolis, France (1992)
17. Ziegler, J., Nickel, K., Stiefelhagen, R.: Tracking of the Articulated Upper Body on Multi-View Stereo Image Sequences. In: Proc. IEEE Conf. on Computer Vision and Pattern Recognition, pp. 774–781 (2006)

Automatic Initialization for Facial Analysis in Interactive Robotics

Ahmad Rabie[1], Christian Lang[1], Marc Hanheide[1],
Modesto Castrillón-Santana[2], and Gerhard Sagerer[1]

[1] Applied Computer Science Group, Fac. of Techn., Bielefeld University, Germany
[2] SIANI, University of Las Palmas de Gran Canaria, Spain
{arabie,clang,mhanheid,mcastril,sagerer}@techfak.uni-bielefeld.de

Abstract. The human face plays an important role in communication as it allows to discern different interaction partners and provides non-verbal feedback. In this paper, we present a soft real-time vision system that enables an interactive robot to analyze faces of interaction partners not only to identify them, but also to recognize their respective facial expressions as a dialog-controlling non-verbal cue. In order to assure applicability in real world environments, a robust detection scheme is presented which detects faces and basic facial features such as the position of the mouth, nose, and eyes. Based on these detected features, facial parameters are extracted using active appearance models (AAMs) and conveyed to support vector machine (SVM) classifiers to identify both persons and facial expressions. This paper focuses on four different initialization methods for determining the initial shape for the AAM algorithm and their particular performance in two different classification tasks with respect to either the facial expression DaFEx database and to the real world data obtained from a robot's point of view.

Keywords: facial analysis, initialization, aam, face detection.

1 Introduction

Fig. 1. Facial expression in interaction

As the face of an interaction partner is one of the most important cues for any interaction, humans evidence very advanced and specialized capabilities to acquire and apply models of human faces. Additionally, when targeting at social robots communicating with humans, the analysis of facial features is a rich source of information for successful and natural interaction. First, the face is considered to be the most discriminant visual feature to identify and discern different interaction partners. This identification is especially important for a robot to provide personalized services and allows for user adaptation in scenarios where it has to cope with several different users as illustrated in Fig. 2(a) for a typical home environment. Second,

A. Gasteratos, M. Vincze, and J.K. Tsotsos (Eds.): ICVS 2008, LNCS 5008, pp. 517–526, 2008.
© Springer-Verlag Berlin Heidelberg 2008

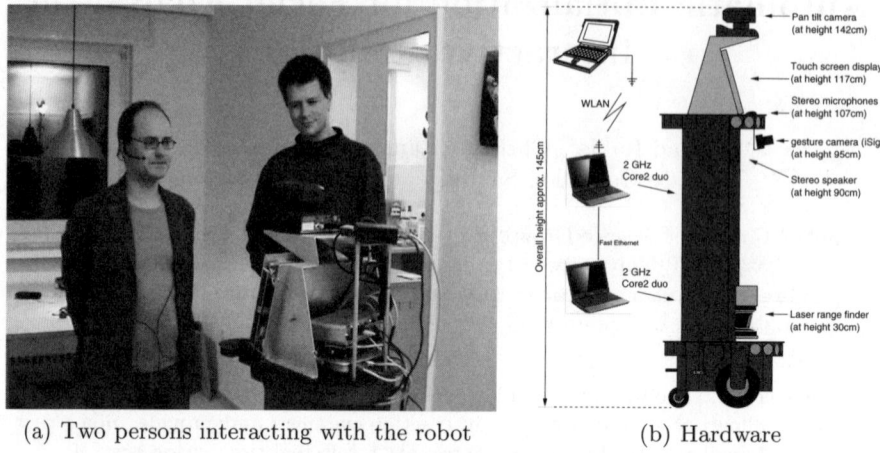

(a) Two persons interacting with the robot   (b) Hardware

Fig. 2. BIRON — the Bielefeld Robot Companion

the robot has to communicate with a person in a most intuitive and natural way. Communication involves not only verbal but also non-verbal feedback cues that yield information about the human's conversational and emotional state during the interaction with a robot in terms of facial expressions [1]. Especially communication problems such as confusion as illustrated in Fig. 1 can often be read from facial expressions [2] and trigger appropriate dialog and classification behavior in the robot. Consequently, this paper presents a system for visual facial analysis embedded as part of the interactive robot companion BIRON [3]. The robot is enabled to focus on its current interaction partner and to detect other persons of interest. Its person attention mechanism [4] allows it to align its pan-tilt camera accordingly (see Fig. 2(b) for a sketch of the robot), and zoom and focus the face of the respective interaction partner. Its goal is to learn about the environment of its users and to provide personalized services. Besides other components the robot system comprises a speech understanding and dialog system [5] including user modeling and adaptation that can directly benefit from face recognition and facial expression analysis as presented in this paper. In this paper we focus on appropriate detection and initialization methods to account for the real-world challenges of varying view points for facial analysis targeting at emotions recognition and face identification.

Although facial analysis has been well studied in computer vision literature [6,7] these approaches have mostly been designed for the still image context and rarely for continuous processing [8]. AAMs [9] are one popular solution of the problem of feature extraction from face images. They have been well studied in this domain and also constitute the basic technology for the system presented here. But in the real world domain of social robotics besides the facial feature extraction and analysis also the face detection in the continuous image stream captured from the robot's camera is important. Furthermore, AAMs are based on an iterative optimization scheme that demands an appropriate initialization.

The alignment and initialization for facial analysis using AAMs is studied in this paper and its relevance for applications in the interactive robot companion is evaluated and discussed.

In a related work that discusses the initialization for AAMs, Sattar et al. [10] focused on the face alignment phase for the AAM, but assumed a fixed pose of the face in contrast to the integrated system presented here. Other researchers in human robot interaction have studied facial features mainly for identification of interaction partners. Wong et al. [11] already presented a robot system that is able to recognize humans on the basis of their faces more than ten years ago. However, their approach is limited to six pre-trained faces and rather sensitive to lighting conditions. The humanoid robot ROBITA has also been equipped with a person attention system comprising face recognition [12] to discern different users. Sakaue et al. [13] presented a face recognition system for a dialog interface robot.

In the following we present the general architecture of the facial analysis sub-system. As this paper is focused on the effect and relevance of appropriate initialization a separate section is dedicated to the detection of faces and basic facial features. Afterwards we present basics of the applied AAMs and discuss different types of initialization. A comprehensive evaluation as well on databases as on real world video material unveils the relevance of the developed initialization schemes. Concluding remarks discuss these results.

2   System

The goal of the facial analysis sub-system as part of the general architecture in BIRON is to (i) discern different interaction partner and (ii) recognize basic emotions that can be used to influence the dialog as one cue of non-verbal feedback [5]. As the basic technique for both goals we apply AAMs. An AAM realizes an iterative optimization scheme, requiring an initialization. Therefore,

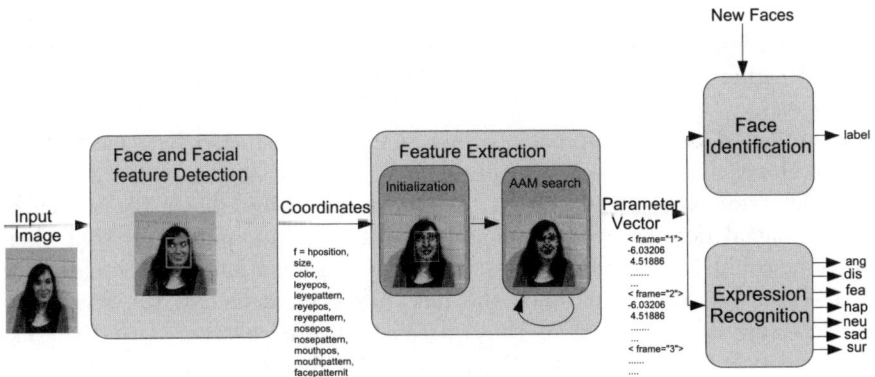

Fig. 3. Architecture of the facial analysis sub-system

the AAM fitting algorithm is embedded in a vision system that consists of four basic components as illustrated in Fig. 3. Face pose and basic facial features (BFFs), such as nose, mouth and eyes, are recognized by the face detection module. The coordinates representing these features are conveyed to the facial feature extraction module. Here, the BFFs are used to initialize the iterative AAM fitting algorithm. A bad alignment of the model drops as well the fitting algorithm as the whole performance of the system [14]. We proposed several methods to initialize the AAM on the basis of detected BFFs and evaluated the results for each of them. After feature extraction the resulting parameter vector for every image frame is either classified to discern different persons or to recognize facial expression related to six basic emotions in addition to the neutral one. Besides the feature vector, AAM fitting also returns a reconstruction error that is applied as a confidence measure to reason about the quality of the fitting and also to reject prior false positives resulting from face detection. For both classifiers, SVMs [15] are applied. However, the requirements derived from the two classification tasks differ for both classifiers. While the identification sub-system is able to learn new faces during the course of interaction when yet unknown persons introduce themselves to the robot, the facial expression classification is trained in advance to work more independently of the person's identity. Both classification schemes can be improved by drawing benefit of the continuous video stream applying a majority voting scheme on the basis of a history of recognition results. The system is applicable in soft real-time, running at a rate of approximate (5) Hz on recent PC hardware.

3   Face Detection

For our facial analysis sub-system, the frontal face and the BFFs have to be detected from the continuous video stream. Face detection has gained the attention of researches in recent years achieving different approaches that solve the problem with great performance [16,17,18]. However, instead of restricting our approach to a single image based technique as the well known [18], we have preferred an approach that makes use of cue combination to get greater robustness and higher processing speed, particularly for our scenario where live video is processed.

In the face detection approach, a face is initially detected by means of Viola and Jones based detectors: frontal face [19] and upper body [20]. This initial detection allows the system to opportunistically trigger the search of its inner facial details: eyes, nose and mouth. Our assumption is that their detection would improve the precision of the initialization and therefore the AAM search process. Thus once the face has been detected, the facial feature detectors are launched in those areas that are coherent with their expected location for a frontal face. Those located will characterize the face as follows: $f = \langle position, size, color, leye_{pos}, leye_{pattern}, reye_{pos}, reye_{pattern}, nose_{pos}, nose_{pattern}, mouth_{pos}, mouth_{pattern}, face_{pattern} \rangle$.

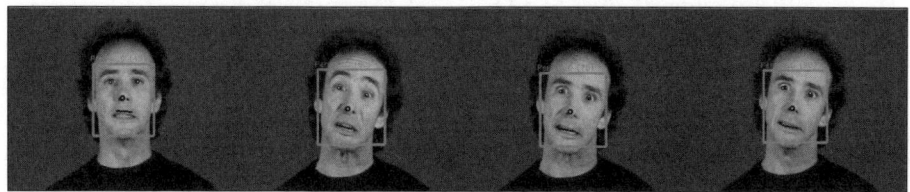

Fig. 4. Face and facial element detection results for some samples of a sequence extracted from DaFEx [21]

Following this idea, an initial detection provides different features that not only characterize the detected face, but are also used in the next frames to speed up and make more robust the detection process, taking into account the temporal coherence enclosed in a video stream. Viola and Jones based detection is therefore combined with facial feature tracking and color segmentation, achieving a cue combination approach that in our context provides faster and more robust performance than the single cue based Viola and Jones approach. Some detection results are presented in Fig. 4. Further details can be found in [22].

4   Features Extraction Using AAMs

The generative AAM approach uses statistical models of shape and texture to describe and synthesize face images. To build these models, a training set of faces with shape-defining landmarks is required. A linear shape model is obtained by first aligning all landmark sets with respect to scale, translation and rotation and applying a principal component analysis (PCA) afterwards. Thus, a parameter vector can be used to generate a shape. A triangulation algorithm and image warping are applied to transform all images to fit a common reference shape, so that all remaining differences are due to texture variations. A further PCA is applied to get a linear texture model, allowing for texture generation by a parameter vector as in the shape case. Applying a third PCA on the combined parameter vectors yields the appearance model. It can describe and generate both shape and texture using a single appearance parameter vector, which is used as feature vector for the classification. The "active" component of an AAM is a search algorithm that can find the appearance parameter vector representing a new image, given an initial estimation of its shape in terms of the respective parameter vector. This is achieved by evaluation of the gray value differences between the new image and the model-generated texture.

4.1   Initialization

The AAM fitting algorithm requires a suitable initial estimation of the face's shape to find a proper landmark matching (see Fig. 5). In our approach this initialization is based on the detected BFFs (see Sec. 2). Basically we use the mean shape $m = \left(\begin{smallmatrix} m_{x1}\cdots m_{xn} \\ m_{y1}\cdots m_{yn} \end{smallmatrix}\right)^T$ of the AAM as initial shape and place it within the detected face bounding box. The mean shape can be adopted to improve the fitting of the landmarks to the BFFs $f = \left(\begin{smallmatrix} f_{x1}\cdots f_{x4} \\ f_{y1}\cdots f_{y4} \end{smallmatrix}\right)^T$ (centers of right and left eye, nose and mouth). For each center of such a feature, there is a corresponding landmark in the mean shape. We refer to these special landmarks as *basic landmarks* $p = \left(\begin{smallmatrix} p_{x1}\cdots p_{x4} \\ p_{y1}\cdots p_{y4} \end{smallmatrix}\right)^T$, whereas all other points of the mean shape are simply called *landmarks*. Fig. 5 depicts the face bounding box as a white rectangle, the BFFs as white crosses, the basic landmarks colored green and all remaining landmarks in blue. Since the detection component will not always robustly find all BFFs, the initialization works flexibly on any partial set given. If, for instance, only the bounding box (no BFFs at all) of the face is detected only a global scaling and positioning is applied. Given detected BFFs, the corresponding basic landmarks are adopted according to one of the following initialization schemes:

- **Linear transformation:** The size and position of the mean shape is linear transformed such that the distance between each BFF and the corresponding basic landmark is minimized: $m' = m \cdot \left(\begin{smallmatrix} s_x & 0 \\ 0 & s_y \end{smallmatrix}\right) + \left(\begin{smallmatrix} d_x\cdots d_x \\ d_y\cdots d_y \end{smallmatrix}\right)^T$ where $s_k = \frac{\sum_{i=1}^{4}\sum_{j=i+1}^{4} f_{ki}}{\sum_{i=1}^{4}\sum_{j=i+1}^{4} p_{ki}}$ and $d_k = \frac{1}{4}\sum_{i=1}^{4} f_{ki} - s_k \cdot \frac{1}{4}\sum_{i=1}^{4} p_{ki}$ with $k \in \{x, y\}$
- **Linear warping:** Each basic landmark is moved to fit the corresponding BFF exactly. The surrounding landmarks are also warped, depending on their distance to the BFF and the basic landmark. The displacement decreases linearly to the distance. Formally, for each landmark i, facial feature j and $k \in \{x, y\}$ do: $m'_{ki} = m_{ki} + d_{kij}$ where $r = (m_{xi} - p_{xj})^2 + (m_{yi} - p_{yj})^2$ and $d_{kij} = (f_{kj} - p_{kj}) \cdot (1 - min\{\frac{\sqrt{r}}{w_k}, 1\})$ where w_k is a weight parameter
- **Gaussian warping:** Likewise to the linear warping, but the decrement of the displacement is Gaussian-based: $d_{kij} = (f_{kj} - p_{kj}) \cdot \exp(-\frac{r}{w_k})$

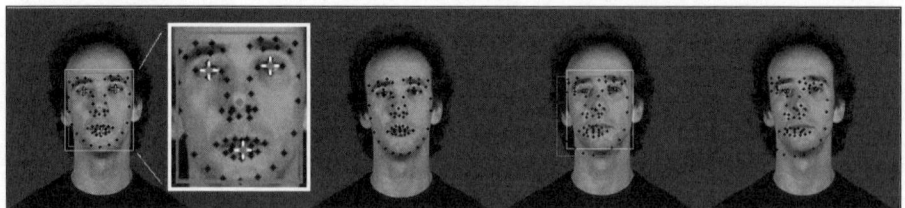

Fig. 5. Initialization based on face bounding box and BFFs (first from left) and landmark matching via AAM search (second) for an image from DaFEx [21]. In cases where the initialization is too poor (third), the AAM search algorithm cannot eventually find a correct matching (fourth).

5   Classification and Evaluation

In the following we present results from evaluation studies carried out with the presented system to assess the appropriateness of the different initialization techniques. For the evaluation a public available database has been chosen to show the general applicability of the system, furthermore data captured from the view point of our robot is analyzed. The chosen DaFEx database [21] comprises videos of different actors performing different emotions either silently or while talking. The robot corpus has been recorded from the robot's point of view and is applied for the identification sub-task. For all evaluation the AAM has been trained in advance to cover most of the variations occurring between individuals and different facial expressions. Basically, a generic AAM can be trained which is not specific to the dedicated classification tasks presented in the following. All results discussed in the following are obtained on a per frame basis, neglecting the positive effect of possible majority voting on a history of frames.

5.1   Face Identification

An one-vs-all SVM-classifier with linear kernel is used to recognize the identity of known persons. The AAM was trained with 1,056 images (non-talking) from block three of the DaFEx and covers 95% of the training set variance, resulting in a 24-dimensional feature vector. For the classification we randomly selected 100 images per person from block six (non-talking) as training data and 100 images from block one (talking) as test data. Testing with talking faces has been conducted to account for the application domain of our interactive robot. In addition to the tests with the eight persons of the DaFEx we also used videos of twelve persons captured from the robot's perspective. Again, we randomly selected 100 images of each person for training and test (both with talking subjects). The right part of table 1 reports the results in terms of recognition rates (column "Rates").

Considering the BFFs for initialization reduces the reconstruction error[1] and consequently leads to a better representation of the face, compared to the bounding box initialization. Surprisingly, this does not always lead to better classification results. In the DaFEx case it yields slightly higher classification rates for linear and Gaussian warping, whereas linear transformation performs slightly worse despite the good reconstruction error. Even the classification with initialization by placing the AAM mean shape central in the image (without face detection) yields a rate above 95%, though the reconstruction error is very poor. That is due to the unvarying backgrounds and face positions in the training and test data, which causes the AAM search to "fail in a similar way" in both training and test, resulting in poor, but similar feature vectors. Thus the SVM can discriminate the persons nevertheless, although the feature vectors might be inapplicable in terms of the AAM representation.

Unlike the faces in the DaFEx videos, the faces in the videos captured by the robot are not always centered and may also differ in scaling due to different distances. Therefore an initialization by simply centering is not applicable at all. As for the DaFEx videos, Gaussian warping performs best and linear transformation yields classification rates poorer than bounding box initialization. Surprisingly,

---

[1] Sum of squared pixel intensity differences between input image and AAM generated image, column "Rec. Err" in table 1.

Table 1. Classification rates and reconstruction errors obtained considering the initialization methods described in section 4.1

	Facial Expression				Face Identification			
	Indiv Model		Gen Model		DaFEx		Robot	
	Rates	Rec Err	Rates	Rec Err	Rates	Rec Err	Rates	Rec Err
Centering	25.70	0.2124	25.31	0.1467	95.38	0.4729	-	-
Bounding Box	71.90	0.0489	67.09	0.0345	99.25	0.0275	95.42	0.1289
Linear Transform	84.30	0.0540	79.04	0.0320	99.00	0.0255	93.25	0.1234
Linear Warping	85.87	0.0485	81.17	0.0186	99.62	0.0236	91.75	0.1180
Gaussian Warping	88.70	0.0472	80.80	0.0180	99.75	0.0224	96.50	0.1104

linear warping yields the worst results though not dramatically bad. Also using different kernels (polynomial, RBF) or an one-vs-one SVM did not improve the performance. Tests with another AAM trained with 333 images of 65 subjects from the Spacek database [23] confirmed the poor performance of linear transformation, but yield better results for linear warping. The classification rates ranked usually between those of bounding box initialization and Gaussian warping, which performed the best in this case, too. However, the differences are minor in most cases and not significant, although Gaussian warping tends to perform best.

5.2   Facial Expression Recognition

In order to evaluate the facial expression recognition DaFEx has been used to train and test the system. The robot data set currently does not contain images of different facial expression. Accordingly, no evaluation of expression recognition is carried out on this data. The third block with non talking video data of each actor from DaFEx is selected to train an individual AAM for each actor and also a generic one covering data from all actors. All AAMs are built covering 99% of the training set variance. The parameter vectors of training data of each actor and of all actors are extracted by using the corresponding AAM and are subsequently conveyed to train support vector machine classifier to perform person-dependent and -independent classification into the seven emotion classes. In both person-dependent and -independent cases an one-vs-all SVM-classifier with RBF kernel is used to evaluate the impact of the different initialization methods on the efficiency of the facial expression recognition subsystem.

Table 1 (left part) indicates that the classification rates using the individual models are better than using generic one. That shows the advantage of individual AAMs although their reconstruction errors are larger than those resulting from the generic one. The reason behind is that the variation of the facial features relevant to the expression of one person are smaller than those of multi-person and the classes of individual models are clustered more compact than of the generic one. The smaller reconstruction error of the generic AAM is expected because a larger train data is used in its constructing than in the individual ones. The largest reconstruction errors and the lowest recognition rates occurred by aligning the model on about the image center (Centering). Coarsely initializing by using the bounding box provided already considerable enhancement of the performance. Minimizing the distance between the facial features and the feature points by using linear transformation initialization offered more adequate AAM fitting and therefore yields better classification results. Moving the basic landmarks and their surrounding to fit the BFFs according to either linear warping or Gaussian warping led to the best performance of the system.

6   Conclusions and Outlook

We presented an integrated vision system for facial analysis and focused on different initialization schemes for AAMs. Our intention was to perform face recognition in the context of human robot interaction to identify the user and also to classify facial expressions occurring in conversation. The presented results show that the information related to the BBFs and especially the way in which they are used improves the AAM fitting process and in consequence the classification performance. The facial expression recognition profits more by the initialization according to the BFFs because the former depends more on the shape recognition, whereas the texture is more important for the latter. The reported results have been achieved by processing single images and should be easily improvable by taking into account the temporal coherence in video. Some authors have used anchoring to combine different modalities in that sense.

In the outlook we expect that sending the information obtained by the AAM fitting process back to the face detector can improve the detection. Furthermore, the classification results have evidenced the benefits of using a person-specific classification model for facial expression recognition. It shall be investigated how an integrated approach directly incorporating the results of identity recognition can improve the recognition of facial expressions. However, this demands online trainable expression models which are therefore in focus of future work similarly as currently already applied for the face identification. Also the surprising result that a good reconstruction error can be paired with low classification rates is worthy to be investigated.

References

1. Darwin, C., Ekman, P.: The Expression of the Emotions in Man and Animals, 3rd edn. Oxford University Press, Oxford (1998)
2. Barkhuysen, P., Krahmer, E., Swerts, M.: Problem detection in human-machine interactions based on facial expressions of users. Speech Communication 45(3), 343–359 (2005)
3. Haasch, A., Hohenner, S., Hüwel, S., Kleinehagenbrock, M., Lang, S., Toptsis, I., Fink, G.A., Fritsch, J., Wrede, B., Sagerer, G.: Biron – the bielefeld robot companion, May 2004, pp. 27–32. Fraunhofer IRB Verlag, Stuttgart, Germany (2004)
4. Fritsch, J., Kleinehagenbrock, M., Lang, S., Plötz, T., Fink, G.A., Sagerer, G.: Multi-modal anchoring for human-robot-interaction. Robotics and Autonomous Systems 43(2–3), 133–147 (2003)

5. Li, S., Wrede, B.: Why and how to model multi-modal interaction for a mobile robot companion. In: AAAI Technical Report SS-07-04: Interaction Challenges for Intelligent Assistants, pp. 71–79. Stanford, AAAI Press, Menlo Park (2007)
6. Chellappa, R., Wilson, C., Sirohey, S.: Human and machine recognition of faces: A survey. Proceedings IEEE 83(5), 705–740 (1995)
7. Zhao, W., Chellappa, R., Phillips, P.J., Rosenfeld, A.: Face recognition: A literature survey. Association for Computing Machinery 35(4), 399–458 (2003)
8. Phillips, P.J., Flynn, P.J., Scruggs, T., Bowyer, K.W., Chang, J., Hoffman, K., Marques, J., Min, J., Worek, W.: Overview of the face recognition grand challenge. In: IEEE Conference on Computer Vision and Pattern Recognition (2005)
9. Cootes, T.F., Edwards, G.J., Taylor, C.J.: Active appearance models. PAMI 23(6), 681–685 (2001)
10. Sattar, A., Aidarous, Y., Gallou, S.L., Seguier, R.: Face alignment by 2.5d active appearance model optimized by simplex. In: ICVS (2007)
11. Wong, C., Kortenkamp, D., Speich, M.: A mobile robot that recognizes people. In: Proc. Int. Conf. on Tools with Artificial Intelligence, p. 346. IEEE Computer Society, Washington, DC, USA (1995)
12. Matsusaka, Y., Tojo, T., Kubota, S., Furukawa, K., Tamiya, D., Fujie, S., Koabyashi, T.: Multi-person conversation via multi-modal interface: A robot who communicate with multi-user. In: Proc. Eurospeech, pp. 1723–1726 (1999)
13. Sakaue, F., Kobayashi, M., Migita, T., Shakunaga, T.: A real-life test of face recognition system for dialogue interface robot in ubiquitous environments. In: ICPR 2006: Proceedings of the 18th International Conference on Pattern Recognition, pp. 1155–1160. IEEE Computer Society, Washington, DC, USA (2006)
14. Huang, X., Li, S.Z., Wang, Y.: Statistical learning of evaluation function for ASM/AAM image alignment. In: Maltoni, D., Jain, A.K. (eds.) BioAW 2004. LNCS, vol. 3087, Springer, Heidelberg (2004)
15. Vapnik, V.: The nature of statistical learning theory. Springer, New York (1995)
16. Li, S.Z., Zhu, L., Zhang, Z., Blake, A., Zhang, H., Shum, H.: Statistical learning of multi-view face detection. In: European Conference Computer Vision, pp. 67–81 (2002)
17. Schneiderman, H., Kanade, T.: A statistical method for 3d object detection applied to faces and cars. In: IEEE Conference on Computer Vision and Pattern Recognition, pp. 1746–1759 (2000)
18. Viola, P., Jones, M.J.: Robust real-time face detection. International Journal of Computer Vision 57(2), 151–173 (2004)
19. Lienhart, R., Kuranov, A., Pisarevsky, V.: Empirical analysis of detection cascades of boosted classifiers for rapid object detection. In: Michaelis, B., Krell, G. (eds.) DAGM 2003. LNCS, vol. 2781, pp. 297–304. Springer, Heidelberg (2003)
20. Kruppa, H., Castrillón Santana, M., Schiele, B.: Fast and robust face finding via local context. In: Joint IEEE Internacional Workshop on Visual Surveillance and Performance Evaluation of Tracking and Surveillance (VS-PETS), October 2003, pp. 157–164 (2003)
21. Battocchi, A., Pianesi, F., Goren-Bar, D.: Dafex, a database of kinetic facial expression. In: ICMI 2005 Doctoral Spotlight and Demo Proceedings, pp. 49–51 (2005)
22. Castrillón Santana, M., Déniz Suárez, O., Hernández Tejera, M., Guerra Artal, C.: ENCARA2: Real-time detection of multiple faces at different resolutions in video streams. Journal of Visual Communication and Image Representation, 130–140 (April 2007)
23. Spacek, L.: Collection of Facial Images WWW (September 2007), Available: http://cswww.essex.ac.uk/mv/allfaces/index.html

Face Recognition Across Pose Using View Based Active Appearance Models (VBAAMs) on CMU Multi-PIE Dataset

Jingu Heo and Marios Savvides

Department of Electrical and Computer Engineering
Carnegie Mellon University, U.S.A
jheo@cmu.edu, msavvid@ri.cmu.edu

Abstract. In this paper we address the challenge of performing face recognition of a probe set of non-frontal images by performing automatic pose correction using Active Appearance Models (AAMs) and matching against a set of enrollment gallery of frontal images. Active Appearance Models are used as a way to register and fitting the model to extract 79 facial fiducial points which are then used to partition the face into a wire-mesh of triangular polygons which are used to warp the facial image to a frontal facial mesh pose. We extend to use View-Based Active Appearance Models (VBAAMs) which are able to represent a preset number of poses better than synthesizing a single AAM to handle all possible pose variations. We demonstrate our approach is able to achieve high performance results on the new larger CMU Multi-PIE dataset using 249 different people with 15 different pose angles and 20 different illumination variations under 2 different expressions (total of 149400 images). We show that our proposed pose correction approach can improve the recognition performance of many baseline algorithms such PCA, LDA, Kernel Discriminant Analysis (KDA) on the CMU Multi-PIE dataset.

Keywords: Active Appearance Models, Face Recognition, Pose Correction.

1 Introduction

Face recognition is a crucial and integral part of many current automatic surveillance systems. However the camera infrastructure is typically deployed at ceiling levels thus faces are at about 45 degrees angle from top and in the case of watchlist application where we look for criminals and terrorists we need to be able to automatically perform pose correction in order to match against an enrollment gallery which was probably taken using a frontal pose, neutral expression. We call this scenario the un-constrained scenario. There have been a lot of work in area of face recognition such as [1][2] including the most common baseline PCA algorithm [3] which was extended to view-based Eigenfaces models [4] in order to handle pose changes for face recognition. However, obtaining training data of subjects at all possible poses is a difficult and unfeasible task to perform in real-world applications thus we must be able to provide some kind of pre-processing module for matching. One way to fix this problem is to use 3D face recognition [5] which can alleviate the

A. Gasteratos, M. Vincze, and J.K. Tsotsos (Eds.): ICVS 2008, LNCS 5008, pp. 527–535, 2008.

problem with 3D facial data, many commercial acquisition devices exist which can obtain a depth map (3D shape) of the face. This can then be used to match shape as well as texture information. However the disadvantage of this approach is that it will typically require the user to be close to the 3D sensor and also require significant co-operation (e.g. standing still for several seconds). Thus type of approach is not feasible for face recognition at longer stand-offs or in automated surveillance applications. Blanz & Vetter [6] developed 3D morphable models to address this problem. They proposed to extract a 3D model from 2D facial image by the use of 3D morphable Models. This approach requires several hundred offline complete 3D facial scans which are then used to build a statistical 3D morphable Model based on texture and 3D shape information. However, they require the manually label 7 facial points from the 2D test input face in order to initialize the 3D morphable Model fitting process. This clearly can not be used in a fully automatic surveillance application as the input from a human operator is required for every single 2D face image detected. The other disadvantage of this approach is that currently it takes too long to form a 3D morphable model given a 2D face image (approx 4.5min on a P4 machine) thus yielding this approach too slow for real-time applications.

In this paper, we apply View-Based Active Appearance Models (VBAAMs) for faces under different poses which are proven to be faster than 3D model based approaches handling pose changes. After fitting with the VBAAMs, it is necessary to use these images to recognize faces. Since most of face recognition systems are frontal-based, we convert all faces to frontal faces without expressions. Evaluation on the CMU Multi-PIE database shows the effectiveness of our proposed method recognition across changes.

2 Active Appearance Models

Active Appearance Models have first been introduced by Cootes [7] with many applications in face tracking and biomedical area. An Active Appearance Model (AAM) is a statistical model to interpret (in this case) images with known parameters. It is compromised of a shape model and an appearance (pixel intensity) model. A compact representation of the trained images and new images can be achieved through training and model fitting. Figure 1 shows examples of shape meshes around texture of the faces. An AAM can be regarded in some sense as a linear modeling method because it uses Principal Component Analysis (PCA) for modeling variations. Matthews et al [8] consider the AAM model and the AAM fitting differently from [7] by mainly focusing on improving the AAM fitting algorithm using a faster non-linear optimization method. In general one can use an AAM for fitting an image with 2D or 3D AAM [9]. New images under different rotations and expressions are interpreted by analyzing the errors between the input images and the reconstructed images.

The AAM model training is based on PCA for shape, appearance, or both models in a combined form. Then an AAM fitting can be done by finding the direction which gives the least square approximation error using these model parameters. The manually labeled shape information is normalized to deal with global geometric transformations such as scale and rotation using a method called **Procrustes Analysis** which is a well-known technique for analyzing the statistical distribution of shapes.

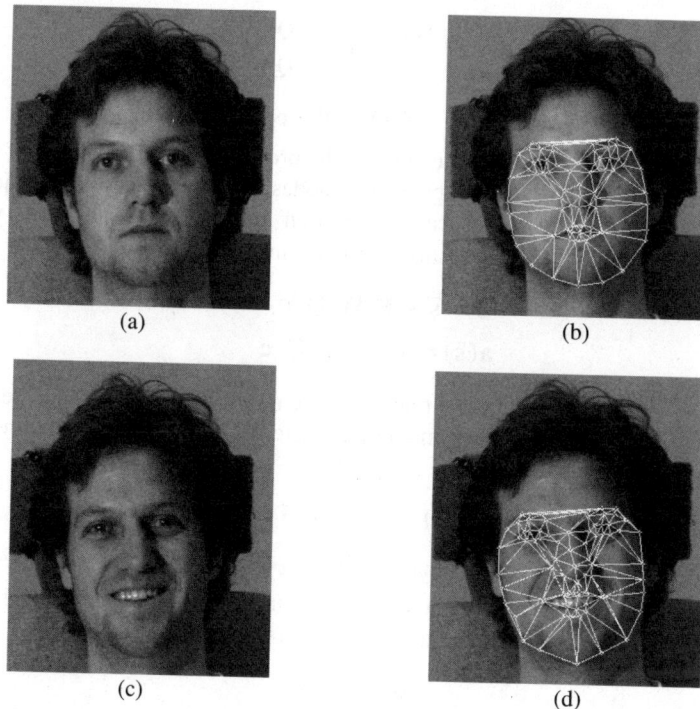

Fig. 1. The shape and texture models of a neutral face in (a) and (b) respectively and similarly shown for a smiling face in (c) and (d)

The normalized shape vector **s** for an AAM model can be expressed as the mean shape vector $\bar{\mathbf{s}}$ added to a linear combination (determined by the projection coefficient vector $\mathbf{p}_s$) of the basis vectors obtained from PCA. This can be shown as

$$\mathbf{s} = \bar{\mathbf{s}} + \mathbf{V}_s \mathbf{p}_s \tag{1}$$

where matrix $\mathbf{V}_s$ holds the the eigenvectors from the resulting eigen analysis on the shape variations. In our process, we warp an original image based on the mean hape, thus we can also model the texture appearance (shape free) model as the mean appearance $\overline{\mathbf{a}(\bar{s})}$ and a linear combination of appearance basis vectors. This can be expressed by:

$$\mathbf{a}(\bar{s}) = \overline{\mathbf{a}(\bar{s})} + \mathbf{V}_a \mathbf{p}_a \tag{2}$$

where $\mathbf{a}(\bar{s})$ indicates an appearance image resulting after the warping based on the mean shape $\bar{s}$ and $\mathbf{V}_a$ indicates the eigenvector matrix of the appearances and $\mathbf{p}_a$ is the projection coefficients vector. We typically retain eigenvectors such that we can reconstruct the training data with 95% reconstruction accuracy. We then perform a second PCA to form a combined AAM model to include both the texture and shape on the set of coefficients ($\mathbf{p}_{s,a}$) which can be denoted by:

$$\mathbf{p}_{s,a} = \begin{pmatrix} \mathbf{W}_s \mathbf{p}_s \\ \mathbf{p}_a \end{pmatrix} = \mathbf{Q}\mathbf{c} = \begin{pmatrix} \mathbf{Q}_s \\ \mathbf{Q}_a \end{pmatrix} \mathbf{c} \tag{3}$$

where $\mathbf{W}_s$ is a weighting matrix and $\mathbf{Q}$ is the eigenvector matrix on the combined texture and shape set. The vector $\mathbf{c}$ denotes the projection coefficient vector which can controls both the shape and appearance modes simultaneously. Consequently the shape and the texture model can be written in the following form where the normalized texture $\mathbf{a}(\overline{s})$ is a function of the mean shape $\overline{s}$.

$$s = \overline{s} + \mathbf{P}_s \mathbf{W}_s \mathbf{Q}_s \mathbf{c} \tag{4}$$
$$\mathbf{a}(\overline{s}) = \mathbf{a}(\overline{s}) + \mathbf{P}_a \mathbf{Q}_a \mathbf{c}$$

Given a new test image, we can fit an AAM by minimizing the distance between new image with and an AAM known model parameters so that the following the objective function is satisfied:

$$e(s) = \|\mathbf{a}(\overline{s}) - \mathbf{t}(s,\overline{s})\|^2 \tag{5}$$

where $\mathbf{t}(s,\overline{s})$ indicates an input image with shape s which is being warped based on the mean shape. The minimization can be done by assuming a linear relationship between residual errors ($\delta\mathbf{t}$) and displacement vectors ($\delta\mathbf{c}$).

$$\delta\mathbf{c} = \mathbf{M}\delta\mathbf{t} \tag{6}$$

where $\mathbf{M}$ can be computed by multivariate linear regression. The model can be iteratively refined using the current residual errors to find the direction which gives the minimum residual error.

3   View-Based Active Appearance Models

Most AAM approaches so far have been developed using a global statistical modeling framework. AAM uses PCA where by warping to a mean shape (if the data exhibits significant variations) may contribute to an unreliable (blurry) model. We can divide a global AAM into view-specific AAMs in detail where we are able to locate the facial feature points more accurately. Based on the feature points from the VBAAMs, we correct all different poses into a frontal pose. Since we use different poses and expressions, the mean shape for the AAM may not be a non-neutral and frontal face. Therefore, we only consider the mean of frontal images without expressions out of the training images used for the AAM. All the tracked images are warped based on the non-neutral and frontal mean shape, and this should be distinguished from the global mean shape used for an AAM. We apply an illumination scheme [10] and the face symmetry property only if the tracked features are non-frontal. By performing these, the intra-variations of the same individuals are greatly reduced, and therefore are more suitable for inputting these images to a frontal face recognition system for robust matching under different pose and illumination conditions. Figure 2 shows the different face normalization results. We normalize the faces based on the eye

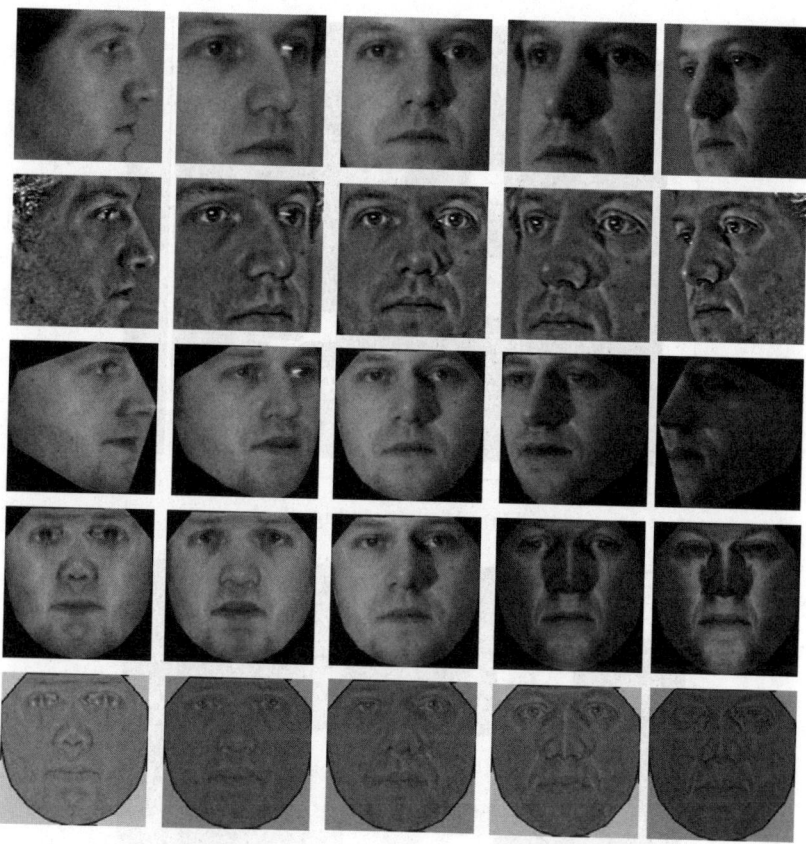

Fig. 2. (a) Sample images of the MultiPIE database. The 1st row shows the view-based face normalization. (b) The 2nd row shows the illumination processed images of the 1st row in the corresponding column. (c) The 3rd row contains the view-based AAM shape normalization, while 4th row shows the pose-corrected representation. (d) The last row contains the illumination processing of the 4th row.

coordinates and processed illumination changes in the first and second row. The 3rd row shows the AAM normalization (Procrustes Analysis) results while the 4th row shows the pose correction and the final row shows illumination normalization results from the above row. For the normalization of the profile faces, we normalize the faces using the coordinates of an eye and the tip of the nose. The size of the images is 100*100.

We used leave k-out cross validation by keeping only one view in the training. Traditional algorithms like PCA, LDA, and Kernel LDA are evaluated on the same dataset. Most algorithms work well under same views in the training set. However, performance degradation has been observed with small deviations from the view in the training as shown in Figure 3. Therefore, handing different poses for face

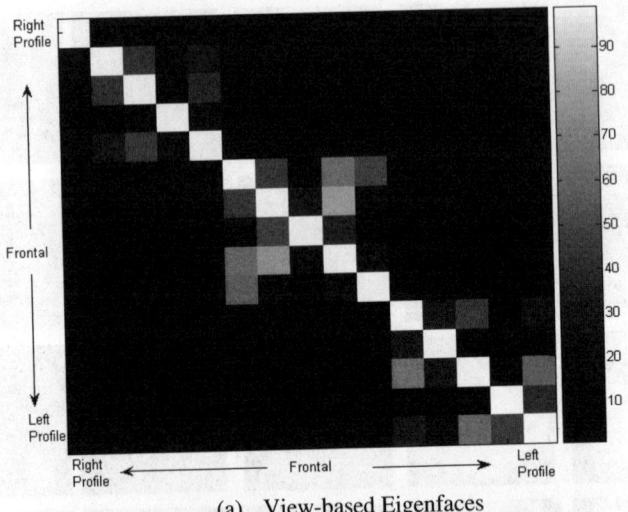

(a)   View-based Eigenfaces

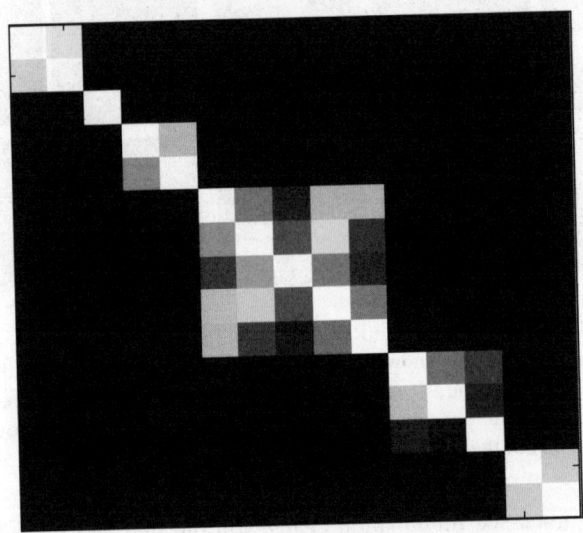

(b) View-based Eigenfaces using AAM normalization

Fig. 3. (a) View-base Eigenfaces which are based on training PCA on different pose views. (b) represents the View-Based AAM normalization which pose normalizes each image according to the View-Based AAM, so it can recognize images within a particular small range of views significantly better compared to View-based Eigenfaces which is not able to match even faces within a particular view.

recognition requires view specific algorithms. On the other hand, by correcting poses into frontal poses, performance has been increased regardless of the algorithms as show in Figure 4.

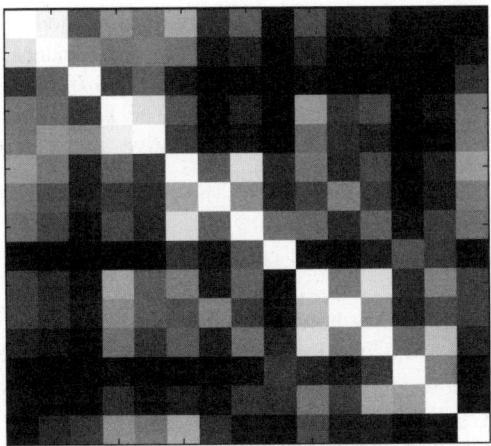

Fig. 4. Pose-Corrected normalization showing good generalization across the 15 different poses compared to the previous results in Figure 3. The similarity matrix shows that significant better matching can be achieved.

4 Results

Considering most of automatic face recognition systems are frontal-based, it may be desirable to process non-frontal images also without redesigning overall configurations of the systems. For example, for handing N different views for both Eigenfaces and an AAM, N different sets of the PCA vectors need to be calculated. Also, we need to store N views per person. If the number of people increases, handling and storing all views might be difficult.

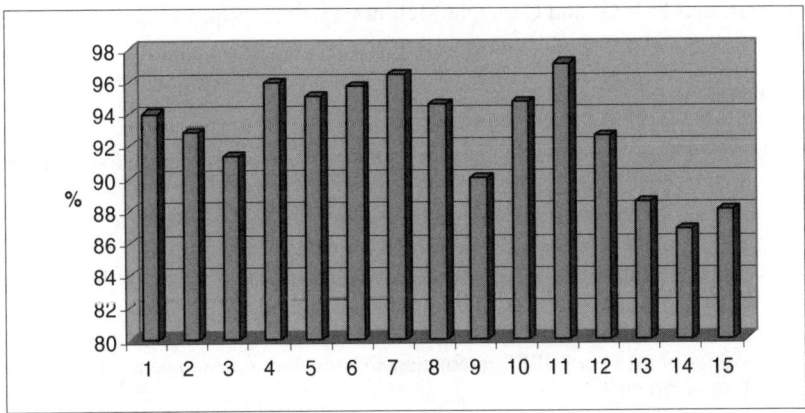

Fig. 5. Bar chart showing the recognition accuracy using Kernel Discriminant Analysis on the CMU Multi-PIE across the 15 different poses matching against frontal neutral pose images

Therefore, dealing with pose changes, our proposed method does not need to store different pose images per person without loss of the performance. Figure 5 shows the performance of Kernel Discriminant Analysis handling different views by using a set of 3 samples per each view in the training set. The kernel representation of LDA handles nonlinearities associated face well, hence gives better performance compared to linear approaches as shown previous figures.

5 Conclusion

In this paper we have shown how our pose correction approach using Active Appearance Models (AAMs) can increase the performance of baseline algorithms when tested on, occlusions can be removed efficiently for better visual quality of the faces as well as for better similarity scores of the face recognition systems while converting into frontal faces. A set of these frontal-neural faces is chosen for the basis and used for reconstructing other face images with occlusions. In addition, we are able to correct missing features while converting into frontal faces. Those corrected faces are used for inputting to a frontal based system which can handle non-frontal faces. Our focus is not evaluating other pose correction algorithms but applying pre-processing schemes such as piece-wise warping and illumination normalization to recognize faces across pose changes.

We demonstrate a frontal based face recognition system which can cover various pose changes after converting non-frontal faces into frontal-neutral faces. The VBAAMs can locate facial feature more precisely since the accuracy of the feature points are essential for warping into frontal faces. We demonstrate the pose correction method showing equivalent performance compared to the view-based Eigenfaces without the need to store images under different poses.

Acknowledgments. We would like to thank the United State Technical Support Working Group (TSWG) and Carnegie Mellon CyLab for supporting this research.

References

[1] Zhao, W., Chellappa, R., Rosenfeld, A., Phillips, P.J.: Face Recognition: A Literature Survey. In: ACM Computing Surveys, pp. 399–458 (2003)
[2] Moghaddam, B., Pentland, A.: Probabilistic visual learning for object recognition. IEEE Transactions on Pattern Analysis and Machine Intelligence 19(7), 696–710 (1997)
[3] Turk, M., Pentland, A.: Eigenfaces for Recognition. Journal of Cognitive Neuroscience 3, 72–86 (1991)
[4] Cootes, T.F., Walker, K., Taylor, C.J.: View-Based Active Appearance Models. In: Proceedings of the Fourth IEEE International Conference on Automatic Face and Gesture Recognition (2000)
[5] Bowyer, K.W., Chang, K., Flynn, P.: Evaluation of Multimodal 2D+3D Face Biometrics. IEEE Trans. on Pattern Analysis and Machine Intelligence 27(4), 619–624 (2005)
[6] Blanz, V., Vetter, T.: Face Recognition Based on Fitting a 3D Morphable Model. IEEE Transactions on Pattern Analysis and Machine Intelligence 25(9), 1063–1074 (2003)

[7] Cootes, T., Edwards, G., Taylor, C.: Active appearance models. Proceedings of the European Conference on Computer Vision 2, 484–498 (1998)

[8] Matthews, I., Baker, S.: Active Appearance Models Revisited. International Journal of Computer Vision 60(2), 135–164 (2004)

[9] Hu, C., Xiao, J., Matthews, I., Baker, S., Cohn, J., Kanade, T.: Fitting a Single Active Appearance Model Simultaneously to Multiple Images. In: Proceedings of the British Machine Vision Conference (September 2004)

[10] Gross, R., Brajovic, V.: An Image Preprocessing Algorithm for Illumination Invariant Face Recognition. In: 4th International Conference on Audio- and Video-Based Biometric Person Authentication (AVBPA), June 2003, Springer, Heidelberg (2003)

Part VIII

Cross Modal Systems

Object Category Detection Using Audio-Visual Cues

Jie Luo[1,2], Barbara Caputo[1,2], Alon Zweig[3],
Jörg-Hendrik Bach[4], and Jörn Anemüller[4]

[1] IDIAP Research Institute, Centre du Parc, 1920 Martigny, Switzerland
[2] Swiss Federal Institute of Technology in Lausanne(EPFL), 1015 Lausanne, Switzerland
[3] Hebrew university of Jerusalem, 91904 Jerusalem, Israel
[4] Carl von Ossietzky University Oldenburg, 26111 Oldenburg, Germany
{jluo,bcaputo}@idiap.ch, zweiga@cs.huji.ac.il,
{joerg-hendrik.bach,joern.anemueller}@uni-oldenburg.de

Abstract. Categorization is one of the fundamental building blocks of cognitive systems. Object categorization has traditionally been addressed in the vision domain, even though cognitive agents are intrinsically multimodal. Indeed, biological systems combine several modalities in order to achieve robust categorization. In this paper we propose a multimodal approach to object category detection, using audio and visual information. The auditory channel is modeled on biologically motivated spectral features via a discriminative classifier. The visual channel is modeled by a state of the art part based model. Multimodality is achieved using two fusion schemes, one high level and the other low level. Experiments on six different object categories, under increasingly difficult conditions, show strengths and weaknesses of the two approaches, and clearly underline the open challenges for multimodal category detection.

Keywords: Object Categorization, Multimodal Recognition, Audio-visual Fusion.

1 Introduction

The capability to categorize is a fundamental component of cognitive systems. It can be considered as the building block of the capability to think itself [1]. Its importance for artificial systems is widely recognized, as witnessed by a vast literature (see [2,3] and references therein). Traditionally, categorization has been studied from an unimodal perspective (with some notable exceptions, see [4] and references therein). For instance, during the last five years the computer vision community has attacked the object categorization problem by *(a)* developing algorithms for detection of specific categories like cars, cows, pedestrian and many others [2,3]; *(b)* collecting several benchmark databases and promoting benchmark evaluations for assessing progresses in the field. The emerging paradigm from these activities is the so-called 'part-based approach', where visual categories are modeled on the basis of local information. This information is then used to build a learning based algorithm for classification. Both probabilistic and discriminative approaches have been used so far with promising results.

Still, an algorithm aiming to work on an autonomous system cannot ignore the intrinsic multimodal nature of categories, and the multi sensory capabilities of the system.

A. Gasteratos, M. Vincze, and J.K. Tsotsos (Eds.): ICVS 2008, LNCS 5008, pp. 539–548, 2008.

For instance, we do recognize people on the basis of their visual appearance and their voice. Linen can be easily recognized because of its distinctive textural visual and tactile properties; and so forth. Biological systems combine information from all the five senses, so to achieve robust perception (see [5] and references therein).

In this paper we propose an audio-visual object category detection algorithm. We consider categories like vehicles (cars, airplanes), instruments (pianos, guitars) and animals (dogs, cows). We assume that the category has been localized, and we focus on how to integrate together effectively the two modalities. We represent visual information using a state of the art part based model (section 2, [3]). Audio information is represented by a discriminative classifier, trained on biologically motivated spectral features (section 3.1, [6]). Following results from psychophysics, we propose to combine the two modalities with a high level fusion scheme that extends previous work on integration of multiple visual cues (section 3.2, [7]). Our approach is compared with single modality classifiers, and with a low level integration approach. Experiments on six different object categories, with increasing level of difficulty, show the value of our approach and clearly underline the existing challenges in this domain (section 3.3).

2   Vision Based Category Detection

In this section we present the chosen vision based category detection algorithm (section 2.1) and experiments showing its strengths and weaknesses (section 2.2).

2.1   Visual Category Detection

To learn object models, we use the method described in [3]. The method starts by extracting interest regions using the Kadir & Brady (KB) [8] feature detector. After their initial detection, selected regions are cropped from the image and scaled down to 11×11 pixel patches, represented using the first 15 DCT (Discrete Cosine Transform) coefficients (not including the DC). To complete the representation, 3 additional dimensions are concatenated to each feature, corresponding to the x and y image coordinates of the patch, and its scale respectively. Therefore each image I is represented using an unordered set $F(I)$ of 18 dimensional vectors. The algorithm learns a generative relational part-based object model, modeling appearance, location and scale. Each part in a specific image I_i corresponds to a patch feature from $F(I_i)$. It is assumed that the appearance of different parts is independent, but this is not the case with the parts' scale and location. However, once the object instances are aligned with respect to location and scale, the assumption of part location and scale independence becomes reasonable. Thus a 3-dimensional hidden variable $C = (C_l, C_s)$, which fixes the location of the object and its scale, is used. The model's parameters are discriminatively optimized using an extended boosting process. For the full derivation of the model and further details, we refer the reader to [3].

2.2   Experiments

We used an extensive dataset of six categories (airplanes, cars, cows, dogs, guitars and pianos). They present different type of challenges: airplanes and cars contain relatively

Fig. 1. Sample images from the datasets. Object images appear on the left, background images on the right.

small variations in scale and location, while cows and dogs have a more flexible appearance and variations in scale and locations. The category images and the background classes were collected from standard benchmark datasets (Caltech Datasets[1] and PASCAL Visual Challenge[2]). For each category we have several corresponding testing backgrounds, containing natural scenes or various distracting objects. Images from the six categories and the background groups are shown in Figure 1. Each category was trained and tested against different backgrounds. Each experiment was repeated several times, with randomly generated training and test sets. Table 1 presents the average results, for different categories and varying backgrounds. These numbers can be compared with those reported in [3], and show that the method delivers state of the art performance. We then run some experiments to challenge the algorithm. Namely, we reduced the training set to roughly 1/3 for some categories (airplanes, cars; results reported in Figure 2) and, for all categories, we collected new test images containing strong occlusions, unusual poses and high categorical variability. Exemplar challenging images are shown in Figure 2. We used the learnt models to classify these challenging images. These results are also reported in Figure 2. We see that, under these conditions, performance drops significantly for all categories. Indeed, these results seem to indicate that the part-based approach might suffer when different categories share similar visual part (dogs and cows sharing legs, cars and airplanes sharing wheels), or when the variability within a single category is very high, as it is for instance for grand pianos and upright pianos, or classic and electric guitars. It is worth stressing that these considerations are likely to apply to *any* part-based visual recognition method. Thus, our multimodal approach for overcoming these issues is of interest for a wide variety of algorithms.

---

[1] Available at http://www.vision.caltech.edu/archive.html
[2] Available at http://www.pascal-network.org/challenges/VOC/

Table 1. Performance of our visual category detection algorithm on six different objects on various background. *False Negative Rate(FNR)* = $\frac{num.\ of\ false\ neg.}{num.\ of\ pos.\ instances}$, *False Positive Rate(FPR)* = $\frac{num.\ of\ false\ pos.}{num.\ of\ neg.\ instances}$ and *Error Rate(ERR)* = $\frac{num.\ of\ false\ prediction}{total\ num.\ of\ instances}$ are reported separately.

Object	Background	FNR	FPR	ERR	Background	FNR	FPR	ERR
Airplanes	Google	2.05	0.81	1.46	Road	1.90	4.96	3.62
Cars	Google	5.70	0.41	2.25	Road	11.39	0.73	3.69
Cows	Site	19.70	2.22	6.91	Road	9.09	0.18	1.14
Dogs	Site	17.00	13.89	15.53	Road	1.90	0.55	0.91
Guitars (Electrical)	Google	9.36	7.59	8.49	Objects	3.69	1.68	2.75
Pianos (Grand)	Google	18.89	1.41	4.23	Objects	6.67	6.56	6.60

Object	Background	Visual		
		FNR	FPR	ERR
Airplane⋆	Road	26.29	13.89	19.97
Car⋆	Road	38.02	1.91	13.54
Cow°	Site	78.33	-	78.33
Dog°	Site	27.00	-	27.00
Piano†	Google	58.48	-	58.48
Guitar†	Google	16.00	-	16.00

⋆: reduced number of training samples;
°: learnt models of cows & dogs to detect new test images with occlusions and strange pose;
†: learnt models of grand pianos & electrical guitars to detect upright piano and classical guitar respectively.

(a) Hard Dog Examples;

(b) Hard Cow Examples;

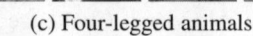

(c) Four-legged animals;

(d) Upright Piano

Fig. 2. Performance of the visual category detection algorithm on various difficulty examples. Some exemplary images are shown on the right of the table.

3   Audio-Visual Category Detection

This section presents our multi-modal approach to object category detection. We begin by illustrating the sound classification method used (section 3.1). We then illustrate our integration method (section 3.2) and show with an extensive experimental evaluation the effectiveness of our approach (section 3.3).

3.1   Audio Category Detection

Real-world audio data is characterized in particular by two properties, spectral characteristics and modulation characteristics. Spectral characteristics are obtained by decomposing the signal into different spectral bands, typically using "Bark-scaled" frequency bands that approximate the spectral resolution of the human ear. Here, we use 17 Bark bands ranging from about 50 Hz to 3800 Hz. Within each spectral band, information about the signal is encoded in changes of spectral energy across time, so-called amplitude modulations (2 Hz to 30 Hz). Grouping both properties in a single diagram, we obtain the "amplitude modulation spectrogram" (AMS, [9]), a 3-dimensional signal representation with dimensions time, (spectral) frequency and modulation frequency. Each 1s long temporal window is represented by $17 \times 29 = 493$ points in frequency/modulation-frequency space. Audio category detection [6] is performed by linear SVM classification based on a subset of the 493 AMS input features, trained to discriminate between audio samples containing only background noise (e.g., street) and samples containing an audio category object (e.g., dog) embedded in background noise at different signal-to-noise ratios (from +20 dB to -20 dB).

3.2 Audio-Visual Category Detection

This section provides a short description of our cue integration scheme. Many cue integration methods have been presented in the literature so far. For instance, one can divide them in *low level* and *high level* integration, where the emphasis is on the level at which integration happens [4]. In *low level* integration, information is combined before any use of classifiers or experts. In *high level* approaches, integration is accomplished by an ensemble of experts or classifiers; on each prediction, a classifier provides a hard decision, an expert provides an opinion. In this paper, we will investigate methods from both approaches.

High Level Integration. There are several methods for fusing multiple classifiers at the decision level [10], such as voting, sum-, product-rule, etc. However, voting could not be easily applied on our setup, since it requires an odd number of classifiers for a two class problem, and more for a multi-class problem. Here we use an extension of the *discriminative accumulation scheme (DAS)* [7]. The basic idea is to consider the margin outputs of any discriminative classifiers (e.g. AdaBoost and SVMs) as a measure of the confidence of the decision for each class, and accumulate all the outputs obtained for various cues with a linear function. The binary class version of the algorithm could be described into two steps:

1. *Margin-based classifiers:* These are a class of learning algorithms which take as input binary labeled training examples $(x_1, y_1), \ldots, (x_m, y_m)$ with $x_i \in \chi$ and $y_i \in \{-1, +1\}$. Data are used to generate a real-valued function or hypothesis $f : \chi \to \Re$, with f belonging to some hypothesis space F. The margin of an example x with respect to f is $f(x)$, which is determined by minimizing: $\frac{1}{m} \sum_{i=1}^{m} L(y_i f(x))$, for some loss function: $L : \Re \to [0, \infty]$ Different choices of the loss function L and different algorithms for minimizing the equation over some hypothesis space lead to various well studied learning algorithms such as Adaboost and SVMs.
2. *Discriminative Accumulation:* After all the margins are collected $\{f_j^p\}_{p=1}^{P}$, for all the P cues, the data x is classified using their linear combination:

$$J = \text{sgn} \left(\sum_{p=1}^{P} w_p f_j^p(x_p) \right).$$

The original DAS method considered only SVM as experts, used multiple visual cues for training and determined the weighting coefficients via cross validation.

Here we generalize the approach in many respects: we take two different large margin classifiers (SVM and AdaBoost) as experts, we train each expert on a different modality, and we determine the weights $\{w_p\}_{p=1}^P$ by training a single-layer artificial neural network (ANN) on a validation set.

A drawback of the original DAS algorithm is that the accumulation function is linear, thus the method is not able to adapt to the special characteristics of the model. For example, one sensor might be suddenly affected by noise, or detect a novel input. Here we will assume that if one sensor is very confident about the presence of a category (i.e. margin above a certain threshold), it is highly probable that this sensor is correct. We thus introduce a threshold before the accumulation, so that if the margin output value of one classifier is larger than the threshold, we will take it directly as the decision.

Low Level Integration. The *low level* fusion is also known as feature level fusion. Features extracted from data provided by different sensors are combined. In case of audio and visual feature vectors, the simple concatenation technique could be employed, where a new feature vector can be built by concatenating two feature vectors together. There are a few drawbacks to this approach: the dimensionality of the resulting feature vector is increased, and the two separate feature vectors must be available at the same time (synchronous acquisition). Due to the second problem, the *high level* integration is usually preferred in the literature for audio-visual fusion [4].

The visual feature vectors are built by concatenating all the P feature descriptors. Each feature consists of a 20-dimensional vector including [3]: the 18 dimensional vector representing each image (see section 2.1), plus a normalized mean of the feature and a normalized logarithm of the feature variance. The training set is then normalized to have unit variance in all dimensions, and the standard deviations are stored in order to allow for identical scaling of the test data. Finally, the visual feature vector is concatenated with audio feature vectors, and a linear SVM is trained for the detection.

3.3   Experiments

Experimental Setup. We evaluated our multi-modal approaches with three series of experiments. Our audio dataset contains a large number of audio clips, manually collected from the internet, corresponding to the six visual categories as well as some other objects. The audio background noise class contains recordings of road traffic and pedestrian zone noise. All audio models were trained with the same background noise but different object sounds, on several combinations of training and test sets, randomly generated. Then each audio file (object/background) was randomly associated with an image (object/background) without repetitions. Audio and visual data were collected separately, and their association was somehow arbitrary. Thus, we repeated the experiments at least 1,000 times, for each setup, so to prevent "lucky" cases. We compared our result on fusion with those obtained by single cues, reporting average results. For DAS, we experimented with the linear and non-linear (i.e. with an additional threshold for

Table 2. Results of each separate audio and visual cues and detection performance of both the high- and low-level integration scheme on six different objects

Object	Background	Audio			Visual			Fusion		
		FNR	FPR	ERR	FNR	FPR	ERR	FNR	FPR	ERR
High-level Airplane	Road	7.53	11.41	9.71	1.55	2.99	2.36	1.36	1.52	1.45
Cars	Road	6.73	3.22	4.20	11.33	0.71	3.67	1.51	0.70	0.93
Cows	Site	4.62	0.47	1.49	19.97	2.21	6.97	2.40	0.62	1.10
Dog	Site	2.09	0.36	1.27	16.78	13.79	15.37	0.36	0.62	0.48
Piano	Google	7.98	0.09	1.36	18.87	1.41	4.21	1.75	0.31	0.54
Guitar	Google	7.53	0.09	3.16	9.32	7.57	8.29	0.48	0.30	0.38
Low-level Airplane	Road	8.12	6.19	7.03	4.63	9.57	7.40	3.49	2.31	2.83
Cars	Road	7.52	1.35	3.06	8.27	1.46	3.35	3.67	0.19	1.16
Cows	Site	5.37	0.03	1.47	16.74	6.44	9.20	5.13	0.00	1.39
Dog	Site	1.96	0.01	0.99	16.93	22.91	19.76	1.83	0.01	0.97
Piano	Google	8.50	0.00	1.37	21.56	0.81	4.16	7.50	0.00	1.21
Guitar	Google	4.15	0.06	2.15	18.5	1.45	10.17	3.80	0.02	1.96

high-confidences input) approaches. However, we did not find significant differences between them. Thus we only report results obtained using the linear method.

Experiments with Clean Data. Table 2 reports the FNR., FPR., and ERR. for different objects, using *high-* and *low-level* fusion schemes. For each object, we performed experiments using various backgrounds. For space reasons we report here only a representative subset. Results show clearly that, for all objects and both fusion schemes, recognition improves significantly when using multiple cues, as opposed to single modalities. Regarding the comparison between the two fusion approaches, it is important to stress that, due to the different classification algorithms, and the differences in statistics in the training data for the different classes, it is not straightforward how to compare the performance of the two fusion schemes. Still, the high-level scheme seems to obtain overall lower error rates, compared to the low-level approach.

Experiments with Difficult/Noisy Data. We tested the robustness of our system with respect to noisy cues or difficult sensory inputs. First, we showed the effects of including audio cues for improving the system performance when there are not enough training examples (see section 2.2); results are reported in Table 3. Then, we used the models trained on clean data and test them on various difficult images (see section 2.2). These results are also shown in Table 3. Finally, the systems were tested against noisy audio inputs. The performance of the audio classifier was deliberately decreased by adding varying amount of street noise on the test object audio (SNR $\in [-20db, 20db]$), and including a varying amount of audio files generated by other objects [3] as part of the test background noise (from 25% to 1% of the total number of testing background samples). Average results on two selected examples, car (less training examples, road background) and dog (site background), are shown in Figure 3.

---

[3] Sounds of other animals, e.g. bear, horse, in case of experiments on cows and dogs, and sounds of artificial objects, e.g. phone, helicopters, in case of vehicles and instruments.

Table 3. Performance of the multimodal system suffering from less visual training examples

	Object	Background	Audio			Visual			Fusion		
			FNR	FPR	ERR	FNR	FPR	ERR	FNR	FPR	ERR
High	Airplane (Less)	Road	8.72	11.90	10.33	26.24	13.89	19.97	6.17	7.62	6.90
	Cars (Less)	Road	6.80	3.31	4.46	38.02	1.91	13.54	3.69	1.76	2.38
Low	Airplane (Less)	Road	5.36	9.65	7.76	3.78	29.16	18.01	2.76	6.96	5.12
	Cars (Less)	Road	7.50	1.57	3.21	14.08	10.01	11.15	4.83	0.50	1.70

Table 4. Performance of the multimodal system in presence of difficult test examples with occlusions, unusual poses and high categorical variability. Since background images were not used during test, only the false negative error rates (FNR) are reported.

Object	Background	High-level			Low-level		
		Audio	Visual	Fusion	Audio	Visual	Fusion
Cows (Hard)	Site	7.24	78.33	7.27	7.54	77.02	7.92
Dog (Hard)	Site	2.69	27.00	2.32	2.56	29.24	2.54
Piano (Upright)	Google	7.21	58.48	16.35	8.43	39.39	8.41
Guitar(Classical)	Google	7.14	16.00	6.40	6.04	29.80	5.93

With respect to the high-level and low-level fusion methods, we see that the low level approach seems to be more robust to noise (Table 3 and Figure 3). This might be due to the nature of the two algorithms, as for the low level fusion method the error rate is linked to the lower error rate between the two cues. The high-level fusion scheme instead weights the confidence estimates from the two sensory channels with coefficients learned during training. Thus, if one modality was weighted strongly during training, but is very noisy during test, the high-level scheme will suffer from that.

Experiments with Missing Audio. An important issue when working on multimodal information processing is the synchronicity of the two modalities, i.e. both audio and visual input must be perceived together by the system. However, unlike the multimodal person authentication scenario [4], in real-world cases the two inputs may not always be synchronized, e.g. a dog might be quiet. We tested our system in the case where some of the object samples were not accompanied by audio. To simplify the problem, we only considered the case where roughly 50% of the object samples are "silent". We considered three different ways to tackle the problem (see Figure 4, caption), and we optimized our system using a validation set under the same setup. Figure 4 reports the average results on the categories car (road background) and dog (site background). We can see that the performance still improves significantly when the missing audio inputs were represented using zero values (roughly the same as results reported in Table 2). For the other two scenarios, the performance on cars still grows, while the performance on dogs drops because the system was biased toward the audio classifier when the visual classifier did not have high accuracy. However, the system was always better than using the visual algorithm alone.

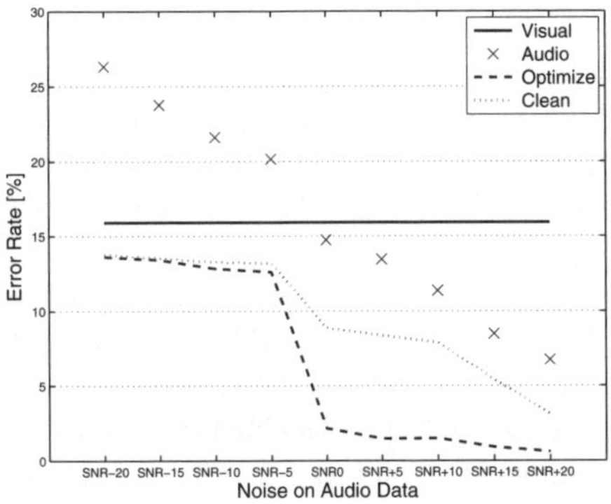

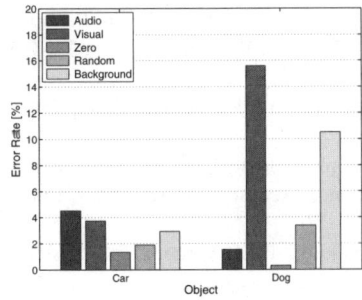

(a) Cars, High-level Fusion. 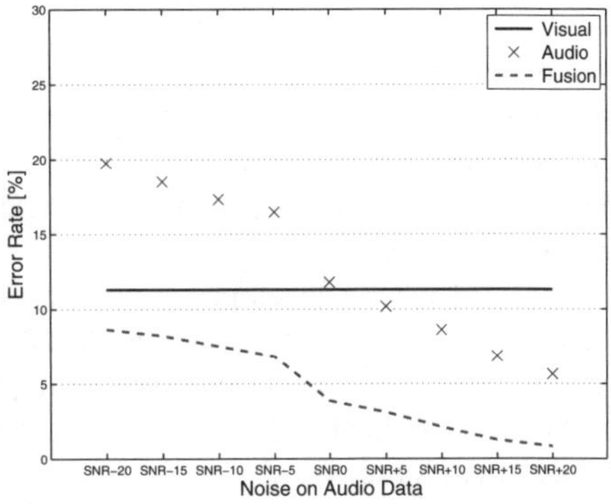   (b) Cars, Low-level Fusion.

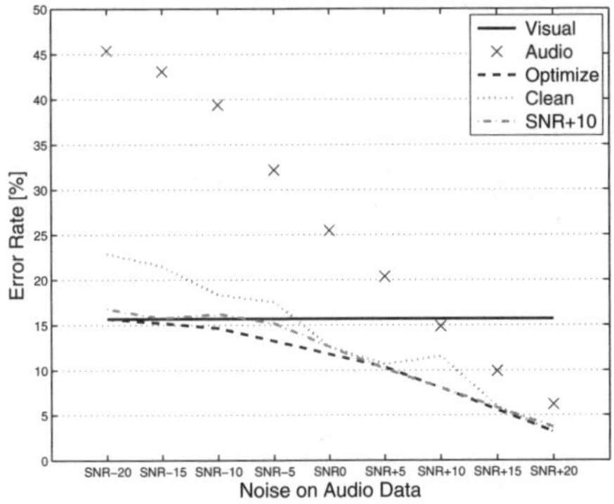

(c) Dogs, High-level Fusion. 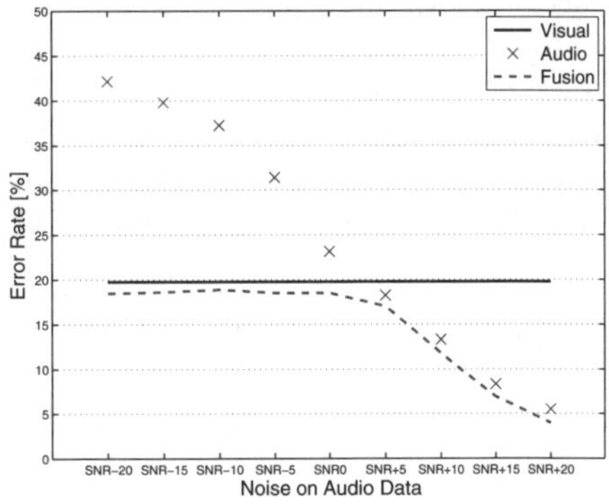   (d) Dogs, Low-level Fusion.

Fig. 3. Performance of the multimodal system in the presence of different level of corrupted audio inputs. For high-level fusion, the accumulating weights were found using different criteria: the weights were determined using clean audio and visual data through previous experiments (Clean), determined using data at current test noisy level (Optimize), or determined using data at fixed noisy level (e.g. SNR+10).

Three ways for representing the missing audio input:
Zero: the input confidences of the audio classifier equal zero, if the audio is missing; thus only the visual classifier will be considered.
Random: the input confidences of the audio classifier equal randomly generated numbers with a zero mean and standard deviation equals one, if the audio is missing;
Background: based on the assumption that the environmental noise was always presented, the test images were associated with a random background audio if the audio input is missing.

Fig. 4. Performance of the multimodal system under asynchronous test conditions

4 Discussion and Conclusions

This paper presented a multimodal approach to object category detection. We considered audio and visual cues, and we proposed two alternative fusion schemes, one high-level and the other low-level. We showed with extensive experiments that using multiple modalities for categorization leads to higher performance and robustness, compared to uni-modal approaches.

This work can be developed in many ways. Our experiments show that the high-level approach might suffer in case of noisy data. This could be addressed by using adaptive weights, related to the confidence of the prediction for each modality. Also, we estimate confidences using the distance from the separating hyperplane, but other solutions should be explored. We also plan to extend our model to a hierarchical representation as in [11]. Finally, these experiments should be repeated on original audio-visual data, so to better address the issues of synchronicity and sound-visual localization. Future work will focus on these issues.

Acknowledgments. This work was sponsored by the EU integrated project DIRAC (Detection and Identification of Rare Audio-visual Cues, http://www.diracproject.org/) IST-027787. The support is gratefully acknowledged.

References

1. Pfeifer, R., Bongard, J.: How the body shapes the way we think. MIT Press, Cambridge (2006)
2. Fergus, R., Perona, P., Zisserman, A.: Weakly supervised scale-invariant learning of models for visual recognition. Int. J. Comput. Vision 71(3), 273–303 (2006)
3. Bar-Hillel, A., Weinshall, D.: Efficient learning of relational object class models. Int. J. Comput. Vision (in press, 2007)
4. Sanderson, C., Paliwal, K.K.: Identity verification using speech and face information. Digital Signal Processing 14(5), 449–480 (2004)
5. Burr, D., Alais, D.: Combining visual and auditory information. Progress in Brain Research 155, 243–258 (2006)
6. Schmidt, D., Anemüller, J.: Acoustic feature selection for speech detection based on amplitude modulation spectrograms. In: 33rd German Annual Conference on Acoustics (2007)
7. Nilsback, M.E., Caputo, B.: Cue integration through discriminative accumulation. In: IEEE Computer Society Conference on Computer Vision and Pattern Recognition, pp. 578–585 (2004)
8. Kadir, T., Brady, M.: Saliency, scale and image description. Int. J. Comput. Vision 45(2), 83–105 (2001)
9. Kollmeier, B., Koch, R.: Speech enhancement based on physiological and psychoacoustical models of modulation perception and binaural interaction. J. Acoust. Soc. Am. 95(3), 1593–1602 (1994)
10. Polikar, R.: Ensemble based systems in decision making. IEEE Circuits and Systems Mag. 6(3), 21–45 (2006)
11. Zweig, A., Weinshall, D.: Exploiting object hierarchy: Combining models from different category levels. In: IEEE 11th International Conference on Computer Vision, pp. 1–8 (2007)

Multimodal Interaction Abilities for a Robot Companion

Brice Burger[1,2,3], Isabelle Ferrané[2,3], and Frédéric Lerasle[1,3]

[1] CNRS ; LAAS ; 7, avenue du Colonel Roche, F-31077 Toulouse, France
[2] IRIT ; 118 route de Narbonne, F-31077 Toulouse, France
[3] Université de Toulouse ; UPS, INSA, INP, ISAE ; LAAS-CNRS : F-31077 Toulouse, France
{burger,ferrane}@irit.fr, lerasle@laas.fr

Abstract. Among the cognitive abilities a robot companion must be endowed with, human perception and speech understanding are both fundamental in the context of multimodal human-robot interaction. In order to provide a mobile robot with the visual perception of its user and means to handle verbal and multimodal communication, we have developed and integrated two components. In this paper we will focus on an interactively distributed multiple object tracker dedicated to two-handed gestures and head location in 3D. Its relevance is highlighted by in- and off- line evaluations from data acquired by the robot. Implementation and preliminary experiments on a household robot companion, including speech recognition and understanding as well as basic fusion with gesture, are then demonstrated. The latter illustrate how vision can assist speech by specifying location references, object/person IDs in verbal statements in order to interpret natural deictic commands given by human beings. Extensions of our work are finally discussed.

Keywords: particle filtering, multiple object tracking, speech understanding, multimodal interaction, personal robotics.

1 Introduction and Framework

The development of socially interactive robots is a motivating challenge, so that a considerable number of mature robotic systems have been developed during the last decade [3]. Moving such robots out of laboratories, *i.e.* in private homes, to become robot companions is a deeper challenge because robots must be endowed with cognitive abilities to perform a unconstrained and natural interaction with non expert users. Besides the verbal information, gestures and reactive body motions stemmed from audio and video stream analysis must also be considered to achieve a successful intuitive communication/interaction with a household autonomous platform. This also raises issues related to efficiency and versatility. Because of the concurrent execution of other embedded functions, only a small percentage of the robot's computational power can be allocated to the interactive system. Meanwhile, as the on-board sensors are moving instead of being static, the interactive system is faced with noisy and cluttered environments.

A. Gasteratos, M. Vincze, and J.K. Tsotsos (Eds.): ICVS 2008, LNCS 5008, pp. 549–558, 2008.
© Springer-Verlag Berlin Heidelberg 2008

On one hand, fusing the interpretation of auditive and visual features improves the system robustness to such environments. On the other hand, their combination, permits to specify parameters related to person/object IDs or location references in verbal statements, typically *"give him a glass"*, *"give this object to me"*, *"put it there"*. Many interactive robotic systems make use of single-hand gesture [7,8,10] and/or object recognition [7,10] to complete the message conveyed by the verbal communication channel. Considering at once the identification of a person's face and pose, as well as two-handed gestures, must clearly disambiguates verbal utterances and so enriches any H/R interaction mechanism. An essential issue that we want to address in this context concerns the design of body and gesture trackers which must be endowed with both properties: visual data fusion (in the vein of [8]) and automatic re-initialization. All this makes our trackers work under a wide range of viewing conditions and aid recovery from transient tracking failure, which are due for instance to out-field of sight when the user is performing gestures.

The paper is organized as follows. Section 2 presents our particle filtering framework for the binocular tracking of multiple targets, namely the user's head and two-handed gestures. Section 3 presents preliminary robotic experiments involving involving this component and the one that is in charge of verbal and multimodal communication. Last, section 4 summarizes our contributions and discuss future extensions.

2   Visual Perception of the Robot User

2.1   3D Tracking of Heads and Hands

Our system dedicated to the visual perception of the robot user includes 3D face and two-hand tracking. Particle filters (PF) constitute one of the most powerful framework for view-based multi-tracking purpose [12]. In the robotics context, their popularity stems from their simplicity, modeling flexibility, and ease of fusion of diverse kinds of measurements. Two main classes of multiple object tracking (MOT) can be considered. While the former, widely accepted in the Vision community, exploits a single joint state representation which concatenates all of the targets' states together [6], the latter uses distributed filters, namely one filter per target. The main drawback of the centralized approach remains the number of required particles which increases exponentially with the state-space dimensionality. The distributed approach, which is the one we have chosen, suffers from the well-known "error merge" and "labeling" problems when targets undergo partial or complete occlusion. In the vein of [12], we develop a interactively distributed MOT (IDMOT) framework which is depicted in Table 1. Recall that Particle filters aim to recursively approximate the posterior probability density function (pdf) $p(\mathbf{x}_t^i | z_{1:t})$ of the state vector $\mathbf{x}_t^i$ for body part i at time t given the set of measurements $z_{1:t}$. A linear point-mass combination

$$p(\mathbf{x}_t^i | z_{1:t}) \simeq \sum_{n=1}^{N} \omega_t^{i,n} \delta(\mathbf{x}_t^i - \mathbf{x}_t^{i,n}), \quad \sum_{n=1}^{N} \omega_t^{i,n} = 1,$$

is determined -with $\delta(.)$ the Dirac distribution- which expresses the selection of a value -or "particle"- $\mathbf{x}_t^{i,n}$ for target i at time t with probability -or "weight"- $\omega_t^{i,n}$. An approximation of the conditional expectation of any function of $\mathbf{x}_t^i$, such as the MMSE estimate $E_{p(\mathbf{x}_t^i | z_{1:t})}[\mathbf{x}_t^i]$, then follows.

In our framework, when two particles $\mathbf{x}_t^{i,n}$ and $\mathbf{x}_t^{j,n}$ for target i and j do not interact one with the other, *i.e.* their relative Euclidian distance exceeds a predefined threshold (annoted d_{TH} in Table 1), the approach performs like multiple independent trackers. When they are in close proximity, magnetic repulsion and inertia likelihoods are added in each filter to handle the aforementioned problems. Following [12], the repulsion "weight" $\varphi_1(.)$ follows

$$\varphi(\mathbf{x}_t^{i,n}, z_t^i, z_t^j) \propto 1 - \frac{1}{\beta_1} \exp\left(-\frac{D_{i,n}^2}{\sigma_1^2}\right), \qquad (1)$$

with β_1 and σ_1 two normalization terms being determined *a priori*. $D_{i,n}$ terms the Euclidian distance between particle $\mathbf{x}_t^{i,n}$ and temporary particle $\mathbf{x}_{t,k}^j$. The principle can be extended to 3-clique $\{z^i\}_{i=1,2,3}$. The inertia "weight" $\varphi_2(.)$ considers the target's motion vector $\overrightarrow{v_1}$ from the states in previous two frames in order to predict its motion vector $\overrightarrow{v_2}$ for the current. The function then follows

$$\varphi(\mathbf{x}_t^{i,n}, \mathbf{x}_{t-1}^{i,n}, \mathbf{x}_{t-2}^{i,n}) \propto 1 + \frac{1}{\beta_2} \exp\left[-\frac{(\|\overrightarrow{v_1}\| - \|\overrightarrow{v_2}\|)^2}{\sigma_{22}^2}\right] \exp\left(-\frac{\theta_{i,n}^2}{\sigma_{21}^2} \cdot \frac{\|\overrightarrow{v_1}\|^2}{\sigma_{22}^2}\right), \qquad (2)$$

with β_2 a normalization term. $\theta_{i,n}$ represents the angle between the above vectors while σ_{21} and σ_{22} characterize the variance of motion vector direction and speed.

Our IDMOT particle filter follows this principle but is extended in three ways. First, the conventional CONDENSATION [4] strategy is replaced by the ICONDENSATION [5] one whose importance function $q(.)$ in step 3 of Table 1 permits automatic (re)-initialization when the targeted human body parts appear or reappear in the scene. The principle consists in sampling the particle according to visual detectors $\pi(.)$, dynamics $p(\mathbf{x}_t|\mathbf{x}_{t-1})$, and the prior p_0 so that, with $\alpha \in [0; 1]$

$$q(\mathbf{x}_t^{i,n}|\mathbf{x}_{t-1}^{i,n}, z_t^i) = \alpha\pi(\mathbf{x}_t^{i,n}|z_t^i) + (1-\alpha)p(\mathbf{x}_t^i|\mathbf{x}_{t-1}^{i,n}). \qquad (3)$$

Secondly, the IDMOT particle filter, devoted initially to the image-based tracking of multiple objects or people, is here extended to estimate the 3D pose of multiple deformable body parts of a single person. The third line of investigation concerns data fusion, as our observation model is based on a robust and probabilistically motivated integration of multiple cues. Fusing 3D and 2D (image-based) information from the video stream of a stereo head - with cameras mounted on a mobile robot - enables to benefit both from reconstruction-based and appearance-based approaches. The aim of our IDMOT approach, named IIDMOT, is to fit the projections all along the video stream of a sphere and two deformable ellipsoids (resp. for the head and the two hands), through the estimation of the 3D location $\mathcal{X} = (X, Y, Z)'$, the orientation $\Theta = (\theta_x, \theta_y, \theta_z)'$, and the axis length [1] $\Sigma = (\sigma_x, \sigma_y, \sigma_z)'$ for ellipsoids. All these parameters are accounted for in the state vector $\mathbf{x}_t^i$ related to target i for the t-th frame. With regard to the dynamics model $p(\mathbf{x}_t^i|\mathbf{x}_{t-1}^i)$, the 3D motions of observed gestures are difficult to characterize over time. This weak knowledge is formalized by defining the state vector as $\mathbf{x}_t^i = [\mathcal{X}_t, \Theta_t, \Sigma_t]'$ for each hand and assuming that its entries evolve according to mutually independent random walk models, viz. $p(\mathbf{x}_t^i|\mathbf{x}_{t-1}^i) = \mathcal{N}(\mathbf{x}_t^i|\mathbf{x}_{t-1}^i, \Lambda)$, where $\mathcal{N}(.|\mu, \Lambda)$ is a Gaussian distribution in 3D with mean μ and covariance Λ being

---

[1] To take into account the hand orientation in 3D.

Table 1. Our IIDMOT algorithm

1: **IF** $t = 0$, **THEN** Draw $\mathbf{x}_0^{i,1}, \ldots, {}^i\mathbf{x}_0^{i,j}, \ldots, \mathbf{x}_0^{i,N}$ i.i.d. according to $p(\mathbf{x}_0^i)$, and set $w_0^{i,n} = \frac{1}{N}$ **END IF**

2: **IF** $t \geq 1$ **THEN** $\{-[\{\mathbf{x}_{t-1}^{i,n}, w_{t-1}^{i,n}\}]_{n=1}^{N}$ being a particle description of $p(\mathbf{x}_{t-1}^i|z_{1:t-1}^i)-\}$

3:    "Propagate" the particle $\{\mathbf{x}_{t-1}^{i,n}\}_{n=1}^{N}$ by independently sampling $\mathbf{x}_t^{i,n} \sim q(\mathbf{x}_t^i|x_{t-1}^{i,n}, z_t^i)$

4:    Update the weight $\{w_t^{i,n}\}_{n=1}^{N}$ associated to $\{\mathbf{x}_t^{i,n}\}_{n=1}^{N}$ according to the formula $w_t^{i,n} \propto w_{t-1}^{i,n} \dfrac{p(z_t^i|\mathbf{x}_t^{i,n})p(\mathbf{x}_t^{i,n}|\mathbf{x}_{t-1}^{i,n})}{q(\mathbf{x}_t^{i,n}|\mathbf{x}_{t-1}^{i,n}, z_t^i)}$,

     prior to a normalization step so that $\sum_n w_t^{i,n} = 1$

5:    Compute the conditional mean of any function of $\hat{x}_t^i$, e.g. the MMSE estimate $\mathrm{E}_{p(\mathbf{x}_t^i|z_{1:t}^i)}[\mathbf{x}_t^i]$, from the approxi-

     mation $\sum_{n=1}^{N} w_t^{i,n}\delta(\mathbf{x}_t^i - \mathbf{x}_t^{i,n})$ of the posterior $p(\mathbf{x}_t^i|z_{1:t}^i)$

6:    **FOR** $j = 1 : i$, **DO**

7:       **IF** $d_{ij}(\hat{\mathbf{x}}_{t,k}^i, \hat{\mathbf{x}}_{t,k}^j) < d_{TH}$ **THEN**

8:          Save link(i,j)

9:          **FOR** k=1:K iterations, **DO**

10:             Compute φ_1, φ_2

11:             Reweight $w_t^{i,n} = w_t^{i,n}.\varphi_1.\varphi_2$

12:             Normalization step for $\{w_t^{i,n}\}_{n=1}^{N}$

13:             Compute the MMSE estimate $\hat{\mathbf{x}}_t^i$

14:             Compute φ_1, φ_2

15:             Reweight $w_t^{j,n} = w_t^{j,n}.\varphi_1.\varphi_2$

16:             Normalization step for $\{w_t^{j,n}\}_{n=1}^{N}$

17:             Compute the MMSE estimate $\hat{\mathbf{x}}_t^j$

18:          **END FOR**

19:       **END IF**

20:    **END FOR**

21:    At any time or depending on an "efficiency" criterion, resample the description $[\{\mathbf{x}_t^{i,n}, w_t^{i,n}\}]_{n=1}^{N}$ of $p(\mathbf{x}_t^i|z_{1:t}^i)$

     into the equivalent evenly weighted particles set $[\{\mathbf{x}_t^{(s^{i,n})}, \frac{1}{N}\}]_{n=1}^{N}$, by sampling in $\{1, \ldots, N\}$ the indexes

     $s^{i,1}, \ldots, s^{i,N}$ according to $P(s^{i,n} = j) = w_t^{i,j}$; set $\mathbf{x}_t^{i,n}$ and $w_t^{i,n}$ with $\mathbf{x}_t^{(s^{i,n})}$ and $\frac{1}{N}$

22: **END IF**

---

determined *a priori*. Our importance function $q(.)$ followed by our multiple cues based measurement function $p(z_t^i|\mathbf{x}_t^i)$ are depicted below. Recall that α percent of the particles are sampled from detector $\pi(.)$ (equation (3)). These are also drawn from Gaussian distribution for head or hand configuration but deduced from skin color blob segmentation in the stereo video stream. The centroids and associated covariances of the matched regions are finally triangulated using the parameters of the calibrated stereo setup. For the weight updating step, each ellipsoid defined by its configuration $\mathbf{x}_t^i$ is then projected in one of the two image planes. Given $Q = \begin{bmatrix} A & b \\ b' & c \end{bmatrix}$ the associated 4×4 symmetric matrix, the set of image points $\mathbf{x}$ that belongs to the projection contours verify the following expression: $\mathbf{x}'.(\mathbf{bb}' - c\mathbf{A}).\mathbf{x} = 0$.

The measurement function fuses skin color information but also motion and shape cues. For each ellipsoid projection, the pixels in the image are partitioned into a set of target pixels O, and a set of background pixels B. Assuming pixel-wise independence, the skin color-based likelihood is factored as

$$p(z_t^{i,c}|\mathbf{x}_t^i) = \prod_{o \in O} p_s(o|\mathbf{x}_t^i) \prod_{b \in B} [1 - p_s(b|\mathbf{x}_t^i)], \qquad (4)$$

where $p_s(j|\mathbf{x}_t^i)$ is the skin color probability at pixel location j given $\mathbf{x}_t^i$. Using only color cue for the model-to-image fitting is not sufficiently discriminant in our robotics context. We also consider a likelihood $p(z_t^{i,s}|\mathbf{x}_t^i)$ which combines motion and shape cues. In some H/R situations, it is highly possible that the targeted limbs be moving, at least intermittently. We thus favor the moving edges (if any) of the target in this likelihood so that

$$p(z_t^{i,s}|\mathbf{x}_t^i) \propto \exp\left(-D^2/2\sigma_s^2\right), \; D = \sum_{j=1}^{N_p} |x(j) - z(j)| + \rho\gamma(z(j)), \qquad (5)$$

which depends on the sum of the squared distances between N_p points uniformly distributed along the ellipsoid contours $\mathbf{x}$ and their nearest image edges z. σ_s is a standard deviation being determined *a priori*. Given $\overrightarrow{f}(z_t(j))$ the optical flow vector at pixel $z(j)$, $\gamma(z(j)) = 0$ (resp. 1) if $\overrightarrow{f}(z(j)) \neq 0$ (resp. if $\overrightarrow{f}(z(j)) = 0$) and $\rho > 0$ terms a penalty. Finally, assuming the cues to be mutually independent, the unified measurement function in step 4 (Table 1) is formulated as

$$p(z_t^{i,c}, z_t^{i,s}|\mathbf{x}_t^i) = p(z_t^{i,c}|\mathbf{x}_t^i).p(z_t^{i,s}|\mathbf{x}_t^i). \qquad (6)$$

2.2   Experimental Results

Prior to their integration on our mobile robot, experiments on a database of 10 sequences (1214 stereo-images) acquired from the robot are performed off-line in order to: (i) determine the optimal parameter values of our strategy, (ii) characterize its performances. This sequence set involves variable viewing conditions, namely illumination changes, clutter, occlusions or out-field of sight. Figure 1 shows snapshots of a typical run for IIDMOT involving sporadic disappearances of some body parts. For each frame, the template depicts the projection of the MMSE estimate for each ellipsoid. The IIDMOT strategy, by drawing some particles according to the detector output, permits automatic re-initialization and aids recovery after loss of observability.

Fig. 1. Tracking scenario involving occlusion and out-field of sight with IIDMOT

Quantitative performance evaluation have been carried out on the sequence set. Since the main concern of tracking is the correctness of the tracker results, location as well as label, we compare the tracking performance quantitatively by defining the false position rate (FR_p) and the false label rate (FR_l). As we have no ground truth, failure situations must be defined. No tracker associated with one of the target in (at least) one image plane will correspond to a position failure while a tracker associated with the wrong target will correspond to a label failure. Table 2 presents the performance using multiple

Table 2. Quantitative performance and speed comparisons

Method	MIPF	IDMOT	IIDMOT
FR_p	29%	18%	4%
FR_l	9%	1%	1%
Speed (fps)	15	12	10

independent particle filters (MIPF) [4], conventional IDMOT [12] strategy, and our IIDMOT strategy with data fusion.

Our IIDMOT strategy is shown to outperform the conventional approaches for a slight additional time consumption. The MIPF strategy suffers especially from "labeling" problem due to lacking modeling of interaction between trackers while the IDMOT strategy doesn't recover the target after transient loss. These results have been obtained for the "optimal" tracker parameter values listed in Table 3.

Table 3. Parameter values used in our IIDMOT tracker

Symbol	Meaning	Value
N	number of particles per filter	100
α	coeff. in the importance function (3)	0.4
K	number of iterations in PF algorithm	4
d_{TH}	Euclidian distance between particles in PF algorithm	0.5
-	image resolution	256×192
-	colorspace for skin-color segmentation	CIE Lab
N_p	number of points along the ellipsoid contours	20
σ_s	standard in likelihood (5)	36
ρ	penalty in equation (5)	0.12
(σ_1, β_1)	coeff. in the repulsion "weight" (1)	$(0.12, 1.33)$
$(\sigma_{21}, \sigma_{22}, \beta_2)$	coeff. in the inertia "weight" (2)	$(1.57, 0.2, 2.0)$
Λ	standard deviation in random walk models	$\begin{pmatrix} 0.07 & 0.07 & 0.07 \\ 0.03 & 0.03 & 0.03 \\ 0.17 & 0.17 & 0.17 \end{pmatrix}$

3   Multimodal System Setup Embedded on the Robot Companion

This section gives some considerations about the integration of the above components in the architecture of our robot, depicts the execution of a target scenario in order to highlight the relevance and the complementarity of this visual component with the one dedicated to verbal and multimodal communication.

3.1   Characteristics of the Robot

Our robot is especially equipped with a 6-DOF arm, a pan-tilt stereo system on a mast, a microphone (hold by the user and cable wire connected to the robot for this first experiment), two laser scanners (figure 2-left-). From these sensors and actuators, the robot has been endowed with a set of basic functions that allows us to carry out scenarios

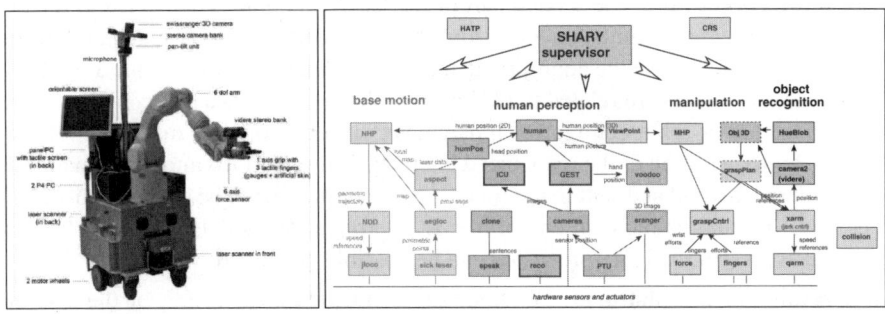

Fig. 2. The robot Jido and its layered software architecture

based on a multimodal interaction between a person and a robot, as the scenario presented in this section. Thanks to these functions, the robot is able to navigate in its environment and to recognize objects. Preliminary developments related to its vision-based functions have concerned face identification implemented through the ICU[2] module (see [11] for more details). Then, a module for gesture tracking, called GEST, has been added. It is based on the method we have described in section 2. The verbal communication mode, that deals with recognition and understanding of the user utterances, is handled by means of a dedicated module called RECO and is briefly presented below. These modules have been integrated on the robot software architecture that relies on sets of communicating modules running under the control of the platform supervisor [2].

3.2 Enabling Verbal and Multimodal Communication and Multimodal Communication

Natural communication between a person and a robot companion requires to recognize speech once uttered by the user and then to understand its meaning in relation to the current context represented by a specific task, a place, an object, an action, a set of objects or some other people involved and in some case a complementary gesture. This is the role of the RECO module integrated on the platform. Only outline and examples of results related to the type of scenarios we want to carry out are presented here.

Speech recognition: To process French utterances, we use a grammar-based speech engine, called Julian (version of the open source engine Julius developed by the Continuous Speech Recognition Consortium [1]). This engine requires essential linguistic resources : a set of acoustic models for French phonetic units (39 models, a lexicon (246 words and 428 pronunciations corresponding to phoneme sequences) drawn up from the French lexical database BDLEX [9], a set of grammars specifically designed to describe sentences related to the subtasks taken into account in our multimodal interaction scenarios : user introducing him/herself, *"Hi Jodo I'm Paul"*, giving basic movement order, *"Turn left"*, or guidance request *"Take me to the hall"*, using *"Please come here"* and other request for object exchange *"Give me this bottle"*, ... They represent 2334 different well-formed sentences, to enable communication with speech and gesture.

---

[2] For the acronym of "I see you".

Speech interpretation: The second part of the RECO module is dedicated to the extraction of the semantic units, directly from the recognizer output. A semantic lexicon has been designed to give the appropriate meaning of relevant words. Some are related to actions while others are related to objects or their own attributes like color or size as well as location or robot configuration parameters (speed, rotation, distance). At last, the global interpretation of the recognized utterance is transformed into a command. To be considered as valid and sent to the robot supervisor in order to be executed this command must be compatible with one of our 31 interpretation models. From the lexicon available at present, 328 interpretations can be possibly generated.

First results on the platform: Without any adaptation step, 77.6% of the 250 utterances processed have been transformed in the right command. Though, recognition and interpretation must be improved, the robot is now endowed with some abilities to interpret the user's verbal message given to him.

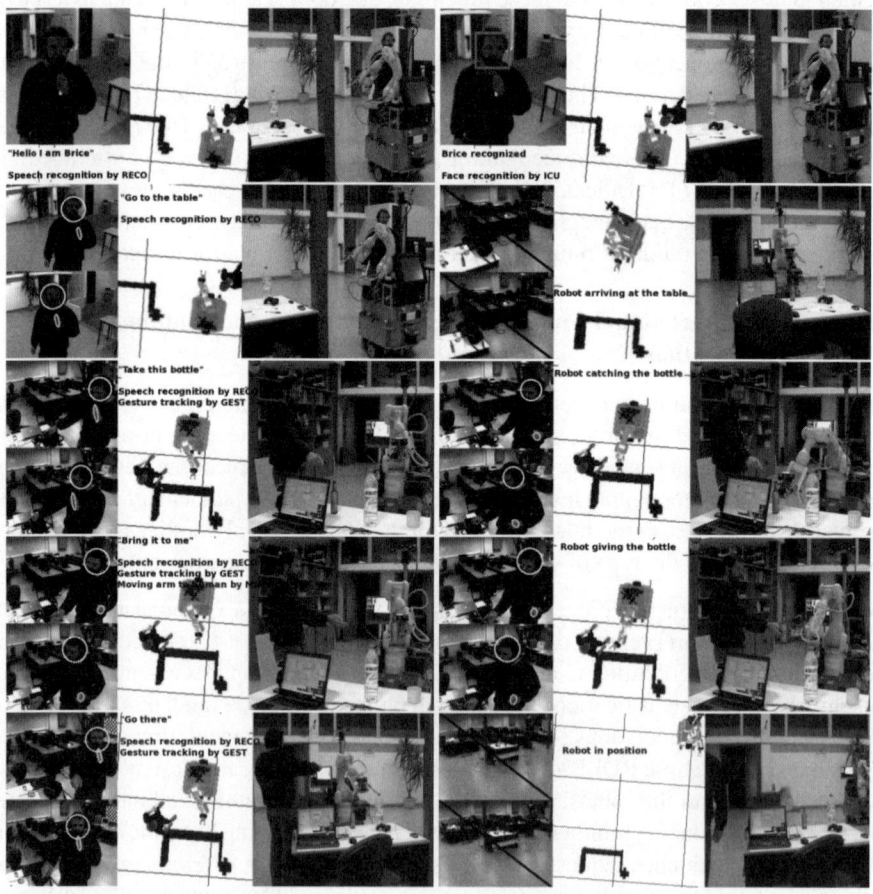

Fig. 3. From top-left to bottom-right : GEST (or ICU) module -left-, virtual 3D scene (yellow cubes represent hands) -middle-, current H/R situation -right-

Fusion with gesture: Deictic can be interpreted by our RECO module. If the object or location designation is precise enough (*"Put the bottle on the table"*) the right parameters are extracted from the sentence (what ? object = bottle ; where ? location = on table) and the underlying command can be generated (put(object(bottle), location(on table))). But in deictic case (*"Put the bottle there"*), the sentence analysis will mark the interpretation as "must be completed by the gesture result" and a late and hierarchical fusion strategy will be applied (put(object(bottle), location(Gesture_result)). In the same manner, for other human-dependent commands such as (*"come on my left-side"*) the same kind of strategie will be applied.

3.3 Target Robot Scenario and Preliminary Experiments

The target scenario focuses on the understanding of natural human peer-to-peer multimodal interaction in a household situation. It depends on the beforehand identification of the robot interlocutor before this one be granted permission to interact with it.

Given both verbal and gesture commands, the identified interlocutor is allowed to make the robot change its position in the environment and/or simply marks some objects the robot must catch and carry,... Figure 3 illustrates a typical run of this scenario where the robot user, after introducing himself or herself, sequences the following commands: *"go to the table"*, *"take this bottle"*, *"bring it to me"*, *"go over there"*. For each step, the left subfigure shows the tracking results while the right one depicts the current H/R situation and the middle one represents the virtual H/R configuration in space (thanks to the outcome of the GEST module). The entire video and more illustrations are available at the URL www.laas.fr/~bburger/.

4 Conclusion

This paper presents a fully automatic distributed approach for tracking two-handed gestures and head tracking in 3D. Two lines of investigations have been pursued. First, the conventional IDMOT strategy, extended to the 3D tracking of two-handed gestures, is endowed with the nice properties of ICONDENSATION and data fusion. The amended particle filtering strategy allows to recover automatically from transient target loss while data fusion principle is shown to improve the tracker versatility and robustness to clutter. The second contribution concerns the merge of the tracker with a continuous speech interpretation process in order to specify parameters of location references and object/person IDs in verbal statements. All the components have been integrated on a mobile platform while a target robot scenario highlights the relevance and the complementarity of verbal and non verbal communication for the detection and interpretation of deictic actions during a natural peer-to-peer H/R interaction.

These preliminary robotic experiments are promising even if quantitative performance evaluations still needs to be carried out. These evaluations are expected to highlight the robot capacity to succeed in performing multimodal interaction. Further investigations will be also to estimate the head orientation as additional features in the gesture characterization. Our robotic experiments report strongly evidence that person tend to look at pointing targets when performing such gestures. Finally, dedicated HMM-based classifiers will be developed to filter more efficiently pointing gestures.

Acknowledgements. The work described in this paper was partially conducted within the EU Projects COGNIRON ("The Cognitive Robot Companion" - www.cogniron.org) and CommRob ("Advanced Robot behaviour and high-level multimodal communication" - www.commrob.eu) under contracts FP6-IST-002020 and FP6-IST-045441.

References

1. Kawahara, T., Lee, A., Shikano, K.: Julius — an open source real-time large vocabulary recognition engine. In: European Conference on Speech Communication and Technology (EUROSPEECH), pp. 1691–1694 (2001)
2. Clodic, A., Montreuil, V., Alami, R., Chatila, R.: A decisional framework for autonomous robots interacting with humans. In: IEEE International Workshop on Robot and Human Interactive Communication (RO-MAN) (2005)
3. Fong, T., Nourbakhsh, I., Dautenhahn, K.: A survey of socially interactive robots. Robotics and Autonomous Systems 42, 143–166 (2003)
4. Isard, M., Blake, A.: CONDENSATION – conditional density propagation for visual tracking. Int. Journal on Computer Vision 29(1), 5–28 (1998)
5. Isard, M., Blake, A.: I-CONDENSATION: Unifying low-level and high-level tracking in a stochastic framework. In: European Conf. on Computer Vision, 1998, pp. 893–908 (1998)
6. Isard, M., Blake, A.: BraMBLe: a bayesian multiple blob tracker. In: Int. Conf. on Computer Vision, Vancouver, pp. 34–41 (2001)
7. Maas, J., Spexard, T., Fritsch, J., Wrede, B., Sagerer, G.: A multi-modal topic tracker for improved human-robot interaction. In: Int. Symp. on Robot and Human Interactive Communication, Hatfield (September 2006)
8. Nickel, K., Stiefehagen, R.: Visual recognition of pointing gestures for human-robot interaction. Image and Vision Computing 3(12), 1875–1884 (2006)
9. Pérennou, G., de Calmès, M.: MHATLex: Lexical resources for modelling the french pronunciation. In: Int. Conf. on Language Resources and Evaluations, Athens, June 2000, pp. 257–264 (2000)
10. Rogalla, O., Ehrenmann, M., Zollner, R., Becher, R., Dillman, R.: Advanced in human-robot interaction. In: Using gesture and speech control for commanding a robot., vol. 14, Springer, Heidelberg (2004)
11. Lerasle, F., Germa, T., Brèthes, L., Simon, T.: Data fusion and eigenface based tracking dedicated to a tour-guide robot. In: Int. Conf. on Computer Vision Systems (2007)
12. Wei, Q., Schonfeld, D., Mohamed, M.: Real-time interactively distributed multi-object tracking using a magnetic-inertia potential model. In: Int. Conf. on Computer Vision, Beijing, October 2005, pp. 535–540 (2005)

Author Index

Printing: Mercedes-Druck, Berlin
Binding: Stein+Lehmann, Berlin

Lecture Notes in Computer Science

Sublibrary 1: Theoretical Computer Science and General Issues

For information about Vols. 1– 4672
please contact your bookseller or Springer

Vol. 4860: G. Eleftherakis, P. Kefalas, G. Păun, G. Rozenberg, A. Salomaa (Eds.), Membrane Computing. IX, 453 pages. 2007.

Vol. 4855: V. Arvind, S. Prasad (Eds.), FSTTCS 2007: Foundations of Software Technology and Theoretical Computer Science. XIV, 558 pages. 2007.

Vol. 4854: L. Bougé, M. Forsell, J.L. Träff, A. Streit, W. Ziegler, M. Alexander, S. Childs (Eds.), Euro-Par 2007 Workshops: Parallel Processing. XVII, 236 pages. 2008.

Vol. 4851: S. Boztaş, H.-F.(F.) Lu (Eds.), Applied Algebra, Algebraic Algorithms and Error-Correcting Codes. XII, 368 pages. 2007.

Vol. 4848: M.H. Garzon, H. Yan (Eds.), DNA Computing. XI, 292 pages. 2008.

Vol. 4847: M. Xu, Y. Zhan, J. Cao, Y. Liu (Eds.), Advanced Parallel Processing Technologies. XIX, 767 pages. 2007.

Vol. 4846: I. Cervesato (Ed.), Advances in Computer Science – ASIAN 2007. XI, 313 pages. 2007.

Vol. 4838: T. Masuzawa, S. Tixeuil (Eds.), Stabilization, Safety, and Security of Distributed Systems. XIII, 409 pages. 2007.

Vol. 4835: T. Tokuyama (Ed.), Algorithms and Computation. XVII, 929 pages. 2007.

Vol. 4818: I. Lirkov, S. Margenov, J. Waśniewski (Eds.), Large-Scale Scientific Computing. XIV, 755 pages. 2008.

Vol. 4800: A. Avron, N. Dershowitz, A. Rabinovich (Eds.), Pillars of Computer Science. XXI, 683 pages. 2008.

Vol. 4783: J. Holub, J. Žďárek (Eds.), Implementation and Application of Automata. XIII, 324 pages. 2007.

Vol. 4782: R. Perrott, B.M. Chapman, J. Subhlok, R.F. de Mello, L.T. Yang (Eds.), High Performance Computing and Communications. XIX, 823 pages. 2007.

Vol. 4771: T. Bartz-Beielstein, M.J. Blesa Aguilera, C. Blum, B. Naujoks, A. Roli, G. Rudolph, M. Sampels (Eds.), Hybrid Metaheuristics. X, 202 pages. 2007.

Vol. 4770: V.G. Ganzha, E.W. Mayr, E.V. Vorozhtsov (Eds.), Computer Algebra in Scientific Computing. XIII, 460 pages. 2007.

Vol. 4769: A. Brandstädt, D. Kratsch, H. Müller (Eds.), Graph-Theoretic Concepts in Computer Science. XIII, 341 pages. 2007.

Vol. 4763: J.-F. Raskin, P.S. Thiagarajan (Eds.), Formal Modeling and Analysis of Timed Systems. X, 369 pages. 2007.

Vol. 4759: J. Labarta, K. Joe, T. Sato (Eds.), High-Performance Computing. XV, 524 pages. 2008.

Vol. 4746: A. Bondavalli, F. Brasileiro, S. Rajsbaum (Eds.), Dependable Computing. XV, 239 pages. 2007.

Vol. 4743: P. Thulasiraman, X. He, T.L. Xu, M.K. Denko, R.K. Thulasiram, L.T. Yang (Eds.), Frontiers of High Performance Computing and Networking ISPA 2007 Workshops. XXIX, 536 pages. 2007.

Vol. 4742: I. Stojmenovic, R.K. Thulasiram, L.T. Yang, W. Jia, M. Guo, R.F. de Mello (Eds.), Parallel and Distributed Processing and Applications. XX, 995 pages. 2007.

Vol. 4739: R. Moreno Díaz, F. Pichler, A. Quesada Arencibia (Eds.), Computer Aided Systems Theory – EUROCAST 2007. XIX, 1233 pages. 2007.

Vol. 4736: S. Winter, M. Duckham, L. Kulik, B. Kuipers (Eds.), Spatial Information Theory. XV, 455 pages. 2007.

Vol. 4732: K. Schneider, J. Brandt (Eds.), Theorem Proving in Higher Order Logics. IX, 401 pages. 2007.

Vol. 4731: A. Pelc (Ed.), Distributed Computing. XVI, 510 pages. 2007.

Vol. 4728: S. Bozapalidis, G. Rahonis (Eds.), Algebraic Informatics. VIII, 291 pages. 2007.

Vol. 4726: N. Ziviani, R. Baeza-Yates (Eds.), String Processing and Information Retrieval. XII, 311 pages. 2007.

Vol. 4719: R. Backhouse, J. Gibbons, R. Hinze, J. Jeuring (Eds.), Datatype-Generic Programming. XI, 369 pages. 2007.

Vol. 4711: C.B. Jones, Z. Liu, J. Woodcock (Eds.), Theoretical Aspects of Computing – ICTAC 2007. XI, 483 pages. 2007.

Vol. 4710: C.W. George, Z. Liu, J. Woodcock (Eds.), Domain Modeling and the Duration Calculus. XI, 237 pages. 2007.

Vol. 4708: L. Kučera, A. Kučera (Eds.), Mathematical Foundations of Computer Science 2007. XVIII, 764 pages. 2007.

Vol. 4707: O. Gervasi, M.L. Gavrilova (Eds.), Computational Science and Its Applications – ICCSA 2007, Part III. XXIV, 1205 pages. 2007.

Vol. 4706: O. Gervasi, M.L. Gavrilova (Eds.), Computational Science and Its Applications – ICCSA 2007, Part II. XXIII, 1129 pages. 2007.

Vol. 4705: O. Gervasi, M.L. Gavrilova (Eds.), Computational Science and Its Applications – ICCSA 2007, Part I. XLIV, 1169 pages. 2007.

Vol. 4703: L. Caires, V.T. Vasconcelos (Eds.), CONCUR 2007 – Concurrency Theory. XIII, 507 pages. 2007.

Vol. 4700: C.B. Jones, Z. Liu, J. Woodcock (Eds.), Formal Methods and Hybrid Real-Time Systems. XVI, 539 pages. 2007.

Vol. 4699: B. Kågström, E. Elmroth, J. Dongarra, J. Waśniewski (Eds.), Applied Parallel Computing. XXIX, 1192 pages. 2007.

Vol. 4698: L. Arge, M. Hoffmann, E. Welzl (Eds.), Algorithms – ESA 2007. XV, 769 pages. 2007.

Vol. 4697: L. Choi, Y. Paek, S. Cho (Eds.), Advances in Computer Systems Architecture. XIII, 400 pages. 2007.

Vol. 4688: K. Li, M. Fei, G.W. Irwin, S. Ma (Eds.), Bio-Inspired Computational Intelligence and Applications. XIX, 805 pages. 2007.

Vol. 4684: L. Kang, Y. Liu, S. Zeng (Eds.), Evolvable Systems: From Biology to Hardware. XIV, 446 pages. 2007.

Vol. 4683: L. Kang, Y. Liu, S. Zeng (Eds.), Advances in Computation and Intelligence. XVII, 663 pages. 2007.

Vol. 4681: D.-S. Huang, L. Heutte, M. Loog (Eds.), Advanced Intelligent Computing Theories and Applications. XXVI, 1379 pages. 2007.